AF785380

Annual Review of
Financial Economics

Editorial Committee (2017)

Tobias Adrian, International Monetary Fund
Yacine Aït-Sahalia, Princeton University
Patrick Bolton, Columbia University
Robert A. Jarrow, Cornell University
Kose John, New York University
Andrew W. Lo, Massachusetts Institute of Technology
Deborah J. Lucas, Massachusetts Institute of Technology
Robert C. Merton, Massachusetts Institute of Technology
Matthew Richardson, New York University
Antoinette Schoar, Massachusetts Institute of Technology

Responsible for the Organization of Volume 9 (Editorial Committee, 2015)

Tobias Adrian
Yacine Aït-Sahalia
Patrick Bolton
Robert A. Jarrow
Kose John
Andrew W. Lo
Deborah J. Lucas
Robert C. Merton
Matthew Richardson
Antoinette Schoar

Production Editor: Andrew Levy
Managing Editors: Linley E. Hall, Nina G. Perry, Maria Duncan
Electronic Content Coordinators: Suzanne K. Moses, Erin H. Lee
Illustration Editor: Savitha Viswanathan

Annual Review of Financial Economics

Volume 9, 2017

Andrew W. Lo, *Co-Editor*
Massachusetts Institute of Technology

Robert C. Merton, *Co-Editor*
Massachusetts Institute of Technology

www.annualreviews.org • science@annualreviews.org • 650-493-4400

Annual Reviews
4139 El Camino Way • P.O. Box 10139 • Palo Alto, California 94303-0139

Annual Reviews
Palo Alto, California, USA

COPYRIGHT © 2017 BY ANNUAL REVIEWS, PALO ALTO, CALIFORNIA, USA. ALL RIGHTS RESERVED. Authorization to make copies of an article for personal or internal use, or for the personal or internal use of specific clients, is granted by Annual Reviews on the condition that the copier pay the per-copy fee through the Copyright Clearance Center, Inc. (http://www.copyright.com/) for copying beyond that permitted by Section 107 or 108 of the U.S. Copyright Law. The per-copy fee also applies to the copying, under the stated conditions, of articles published in any *Annual Review* serial before January 1, 1978. Individual readers, and nonprofit libraries acting for them, are permitted to make a single copy of an article without charge for use in research or teaching. This consent does not extend to other kinds of copying, such as copying for general distribution, for advertising or promotional purposes, for creating new collective works, or for resale. For such uses, written permission through Copyright Clearance Center, Inc. is required.

International Standard Serial Number: 1941-1367
International Standard Book Number: 978-0-8243-4809-0
Library of Congress Control Number: 2008214324

All Annual Reviews and publication titles are registered trademarks of Annual Reviews.

♾ The paper used in this publication meets the minimum requirements of American National Standards for Information Sciences—Permanence of Paper for Printed Library Materials, ANSI Z39.48-1992.

Annual Reviews and the Editors of its publications assume no responsibility for the statements expressed by the contributors to this *Annual Review*.

TYPESET BY APTARA
PRINTED AND BOUND BY SHERIDAN BOOKS, INC., CHELSEA, MICHIGAN

Annual Review of
Financial Economics

Volume 9, 2017

Contents

Indexes

Errata

An online log of corrections to *Annual Review of Financial Economics* articles may be found at http://www.annualreviews.org/errata/financial

Related Articles

From the ***Annual Review of Economics***, Volume 9 (2017)

Agricultural Insurance and Economic Development
Shawn A. Cole and Wentao Xiong

The Formation of Consumer Brand Preferences
Bart J. Bronnenberg and Jean-Pierre Dubé

Health, Health Insurance, and Retirement: A Survey
Eric French and John Bailey Jones

Large-Scale Global and Simultaneous Inference: Estimation and Testing in Very High Dimensions
T. Tony Cai and Wenguang Sun

How Do Patents Affect Research Investments?
Heidi L. Williams

Mobile Money
Tavneet Suri

The History and Economics of Safe Assets
Gary Gorton

Global Liquidity: A Selective Review
Benjamin H. Cohen, Dietrich Domanski, Ingo Fender, and Hyun Song Shin

From the ***Annual Review of Resource Economics***, Volume 9 (2017)

Household Response to Time-Varying Electricity Prices
Matthew Harding and Steven Sexton

Life Cycle Assessment for Economists
Deepak Rajagopal, Caroline Vanderghem, and Heather L. MacLean

Index Insurance for Developing Country Agriculture: A Reassessment
Michael Carter, Alain de Janvry, Elisabeth Sadoulet, and Alexandros Sarris

From the ***Annual Review of Statistics and Its Application***, Volume 4 (2017)

p-Values: The Insight to Modern Statistical Inference
D.A.S. Fraser

Risk and Uncertainty Communication
David Spiegelhalter

Annual Reviews is a nonprofit scientific publisher established to promote the advancement of the sciences. Beginning in 1932 with the *Annual Review of Biochemistry*, the Company has pursued as its principal function the publication of high-quality, reasonably priced *Annual Review* volumes. The volumes are organized by Editors and Editorial Committees who invite qualified authors to contribute critical articles reviewing significant developments within each major discipline. The Editor-in-Chief invites those interested in serving as future Editorial Committee members to communicate directly with him. Annual Reviews is administered by a Board of Directors, whose members serve without compensation.

2017 Board of Directors, Annual Reviews

Richard N. Zare, *Chairperson of Annual Reviews, Marguerite Blake Wilbur Professor of Natural Science, Department of Chemistry, Stanford University*
Karen S. Cook, *Vice-Chairperson of Annual Reviews, Ray Lyman Wilbur Professor of Sociology, Director of the Institute for Research in the Social Sciences, Vice Provost for Faculty Development and Diversity, Stanford University*
Sandra M. Faber, *Vice-Chairperson of Annual Reviews, Professor Emerita of Astronomy and Astrophysics, University of California, Santa Cruz*
John I. Brauman, *J.G. Jackson-C.J. Wood Professor of Chemistry, Emeritus, Stanford University*
Peter F. Carpenter, *Founder, Mission and Values Institute, Atherton, California*
Susan T. Fiske, *Eugene Higgins Professor, Psychology and Public Affairs, Princeton University*
Richard Gallagher, *President and Editor-in-Chief, Annual Reviews*
Steven E. Hyman, *Director, Stanley Center for Psychiatric Research, Broad Institute of MIT and Harvard; Distinguished Service Professor of Stem Cell and Regenerative Biology, Harvard University*
Roger D. Kornberg, *Mrs. George A. Winzer Professor in Medicine, Stanford University School of Medicine*
Sharon R. Long, *William C. Steere, Jr.–Pfizer Inc. Professor in Biological Sciences, Stanford University*
J. Boyce Nute, *Former CEO, Mayfield Publishing Company*
Michael E. Peskin, *Professor of Particle Physics and Astrophysics, SLAC, Stanford University*
Harriet A. Zuckerman, *Professor Emerita, Columbia University*

Management of Annual Reviews

Richard Gallagher, President and Editor-in-Chief
Liz Allen, Director of MarCom and Strategic Development
Paul J. Calvi Jr., Director of Technology
Steven J. Castro, Chief Financial Officer
Jennifer L. Jongsma, Associate Editor-in-Chief and Director of Production
Natalie D. DeWitt, Associate Editor-in-Chief and Corporate Secretary
Andrea Lopez, Director of Sales
Lisa R. Wucher, Director of Human Resources

Annual Reviews of

Analytical Chemistry
Animal Biosciences
Anthropology
Astronomy and Astrophysics
Biochemistry
Biomedical Engineering
Biophysics
Cancer Biology
Cell and Developmental Biology
Chemical and Biomolecular Engineering
Clinical Psychology
Condensed Matter Physics
Earth and Planetary Sciences
Ecology, Evolution, and Systematics
Economics
Entomology
Environment and Resources
Financial Economics
Fluid Mechanics
Food Science and Technology
Genetics
Genomics and Human Genetics
Immunology
Law and Social Science
Linguistics
Marine Science
Materials Research
Medicine
Microbiology
Neuroscience
Nuclear and Particle Science
Nutrition
Organizational Psychology and Organizational Behavior
Pathology: Mechanisms of Disease
Pharmacology and Toxicology
Physical Chemistry
Physiology
Phytopathology
Plant Biology
Political Science
Psychology
Public Health
Resource Economics
Sociology
Statistics and Its Application
Virology
Vision Science

Do the Effects of Accounting Requirements on Banks' Regulatory Capital Adequacy Undermine Financial Stability?

Stephen G. Ryan

Stern School of Business, New York University, New York, NY 10012;
email: sryan@stern.nyu.edu

Annu. Rev. Financ. Econ. 2017. 9:1–20

First published as a Review in Advance on August 11, 2017

The *Annual Review of Financial Economics* is online at financial.annualreviews.org

https://doi.org/10.1146/annurev-financial-110716-032340

Copyright © 2017 by Annual Reviews.
All rights reserved

JEL codes: G01, G21, G28, M41, M48

Keywords

incurred loss model, fair value, securitization, accounting, regulatory capital, financial stability

Abstract

During the 2007–2009 financial crisis, many parties criticized aspects of accounting requirements for banks as undermining financial stability. These criticisms generally reflect the view that these requirements primarily affect stability through their effects on banks' regulatory capital adequacy. I critically evaluate whether this idea can be sustained on logical and evidential grounds. I explain how accounting requirements typically have quite small effects on banks' regulatory capital adequacy. I discuss the plausibility of the alternative view that accounting requirements primarily affect stability by improving banks' understanding of their risks and their transparency to markets and regulators. Because securitization is the setting in which banks' regulatory capital adequacy is most likely to be significantly affected by accounting requirements, I describe empirical research on significant changes in securitization accounting effective in 2010. I explain how even in this setting regulatory capital adequacy incompletely explains how accounting requirements for banks affect stability.

1. INTRODUCTION

During the 2007–2009 financial crisis (hereafter, crisis), three areas of US generally accepted accounting principles (GAAP) applicable to banks were criticized as significantly contributing to or even causing the crisis. First, parties claimed that loan loss provisioning under FAS 5's incurred loss model (FASB 1975) prevented banks from adequately reserving for loan losses in the economic good times prior to the crisis. As a consequence, banks had to sharply and substantially increase their loan loss reserves during the crisis. These increases reduced banks' regulatory capital adequacy at a time when it was costly for them to issue equity or to sell illiquid assets.[1]

Second, parties claimed that fair value accounting requirements—both the rules governing fair value accounting for specific types of financial instruments and FAS 157's overarching fair value measurement guidance (FASB 2006)—required banks to record losses[2] on financial assets that became illiquid during the crisis. Assets whose liquidity deteriorates typically experience increases in the relevant (i.e., instrument-specific) market discount rates. These increases reduce the estimated fair values of the assets. Banks willing and able to hold assets to maturity or the recovery of their amortized cost bases, whichever comes first, will not realize losses[3] of fair value resulting from increases in the relevant market discount rates. Recording such losses as reductions of net income reduces banks' regulatory capital. These reductions may induce banks to sell illiquid assets, further depressing their prices, among other adverse feedback effects.[4]

Third, prior to the crisis banks readily obtained sale accounting for securitizations and nonconsolidation of securitization vehicles under FAS 140 and FIN 46(R), respectively (FASB 2000, 2003). The combination of sale accounting and nonconsolidation yielded off-balance-sheet treatment for the securitized assets and associated debt as well as the recording of gains on sale, both of which work to increase banks' regulatory capital. Parties claimed that this accounting treatment motivated banks to originate and securitize low-quality assets while retaining much of the assets' risk. During the crisis and its aftermath, banks bore sizable securitization-related losses through their provision of contractually required, voluntary, or court-imposed credit and liquidity support to securitization vehicles or investors.[5]

[1]For example, Dugan (2009) states, "in the booming part of the economic cycle in the earlier part of this decade, the ratio of loan loss reserves to total loans went down, not up—even though there was broad recognition that the cycle would soon have to turn negative. Conversely, when the turn finally did come, and the tidal wave of losses began hitting shore, banks have had to recognize losses through a sudden series of increased provisions to the loan loss reserve, which in turn has more than offset earnings and eaten into precious capital. Stated differently, rather than being counter-cyclical, loan loss provisioning has become decidedly procyclical, magnifying the impact of the downturn." To remedy this alleged problem, Dugan asks "whether there ought to be changes made to the incurred loss model."

[2]In accounting, recording a loss on a position means giving accounting effect to the loss. Depending on the type of position, this effect can be to reduce net income or other comprehensive income. Recording a loss is not the same thing as realizing the loss (see Footnote 3).

[3]In accounting, realizing a loss on a position generally means experiencing a cash shortfall associated with the loss through sale of the position or various other means. (An exception is that other-than-temporary impairment losses are treated as realized losses despite the associated cash shortfalls not yet being experienced.) Realizing a loss is not the same thing as recording the loss (see Footnote 2).

[4]For example, the International Monetary Fund (2008, p. 127) states that although "fair value accounting gives the most comprehensive picture of a firm's financial health . . . investment decision rules based on fair value accounting outcomes could lead to self-fulfilling forced sales and falling prices when valuations fell below important thresholds (either self-imposed by financial institutions or by regulation)."

[5]For example, Senate Banking Committee Chairman Jack Reed (2008) states: "The drivers of the subprime crisis . . . [include] accounting rules that allowed mortgage-backed securities be held off the balance sheet. The securities packaged from these

These criticisms all reflect the view that accounting requirements for banks have systemically adverse effects in large part owing to their effects on banks' regulatory capital adequacy.[6] In this article, I argue that this view is difficult to sustain on both logical and evidential grounds. I explain how the incremental effects of timelier or otherwise more conservative loan loss provisioning on banks' regulatory capital adequacy are too small in absolute terms and relative to the variation in their loan losses across the cycle to be the primary driver of banks' investment and financing decisions. The effects of fair value accounting are smaller still, owing to the small amount of mostly low credit risk assets that banks account for at fair value. Although on-balance-sheet treatment for securitizations has appreciable effects on regulatory capital adequacy for relatively few, but typically very large, securitizing banks, these banks generally remain very well capitalized throughout the cycle even with that treatment. Moreover, large banks should be sophisticated enough to anticipate most of the average differential effects of alternative accounting requirements across the phases of the cycle and to make their investment and financing decisions accordingly.

I emphasize that I do not argue against the widely held view that increasing banks' regulatory capital adequacy enhances financial stability. I argue only that in most settings accounting requirements for banks have relatively little effect on banks' regulatory capital adequacy and that two alternative channels more plausibly link accounting requirements for banks to stability. Both of these channels reflect the fact that improved accounting requirements for banks or better compliance with existing requirements by banks typically involves banks more fully modeling their individual and aggregate risk exposures. Fuller modeling enhances banks' decidedly imperfect understanding of their risks, thus enabling them to make better investment and financing decisions (the first channel). Such modeling also increases the transparency of banks' financial and regulatory reports to market participants and bank regulators, thus increasing market and regulatory discipline on banks (the second channel).

To address the criticisms of accounting requirements for banks discussed above, during and after the crisis the Financial Accounting Standards Board (FASB) made three sets of changes to these requirements. First, in June 2016, FASB issued ASU 2016-13 (FASB 2016a). When effective in 2020, this standard will replace FAS 5's incurred loss model—which banks currently use to reserve for credit losses on loans, other assets, and off-balance-sheet loan commitments—with an expected loss model. ASU 2016-13 constitutes a significant change in accounting requirements for banks.

Second, FASB made modest changes in FAS 157's fair value measurement guidance as well as various targeted expansions and restrictions of fair value accounting for financial instruments. These expansions and restrictions reflect FASB's acceptance of the view that fair value accounting should record unrealized gains and losses only when firms expect to realize these gains and losses through sale or other means. The primary expansion is ASU 2016-01's requirement, effective in 2018, of full fair value accounting for investments in equity securities (FASB 2016b). FASB explained this expansion as attributable to equity securities having no maturity, so firms primarily realize fair value gains and losses on these securities by selling them for fair value.

mortgages, many of them risky subprime mortgages, remain far from the view of investors and less closely reviewed by regulators."

[6]This common theme appears to stem in part from the requirement of the Federal Deposit Insurance Corporation Improvement Act of 1991 (FDICIA) that banks' regulatory accounting principles, which underlie banks' regulatory capital ratios, be "no less stringent" than GAAP. However, this restriction does not appear to bind in practice. For example, regulatory accounting principles differ from GAAP in various significant ways that arguably render regulatory accounting principles less stringent than GAAP. For example, unrealized gains and losses on available-for-sale debt securities recorded in other comprehensive income do not affect regulatory capital for most US banks under the US implementation of Basel III. Moreover, the US Congress could easily repeal this provision of FDICIA.

The primary restriction of fair value accounting is FASB Staff Position (FSP) FAS 115-2 and FAS 124-2's April 2009 reduction of the amounts of write-downs of other-than-temporarily impaired debt investment securities that are recorded in net income (FASB 2009d). Under prior GAAP, these amounts equaled the entire decreases in the fair values of the securities below their amortized cost bases. Under FSP FAS 115-2 and FAS 124-2, holders of other-than-temporarily impaired debt securities, if they intend to and more likely than not can hold the securities to recovery of their amortized cost bases, record only losses attributable to the decreases in expected cash flows for the securities in net income. They record losses attributable to the increases in the relevant market discount rates for the securities in other comprehensive income. For all US banks during the crisis, and for most US banks today under the US implementation of Basel III, regulatory capital is unaffected by losses recorded in other comprehensive income.[7] This restriction of fair value accounting is of modest significance for most banks, owing to the small amounts (compared with loans) and typically low credit risk of their debt investment securities.

ASU 2016-1 also contains the less significant restriction that changes in the fair values of optionally fair-valued liabilities attributable to changes in instrument-specific credit risk be recorded in other comprehensive income rather than in net income. FASB explains this restriction as motivated by firms' limited ability to realize gains and losses on liabilities, because firms typically must obtain counterparty approval to transfer liabilities.

Third, in June 2009 FASB issued FAS 166 and FAS 167, both of which became effective in 2010 (FASB 2009a,b). FAS 166 modestly tightens the conditions that must be met to account for securitizations as sales. More importantly, FAS 166 and FAS 167 together eliminate the notion of qualifying special purpose entities (QSPEs) that had been exempt from consolidation under prior GAAP. FAS 167 requires banks that securitize their own assets or that sponsor securitizations of the assets of their clients (hereafter, securitizing banks) to consolidate any securitization vehicles that they control and in which they bear a reasonable possibility of significant loss. In practice, these standards have led securitizing banks primarily to consolidate credit card master trusts and asset-backed commercial paper conduits, owing to the banks' control over and retention of risk in these vehicles. These changes constitute significant changes in accounting requirements for relatively few, typically very large, securitizing banks.

I have previously written at length on the association between banks' financial reporting and financial stability, mostly targeting accounting researchers (Acharya & Ryan 2016). To avoid repetition and to target the financial economists reading this journal, the remainder of this article is devoted to the following topics: In Section 2, I intuitively explain the changes in accounting requirements for banks described above. In Section 3, I describe the typically quite small magnitude of the effects of alternative accounting requirements for financial instruments on banks' regulatory capital adequacy. In Section 4, I discuss the plausibility of banks' internal understanding of their risks and transparency to outsiders as alternative channels by which accounting requirements for banks affect stability. In Section 5, I describe recent empirical research on the setting in which banks' regulatory capital adequacy is most likely to constitute a significant channel. This research examines the effects of on-balance-sheet treatment of securitizations under FAS 166 and FAS 167 on the volume and mix of securitizing banks' loan originations and sales, overall asset quality and liquidity, and information asymmetry. Even in this setting, I argue that banks' regulatory capital

[7]Subsequent to the crisis, Basel III specifies the inclusion of unrealized gains and losses recorded in other comprehensive income in banks' regulatory capital. In July 2013, however, US bank regulators decided to require this aspect of Basel III only for the few very large US banks that apply Basel III's advanced methods.

adequacy is unlikely to fully explain the effects of banks' accounting requirements on stability. Section 6 concludes this review.

2. RECENT CHANGES IN ACCOUNTING REQUIREMENTS FOR BANKS

2.1. Loan Loss Reserving

The loan loss allowance (which reduces loans outstanding) and the loan loss provision (which reduces net income) are by far the most important and judgmental accrual estimates for most banks.[8] For simplicity, I refer to the loan loss allowance and provision collectively as loan loss reserves. In this section, I first describe banks' loan loss reserving under FAS 5's current incurred loss model. I then describe how that reserving will change under ASU 2016-13's expected loss model.

Under FAS 5's incurred loss model, banks reserve for future credit losses on loans only when the losses are "incurred," "probable," and "capable of reasonable estimation." These three requirements, all of which must be met, tend to delay banks' reserving for loan losses.

The "incurred" requirement is rather vaguely specified in FAS 5, which allows accruals for loss contingencies only if there is "an existing condition, situation, or set of circumstances involving uncertainty as to possible . . . loss . . . to an enterprise" (FASB 1975, paragraph 1). "Existing" is the critical word in this specification. To meet the requirement that loan losses be incurred, banks must clearly root these losses in current conditions, not simply in the ever-present potential for conditions to deteriorate in the future.[9]

To illustrate the effect of the "incurred" requirement, consider a bank with a pool of consumer loans that are 60 days past due and for which current economic conditions are good. The bank generally should predict that the loans will migrate to default (typically defined as 120 or 180 days past due, depending on the type of consumer loan) with some probability based on historical experience or other information, because this probability is clearly rooted in the current delinquency status of the loans. That is, the losses that will be realized from this expected migration are incurred.[10] The bank generally should not predict that economic conditions will deteriorate with some probability, however, because future economic conditions are not as clearly rooted in the current economic conditions. Hence, these losses are not yet incurred.

To meet the "probable" requirement, banks must determine that loan losses are "more likely than more likely than not" to be realized. In practice, banks typically define probable as 70% or

[8]Banks' allowances and provisions for loan losses are linked by the operation of double-entry bookkeeping. Double-entry bookkeeping makes changes to balance-sheet items, such as the loan loss allowance, consistently with changes to the corresponding income statement or cash flow statement items, such as the loan loss provision. The change in the loan loss allowance over a period equals the loan loss provision for the period less net loan charge-offs for the period. Loan charge-offs are recorded when loans are deemed uncollectible.

[9]Standard models represent credit losses as the product of three components: the probability of default, the loss given default, and the expected loss at default. Although not stated explicitly in FAS 5 or other GAAP, the requirement that loan losses be incurred applies to all these components.

[10]Because banks often cannot directly observe incurred losses, they employ practical expedients, most notably "loss emergence periods," to estimate these losses. A loss emergence period extends forward from the balance-sheet date. For example, if a bank is preparing its financial report for the fiscal year ending December 31, 2006, and it uses a 1-year loss emergence period, that period extends from January 1, 2007, to December 31, 2007. If, on the basis of statistical analysis of historical loan performance data or other evidence, the bank expects a loss to be realized during the loss emergence period, it assumes the loss is incurred at the balance-sheet date of December 31, 2006. On the basis of bank regulatory guidance, banks typically use a 1-year loss emergence period for nonclassified (i.e., not severely delinquent) consumer loans. For most types of consumer loans, a 1-year loss emergence period is less than the expected remaining life of the loans, so this period does not capture all currently expected loan losses.

more likely, a high probability threshold. To meet the "can be reasonably estimated" requirement, banks must have statistical or other evidential bases to reliably estimate their losses. Banks typically find it relatively easy to meet the "probable" and "can be reasonably estimated" requirements for homogeneous loan types (e.g., consumer loans), for which they primarily reserve for loan losses at the pool level using statistical analysis of historical loan performance data. Banks typically find it relatively difficult to meet these requirements for heterogeneous loan types (e.g., commercial and industrial loans), however, for which they primarily reserve for loan losses at the individual loan level relying on the imperfect and potentially conflicted judgments of the loan officers responsible for the loans (Berger & Udell 2002, Udell 1989).

To summarize, banks' loan loss reserves do not reflect losses that are not currently incurred. Determining whether or not a loss is incurred is somewhat easier using statistics for a pool of homogeneous loans than it is using the loan officer's judgment for an individual heterogeneous loan. The main difference between the two types of loan, however, is that it is much easier to meet the "probable" and "can be reasonably estimated" conditions for homogeneous loan types than for heterogeneous loan types. Hence, banks' loss reserves for homogeneous loan types incorporate most incurred losses, whereas banks' loss reserves for heterogeneous loan types incorporate only a potentially quite small portion of incurred losses. As a consequence, criticisms of FAS 5's incurred loss model apply more strongly to its use in loss reserving for heterogeneous loan types.

When ASU 2016-13 becomes effective in 2020, banks will apply the standard's expected loss model to account for credit losses on loans, most other types of financial assets, and off-balance-sheet loan commitments. This model will require banks to reserve for expected future credit losses on outstanding loans over their remaining lives. The model substantially weakens the "incurred" and "can be reasonably estimated" requirements and eliminates the "probable" requirement that must be met to reserve for loan losses under FAS 5's incurred loss model. Most notably, ASU 2016-13 requires banks' loan loss reserves to incorporate all "reasonable and supportable forecasts" over the remaining lives of loans outstanding that are expected to affect the collectibility of the carrying amount of loans on the balance sheet. Naturally, banks may exercise discretion over what they deem "reasonable and supportable" forecasts. Such exercise of discretion likely will affect the level and timeliness of banks' loan loss reserves.

To illustrate the effect of ASU 2016-13, I return to the above example involving a pool of 60-day delinquent consumer loans for which current economic conditions are good. Unlike under FAS 5's incurred loss model, under ASU 2016-13 the bank generally should predict that economic conditions will deteriorate with some probability and expected severity over the remaining life of the loans. That is, the bank will accrue for the losses on these outstanding loans that will result from the predicted economic deterioration, because these losses are expected despite not yet being incurred.

Compared with FAS 5, ASU 2016-13 will require banks to reserve more for loan losses in economic good times, both because banks will reserve for losses over the entire life of loans and because their forecasts typically will be for economic conditions to mean revert and thus to deteriorate. One might think that banks reserving more for loan losses in good times implies that they must reserve less for loan losses in bad times, because the cumulative amount of credit losses that will be realized (i.e., loan charge-offs) is fixed. However, because loan loss reserving occurs in advance of loan charge-offs, more so under ASU 2016-13 than under FAS 5, it actually is unclear what the directional effect of ASU 2016-13 on banks' loan loss reserving is in bad times. The two effects that work in the same direction during good times offset in bad times. Specifically, the requirement to reserve for losses over the expected remaining life of loans will increase loan loss reserves, but reasonable and supportable forecasts typically will be for economic conditions to mean revert and thus to improve, decreasing loan loss reserves. If the former effect dominates the latter effect, then it is possible that banks' incremental loan loss reserves in bad times exceed their incremental reserves in good times. If so, banks' loan loss reserves, and thus regulatory capital adequacy, will be less smooth across the cycle under ASU 2016-13 than they are under FAS 5.

I note that ASU 2016-13's expected loss model is neither fair value accounting nor the bank regulatory notion of dynamic loan loss reserving. Changes in the fair value of a position after its inception reflect changes in both expected cash flows and the relevant market discount rate. In contrast, changes in the expected loss on a position as defined ASU 2016-13 reflects only changes in expected cash flows, not changes in the relevant market discount rate. Dynamic loan loss reserves incorporate "through the cycle" loss rates. In contrast, expected losses under ASU 2016-13 reflect reasonable and supportable forecasts of loss rates only over the remaining life of currently outstanding positions, which often is less than a complete cycle.

2.2. Fair Value Accounting and Measurement

Fair value accounting for financial instruments and fair value measurement constitute a broad swath of accounting requirements for banks that I discuss at length elsewhere (Ryan 2007, 2011). In this section, I describe only the relatively few and modest changes that FASB has made to these requirements during and after the crisis. The limited scope of these changes contrasts (unfortunately, in my view) with FASB's repeated statements during the decade or so preceding the crisis that it intended to extend fair value accounting to essentially all financial instruments after resolving the conceptual and measurement issues (e.g., FASB 1999). This scope reflects FASB's acceptance of the view that fair value accounting should record unrealized gains and losses only when firms expect to subsequently realize these gains and losses through sale or other means.

I divide these changes in accounting requirements for banks into the following three areas, which are then discussed in sequence:

1. fair value measurements when markets are illiquid;
2. other-than-temporary impairments of available-for-sale and held-to-maturity debt securities; and
3. expansion of fair value accounting for investments in equity securities and restriction of fair value accounting for optionally fair valued liabilities.

First, FAS 157's fair value measurement guidance "prioritizes" the use of observable but imperfect market (Level 2) inputs, such as prices in inactive markets, over reporting firms' unobservable internally generated (Level 3) inputs, such as banks' historical loss rates. The standard does not require the use of Level 2 over Level 3 inputs, however, if market participants would use Level 3 over Level 2 inputs to fair value items. During the crisis, the market prices of many types of financial assets were depressed by illiquidity. Some parties claimed that FAS 157's prioritization of these Level 2 inputs over Level 3 inputs caused firms to report losses in excess of those they expected to realize through holding the securities to maturity or recovery of market liquidity (for example, see Johnson 2008a,b; Rummell 2008; The Economist 2008). While arguably unnecessary, FASB addressed these criticisms in two FSPs issued during the crisis. FSP FAS 157-3 (FASB 2008), issued in October 2008, indicates that Level 2 inputs should be used over Level 3 inputs only if the former are "relevant." FSP FAS 157-4 (FASB 2009c), issued in April 2009, provides a list of indicators as to when the volume of activity for an asset or liability has significantly decreased and transactions are not orderly, thereby providing more concrete grounds for firms to use Level 3 inputs instead of low-quality Level 2 inputs. These FSPs are entirely consistent with and at most modest elaborations on FAS 157's fair value measurement guidance.

Second, prior to April 2009, FAS 115 (FASB 1993) required that the amortized cost bases of other-than-temporarily impaired available-for-sale and held-to-maturity debt securities[11] be written down to their fair values, with the entire decreases in the cost bases recorded as losses in net income. For much the same reasons as just discussed, parties criticized this requirement as requiring firms to record other-than-temporary impairment losses in net income in excess of the losses they expected to realize through holding the securities to maturity or recovery of their amortized cost bases, whichever comes first. FASB addressed this criticism in April 2009 by issuing FSP FAS 115-2 and FAS 124-2 (FASB 2009d), which amends FAS 115's other-than-temporary impairment requirements. This FSP allows holders of other-than-temporarily impaired debt securities, if they intend to and more likely than not can hold the securities to maturity or recovery of their cost bases, to write down the cost bases of the securities to the present values of the expected future cash flows discounted at the preexisting effective interest rates. These present values exceed the corresponding fair values when current relevant market interest rates for the securities are higher than the preexisting effective interest rates. Only the decreases in the cost bases, referred to as credit losses, are recorded in net income. Decreases in fair value below the written-down cost bases, often referred to as noncredit losses, are recorded in other comprehensive income. Because banks' regulatory capital was unaffected by other comprehensive income in April 2009, FSP FAS 115-2 and FAS 124-2 increased the regulatory capital adequacy of banks that recorded other-than-temporary impairments of available-for-sale and held-to-maturity debt securities (Badertscher, Burks & Easton 2014).[12]

Third, the only significant expansion of fair value accounting since the crisis involves the accounting for investments in equity securities. Under FAS 115, equity securities can be classified either as trading or available for sale. Trading securities are recognized on the balance sheet at fair value with both realized and unrealized gains and losses recorded in net income. Available-for-sale securities are recognized on the balance sheet at fair value with realized gains and losses recorded in net income and with unrealized gains and losses recorded in other comprehensive income. Effective in 2018, ASU 2016-01 will require that all investments in equity securities be recognized at fair value with both realized and unrealized fair value gains and losses recorded in net income, i.e., the accounting for trading securities. FASB explains this expansion as attributable to equity securities having no maturity, so firms primarily realize gains and losses by selling the securities.

The most significant crisis-motivated restrictions of fair value accounting are FSP FAS 115-2 and FAS 124-2 discussed above. ASU 2016-01 contains one additional restriction effective in 2018. Under current GAAP firms recognize most financial liabilities at amortized cost. An exception is that under FAS 159 (FASB 2007) firms may irrevocably elect at the inception of individual financial instruments to recognize the instruments at fair value throughout their lives, recording both realized and unrealized gains and losses in net income. Banks relatively infrequently elect

[11]The criteria under which available-for-sale and held-to-maturity securities are other-than-temporarily impaired have changed over time. Simplifying somewhat, the main criteria and how they changed over time are as follows: Prior to April 2009, under FAS 115 securities were other-than-temporarily impaired when it was probable that the securities would not generate the promised cash flows or, for previously impaired securities, the expected cash flows at the most recent prior impairment. Effective in April 2009, under FSP FAS 115-2 and FAS 124-2 securities are other-than-temporarily impaired when, because of decreases in expected cash flows, the holder expects not to recover the amortized cost bases of the securities. The decreases in expected cash flows need not be probable.

[12]FSP FAS 115-2 and FAS 124-2 requires firms to apply its guidance retroactively upon adoption. Hence, banks that had previously recorded other-than-temporary impairments entirely as reductions of net income under prior GAAP restated these impairments upon adoption of this FSP. These restatements retroactively reclassified portions of prior other-than-temporary impairment losses from net income to other comprehensive income, immediately increasing the banks' regulatory capital adequacy.

this "fair value option" for liabilities; when they do, they typically elect the option either for their economically hedged debt (as a substitute for hedge accounting) or for the asset-backed securities issued by their consolidated securitization vehicles (to match the accounting for the assets of the vehicles).

FAS 157's fair value measurement guidance requires that the fair values of liabilities incorporate the reporting firm's own credit risk. When the reporting firm's own credit risk increases, the fair value of liabilities decreases, yielding gains that are recorded in net income, and vice versa. These net income effects can be significant in periods that the reporting firm's own credit risk changes sharply. These effects are often referred to as misleading or counterintuitive, because firms record gains when they perform poorly and losses when they perform well (see ASU 2016-01, paragraph BC100; also see Am. Account. Assoc. Financ. Account. Stand. Comm. 2007; Barth, Hodder & Stubben 2008). The effects result from the fact that firms' liabilities are claims on their economic assets. These assets should experience economic losses when firms perform poorly and economic gains when they perform well that more than offset the corresponding gains and losses on liabilities. Accounting may or may not record some or all of the economic losses and gains on economic assets, however, depending on the types of those assets. For example, GAAP require firms to immediately expense the costs of most internally developed intangible assets, so firms cannot subsequently record impairment losses on those assets when they perform poorly.

For liabilities for which firms elect FAS 159's fair value option, ASU 2016-01 will require changes in the fair value of the liabilities attributable to changes in firms' own (referred to as instrument-specific) credit risk to be recorded in other comprehensive income rather than in net income. FASB presumably made this change in part to assuage concerns about the potentially misleading net income effects described above. However, FASB primarily explains this restriction of fair value accounting as attributable to firms' limited ability to realize gains and losses on their liabilities, because firms typically must obtain counterparty approval to transfer liabilities.

2.3. Securitization Accounting

In this section, I first describe the accounting by banks that securitize their own assets, referred to as transferors, for securitizations under GAAP prior to 2010. I then describe transferors' accounting for securitizations under the GAAP beginning in 2010. I allude at various points to the accounting by banks that sponsor securitizations of their clients' assets.

Transferors' accounting for securitizations involves two questions. First, should transferors account for their transfers of assets to securitization vehicles as sales or secured borrowings? Prior to 2010, FAS 140 governed this question. Effective in 2010, FAS 166 amended FAS 140, although the earlier standard continues to govern most aspects of this question. Second, should transferors or other parties, such as banks that sponsor securitizations of their clients' assets, consolidate the securitization vehicles? Prior to 2010, FIN 46(R) governed this question. Effective in 2010, FAS 167 amended FIN 46(R), although the earlier standard continues to govern some aspects of this question.

FAS 140 requires that transferors account for securitizations as sales or secured borrowings depending on whether they surrender or retain control over the assets, respectively. For the transferor to be deemed to have surrendered control of the securitized assets under FAS 140, (*a*) the assets must be (legally) isolated from the transferor, (*b*) the transferee must be able to pledge or exchange the assets, and (*c*) the transferor must not retain effective control over the assets. Under sale accounting prior to 2010, the transferor (*a*) derecognized the securitized assets, (*b*) recognized the cash and other consideration received from securitization investors as well as retained servicing rights and liability interests in the securitized assets at fair value, (*c*) recognized any other retained interests in the securitized assets at an allocation of the prior carrying value of the assets, and (*d*) recorded a gain (loss, if negative) on sale for the fair value of the cash and other consideration received plus the fair value of retained servicing rights minus the fair value of retained liabilities plus the allocated carrying value of the other retained interests in the securitized assets minus the carrying value of the securitized assets at the time of securitization. As discussed below, sale accounting is necessary but not sufficient for the securitized assets and associated debt (i.e., asset-backed securities) to be off balance sheet for the transferor.

Under secured borrowing accounting, the transferor (*a*) continues to recognize the securitized assets, (*b*) recognizes the fair values of the cash and any other consideration received as additional assets, and (*c*) recognizes debt in the amount of the fair value of the cash and other consideration received as a liability. The debt essentially represents the asset-backed securities issued by the securitization vehicle. Securitizations accounted for as secured borrowings are on balance sheet for the transferors.

To attain off-balance-sheet treatment for securitizations accounted for as sales, the transferor must also not consolidate the securitization vehicle. Consolidation reverses the accounting for all intercompany transactions, including intercompany sales. Prior to 2010, FAS 140 specified three characteristics of special purpose entities—passive, with limited activities, and distinct from their transferors—necessary for the entities to be deemed QSPEs. FAS 140 exempted QSPEs from consolidation by their transferors, and FIN 46(R) further exempted QSPEs from consolidation by most other parties, such as their sponsors. Owing to this exemption, securitizations that met FAS 140's control conditions for sale accounting and for which the securitization vehicles were deemed QSPEs were off balance sheet for the transferors. This was the case for the vast majority of banks' securitizations prior to 2010.

For the few securitization vehicles that were not deemed QSPEs (e.g., multiseller asset-backed commercial paper conduits), FIN 46(R) governed the consolidation of the vehicles. FIN 46(R) required transferors or other parties to consolidate non-QSPE securitization vehicles if they bore more than 50% of the expected risks and rewards of the vehicles. To avoid consolidation of non-QSPE securitization vehicles, securitizing banks typically arranged for these vehicles to sell first-loss "expected loss notes" to risk-tolerant third parties such as hedge funds. The banks sized these notes just large enough to bear slightly more than 50% of variability of the unexpected gains and losses of the vehicles according to the banks' models, thereby avoiding consolidation of the vehicles. As a consequence primarily of securitization vehicles being determined to be QSPEs, and to a lesser extent of bright-line structuring of non-QSPE vehicles, prior to 2010 almost all these vehicles were not consolidated by the securitizing banks. Sale accounting and nonconsolidation together yield off-balance-sheet treatment and the recognition of gains on sales, both of which increase banks' regulatory capital adequacy. However, off-balance-sheet treatment was not necessary for asset-backed commercial paper conduits to receive favorable regulatory capital treatment, owing to the regulatory exclusion of these conduits (Acharya, Schnabl & Suarez 2013).

In my observation, knowledgeable accounting observers understood long before the crisis that securitization vehicles that transferors deemed to be QSPEs—i.e., passive, with limited activities, and distinct from the transferors—would be actively managed by their transferors or sponsors during severely adverse times, when these parties would have strong incentives to support their securitizations. This turned out be the case during the crisis and its aftermath, when banks contractually, voluntarily, or by court order provided liquidity or credit support to securitization vehicles or investors. Types of vehicles that frequently received voluntary support (referred to as implicit recourse) from banks include structured investment vehicles, asset-backed commercial paper conduits, and credit card master trusts.

The accounting for securitizations changed significantly in 2010, when FAS 166 and FAS 167 became effective. FAS 166 modestly restricts sale accounting for securitizations, primarily by making the effective control condition somewhat broader and less explicit and thus harder to meet. More importantly, FAS 166 and FAS 167 together eliminate QSPEs exempt from consolidation by transferors and most other parties, so all securitization vehicles are now evaluated for consolidation. FAS 167 significantly changed the criteria for consolidation of special purpose entities, requiring banks to consolidate entities over which they have "the power to direct the activities . . . that most significantly impact the entity's economic performance" and the "obligation to absorb losses of the entity that could potentially be significant." This significantly control-based and qualitative approach to variable interest entity consolidation contrasts with FIN 46(R)'s entirely risk-and-rewards-based and quantitative approach described above. In particular, under FAS 166 issuance of minimalistic expected loss notes to third parties no longer suffices to avoid consolidation of securitization vehicles. Bonsall et al. (2017) find that FAS 167 leads to other types of structuring, however, such as sale of controlling special servicing rights to third parties.

3. REGULATORY CAPITAL ADEQUACY AS THE CHANNEL BY WHICH ACCOUNTING REQUIREMENTS FOR BANKS AFFECT FINANCIAL STABILITY

In this section, I argue that in most settings banks' regulatory capital adequacy is not plausibly the primary channel by which accounting requirements for banks affect financial stability. The effects of alternative accounting approaches or alternative implementations of given accounting approaches on banks' regulatory capital adequacy are not large enough to drive banks' stability-related investment and financing decisions. This is particularly true in economic good times when banks' regulatory capital is far beyond the well-capitalized threshold.

I separately discuss the settings of loan loss reserving, fair value accounting, and securitization accounting, which have been subject to the criticisms described in Section 1. I describe stability-related accounting research on these settings. I discuss loan loss reserving in the most detail, because this setting has the largest and most pervasive effects on banks and has been subject to the most intensive and influential stability-related accounting research.

As discussed at length in Acharya & Ryan (2016) and so only briefly acknowledged here, all the research I describe must overcome various nontrivial problems of inference to provide credible evidence of causal links between accounting requirements for banks and financial stability. For example, it is necessary for this research to distinguish the effects of changes in these requirements over time or variation in the application of these requirements across banks from economic changes occurring around the same time and correlated bank characteristics, respectively. To illustrate, the crisis directly motivated the standards that changed securitization accounting discussed in Section 2.3. Hence, it is necessary to distinguish the effects of these standards from the effects of the crisis. Similarly, stronger and better-managed banks tend to make both better accounting choices and stability-enhancing decisions. Hence, it is necessary to distinguish the effects of accounting choices from the effects of bank characteristics that drive those choices.

3.1. Loan Loss Reserving

Loan loss reserves are by far the largest accounting accruals for most banks. Hence, if any accounting approach should have widespread and appreciable effects on banks' regulatory capital adequacy, it is the approach they use for loan loss reserving. All else being equal, timelier loan loss reserving reduces banks' cumulative net income and thus regulatory capital adequacy.

Extant research results suggest that this accounting-driven reduction of banks' regulatory capital adequacy leads banks to make economic decisions that enhance financial stability. In their seminal paper, Beatty & Liao (2011) distinguish banks that reserve on above- versus below-median timely bases for loan losses.[13] They measure the timeliness of quarterly loan loss provisions relative to quarterly changes in nonperforming loans, a commonly used proxy for loan performance, using a firm-level regression approach. Beatty & Liao (2011) show that banks that reserve on an above-median timely basis issue more capital during both nonrecession and recession periods than do banks that reserve on a below-median timely basis. Reflecting the enhanced financial strength resulting from these capital issuances, Beatty & Liao (2011) find that the more timely banks originate more loans during recessions than do the less timely banks. Additional lending by financially stronger banks during recessions should enhance stability.

One way to evaluate the extent to which regulatory capital adequacy could be the channel by which banks' loan loss provision timeliness affects financial stability is to calculate how much variation in regulatory capital adequacy results from variation in the measures of loan loss provision timeliness used in the extant literature. I make these calculations using the descriptive statistics in Bushman & Williams (2012), because these statistics are sufficiently complete to allow the calculations. I note, however, that this study examines variation in loan loss provision timeliness across countries, not individual banks, and so is not ideal for this purpose. Bushman & Williams (2012) measure loan loss provision timeliness in each country by regressing the annual loan loss provision divided by loans on the next year change in nonperforming loans divided by total assets and other variables for the pooled sample of banks in each country. A larger coefficient on the next year change in nonperforming loans indicates timelier loan loss provisioning. Statistics in Bushman & Williams (2012) imply that a one standard deviation increase in this coefficient (0.153), i.e., considerably timelier loan loss provisioning, times the mean of the change in nonperforming loans divided by assets (0.0007), yields only a $0.01\% = 0.153 \times 0.0007$ increment to the loan loss provision divided by loans. Moreover, a one standard deviation increase in the coefficient times a one standard deviation increase in next year's change in nonperforming loans divided by assets (0.0129), i.e., a sizable adverse change in loan performance, yields only a $0.2\% = 0.153 \times 0.0129$ increment to the loan loss provision divided by loans. These incremental provisions are too small to meaningfully reduce banks' regulatory capital adequacy. Moreover, these provisions cannot cumulate over time to yield much larger loan loss allowances. For any closed portfolio of loans, banks' loan loss reserves must reflect all loan defaults no later than the end of the life of the loan with the longest remaining life. This fact limits the incremental allowances for loans recorded by timelier banks.

Admittedly, the above calculations, which are based on regression coefficients that likely are attenuated and do not reflect within-country variation, probably are downward biased. However, cruder calculations indicate that even very large increases in banks' allowances for loan losses during economic good times—much larger than those that would plausibly result from alternative loan loss reserving approaches or from better application by individual banks of given reserving approaches—do not reduce banks' regulatory capital adequacy sufficiently to constrain their lending or induce them to issue capital during those times.[14] For example, in 2006, the last year prior to the crisis, the average ratio of equity to assets for US commercial bank holding companies was

[13] Beatty & Liao (2011) also conduct analysis and find similar results using a measure of the conservatism of banks' allowances for loan losses. For brevity, I discuss only their analysis using banks' loan loss provision timeliness.

[14] This statement may not hold for dynamic loan loss reserving, which uses "through the cycle" loss rates to reserve for loan losses. However, this approach raises other issues, and FASB and international standards setters have rejected it as inconsistent with accounting concepts (see Acharya & Ryan 2016, pp. 280–81, 289–90).

10.16%, indicating a banking system with approximately twice the regulatory capital necessary to be deemed well capitalized, and the average ratio of the loan loss allowance to assets was 0.71% (statistics from Lee & Rose 2010, table A.1). Doubling the loan loss allowance would have reduced the ratio of equity to assets by 0.71% $\times$ (1 – the marginal tax rate), or approximately 0.5%, which would have reduced the average ratio of equity to assets for these holding companies to a still extremely well-capitalized 9.66%. Moreover, this doubling of the loan loss allowance would have gone only a very small way toward reserving for the huge and persistent increase in net loan charge-offs that occurred from 2006 to the years of the crisis and its aftermath. For example, annualized and seasonally adjusted net loan charge-offs (divided by loans) were 0.49% in 2006 Q4 compared with 0.75% in 2007 Q4, 1.92% in 2008 Q4, 3.14% in 2009 Q4, 2.27% in 2010 Q4, 1.34% in 2011 Q4, and 0.92% in 2012 Q4 (statistics from Board Gov. Fed. Reserve Syst. 2017).[15] These statistics strongly suggest that the possibility of dramatic changes in banks' loan performance when economic conditions deteriorate, not modest differences in their regulatory capital adequacy during economic good times, primarily drives banks' stability-related investment and financing decisions.

At least three alternative channels plausibly explain the documented association between banks' loan loss provision timeliness and financial stability. First, better-managed banks reserve for loan losses on a timelier basis (this is a selection effect). Second, banks with information systems that provide them with timelier and more detailed information about loan losses better understand their risks. Third, banks that record timelier loan loss provisions are subject to greater discipline from markets and regulators.

3.2. Fair Value Accounting

In contrast to loan loss reserving, fair value accounting generally cannot have much effect on banks' regulatory capital adequacy, because banks do not hold many financial instruments that they account for at fair value. Their main asset (loans) and main liability (deposits) are recognized at amortized cost. For most banks, the only appreciable financial instrument recognized at fair value is available-for-sale debt securities. However, unrealized gains and losses on these securities are recorded in other comprehensive income and so, as discussed above, have little or no effect on banks' regulatory capital adequacy. Moreover, Xie (2016) shows that, because banks tend to hold very low credit risk debt securities, unrealized gains and losses on these securities tend to be driven by changes in near-riskless interest rates and are thus countercyclical. Even other-than-temporary impairment losses on these securities, which are more properly thought of as impairment accounting than as fair value accounting, were much smaller for banks than were their excess loan loss provisions during the crisis (Badertscher, Burks & Easton 2012, 2014).

3.3. Securitization Accounting

Relatively few, typically very large, banks directly engage in securitizations and so can be affected by securitization accounting requirements. For these few banks, however, on- rather than off-balance-sheet treatment moderately decreases regulatory capital adequacy. For example, Dou,

[15]Despite these sizeable loan charge-offs during the crisis and its aftermath, the vast majority of banks remained well capitalized, in part owing to capital infusions from parents and governmental sources. For example, "the share of assets at well-capitalized banks remained above 99 percent in 2007, although the average margin by which banks remained well capitalized slipped to 1.84 percent" (Bassett & King 2008, p. A12); "a large majority of banks remained well capitalized at year-end 2008" (Bech & Rice 2009, p. A63); and "all three regulatory capital ratios increased to record levels" during 2009 (Lee & Rose 2010, p. A19).

Ryan & Xie (2017) estimate that 27 publicly listed banks reported mostly newly consolidated securitization entities holding assets of $765 billion at the end of 2010, 5.3% of the US banking industry total assets. This increase corresponds to an average decrease in the leverage capital ratio of almost 0.5%, approximately the same magnitude as an (implausible) doubling of the loan loss allowance during economic good times and concentrated in relatively few securitizing banks. The most affected banks are those that securitize credit card receivables. Tian & Zhang (2016) estimate that consolidation of securitization reduced eight credit card securitizing banks' tier 1 risk-based capital by 2.49% in 2010.

4. BANKS' UNDERSTANDING AND TRANSPARENCY AS CHANNELS BY WHICH ACCOUNTING REQUIREMENTS FOR BANKS AFFECT FINANCIAL STABILITY

As discussed in Section 3.1 above, banks' net loan charge-offs during severe downturns such as the crisis generally far exceed the allowances for loan losses that they record in economic good times under FAS 5's incurred loss model. One way for banks to be prepared to absorb the losses during such downturns would be for them to issue more equity financing instruments, i.e., to deleverage, as urged by Admati & Hellwig (2013) and others. However, banks' virtually universal decisions to issue mostly debt financing instruments indicate that they believe it is too costly to prophylactically protect themselves by issuing sufficient equity in good times to see them through severe downturns. Accepting this belief as unlikely to change, I argue the most useful roles that accounting can play is to provide banks and the external parties that discipline them, e.g., market participants and bank regulators, with timelier information about banks' increasing risk of loss as downturns approach. Timelier information should enhance banks' ability and incentives to issue equity or sell assets on acceptable terms when cracks begin to appear in good times or at least before the depths of downturns arrive. After this time, these regulatory-capital-increasing options become considerably less attractive and perhaps even infeasible.

In this section, I provide support for this argument by summarizing three studies that examine the associations of the timeliness and other attributes of banks' loan loss reserving with the procyclicality or overall risk-management quality of their investment and financing decisions. This research shows that timelier loan loss provisions are associated with less procyclical and overall better investment and financing decisions by banks. In contrast, less informative loan loss provisions are associated with more procyclical and overall worse decisions by banks.

First, Bushman & Williams (2012) examine two attributes of banks' loan loss reserving: (*a*) the timeliness of annual loan loss provisions, measured relative to the next-year change in nonperforming loans, and (*b*) the use of annual loan loss provisions to smooth annual earnings, measured as a positive correlation between loan loss provisions and earnings before loan loss provisions. The first (second) attribute should render loan loss provisions more (less) informative. Bushman & Williams (2012) estimate these attributes at the country level for 27 different countries. They examine the associations of these loan loss reserving attributes with two measures of banks' risk-taking: (*a*) the change in financial leverage and (*b*) the change in the value of actuarially fair deposit insurance premia. Bushman & Williams (2012) hypothesize that banks with more informative loan loss provisions make better risk-management decisions, as indicated by more strongly offsetting changes in their underlying risk and their risk-taking, and vice versa. More strongly offsetting changes in these variables suggest banks more actively manage risks to stay within predetermined risk tolerances. To test these hypotheses, Bushman & Williams (2012) estimate how these country-level attributes of loan loss provisioning interactively influence the associations between a measure of the change in banks' underlying risk, the change in asset volatility, and the two measures of changes in bank's risk-taking. Bushman & Williams (2012) provide evidence that greater loan loss provision timeliness is associated with better risk-management decisions, whereas the use of loan loss provisions to smooth earnings is associated with worse risk-management decisions.

Second, and relatedly, Bushman & Williams (2015) examine the association of banks' loan loss provision timeliness with three measures of their systemic risk: (*a*) covariance of banks' illiquidity with banking industry illiquidity and market returns, (*b*) banks' downside tail risk, and (*c*) covariance of banks' downside tail risk with the banking industry downside tail risk. They find that banks with timelier loan loss provisions exhibit lower levels of all three systemic risk measures, again consistent with better risk management.

Third, Bhat, Ryan & Vyas (2017) examine the associations of financial-report-disclosure-based proxies for the extent of banks' credit risk modeling, which informs banks about their risk of loan losses, with banks' loan loss provision timeliness and loan origination procyclicality. They find that banks that more actively engage in credit risk modeling exhibit more timely loan loss provisions and less procyclical loan origination. Moreover, Bhat, Ryan & Vyas (2017) identify and examine two distinct types of credit risk modeling based on banks' financial report disclosures: (*a*) statistical analysis of the association of historical data on loan and borrower attributes, loan statuses, and other variables with the probability of default and loss given default on loans and (*b*) stress tests of future loan losses to unlikely adverse scenarios. They find that the effects of statistical credit risk modeling are particularly strong for homogeneous loans, for which banks reserve for loan losses at the loan-pool level using statistics, and in stable periods when credit loss parameters change gradually. They find that the effects of stress testing are strongest for heterogeneous loans, which typically default at much higher rates during downturns than during stable periods, and at sharp turns in economic cycles when credit loss parameters change rapidly.

The most natural interpretation of the findings of Bushman & Williams (2012, 2015) regarding banks' loan loss provision timeliness and of Bhat, Ryan & Vyas (2017) regarding banks' credit risk modeling is that more informative loan loss provisions alert banks, market participants, and regulators to changes in banks' risk. This allows and incentivizes banks to take appropriate actions to keep their risks within predetermined tolerances. In contrast, the most natural interpretation of the findings of Bushman & Williams (2012) regarding loan loss provisions that smooth earnings is that these provisions suppress the awareness of banks, market participants, and regulators about changes in banks' risk.

5. RESEARCH ON THE EFFECTS OF FAS 166 AND FAS 167

Based on logic and empirical evidence to date, the accounting for securitizations, including the consolidation of securitization entities, is the setting in which regulatory capital adequacy is most likely to be a significant channel linking accounting requirements for banks to financial stability. There are two primary bases for this statement. First, as discussed in Section 3.3, the reduction of regulatory capital adequacy from on- rather than off-balance-sheet treatment of securitizations is quite large for securitizing banks, particularly those that securitize credit card receivables. Moreover, securitizing banks tend to be very large and thus relatively likely to impose risk on the financial system. Second, despite the prominent financial statement presentation of on-balance-sheet loans and debt, it is not clear that securitizing banks, knowledgeable market participants, or regulators produce or are provided with much different information under the two accounting treatments. In particular, off-balance-sheet accounting is accompanied by extensive, albeit less prominent, standardized tabular disclosures in banks' financial and regulatory reports. These disclosures indicate the amounts and types of off-balance-sheet securitized loans, the principal amounts and credit quality of "managed" loans (i.e., off-balance-sheet securitized loans plus on-balance-sheet loans), and the risk of retained interests in the securitized assets (see FASB 2000, paragraph 17). Credit rating agencies indicate that they analytically treat off-balance-sheet securitizations in which securitizing or sponsoring banks provide recourse as on-balance-sheet securitizations (e.g., Standard & Poor's 2008, pp. 89–90). These facts should limit differences in securitizing banks' understanding and in market and regulatory discipline resulting from on- versus off-balance-sheet treatment of securitizations.

Dou (2017); Dou, Ryan & Xie (2017); and Tian & Zhang (2016) provide evidence about the effects of expanded on-balance-sheet treatment of securitizations under FAS 166 and FAS 167 on banks' loan originations, loan sales, and other decisions. These studies are motivated in significant part or whole by the decrease in securitizing banks' regulatory capital adequacy that results from on- rather than off-balance-sheet treatment of securitized loans. All three studies find that on-balance-sheet treatment is associated with risk-reducing decisions by securitizing banks and that these findings are stronger for banks with lower regulatory capital. The studies conclude that banks' regulatory capital adequacy is a significant channel linking banks' accounting for securitizations to financial stability. As discussed below, Dou (2017) and Dou, Ryan & Xie (2017) also provide evidence that on-balance-sheet treatment has stronger effects when market discipline is higher.

The studies collectively exhibit four research design features that enhance confidence in that conclusion. First, the studies examine various types of loans, some of which are frequently securitized (e.g., mortgages and credit card receivables) and some of which are not (e.g., small business loans). Second, the studies that examine frequently securitized loan types distinguish types that typically receive on-balance-sheet treatment under FAS 166 and FAS 167 (e.g., credit card receivables) versus types that typically receive off-balance-sheet treatment under the standards (e.g., mortgages). Third, the second feature enables the studies to employ difference-in-differences research designs that control for changes in economic conditions affecting securitizations, thereby isolating the differential effects of on- versus off-balance-sheet treatment of securitized loans. Such control is critical given the close proximity of the end of the crisis in 2009 Q2 to the 2010 effective date of FAS 166 and FAS 167. Fourth, the studies employ falsification tests, cross-sectional partitions, and other research design features that further enhance confidence that the results are not attributable to contemporaneous changes in economic conditions, omitted bank characteristics, or other correlated omitted variables.

Dou (2017) examines the differential origination of small business loans, which are rarely securitized, by matched samples of 43 treatment banks that are affected by FAS 166 and FAS 167 and control banks that are not affected by the standards but that originate small business loans in the same county. He includes county-year fixed effects in his empirical models. These research design features yield a high degree of control for local loan demand and economic conditions. Dou (2017) provides evidence that, in 2010 and subsequent years, but not before (based on falsification tests), the treatment banks exhibit significantly lower small business lending than the matched control banks. He finds that this result is stronger for the treatment banks with lower regulatory capital adequacy. He also finds that this result is stronger for the treatment banks with more uninsured deposits, a proxy for market discipline. Lastly, Dou (2017) finds that counties with higher proportions of banks affected by the standards reduce small business lending compared with counties with lower proportions of affected banks. Hence, the reduction of local loan supply by affected banks is not fully offset by increased supply by unaffected banks.

Using a difference-in-differences research design, Dou, Ryan & Xie (2017) examine the differential associations of 33 banks' on-balance-sheet securitized loans under FAS 166 and FAS 167 versus all securitizing banks' off-balance-sheet securitized loans under those and prior standards on banks' loan-level mortgage loan origination and sale decisions. The study exploits the availability of loan-level loan application, loan origination, and loan sale data from the Home

Mortgage Disclosure Act database (**https://www.ffiec.gov/hmda/**). These data enable potential borrowers' expressed loan demand (i.e., applications) to be distinguished from banks' loan supply satisfying that demand (i.e., originations). In contrast, most other studies examine loan growth, which reflects both loan demand and loan supply. Dou, Ryan & Xie (2017) provide evidence that in 2010 and subsequent years, but not before (based on falsification tests), banks with greater on-balance-sheet treatment of securitized (almost entirely nonmortgage) loans under FAS 166 and FAS 167 exhibit reduced mortgage supply and increased mortgage sales, both of which work to increase the affected banks' regulatory capital adequacy. Similar to Dou (2017), Dou, Ryan & Xie (2017) further find that their results are stronger for banks with lower regulatory capital adequacy and with higher uninsured short-term funding.

Tian & Zhang (2016) examine eight treatment banks that securitize credit card receivables and nine control banks that hold but do not securitize these receivables. Credit card receivables are a loan type that is frequently securitized, and these receivables are the only significant loan type for which securitized loans typically receive on-balance-sheet treatment under FAS 166 and FAS 167 and off-balance-sheet treatment under prior GAAP.[16] Using a difference-in-differences research design, they examine managed credit card receivable growth and credit quality for the securitizing banks affected by FAS 166 and FAS 167 versus the nonsecuritizing banks unaffected by the standards. Tian & Zhang (2016) provide evidence that the securitizing banks exhibit significantly higher managed credit card receivable growth in the period prior to the effective date of FAS 166 and FAS 167 and a significantly larger (and close to offsetting) reduction of managed credit card receivable growth after that date. They further provide evidence that the credit quality of securitizing banks' managed credit card receivables increased after the adoption of the standards. Similar to Dou (2017) and Dou, Ryan & Xie (2017), Tian & Zhang (2016) further find stronger results for securitizing banks with lower regulatory capital adequacy.

In summary, the results of all three studies are consistent with banks' regulatory capital adequacy being a significant channel by which securitizing banks' increased on-balance-sheet treatment of securitizations under FAS 166 and FAS 167 affects banks' decision making regarding loan origination, loan sale, and loan quality. However, the treatment banks generally remain very well capitalized even with on-balance-sheet accounting for securitized loans, although it is possible that their reported capital exceeds their economic capital owing to other limitations of their accounting, e.g., their minimal use of fair value accounting. Moreover, these typically large banks should be sophisticated enough to anticipate the average effects of accounting requirements across the cycle, and so make appropriate investment and financing decisions. Hence, it remains a puzzle why securitizing banks' regulatory capital adequacy would drive the banks' stability-related decisions.

A plausible alternative explanation for the results of these and other studies is that the banks care about their regulatory capital adequacy less because they are concerned with violating capital requirements, and more because they believe, perhaps incorrectly, that regulatory capital adequacy affects how market participants and regulators perceive them. The findings of Dou (2017) and Dou, Ryan & Xie (2017) that the effect of on-balance-sheet treatment of securitizations is stronger when market discipline is higher are consistent with this alternative explanation. I encourage future researchers to consider how to disentangle these explanations.

[16]Some credit card securitizing banks provided implicit recourse to their credit card master trusts during the financial crisis, typically to avoid triggering early amortization of the securitizations. This provision of implicit recourse led the banks to consolidate the trusts at the time of the provision of implicit recourse under prior GAAP. For example, JPMorgan Chase did this for its (recently acquired) Washington Mutual trust in 2009 Q2.

6. CONCLUSION

During the crisis, various parties criticized the incurred loss model, fair value accounting, and securitization accounting as undermining financial stability because of their effects on banks' regulatory capital adequacy. In this article, I evaluate the logical and evidential merits of these criticisms. I conclude that the effects of the incurred loss model and especially of fair value accounting on banks' regulatory capital adequacy are too small to be the primary driver of banks' stability-related decisions. This is despite the fact that a body of prior research beginning with Beatty & Liao (2011) consistently shows that banks that record timelier loan loss reserves tend to make decisions that favorably affect stability and that these associations are stronger in settings where banks' regulatory capital is more likely to be constrained. (In contrast, most extant research finds little or no association between banks' use of fair value accounting and their stability-related decisions.) I propose that the primary channels operating in these settings are that timelier loan loss provisioning results from (better) banks better modeling their individual and aggregate risk exposures and that fair value accounting requires such modeling of banks. Hence, banks' internal, market, and regulatory discipline increase with timelier loan loss provisioning and fair value accounting.

In contrast, I conclude that the effects of securitization accounting on securitizing banks' regulatory capital adequacy are large enough to affect these banks' stability-related decisions. I conclude that the internal, market, and regulatory discipline channels are less in operation owing to extensive required financial and regulatory report disclosures by banks about their securitizations accounted for as sales. Even in the securitization accounting setting, however, banks' regulatory capital adequacy does not appear to be the complete story. Securitizing banks typically remain well capitalized even with on-balance-sheet treatment for securitization. Dou (2017) and Dou, Ryan & Xie (2017) provide evidence that the effect of on-balance-sheet treatment is stronger when market discipline is higher, consistent with the market discipline channel also operating.

I caveat these conclusions with the following issue about which I have not yet been able to formulate an opinion, and which I believe merits considerable thought and research. The combination of (*a*) the 2014 implementation of Basel III in the United States for the typically very large banks following Basel III's advanced approaches and (*b*) the similarly timed implementation of the Dodd-Frank Act requirements for systematically important financial institutions has recently created numerous more onerous regulatory capital and liquidity requirements for affected banks. Though I tend to doubt that any single requirement is a major constraint on these banks, it is plausible and perhaps even likely that these requirements collectively are constraints or will become so in an economic downturn. Regardless, these requirements became effective well after the crisis had eased and the time frames of the research described in this paper, in particular, 2010, for the changes in securitization accounting.

DISCLOSURE STATEMENT

The author is not aware of any affiliations, memberships, funding, or financial holdings that might be perceived as affecting the objectivity of this review.

ACKNOWLEDGMENTS

I am grateful to Deborah Lucas (reviewing editor), Anne Beatty (discussant), Yiwei Dou, Xi Wu, Biqin Xie, and Chenqi Zhu for useful comments.

LITERATURE CITED

Acharya V, Ryan S. 2016. Banks' financial reporting and financial system stability. *J. Account. Res.* 54:277–340

Acharya V, Schnabl P, Suarez G. 2013. Securitization without risk transfer. *J. Financ. Econ.* 107:515–36

Admati A, Hellwig M. 2013. *The Bankers' New Clothes: What's Wrong with Banking and What To Do about It.* Princeton, NJ: Princeton Univ. Press

Am. Account. Assoc. Financ. Account. Stand. Comm. 2007. Response to FASB exposure draft, "The Fair Value Option for Financial Assets and Financial Liabilities, Including an Amendment of FASB Statement No. 115." *Account. Horiz.* 21(2):189–200

Badertscher B, Burks J, Easton P. 2012. A convenient scapegoat: fair value accounting by commercial banks during the financial crisis. *Account. Rev.* 87:59–90

Badertscher B, Burks J, Easton P. 2014. The market pricing of other-than-temporary impairments. *Account. Rev.* 89:811–38

Barth M, Hodder L, Stubben S. 2008. Fair value accounting for liabilities and own credit risk. *Account. Rev.* 83(3):629–64

Bassett W, King T. 2008. Profits and balance sheet developments at U.S. commercial banks in 2007. *Fed. Res. Bull.* 94:A1–39

Beatty A, Liao S. 2011. Do delays in expected loss recognition affect banks' willingness to lend? *J. Account. Econ.* 52:1–20

Bech M, Rice T. 2009. Profits and balance sheet developments at U.S. commercial banks in 2008. *Fed. Res. Bull.* 95:A57–97

Berger A, Udell G. 2002. Small business credit availability and relationship lending: the importance of bank ownership structure. *Econ. J.* 112(477):F32–53

Bhat G, Ryan S, Vyas D. 2017. *The implications of credit risk modeling for banks' loan loss provisions and loan origination procyclicality.* Work. Pap., New York Univ., New York

Board Gov. Fed. Reserve Syst. 2017. *Charge-off and delinquency rates on loans and leases at commercial banks.* Stat. Release, US Fed. Reserve, May 17. **https://www.federalreserve.gov/releases/chargeoff/**

Bonsall S, Bozanic Z, Dou Y, Richardson G, Vyas D. 2017. *Have FAS 166 and FAS 167 improved the financial reporting for securitizations?* Work. Pap., Ohio State Univ., Columbus

Bushman R, Williams C. 2012. Accounting discretion, loan loss provisioning, and discipline of banks' risk-taking. *J. Account. Econ.* 54:1–18

Bushman R, Williams C. 2015. Delayed expected loss recognition and the risk profile of banks. *J. Account. Res.* 53:511–53

Dou Y. 2017. *The spillover effects of consolidating securitization entities on small business lending.* Work. Pap., New York Univ., New York

Dou Y, Ryan S, Xie B. 2017. *The real effects of FAS 166/167 on banks' mortgage approval and sale decisions.* Work. Pap., Penn. State Univ., University Park

Dugan J. 2009. *Loan loss provisioning and pro-cyclicality.* Remarks before the Inst. Int. Bank., Mar. 2, New York

FASB (Financ. Account. Stand. Board). 1975. *Accounting for contingencies.* Statement Financ. Account. Stand. 5, FASB, Norwalk, CT

FASB (Financ. Account. Stand. Board). 1993. *Accounting for certain investments in debt and equity securities.* Statement Financ. Account. Stand. 115, FASB, Norwalk, CT

FASB (Financ. Account. Stand. Board). 1999. *Preliminary views on major issues related to reporting financial instruments and certain related assets and liabilities at fair value.* Dec. Statement, FASB, Norwalk, CT

FASB (Financ. Account. Stand. Board). 2000. *Accounting for transfers and servicing of financial assets and extinguishments of liabilities: a replacement of FASB statement no. 125.* Financ. Account. Stand. 140, FASB, Norwalk, CT

FASB (Financ. Account. Stand. Board). 2003. *Consolidation of variable interest entities (revised December 2003)—an interpretation of ARB no. 51.* FASB Interpret. 46(R), FASB, Norwalk, CT

FASB (Financ. Account. Stand. Board). 2006. *Fair value measurements.* Statement Financ. Account. Stand. 157, FASB, Norwalk, CT

FASB (Financ. Account. Stand. Board). 2007. *The fair value option for financial assets and financial liabilities—including an amendment of FASB statement no. 115.* Statement Financ. Account. Stand. 159, FASB, Norwalk, CT

FASB (Financ. Account. Stand. Board). 2008. *Determining the fair value of a financial asset when the market for that asset is not active.* FASB Staff Position FAS 157-3, FASB, Norwalk, CT

FASB (Financ. Account. Stand. Board). 2009a. *Accounting for transfers of financial assets—an amendment of FASB statement no. 140.* Statement Financ. Account. Stand. 166, FASB, Norwalk, CT

FASB (Financ. Account. Stand. Board). 2009b. *Amendments to FASB interpretation no. 46(R).* Statement Financ. Account. Stand. 167, FASB, Norwalk, CT

FASB (Financ. Account. Stand. Board). 2009c. *Determining fair value when the volume and level of activity for the asset or liability have significantly decreased and identifying transactions that are not orderly.* FASB Staff Position FAS 157-4, FASB, Norwalk, CT

FASB (Financ. Account. Stand. Board). 2009d. *Recognition and presentation of other-than-temporary impairments.* FASB Staff Position FAS 115-2 and FAS 124-2, FASB, Norwalk, CT

FASB (Financ. Account. Stand. Board). 2016a. *Financial instruments—credit losses (Topic 326): measurement of credit losses on financial instruments.* Account. Stand. Update 2016-13, FASB, Norwalk, CT

FASB (Financ. Account. Stand. Board). 2016b. *Financial instruments—overall (Subtopic 825-10).* Account. Stand. Update 2016-01, FASB, Norwalk, CT

Int. Monet. Fund. 2008. *Containing systemic risks and restoring financial soundness.* Glob. Financ. Stab. Rep., Apr., World Econ. Financ. Surv., Washington, DC

Johnson S. 2008a. How far can fair value go? *CFO.com*, May 6

Johnson S. 2008b. The fair-value blame game. *CFO.com*, Mar. 19

Lee S, Rose J. 2010. Profits and balance sheet developments at U.S. commercial banks in 2009. *Fed. Res. Bull.* 96:A1–37

Reed J. 2008. *How assets held off of the balance sheet contributed to the securitization of risky assets.* Chairm. Open. Statement, US Senate Comm. Bank. Hous. Urban Aff., Sept. 18, Washington, DC

Rummell N. 2008. Fair-value rules get more blame for crunch. *Financial Week*, Mar. 24.

Ryan S. 2007. *Financial Instruments and Institutions: Accounting and Disclosure Rules.* Hoboken, NJ: John Wiley & Sons. 2nd ed.

Ryan S. 2011. Financial reporting for financial instruments. *Found. Trends Account.* 6:187–354

Standard & Poor's. 2008. RatingsDirect, corporate ratings criteria 2008. *S&P Global Ratings*, Apr. 15. **https://www.standardandpoors.com/en_US/web/guest/ratings/ratings-criteria/-/articles/criteria/requests-for-comment/filter/all**

The Economist. 2008. All's fair. *The Economist*, Sept. 18. **http://www.economist.com/node/12274096**

Tian X, Zhang H. 2016. *Impact of FAS 166/167 on credit card securitization.* Work. Pap., Ohio State Univ., Columbus

Udell G. 1989. Loan quality, commercial loan review and loan officer contracting. *J. Bank. Finance* 13(3):367–82

Xie B. 2016. Does fair value accounting exacerbate the pro-cyclicality of bank lending? *J. Account. Res.* 54:235–74

What to Do About the GSEs?

Matthew P. Richardson,[1,2] Stijn Van Nieuwerburgh,[1,2] and Lawrence J. White[1]

[1] Stern School of Business, New York University, New York, NY 10012; email: mrichar0@stern.nyu.edu

[2] National Bureau of Economic Research, Cambridge, Massachusetts 02138

Annu. Rev. Financ. Econ. 2017. 9:21–41

First published as a Review in Advance on September 20, 2017

The *Annual Review of Financial Economics* is online at financial.annualreviews.org

https://doi.org/10.1146/annurev-financial-121415-033047

Copyright © 2017 by Annual Reviews. All rights reserved

JEL codes: G21, G23, G28

Keywords

Fannie Mae, Freddie Mac, government-sponsored enterprises, mortgages, mortgage-backed securities, secondary mortgage markets, residential mortgage finance, housing finance reform

Abstract

Fannie Mae and Freddie Mac, the two large government-sponsored enterprises (GSEs) that are at the center of US residential mortgage finance, are "elephants in the room" that are being ignored as part of broad-brush financial sector reform. Neither the Dodd–Frank Act nor recently proposed overhauls of Dodd–Frank have addressed reform of the GSEs' structures, although the GSEs were placed in government conservatorships in early September 2008 and have remained in that state since then. In this article, we review what the GSEs do and how they got themselves into financial difficulties, and we provide an overview of some of the major proposals for reforming the US residential mortgage finance system. We conclude with our own ideas and suggestions for how housing finance, as well as housing policy more generally, should be reformed.

1. INTRODUCTION

Fannie Mae and Freddie Mac, the two large government-sponsored enterprises (GSEs) that are at the center of US residential mortgage finance,[1] are "elephants in the room" that are being ignored as part of broad-brush financial sector reform. Neither the Dodd–Frank Act nor recently proposed overhauls of Dodd–Frank, such as the House Republicans' Financial CHOICE Act, have addressed reform of the GSEs' structures, although the GSEs were placed in government conservatorships in early September 2008 and have remained in that state since then.

Nevertheless, as we argue in this article, reform of the GSEs is essential for a more efficient housing finance system. Accordingly, there are two central issues for financial reform with respect to the GSEs: first, the immediate issue of what should be done about the GSEs; and second, larger questions of how residential mortgages should be financed and how US public policy toward housing finance and toward housing in general should be structured.

2. WHAT THE GSES DO

Fannie Mae and Freddie Mac are large financial institutions that operate in the secondary mortgage market (for details, see Frame & White 2005, Acharya et al. 2011b; see also Jaffee et al. 2009, Acharya et al. 2011a). They buy residential mortgages[2] from mortgage originators, i.e., from banks (meaning commercial banks and other depository institutions, such as savings institutions and credit unions, unless otherwise indicated) and mortgage companies (sometimes called mortgage banks, these are companies that originate mortgages and immediately sell them in the secondary market), and bundle the mortgages into mortgage-backed securities (MBSs) that are sold in the capital markets; the MBSs can be structured as simple pass-through securities, or they can take more complex forms. These MBSs carry the GSEs' guarantees to MBS investors against losses resulting from credit risks on the underlying mortgages.[3] The GSEs charge a small fee to the mortgage originators for this guarantee and, at least in the past, were required to hold \$0.45 of capital for every \$100 of mortgage face value guaranteed.

In addition, both banks and the GSEs keep some of the mortgages on their own balance sheets, financing these retained mortgages with deposits (for banks) and debt (for the GSEs).[4] During the financial crisis, banks and GSEs purchased large amounts of both prime and nonprime (Alt-A and subprime) MBSs. Whereas the GSEs were required to hold just \$2.50 in capital for every \$100, banks were required to hold an even smaller amount, \$1.60, if the MBSs were guaranteed by the

[1]There is one additional large GSE, the Federal Home Loan Bank System (FHLBS), that we do not address. The FHLBS is a group of 11 large wholesale banks that collectively borrow in the capital markets and provide wholesale financing for banks and other depository institutions. As of year-end 2015, the FHLBS had \$969 billion in assets. Any legislative reform of Fannie Mae and Freddie Mac would likely—and should—include reform of the FHLBS. More detail on the FHLBS is provided by Frame & White (2011). We use the term GSEs to refer only to Fannie Mae and Freddie Mac, except where otherwise indicated.

[2]The mortgages that they buy must conform to specified standards and are thus described as conforming loans: There are limits on the size of the mortgage that can be bought, and the mortgage borrowers are expected to make a 20% down payment (unless they obtain private mortgage insurance or there is some other support for the mortgage) and to have credit scores that make them good credit risks.

[3]The GSEs charge an annual guarantee fee (g-fee) for that credit-risk guarantee. For a discussion of the mispricing of the GSEs' guarantees, see, for example, Lucas & McDonald (2006, 2010). Elenev, Landvoigt & Van Nieuwerburgh (2016) argue that an increase in g-fees would crowd in the private sector and lead to a system with a less fragile financial system and with fewer but safer mortgage loans and less leverage in the financial sector.

[4]The GSEs financed these asset purchases by issuing debt (so-called agency debt). Because of the implicit government guarantee (which has now become an explicit guarantee), the GSEs are able to borrow at below-market interest rates, i.e., rates below those that an otherwise similar company (but without the guarantee) would have to pay.

GSEs. Coupled with the aforementioned \$0.45 capital requirement for GSE guarantees, the total capital required in the system was then a paltry \$2.05. This is approximately half of the \$4.00 per \$100 of mortgage assets that banks were required to hold on their balance sheets for the exact same mortgage loans without involvement of the GSEs.

With both the implicit guarantee of the US Government (resulting in a below-market cost for debt financing; see, e.g., Ambrose & Warga 2002) and favorable capital requirements, the GSEs grew rapidly for decades. From the last major GSE legislation in 1992, for example, Fannie Mae and Freddie Mac combined went from holding \$153 billion in mortgages and guaranteeing the credit risk of another \$714 billion to holding \$1.4 trillion and guaranteeing \$3.5 trillion, respectively, by the end of 2007.

The GSEs still play a major role in housing finance. During 2016, the GSEs' mortgage purchases accounted for 45.9% of all single-family mortgage originations; their outstanding MBS guarantees accounted for 59.2% of all single-family residential mortgages.[5]

To understand their outsize importance, note that the GSEs are hybrid organizations. They each have corporate structures, with private shareholders and boards of directors. But their charters come from congressional legislation (and not, for example, from the state of Delaware, where many large corporations are chartered); the President had the power to appoint 5 of the 18 directors on their respective boards; and they have had special access to US Treasury financing and other special government-related privileges. This is why they are described as government-sponsored.

The problem with the GSEs is that capital markets have always treated them as special, with the strong expectation that the Federal Government would support their creditors if the GSEs had financial difficulties; thus, as mentioned above, the GSEs have been able to finance themselves at a lower cost than their financial structures would otherwise have warranted. In return for this special status, the GSEs' charters call for them to maintain liquidity in the mortgage markets and ensure access to the mortgage markets by borrowers. Since 1992, the GSEs have been expected to meet various housing affordability targets.

2.1. The Conservatorships

Although the GSEs initially operated conservatively (at least, with respect to credit risk; concerning the substantial questions as to their exposure to interest rate risk, see, e.g., Jaffee 2003) and profitably, this discipline broke down in the early 2000s: The private-label (i.e., non-GSE) MBS (PLMBS) sector grew rapidly, and, to protect their market shares, the GSEs expanded their operations into buying and securitizing riskier mortgages. However, the aforementioned levels of equity financing that they were required to maintain—only 0.45% against their MBS credit-risk guarantees and 2.5% against the mortgages that they held on their balance sheets—were not sufficient to protect them against the potential credit losses of these riskier mortgages.

The GSEs' profitability fell in 2006, and they ran losses in 2007 and the first half of 2008. By late summer 2008, they were approaching insolvency, and on September 6, 2008, they were placed into government conservatorships. [The conservatorships were authorized by Congress through the Housing and Economic Recovery Act (HERA) of 2008. The conservatorship decision and

[5]The GSEs also operate in the secondary mortgage market for multifamily housing, but that is a far less important part of their operations; the mortgage market for multifamily housing is about one-tenth the size of the single-family mortgage market. In addition to the GSEs, Ginnie Mae (which is an agency within the US Department of Housing and Urban Development) securitizes mortgages that are insured by the Federal Housing Administration (FHA), the Department of Veterans Affairs (VA), and the Department of Agriculture. Banks also hold some residential mortgages—typically those that exceed the conforming loan value limit and/or that do not meet the documentation or other criteria of the GSEs—on their own balance sheets.

processes are discussed by Frame et al. 2015; see also Sorkin 2009, Paulson 2010, Morgenson & Rosner 2011, Hagerty 2012, Howard 2014, and McLean 2015.] In essence, they were placed under the direct control of their regulator, the Federal Housing Finance Agency (FHFA), where they remain today. As their majority shareholder, the Department of the Treasury also exerts substantial control over the functioning of the GSEs.[6]

The capital markets' expectations that the GSEs' creditors would remain whole in the event of financial difficulties proved to be accurate: The direct creditors (bondholders) to the GSEs, including subordinated debt holders, have not suffered losses as a consequence of the conservatorships, and the GSEs' guarantees to their MBS investors have been honored as well.

2.2. Important Changes During the Conservatorships

Prior to the conservatorships, the GSEs' critics worried that their on-balance-sheet holdings of mortgages had ballooned because of their favorable financing from the capital markets (resulting from their GSE status) and because their equity financing requirement for these mortgages was only 2.5%. In essence, they worried that the GSEs had become very large, highly leveraged, and (possibly) maturity-mismatched hedge funds for the benefit of their shareholders. Subsequent to the conservatorship, there was the realization that their credit-risk guarantees on their MBSs also posed a risk to the Federal Government, again because of the GSEs' special status and the belief of the capital markets that the Federal Government would cover the GSEs' losses at a time of financial difficulties, as had actually happened in 2008 and would likely happen again.

The FHFA has taken actions, authorized by the HERA, to address both of these concerns. First, the size of the GSEs' balance sheets has shrunk. Whereas, at year-end 2008 (shortly after the onset of the conservatorships), Fannie Mae had on-balance-sheet mortgage holdings of $768 billion and Freddie Mac had on-balance-sheet mortgage holdings of $749 billion, as of the first quarter of 2017, their on-balance-sheet mortgage holdings were $268 billion and $291 billion, respectively.

Second, the GSEs have been reducing the credit risks on the mortgages that they own and have guaranteed through two mechanisms: (*a*) They have been buying insurance against credit losses on the mortgages, and (*b*) they have issued the rough equivalent of catastrophe bonds, whereby the bond buyer is repaid less principal in the event of credit losses on the underlying mortgages. (For further discussion of these risk reduction processes, see FHFA 2016; for the most recent numbers, see Urban Inst. 2017.) In essence, the GSEs have privatized some credit risks through these front-end (insurance) and back-end [credit risk transfer (CRT)] transactions. As of May 2017, the risks on 29% of Fannie Mae's guarantees and 42% of Freddie Mac's guarantees have been privatized in this way. In addition, the annual guarantee fees on the GSEs' MBSs, which had been in the range of 20–25 basis points, have more than doubled to 50–60 basis points. In conjunction with the privatization of some of the GSEs' risks (which, as we discuss below, we strongly endorse), these higher g-fees have meant that the GSEs may currently be earning more in compensation for default risk than they have been paying for insurance and paying to investors in catastrophe bonds.[7]

[6]Upon conservatorship, common equity shareholders were wiped out and preferred shareholders were diluted—with the US Treasury acquiring a 79.9% ownership—but not eliminated. The preferred shareholders, which are now largely hedge funds and private equity funds, are currently suing the Federal Government over the legality of the continued conservatorships and the Treasury's absorption of all of the current operating profits of the GSEs.

[7]A back-of-the-envelope calculation on the first Fannie Mae and Freddie Mac CRT deals from 2013 by Goodman (2014) reveals that the CRT bond yields imply a guarantee fee below 40 basis points, whereas the GSEs charged a 60-basis-point guarantee fee on the loans in this vintage. These calculations ignore that the government continues to bear the catastrophic

3. LITERATURE REVIEW

The collapse of the GSEs and the ensuing discussion on the redesign of the US housing finance system have prompted a growing academic literature. Several recent papers study the effects of a policy that would abolish the GSEs. Because of the large role the GSEs play in the overall mortgage and housing markets, such a counterfactual analysis requires a general equilibrium model. In addition to exploring the effects on house prices, mortgage credit provision, and mortgage interest rates, these studies emphasize the distributional implications of a GSE phaseout.

Jeske, Krueger & Mitman (2013) analyze mortgage guarantees in a model with heterogeneous agents and idiosyncratic risk. They model the GSEs as enjoying a funding subsidy that lowers the cost of mortgage credit to all households. They conclude that eliminating the mortgage default guarantees provided by the GSEs is a progressive policy that would hurt high-income, high-wealth households the most. After all, these households buy larger houses with larger mortgages and receive greater subsidies. Abolishing the GSEs reduces overall mortgage origination in the authors' model. The policy increases aggregate welfare by 0.5% in consumption equivalence units. The welfare gain arises from a reduced fiscal burden once the GSE subsidy no longer needs to be financed by taxpayers. Eliminating the GSEs reduces wealth inequality.

Gete & Zecchetto (2017) use a similar framework but instead model the GSEs as a credit risk subsidy. The risk of the borrower, rather than the size of the mortgage, determines the size of the subsidy. Low-income mortgage borrowers receive the largest GSE subsidies because they have the largest default risk. The distributional implications reverse: Poor, high-risk borrowers are hurt most by the elimination of the GSEs. The higher cost of mortgage credit for low-income households increases wealth inequality. Higher mortgage payments reduce these households' ability to accumulate wealth. Equilibrium safe interest rates fall to discourage the supply of savings in the wake of the fall in demand for mortgage credit. This further hampers the accumulation of wealth, especially for renters. The elimination of the GSEs reduces the home ownership rate. The equilibrium price of housing falls while rents rise. The higher rents and lower interest rates hurt poor renters. Rich households shift wealth from safe assets to housing, as the returns to becoming a landlord have increased. In this model, the majority of households oppose the removal of the GSEs, which may explain the observed resistance to change.

Elenev, Landvoigt & Van Nieuwerburgh (2016) emphasize the effect of the underpriced government mortgage guarantee on the fragility of the mortgage banking sector. They study a general equilibrium model with aggregate shocks and an explicit role for the financial sector, but without heterogeneity among borrowers or rental markets. Their model features borrowers, depositors, bankers, and a government that, in addition to subsidizing mortgage credit risk, provides a bailout guarantee to the banks. Phasing out the GSEs is modeled as an increase in the g-fee that banks have to pay the government in return for the mortgage guarantee. Raising the cost of the insurance induces banks to reduce their purchases of the guarantee. As the private sector is crowded in, the cost of mortgage credit starts to accurately reflect the default risk. Banks make fewer and less risky loans. Equilibrium mortgage defaults are lower, as are the associated deadweight losses. The reduction in foreclosure risk lowers the fragility of the banking system and reduces macroeconomic risk (aggregate consumption growth volatility). Risk-free interest rates go up, which is consistent with a weakened precautionary savings motive. The overall effect of phasing out the GSEs is a

default risk. Also, it may be prudent to build up some reserves in good times for future states of the world in which private CRT investors demand much higher compensation for bearing mortgage default risk.

reduction in house prices, a reduction in mortgage credit outstanding, a small reduction in the mortgage interest rate, and similarly stable mortgage credit provision as under the status quo. There is an increase in economy-wide welfare of 0.63% in consumption equivalence units. Borrower welfare increases only marginally (+0.04%), whereas depositors (+1.30%) and intermediaries (+1.69%) gain substantially. Although this is a Kaldor–Hicks potential Pareto improvement, the abolition of the GSEs would increase wealth inequality. Allen et al. (2017) also study the moral hazard implications of government guarantees in a model with bank runs.

A closely related literature quantifies the effect of the mortgage interest rate deduction (MID) with respect to personal income taxes and the tax exemption of imputed rental income of owner-occupied housing. Examples include the work of Gervais (2002); Chambers, Garriga & Schlagenhauf (2009b, 2014); Floetotto, Kirker & Stroebel (2016); and Sommer & Sullivan (2016). When house and rental prices are determined endogenously, abolishing the MID lowers house prices and price–rent ratios. This would cause an increase in home ownership rates. This literature generally finds that abolishing the favorable tax treatment of owner-occupied housing is good for society. The reduced tax expenditures allow for a reduction in distortionary labor income taxation, which increases economic output.

Although the GSEs adjust the g-fee for differences in borrower characteristics, such as loan-to-value (LTV) ratio, debt-to-income (DTI) ratio, and FICO score, they do not account for regional variation in labor income or unemployment risk. Hurst et al. (2016) focus on the redistributive implications of this policy. Exploiting discontinuities around the conforming loan limit, they provide empirical evidence that borrowers in regions with below-average default risk pay higher mortgage rates, which cross-subsidizes borrowers in regions with above-average default risk. The fiscal implications of this policy are on the same order of magnitude as the Bush tax cuts in 2008.

Fieldhouse & Mertens (2017a) use a narrative approach to identify regulatory shocks to the supply of mortgage credit, similar to approaches used to classify monetary and fiscal policy shocks. These shocks pick up changes in GSE policies and other housing policy changes, whose effects on the rest of the macroeconomy are studied by Fieldhouse & Mertens (2017b).

This literature fits in a broader literature that explores the causes and consequences of the housing boom and bust. Examples of quantitative papers include those of Chambers, Garriga & Schlagenhauf (2009a); Arslan, Guler & Taskin (2015); Chatterjee & Eyigungor (2015); Corbae & Quintin (2015); Landvoigt, Piazzesi & Schneider (2015); Hedlund (2016); Kaplan, Mitman & Violante (2016); Favilukis, Ludvigson & Van Nieuwerburgh (2017); and Landvoigt (2017). For a recent review of this literature, see Davis & Van Nieuwerburgh (2015). Greenwald (2016) and Elenev (2016) investigate the implications for conventional and unconventional monetary policy.

In addition, a large empirical literature has studied the role of changes in mortgage credit supply, including those caused by the GSEs, in the housing boom and bust. Examples include the work of Gerardi et al. (2008); Foote et al. (2008); Mian & Sufi (2009, 2011); Foote, Gerardi & Willen (2012); Keys, Seru & Vig (2012); Mian, Rao & Sufi (2013); Mian, Sufi & Trebbi (2013); Ghent, Hernandez-Murillo & Owyang (2015); and Adelino, Schoar & Severino (2016). Related empirical work studies the effects of housing policies enacted after the financial crisis, e.g., Agarwal et al. (2017) and Di Maggio et al. (2017). Several of these policies relied on the GSEs for implementation. Campbell (2013) discusses broader implications for mortgage market design.[8]

[8]Relevant policy analyses can also be found in studies that have been done by the Congressional Budget Office (CBO 2014) and by the Urban Institute (2016).

4. THE GSES: WHAT DODD–FRANK DID AND WHAT THE CHOICE ACT PROPOSES TO DO

As mentioned above, Dodd–Frank did nothing substantive with respect to the GSEs. Section 1074 of Dodd–Frank mandated a report by the Treasury on what should be done about the GSEs. The Obama Administration delivered its report in February 2011 (US Dep. Treas. & US Dep. Hous. Urban Dev. 2011). That report provided a range of choices as to possible actions, but did not indicate what course of action the Obama Administration endorsed. Dodd–Frank devoted a considerable amount of attention to regulation with respect to residential mortgages, which has some indirect consequences, mostly favorable, for the GSEs.

The proposed Financial CHOICE Act, which has recently been put forward to roll back many of the provisions of Dodd–Frank, similarly avoids any substantive action with respect to the GSEs. Like Dodd–Frank, it requires the Treasury to report to Congress; however, Section 336 of the CHOICE Act requires annual reports rather than the single report specified in Dodd–Frank.

5. WHY HAVE THE GSES BEEN THE "ELEPHANTS IN THE ROOM"?

Before we offer our recommendations for the disposition of the GSEs and for housing finance and housing policy more generally, it is worth considering why the GSEs were ignored by Dodd–Frank and seem likely to be ignored by reforms of Dodd–Frank such as the proposed CHOICE Act.

First, the crisis that precipitated the conservatorships of the GSEs has passed. The GSEs are not currently in the risky position that brought them to the brink of insolvency in 2008. Although the GSEs in conservatorships jointly had to draw on the Treasury for $188 billion to avoid insolvency, they have subsequently produced positive earnings and are currently making payments to the Treasury.[9] That the GSEs are currently making positive contributions to the Treasury is no small thing when the overall federal budget continues to run substantial annual deficits.

In addition, as discussed above, the FHFA (as authorized by the HERA) has required the GSEs to take actions—shrink their balance sheets, offload some of their risks to the private sector, double their annual guarantee fees—that have reduced the Federal Government's exposure to the downside risks of the GSEs' actions. Again, the crisis has passed.

Second, broadly encouraging and subsidizing home ownership (and also rental housing, which the GSEs also finance) has been a politically popular activity. It is even more popular when the subsidy is implicit and off-budget, as has been true because of the special status of the two GSEs. (It is worth remembering, however, that the charters of the GSEs do not mention subsidy; instead, the goals of the GSEs should be to maintain liquidity in mortgage markets and to ensure access. Even the housing affordability goals that have been present since 1992 do not mention subsidy.) Lobbying and campaign contributions by companies and their trade associations that are directly or indirectly involved in housing, such as real estate agents, mortgage companies, home builders, appliance manufacturers, etc., enhance the political popularity of subsidizing housing.

[9]Their payments to the Treasury have totaled over $250 billion. This fact, however, deserves two comments: First, these are nominal sums and do not take into account the time value of money. Whether one believes that the GSEs have completely paid back their original draws on the Federal Government depends on what one thinks the appropriate interest rate on the government investment in the GSEs should be. It is worth recalling that at the time of the conservatorships, the GSEs were unable to raise funds in the capital markets—i.e., private investors were unwilling to lend to them. Second, these earnings do not incorporate potential losses from future mortgage defaults that may arise if another widespread housing collapse occurs. Since the financial crisis of 2007–2009, housing prices have mostly recovered, and therefore there have been far fewer defaults. Extensive defaults take place only during periods when housing prices fall, so earnings of the GSEs will tend to be asymmetric.

Any proposed reform of the GSEs would likely reduce the extent of government backing for them and thereby raise mortgage costs for their future borrowers. A substantial fraction of Congress (encouraged, of course, by the lobbyists mentioned above) would immediately object.

Third, any proposals to reform Fannie Mae and Freddie Mac would raise the question of whether the other large GSE, the FHLBS, should also be reformed. That prospect adds an extra set of issues and controversies.

In consequence of all of this, in addition to the silence of Dodd–Frank and the CHOICE Act with respect to the reform of the GSEs, there have been very few specific legislative proposals aimed at addressing the GSEs. During 2013 and 2014, there were a few exceptions, such as the Corker–Warner Act, the Johnson–Crapo Act, and the Protecting American Taxpayers and Homeowners (PATH) Act,[10] that gained some media attention but then lost momentum without being passed by Congress. We comment on these proposals in Section 7.

6. WHAT SHOULD BE DONE?

The consequences of the financial crisis of 2007–2009 put into question the housing finance system of the United States and the role the GSEs played in its development. Though not unanimous in its thinking, the aforementioned literature generally finds welfare gains from phasing out the GSEs.

In earlier writings we laid out the principles that should guide a system of housing finance (see, for example, Jaffee et al. 2009; Acharya et al. 2011a,b). In essence, the goal of reforming housing finance should be to ensure an efficient mortgage market, both in primary (origination) as well as in secondary mortgage markets, while maintaining financial stability. We have in mind an efficient housing finance system that corrects any government and market failures if they exist, notably, in this case: (*a*) unpriced government guarantees that destroy market discipline and lead to below-market borrowing rates, encouraging excess leverage and risk taking; and (*b*) the externality from undertaking too much credit and interest rate risk, as this risk is inherently systemic in nature.[11]

Moreover, the bulk of the mortgage finance system should not have national housing policy injected into it, as mortgage finance generally is an inefficient way of addressing the affordability and income-redistribution goals that are usually at the center of housing policies.[12]

As a general matter, given the difficulties in pricing government guarantees and maintaining a level playing field between the different financial players in the mortgage market to limit a concentrated buildup of systemic risk, the mortgage finance system should be one that is primarily private in nature. In this regard, there are two important questions. The current US mortgage finance system is heavily based on capital market financing implemented through securitization. Is such a system efficient relative to bank-financed systems that exist nearly everywhere else in the world? Is the system consistent with the goal of financial stability?

---

[10]For detailed summaries of all three bills, see **http://www.housingwire.com/ext/resources/files/Editorial/GSELegislativeProposalsComparison.pdf**.

[11]The negative externality arises when individual firms acting optimally in their own self-interest choose leverage and risk-taking activities that, in aggregate, can lead to capital shortfalls during severe downturns, leading to aggregate financial disintermediation and therefore knock-on effects to the real economy. Note that although government guarantees amplify this externality, it still exists even if guarantees are correctly priced or nonexistent.

[12]As we discuss below, we believe that any subsidy that does remain for housing finance should be on-budget and transparent, e.g., through FHA and VA. For an early essay that shows the GSEs' lack of achievement in addressing affordability, see Brown (2001).

Specifically, we argue below that at the center should be the securitization of mortgages that conform to reasonable credit quality and are standardized,[13] with the underlying credit risk being borne by investors, perhaps with some support from private guarantors—in other words, with few guarantees (if any) from the government. We maintain the view that the system can be based on the capital markets (i.e., relying on securitization), instead of on banks. The institutions involved in this endeavor should not be housed in government; also, to the extent that securitization requires government guarantees of tail credit risk, these guarantees must be priced by the market.

6.1. An Efficient Housing Finance System

In comparing the bank financing model for housing versus the securitization model, the discussion is appropriately framed as a trade-off between better aligned incentives associated with banking versus greater cost efficiencies and superior risk allocation using capital markets.

For example, there is some evidence, primarily focused on the financial crisis, that banks are better than lenders and servicers in the residential MBS process at screening borrowers, structuring bespoke mortgages, and modifying mortgages in default (see, for example, Loutskina & Strahan 2009; Keys et al. 2010; Piskorski, Seru & Vig 2010; Loutskina 2011; Purnanandam 2011; Dell'Ariccia, Igan & Laeven 2012). Some of this evidence, however, is contested by Adelino, Gerardi & Willen (2010, 2013) and Black, Krainer & Nichols (2014).

To this point about bank financing, in mortgage finance systems in countries outside the United States, lenders retain the risk of mortgages (skin in the game). In particular, the cross section of mortgage funding models across various developed countries shows that few countries have any entities that resemble Fannie Mae or Freddie Mac (see, e.g., Campbell 2013). The majority of countries rely on a bank-based system in which mortgage lenders retain the mortgage loans on their books. These institutions are subject to prudential regulation just like any other bank. And the argument cannot be that this has a major negative impact on homeownership rates. Of the 25 most developed countries, the United States ranks 17th in homeownership rate. What is unique about US mortgage finance is that almost two-thirds of all mortgages are securitized, whereas for the next largest securitizers abroad—Australia and Canada—this figure is only about 20%.[14]

Yet there are reasonable economic grounds for preferring the US mortgage finance system of securitization. Securitization truly can "turn lead into gold": Securitization takes illiquid mortgage loans and pools them to form liquid MBSs that trade on the secondary market. Because illiquidity commands a risk premium, the more liquid mortgage assets from securitization command better prices and thus a reduced mortgage rate. An additional benefit is that the credit risk gets transferred out of the systemically risky banking sector to the capital markets at large. In other words, if securitization works the way it is supposed to, the banking sector can better share its mortgage risks with rest of the economy. Finally, MBSs provide banks with access to investors worldwide, which diversifies their funding base.

Although the debate continues as to whether a bank-financed mortgage finance system is preferred to one based on capital markets, it should be noted that the US securitization framework, with its broad-based groups of investors, has developed over the past 30 years. The costs of turning

[13] Without mispriced government guarantees, good-quality, standardized mortgages should constitute the bulk of securitizations. Banks, with soft information about borrowers, are likely to be the natural home for apparently lesser-quality mortgages; we are agnostic as to whether a securitization market for lesser-quality mortgages can be revived.

[14] Denmark's mortgage market relies, for 90% of financing, on covered bonds, which are a close cousin of MBSs, but which provide investors with full recourse not only to the mortgage loans but also to the bank's capital. Several other European countries, such as Germany, the United Kingdom, and Spain, have substantial covered bond market shares.

back on such a system would be substantial. Moreover, although bank-financed mortgages are still important in the United States, the strong American preference for long-term (e.g., 30-year) fixed-rate mortgages means that a bank-centered system would involve substantial interest rate risk (as the savings and loan industry and Fannie Mae and Freddie Mac themselves experienced 30–40 years ago). These risks can have systemic consequences.[15]

6.2. Government Guarantees and Private Securitization

The question is: How does one effectively get to a model of securitization without government guarantees, given the current state of mortgage finance? We call this the "genie in the bottle" problem. Twenty-five years ago, the proverbial genie was let out of the bottle when mortgage markets were exposed to wider market forces, yet the government guarantees and special treatment of Fannie Mae and Freddie Mac were left in place.[16] Capital markets over the past 25 years have come to rely on these ever-growing guarantees. To wean the system off these guarantees—to put the genie back in the bottle—we need to transition away from a government-backed system to a private-based one. The problem is that the transitional process will succeed only if private markets are not crowded out, regulatory capital arbitrage by private guarantors is averted, and the systemic risk that is inherent in mortgage credit and interest rate risks is managed.

There has been some limited success at moving in this direction. Although the GSEs remain at the front and center of the mortgage market, they have been shrinking their portfolio of mortgages, effectively reducing their footprint. Also, the GSEs' guarantee fees were increased after the crisis, thus reducing the market subsidy and, in theory, increasing market discipline. Moreover, a report by the FHFA (2015) argued that the guarantee fees were consistent with the pricing implied by the GSEs' CRT transactions. Nevertheless, these GSE reforms do not seem to have led to a significant re-emergence of PLMBSs.

In the aftermath of the 2006 collapse of the housing market and the concomitant collapse of the PLMBS market, there has been no revival of significant PLMBS activity. The reasons for this absence are not entirely clear. Among the possibilities are: fears of a renewal of moral hazard behavior by mortgage originators and securities packagers; continued uncertainty over the legal liabilities of private issuers and originators (with respect to their representations and warranties); distrust of the credit rating agencies' ratings for PLMBSs; continued favorable capital treatment (a 1.6% equity financing requirement) that applies to the GSEs' MBSs when they are bought by banks; g-fees by the GSEs that may still be too low (e.g., Lucas & MacDonald 2010); and a lack of comfort and familiarity on the part of insurance companies and pension funds (which would be the natural buyers of long-lived MBSs that are based on 30-year fixed-rate mortgages) for PLMBSs.

However, because mortgage default guarantees were an essential element of the development and liquidity of the mortgage securitization market, it seems likely that investors would continue

[15] Of course, this interest rate risk, if acted on, can be hedged out using interest rate swaps. Nevertheless, hedging prepayment risk is more difficult and costly than hedging duration risk. Moreover, there is the risk that banks will choose not to hedge fully to take advantage of the interest rate carry. In the most recent financial crisis, banks engaged in a related carry trade centered on small credit risk by holding large amounts of AAA-rated asset-backed securities which suffered large losses, leading to capital shortfalls in the sector (see, e.g., Acharya et al. 2010).

[16] Government involvement in housing finance, of course, extends much farther back in history, at least to the early 1930s: The FHLBS was established in 1932; federal deposit insurance was extended to the (mortgage-financing) savings and loan industry in 1934; the FHA was created in 1935; and Fannie Mae was created (within the FHA) in 1936. Indeed, one could argue that government guarantees of some sort, both in the United States and in bank-financed systems abroad, have been part of mortgage finance for many years because of bank deposit insurance.

to demand mortgage default insurance in some form (at least in the short term).[17] A particular reason is the efficacy of the highly successful "to be announced (TBA)" market for forward trading of MBSs issued by the GSEs. The TBA market allows mortgage lenders to hedge and substantially reduce risks inherent in the origination process. Because TBA securities are governed by a set of specific characteristics, their pricing is standardized with high liquidity, leading to broad investor participation. There is a widespread belief that this market cannot exist without guarantees of the cash flows of mortgage principal and interest (see, for example, Vickery & Wright 2010). The problem is that the private sector cannot be the sole provider of these guarantees, as this insurance is systemic because of its dependence on macroeconomic events, resulting in mispriced negative externalities. This argues for some form of governmental intervention.[18] Given the strong political considerations discussed above, however, there is a high likelihood that any government guarantees will be mispriced so as to subsidize housing (as was clearly the case for the GSEs).

Acharya et al. (2011b) argue for a public–private partnership in which the private sector prices the mortgage guarantees and insures a small X% fraction, whereas the government is a silent partner, insuring the majority of the remainder (100 – X%) and receiving the corresponding premiums.[19] Market pricing of the guarantees would ensure that: (*a*) a competing private-sector mortgage market (without guarantees) would not be crowded out; and (*b*) market discipline would return to the mortgage market. Interestingly, a similar proposal, the Partnership to Strengthen Homeownership Act, was offered in 2014 by Congressmen John Carney, John Delaney, and Jim Himes, along with a number of bipartisan cosponsors (for the text of the bill, see **https://delaney.house.gov/sites/delaney.house.gov/files/Partnership%20to%20Strengthen%20Homeownership.pdf**).

6.3. Transitioning the GSEs

We argue above that the initial phase of a transition to a new mortgage finance system would preserve mortgage default insurance via the aforementioned public–private partnership, primarily because such guarantees have been essential for the way that the securitization market for mortgages has developed. This way, the private sector would be encouraged to shrug off any regulatory uncertainty and allowed to flourish. Financial innovation in these markets could return. New investors focused on the credit risk of mortgage pools would emerge. As a result, mortgages would likely become more standardized, and underwriting standards would improve.

What would be the role for the existing GSEs? To help the transition process, reliance on the GSEs' guarantees should be mandated to end, and their mortgage portfolios should continue to shrink. One example of such a mandate would be a gradual reduction of the size limit for conforming mortgages; another would be an increase in the fees that the GSEs charge for their

[17]This statement is controversial. There are other parts of the capital markets, albeit smaller and less liquid, that function without guarantees of the underlying credit risk. Two examples include corporate bonds and commercial MBSs.

[18]Scharfstein & Sunderam (2011) offer a novel solution in which government guarantees of newly issued MBSs are provided during crisis times to keep the market going, but no such government support is provided for MBSs during normal periods. Importantly, previously issued MBSs are not supported during crisis times. The question of whether such a regulatory approach would negatively impact the TBA market remains.

[19]The private sector firm/subsidiaries would be well-capitalized and, if large enough, would be subject to the nonbank SIFI (systemically important financial institution) designation. An example of one such private–public program is the Terrorism Risk Insurance Act (TRIA) of 2002. Note that, given the aforementioned development of the market for mortgage credit risk sold off by the GSEs, it is possible that the public–private partnership is required only for tail or catastrophe risk. Also, over time, as the private sector's comfort with this arrangement grew, the X% could well expand, which would concomitantly reduce the government's role.

guarantees (as was done after the financial crisis).[20] Keeping the GSEs in conservatorships and thereby as wards of the Federal Government is concerning because of the way g-fees are set. If there are efficiency gains and/or innovation possibilities that would accompany their operation as private, for-profit companies, these advantages are forgone by their continued operation as government wards.

Further, their continued operation as government wards makes them prime candidates for mission creep and the diversion of their revenues and activities to other purposes. For example, within the past few years, 4.2 basis points of their annual guarantee fees has been earmarked for an affordable housing fund, and 10 basis points has been earmarked for transfers to the Social Security Trust Fund to offset reduced payroll taxes. In addition, affordable housing goals for their securitization activities remain likely.[21]

A reasonable question is whether the two GSEs have significant going-concern value, e.g., whether their brand names have worth and/or whether their organizations and technologies have value if kept intact. It may be a waste, therefore, to shutter them, and instead the GSEs should be privatized. Indeed, given that they currently securitize large chunks of the mortgage market, guarantee the mortgage payments, and sell off an increasing fraction of the credit risk to private investors, the GSEs might be good candidate firms to handle the residual catastrophe risk guarantees of the aforementioned public–private partnership.

If this is the case, then the Federal Government's 79.9% stake in the companies should be sold to the public in an initial public offering (IPO), and the companies should be structured (to the greatest extent possible) as normal companies (i.e., not as GSEs) with normal charters (e.g., from the state of Delaware) and normal bylaws, etc. The Federal Government's IPO of Conrail in 1987 could serve as an example. In the IPO of the GSEs, however, the Federal Government should be clear that the resulting private-sector entities will be required to be well financed with equity and that they (along with other residential mortgage securitizers) would be subject to bank-like rigorous prudential regulation, so that the likelihood that they would (again) require bailouts from the Federal Government would be quite small.

If the two GSEs were privatized, or even if they were wound down and replaced by other securitizers, it is clear that the maintenance of adequate levels of equity financing for private residential mortgage securitizers (relative to the risks of the mortgages that are securitized) would be a key feature. It was clear in 2008 that the two GSEs were systemic and could not be allowed to simply fail and cause their creditors to suffer losses. The same would continue to be true if the two organizations were privatized and maintained roughly their current sizes, or even if they were wound down and replaced by somewhat smaller organizations.

For such systemic organizations, any ex ante government statements about refusals to bail out the organizations (or, in reality, their creditors) are likely to lack credibility ex post at times of financial difficulties. (It is worth recalling that all of the GSE debt securities explicitly stated that these were not obligations of the US Government; nevertheless, in September 2008, those securities did become obligations of the US Government.) It follows, then, that to reduce the likelihood of such situations arising, the organizations should be required to maintain adequate

[20]From 2006 to 2016, the conforming loan limit for most parts of the United States was $417,000, with higher amounts allowed in high–housing price areas. For 2017, however, the conforming loan limit has been raised to $424,100, which is the opposite direction from what we believe is appropriate.

[21]Of course, even before the conservatorships, the GSEs (starting in 1992) were subject to explicit (and rising) affordable housing goals, and commercial banks and savings institutions have been subject to obligations to support their local communities by the Community Reinvestment Act of 1977. Nevertheless, the temptations and likelihoods of mission creep and diversions are surely greater when an organization is the direct ward of the government.

levels of equity financing relative to the risk characteristics of the mortgages that they are securitizing. They would therefore have adequate loss-absorbing capacities (i.e., equity) that would allow them to continue to operate and (until the equity is wholly depleted) avoid the disruptions and uncertainties of insolvency.[22] In the determination of appropriate levels of equity financing for these organizations, the same kind of stress testing that is conducted for banks should be applied to these organizations, as well.

In addition, whatever resolution authority is in place—i.e., the orderly liquidation authority (OLA) in Dodd–Frank or a revised bankruptcy code for systemically important financial institutions (SIFIs) in the Financial CHOICE Act—the GSEs or the next generation of GSEs should be subject to this authority. One of the important features of the OLA or bankruptcy is that it eliminates the existing shareholder-owners, which was not true of the conservatorships of the GSEs. Neither the OLA nor bankruptcy necessarily implies liquidation of the insolvent entity: As is true for banks, if there is sufficient going-concern value (which would disappear in a liquidation), the OLA or bankruptcy judge can try to find new owners quickly, or even operate the entity for an interim period while finding those new owners.

GSEs aside, even if PLMBSs return to pre-crisis levels, given that the tranching/subordination structure was supposed to—but did not—provide safety for the holders of the safe PLMBS tranches, the provision of guarantees (similar to those that have been offered by the GSEs) may be necessary. (Indeed, if privatization of the GSEs occurs along the lines that we have described above, then their MBSs ought to be considered as PLMBSs.) Whether those guarantees are offered by the securitizers themselves (as was true for the GSEs) or by a set of third-party guarantors seems less important than the issue of who will back up the guarantors.

Rigorous prudential regulation of the guarantors is surely part of the answer. But the provision of a government backstop for the guarantors—in essence, government coverage of catastrophic risk, much like the role that government-provided deposit insurance plays for bank depositors—may be important as well. (Once the government enters the role of a backstop for the guarantors, the system of prudential regulation can be seen as protection for the government and, ultimately, taxpayers.) But the pricing of the risk to which the government is thereby exposed is a difficult problem by itself; there will always be intense political pressures to underprice that risk and thereby provide an implicit subsidy for mortgage finance. As described above, to address these problems, we propose a system of guarantees whereby the Federal Government would provide PLMBS guarantees that would stand side-by-side with those of private guarantors. The Federal Government could thereby price its guarantees on a par with the pricing of the private guarantors.

7. OTHER PROPOSALS

Despite the absence of successful legislation—or, perhaps, because of that absence—there have been a plethora of policy papers and blueprints for GSE reform and more general reform of the residential mortgage finance system that have been offered by individuals and policy think tanks.[23]

[22]Equivalently, adequate equity financing will mean that the equity holders/owners of these organizations will bear most of the losses, as well as enjoy all of the gains. The pre-2008 GSE structure, with inadequate equity financing, meant that the GSEs' gains were privatized, while their losses were socialized.

[23]For a recent effort under the auspices of the Urban Institute that offers a diversity of proposals, see: **http://www.urban.org/policy-centers/housing-finance-policy-center/projects/housing-finance-reform-incubator**. The New York University Center for Real Estate Finance Research hosted a discussion of recent reform proposals, a summary of which can be found here: **http://www.stern.nyu.edu/experience-stern/about/departments-centers-initiatives/centers-of-research/center-real-estate-finance-research/research/gse-reform-will-it-happen-and-what-form-will-it-take**.

As mentioned above, various bills have also been proposed over the past several years. Scharfstein & Swagel (2016) provide a detailed analysis of various legislative approaches to GSE reform.

We discuss some of these legislative bills and think tank proposals below. Before we provide this discussion, however, note that these proposals describe specific mechanisms whereby government catastrophic risk insurance is provided in conjunction with securitization and first-loss private-sector guarantee processes. Regardless of the details, we reiterate that rigorous prudential regulation of the securitizers and guarantors—with adequate levels of equity financing, so as to provide private-sector first-loss and second-loss capacity that will protect the ultimate government (and thus taxpayer) guarantor—is an essential first step for any such plan.

7.1. The Johnson–Crapo Act

Building on an earlier proposal by Senators Bob Corker and Mark Warner, Senators Tim Johnson and Mike Crapo put forth a bill, the Johnson–Crapo Act, that passed the Senate Banking Committee in 2014 but never came up for vote on the Senate floor. The Act essentially created a government insurance program for MBSs for qualified mortgages, with first losses to be borne by new mortgage securitization companies. The Act had several notable features: First, the existing GSEs would be wound down. Second, these new mortgage securitization companies would bundle together the mortgages, securitize them, and guarantee the principal. The firms themselves would receive no government guarantees, but the government would instead guarantee the MBSs for a fee. The firms would have to hold capital equal to 10% of the underlying MBS value. The government would step in only after the mortgage firm's capital was fully depleted. The new government entity would be called the FMIC (Federal Mortgage Insurance Corporation) and would be akin to the FDIC (Federal Deposit Insurance Corporation). Some government fees would be earmarked for affordable housing.

The Johnson–Crapo Act provides a major contribution to the GSE debate because, in contrast to the current formulation of the GSEs, the Act requires a much higher level of capital (10%) to be held by these firms. Whether 10% is the right level is up for debate, but, regardless, the capital requirement should be consistent with capital requirements required elsewhere in the financial system for such risks. This condition would allow for a more competitive market to develop and presumably encourage greater amounts of innovation.

However, the Johnson–Crapo Act has some unfortunate similarities with the existing system: (*a*) The government provides guarantees (now explicit) for MBS principal repayment without market pricing (and without the side-by-side sharing that, as we argued above, could encourage market pricing); (*b*) housing policy is still injected into the system, enabling possible future mission creep; and (*c*) because of all this, the proposed legislation likely leads to an unlevel playing field and a buildup of systemic risk at the new mortgage securitization institutions that would replace the GSEs.

7.2. The PATH Act

The Protecting American Taxpayers and Homeowners (PATH) Act put forth by Congressman Jeb Hensarling also passed its House committee (in 2013) but failed to be voted on in the full House of Representatives. [This should not be confused with the Protecting Americans from Tax Hikes (PATH) Act of 2015, which was passed by both houses of Congress and signed into law.] The bill proposed to eliminate Fannie Mae and Freddie Mac entirely, yet leave the FHA/GNMA (Ginnie Mae) combination in place as guarantors of mortgages of low-income families and first-time buyers. Two additional provisions, however, limit the amount of government support. The first was a generally lower maximum on the size of the loans insured by the FHA relative to current limits on Fannie Mae and Freddie Mac. The second was that 10% of new loans should be held privately.

As discussed above, any legislative reform of Fannie Mae and Freddie Mac should include the FHLBS. The PATH Act essentially leaves only Ginnie Mae in place as the government securitizer of residential mortgages. From the perspective of the discussion in Section 5, the PATH Act certainly reduces the amount of mispriced government guarantees and resulting moral hazard, assuming appropriate levels of regulation of financial firms that issue PLMBSs or directly carry mortgage loans. As posed in Section 5, the question is whether mortgage default guarantees are essential to the operation of the mortgage securitization market and whether these guarantees are credible without some government backing. To the extent there is government involvement, we call for these guarantees to be market priced.

7.3. The Bright–DeMarco Plan (Milken Institute Center for Financial Markets) (2016)

The basic idea behind the proposal of Michael Bright and Edward DeMarco is to simply amend the charters of the GSEs (Fannie Mae, Freddie Mac, and Ginnie Mae) to restructure the housing finance system. In their plan, Fannie Mae and Freddie Mac would become lender-owned mutuals, providing credit enhancement much as they do now and continuing to build out the CRT transactions discussed in Section 2. Other than being approved by the FHFA as a credit enhancer, these GSEs would no longer have any government role. Ginnie Mae would become a stand-alone government corporation akin to the FDIC, providing guarantees on MBSs with credit enhancement from either government programs (such as the FHA) or approved credit enhancers (such as the newly reconstituted GSEs).

On the positive side, the GSEs would no longer have government backing and would essentially be selling credit support for MBSs through the mutual ownership. Presumably, this credit risk would be priced by the market. A major concern, however, is whether such a mutual ownership of potentially systemic financial institutions can survive a severe downturn. There is a history of failures of such institutions in the banking system prior to the creation of the Federal Reserve. Moreover, on the negative side, there is the question of how the government guarantees are priced by Ginnie Mae and the extent to which Ginnie Mae takes on increasing amounts of risk, looking increasingly like the previous GSEs. The PATH Act, through its loan limits, provides some control over Ginnie Mae's growth. The devil would be in the details.

7.4. Dechario–Mosser–Tracy–Vickery–Wright Plan (New York Federal Reserve) (2010)

Similar to the above plan from the Milken Institute, the one proposed by economists at the New York Federal Reserve also calls for Fannie Mae and Freddie Mac to be replaced by a mutual owned by lenders, albeit with a different structure. In this plan, the private mutual is called a financial market utility (FMU). The FMU securitizes standardized residential mortgages, forming typical MBSs and guaranteeing their credit risk. The FMU prices and manages the risk of the MBSs, subject to prudential capital regulation, and buys catastrophic reinsurance from the government. The success of the CRT transactions, albeit so far only in normal times, suggests that the FMU can sell off substantial parts of the credit risk to the marketplace.[24]

[24]As implied by Scharfstein & Sunderam (2011), there is a question of whether the market for CRT transactions will be viable during a crisis period. Presumably, the prices of credit risk inherent in the CRT transactions will map closely with the offered mortgage rates in the market.

Like the Milken Institute plan, the New York Fed proposal has the nice feature of removing the GSEs from government's reach. The incentive to innovate and be efficient remains. However, depending on the degree of financial regulation, the question is whether the FMU produces systemic risk or not. Does the mutual form lead to more or less systemic risk? On a positive note, the FMU aligns incentives across mortgage lenders. On a negative note is a question of whether the government can credibly commit to not bailing out the FMU and its members. And, of course, the pricing issue underlying the government guarantee persists.

7.5. Parrott–Ranieri–Sperling–Zandi–Zigas Plan (Promising Road Proposal) (2015)

The Promising Road proposal would combine Fannie Mae and Freddie Mac into a single government corporation called the National Mortgage Reinsurance Corporation (NMRC). The NMRC would essentially be run similarly to how the current GSEs are run: The NMRC would: (*a*) purchase mortgage loans from lenders; (*b*) issue securities backed by these loans; (*c*) guarantee the payment of interest and principal of these securities; and (*d*) sell off noncatastrophic credit risk, like the aforementioned CRT transactions, to the market. Like the previous mandates of the GSEs, the NMRC would ensure access to credit in compliance with housing policy goals.

Although it is in many ways similar to the New York Federal Reserve plan, the Promising Road proposal offers one major difference: The utility would be housed in government, as opposed to in a mutual owned by a collection of lenders. Government ownership can lead to mission creep; indeed, the plan calls for explicit attention to housing policy goals. This would seem to increase the likelihood of larger losses down the road. Moreover, innovation and efficiency are unlikely to occur in these government-supported markets. Of course, a counterargument is that, without adequate regulation, the more market-oriented proposals increase the systemic risk in the financial sector by again creating large private mortgage insurers. To a first approximation, these new entities would resemble the old GSEs, albeit without the government's special status.

8. HOUSING FINANCE REFORM IN GENERAL

Any discussion of reform of the GSEs should acknowledge the larger policy context in which the GSEs are embedded: Public policy in the United States broadly favors housing—encouraging the construction, financing, and consumption of housing—through a broad range of explicit and (all too often) implicit policy tools at all levels of government. In addition to the GSEs,[25] the FHA, VA, and USDA provide government-backed mortgage insurance, and the mortgages that are insured by these three agencies are securitized by another government agency: Ginnie Mae. With respect to personal income taxes, the Federal Government and the states encourage housing through the MID and the exemption of most capital gains on housing from reported income; the Federal Government also allows deductions for the state and local property taxes that home owners pay. The Federal Government and the states provide subsidies to builders to build multifamily housing; the Federal Government provides rental vouchers to low-income households; and public housing continues to be provided to low-income households by various levels of government.

[25] Also, the FHLBS was established in 1932 as a wholesale bank for savings institutions, which at that time were focused almost entirely on making residential mortgages. Although the FHLBS has broadened in terms of its institutional members and the kinds of lending that it supports, the support of residential mortgage lending is still an important part of its mission.

United States public policy is heavily embedded in the housing market. In that context, then, along with the above suggestions for reforming the GSEs, we discuss changes in mortgage finance and housing policy more generally.

8.1. Subsidies for Home Ownership Should Not Be Done Through a Revived Private-Label Mortgage-Backed Securities Market

Whether the GSEs survive and are privatized or instead are wound down and replaced, Acharya et al. (2011b) argue that the resulting PLMBS market should not be the vehicle for subsidies for home ownership and/or for income redistribution that favors lower-income households, for three reasons.

First, any subsidies should be transparent, explicit, and on-budget; none of those characteristics apply to the cross-subsidies that would occur through a distorted PLMBS market. The FHA and Ginnie Mae, as on-budget entities of the Federal Government, are arguably better vehicles for such subsidies.

Second, it can be argued that home ownership is an overvalued feature of US housing policy. A house is a large, illiquid asset with large transaction costs for buying and selling. Home ownership, with its accompanying mortgage finance, is not for everyone; it requires a relatively steady (and adequate) income and budgetary discipline on the part of the owning household. Those large transaction costs can impede job mobility when better employment opportunities would require moving to a different community. Also, given the experience of the steep decline in house prices after their 2006 peak, the idea that home ownership is a sure road to building household wealth should have been dispelled.[26]

Any de-emphasis of home ownership should reasonably include a de-emphasis of the importance of national home ownership rates. In essence, renting should be promoted in respectability.

Third, trying to redistribute income through housing policy, whether explicitly (e.g., through rent vouchers) or implicitly (e.g., through the GSEs), is a distinctly inferior method compared with direct income transfers (e.g., through refundable tax credits for low-income households).[27]

There may well be some modest positive externalities from home ownership and from encouraging low-income households to move to better neighborhoods through vouchers; for a recent study on the benefits of home ownership, see Sodini et al. (2016) and the references therein. Again, these goals should be pursued through transparent, explicit, on-budget means and vehicles.

8.2. Reforming Housing Policies More Generally

Not unlike other economists, we have argued elsewhere that US public policy has encouraged too much investment in housing. Concomitantly, other forms of investment—whether in physical production capital, such as plants and machinery; in community capital, such as schools, hospitals, roads, airports, etc.; or in human capital, such as more and better education and skill development for children and adults alike—have been neglected. Similarly, US GDP has surely suffered. The

[26]To the extent that the paying off of mortgage principal is a form of forced saving for a household, there may be some wealth building. But, again, the transactions costs of buying and selling are large, and the variance in house prices can also wipe out the forced saving.

[27]If one thinks of the GSEs as providing a subsidy for borrowing, they encourage greater leverage by home-owning households. And, to the extent that lower-income households are more leveraged, there may be income-distribution consequences from the termination of subsidies through the GSEs; see Gete & Zecchetto (2017). As they point out, and as we discuss below, a ready offset would be the termination of the income tax deduction for residential mortgage interest.

specific tools that are used to encourage investment in housing are often inefficient and have perverse consequences for income distribution.

The personal income tax deduction for mortgage interest is a prime example. Notionally, it is intended to encourage home ownership by reducing the personal cost of a mortgage that is used to purchase a house. But it is explicitly a subsidy for borrowing, which encourages households to become more leveraged than would otherwise be the case. Next, it is far more likely to provide benefits to high-income households, who are more likely to itemize on their income tax filing and who are far more likely to take out a larger mortgage on a more expensive house and thereby get a larger deduction, than to low-income households (see, e.g., Poterba & Sinai 2008). Because high-income households are more likely to buy even in the absence of a mortgage subsidy, the MID largely encourages those who would buy anyway to buy a larger and better-appointed house. We fail to see the social value of such outcomes. Finally, we question the goal of broadly encouraging home ownership, even if the mortgage interest deduction were effective in doing so, which it largely is not.

8.3. Better Ways to Reduce the Cost of Housing

There are likely better ways to reduce the cost of housing. They involve attacking the issue from the supply side, instead of through the demand side, through subsidies; builder subsidies for multifamily housing appear to be the sole existing policy that operates through the supply side. There are at least three such ways.

First, the Federal and state governments could limit the ability of local (suburban) communities to restrict the supply of land for rental housing and for smaller houses (that tend to be on smaller lots) through those communities' restrictive zoning ordinances. Second, the Federal Government could undo protectionist trade measures that have limited supplies of building materials, such as cement and lumber. Third, the Federal and state governments could limit the ability of local communities generally to impose local building codes that raise costs without providing commensurate benefits. In sum, there are ways of reducing the cost of housing that are consistent with improved efficiency—and with improved social equity.

9. CONCLUSION

It has been more than 8 years since Fannie Mae and Freddie Mac were put into government conservatorships. The Dodd–Frank Act largely ignored them. The proposed Financial CHOICE Act does the same. Thus, the GSEs remain in those conservatorships. The US system of financing residential housing is badly in need of reform. Keeping the GSEs in conservatorships is surely not an element of any sensible reform.

In this article, we have laid out some ideas for moving the system of financing residential housing in the direction of greater efficiency and greater equity. Because current efforts at financial reform are still at the stage of proposed legislation, there is plenty of time for its drafters to address the GSEs and develop a blueprint for a better financial system for residential housing. We hope that this analysis can be useful in that process.

DISCLOSURE STATEMENT

The authors are not aware of any affiliations, memberships, funding, or financial holdings that might be perceived as affecting the objectivity of this review.

ACKNOWLEDGMENTS

We would like to thank Deborah Lucas for valuable comments on an earlier draft of this essay, as well as our colleagues at the NYU Stern School of Business for their input on this topic, with a special acknowledgment to Viral Acharya, who has coauthored on many of these ideas in the past.

LITERATURE CITED

Acharya VV, Cooley T, Richardson M, Walter I. 2010. Manufacturing tail risk: a perspective on the financial crisis of 2007–2009. *Found. Trends Finance* 4(4):247–325

Acharya VV, Oncu TS, Richardson M, Van Nieuwerburgh S, White LJ. 2011a. The government-sponsored enterprises. In *Regulating Wall Street: The Dodd–Frank Act and the New Architecture of Global Finance*, ed. VV Acharya, TF Cooley, M Richardson, I Walter, pp. 429–42. Hoboken, NJ: Wiley

Acharya VV, Richardson M, Van Nieuwerburgh S, White LJ. 2011b. *Guaranteed to Fail: Fannie Mae, Freddie Mac and the Debacle of Mortgage Finance*. Princeton, NJ: Princeton Univ. Press

Adelino M, Gerardi K, Willen P. 2010. *What explains differences in foreclosure rates? A response to Piskorski, Seru, and Vig*. Work. Pap. 10-2, Fed. Reserve Bank Boston, Boston, MA

Adelino M, Gerardi K, Willen PS. 2013. Why don't lenders renegotiate more home mortgages? Redefaults, self-cures and securitization. *J. Monet. Econ.* 60(7):835–53

Adelino M, Schoar A, Severino F. 2016. Loan originations and defaults in the mortgage crisis: the role of the middle class. *Rev. Financ. Stud.* 29(7):1635–70

Agarwal S, Amromin G, Ben-David I, Chomsisengphet S, Piskorski T, Seru A. 2017. Policy intervention in debt renegotiation: evidence from the Home Affordable Modification Program. *J. Political Econ.* 125(3):654–712

Allen F, Carletti E, Goldstein I, Leonello A. 2017. *Government guarantees and financial stability*. Work. Pap., Wharton Sch., Univ. Pa.

Ambrose BW, Warga A. 2002. Measuring potential GSE funding advantages. *J. Real Estate Finance Econ.* 25(2–3):129–50

Arslan Y, Guler B, Taskin T. 2015. Joint dynamics of house prices and foreclosures. *J. Money Credit Bank.* 47(51):133–69

Black L, Krainer J, Nichols J. 2014. From origination to renegotiation: a comparison of portfolio and securitized commercial real estate loans. *J. Real Estate Finance Econ.* 55(1):1–31

Brown J. 2001. Reform of GSE housing goals. In *Serving Two Masters, Yet Out of Control: Fannie Mae and Freddie Mac*, ed. PJ Wallison, pp. 153–68. Washington, DC: Am. Enterpr. Inst. Press

Campbell JY. 2013. Mortgage market design. *Rev. Finance* 17(1):1–33

CBO (Congr. Budg. Off.). 2014. *Transitioning to alternative structures for housing finance*. Publ. 49765, CBO, Washington, DC

Chambers M, Garriga C, Schlagenhauf DE. 2009a. Accounting for changes in the homeownership rate. *Int. Econ. Rev.* 50(3):677–726

Chambers M, Garriga C, Schlagenhauf DE. 2009b. Housing policy and the progressivity of income taxation. *J. Monet. Econ.* 56(8):1116–34

Chambers M, Garriga C, Schlagenhauf DE. 2014. Did housing policies cause the post-war housing boom? A general equilibrium analysis. In *Housing and Mortgage Markets in Historical Perspective*, ed. P Fishback, K Snowden, E White, pp. 351–86. Chicago: Chic. Univ. Press

Chatterjee S, Eyigungor B. 2015. A quantitative analysis of the US housing and mortgage markets and the foreclosure crisis. *Rev. Econ. Dyn.* 18(2):165–84

Corbae D, Quintin E. 2015. Leverage and the foreclosure crisis. *J. Political Econ.* 123(1):1–65

Davis MA, Van Nieuwerburgh S. 2015. Housing, finance, and the macroeconomy. In *Handbook of Regional and Urban Economics*, Vol. 5, ed. G Duranton, JV Henderson, WC Strange, pp. 753–811. Amsterdam: North-Holland

Dell'Ariccia G, Igan D, Laeven LUC. 2012. Credit booms and lending standards: evidence from the subprime mortgage market. *J. Money Credit Bank.* 44(2–3):367–84

Di Maggio M, Kermani A, Keys B, Piskorski T, Ramcharan R, et al. 2017. Interest rate pass-through: mortgage rates, household consumption and voluntary deleveraging. *Am. Econ. Rev.* In press

Elenev V. 2016. *Mortgage credit, aggregate demand, and unconventional monetary policy*. Work. Pap., Stern Sch. Bus., N.Y. Univ.

Elenev V, Landvoigt T, Van Nieuwerburgh S. 2016. Phasing out the GSEs. *J. Monet. Econ.* 81:111–32

Favilukis J, Ludvigson SC, Van Nieuwerburgh S. 2017. The macroeconomic effects of housing wealth, housing finance and limited risk sharing in general equilibrium. *J. Political Econ.* 125(1):140–223

FHFA (Fed. Hous. Finance Agency). 2015. *Results of Fannie Mae and Freddie Mac guarantee fee review*. Fact Sheet, April 17. **https://www.fhfa.gov/media/publicaffairs/pages/results-of-fannie-mae-and-freddie-mac-guarantee-fee-review.aspx**

FHFA (Fed. Hous. Finance Agency). 2016. *Single-family credit risk transfer progress report, June 2016*. Div. Hous. Mission Goals, FHFA, Washington, DC

Fieldhouse AJ, Mertens K. 2017a. *A narrative analysis of mortgage asset purchases by federal agencies*. Work. Pap., Cornell Univ.

Fieldhouse AJ, Mertens K. 2017b. *The macroeconomic effects of government asset purchases: evidence from postwar US housing credit policy*. Work. Pap., Cornell Univ.

Floetotto M, Kirker M, Stroebel J. 2016. Government intervention in the housing market: Who wins, who loses? *J. Monet. Econ.* 80:106–23

Foote CL, Gerardi K, Goette L, Willen PS. 2008. Just the facts: an initial analysis of subprime's role in the housing crisis. *J. Hous. Econ.* 17(4):291–305

Foote CL, Gerardi K, Willen PS. 2012. *Why did so many people make so many ex-post bad decisions? The causes of the foreclosure crisis*. Public Policy Discuss. Pap. 12-2, Fed. Reserve Bank Boston, Boston, MA

Frame WS, Fuster A, Tracy J, Vickery J. 2015. The rescue of Fannie Mae and Freddie Mac. *J. Econ. Perspect.* 29(2):25–52

Frame WS, White LJ. 2005. Fussing and fuming at Fannie and Freddie: how much smoke, how much fire? *J. Econ. Perspect.* 19(2):159–84

Frame WS, White LJ. 2011. The Federal Home Loan Bank system: current issues in perspective. In *Reforming Rules and Regulations*, ed. V Ghosal, pp. 255–75. Cambridge, MA: MIT Press

Gerardi K, Lehnert A, Sherlund SM, Willen P. 2008. Making sense of the subprime crisis. *Brookings Pap. Econ. Act.* 2008(2):69–145

Gervais M. 2002. Housing taxation and capital accumulation. *J. Monet. Econ.* 49(7):1461–89

Gete P, Zecchetto F. 2017. Distributional implications of government guarantees in mortgage markets. *Rev. Financ. Stud.* In press

Ghent AC, Hernandez-Murillo R, Owyang MT. 2015. Did affordable housing legislation contribute to the subprime securities boom? *Real Estate Econ.* 43(4):820–54

Goodman L. 2014. Risk-sharing deals support reduction in Freddie and Fannie guarantee fees. *Urban Wire: Housing and Housing Finance*, Dec. 3

Greenwald D. 2016. *The mortgage credit channel of macroeconomic transmission*. Work. Pap., MIT

Hagerty JR. 2012. *The Fateful History of Fannie Mae: New Deal Birth to Mortgage Crisis Fall.* Charleston, SC: History Press

Hedlund A. 2016. The cyclical dynamics of illiquid housing, debt, and foreclosures. *Quant. Econ.* 7(1):289–328

Howard T. 2014. *The Mortgage Wars*. New York: McGraw-Hill

Hurst E, Keys BJ, Seru A, Vavra J. 2016. Regional redistribution through the US mortgage market. *Am. Econ. Rev.* 106(10):2982–3028

Jaffee D. 2003. The interest rate risk of Fannie Mae and Freddie Mac. *J. Financ. Serv. Res.* 24(1):5–29

Jaffee D, Richardson M, Van Nieuwerburgh S, White LJ, Wright R. 2009. What to do about the government sponsored enterprises? In *Restoring Financial Stability: How to Repair a Failed System*, ed. VV Acharya, M Richardson, pp. 131–37. Hoboken, NJ: Wiley

Jeske K, Krueger D, Mitman K. 2013. Housing, mortgage bailout guarantees and the macro economy. *J. Monet. Econ.* 60(8):917–35

Kaplan G, Mitman K, Violante G. 2016. *Consumption and house prices in the Great Recession: Model meets evidence*. Work. Pap., N.Y. Univ.

Keys BJ, Mukherjee T, Seru A, Vig V. 2010. Did securitization lead to lax screening? Evidence from subprime loans. *Q. J. Econ.* 125(1):307–62

Keys BJ, Seru A, Vig V. 2012. Lender screening and the role of securitization: evidence from prime and subprime mortgage markets. *Rev. Financ. Stud.* 25(7):2071–108

Landvoigt T. 2017. Housing demand during the boom: the role of expectations and credit constraints. *Rev. Financ. Stud.* 30(6):1865–902

Landvoigt T, Piazzesi M, Schneider M. 2015. The housing market(s) of San Diego. *Am. Econ. Rev.* 105(4):1371–407

Loutskina E. 2011. The role of securitization in bank liquidity and funding management. *J. Financ. Econ.* 100(3):663–84

Loutskina E, Strahan PE. 2009. Securitization and the declining impact of bank finance on loan supply: evidence from mortgage originations. *J. Finance* 64(2):861–89

Lucas DJ, McDonald RL. 2006. An options-based approach to evaluating the risk of Fannie Mae and Freddie Mac. *J. Monet. Econ.* 53(1):155–76

Lucas DJ, McDonald RL. 2010. Valuing government guarantees: Fannie and Freddie revisited. In *Measuring and Managing Federal Financial Risk*, ed. DJ Lucas, pp. 131–54. Chicago: Univ. Chic. Press

McLean B. 2015. *Shaky Ground: The Strange Saga of the U.S. Mortgage Giants.* New York: Columbia Global Rep.

Mian A, Rao K, Sufi A. 2013. Household balance sheets, consumption, and the economic slump. *Q. J. Econ.* 128(4):1687–726

Mian A, Sufi A. 2009. The consequences of mortgage expansion: evidence from the U.S. mortgage default crisis. *Q. J. Econ.* 124(4):1449–96

Mian A, Sufi A. 2011. House prices, home equity-based borrowing, and the U.S. household leverage crisis. *Am. Econ. Rev.* 101(5):2132–56

Mian A, Sufi A, Trebbi F. 2013. The political economy of the subprime mortgage credit expansion. *Q. J. Political Sci.* 8(4):373–408

Morgenson G, Rosner J. 2011. *Reckless Endangerment.* New York: Times Books

Paulson HM Jr. 2010. *On the Brink: Inside the Race to Stop the Collapse of the Global Financial System.* New York: Hachette

Piskorski T, Seru A, Vig V. 2010. Securitization and distressed loan renegotiation: evidence from the subprime mortgage crisis. *J. Financ. Econ.* 97(3):369–97

Poterba J, Sinai T. 2008. Tax expenditures for owner-occupied housing: deductions for property taxes and mortgage interest and the exclusion of imputed rental income. *Am. Econ. Rev.* 98(2):84–89

Purnanandam A. 2011. Originate-to-distribute model and the subprime mortgage crisis. *Rev. Financ. Stud.* 24(6):1881–915

Scharfstein D, Sunderam A. 2011. The economics of housing finance reform. In *Future Housing Finance: Restructuring the US Residential Mortgage Market*, ed. MN Baily, pp. 146–98. Washington, DC: Brookings Inst.

Scharfstein D, Swagel P. 2016. Legislative approaches to housing finance reform. In *Principles of Housing Finance Reform*, ed. SM Wachter, J Tracy, pp. 7–31. Philadelphia: Univ. Pa. Press

Sodini P, Van Nieuwerburgh S, Vestman R, von Lilienfeld-Toal U. 2016. *Identifying the benefits from home ownership: a Swedish experiment.* NBER Work. Pap. 22882

Sommer K, Sullivan P. 2016. *Implications of U.S. tax policy for house prices, rents and homeownership.* Work. Pap., Fed. Reserve Board Gov., Washington, DC

Sorkin AR. 2009. *Too Big to Fail: The Inside Story of How Wall Street and Washington Fought to Save the Financial System—and Themselves.* New York: Viking Penguin

Urban Inst. 2016. *Housing Finance Reform Incubator, July 2016.* Washington, DC: Urban Inst.

Urban Inst. 2017. *Housing Finance at a Glance: A Monthly Chartbook, May 2017.* Washington, DC: Urban Inst.

US Dep. Treas., US Dep. Hous. Urban Dev. 2011. *Reforming America's housing finance market. February 2011.* Rep. Congr., Dep. Treas., Dep. Hous. Urban Dev., Washington, DC

Vickery J, Wright J. 2010. *TBA trading and liquidity in the agency MBS market.* Staff Rep. 468, Fed. Reserve Bank N.Y., New York

Market Liquidity After the Financial Crisis

Tobias Adrian,[1] Michael Fleming,[2] Or Shachar,[2] and Erik Vogt[3]

[1]International Monetary Fund, Washington, DC 20431; email: tadrian@imf.org

[2]Federal Reserve Bank of New York, New York, NY 10045; email: michael.fleming@ny.frb.org, or.shachar@ny.frb.org

[3]Citadel LLC, Chicago, Illinois 60603; email: erikvogt.econ@gmail.com

Annu. Rev. Financ. Econ. 2017. 9:43–83

The *Annual Review of Financial Economics* is online at financial.annualreviews.org

https://doi.org/10.1146/annurev-financial-110716-032325

Copyright © 2017 by Annual Reviews. All rights reserved

JEL codes: G12, G21, G28

Keywords

liquidity, market making, regulation, Treasury securities, corporate bonds

Abstract

This article examines market liquidity in the postcrisis era in light of concerns that regulatory changes might have reduced dealers' ability and willingness to make markets. We begin with a discussion of the broader trading environment, including an overview of regulations and their potential effects on dealer balance sheets and market making, but also considering additional drivers of market liquidity. We document a stagnation of dealer balance sheets after the financial crisis of 2007–2009, which occurred concurrently with dealer balance sheet deleveraging. However, using high-frequency trade and quote data for US Treasuries and corporate bonds, we find only limited evidence of a deterioration in market liquidity.

1. INTRODUCTION

In the years since the financial crisis of 2007–2009, market participants have expressed concerns about worsening liquidity in certain markets (for media reports, see, e.g., Krouse 2015a,b; Levine 2015; Wigglesworth 2015; Bloomberg 2016a,b; Marriage & Mooney 2016). Market liquidity, broadly defined, refers to the cost of exchanging assets for cash. Liquidity considerations feature prominently in real and financial investment decisions because liquidity is priced, with investors demanding higher returns for less liquid assets (Amihud & Mendelson 1986). Moreover, asset illiquidity deters trade and hence investment, impeding the efficient allocation of risk and capital in the economy.

Frequently cited causes for the ostensibly worsening liquidity are the Dodd–Frank Act and the Basel III regulatory framework. In an effort to address the solvency and liquidity problems that arose during the crisis, this regulatory framework includes provisions that tighten banks' capital requirements, introduce leverage ratios, and establish liquidity requirements. Although these regulations are intended to make the global financial system more resilient to shocks, market participants argue that they also increase the cost of market making by raising the cost of capital and restricting dealers' risk taking. The differing perspectives of regulators and market participants suggest a trade-off in which the banking sector can draw on enhanced capital and liquidity buffers to maintain its market-making functions in times of stress but potentially provides less liquidity in normal times.

This article examines the evidence surrounding market liquidity in the postcrisis era. We begin with a discussion of the broader trading environment in an effort to outline potential drivers of market liquidity since the crisis. This includes a discussion of regulations and their potential effects on dealer balance sheets and market making, as well as other plausible determinants of market liquidity. The drivers that we discuss include:

1. the postcrisis regulatory framework, reflecting the Dodd–Frank Act and the Basel III capital and liquidity requirements;
2. voluntary changes in dealer risk-management practices and balance sheet composition following the housing market boom and bust;
3. changes in market structure with the growth of electronic trading;
4. the changing landscape of institutional investors, including the evolving liquidity demands of large asset managers; and
5. changes in expected returns associated with the economic environment.

We argue that because these factors were all at play in the years immediately following the crisis, identification of the causal effects of any single factor must control for the others. Identification is further complicated by the fact that most (if not all) of these drivers are highly interrelated and endogenous.

We document the striking fact that dealer balance sheets stagnated after the crisis. In the years running up to the crisis, dealer assets grew at an exponential pace, peaking at about $5 trillion in early 2008. In late 2008, assets contracted sharply to $3.5 trillion, a level that was first breached in 2005. After that, through mid-2016, dealer assets were stagnant around this $3.5 trillion level. This balance sheet stagnation coincided with dealer deleveraging. Curbing dealer leverage is of course an intended consequence of tighter capital regulation. However, the stagnation and deleveraging of dealer balance sheets raises the questions of whether regulations might have had unintended consequences for market liquidity and whether liquidity in dealer-intermediated markets can still be provided efficiently. To get at this question, we analyze market liquidity empirically.

Our main empirical exercise consists of assessing the evolution of market liquidity in the US Treasury and US corporate bond markets. Market participants' concerns about liquidity center on fixed-income markets that are dealer intermediated, and these are the most important of these markets. Given the multifaceted nature of market liquidity, we compute a variety of liquidity measures, including bid-ask spreads, depth, price impact, and trade size. The measures are based on tick-level order book and transactions data from the interdealer Treasury market and on corporate bond transactions data from the Trade Reporting and Compliance Engine (TRACE) database of the Financial Industry Regulatory Authority (FINRA).

Overall, we do not find strong quantitative evidence of a widespread deterioration in bond market liquidity in the years after the crisis. As of mid-2016, average bid-ask spreads for benchmark notes in the interdealer Treasury market were narrow and stable. Moreover, Treasury market depth and price impact, though suggesting reduced liquidity, were within historical variation and far from crisis levels. For corporate bonds, average bid-ask spreads and price impact declined after the crisis, albeit to levels higher than those before the crisis for institutional trades (i.e., trades of $100,000 and above). Moreover, corporate bond trading volume and issuance were at record highs.

Our empirical findings on market liquidity are broadly consistent with those of others. Analyzing TRACE corporate bond transactions data from 2003 to 2015, Mizrach (2015, p. 1) concludes that "most measures suggest a healthy market" with rising transaction volumes, narrowing bid-ask spreads, and falling price impact of trades. Looking at price impact, round-trip costs, and other measures, Trebbi & Xiao (2015, p. 5) report "a lack of any form of systematic evidence of deterioration in liquidity levels or breaks in liquidity risk for corporate bonds." Bessembinder et al. (2016) further find lower transaction costs during the 2012–2014 Dodd–Frank phase-in period than in the 2003–2007 precrisis period. Anderson & Stulz (2017) report lower average transaction costs and price impact postcrisis versus precrisis for all corporate bond transactions, but also report somewhat worse liquidity for large (≥$100,000) trades, in line with our findings.

In contrast to these studies on broad liquidity trends, several studies have documented worsening liquidity along some dimension. Bao, O'Hara & Zhou (2016) find that price impact increased among recently downgraded corporate bonds when comparing the periods before and after implementation of the Volcker rule. Similarly, Dick-Nielsen & Rossi (2016) use bond index exclusions as a natural experiment during which index-tracking investors demand immediacy from dealers; the authors find that the price of immediacy significantly increased postcrisis versus precrisis. Choi & Huh (2016) show that dealers are providing liquidity for a decreasing share of trades over time and that transaction costs have increased for this subset of trades. Furthermore, although Bessembinder et al. (2016) estimate lower transaction costs after the crisis, they also document a structural break that suggests a decline in dealers' capital commitment relative to the precrisis period. Adrian, Boyarchenko & Shachar (2017) find that corporate bond liquidity provision declined significantly in recent years for dealers that are relatively more constrained by regulations.

We also present three case studies on the resilience of market liquidity to shocks in the postcrisis era. The first analyzes dealer balance sheet behavior during the 2013 taper tantrum, when Treasury yields rose by more than 100 basis points within a 10-week period. The second looks at the October 2014 flash rally in the US Treasury market, when yields rose and fell rapidly within a 12-minute event window. The third reviews the extent to which the liquidation of Third Avenue's high-yield bond fund in December 2015 affected market liquidity. In all three cases, the degree of deterioration in market liquidity was within historical norms, suggesting that liquidity remained resilient.

Although we do not uncover clear indications of a widespread worsening of bond market liquidity, our analysis faces several limitations. Most importantly, our review of corporate bond liquidity relies on trades that have occurred and does not account for any trades that have not taken place due to changes in the regulatory environment or other factors. Future work should thus consider both a wider range of data and methodological improvements to better exploit existing data. Moreover, dealer balance sheets have undergone dramatic changes, reflecting macroeconomic trends and the evolution of the market-making business model, and some funding cost metrics, such as interest rate swap spreads and the credit default swap (CDS)-bond basis, imply increased balance sheet costs. Further researching the determinants of these funding cost metrics is a promising avenue of future research, particularly given the close relationship between funding liquidity and market liquidity (Brunnermeier & Pedersen 2009). Additional topics for future research include endogeneities in the data-generating process and the concept of liquidity risk.

This article proceeds as follows. Section 2 discusses the evolving trading environment for broker/dealers as well as the broader trading environment. Section 3 presents our main empirical findings on market liquidity and their relation to the recent literature. Section 4 discusses directions for future research, and Section 5 concludes.

2. THE POSTCRISIS TRADING ENVIRONMENT

Security broker/dealers (or simply dealers) trade securities on behalf of their customers and for their own accounts, using their balance sheets primarily for trading operations, particularly market making. The dealer business model has changed rapidly in recent years, as we illustrate through dealer balance sheet size. A priori, we would expect the size of dealers' balance sheets to expand exponentially over time, similar to gross domestic product or population.

Figure 1 shows dealer balance sheet size from 1990 to 2016. Dealer size grew exponentially from 1990 through 2008, with a peak close to \$5 trillion. Dealer assets then collapsed after Lehman Brothers' failure and remained stalled at about \$3.5 trillion, the level of 2005. If the previous trend of exponential growth had continued, the balance sheet size of dealers would have been several times larger in 2016 than it was. The stagnation of the balance sheet size of dealers after the crisis raises the questions of whether the \$5 trillion peak was excessive, whether the precrisis growth

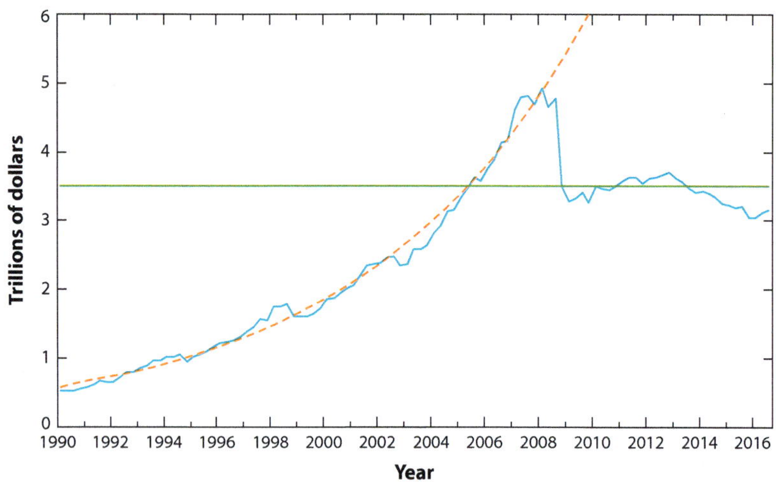

Figure 1

Dealers' assets. This figure plots the total financial assets of security broker/dealers at the subsidiary level. The orange dashed curve shows the computed exponential growth trend of the 1990–2008 period. The green line is set at \$3.5 trillion. Data are from the Financial Accounts of the United States published by the Board of Governors of the Federal Reserve System.

was sustainable, and whether the 2016 level was, in some sense, depressed. The stagnation also raises the concern that dealers' market-making capacity could be constrained, adversely affecting market liquidity (Adrian et al. 2015g).

One possible explanation for the stagnation of the balance sheet size of dealers is regulation. In fact, tighter capital regulation explicitly seeks to limit balance sheet leverage, and deleveraging can occur through either an increase in capital or a reduction in assets. However, the extent to which the stagnation of dealer balance sheet size has been caused by regulation is difficult to quantify because dealers continuously adjust the size and composition of their balance sheets during the normal course of business. Recent research (Adrian & Shin 2014) suggests that dealers expand their balance sheets in booms and contract them in busts, primarily by adjusting leverage. Dealers' balance sheets and risk appetite are highly correlated, because (other things being equal) higher leverage mechanically exposes dealers to more risk by amplifying potential losses. It is therefore not uncommon to see dealers rationally deleverage to reduce risk taking during downturns as potential losses are realized.

Figure 2 shows that the private incentives of dealers to deleverage and the social incentives of regulators to impose limits on leverage coincided in the wake of the housing market boom and bust. Leverage peaked at 48 in the first quarter of 2008, just prior to the near failure of Bear Stearns, but then dropped to 25 by June 2009, roughly a year before the passage of Dodd–Frank and the announcement of the Basel III banking capital regulations in July 2010. Most deleveraging thus occurred prior to the announcement of potentially constraining regulation. Dodd–Frank and Basel III regulations may help explain the deleveraging since 2010, but it is unclear to what extent regulations constrain growth in dealer leverage and risk taking today.

As mentioned, there are a number of possible explanations for the remarkable change in dealer balance sheets, including the postcrisis regulatory framework, voluntary changes in dealer

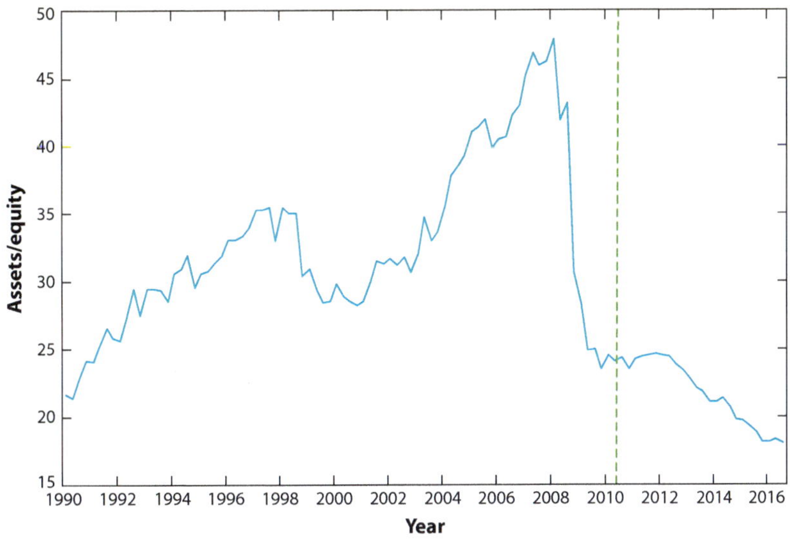

Figure 2

Procyclical dealer leverage. This figure shows the leverage of security broker/dealers at the subsidiary level. Leverage is defined as (total assets)/(book equity capital). The green dotted line marks the passage of the Dodd–Frank Act and the announcement of the Basel III capital reforms in July 2010. Data are from the Financial Accounts of the United States published by the Board of Governors of the Federal Reserve System.

risk-management practice and balance sheet composition, the growth of electronic trading, the evolving liquidity demands of large asset managers, and changes in expected returns. We discuss each of these factors in detail.

2.1. Postcrisis Regulatory Framework

Regulations affecting the dealer sector tightened markedly after the financial crisis of 2007–2009. The five major independent US dealers were outside of the safety net prior to the crisis and were regulated under Basel II capital rules, and all of them either failed (Lehman), were acquired by banking organizations (Bear Stearns and Merrill Lynch), or became bank-holding companies (BHCs) themselves (Goldman Sachs and Morgan Stanley). All major US dealers are now subject to the Federal Reserve's stress tests and enhanced capital and liquidity requirements, as well as the more stringent Basel III rules.

Regulatory reform after the crisis stems directly from shortcomings in the regulatory framework uncovered during the crisis. During the crisis, banks, dealers, financial market utilities, and other systemically important market participants experienced both solvency and liquidity problems. That motivated subsequent tightening of capital and liquidity requirements. In addition, some regulations directly restrict certain activities, such as the Volcker rule, which prohibits proprietary trading by banks. The regulations have substantially affected institutions' business models. We briefly review these regulatory changes and provide further references.

2.1.1. Basel 2.5 market risk amendment. In 2010, the Basel Committee on Banking Supervision (BCBS 2010) put forth the market risk amendment, recognizing that the existing capital framework for market risk did not capture some key risks. The value-at-risk (VaR)-based trading book framework was supplemented with an incremental risk capital charge that accounted for default and migration risk for credit products. The incremental risk capital charge aims to reduce the incentive for regulatory arbitrage between banking and trading books. In addition, this framework introduced a stressed VaR requirement. The incremental risk capital charge and the stressed VaR requirement significantly affect balance sheet costs, particularly for corporate bonds and bespoke credit derivatives [Committee on the Global Financial System (CGFS) 2014].

2.1.2. Basel III capital requirements. The 2010 Basel III capital framework (BCBS 2011) aims to strengthen the resilience of the banking sector through enhanced capital requirements. The reforms raise both the quality and quantity of the regulatory capital base and enhance the risk coverage of the capital framework. The BCBS also introduced several macroprudential elements into the capital framework to help contain systemic risk arising from procyclicality and the interconnectedness of financial institutions.

In order to improve the quality of capital, Basel III requires the preponderance of tier 1 capital to be in the form of common shares and retained earnings. Common tier 1 equity has to be at least 4.5% of risk-weighted assets at all times. The BCBS also introduced a capital conservation buffer of 2.5% that can be drawn down in periods of stress. Furthermore, the committee introduced a countercyclical capital buffer that can be set by regulators in a range of 0–2.5%, depending on the state of the credit cycle.

Basel III introduced measures to strengthen the capital requirements for counterparty credit exposures arising from banks' derivatives, repurchase agreement (repo), and securities financing activities. Banks must determine their capital requirement for counterparty credit risk using stress assumptions in order to address concerns about capital charges becoming too low during periods of compressed market volatility, thereby helping mitigate the effects of the procyclicality of leverage.

Banks are subject to a capital charge for potential mark-to-market losses, referred to as a credit valuation adjustment, associated with a deterioration in counterparty creditworthiness.

The BCBS also introduced a leverage ratio requirement to constrain leverage in the banking sector. The leverage ratio provides an additional safeguard against model risk and measurement error by supplementing the risk-based capital measure with a simple, transparent, independent measure of risk. The leverage ratio requirement is 3%, with an additional 2% supplement for the largest US institutions. The requirement increases balance sheet costs relatively more for low-margin businesses such as market making in repo and highly rated sovereign bonds (CGFS 2014).

The BCBS additionally introduced a macroprudential surcharge to reduce the probability of failure of global systemically important banks (GSIBs) by increasing their going-concern loss absorbency, as well as to reduce the cost of failure of GSIBs by improving global recovery and resolution frameworks (BCBS 2013b). The systemic importance of GSIBs is assessed using an indicator-based measurement approach. The selected indicators are chosen to reflect the different aspects of what generates negative externalities and what makes a bank critical for the stability of the financial system, and include size, cross-jurisdictional activity, interconnectedness, substitutability/financial institution infrastructure, and complexity.

2.1.3. Liquidity regulation. To bolster the liquidity positions of banks, the BCBS developed the liquidity coverage ratio (LCR) and the net stable funding ratio (NSFR; see BCBS 2013a, 2014). The objective of the LCR is to promote the short-term resilience of banks' liquidity risk profiles by ensuring that banks have an adequate stock of liquid assets to meet liquidity needs for a 30-day stress scenario. The objective of the NSFR is to reduce banks' funding risk over a longer time horizon by requiring banks to maintain sufficiently stable sources of funding. The NSFR is defined as the amount of available stable funding relative to the amount of required stable funding and must equal or exceed 100% on an ongoing basis.

2.1.4. Total loss-absorbing capacity. In 2013, G20 leaders asked regulators to assess and develop proposals to ensure the adequacy of global systemically important financial institutions' loss-absorbing capacity when they fail. The aim is to reduce both the probability and impact of failure of GSIBs by requiring sufficient loss-absorbing and recapitalization capacity in resolution to implement an orderly resolution that minimizes effects on financial stability, ensures the continuity of critical functions, and avoids exposing public funds to loss. A total loss-absorbing capacity requirement thus imposes a minimum level of bail-in-able debt, which can be transformed into equity during the resolution of a GSIB. The Financial Stability Board (FSB 2015) provides an overview.

2.1.5. Stress tests. In the United States, the Federal Reserve conducts annual stress tests for the largest BHCs and designated systemically important financial institutions (SIFIs). The Dodd–Frank Act requires such tests in order to ascertain whether BHCs and SIFIs have sufficient capital to absorb losses resulting from adverse economic conditions. The tests are based on a hypothetical, severely adverse scenario designed by the Federal Reserve, incorporate detailed information about the risk characteristics and business activities of each BHC, and are estimated using a consistent approach across BHCs. The projected losses under the scenario thereby provide a unique perspective on the robustness of the capital positions of these firms and provide comparable results across firms.

The Federal Reserve's annual Comprehensive Capital Analysis and Review (CCAR) is an intensive assessment of the capital adequacy and capital planning processes of large US BHCs based on the stress tests. Through CCAR, the Federal Reserve seeks to ensure that large BHCs have strong processes for assessing their capital needs supported by effective firm-wide practices to identify, measure, and manage their material risks; strong internal controls; and effective oversight by boards of directors and senior management. CCAR helps promote greater resiliency at firms by requiring each BHC to support its capital management decisions with forward-looking comprehensive analysis that takes into account the BHC's unique risk profile and activities as well as the effect of highly stressful operating environments on financial performance.

2.1.6. Volcker rule. Section 619 of the Dodd–Frank Act, referred to as the Volcker rule, prohibits insured depository institutions and any company affiliated with an insured depository institution from engaging in proprietary trading and from acquiring or retaining ownership interests in, sponsoring, or having certain relationships with a hedge fund or private equity fund. The rule, aiming to rein in excessive risk taking in over-the-counter (OTC) markets, essentially prohibits proprietary trading by banks except for market-making activities. Although the rule directly affects market makers' capacity to provide liquidity, Duffie (2012) argues that overall market liquidity might not be hampered if lost market-making capacity is filled by nonbank firms such as hedge funds or insurance companies. US Treasuries, agency mortgage-backed securities (MBS), and agency debt securities are exempt from the Volcker rule.

2.1.7. Impact of the regulatory reforms for dealers. CGFS (2014) considers the effects of these regulations for dealers' business models and market making more generally. Regulatory changes after the crisis likely affect dealers' balance sheets and profitability, and market participants assert that they raise market-making costs. Risk weights and credit risk charges make trading of corporate bonds and credit derivatives more expensive. In particular, the incremental risk capital charge and the stressed VaR increase holding costs of corporate bonds. Furthermore, less liquid corporate bonds are ineligible for the LCR, which is thought to reduce the willingness of banks to warehouse these assets. Moreover, the leverage ratio increases the balance sheet cost of repos, including those backed by corporate bonds and structured credit, increasing dealers' financing costs.

CGFS (2016) provides results of an informal survey of market participants on the effects of regulatory reforms. Respondents provided estimates of the relative importance of different cost drivers, including regulatory capital requirements as well as trading and operational costs, using two highly stylized portfolios: one of sovereign bonds and one of corporate bonds. The survey results suggest that the effects of postcrisis regulatory changes are differentiated. For sovereign bonds, the Basel III leverage ratio and higher risk-weighted capital requirements are thought to have the largest effect on regulatory capital charges and, hence, on dealers' profits. For corporate bonds, by comparison, revisions to the Basel II market risk framework (Basel 2.5) are thought to have the largest effect on regulatory charges. The survey responses imply that the gross revenue required to yield a return on capital of 8% under a fully phased-in Basel III framework would have resulted in returns above 20% under Basel II.

The academic evidence on the effects of regulatory reforms is mixed, at least partially reflecting the challenges in estimating effects of regulations considered, approved, and implemented over extended periods amid numerous other developments. As noted earlier, Mizrach (2015), Bessembinder et al. (2016), and Anderson & Stulz (2017) find that corporate bond liquidity overall is better in the postcrisis period than in the precrisis period, although Anderson & Stulz (2017) find higher transaction costs and price impact for large (≥$100,000) trades, a finding that we discuss further below. Trebbi & Xiao (2015) test for break points in various liquidity measures and find that none of their estimated structural breaks occur around the approval of Dodd–Frank, the occurrence of major bank proprietary trading desk closures, or the Volcker rule finalization, and conclude that postcrisis regulatory changes have not produced a structural deterioration in bond market liquidity.

In contrast, Bao, O'Hara & Zhou (2016) find that price impact increased among recently downgraded corporate bonds when comparing the periods before and after implementation of the Volcker rule. Similarly, Dick-Nielsen & Rossi (2016) find that the price of immediacy (which they measure around bond index inclusions) significantly increased postcrisis versus precrisis. Moreover, Choi & Huh (2016) show that dealers are providing liquidity for a decreasing share of trades over time and that transaction costs have increased for this subset of trades. Bessembinder et al. (2016) also find that dealers' propensity to intermediate on an agency basis increases at times of market stress and that dealers appear less willing to commit capital on a principal basis in the postcrisis period. Although their study does not rule out other explanations, they note that the timing of these changes is consistent with dealers' behavior having been affected by the implementation of Dodd–Frank.

Adrian, Boyarchenko & Shachar (2017) study the relationship between bond-level liquidity and financial institutions' balance sheet constraints. They first document that there is a relationship between institutional constraints and bond liquidity. Bonds traded by more levered and systemic institutions (those with higher leverage, a higher ratio of securities bought under repurchase agreements to assets, and higher financial vulnerability), as well as bonds traded by institutions more akin to investment banks (BHCs with smaller ratios of risk-weighted assets to assets, smaller allocations to loans, and higher trading revenues), are less liquid. These results hold across bonds with different credit ratings, issued by companies in different industries, with different issuance sizes, and with different prior levels of liquidity.

The relationship between bond liquidity and institution-level constraints does, however, change significantly over time. Adrian, Boyarchenko & Shachar (2017) find that, prior to the crisis, bonds traded by institutions with higher leverage, higher return on assets, lower risk-weighted assets, lower reliance on repo funding, and lower vulnerability were more liquid. During the rule implementation period (starting in January 2014), these relationships reversed: Bonds traded by institutions with lower leverage, higher risk-weighted assets, more reliance on repo funding, and lower return on assets were more liquid. That is, the relationship between bond liquidity and dealer constraints that we see in the full sample is primarily driven by that same relationship in the postcrisis period. These findings are consistent with more stringent leverage regulation and greater regulation of dealer banks reducing institutions' ability to provide liquidity to the market overall.

2.2. Consequences of the Housing Market Boom and Bust

Dealers' balance sheet management is reflective of their risk appetite. Adrian & Shin (2010, 2014) thus document that dealers' risk taking is closely tied to their risk-management constraints, particularly balance sheet VaR. In booms, when volatility tends to be compressed, dealers have loose VaR constraints, allowing them to expand their balance sheets by increasing leverage. When an adverse shock hits, such as a sudden decline in housing prices, the VaR constraints can act as an amplification mechanism: Declining asset prices are associated with increased measured risk, forcing dealers to sell, thus inducing further price declines. The tightness of dealer VaR constraints thus determines dealers' risk appetite.

To investigate the effect of risk appetite on dealers' balance sheet contraction, we examine whether the cross section of dealers' risk-taking behavior during the housing boom shaped their growth in the subsequent housing bust. In **Figure 3**, we show that dealers that expanded their balance sheets more in the period before the financial crisis (2002–2007) tended to contract

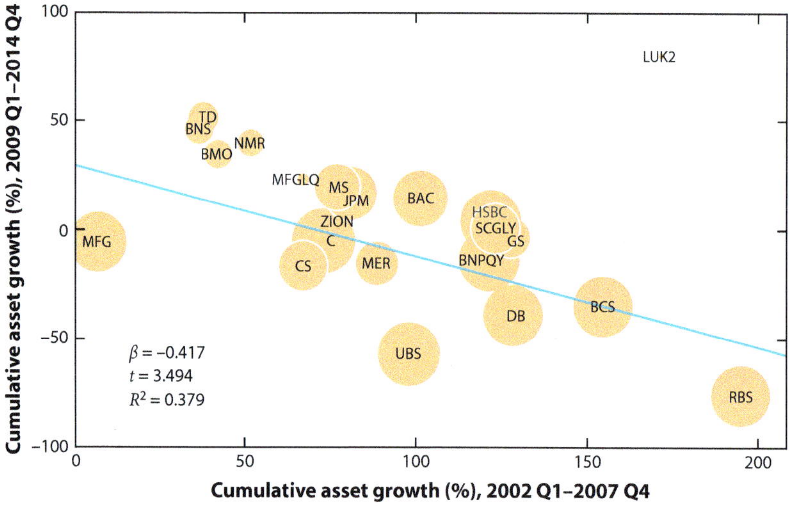

Figure 3

Dealers' balance sheet expansions and contractions. This figure compares asset growth precrisis to asset growth postcrisis for the primary dealers for which data are available. Dots are labeled with each dealer's stock market ticker and are scaled to reflect dealer size as measured by average total assets from 2002 to 2007. The asset-weighted least squares regression line is in blue. Data are from Compustat.

their balance sheets more after the crisis (2009–2014). This finding is a cross-sectional version of the procyclicality of dealers' balance sheets documented by Adrian & Shin (2010, 2014).

Adrian et al. (2015g) further investigate the cross section of risk taking using the realized volatility of equity returns over the precrisis period as a measure of risk taking. They find that riskier dealers tended to have larger losses during the crisis. (A related academic study shows that the propensity to take risk across firms persists over time; see Cheng, Hong & Scheinkman 2015.) Furthermore, greater risk taking during the crisis—as measured by dealers' VaR—predicts greater contraction of assets postcrisis. These findings are consistent with the interpretation that dealers' propensity to take risk amplified the growth of dealers' balance sheets going into the crisis, causing crisis losses and a subsequent sharp contraction of balance sheets after the crisis.

This evidence is thus suggestive of balance sheet contraction being related to dealers' risk-taking behavior in the run-up to the crisis. In particular, many European banking organizations aggressively entered the US investment banking market in the late 1990s and early 2000s, fueling the increase in aggregate balance sheet size. Furthermore, many major dealers significantly expanded their securitization activities and holdings of securitized assets. Both factors likely increased balance sheet growth before the crisis, and both factors are (cross-sectionally) associated with losses during the crisis and balance sheet reduction after the crisis.

2.3. Electronification

Another key development in recent years is the electronification of fixed-income markets. Electronification refers to the shift toward trading through computer systems, increased automated trading (which relies on algorithms for trading decisions and executions), and the reliance on speed to identify and act upon trading opportunities [that is, high-frequency trading (HFT)]. The growth of electronic trading has likely reduced dealers' profits from intermediating customer order flow, causing dealers to step back from making markets and reducing their need for large balance sheets. The Joint Staff Report on the US Treasury market on October 15, 2014 (Joint Staff 2015) showed that trading in the interdealer cash and futures markets is now dominated by principal trading firms (PTFs), which typically execute HFT strategies.

The Bank for International Settlements (BIS 2016) provides an overview of electronic trading in fixed-income markets and argues that electronic and automated trading tends to have a positive impact on market quality. Indeed, academic studies show that automated trading is associated with a compression in bid-ask spreads, an increase in trading volume, and smaller trade sizes, on average (see the surveys by Jones 2013 and Menkveld 2016).[1] Hasbrouck & Saar (2013) show that low latency reduces bid-ask spreads, the total price impact of trades, and short-term volatility; Hendershott, Jones & Menkveld (2011) find that algorithmic trading narrows bid-ask spreads and enhances price discovery. Menkveld (2013) studies the trading strategy of a large high-frequency trader whose entry coincided with a 50% drop in the bid-ask spread.

However, automated trading may also be associated with an increase in liquidity risk, as suggested by the BIS (2016). Some have thus linked the flash events in the equity market on May 6, 2010, in the US Treasury market on October 15, 2014, and in the foreign exchange market on March 18, 2015, to the presence of automated trading [see Securities and Exchange Commission (SEC) 2010, Joint Staff 2015, Schaumburg & Yang 2015]. Automated trading might therefore be beneficial on average, but associated with costs in some states of the world.

To gauge the effects of electronification on market making, we estimate market-making returns in equity and corporate bond markets, following Adrian et al. (2015a). We first calculate minute-by-minute returns from a reversal strategy for the 30 firms in the Dow Jones Industrial Average, using the methodology described by Khandani & Lo (2007) and Nagel (2012). Returns are based on an investment portfolio that is long past losers and short past winners, thus betting on the reversal of past trends. The literature uses such reversal profits as proxies for expected returns to market making, as market makers tend to manage their trading book in a similar fashion. As shown in **Figure 4**, profits on this reversal strategy declined precipitously between the mid-1990s and mid-2000s and then stabilized at historically low levels, except for a temporary increase during the financial crisis. Although market-making returns were highly correlated with the Chicago Board Options Exchange Volatility Index (VIX) through 2004, they were more stable than the VIX after that, except during the crisis, when both the VIX and the returns increased sharply.

The decline in high-frequency market-making returns occurred against a backdrop of increasing competition. The expected returns to high-frequency trading in the 1990s encouraged large investments in speed and led many new firms to enter the sector, as documented by Budish, Cramton & Shim (2015). The sharp decline in high-frequency profits over the first 10 years of our sample suggests that these profits were gradually eroded by competition as the HFT sector developed. Importantly, market-making profits did not increase after capital and liquidity regulations were tightened following the crisis.

Figure 5 shows that a somewhat different picture emerges for day-to-day market-making returns. Daily reversal trading returns for the firms tracked in the Center for Research in Security Prices (CRSP) database declined between the mid-1990s and the mid-2000s and increased sharply during the crisis, with no discernible trend after the crisis. However, **Figure 5** also shows a high correlation between day-to-day market-making profits and the evolution of market volatility after the mid-2000s, a relationship not observed for higher-frequency market making. The interpretation is that higher market volatility tightens dealers' funding constraints, contributing to

[1]In contrast, Biais, Foucault & Moinas (2015) show that high-speed technology enables fast traders to retrieve information before slow traders, generating adverse selection and thus negative externalities.

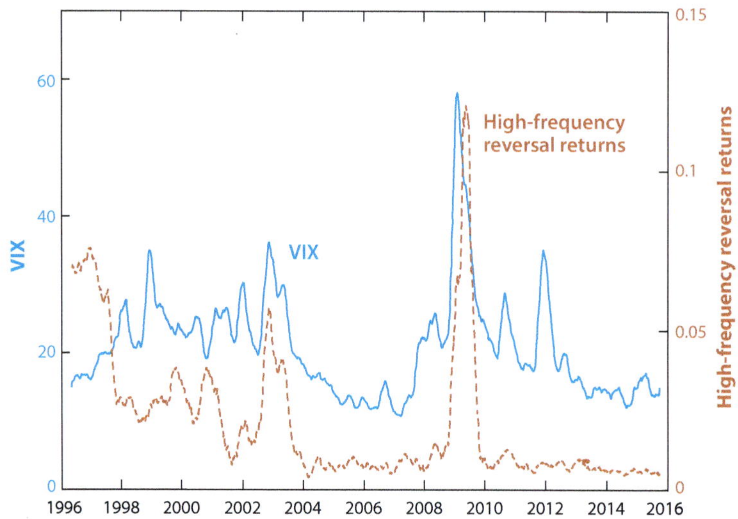

Figure 4

High-frequency equity market returns. This figure plots the Chicago Board Options Exchange (CBOE) Volatility Index (VIX) alongside a proxy for high-frequency market-making returns in equities as calculated by the daily returns to a minute-by-minute reversal strategy for the 30 firms in the Dow Jones Industrial Average as described by Khandani & Lo (2007) and Nagel (2012). Three-month moving averages are shown for both series. The equity data from which the market-making returns are calculated are from the Thomson Reuters tick history; VIX data are from the CBOE.

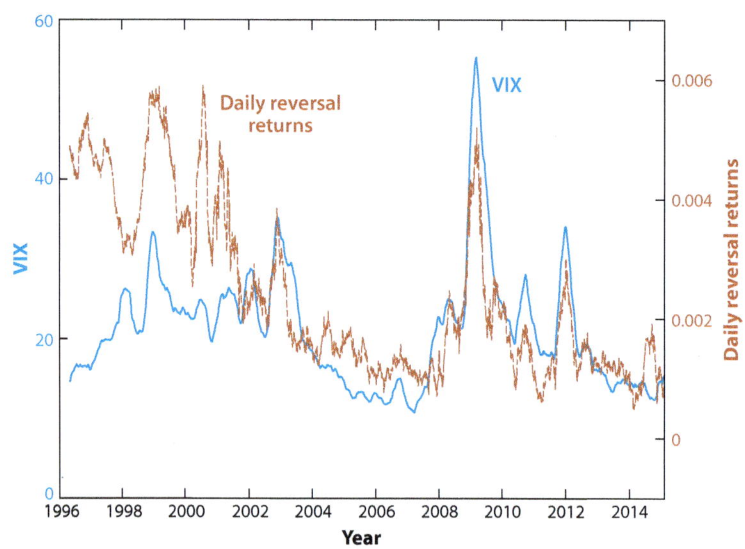

Figure 5

Day-to-day equity market returns. The figure plots the Chicago Board Options Exchange (CBOE) Volatility Index (VIX) alongside a proxy for daily market-making returns in equities as calculated by a day-by-day reversal strategy for the 30 firms in the Dow Jones Industrial Average as described by Khandani & Lo (2007) and Nagel (2012). Three-month moving averages are shown for both series. The equity data from which the market-making returns are calculated are from the Thomson Reuters tick history; VIX data are from the CBOE.

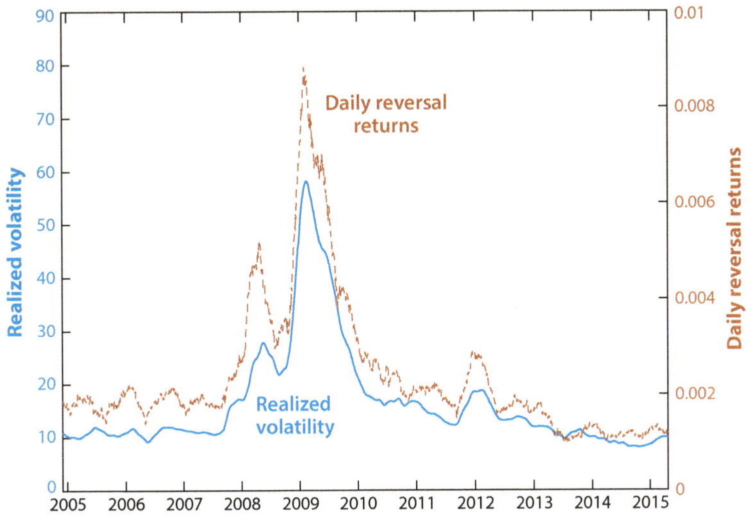

Figure 6

Day-to-day corporate bond market returns. This figure plots the cross-sectionally averaged monthly realized volatility of Markit's North American Investment Grade CDX Index constituents alongside a proxy for daily market-making returns as calculated by the daily returns to a reversal strategy as described by Khandani & Lo (2007) and Nagel (2012). The reversal strategy is applied to the same index constituents. Three-month moving averages are shown for both series. The daily returns are from FINRA's TRACE database and the realized volatilities are from Markit.

a widening of market-making returns. Risk-management techniques that rely directly on market volatility, such as VaR limits, can cause such funding constraints to bind and create a link between funding liquidity and market liquidity (Brunnermeier & Pedersen 2009, Adrian & Shin 2014).

Whereas dealers play a modest role in equity markets, they remain the predominant market makers in the corporate bond market. Moreover, although electronification has become more prevalent in corporate bond trading, such trading does not involve HFT strategies. **Figure 6** shows that reversal returns for corporate bonds at the daily frequency exhibit no increase in market-making profits and thereby do not suggest a withdrawal of market-making activity in this market. The figure also reveals a close relationship between returns to market making and corporate bond realized volatility, with returns to market making highest during high-volatility periods.

Overall, this evidence suggests that expected returns to market making remained compressed after the crisis, both in equity markets, where electronic HFT is predominant, and in credit markets, where electronification is not yet associated with HFT. Adrian et al. (2015a) present complementary evidence by investigating the profitability of dealers. They find that postcrisis trading revenue for dealers listed on the New York Stock Exchange (NYSE) was very close to precrisis levels, whereas the volatility of trading revenue was much lower. It follows that the Sharpe ratio of trading revenue (aggregate revenue of dealers divided by the volatility of revenue) was considerably higher postcrisis. Net income for the five largest US dealers in particular—Bank of America, Citigroup, Goldman Sachs, J.P. Morgan, and Morgan Stanley—was also much higher and less volatile after the crisis than before, and the Sharpe ratio of net income was nearly twice as high. These trading revenue and income figures suggest that dealers continue to play a key role in liquidity provision. This is particularly important for less liquid securities in which HFT firms are less active, such as corporate bonds and off-the-run Treasury securities, and at times

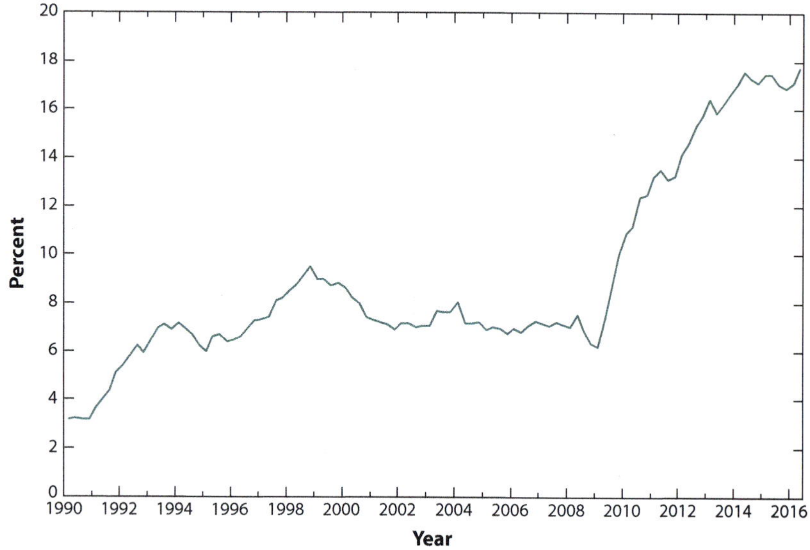

Figure 7

Mutual fund ownership of corporate bonds. This figure plots corporate and foreign bonds outstanding (held in the United States) owned by mutual funds and exchange-traded funds as a fraction of the total amount of corporate and foreign bonds (held in the United States) outstanding. Data are from the Financial Accounts of the United States published by the Board of Governors of the Federal Reserve System.

of stress, when dealers have greater incentive to provide liquidity because of their customer relationships. The picture that emerges is of a change in the risk-sharing arrangement among trading institutions.

2.4. Evolving Liquidity Demands of Large Asset Managers

As of mid-2016, mutual funds owned about 18% of corporate bonds, up from about 3% in 1990, as shown in **Figure 7**. The surge in ownership was strikingly rapid after 2008, suggesting that the channels of credit intermediation changed with the financial crisis. Before the crisis, shadow credit intermediation was widespread, involving maturity transformation by money market funds that funded credit. After the crisis, money market fund investments in credit vehicles such as asset-backed commercial paper conduits shrank sharply, and market-based credit intermediation shifted to bond funds. Although credit intermediation by bond funds still involves some maturity transformation, such maturity transformation is far smaller than the maturity transformation of lengthy shadow credit intermediation chains that was common before the crisis.

Mutual funds' increased ownership of corporate bonds raises concerns about redemption risk. When mutual funds are subject to large redemptions, they can be forced to sell some of their holdings, which can cause price declines, especially for relatively illiquid bonds. Such redemption risk is reinforced when redemptions are correlated across funds. Adverse pricing conditions in secondary markets can in turn lead to a deterioration of primary markets. However, Adrian et al. (2015d) find that net bond fund flows (fund share purchases minus fund share redemptions) as a fraction of corporate bonds outstanding have not increased over time, suggesting that redemption risk has not necessarily increased.

Even if redemption risk has not increased, the price riskiness of corporate bonds could have increased owing to self-reinforcing dynamics: When adverse news leads to lower returns, redemptions might force mutual funds to sell assets, which might reinforce the negative returns, thus generating additional redemptions (Feroli et al. 2014). Negative returns tend to be followed by net bond fund redemptions, and positive returns by net bond fund purchases, giving rise to a positive flow-performance relationship.

The flow-performance relationship for equity mutual funds is generally found to be convex: Strong positive performance tends to generate an increasingly strong response of flows (Chevalier & Ellison 1999). In contrast, Goldstein, Jiang & Ng (2015) find a concave relationship for bond funds, so that flows react more strongly when returns are low. The concavity is more pronounced for illiquid bonds and is stronger when market returns are negative. Moreover, the flow-performance relationship for bond funds is both statistically and economically larger than that for equity funds. These results suggest that the illiquidity of corporate bonds may generate incentives to sell quickly in response to bad news, which might amplify adverse price changes. These incentives might also give rise to self-reinforcing redemption dynamics as investors might anticipate that it pays to redeem early. In equilibrium, redemption risk might lead to higher secondary market volatility and more costly intermediation.

In contrast to mutual funds' increased ownership share of corporate bonds, dealers' ownership share of corporate bonds declined during and after the crisis, averaging 2.7% from 1990 to 2008, but just 1.2% from 2009 to 2016. The reduced ownership share raises the concern that dealers may no longer be able or willing to absorb selling pressure when redemptions force mutual funds to sell. Adrian et al. (2015d) explore this issue by regressing weekly bond fund flows on past returns and the weekly change in dealer corporate bond positions between January 2007 and August 2015. They find that dealer positioning tends to evolve in the same direction as bond fund flows, suggesting that dealers do not typically absorb the aggregate selling pressure of bond funds. Given that dealers tend not to trade against bond fund flows, they surmise that dealers' falling corporate bond ownership share is unlikely to exacerbate redemption risk.

2.5. Changes in Expected Returns

Dealer positioning reflects the proprietary trading and risk-management motives of dealers as well as the positioning of dealer clients. To illustrate dealers' positioning, we examine the composition of dealers' assets. **Figure 8** shows dealers' net positions in Treasury securities and corporate bonds from 1990 to 2016. The plot reveals three key features:

1. Dealers' net corporate positions grew quickly in the years preceding the crisis, plunged during the crisis, and stagnated after the crisis.
2. Dealers' net Treasury positions fluctuated between positive and negative between 1990 and 2016 and were negative for an extended period from 2004 to 2008.
3. In the roughly 15 years between 2001 and 2016, changes in net Treasury and corporate bond positions were negatively correlated and tended to offset, suggesting that dealers trade the credit spread.

The sharp decline in net corporate positions, in particular, raises the concern that dealers have reduced their capital commitment to market making, with potentially adverse effects on market liquidity. Traditionally, dealers acted as principal, buying bonds from their customers when they wanted to sell, and holding them on their balance sheet until offsetting trades were found later, thus bearing the risk that prices fell in the interim. More recently, however, they may have shifted toward an agency model, as suggested by Barclays (2016), Bessembinder et al. (2016), and Choi &

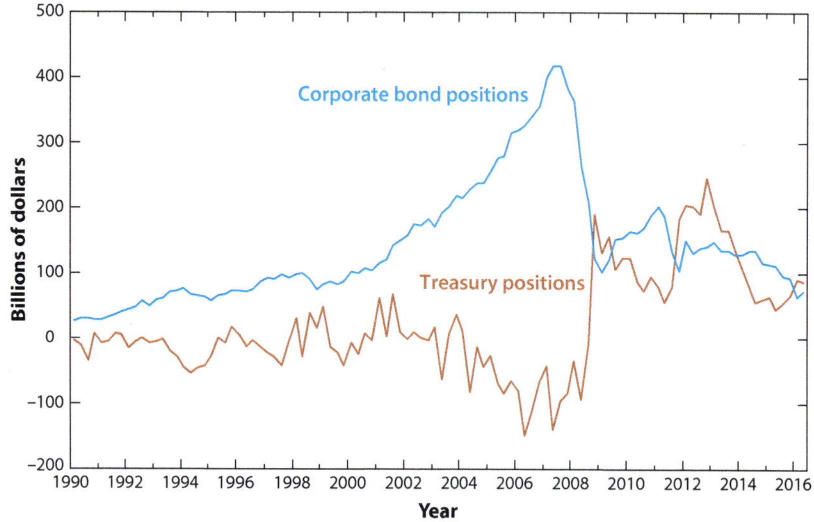

Figure 8

Dealers' corporate bond and Treasury positions. This figure plots corporate bond (domestic and foreign) and Treasury security positions (held in the United States) of security broker/dealers. Data are from the Financial Accounts of the United States published by the Board of Governors of the Federal Reserve.

Huh (2016), in which dealers match offsetting orders so as to avoid holding bonds on their balance sheets. Although such a shift could explain the decline in net positions, it leaves open the question as to whether liquidity is adversely affected. There are tens of thousands of outstanding corporate bond issues with varying maturity, seniority, and optionality characteristics, making it difficult to match demand and supply.

Across all debt securities, dealer positioning is likely managed to maximize expected returns and hence varies over time. In **Figure 9**, we plot debt securities as a share of dealer financial assets together with a measure of expected fixed-income returns: the sum of the 10-year Treasury term premium and the credit risk premium. The 10-year Treasury term premium, computed by Adrian, Crump & Moench (2013), measures the interest rate risk premium embedded in a Treasury bond portfolio with a 10-year duration. The credit risk premium is measured by Moody's Baa-Aaa spread. The figure shows a tight correlation (55%) between expected fixed-income returns and dealer fixed-income positioning, with periods of sharp changes in asset valuations typically accompanied by sharp adjustments in positions. The low level of debt securities as a share of total assets prior to the financial crisis was thus associated with a compression of expected returns at that time. Similarly, the sharp rise in debt securities during the crisis corresponded with a period when expected returns were unusually high. For further analysis, see Adrian, Fleming & Vogt (2015).

Figure 9 does suggest one exceptional period in 2012 and early 2013, when dealer positions were increasing despite ever more compressed expected returns in the bond market. Governor Jeremy Stein (2013) warned that fixed-income markets might be overheating, and the Financial Stability Oversight Council (FSOC 2013) issued a similar warning in its annual report. That episode ended with the bond market sell-off in mid-2013 (the taper tantrum), when yields rose abruptly and dealers quickly shed fixed-income positions (Adrian & Fleming 2013). In 2014, the tight link between dealer positions and expected returns returned, with both declining sharply.

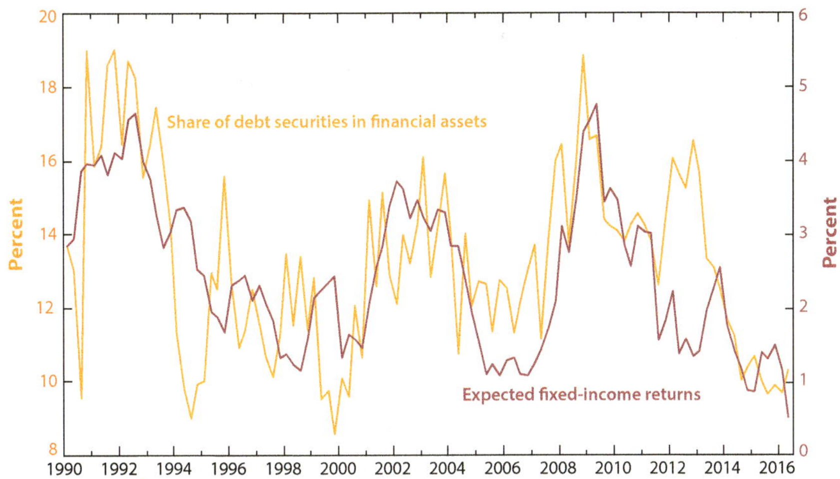

Figure 9

Dealers' debt security positions and expected returns. This figure shows dealers' debt securities as a percentage of their total financial assets together with a measure of expected fixed-income returns. Debt securities comprise US Treasury securities, corporate and foreign bonds, agency mortgage-backed securities, commercial paper, and municipal bonds. Expected returns to fixed-income securities are computed as the 10-year Treasury term premium from Adrian, Crump & Moench (2013) plus Moody's Baa-Aaa credit spread. Data on dealer debt securities and total financial assets are from the Financial Accounts of the United States published by the Board of Governors of the Federal Reserve. Term premium data are from the Federal Reserve Bank of New York. Credit spread data are from the Board of Governors of the Federal Reserve.

3. EMPIRICAL EVIDENCE ON MARKET LIQUIDITY

We proceed to assess the extent to which the changes that have roiled dealers' balance sheets have affected liquidity in the US Treasury and corporate bond markets. Not only do market participants' liquidity concerns center on bond markets, but the US government and corporate bond markets are the largest of their kind, with debt outstanding of $13.4 trillion and $8.4 trillion, respectively, as of June 30, 2016. Liquidity is of critical importance to both markets, given their roles in financing the US government and corporations; as investment vehicles; and (in the case of the Treasury market) as a hedging vehicle, risk-free benchmark for pricing other financial instruments, and key instrument of monetary policy.

We define market liquidity as the cost of quickly converting an asset into cash (or vice versa). Liquidity has multiple dimensions, so we examine several measures for each market. We first review the time-series evolution of liquidity in these markets using data from 2005 to 2016. We then consider three case studies of market stress in the postcrisis era to shed light on the resilience of market liquidity.

3.1. Evidence from the US Treasury Market

We consider four common liquidity measures for the Treasury market, all calculated using high-frequency data from the interdealer market.[2] Our measures are for the most recently issued

[2]This section draws on the work of Adrian et al. (2015f) and reports measures calculated using data from BrokerTec, the larger of two interdealer trading platforms for Treasuries. We first reconstruct the BrokerTec limit order book for each day and security from the platform message data. Our measures are calculated for 7 AM–5 PM Eastern time and thus exclude the

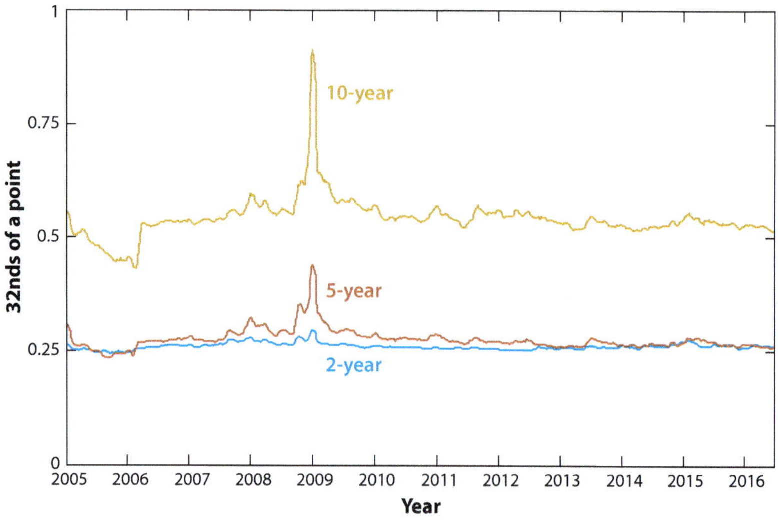

Figure 10

Bid-ask spreads of US Treasury securities. The figure plots 21-day moving averages of average daily bid-ask spreads for the on-the-run notes in the interdealer market. Spreads are measured in 32nds of a point, where a point equals 1% of par. Data are from BrokerTec.

(on-the-run or benchmark) 2-, 5-, and 10-year notes, the three most actively traded Treasury securities. Our sample runs from the beginning of 2005 through June 2016, so it covers the 2007–2009 financial crisis, the 2013 taper tantrum, and the flash rally of October 15, 2014.

One of the most direct liquidity measures is the inside bid-ask spread: the difference between the highest bid price and the lowest ask price for a security. The spread directly measures the cost of executing a trade of limited size, with the cost typically calculated as one-half of the bid-ask spread. As shown in **Figure 10**, average bid-ask spreads widened markedly during the crisis, but were narrow and stable in the years after the crisis.

Although the bid-ask spread directly measures transaction costs and hence liquidity, it does not account for the depth of the market and hence how costs might vary for multiple trades or for trades above the minimum size. Another limitation of the measure is that the minimum tick size (one-half of one 32nd of a point for the 10-year note and one-quarter of one 32nd for the 2- and 5-year notes) is frequently constraining, limiting variation in the spread.[3]

The quantity of securities that can be traded at various bid and offer prices helps account for the depth of the market and complements the bid-ask spread as a measure of market liquidity. We estimate depth as the quantity of securities that are explicitly bid for or offered for sale at the best five bid and offer prices in the BrokerTec limit order book. **Figure 11** shows that average depth rebounded healthily after the crisis, but declined markedly during the taper tantrum and around the October 2014 flash rally, thus painting a less sanguine picture of Treasury market liquidity.

A key limitation of the depth measure is that it does not consider the spread between quoted prices, including the inside bid-ask spread, and as such does not directly capture the cost aspect of

less liquid overnight period (Fleming 1997). Engle et al. (2012) and Fleming & Nguyen (2013) plot time series of many of the same liquidity measures, also using BrokerTec data.

[3]Using BrokerTec tick data for 2010–2011, Fleming, Mizrach & Nguyen (2017) find that 97% of inside spreads for the on-the-run 2-year note are at the minimum tick size.

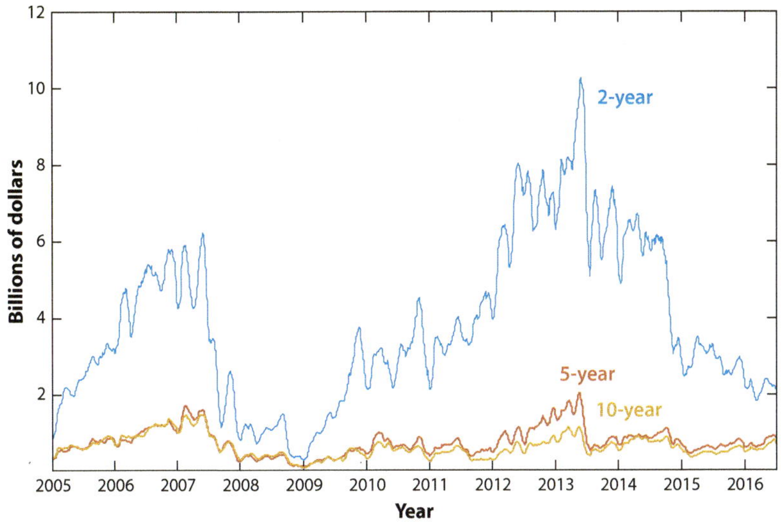

Figure 11

Depth of US Treasury securities. This figure plots 21-day moving averages of average daily depth for the on-the-run notes in the interdealer market. Depth is summed across the top five levels of both sides of the order book. Data are from BrokerTec.

liquidity. Another important drawback of quoted depth is that market participants often do not reveal the full quantities they are willing to transact at a given price, so that measured depth may underestimate true depth (Boni & Leach 2004, Fleming & Nguyen 2013). Conversely, because of the speed with which orders can be withdrawn from the market, actual depth may instead be lower than what is posted in the limit order book.

An alternative measure of market depth is trade size. Trade size is an ex-post measure of the quantity of securities traded at the bid or offer price, reflecting any negotiation over quantity that takes place. Average trade size declined sharply during the crisis, increased markedly after, and then declined again during the taper tantrum and around the flash rally of October 2014, as shown in **Figure 12**.

One difficulty in interpreting trade size is that it underestimates market depth because the quantity traded is often less than the quantity that could have been traded at a given price. The decline in trade size compared with the precrisis period, in particular, may reflect the increasing prevalence of HFT in the interdealer market, and not necessarily reduced liquidity. In addition, trade size does not consider the actual prices at which trades are executed and hence, like depth, does not directly measure transaction costs.

A popular measure of liquidity, suggested by Kyle (1985), considers the rise (or fall) in price that typically occurs with a buyer-initiated (or seller-initiated) trade. The Kyle lambda, or price impact, is defined as the slope of the line that relates the price change to trade size and is often estimated by regressing price changes on net signed trading volume (positive for buyer-initiated volume and negative for seller-initiated volume) for intervals of fixed time. The measure is relevant to those executing large trades or a series of trades and, together with the bid-ask spread and depth measures, provides a fairly complete picture of market liquidity.

Measures of price impact also suggest some deterioration of liquidity over the 2013–2015 period. **Figure 13** plots the estimated price impact per $100 million net order flow as calculated

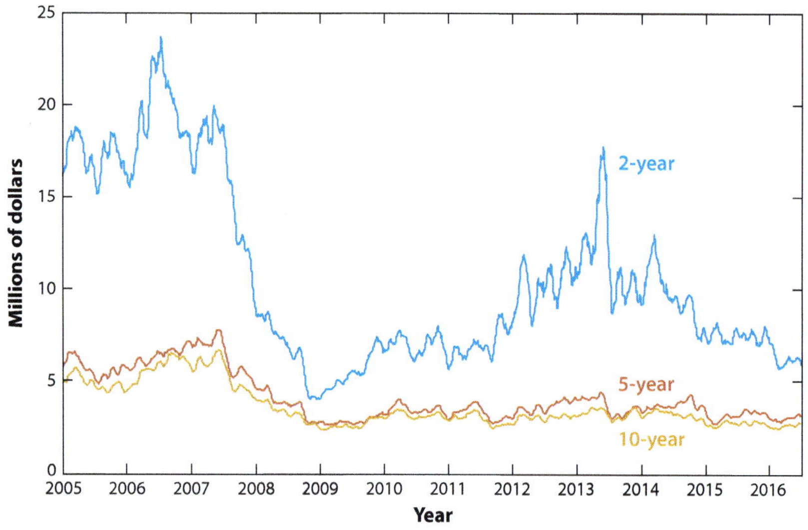

Figure 12

Trade sizes of US Treasury securities. This figure shows 21-day moving averages of average daily trade sizes for on-the-run notes in the interdealer market. Data are from BrokerTec.

weekly from regressions of 5-minute price changes (calculated using bid-ask midpoints) on net trading volume over the same 5-minute interval. Price impact rose sharply during the crisis, declined markedly after, and then increased during the taper tantrum and in the week including October 15, 2014. The measure remained somewhat elevated after October 15, 2014, but was not especially high in 2015 and 2016 by historical standards.

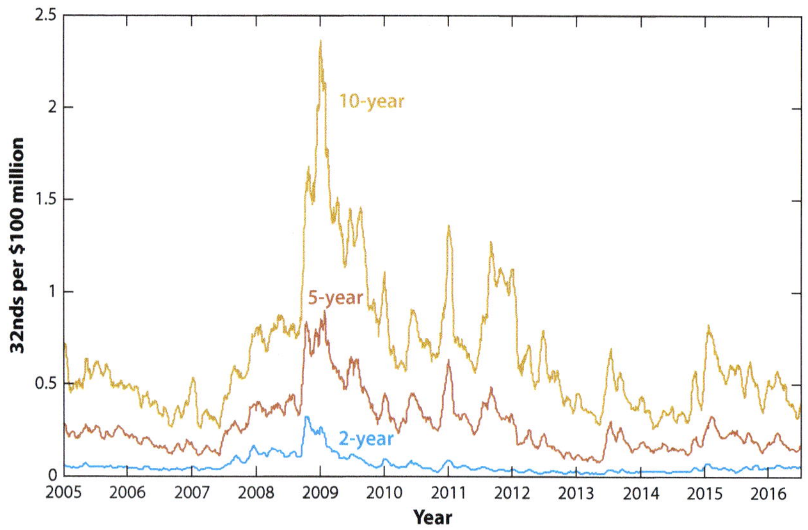

Figure 13

Price impact of US Treasury securities. This figure plots 4-week moving averages of slope coefficients from weekly regressions of 5-minute price changes (calculated using bid-ask midpoints) on 5-minute net order flow for on-the-run notes. Data are from BrokerTec.

Overall, we find mixed evidence on Treasury market liquidity in the postcrisis era. The appreciable declines in quoted depth in mid-2013 and late 2014 may be the strongest evidence of worsening liquidity. However, the price impact coefficients suggest a more modest deterioration, and bid-ask spreads, which directly measure the cost of trading, remained narrow by recent historical standards as of mid-2016. Trade sizes declined considerably from levels observed before the crisis, but may reflect the growth of automated trading and associated changes in order submission strategies, and are not necessarily indicative of worse liquidity.

3.2. Evidence from the US Corporate Bond Market

In this section, drawing on the work of Adrian et al. (2015c, 2016a), we analyze some of the same measures for the US corporate bond market as for the US Treasury market, but our analysis is necessarily limited by the market's structure and the associated data. Secondary market trading of corporate bonds is conducted over the counter, with most trading intermediated by dealers. There is no central limit order book, and hence information on quoted bid-ask spreads or depth is limited. We therefore infer liquidity from the record of transactions as reported in FINRA's TRACE database, introduced in 2002.[4]

We calculate realized bid-ask spreads for each bond and day as the difference between the average price at which customers buy from dealers and the average price at which customers sell to dealers. We then calculate the average of these realized bid-ask spreads across bonds for each day. As shown in **Figure 14**, average bid-ask spreads widened sharply during the crisis, but then narrowed to levels lower than precrisis levels.

The evolution of realized bid-ask spreads is broadly robust to the subsample and to the estimation approach. We find generally similar patterns when we condition on trade size, for example, as seen in **Figure 15**, which Edwards, Harris & Piwowar (2007) show (and which our findings confirm) is negatively correlated with transaction costs. Similar patterns are also observed when we condition on credit rating (investment grade versus high yield) and trading frequency. Moreover, weighting by trading volume across bonds instead of weighting equally across bonds results in appreciably lower spreads, but the same general pattern. That said, a notable distinction in **Figure 15** is that spreads are narrower after the crisis than before the crisis for retail (<\$100,000) trades, but are wider for institutional (≥\$100,000) trades, a difference also noted by Anderson & Stulz (2017).

Although we cannot calculate order book depth for the corporate bond market, we can look at trade size. Average trade size declined sharply during the crisis and had not recovered as of mid-2016 (see **Figure 16**). Some market commentators see this trend as evidence that investors find it more difficult to execute large trades and so are splitting orders into smaller trades to lessen their price impact.

In fact, there is evidence of higher price impact after the crisis versus before the crisis. We calculate price impact for each institutional trade as the price change from the previous institutional trade divided by the signed trade size (positive when the customer buys and negative when the customer sells). We average these estimates for each bond and day and then average across bonds for each day. As shown in **Figure 17**, average price impact increased sharply during the crisis and then declined, but remained above precrisis levels. Anderson & Stulz (2017) also find somewhat higher price impact for large trades after the crisis than before.

---

[4]In our analysis, we account for erroneous trade records, remove duplicated interdealer trade records, and exclude trades of Rule 144a issues, trades on weekends and holidays, and trades associated with price outliers (price < \$50 or price > \$200) or trade size outliers (size < \$1,000 or size > \$100 million).

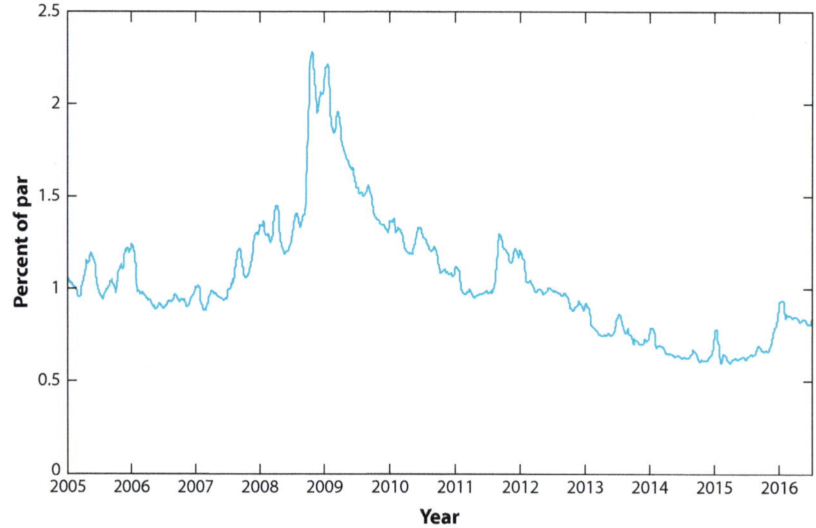

Figure 14

Corporate bond bid-ask spreads. This figure shows the 21-day moving average of realized bid-ask spreads for corporate bonds. The spreads are computed daily for each bond as the difference between the average (volume-weighted) dealer-to-client buy price and the average (volume-weighted) dealer-to-client sell price and then averaged across bonds using equal weighting. Data are from FINRA's TRACE database.

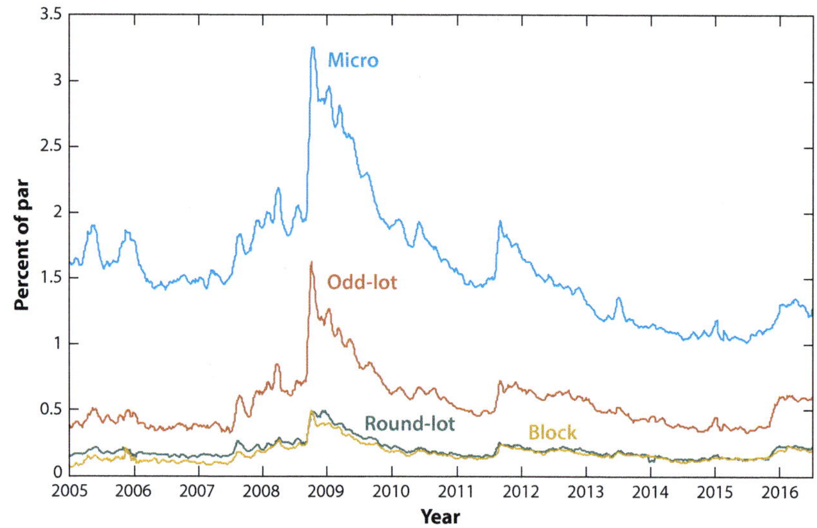

Figure 15

Corporate bond bid-ask spreads by trade size. This figure shows 21-day moving averages of realized bid-ask spreads for four different trade size groupings: micro (<\$100,000), odd-lot (\$100,000–1 million), round-lot (\$1–5 million), and block (>\$5 million). The spreads are computed daily for each bond and trade size category as the difference between the average (volume-weighted) dealer-to-client buy price and the average (volume-weighted) dealer-to-client sell price and then averaged across bonds using equal weights. Data are from FINRA's TRACE database.

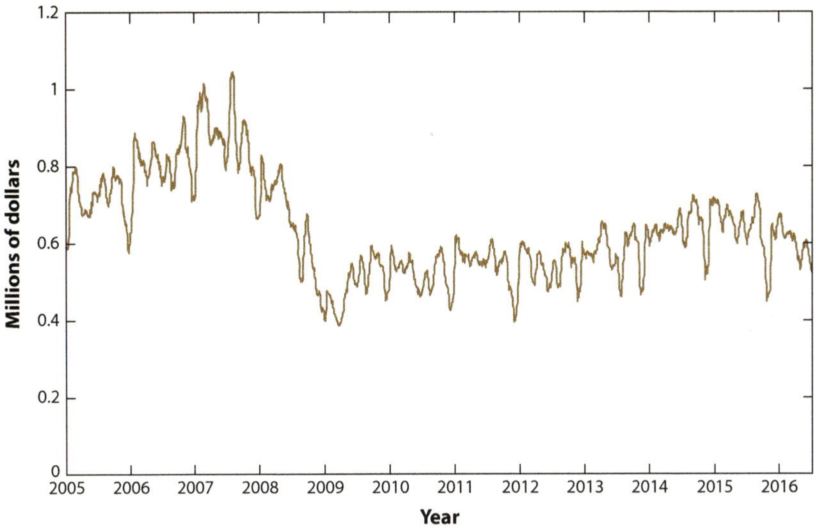

Figure 16

Corporate bond trade size. This figure shows the 21-day moving average of average trade size. Average trade size is calculated daily as total trading volume divided by the number of trades. Data are from FINRA's TRACE database.

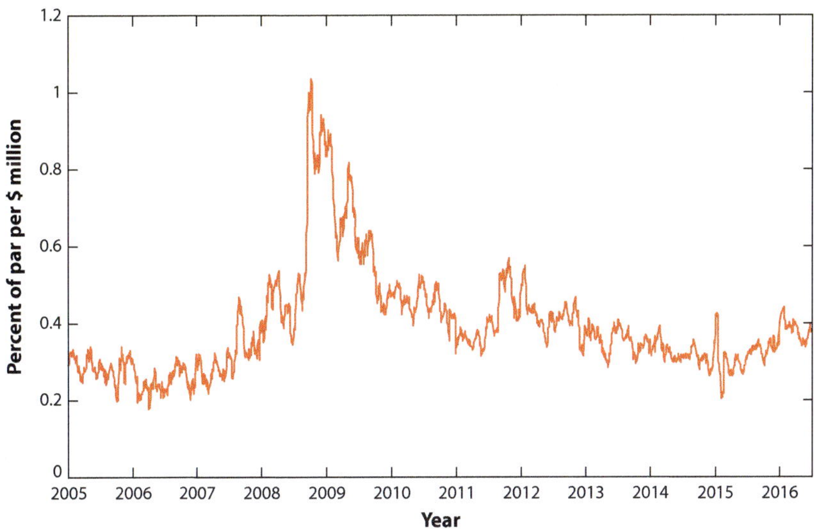

Figure 17

Corporate bond price impact. This figure shows the 21-day moving average of price impact for institutional (≥$100,000) trades. Price impact is calculated for each such trade as the price change from the previous institutional trade divided by the signed trade size (positive when the customer buys and negative when the customer sells). These are averaged daily for each bond using equal weighting and then averaged across bonds using equal weighting. Data are from FINRA's TRACE database.

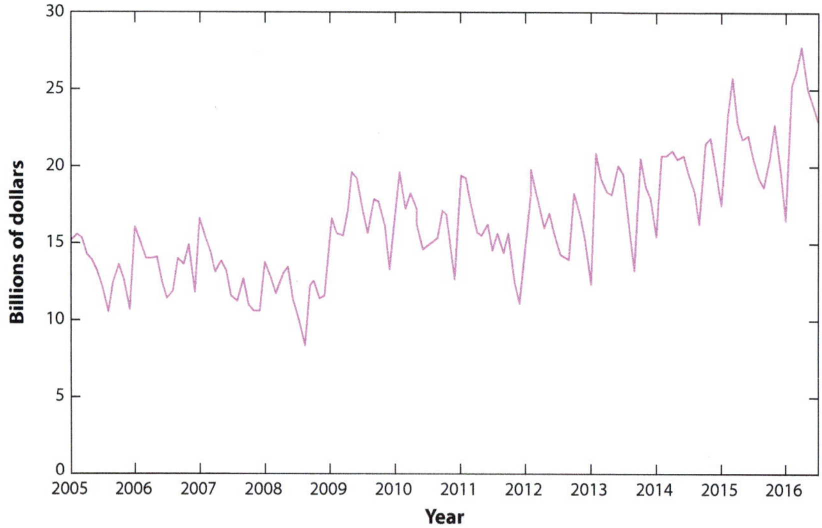

Figure 18

Corporate bond trading volume. This figure shows average daily trading volume by month across all publicly traded nonconvertible corporate debt, medium-term notes, and Yankee bonds (excluding issues with maturities of 1 year or less and certificates of deposit). Data are from the Securities Industry and Financial Markets Association and are based on data from FINRA's TRACE database.

Additional measures suggest ample corporate bond market liquidity. Trading volume, for example, declined during the crisis but rebounded to record highs after (see **Figure 18**). Corporate bond issuance similarly plunged during the crisis but rebounded sharply after, reaching record highs in each year from 2012 through 2016 and driving debt outstanding to ever higher levels. Some analysts note that the corporate bond turnover rate—the ratio of trading volume to debt outstanding—remains below precrisis levels, but it is not obvious that declining turnover amid growing volume indicates worse liquidity.

As for the Treasury market, the overall evidence on liquidity in the corporate bond market in the postcrisis era is mixed. Bid-ask spreads for retail trades declined after the crisis to levels lower than those observed before the crisis. Moreover, trading volume and issuance rose to record highs. However, trade size declined during the crisis and did not quickly rebound after, consistent with the hypothesis that reduced liquidity has made it harder to execute large trades. Moreover, bid-ask spreads and price impact for institutional trades remained higher after the crisis than before, suggesting somewhat worse liquidity for these larger trades.

3.3. Case Studies of Market Liquidity Events

We present three case studies of market behavior during times of stress in the postcrisis era to better understand the resilience of market liquidity. The first is the 2013 taper tantrum, when fixed-income markets sold off, reportedly in anticipation of the end of the Federal Reserve's large-scale asset purchases. The second is the flash rally in the US Treasury market on October 15, 2014, when Treasury yields declined sharply and then rebounded within a 12-minute window. The third is the liquidation of Third Avenue's high-yield Focused Credit Fund (FCF) in December 2015.

3.3.1. Dealers' balance sheet capacity and market liquidity during the taper tantrum. Long-term interest rates increased substantially in 2013 after hitting record lows in 2012. The sharpest increase occurred between May 2 and July 5, 2013, with the 10-year Treasury yield rising from 1.63% to 2.74% (Adrian & Fleming 2013). Market liquidity deteriorated during this episode, as shown in **Figures 11** and **13** by the sharp drop in market depth and increase in price impact between May and June 2013, especially following Federal Reserve Chairman Ben Bernanke's testimony before the Joint Economic Committee on May 22 and the Federal Open Market Committee meeting on June 18 and 19. Some market participants suggested that constraints on dealer balance sheet capacity impaired liquidity during the sell-off, increasing the magnitude and speed of the rise in interest rates and volatility (see, e.g., Cameron & Becker 2013). Dealers intermediate between buyers and sellers, putting capital at risk in order to absorb changes in client supply and demand. The less capacity a dealer has to absorb supply and demand imbalances, the higher volatility and the lower market liquidity are likely to be. In this section, we review the evidence on what motivated dealer behavior during the episode and whether dealer balance sheet capacity amplified the sell-off.

To gauge dealer willingness to add interest rate risk exposure and buffer the selling pressures from their customers, Adrian et al. (2013) examine dealers' positions in US Treasury securities, agency debt, agency MBS, and corporate securities, as reported to the Federal Reserve by primary dealers. During the sell-off, dealers markedly reduced their net positions (the difference between long and short positions) in these securities, particularly agency debt and agency MBS, suggesting that they had decided to limit their outright exposures rather than absorb inventory from customers looking to sell. Moreover, the biggest decline in dealers' long positions in 2013 occurred between May 8 and July 17, suggesting that dealers reduced their market-making activities during the sell-off. Outside of 2013, instances since 1990 in which there were larger changes in both long and short positions are limited to a small number of periods at the height of the financial crisis in 2008, during the bond market sell-off of 1994, and around the financial market turmoil of 1998.

Another indicator of risk taking is VaR, which measures the worst expected loss over a given time horizon at a given confidence level. **Figure 19** shows that the sum of firm-wide VaR across eight large US dealers trended downward after the crisis.[5] The figure also shows that VaR tends to move in tandem with market volatility, as proxied by the Merrill Lynch Option Volatility Estimate (MOVE) index, so that the decline in VaR after the crisis is associated with the decline in volatility.

Interestingly, dealer VaR did not increase during the 2013 sell-off, although volatility rose sharply, suggesting that dealers might have actively managed their risk exposures to insulate their firm-wide VaR from price movements. In fact, an analysis of the cross-sectional behavior of dealers highlights the observation that firms that reduced their net fixed-income positions more during the sell-off tended to experience a larger decline in their interest rate VaR, as shown in **Table 1**. Furthermore, dealers that reduced their positions more experienced larger increases in their tier 1 capital and tier 1 leverage ratios in the second quarter of 2013. That is, a reduction in net positions by some dealers appears to have been associated with a reduction in risk taking.

The finding that dealers reduced their fixed-income positions during the sell-off and that the reduction was associated with reduced risk taking as measured by VaR and regulatory capital ratios is compatible with two alternative explanations. The first is that dealers were unable to provide market liquidity because of capital constraints. The second is that dealers decided to

[5]VaR is reported at either the 95% or 99% level, depending on the firm. For those firms for which the 95% confidence level is reported, we scale the VaR to the 99% level using the Gaussian assumption, as in Adrian & Shin (2014).

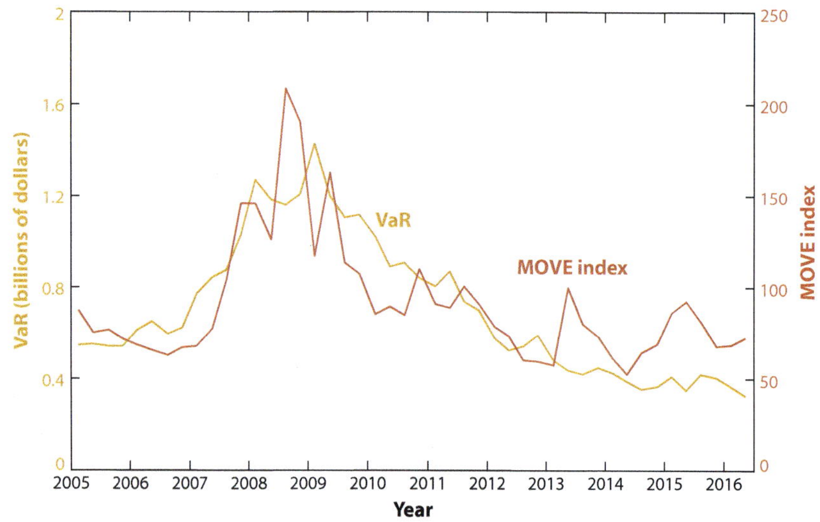

Figure 19

Dealer value at risk (VaR) and interest rate volatility. This figure plots the sum of firm-wide VaR across eight large US firms (Bank of America, Bear Stearns, Citibank, Goldman Sachs, J.P. Morgan, Lehman Brothers, Merrill Lynch, and Morgan Stanley) and the Merrill Lynch Option Volatility Estimate (MOVE) index, a measure of implied interest rate volatility. Data are from Bloomberg.

manage their balance sheets more conservatively at a time when investors were repricing interest rate risk rapidly. That is, dealers may have been able but unwilling to provide market liquidity.

If the constraints explanation were correct, then dealers facing tighter balance sheet constraints before the sell-off would have been expected to reduce their net positions more than other dealers during the sell-off. The evidence presented in **Table 2** is not consistent with that hypothesis. In particular, US dealers with a higher VaR gap (which measures the difference between a dealer's VaR and its VaR limit), a higher Basel III tier 1 common ratio buffer (which measures the difference between a dealer's measured ratio and proposed ratio requirement), and higher tier 1 capital and tier 1

Table 1 Dealers' net positions and balance sheet constraints during the 2013 sell-off

Measure of dealer constraint (Period over which constraint changes)	Correlation between change in net position and change in dealer constraint
Change in interest rate VaR (May 1 to July 10, 2013)	63%
Change in tier 1 capital ratio (March 31 to June 30, 2013)	−34%
Change in tier 1 leverage ratio (March 31 to June 30, 2013)	−87%

The table presents pairwise correlations between dealers' changes in net positions in US Treasury securities, agency debt, agency mortgage-backed securities, and corporate securities during the May–July 2013 sell-off and dealers' changes in balance sheet constraints over the same period. Calculations are based on Federal Reserve supervisory value-at-risk (VaR) data, company reports for major US chartered bank-holding company affiliated dealers, and the Federal Reserve's FR2004 statistical release.

Table 2 Dealer changes in net positions and balance sheet constraints prior to the 2013 sell-off

Measure of dealer constraint (Date prior to sell-off)	Correlation between change in net position and constraint prior to sell-off
VaR gap (May 1, 2013)	−60%
Basel III tier 1 common ratio buffer (March 31, 2013)	−83%
Tier 1 capital ratio (March 31, 2013)	−74%
Tier 1 leverage ratio (March 31, 2013)	−6%

The table presents pairwise correlations between dealers' changes in net positions in US Treasury securities, agency debt, agency mortgage-backed securities, and corporate securities during the May–July 2013 sell-off and dealers' constraints shortly before the sell-off. Calculations are based on Federal Reserve supervisory value-at-risk (VaR) data, company reports for major US chartered bank-holding company affiliated dealers, and the Federal Reserve's FR2004 statistical release.

leverage ratios before the sell-off tended to reduce their net positions more during the sell-off. That is, dealers with greater ability to take on risk prior to the sell-off actually sold off more. This relationship suggests that dealer behavior during the sell-off was not driven by regulatory constraints.

Instead, the evidence supports the second hypothesis: Dealers were less willing to employ their balance sheets as market participants reassessed fixed-income valuations and repriced interest rate risk in response to heightened uncertainty around the stance of monetary policy. Prior to the sell-off, the term premium—the risk premium investors demand for bearing duration risk—had been very low, or even negative, for some time, and interest rate volatility had been at historically low levels. Some investors (including dealers) may have viewed valuations as stretched and may have been waiting for a trigger for the market to reverse. Events in May and June 2013 may have provided the trigger, and dealers responded by cutting their risk exposures and shrinking their inventories.

3.3.2. The Treasury flash event of October 15, 2014.

On October 15, 2014, the US Treasury securities market experienced an unusually high level of volatility and a rapid round-trip in prices. The benchmark 10-year Treasury note traded in a 37-basis-point range, only to close 6 basis points below its opening level. Moreover, between 9:33 and 9:45 AM Eastern time, without a clear cause, the 10-year yield declined 16 basis points and then rebounded. Such a large price change and reversal in so short a time with no obvious catalyst are unprecedented in the recent history of the Treasury market.

As explained in the report of the Joint Staff (2015), PTFs and bank-dealers, in that order, accounted for the largest shares of trading volume in both the cash and futures markets on both October 15 and control days. Moreover, during the event window, the relative share of PTF trading activity increased as prices and volume rose sharply. Although the share of trading shifted toward PTFs, both PTFs and bank-dealers experienced an increase in trading volume, given the sharp increase in overall volume. As the prices quickly retraced their previous increases, the share of PTF trading activity declined somewhat from its elevated levels and the share of bank-dealer activity rose.

PTFs and bank-dealers took actions to reduce their risk exposure to volatility during the event window. PTFs continued to provide the majority of order book depth and tight bid-ask spreads, but reduced their limit order quantities (**Figure 20**). In contrast, bank-dealers widened their bid-ask spreads such that they provided limit orders only at some distance from the top of the book.

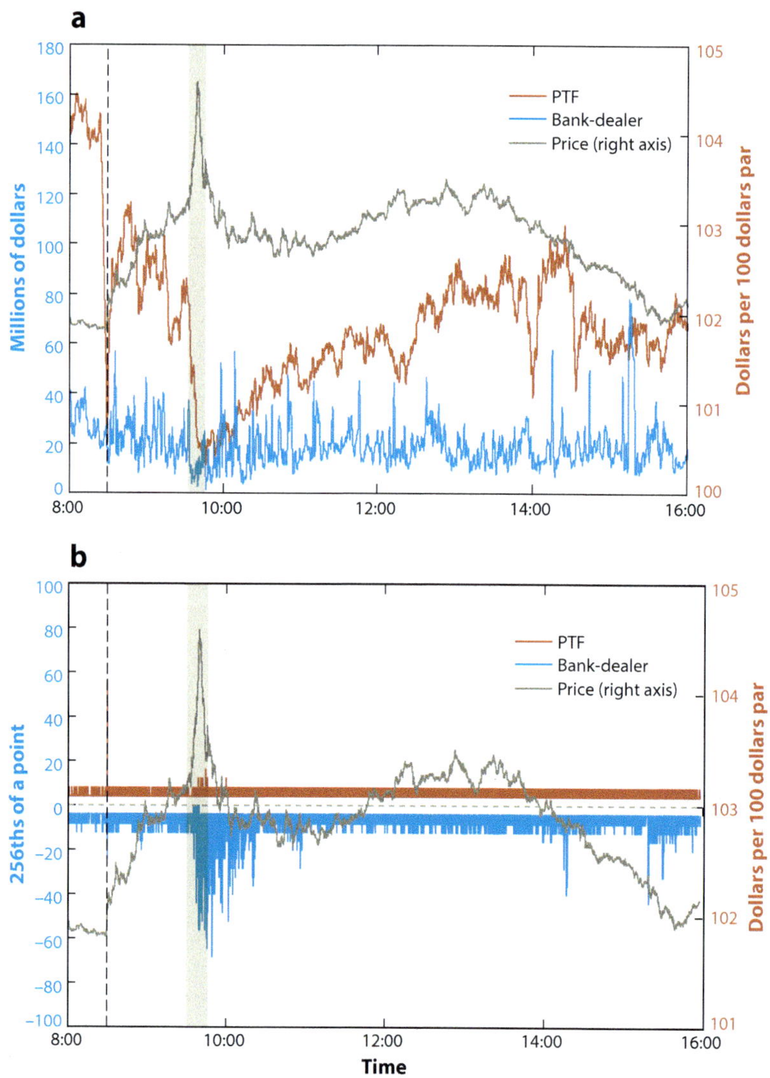

Figure 20

Liquidity during the October 15, 2014, Treasury flash event. (*a*) Limit order book depth at the top three levels in the on-the-run 10-year note as provided by principal trading firms (PTFs) and bank-dealers. (*b*) Bid-ask spreads in the 10-year note as calculated separately for quotes provided by PTFs and bank-dealers. Figure reproduced from the report of the Joint Staff (2015); data are from BrokerTec.

Despite the surge in trading volume during the event window, available data do not show a large change in net position of any specific participant type at that time. However, an imbalance between the volume of buyer-initiated trades and seller-initiated trades is observed, primarily driven by PTFs, with more buyer-initiated trades as prices rose and more seller-initiated trades as prices fell (see **Figure 21*a***). A similar breakdown of the net passive trade flow by participant type shows that PTFs were large net passive sellers during the first part of the event window and large net passive buyers during the second part of the window (see **Figure 21*b***). Notably, the PTF pattern of passive flows closely mirrors the pattern of PTF aggressive flows, so that, as a group,

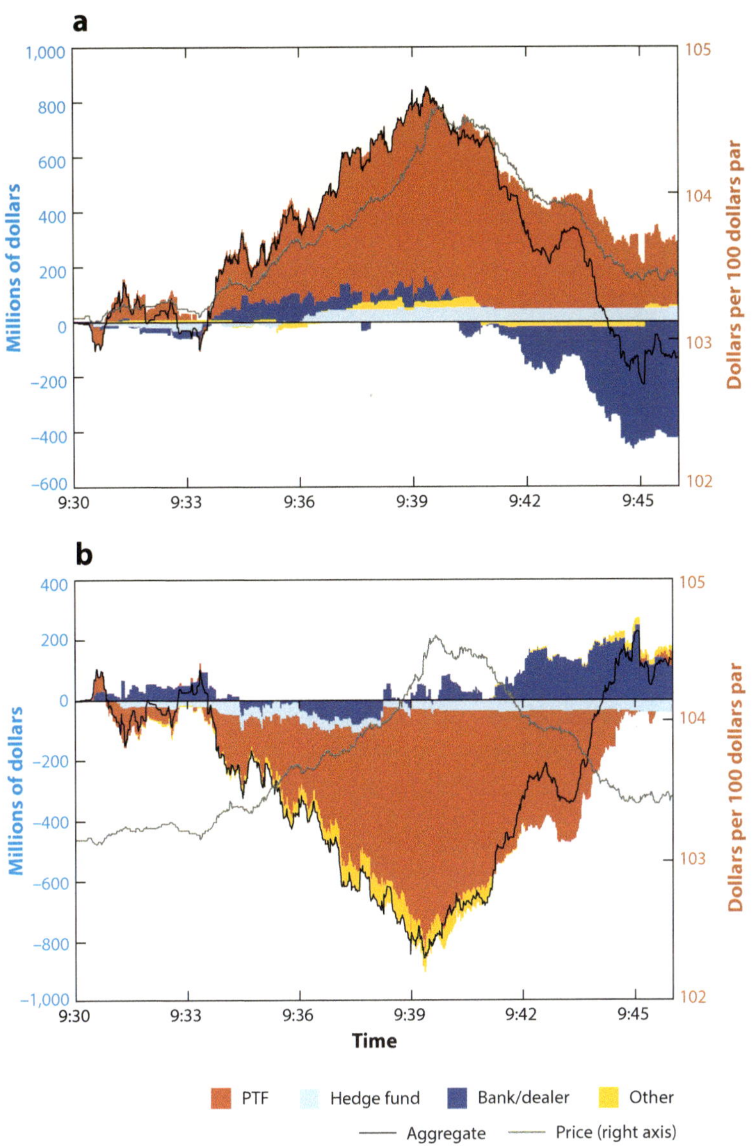

Figure 21

Net trading volume during the October 15, 2014, Treasury flash event. (*a*) Cumulative net aggressive trading volume in the on-the-run 10-year Treasury note by participant type during the 9:30–9:45 AM event window. (*b*) Cumulative net passive trading volume in the note over the same interval. Figure reproduced from the report of the Joint Staff (2015); data are from BrokerTec. Abbreviation: PTF, principal trading firm.

PTFs' net position remained largely unchanged throughout the event window, suggesting that they were deploying multiple types of trading strategies. In contrast, net passive bank-dealer flows are not indicative of significant market-making activity during the event window.

Although the report of the Joint Staff (2015) revealed no single cause for the price behavior during the event window, it did highlight a number of important developments in the market before and during the event window, including a significant increase in trading volume, sizeable changes in market participation, a decline in market depth, and shifts in net order flow, which together provide insight into the nature of the event. The analysis also revealed that changes to the Treasury market structure in recent years have been significant. These changes are likely important context for understanding the unusual volatility that day and for assessing the risk of such an event recurring.

3.3.3. Third Avenue's liquidation and corporate bond liquidity in 2015. Third Avenue's high-yield FCF announced liquidation on December 9, 2015, drawing widespread attention in asset markets. Events of this kind have the potential to increase the demand for market liquidity, as investors revise expectations, reassess risk exposures, and fulfill the need to trade. Moreover, portfolio effects and general fears of contagion may increase the demand for liquidity in assets only remotely related to a liquidating firm's direct holdings. In this section, we examine whether FCF's announced liquidation affected liquidity and returns in broader corporate bond markets.

In the weeks and months preceding its liquidation, FCF experienced an ever-increasing outflow of investor assets, similar to a run. The investor redemptions followed poor fund performance and forced FCF to try to sell assets to meet those redemptions. This created a direct and mechanical need for immediacy in the segment of the corporate bond market in which FCF specialized. There are at least two reasons to think that the corporate bond market in aggregate might experience liquidity strains in such a scenario.

First, a publicized risk event like FCF's announced liquidation may raise expectations of redemptions at other funds. To meet those expected redemptions, fund managers (all else equal) may prefer more liquid bonds, which they can sell at a moment's notice and with low cost. Similarly, these managers may have a preference for safe bonds that can prevent their funds' values from declining further during a flight to safety. If fund managers have these motives in aggregate, the market can become temporarily one-sided, leading to shortages of safe and liquid bonds and, hence, to strains on market liquidity more broadly.

Second, FCF's liquidation occurred against a backdrop of heightened uncertainty in corporate bond markets. Rising credit spreads, increased costs for default insurance, declining commodity prices, uncertainty about global demand, and a possible change in the Federal Reserve's monetary policy stance were all common themes affecting markets at the time. Against that backdrop, a highly observable shock like FCF's liquidation could lead to a broad-based repricing of risk and a subsequent need to hedge and reduce exposures, further increasing the demand for immediacy.

To assess how FCF's closure affected broader market liquidity, Adrian et al. (2016b) examine the corporate bond market liquidity measures discussed above. They first sort bonds into quintiles of performance, as measured by their returns on December 11, 2015, to group bonds by their price sensitivity to news about Third Avenue.[6] Bonds with the worst returns on December 11 tended to (*a*) have higher spreads to Treasury securities, (*b*) have higher yields at issuance, and (*c*) be high yield to a greater extent. These findings support the view that FCF's announced closure triggered a wider sell-off of risky assets.

Bonds with the worst returns on December 11 also exhibited somewhat worse liquidity that day, with wider bid-ask spreads and higher price impact. However, in the months prior, this group of bonds had already been suffering steady losses and was consistently less liquid than bonds in

[6]Note that although FCF's liquidation was announced on December 9, the news did not become public until late on December 10, and market commentary suggests that the initial market reaction came on December 11.

the other performance quintiles. Thus, the event appeared to have the greatest (negative) effects on price and bid-ask spreads for bonds that were less liquid to begin with. Moreover, the liquidity effects were modest in magnitude and did not spill over into the broader universe of corporate bonds.

4. DIRECTIONS FOR FURTHER RESEARCH

Although we do not uncover strong evidence of a widespread worsening of market liquidity, our findings are not unqualified because of data and methodological limitations. We therefore consider directions for future research that could help overcome these shortcomings. Our discussion focuses on five areas: (*a*) additional data, (*b*) methodological improvements, (*c*) endogeneity, (*d*) liquidity risk, and (*e*) funding liquidity.

4.1. Additional Data

A major challenge in accurately measuring market liquidity is inadequate data. For example, in the corporate bond market, trade prices and limited trade size information are publicly disseminated through FINRA's TRACE system, but the aggregate corporate bond limit order book is mostly latent. Thus, information on the quantity that could have been traded at the transaction price or other prices is not reported. Moreover, buyer and seller search costs as well as interactions that did not result in a trade are not reported. In recent years, electronic trading venues for corporate bonds have started to collect such data, but these venues represent only a small portion of total corporate bond trading volume and hence may not be representative of broader liquidity conditions.

Fragmented markets present a further challenge to obtaining comprehensive liquidity data. A given asset may trade in scattered liquidity pools or trading venues, each with different order types or trading environments designed to attract various clienteles. Data on liquidity conditions in one liquidity pool may not be representative of liquidity conditions elsewhere. In the interdealer Treasury market, for example, on-the-run securities trade on well-lit interdealer brokerage (IDB) platforms with extraordinary liquidity and data. However, significant trading in the full range of Treasuries occurs in the dealer-to-customer (DtC) market, which is known to be less liquid, but for which liquidity data are less readily available (Fleming, Keane & Schaumburg 2016). Thus, although high-quality liquidity measures can be calculated in the IDB market for on-the-run Treasury securities, these may not be representative of liquidity conditions in the DtC market, particularly for off-the-run securities.

Along similar lines, derivatives markets offer alternative methods for replicating cash flows and creating synthetic risk exposures. Thus, liquidity challenges in cash markets may be mitigated by creating synthetic positions through futures, options, or swaps. The effect of including these alternative channels for transferring risk directly affects certain liquidity measures. For instance, the price impact measure of Amihud (2002) represents illiquidity as the ratio of absolute returns to dollar trading volume, so the omission of, say, Treasury futures trading volume may lead to an underestimate of liquidity. A comprehensive study of liquidity conditions should consider the joint liquidity, or coliquidity, of a given asset and its close substitutes.

4.2. Methodological Improvements

Liquidity measures that work well in some markets do not necessarily extend to other markets. As an example, consider the problem of computing depth in the corporate bond market.

The equivalent of top-of-book depth in this setting is the largest quantity an investor can trade at the best bid or offer price. Although an investor may assess this quantity by inquiring with individual dealers, the investor's assessment is neither publicly recorded nor disseminated to other market participants. The problem is compounded by the fact that depth available to investor A for a specific security may not be the same depth available to investor B at roughly the same time. Such differences can arise in the absence of anonymous limit order book trading and may reflect investors' differential information content of order flow or varying treatment from dealers, reflecting client relationships (Di Maggio, Kermani & Song 2015).

Facing limited information, researchers construct proxies from observable data to infer properties of unobservable data. For example, Dick-Nielsen, Feldhütter & Lando (2012) impute round-trip costs from TRACE trades to indirectly infer information akin to bid-ask spreads. Similarly, Bessembinder et al. (2016) use indicator variable regressions to estimate unobserved liquidity variables. However, these methods necessarily require securities to trade, which poses a sample selection problem: If only liquid securities trade, then only liquid securities make it into the liquidity calculations and estimates are biased toward higher liquidity.

It follows that broad aggregates of standard market liquidity measures may mask pockets of illiquidity. Adrian et al. (2016c) attempt to address this concern in the corporate bond market by computing liquidity metrics conditional on certain bond characteristics. They find that retail bid-ask spreads were narrower after the crisis than before, on average, but that institutional bid-ask spreads were wider. In terms of credit rating, they find that price impact and spreads improved for investment-grade bonds, but were essentially unchanged for high-yield bonds, on average. Sommer & Pasquali (2016) provide guidance on which bond characteristics tend to correlate with liquidity, including credit quality, maturity, amount issued, age, coupon rate, price volatility, and central bank eligibility.

Market participants have informally referred to the concentration of liquidity in certain subsets of the bond market as a liquidity bifurcation, with trading conditions favorable only for the largest, most recognizable issuers and for the most recently issued bonds. More closely studying the causes and consequences of liquidity bifurcation could be an interesting area of research. For example, liquidity bifurcation can potentially be rationalized by a model of capital-constrained investors (Brunnermeier & Pedersen 2009) who seek to avoid capital-intensive positions in high-margin securities. Because margins for high-yield bonds tend to be larger than those for investment-grade bonds, a higher concentration of liquidity in investment-grade bonds is consistent with this theory, but this is in need of further investigation.

Another important issue concerns strategic quoting. There are indications that certain cross-venue HFT firms display depth in related markets without the intention of delivering the total quantity displayed. For instance, Dobrev & Schaumburg (2015) present evidence that trades against resting quotes in the Treasury futures market are followed by almost instantaneous reductions in depth in the Treasury cash market. Their analysis implies that depth is not summable across trading venues, in the sense that the displayed total depth across trading venues is not the actual quantity available for trade. This type of behavior reinforces the need to further study traditional liquidity measures such as market depth in light of recent changes in market structure and investor composition.

4.3. Endogeneity

The endogenous response of market participants to changing liquidity conditions can also create biases in traditional liquidity measures. Both academic and private-sector researchers note that postcrisis regulations may have induced dealers to shift from a principal model of market making to an agency model (e.g., Barclays 2016, Bessembinder et al. 2016, and Choi & Huh 2016). In a principal model, dealers intermediate buyers and sellers through time by temporarily warehousing securities in their inventory and are compensated for the opportunity cost of capital and the inventory risks incurred through the bid-ask spread. In an agency model, no inventory risks are incurred because buyers and sellers are directly matched and the bid-ask spread is presumably narrower. Thus, in a regime where capital-constrained dealers endogenously avoid carrying large inventories, bid-ask spreads may narrow, suggesting an improvement of liquidity conditions. However, in this setting, the investor now bears inventory risk during the time it takes the market maker to locate the other side of the trade, suggesting that liquidity has not improved. Traditional liquidity measures may therefore need to be adjusted for biases or at least interpreted with caution.

A further challenge to measuring future, or expected, liquidity comes from the observation that liquidity can endogenously appear during risk events. When a shock arrives, investors with different risk appetites, constraints, opinions, and mandates enter the market to fulfill the need to trade. During such episodes, liquidity can improve as buyers and sellers arrive in the market at the same time, essentially offsetting the demand for immediacy on both sides of the market. An example of this phenomenon occurs regularly as a result of Treasury auctions, which lead to higher volatility and also trigger trading. These observations have several implications. First, not all increases in volatility necessarily correspond to a deterioration in liquidity, although the effect may be nonlinear: Moderate increases in volatility may come with higher liquidity, whereas large increases in volatility may result in worse liquidity. Second, the argument that a poor liquidity environment will necessarily exacerbate volatility is perhaps oversimplified, as it assumes that liquidity provision, if low, remains exogenously low. Third, current measures of liquidity may not be indicative of future levels of liquidity, as liquidity is time-varying and responsive to the economic environment.

Conversely, in the absence of a shock, investors may wait to transact, suggesting that investors' decision to pay for immediacy services or to wait to trade at a later date is endogenous. This mechanism is described by Grossman & Miller (1988), who show theoretically that realized trades are the equilibrium outcome determined by the supply and demand for immediacy. Thus, in environments in which investors can afford to wait to trade (e.g., when expected volatility is low), the price for immediacy services (and hence the returns to providing liquidity) can decline. An implication is that infrequent trading may simply reflect low expected volatility, which will affect the reliability of intertrade durations as a measure of liquidity.

4.4. Liquidity Risk

The October 15, 2014, flash rally in the US Treasury market and the May 2010 equity market flash crash highlight that market liquidity and pricing are subject to infrequent but significant disruptions [see, e.g., Commodity Futures Trading Commission (CFTC) & SEC 2010, Joint Staff 2015]. Adrian et al. (2015e,b) model illiquidity dynamics as consisting of a continuous Gaussian component plus an infrequent jump component (capturing liquidity risk) and find that jump-like changes in illiquidity tend to occur at times of high volatility. The authors also find somewhat elevated liquidity risk, as measured by the illiquidity jump intensity, in equities and Treasuries but not corporate bonds. These disparate findings may be reconciled by the fact that HFT, which is a common feature in markets that experience flash events, has not taken hold in the corporate bond market as it has in the US Treasury and equity markets. The authors' method for classifying liquidity jumps is based on daily measures of liquidity and may be improved by using higher-frequency intraday measures.

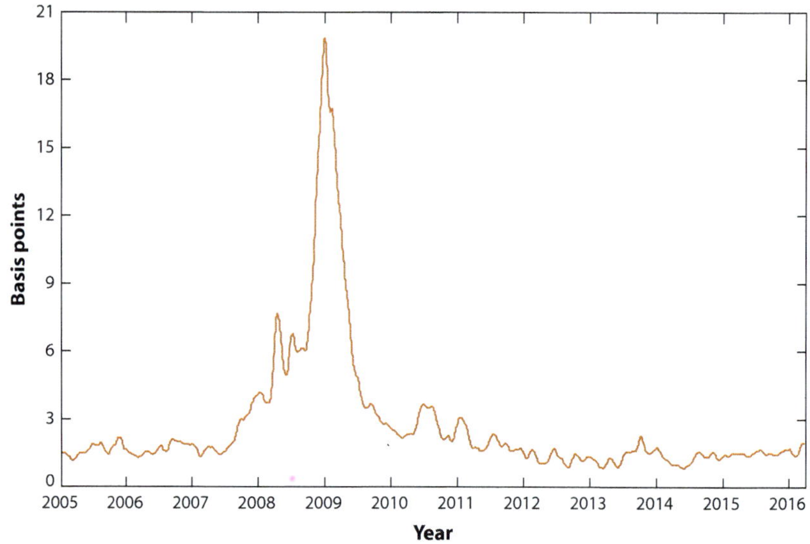

Figure 22

Spline errors of US Treasury securities. This figure shows the 21-day moving average of absolute yield curve fitting errors for 2- to 10-year coupon securities from the Nelson–Siegel–Svensson model of Gürkaynak, Sack & Wright (2007). Data are from the Board of Governors of the Federal Reserve System.

4.5. Funding Liquidity

Theoretical asset pricing models, such as the one proposed by Brunnermeier & Pedersen (2009), suggest a feedback loop or "spiral" connecting market liquidity and funding liquidity: Good funding liquidity allows increased trading, which in turn improves market liquidity and lowers volatility. Lower volatility then allows lenders to lower margin requirements or haircuts applied to collateral in repo transactions, which then further improves funding liquidity. Conversely, tightened funding liquidity dissuades capital-constrained investors from taking positions, adversely affecting market liquidity. A potential consequence is an increased concentration of market liquidity in the least capital-intensive assets. From a measurement perspective, the tight link between funding liquidity and market liquidity suggests further study of their joint evolution, as opposed to study of each in isolation.

One measure in the Treasury market closely linked to both market liquidity and funding liquidity gauges the noisiness of Treasury yields around a smoothed yield curve, as described by Hu, Pan & Wang (2013) (see also Fleming 2000). We calculate this measure as the average absolute yield curve fitting error for coupon-bearing securities from the Nelson–Siegel–Svensson model of Gürkaynak, Sack & Wright (2007). Large pricing differences suggest unexploited profit opportunities, which could reflect constraints on market-making capacity and/or poor liquidity. As shown in **Figure 22**, such pricing differences spiked during the crisis, but were relatively low and stable in the years after the crisis.

A second measure closely tied to both market liquidity and funding liquidity is the RefCorp spread: the yield spread between bonds of the Resolution Funding Corporation and Treasury securities with similar cash flows. Longstaff (2004) argues that because RefCorp bonds and Treasury securities are equally creditworthy, but RefCorp bonds are less liquid, the RefCorp spread solely reflects the value of the liquidity difference. As shown in **Figure 23**, the RefCorp spread also

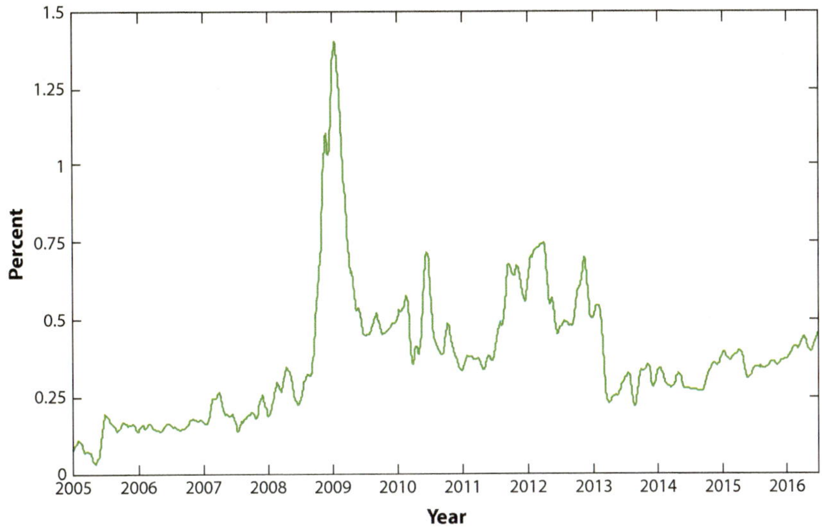

Figure 23

The RefCorp–US Treasury spread. This figure shows the 21-day moving average of the RefCorp spread, which is the difference in yield between a 10-year Resolution Funding Corporation zero-coupon bond and a 10-year zero-coupon Treasury bond. Data are from Bloomberg.

spiked during the crisis and was close to postcrisis lows in the 2013–2016 period, albeit somewhat above precrisis levels.

Alternative funding liquidity measures also warrant attention. **Figure 24** plots the spread between the 10-year interest rate swap and the 10-year Treasury yield. Swap rates represent the value of a stream of payments indexed to LIBOR (London Interbank Offered Rate), so their pricing depends on the credit risk of LIBOR-panel banks. Treasuries, in contrast, price in the credit risk of the US government, and should therefore command lower yields. Indeed, the swap spread has typically been positive. However, such spreads were negative at times in 2010 and also turned negative in late 2015 (remaining so through mid-2016). Such negative swap spreads are often cited as evidence of less plentiful funding liquidity (Dudley 2016) and are sometimes attributed to regulatory balance sheet constraints on banks, hedging demands, and foreign central bank activities.

Figure 24 shows another measure of market dislocation based on the CDS-bond basis. The CDS-bond basis is calculated for investment-grade bonds as the average difference between each bond's market CDS spread and the theoretical CDS spread implied by the bond yield. The basis was close to zero, but generally positive, before the crisis; plunged to extreme negative values during the crisis before rebounding; and has generally been at moderate negative levels since the crisis. Boyarchenko et al. (2016) find that increased funding costs tied to balance sheet constraints are an important determinant of this apparent arbitrage opportunity, with regulatory changes forcing dealers to hold more capital against such trades.

A potential link between market liquidity and funding liquidity is illustrated in **Figure 25**. We use primary dealers' total financing of US Treasury securities, agency debt securities, and agency MBS as an indicator of funding liquidity, and we use Treasury security bid-ask spreads as an indicator of market liquidity. The figure suggests that the two metrics were correlated during the financial crisis, with bid-ask spreads rising as securities financing declined. The metrics otherwise show little comovement, although this may reflect the fact that Treasury bid-ask spreads are often

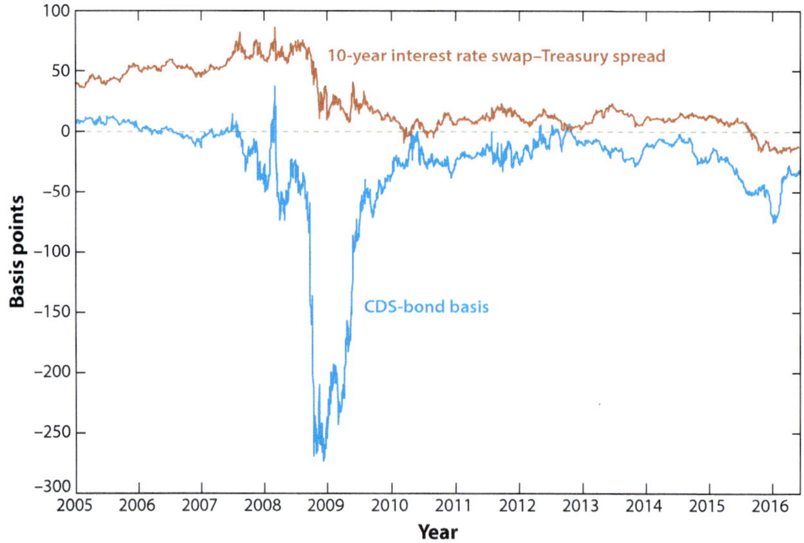

Figure 24

Funding cost measures. This figure plots the 10-year interest rate swap spread and the credit default swap (CDS)-bond basis for investment-grade bonds. The 10-year swap spread is computed as the difference between the 10-year swap rate and the 10-year constant maturity Treasury yield, both from the Board of Governors of the Federal Reserve System. The CDS-bond basis is from J.P. Morgan and is computed for investment-grade corporate bonds as the average difference between each bond's market CDS spread (interpolated to the bond maturity) and the theoretical CDS spread implied by the bond yield. Information has been obtained from sources believed to be reliable, but J.P. Morgan does not warrant its completeness or accuracy. The CDS-bond basis index is used with permission and may not be copied, used, or distributed without J.P. Morgan's prior written approval. Copyright 2017 J.P. Morgan Chase & Co. All rights reserved.

constrained by the minimum tick size, especially during normal times. Note that this evidence of a relationship is only suggestive; there are many ways of measuring funding and market liquidity, and many theoretically plausible arguments for their linkages.

5. CONCLUSION

Dealers' business models have changed markedly since the financial crisis, as reflected in the total balance sheet size of the dealer sector. Whereas dealers' total assets grew exponentially prior to the crisis, they declined sharply during the crisis and then stagnated, in concurrence with the deleveraging of dealers' balance sheets. Although deleveraging is an intended consequence of tighter capital regulations, the associated contraction of dealers' assets could have adverse effects for market liquidity. Identification of causal effects is challenging, however, because the regulations were announced and implemented at a time when dealers' risk-management practices were changing, liquidity demands of asset managers were evolving, the electronification of markets was increasing, and expected returns to market making were changing.

Despite the many factors affecting dealer business models, we do not uncover clear evidence of a widespread worsening of liquidity in two markets in which dealers remain important market makers. Bid-ask spreads in the interdealer Treasury market thus remained narrow and stable in the years after the crisis. Order book depth and price impact showed signs of reduced liquidity after early 2013, but remained within normal historical ranges and far from crisis levels. In the

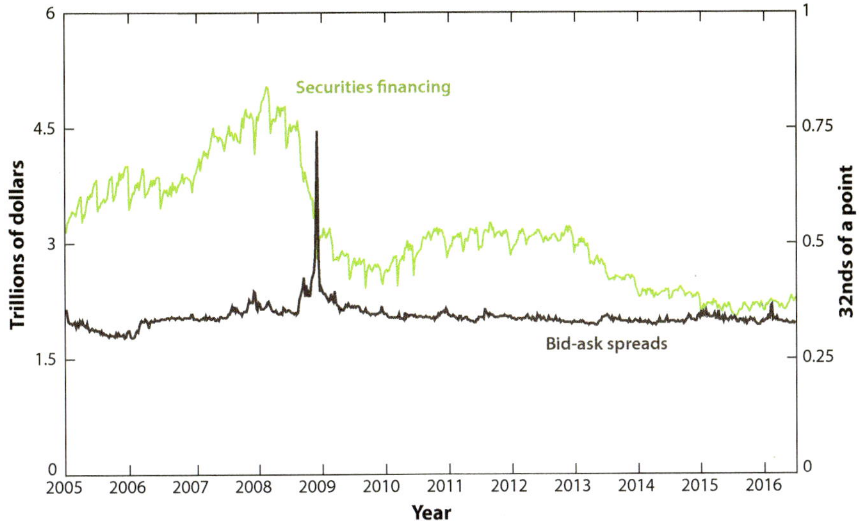

Figure 25

Dealer securities financing and Treasury bid-ask spreads. This figure plots aggregate primary dealer securities financing (defined as securities out) for US Treasury securities, agency debt securities, and agency mortgage-backed securities as well as a geometric average of the 5-day moving averages of average daily bid-ask spreads for on-the-run 2-, 5-, and 10-year Treasury notes in the interdealer market. Financing data are from the Federal Reserve's FR2004 statistical release; data on bid-ask spreads are from BrokerTec.

corporate bond market, bid-ask spreads narrowed after the crisis to levels lower than those before the crisis for retail trades, whereas trading volume and issuance increased to record highs. In contrast, bid-ask spreads and price impact for institutional trades remained above precrisis levels in the years after the crisis. In response to three market shocks in the postcrisis era, we find that bond market liquidity remained resilient and within historical norms.

Our analysis therefore suggests that the postcrisis stagnation of dealer balance sheets has not markedly impaired bond market liquidity. We caution, however, that this inference is not beyond question because of data and methodological limitations. We discuss directions for future research that could potentially overcome these shortcomings. First, we review the need for additional data sources to deepen and broaden coverage of fragmented bond markets. Second, we outline the importance of new methods for drawing inferences about liquidity in the presence of incomplete data. Third, we explain how endogeneities can lead to biases in traditional liquidity measures such as bid-ask spreads and depth. Finally, we discuss distinctions and interactions between market liquidity, liquidity risk, and funding liquidity.

DISCLOSURE STATEMENT

The authors are not aware of any affiliations, memberships, funding, or financial holdings that might be perceived as affecting the objectivity of this review.

ACKNOWLEDGMENTS

An earlier version of this article circulated in May 2015 under the title "Vol-of-Vol and Market Making." We thank Amias Gerety, Frank Keane, Nellie Liang, Lorie Logan, Jamie McAndrews,

Fabio Natalucci, Ernst Schaumburg, Jonathan Sokobin, and Nate Wuerffel, as well as workshop and conference participants at Columbia University; the Commodity Futures Trading Commission; the Conference on the Evolving Structure of the US Treasury Market; the FINRA/Columbia Conference on Corporate Debt Market Structure, Liquidity and Volatility; the Fixed Income Analysts Society; the FSB Workshop on Evaluating the Post-Implementation Effects of the G20 Financial Regulatory Reforms; the New York Society of Security Analysts; Sacred Heart University; SIFMA; the US Treasury Department; and the University of Maryland for helpful comments. We also thank Collin Jones, Daniel Stackman, Zachary Wojtowicz, and Ron Yang for excellent research assistance. At the time of writing, Erik Vogt was with the Federal Reserve Bank of New York. The views expressed in this paper are those of the authors and do not necessarily reflect the position of the International Monetary Fund, its board, or its management, or the position of the Federal Reserve Bank of New York or the Federal Reserve System.

LITERATURE CITED

Adrian T, Boyarchenko N, Shachar O. 2017. Dealer balance sheets and bond liquidity provision. *J. Monet. Econ.* 89:92–109

Adrian T, Crump RK, Moench E. 2013. Pricing the term structure with linear regressions. *J. Financ. Econ.* 110(1):110–38

Adrian T, Fleming M. 2013. The recent bond market selloff in historical perspective. *Fed. Reserve Bank N.Y. Liberty Street Economics*, Aug. 5. **http://libertystreeteconomics.newyorkfed.org/2013/08/the-recent-bond-market-selloff-in-historical-perspective.html**

Adrian T, Fleming M, Goldberg J, Lewis M, Natalucci F, Wu J. 2013. Dealer balance sheet capacity and market liquidity during the 2013 selloff in fixed-income markets. *Fed. Reserve Bank N.Y. Liberty Street Economics*, Oct. 21. **http://libertystreeteconomics.newyorkfed.org/2013/10/dealer-balance-sheet-capacity-and-market-liquidity-during-the-2013-selloff-in-fixed-income-markets.html**

Adrian T, Fleming M, Shachar O, Stackman D, Vogt E. 2015a. Changes in the returns to market making. *Fed. Reserve Bank N.Y. Liberty Street Economics*, Oct. 7. **http://libertystreeteconomics.newyorkfed.org/2015/10/changes-in-the-returns-to-market-making.html**

Adrian T, Fleming M, Shachar O, Stackman D, Vogt E. 2015b. Has liquidity risk in the corporate bond market increased? *Fed. Reserve Bank N.Y. Liberty Street Economics*, Oct. 6. **http://libertystreeteconomics.newyorkfed.org/2015/10/has-liquidity-risk-in-the-corporate-bond-market-increased.html**.

Adrian T, Fleming M, Shachar O, Vogt E. 2015c. Has US corporate bond market liquidity deteriorated? *Fed. Reserve Bank N.Y. Liberty Street Economics*, Oct. 5. **http://libertystreeteconomics.newyorkfed.org/2015/10/has-us-corporate-bond-market-liquidity-deteriorated.html**

Adrian T, Fleming M, Shachar O, Vogt E. 2015d. Redemption risk of bond mutual funds and dealer positioning. *Fed. Reserve Bank N.Y. Liberty Street Economics*, Oct. 8. **http://libertystreeteconomics.newyorkfed.org/2015/10/redemption-risk-of-bond-mutual-funds-and-dealer-positioning.html**.

Adrian T, Fleming M, Stackman D, Vogt E. 2015e. Has liquidity risk in the Treasury and equity markets increased? *Fed. Reserve Bank N.Y. Liberty Street Economics*, Oct. 6. **http://libertystreeteconomics.newyorkfed.org/2015/10/has-liquidity-risk-in-the-treasury-and-equity-markets-increased.html**

Adrian T, Fleming M, Stackman D, Vogt E. 2015f. Has US Treasury market liquidity deteriorated? *Fed. Reserve Bank N.Y. Liberty Street Economics*, Aug. 17. **http://libertystreeteconomics.newyorkfed.org/2015/08/has-us-treasury-market-liquidity-deteriorated.html**

Adrian T, Fleming M, Stackman D, Vogt E. 2015g. What's driving dealer balance sheet stagnation? *Fed. Reserve Bank N.Y. Liberty Street Economics*, Aug. 21. **http://libertystreeteconomics.newyorkfed.org/2015/08/whats-driving-dealer-balance-sheet-stagnation.html**

Adrian T, Fleming M, Vogt E. 2015. Dealer positioning and expected returns. *Fed. Reserve Bank N.Y. Liberty Street Economics*, Dec. 7. **http://libertystreeteconomics.newyorkfed.org/2015/12/dealer-positioning-and-expected-returns.html**

Adrian T, Fleming M, Vogt E, Wojtowicz Z. 2016a. Corporate bond market liquidity redux: more price-based evidence. *Fed. Reserve Bank N.Y. Liberty Street Economics*, Feb. 9. **http://libertystreeteconomics.newyorkfed.org/2016/02/corporate-bond-market-liquidity-redux-more-price-based-evidence.html**

Adrian T, Fleming M, Vogt E, Wojtowicz Z. 2016b. Did Third Avenue's liquidation reduce corporate bond market liquidity? *Fed. Reserve Bank N.Y. Liberty Street Economics*, Feb. 19. **http://libertystreeteconomics.newyorkfed.org/2016/02/did-third-avenues-liquidation-reduce-corporate-bond-market-liquidity.html**

Adrian T, Fleming M, Wojtowicz Z, Vogt E. 2016c. Further analysis of corporate bond market liquidity. *Fed. Reserve Bank N.Y. Liberty Street Economics*, Feb. 10. **http://libertystreeteconomics.newyorkfed.org/2016/02/further-analysis-of-corporate-bond-market-liquidity.html**

Adrian T, Shin HS. 2010. Liquidity and leverage. *J. Financ. Intermed.* 19(3):418–37

Adrian T, Shin HS. 2014. Procyclical leverage and value-at-risk. *Rev. Financ. Stud.* 27(2):373–403

Amihud Y. 2002. Illiquidity and stock returns: cross-section and time-series effects. *J. Financ. Markets* 5(1):31–56

Amihud Y, Mendelson H. 1986. Asset pricing and the bid-ask spread. *J. Financ. Econ.* 17(2):223–49

Anderson M, Stulz RM. 2017. *Is post-crisis bond liquidity lower?* NBER Work. Pap. 23317

Bao J, O'Hara M, Zhou X. 2016. *The Volcker rule and market-making in times of stress.* Work. Pap., Fed. Reserve Board, Washington, DC

Barclays. 2016. *Behavior modification*. Barclays Credit Res., New York

BCBS (Basel Comm. Bank. Superv.). 2010. *Revisions to the Basel II Market Risk Framework*. Basel, Switz.: BCBS

BCBS (Basel Comm. Bank. Superv.). 2011. *Basel III: A Global Regulatory Framework for More Resilient Banks and Banking Systems.* Basel, Switz.: BCBS

BCBS (Basel Comm. Bank. Superv.). 2013a. *Basel III: The Liquidity Coverage Ratio and Liquidity Risk Monitoring Tools.* Basel, Switz.: BCBS

BCBS (Basel Comm. Bank. Superv.). 2013b. *Global Systemically Important Banks: Updated Assessment Methodology and the Higher Loss Absorbency Requirement.* Basel, Switz.: BCBS

BCBS (Basel Comm. Bank. Superv.). 2014. *Basel III: The Net Stable Funding Ratio.* Basel, Switz.: BCBS

Bessembinder H, Jacobsen S, Maxwell W, Venkataraman K. 2016. *Capital commitment and illiquidity in corporate bonds.* Work. Pap., South. Methodist Univ., Dallas

Biais B, Foucault T, Moinas S. 2015. Equilibrium fast trading. *J. Financ. Econ.* 116(2):292–313

BIS (Bank Int. Settl.). 2016. *Electronic trading in fixed income markets*. Rep., Markets Comm., BIS, Basel, Switz.

Bloomberg. 2016a. Cracks exposed in US bond market as liquidity woes warp prices. *Bloomberg News*, Jan. 25

Bloomberg. 2016b. US Treasury sees bond liquidity, but not as we know it. *Bloomberg News*, July 7

Boni L, Leach C. 2004. Expandable limit order markets. *J. Financ. Markets* 7(2):145–85

Boyarchenko N, Gupta P, Steele N, Yen J. 2016. *Trends in credit market arbitrage*. Staff Rep. 784, Fed. Reserve Bank N.Y.

Brunnermeier MK, Pedersen LH. 2009. Market liquidity and funding liquidity. *Rev. Financ. Stud.* 22(6):2201–38

Budish E, Cramton P, Shim J. 2015. The high-frequency trading arms race: frequent batch auctions as a market design response. *Q. J. Econ.* 130(4):1547–621

Cameron M, Becker L. 2013. The great unwind: buy-side fears impact of market-making constraints. *Risk*, July 30

CFTC (Commod. Futures Trading Comm.), SEC (Secur. Exch. Comm.). 2010. *Findings regarding the market events of May 6, 2010.* Staff Rep., CFTC, SEC, Washington, DC. **https://www.sec.gov/news/studies/2010/marketevents-report.pdf**

CGFS (Comm. Global Financ. Syst.). 2014. *Market-making and proprietary trading: industry trends, drivers and policy implications.* Pap. 52, CGFS, Basel, Switz.

CGFS (Comm. Global Financ. Syst.). 2016. *Fixed income market liquidity.* Pap. 55, CGFS, Basel, Switz.

Cheng I-H, Hong H, Scheinkman JA. 2015. Yesterday's heroes: compensation and risk at financial firms. *J. Finance* 70(2):839–79

Chevalier J, Ellison G. 1999. Career concerns of mutual fund managers. *Q. J. Econ.* 114(2):389–432

Choi J, Huh Y. 2016. *Customer liquidity provision: implications for corporate bond transaction costs.* Work. Pap., Div. Res. Stat., Board Gov. Fed. Reserve Syst., Washington, DC

Di Maggio M, Kermani A, Song Z. 2015. *The value of trading relationships in turbulent times.* Res. Pap., Columbia Bus. Sch.

Dick-Nielsen J, Feldhütter P, Lando D. 2012. Corporate bond liquidity before and after the onset of the subprime crisis. *J. Financ. Econ.* 103(3):471–92

Dick-Nielsen J, Rossi M. 2016. *The cost of immediacy for corporate bonds.* Work. Pap., Copenhagen Bus. Sch.

Dobrev D, Schaumburg E. 2015. The liquidity mirage. *Fed. Reserve Bank N.Y. Liberty Street Economics,* Oct. 15. **http://libertystreeteconomics.newyorkfed.org/2015/10/the-liquidity-mirage-.html**

Dudley W. 2016. *Market and funding liquidity: an overview.* Remarks at Fed. Reserve Bank Atlanta Financ. Markets Conf., May 1–3, Amelia Island, FL

Duffie D. 2012. *Market making under the proposed Volcker rule.* Work. Pap. 106, Rock Cent. Corp. Gov., Stanford Univ.

Edwards A, Harris L, Piwowar M. 2007. Corporate bond market transaction costs and transparency. *J. Finance* 62(3):1421–51

Engle RF, Fleming MJ, Ghysels E, Nguyen G. 2012. *Liquidity, volatility, and flights to safety in the US treasury market: evidence from a new class of dynamic order book models.* Staff Rep. 590, Fed. Reserve Bank N.Y.

Feroli M, Kashyap A, Schoenholtz K, Shin HS. 2014. *Market tantrums and monetary policy.* Res. Pap. 14-09, Booth Sch. Bus., Univ. Chic.

Fleming M. 1997. The round-the-clock market for US Treasury securities. *Fed. Reserve Bank N.Y. Econ. Policy Rev.* 3(2):9–32

Fleming M. 2000. The benchmark US Treasury market: recent performance and possible alternatives. *Fed. Reserve Bank Econ. Policy Rev.* 6(1):129–45

Fleming M, Keane F, Schaumburg E. 2016. Primary dealer participation in the secondary US Treasury market. *Fed. Reserve Bank N.Y. Liberty Street Economics,* Feb. 12. **http://libertystreeteconomics.newyorkfed.org/2016/02/primary-dealer-participation-in-the-secondary-us-treasury-market.html**

Fleming M, Mizrach B, Nguyen G. 2017. The microstructure of a US Treasury ECN: the BrokerTec platform. *J. Financ. Markets.* In press

Fleming M, Nguyen G. 2013. *Order flow segmentation and the role of dark trading in the price discovery of U.S. Treasury securities.* Staff Rep. 624, Fed. Reserve Bank N.Y.

FSB (Financ. Stab. Board). 2015. *Principles on Loss-absorbing and Recapitalisation Capacity of G-SIBs in Resolution.* FSB: Basel, Switz.

FSOC (Financ. Stab. Overs. Counc.). 2013. *2013 Annual Report.* Washington, DC: FSOC

Goldstein I, Jiang H, Ng D. 2015. *Investor flows and fragility in corporate bond funds.* Work. Pap., Wharton Sch., Univ. Pa.

Grossman S, Miller M. 1988. Liquidity and market structure. *J. Finance* 43(3):617–33

Gürkaynak RS, Sack B, Wright JH. 2007. The US Treasury yield curve: 1961 to the present. *J. Monet. Econ.* 54(8):2291–304

Hasbrouck J, Saar G. 2013. Low latency trading. *J. Financ. Markets* 16:646–79

Hendershott T, Jones C, Menkveld A. 2011. Does algorithmic trading improve liquidity? *J. Finance* 66:1–33

Hu GX, Pan J, Wang J. 2013. Noise as information for illiquidity. *J. Finance* 68(6):2341–82

Joint Staff. 2015. *The US Treasury market on October 15, 2014.* Joint Staff Rep., U.S. Dep. Treas., Board Gov. Fed. Reserve Syst., Fed. Reserve Bank N.Y., U.S. Secur. Exch. Commis., U.S. Commod. Futures Trad. Commis. **https://www.treasury.gov/press-center/press-releases/Documents/Joint_Staff_Report_Treasury_10-15-2015.pdf**

Jones C. 2013. *What do we know about high-frequency trading?* Res. Pap. 13–11, Columbia Bus. Sch.

Khandani A, Lo A. 2007. What happened to the quants in August 2007? (Digest summary). *J. Invest. Manag.* 5(4):29–78

Krouse S. 2015a. Wall Street bemoans bond market liquidity squeeze. *Wall Street Journal,* June 2

Krouse S. 2015b. Who will fare best in a bond-market liquidity crunch? *Wall Street Journal,* July 1

Kyle AS. 1985. Continuous auctions and insider trading. *Econometrica* 53:1315–35

Levine M. 2015. People are worried about bond market liquidity. *Bloomberg View*, June 3
Longstaff FA. 2004. The flight-to-liquidity premium in US Treasury bond prices. *J. Bus.* 77(3):511–26
Marriage M, Mooney A. 2016. Crunch elevates bond traders. *Financial Times*, March 20
Menkveld A. 2013. High frequency trading and the new market makers. *J. Financ. Markets* 16(4):712–40
Menkveld A. 2016. The economics of high-frequency trading: taking stock. *Annu. Rev. Financ. Econ.* 8:1–24
Mizrach B. 2015. *Analysis of corporate bond liquidity*. Res. Note, Off. Chief Econ., Financ. Ind. Regul. Auth., Washington, DC
Nagel S. 2012. Evaporating liquidity. *Rev. Financ. Stud.* 25(7):2005–39
Schaumburg E, Yang R. 2015. Liquidity during flash events. *Fed. Reserve Bank N.Y. Liberty Street Economics*, Aug. 18. **http://libertystreeteconomics.newyorkfed.org/2015/08/liquidity-during-flash-events.html**
Sommer P, Pasquali S. 2016. Liquidity—how to capture a multidimensional beast. *J. Trad.* 11(2):21–39
Stein J. 2013. *Overheating in credit markets: origins, measurement, and policy responses*. Speech at Res. Symp., Restoring Household Financial Stability After the Great Recession: Why Household Balance Sheets Matter, Feb. 7, St. Louis, MO
Trebbi F, Xiao K. 2015. *Regulation and market liquidity*. NBER Work. Pap. 21739
Wigglesworth R. 2015. Bond market liquidity dominates conversation. *Financial Times*, June 12

Agent-Based Models for Financial Crises

Richard Bookstaber

Office of the Chief Investment Officer, University of California, Oakland, California 94607; email: rbookstaber@gmail.com

Annu. Rev. Financ. Econ. 2017. 9:85–100

First published as a Review in Advance on August 30, 2017

The *Annual Review of Financial Economics* is online at financial.annualreviews.org

https://doi.org/10.1146/annurev-financial-110716-032556

Copyright © 2017 by Annual Reviews. All rights reserved

Keywords

agent-based model, financial crisis, complexity, representative agent, heuristics, leverage, liquidity, contagion

Abstract

This article describes the agent-based approach to modeling financial crises. It focuses on the interactions of agents and on how these interactions feed back to change the financial environment. It explains how these models embody the contagion and cascades that occur owing to the financial leverage and market concentration of the agents and the liquidity of the markets. This article also compares agent-based models to the standard economic approach to crises and shows the ways in which agent-based models overcome limitations of economic models when dealing with financial crises. In particular, this article demonstrates how agent-based models replace homogeneous, representative agents with heterogeneous agents and optimization with heuristics, and how such models move away from a focus on equilibrium, allowing non-ergodic dynamics that are manifest during financial crises to emerge.

INTRODUCTION

The performance of economics during crises is a litmus test for its performance during other times, when limitations might be ignored and cast aside as rounding errors. Crises are a testing ground for economic models, a stress test for economic theory. Understanding the performance of a model during periods of crisis provides us a window into any broader weaknesses. If an economic model fails in crises, we are left to wonder what failings exist in the non-crisis state, failings that might not be so apparent or that can be covered by a residual error term that appears, to use Lucas's (2009) phrase, "too small to matter."

Looking at our recent experience, economics does not seem to fare too well in times of crisis. Despite having an army of economists and all the financial and economic data one could hope for, on March 28, 2007, Ben Bernanke, then Chairman of the Federal Reserve, stated to the US Joint Economic Committee that "the impact on the broader economy and financial markets of the problems in the subprime market seems likely to be contained." Less than 3 months later, this containment ruptured when two Bear Stearns hedge funds that had held a portfolio of more than $20 billion failed, marking a course that blew through one financial market after another over the following 6 months. In February, 2008, as the market turmoil raged, Bernanke gave his semiannual testimony before the US Senate Committee on Banking, Housing, and Urban Affairs. He said there might be failures within the ranks of the smaller banks, but "I don't anticipate any serious problems of that sort among the large internationally active banks that make up a very substantial part of our banking system." That September, Washington Mutual became the largest financial institution in US history to fail. Another bastion of economic brainpower, the International Monetary Fund (IMF), fared no better. In its spring 2007 *World Economic Outlook*, the IMF (2007) forecast that the storm clouds would pass: "Overall risks to the outlook seem less threatening than 6 months ago."

It is not surprising that economics fails during financial crises when, as Trichet (2010) noted, "the serious limitations of existing economic and financial models immediately became apparent. Arbitrage broke down in many market segments, as markets froze and market participants were gripped by panic." Economic models do not incorporate the panics, and they do not have mechanisms that allow markets to freeze. Rather, economics thrives in a world of equilibrium; indeed, most economic models impose regularity conditions to assure that movements away from equilibrium and stability rebound. Lucas (2009) recognized that economics is ill-suited to dealing with crises when he stated that "the simulations were not presented as assurance that no crisis would occur, but as a forecast of what could be expected conditional on a crisis not occurring."

In this article I discuss a recent approach to modeling crises that has been proposed to overcome the limitations of standard economic tools and models (Helbing & Kirman 2013, Haldane 2016, Bookstaber 2017). The methods to do this are drawn from complexity science and employ computer simulations to take a bottom-up approach of examining the behavior of the many heterogeneous individuals that compose the financial system and seeing what emerges from their activities for the system overall. The specific application of the simulations to problems like this is known as agent-based modeling.

Agent-based modeling starts with the agents of the system. In the case of the financial system, these are the investors, providers of funding, and market makers. The model follows the interactions of the agents and examines how the interactions alter the environment and the future actions of one another. The agents operate in their own microenvironments, having no more of a view of the state or the dynamics of the overall system than a driver has of the traffic across a network of roads. The result is a dynamic that can lead to complex outcomes that often do not seem related to the actions of the individuals and from which a crisis emerges.

Figure 1

An illustration of Conway's Game of Life. The periods move from left to right. Dark cells are alive; white cells are dead. A cell is determined to be alive or dead on the basis of its local environment:

1. Each living cell with four or more living neighbors dies.
2. Each living cell with only one living neighbor or no living neighbor dies.
3. Each living cell with two or three living neighbors continues to live.
4. Each cell that is dead and that has exactly three living neighbors becomes alive in the next period.

WHAT ARE AGENT-BASED MODELS?

A Simple Agent-Based Model: Conway's Game of Life

Conway's Game of Life (Gardner 1970) is a zero-player game (because once the initial conditions of the cells are set, there is no further interaction or input as the process evolves) with a simple set of rules. Each cell on a grid can be either alive (dark) or dead (white). Each cell on a grid has eight neighboring cells, and the fate of each cell for the next period is determined by the number of neighboring cells that are alive in the current period:

1. Each living cell with four or more neighbors that are alive dies because of overpopulation.
2. Each living cell with only one neighbor alive or with no neighbor alive dies because of isolation.
3. Each living cell with two or three neighboring cells that are alive survives to the next period.
4. Each cell that is currently dead and has exactly three neighbors that are alive is in just the right nurturing environment to be a birth cell, and becomes alive in the next period.

Figure 1 shows how one initial configuration plays out over a few periods.

The game starts by distributing living automata on a grid. Once the initial state of the grid is set with the various alive and dead cells, the process might end after a few periods, with all the cells having died off, or it might continue, with all sorts of structures emerging and changing.

The Game of Life is one of the simplest examples of an agent-based model. The living cells are agents that operate according to a simple heuristic laid out by the four rules. All the agents use the same rules, and this homogeneity simplifies away from one of the key elements of an agent-based model. But as an agent-based model, the Game of Life still presents two key characteristics that differentiate agent-based models from standard neoclassical models.

First, simple rules can lead to complex, unexpected outcomes, including outcomes that do not seem to relate in any natural or predictable way to the individual agents that are acting on the basis of those rules. Any one cell/agent reacts only to eight other agents and can act only in one of two ways, yet the aggregate result of the individual actions is rich and complex. That is, the Game of Life displays emergence. Emergence means the overall effect of individuals' actions is different from what the individuals are doing. The actions of the system differ from the actions of the agents that comprise the system, sometimes in a dramatic way, such as when a crowd exiting a stadium suddenly turns into a stampede. Any individual is doing what seems innocuous or unavoidable given the immediate surroundings. No individual knows what is happening or why it is happening except as it affects them and those in close proximity, and there is no governing force or body or mind that has that knowledge (Helbing, Farkas & Vicsek 2000).

If we have an emergent phenomenon, then although each agent is acting according to the world around them, and perhaps can know perfectly their part of the world, the overall effect is something different and cannot be determined by what any agent observes. The model for the system as a whole needs to examine the decisions of each agent on the basis of what each agent individually observes, change the agents and the environment accordingly, and then proceed to do the same period by period. This is the essence of the procedure of an agent-based model.

Emergence explains why we can all be doing what we think makes sense and indeed be doing what manages our risk, but with an end result that is disastrous. Our individual worlds can look stable, yet the system can be globally unstable; what is locally prudent can be globally imprudent.

Second, even though the Game of Life is the essence of simplicity, in general it is impossible to predict whether a configuration will die off at a given period. That is, the Game of Life is computationally irreducible (Davis 1958). A computationally irreducible problem is one without mathematical shortcuts; the only way to determine the outcome is to perform each step of the program. If you want to see what a system will be like at a distant time, the computer program that is modeling the system must be run step by step from now until that distant time. By contrast, a computationally reducible system can be described by mathematical formulas that give the outcome at any chosen instant of time without working through all the time steps. Computational reducibility is a critical property for standard economic methods, and absent it, we must rely on simulation methods that follow the path as it occurs.

Components of an Agent-Based Model

Moving from an agent-based model as a game to an agent-based model as a tool, consider modeling traffic (Zheng et al. 2013). Traffic has readily identifiable agents: the drivers and their cars. It is a great laboratory for emergent phenomena, as anyone who has seen the inexplicable and broad variations in congestion can attest.

Drivers operate in their own microenvironments, seeing a small subset of the other cars on the roadway. One minute they might be part of a coordinated, smoothly flowing stream of traffic; another, they are unaccountably contributing to the ripple effect of congestion. It is no wonder that agent-based modeling is a popular tool for evaluating traffic flows. Each driver uses different heuristics. They drive at different speeds; some switch lanes to avoid lane-specific congestion, others go slowly in the left lane.

Think about what is happening on the roadway:

- Agents (cars, drivers) are typically heterogeneous and employ various heuristics to act with some degree of independence or autonomy, so there is no centralized control of the system.
- At the start of each time period each agent observes its environment and acts according to its heuristic. The agent's environment is only a local view of the overall system.
- The agents' actions change the environment.
- In the next period, each agent sees its new environment, altered on the basis of the actions of the previous period, and takes action again. Thus, there is an interaction between the agents and the environment, and between one agent and another.

These are the threads of agent-based models.

In applying agent-based models to study the nature of traffic congestion, the precise nature of the cars on the roadway, including their location and heuristics (that is, individual driving characteristics), is unknown. So the model is run many times, with the agents drawn repeatedly from a distribution of drivers with various heuristics. Sometimes traffic will move along smoothly, sometimes not. The end result will be a distribution of roadway characteristics such as incidents of emergent congestion. The model can be run to test the effects of different configurations of exit and entrance ramps or to determine how best to cycle a traffic light.

The end result is derived from the dynamics of interactions driven by the environment and heuristics the various agents apply in that environment. A heuristic is a decision rule that could be based on optimization, but usually it is not. More typically, a heuristic is based on simple rules of thumb and might ignore information in the process. Heuristics are where issues from behavioral economics can find their home within an agent-based model, because the heuristics can be structured to take biases and idiosyncrasies into account. Heuristics do not try to capture all the nuances of the possible states and their probabilities but, in their simple approach, might be robust with respect to changes in states or to new, unanticipated states.

Take the well-known gaze heuristic for catching a fly ball (Gigerenzer & Brighton 2009). One way to catch the ball is to measure the velocity and spin of the ball immediately after it leaves the bat, take into account air resistance and wind, feed these factors into a differential equation, and then identify the spot on the field that corresponds to the output. Another way to catch the ball is the way ballplayers actually go about the task. If the ball is already high in the air by the time you react, fix your gaze on the ball, start running, and adjust your running speed so that the angle of gaze remains constant.

Another example is to examine how heuristics are used in the animal world (Bookstaber & Langsam 1985, Gigerenzer & Brighton 2009, Gigerenzer & Gaissmaier 2011). Many creatures that use simple heuristics nonetheless have great records of survival. For instance, the survival of the cockroach comes from a basic and seemingly suboptimal escape heuristic: The cockroach simply scurries away when little hairs on its legs vibrate from puffs of air, which might signal an approaching predator. Heuristics are also used in other decisions critical to survival such as foraging and mate selection. For foraging, we can refer to the gaze heuristic. Dragonflies and other species use a variant of it to catch prey (Olberg, Worthington & Venator 2000). For mate selection, the peahen uses a take-the-best heuristic, in which she looks at three or four males and then selects the one with the most eyespots.

COMPARING NEOCLASSICAL AND AGENT-BASED APPROACHES

The behavior described above is at the opposite end of the spectrum from the rational expectations theory that dominates economics, about which Thomas Sargent (quoted by Evans & Honkapohja 2005, pp. 566–67) has said: "Agents inside the model, the econometrician, and God share the same model." Sargent calls this the "communism of models" within the rational expectations hypothesis, and it comes from the fundamental view that those who are being modeled must act in a way that is consistent with the model that is being used to model them.

Agent-based models present an alternative paradigm to neoclassical economics. Whereas neoclassical economics seeks its roots in the mechanics of physics, agent-based modeling is spawned from dynamic networks and complexity theory (Arthur 1999, Colander et al. 2009, Kirman 2010, Page 2011). It is short on theoretical structure and is a slippery subject for parametric testing. It is more of a direct approach, serving as a quantitative basis for developing and inspecting a narrative rather than as a deductive model that gives a solution to the world. Notable distinctions between the two approaches are discussed in detail below.

Interactive Heterogeneity Versus the Representative Agent

To allow for mathematical tractability, economics holds to homogeneous agents, even to using one representative agent. Gathering all the agents in a system into a representative agent prevents a meaningful analysis of interactions, which is at the core of the agent-based approach. Groups of people display patterns and structures of behavior (such as emergent behavior) that are not present in the behavior of the individual members, which is of obvious importance throughout the social sciences. These are the characteristics agent-based models display (Scarf 1960, Kirman 1992, US House 2010).

But the representative agent is used nonetheless, because it is hard to harness the machinery of mathematical economics without it. If one is going to assume the homogeneity that is implicit in a rational expectations model, in which all agents are acting in a lockstep, consistent manner using the same (and correct) model, then one may as well collapse the world into one representative agent.

Complexity and Computational Irreducibility Versus Mathematical Tractability

The interactions that come from our social nature and the shifting preferences that come from experience and context are inherent to humanity. We interact in society, and certainly within markets, and all the more so during periods of crisis, when we are anything but robots with fixed, mechanistic responses to inputs. We face a changing world, which in turn changes the context in which we view the world, and that changes us, again all the more so during periods of crisis. The critical implication is that we cannot plug numbers into a model and solve for the future. We cannot know where we will end up until we take the journey.

Emergence Versus Equilibrium

Complex dynamics result from the agents' interactions, which can lead to emergent phenomena and the prospect of surprises. These surprises include point-of-no-return disruptions from equilibrium, in contrast to perturbations around equilibrium, which are perturbations with stability that are built into most economic models; equations of equilibrium constitute the center of the economic discipline.

Owing to the complexity of interactions, the behavior of the system cannot be constructed as the aggregate of the models of the individuals (Saari 1995, 1996; Kirman 1989). Although a statement such as "assume everyone knows sufficient data to understand the implications of interactions" might be taken as a starting point, that is not how things really work. Keynes (1978) wrote that the material to which economics is applied "is, in too many respects, not homogeneous through time." If this is ever the case, it is during crises.

In addition to computational irreducibility and emergence, another characteristic at variance with the assumptions required for economics is that the world is not ergodic. The future is unknown, and the past does not provide a dependable guide to the future.

Heuristics Versus Optimization

We are seeking reality, and the agents in an agent-based model, rather than being mathematicians or logicians, are rooted in the real world; they are experienced and savvy professionals, working together to determine the best rules and heuristics to perform their job. This remains the case as the crisis emerges. That is, if a heuristic and an objective function with its optimization were placed before financial professionals, they would likely find the heuristic more reflective of how they think and what they do. Indeed, the professional might not even recognize as rational the formalized notions of optimal behavior or the rationality that the economists are presenting.

A Narrative Versus a Solution

Neoclassical models work toward a solution. They are constructed to ensure a straight, unambiguous answer. The final step in building these models is what is termed closing the model, finding a way to tie everything together so that solving for any x results in a unique y. As Romer (2016) has pointed out, the economist's unwavering drive to this end can lead to severe, often opaque assumptions and restrictions. By contrast, an agent-based model, with its host of heterogeneous agents, is not closed—it can be overidentified. To the economic theorist who seeks elegance and parsimony, an agent-based model might look like a scrum. But clearly, the financial system is overspecified, with hundreds, or even thousands, of entities. Many worlds might come out of its dynamics, and the simulation presents a distribution for these possible worlds. The result is not a number, but more like a story line or narrative of the ways the world might evolve. And it is narratives, not numbers, that dominate the high-level meetings on trading floors and board rooms over the course of a crisis.

AGENT-BASED MODELS FOR FINANCIAL CRISES

The underpinnings of agent-based models in finance, heuristics, interaction, and heterogeneity go as far back as 1908, as described by Henri Poincaré (quoted by Helbing & Kirman 2013, p. 9):

> When people are in close contact they do not act randomly and independently of each other; they react to each other. Many factors come into play, and they perturb people, and move them right and left.

In finance, agent-based models were first applied to the dynamics of trading (Zeeman 1974, Rieck 1994). A notable early effort in applying agent-based models of finance is the Santa Fe Institute's Artificial Stock Market project in the 1990s (Palmer et al. 1994; LeBaron, Arthur & Palmer 1999; Ehrentreich 2008), which was an offshoot of a broader, interdisciplinary project centered at the Santa Fe Institute examining economies as complex systems (Anderson, Arrow & Pines 1988). These models had markets that were populated by agents with varying trading strategies and exhibited peaks and troughs that belied the simplicity of the heuristics of the underlying agents.

From there, the work on agent-based models expanded to include, for example, models of mortgages and the housing market (Geanakoplos et al. 2012), the effects of leverage on volatility (Thurner, Farmer & Geanakoplos 2012), and liquidity in the face of capital constraints (Cifuentes, Ferrucci & Shin 2005). The work on agent-based models through the decade after the Artificial Stock Market effort is surveyed by LeBaron (2006a). Leigh Tesfatsion maintains a website for agent-based models used in economics and finance: **http://www2.econ.iastate.edu/tesfatsi/ace.htm**.

Interest in agent-based models has been spurred in the wake of the 2008 crisis (Buchanan 2009, Farmer & Foley 2009, Farmer & Geanakoplos 2009) for the very arguments that standard economic models failed and that the agent-based models can shed light where the standard models struggle, dealing with the complexity, interactions, and emergence that were manifest over the course of the crisis.

To explain how agent-based models can deal with crisis risk, I analogize the sources of a stampede as people escape from a fire—an example to which agent-based models have been applied (Shi, Ren & Chen 2009)—to the components of a market crisis. For a fire marshal the critical question is whether people can get out in the case of fire, and the answer depends on three factors: the number of people in the space, how many people can exit per minute based on the number and size of places of egress, and the time available to exit based on the flammability of the space. Modeling the number of people that can exit per minute is difficult because people are not walking through the exit in an orderly way. There is the potential for panic and stampedes. So this needs to be modeled on the basis of how people behave in a crisis—a role for agent-based models.

Using this example as an analogy for the financial system, market concentration measures the number of people in the market; liquidity determines the rate at which people can exit; and leverage, or more generally, the potential for forced selling, determines the flammability of the market and thus the number of minutes available to exit.[1] For financial markets, the situation gets more complicated. The exits shrink as investors push through them to liquidate. That is, liquidity dries up during a crisis. And for financial markets it is as if the building becomes more flammable as the exits become smaller, because a drop in liquidity can fuel cascades.

So a crisis-focused agent-based model feeds off of concentration, leverage, and liquidity. But the first ingredient of a crisis is the environment in which the agents interact, which is affected by their actions.

The Environment

If you want to follow a crisis, you need to follow the money. The money flows along a course to be processed into assets, to be delivered to those who need funding to transform into securities, and to be sent as collateral. If one of the pipes gets clogged or breaks under pressure, we have the makings of a crisis. If it fails to feed what is downstream, or backs up to spill into other systems, that crisis will spread.

If we keep things abstract and general, the mechanics of a crisis are not so difficult. But abstraction does not get us far. We need to start with a schematic of this plumbing. For an agent-based approach, or for almost any simulation approach, the key is to understand the structure: where the agents are operating, their environment, their heuristics, and the resulting dynamics, all of which are specific to the financial system.

The fastest way to appreciate the real world of the financial system and the degree to which economics has abstracted it away is to look at how funds travel, where cash is borrowed, how assets are bought and then used as collateral, and how the collateral is then used a second time to borrow even more cash (Aguiar, Bookstaber & Wipf 2014). As assets are moved from one institution to another, things change, much as the flows within a chemical plant are altered as they pass into the various processing units. Flows moving from depositors to long-term borrowers are subject to a maturity transformation. The flows of funding from cash providers through secured funding and prime brokers to hedge funds undergo a credit transformation. The flows between the financial institutions on either side of the bank or dealer's trading desk are subject to a liquidity transformation. Finally, the participants in the derivatives area are subject to risk transformations. Interactions matter.

The Agents and Their Heuristics

Syll (2016) asks why economists "consider it worthwhile and interesting to make evaluations of real economies based on abstract imaginary fantasy worlds," which he likens to "telling physiologists to

[1] Although I am focused on forced selling because of leverage, other avenues for forced selling include risk limits that force selling when breached (and that are more likely to be breached when there is a market shock and volatility increases) and preprogrammed selling strategies, such as portfolio insurance, volatility targeting, and risk parity strategies.

evaluate the human body from the perspective of unicorns." An agent-based approach can do away with abstraction, homogeneity, and generalization. It can start with the decisions of real-world, individual agents. Why start off by saying, "Assume there are N banks and K asset managers" when we know those banks and asset managers? Banks such as JPMorgan Chase (JPM) and Citi are the agents, as are hedge funds such as Citadel and Bridgewater, not to mention the various security lenders, asset managers, pension funds, and money market funds.

Each agent interacts with others. Some agents are sources of funding; others use funding. Some are intermediaries and market makers. Some act as conduits for collateral; others take on counterparty risk. Each agent has its own business model, a different level of risk taking, and a different culture. Each agent has its own set of heuristics. Some of the heuristics are spelled out in their governance structure and policies and procedures, and some are communicated to their investors. During times of crisis, some of the heuristics are hardwired; the agents unable to alter their course, most notably when the heuristics relate to margin calls or forced liquidations due to reduced availability of funding.

Interactions

The agent-based approach allows agents' actions to change the environment, and the changed environment changes their actions. What one agent does next depends on what it and other agents have just done. The result is a system imbued with complex dynamics that can defy direct mathematical analysis and trigger emergent phenomena. Financial crises envelop a wide swath of the landscape; therefore, the financial system, including the roles of the various participants and the interrelationships between the various financial functions, needs to be well mapped.[2] There are various types of agents in this system.

1. **Bank/dealers.** The term bank/dealer refers to both banks and broker-dealers, most of which have become aligned with banks post-2008. The bank/dealer can be considered a singular agent in the financial system, but it contains various agents, such as the prime broker, trading desk, and financing desk, such that each agent interacts with different agents and operates with a share of independence.
2. **Hedge funds.** Hedge fund agents borrow from the bank/dealer's prime broker to support their long and short trading positions. Hedge funds trade with the bank/dealer's trading desk, as well as with various exchanges.
3. **Cash providers.** Cash providers are agents that include asset managers, pension funds, insurance companies, securities lenders and money market funds.
4. **Institutional investors.** The institutional investors encompass agents ranging from asset managers to pension funds, sovereign wealth funds, and insurance companies. These agents are critical for providing liquidity to the market.[3]

The agents have various roles related to liquidity and can be recast in those terms (Preis et al. 2006, Tirole 2011). Returning to the fire marshal analogy, liquidity is the means of egress for financial environments. Consistent with the dictum that the markets operate to extract the

[2]The central bank and other government entities can be added as other agents. Here, we focus strictly on the agents within the financial system.

[3]Because of their tendency to become embroiled in forced selling, thus having a special role in fostering crises, hedge funds are presented here as a specific agent type, but hedge funds really are a special class of institutional investor that can borrow money to put on leveraged positions, take on short positions, and enter into illiquid and unusual investment opportunities.

maximum pain, when investors really need to get out, the door to liquidity begins to close. There are three types of agents when it comes to liquidity: liquidity demanders, which buy or sell, the archetype being leveraged investors such as hedge funds; liquidity suppliers, which meet the liquidity demand—for a price—such as asset managers and pension funds; and market makers, which adjust the price to meet the demand with supply.

Modeling liquidity during market crises is difficult because of the complex, nonlinear dynamics of the interactions among market participants. Measuring relatively small transactions does not provide much insight. Liquidity can be subject to emergent phenomena. This arises from the feedback that occurs during periods of market shock and illiquidity. Liquidity becomes an endogenous element of the broader market behavior, and it cannot be analyzed without attention to issues of leverage, funding, and the resulting changes in investor behavior. The complexity also arises from the heterogeneous decision cycles among those in the market, specifically the difference in time frames between the liquidity demanders, which require immediacy, and the liquidity suppliers, which do not (Duffie 2010; Bookstaber, Foley & Tivnan 2016; Leal et al. 2016).

DYNAMICS

The end result of the agents interacting in the environment creates the dynamics of the agent-based model. Each agent in the financial system observes the environment in its purview, which includes the effects of other agents' actions, and acts on the basis of its own heuristics. The agent does this without integrating how all others in the world are operating, much less how all of what it and all others are doing will add up in aggregate. We are developing a methodology that examines the activities of the individual participants and uncovers the global phenomena that emerge.

Once we have laid out the environment through the system map and the agents of the system, we can turn the model on and see how the dynamics unfold. The key dynamic of market crises is the fire sale, which is induced by asset shocks or funding runs, each of which can feed into the other (Brunnermeier & Pedersen 2009, Shleifer & Vishny 2011).

The fire sale dynamic is driven by the anvil and hammer of leverage and liquidity. If the markets are highly liquid, selling can be accommodated without a notable price decline, and there will be no cascades or contagion. If there is little leverage in the market, there will not be a need for substantial deleveraging, even in the face of a market event. Because forced deleveraging leads to asset sales and asset sales lead to price declines (which then lead to further deleveraging), both leverage and illiquidity are essential components of a market crisis.

I illustrate the objectives of the agent-based model by showing how the model can trace a shock as it reverberates through the system (Bookstaber, Paddrik & Tivnan 2017). Despite my comments arguing for agent-based models to be oriented toward the detailed reality, here I use a simplified, stylized example. The model can be applied to a system with many agents, but here I apply it to a tractable network of three assets, two hedge funds, two bank/dealers, and a single cash provider.

Figure 2 shows the progression of one simulation run of the agent-based model with five agents operating in three assets: two hedge funds, HF1 and HF2; two bank/dealers, BD1 and BD2; three assets, A1, A2, and A3; and a cash provider, CP. HF1 and BD1 hold A1 and A2, and HF2 and BD2 hold A2 and A3. The CP holds collateral in all three assets. BD2 is exposed to counterparty risk from BD1.

The first stage begins with an initial shock: A1 drops in price, which affects the three agents that hold this asset. Each stage in the figure, which is a snapshot of the model at different points in the progression from the initial shock, is depicted by showing which agents influence other agents.

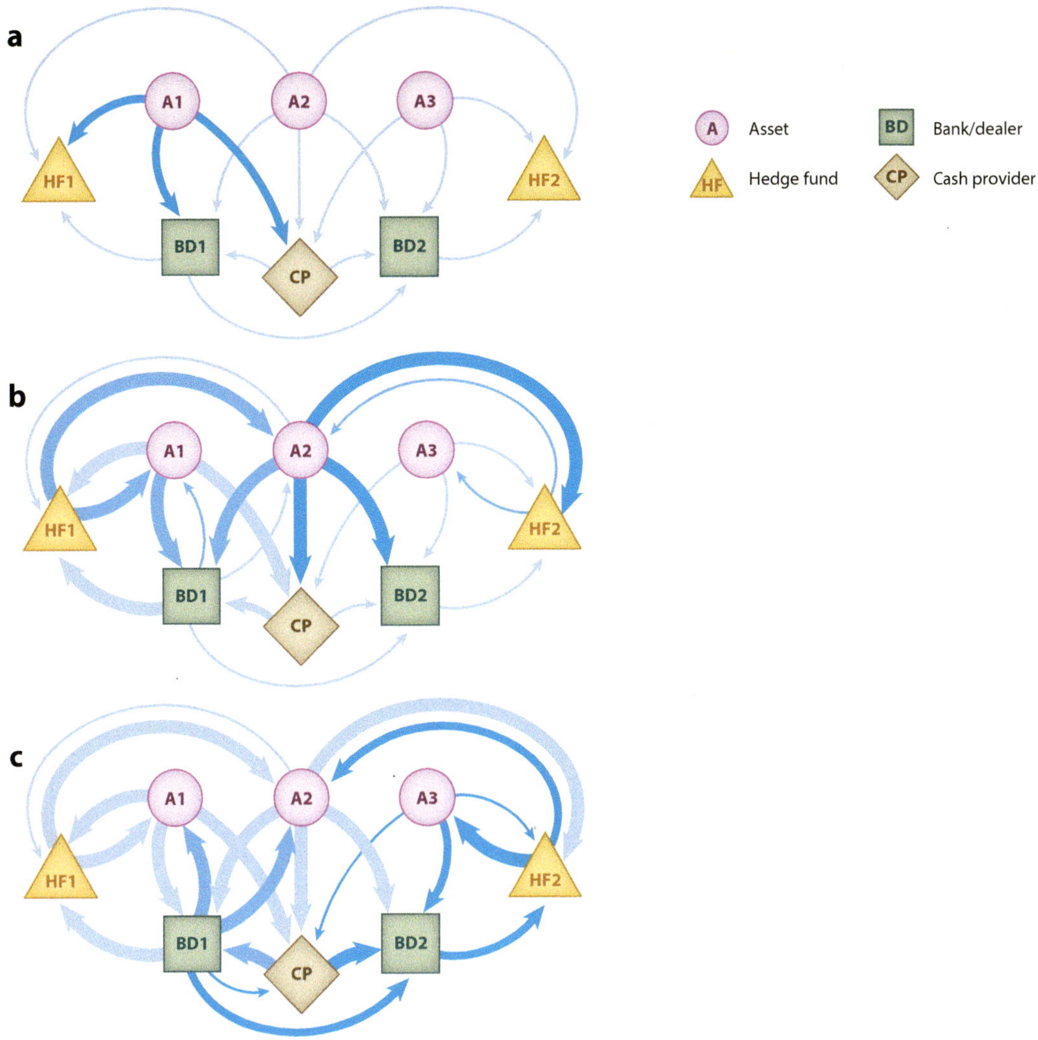

Figure 2

(*a*) The first stage shows the effects of a price shock to asset 1 (A1). The shock affects hedge fund 1 (HF1) and bank/dealer 1 (BD1) because they have exposure to A1. It also affects the cash provider (CP) because it holds A1 as collateral. A new pathway of effects is indicated by a dark blue line, and continuation of a shock along a pathway is indicated by a lighter line, the shading being indicative of the intensity of the effect. (*b*) The second stage shows the propagation to A2, which is also held by HF1 and BD1, and to HF2 and BD2, which, although not holding A1, have exposure to A2. The CP is further affected because of the pressure on A2. (*c*) The third stage shows the feedback, which creates a cascade for A1 and A2. It also shows A3 embroiled because it is held by HF2, BD2, and the CP. Counterparty exposure from BD1 to BD2 creates a further route for propagation. Figure adapted from Bookstaber, Paddrik & Tivnan (2017).

In the second stage, the effects of the initial shock propagate to affect A2 because both HF1 and BD1 sell positions in their portfolio to meet margin calls. A2 also drops in price. This has the same sort of effect on HF2 and BD2 that the shock in A1 had on HF1 and BD1. And A1 will drop further owing to continued pressure on HF1 and BD1. The value of CP's collateral drops even further, and because BD2 has used its assets as collateral, it is now also affected by reductions in funding from the CP.

By the third stage, A3 is embroiled in the effects from the initial shock, because HF2 and BD2 have exposure to A3. In the face of forced selling, HF2 and BD2 will start to liquidate their holdings of A3. Also, with funding restricted for the two bank/dealers, a new channel of contagion opens. The credit relationships between the bank/dealers weaken. BD2 observes BD1 weaken from the drop in its asset holdings and the reduction in funds. From the first stage through the third, the initial shock washes throughout the system, affecting all the assets and all the agents, creating the financial equivalent of a multicar pileup.

Each period in the agent-based model simulation can be represented by a network with the agents as nodes. The links can represent market flows and contractual relationships. The markets are part of the environment, and contractual relationships, most notably for lending, collateral and margin requirements, and counterparty arrangements, are generally embodied in the heuristics. But the network is only a snapshot; nodes and links change, and may even disappear, from one period to the next.[4]

Imagine a hedge fund that invests only in A3. It does not have any exposure to A1, where the initial shock occurs, and it does not even have exposure to agents that share the same assets as those that hold A1. Yet the hedge fund's portfolio drops as a result of the initial shock. That is real collateral damage!

ESTIMATION

The structure of an agent-based model allows estimation and calibration to occur at two levels, the heuristics of the agents and the dynamics of the resulting system. The model is evaluated by comparing its results to stylized facts, characteristics that are considered essential to properly reflect the target dynamics. LeBaron (2006b) illustrates calibration and testing in a market application, where the stylized facts include distributional properties such as the kurtosis, volatility clustering, and autocorrelation of market prices. Ashraf, Gershman & Howitt (2016) calibrate their macroeconomic model using a multistage approach that matches the model to stylized facts regarding economic variables and to measures of internal model consistency. The housing model of Geanakoplos et al. (2012) compares the model output to the pattern of actual housing foreclosures and related housing metrics.

Using stylized facts and internal consistency may be more akin to the methods of estimation for deep-learning artificial intelligence (AI) systems than to the parametric methods of most economic models, although an agent-based model does provide more structure than neural network–driven AI models. This structure no doubt is less than satisfying for researchers who enjoy the rigorous statistical foundations of econometric methods. But for the application of crisis modeling, stylized facts and consistency may be the best researchers can do. Historical data are of limited value when evaluating a present crisis, which is different not only from the more stable pre-crisis world but also from past crises. People are inventive; they construct new financial instruments and strategies (which, being untested and aggressively marketed, often are in the middle of a crisis). People adjust to the past crisis with new governance principles, risk management structures, and refined heuristics. And the path of a new crisis will bypass newly formed pockets of resistance that come from regulations that have been set up in the wake of the previous crisis.

[4]Monin & Bookstaber (2017) show the relationship between agent-based models and dynamic networks, and demonstrate that under suitable conditions both of them are representations of a Markov chain. Additional insight into the network representation can come from considering it as a multilayer network, with the layers being execution, financing, and collateral. Bookstaber & Kenett (2016) construct such a network.

CONCLUSION

A crisis is neither an equilibrium state nor a little nudge from that state. A crisis is not a bad draw from the urn. It is a draw from a new urn, a new distribution. A crisis cannot be pinned down if it is not ergodic, and it cannot be mechanistically predetermined if there is computational irreducibility. A crisis also is not a regime shift except in the obvious, tautological sense in that it is a new dynamic, where "regime shift" dresses up the statement "sometimes things are normal, and sometimes they are not" in the same way that "fat-tailed event" gives a more scientific ring than saying "something really bad happened."

Lucas (1981, p. 8) wrote: "In general, I believe that one who claims to understand the principles of flight can reasonably be expected to be able to make a flying machine, and that understanding business cycles means the ability to make them too, in roughly the same sense." In other words, if you want to understand crises, you have to develop a system that can create one. And to create one, you should note and address the following points.

- The dynamics are likely to be computationally irreducible, so follow the paths rather than trying to find a mathematical shortcut for getting to the end of the story.
- Interaction matters, so allow interaction (which means do not compress the world into representative agents).
- Interactions are based on heuristics, so understand the (heterogeneous) agents' heuristics.
- The interactions can change the environment and lead to emergent phenomena, so be sure the model is constructed in such a way that emergence is not smothered.

How a shock propagates and cascades, including how it changes the environment, our perceptions, and our experience, creates a dynamic for the future course of events, and this dynamic is at the core of agent-based modeling methodology. Agent-based models allow us to recognize some essential aspects of the world that are particularly apparent during crises.

There Is a Real World

The real world is rich and complex. There are many different players and institutions, and many different components have a bearing on how people act. Each person operates according to their particular heuristics, which likely differ from those of others and differ by more than the setting of some parameters. People interact in complex and sometimes unexpected ways, and actions work through the system with surprising and nonlinear results. Institutions such as Morgan Stanley, Goldman, Citadel, Bridgewater, Fidelity, and BlackRock bring their own idiosyncrasies. Inelegant regulations (e.g., Dodd–Frank, Volcker, and the Basel Accords) affect the agents' heuristics; they might reduce risk and constrain activities, but they also can lead to collateral damage and create vulnerabilities.

Using agent-based models, researchers are not starting with axioms and deriving a top-down deductive theory. They are not trying to build a general, abstract model that would work for some economy that might be discovered on Mars.

Agents Are Different

The real world requires us to understand real financial entities and the actual structure in which they operate. Homogeneity cannot be assumed nor can all agents be lumped together into a single representative agent, especially if the goal is to model interactions and emergent phenomena.

Agents Affect the Environment

Large financial institutions cannot take meaningful action in the face of a crisis without affecting the broader system, owing to their liquidation of large positions and their effect on the funding market and related counterparty and credit risk. They can take actions that are locally prudent but imprudent when the effect is extended to the broader system. Sometimes actions are taken to deliberately alter the environment. And a changing environment changes how agents act.

Agents Affect One Another

Contrary to the notion of a representative agent, many forces are interacting. Even similar forces, which we would think could be compressed into a representative agent, generate a complex and unpredictable world. If these forces affect the environment, and the environment affects them, then they all affect each other.

All these characteristics reside within the critical limit to knowledge that we only know the future as we live it. If we alter the environment on the basis of our actions, and if that in turn affects others who then change the environment further, and if all this occurs within actions that depend on the resulting changes in context, the deductive approach of neoclassical economics needs to be reconsidered. It will work some of the time, such as when people are atomistic and mostly the same, and do the same sorts of things as they always do. But they are not, and they do not, especially during periods of crisis.

DISCLOSURE STATEMENT

The author is not aware of any affiliations, memberships, funding, or financial holdings that might be perceived as affecting the objectivity of this review.

ACKNOWLEDGMENTS

This review is derived from Bookstaber (2017).

LITERATURE CITED

Aguiar A, Bookstaber R, Wipf T. 2014. *A map of funding durability and risk*. Work. Pap. 14-03, Off. Financ. Res.

Anderson PW, Arrow KJ, Pines D, eds. 1988. *The Economy as an Evolving Complex System*. Redwood City, CA: Addison-Wesley

Arthur WB. 1999. Complexity and the economy. *Science* 284:107–9

Ashraf Q, Gershman B, Howitt P. 2016. How inflation affects macroeconomic performance: an agent-based computational investigation. *Macroecon. Dyn.* 20:558–81

Bookstaber R. 2017. *The End of Theory: Financial Crisis, the Failure of Economics, and the Sweep of Human Interaction*. Princeton, NJ: Princeton Univ. Press

Bookstaber R, Foley M, Tivnan B. 2016. Toward an understanding of market resilience: market liquidity and heterogeneity in the investor decision cycle. *J. Econ. Interact. Coord.* 11:205–27

Bookstaber R, Kenett D. 2016. *Looking deeper, seeing more: a multi-layer map of the financial system*. Brief Ser. 16-06, Off. Financ. Res.

Bookstaber R, Langsam J. 1985. On the optimality of coarse behavior rules. *J. Theor. Biol.* 116:161–93

Bookstaber R, Paddrik M, Tivnan B. 2017. An agent-based model for financial vulnerability. *J. Econ. Interact. Coord.* In press

Brunnermeier M, Pedersen LH. 2009. Market liquidity and funding liquidity. *Rev. Financ. Stud.* 22:2201–38

Buchanan M. 2009. Meltdown modeling: Could agent-based computer models prevent another financial crisis? *Nature* 460:680–82

Cifuentes R, Ferrucci G, Shin HS. 2005. Liquidity risk and contagion. *J. Eur. Econ. Assoc.* 3:556–66

Colander D, Goldberg M, Haas A, Juselius K, Kirman A, et al. 2009. The financial crisis and the systemic failure of the economics profession. *Crit. Rev.* 21:249–67

Davis M. 1958. *Computability and Unsolvability*. New York: McGraw-Hill

Duffie D. 2010. Presidential address: asset price dynamics with slow-moving capital. *J. Finance* 65:1237–67

Ehrentreich N. 2008. *Agent-Based Modeling: The Santa Fe Institute Artificial Stock Market Model Revisited*. Berlin: Springer-Verlag

Evans GW, Honkapohja S. 2005. An interview with Thomas J. Sargent. *Macroecon. Dyn.* 9:561–83

Farmer JD, Foley D. 2009. The economy needs agent-based modelling. *Nature* 460:685–86

Farmer JD, Geanakoplos J. 2009. The virtues and vices of equilibrium and the future of financial economics. *Complexity* 14:11–38

Gardner M. 1970. Mathematical games: the fantastic combinations of John Conway's new solitaire game 'Life.' *Sci. Am.* 223:120–23

Geanakoplos J, Axtell R, Farmer DJ, Howitt P, Conlee B, et al. 2012. Getting at systemic risk via an agent-based model of the housing market. *Am. Econ. Rev.* 102:53–58

Gigerenzer G, Brighton H. 2009. Homo heuristics: why biased minds make better inferences. *Top. Cogn. Sci.* 1:107–43

Gigerenzer G, Gaissmaier W. 2011. Heuristic decision making. *Annu. Rev. Psychol.* 62:451–82

Haldane A. 2016. *The dappled world*. Speech at GLS Shackle Bien. Mem. Lect., Bank Engl., Nov. 10, London. **http://www.bankofengland.co.uk/publications/Pages/speeches/2016/937.aspx**

Helbing D, Farkas I, Vicsek T. 2000. Simulating dynamical features of escape panic. *Nature* 407:487–90

Helbing D, Kirman A. 2013. Rethinking economics using complexity theory. *Real-World Econ. Rev.* 64:23–51

Int. Monet. Fund. 2007. *World Economic Outlook: Globalization and Inequality*. Washington, DC: Int. Monet. Fund

Keynes JM. 1978. Letter to Harrod, 4 July 1938. In *The Collected Writings of John Maynard Keynes*, Vol. 14: *The General Theory and After: Part II. Defence and Development*, ed. E Johnson, D Moggridge, pp. 295–97. Cambridge, UK: Cambridge Univ. Press. **http://economia.unipv.it/harrod/edition/editionstuff/rfh.346.htm**

Kirman A. 1989. The intrinsic limits of modern economic theory: The emperor has no clothes. *Econ. J.* 99:126–39

Kirman A. 1992. Whom or what does the representative individual represent? *J. Econ. Perspect.* 6:117–36

Kirman A. 2010. The economic crisis is a crisis for economic theory. *CESifo Econ. Stud.* 56:498–535

Leal SJ, Napoletano M, Roventini A, Fagiolo G. 2016. Rock around the clock: an agent-based model of low- and high-frequency trading. *J. Evol. Econ.* 26:49–76

LeBaron B. 2006a. Agent-based computational finance. In *Handbook of Computational Economics*, Vol. 2: *Agent-Based Computational Economics*, ed. L Tesfatsion, KL Judd, pp. 1187–227. Amsterdam: North-Holland/Elsevier

LeBaron B. 2006b. Agent-based financial markets: matching stylized facts with style. In *Post Walrasian Macroeconomics*, ed. D Colander, pp. 221–35. New York: Cambridge Univ. Press

LeBaron B, Arthur WB, Palmer R. 1999. Time series properties of an artificial stock market model. *J. Econ. Dyn. Control* 23:1487–516

Lucas R Jr. 1981. *Studies in Business-Cycle Theory*. Cambridge, MA: MIT Press

Lucas R Jr. 2009. In defence of the dismal science. *The Economist*, Aug. 6. **http://www.economist.com/node/14165405**

Monin P, Bookstaber R. 2017. *Information flows, the accuracy of opinions, and crashes in a dynamic network*. Staff Discuss. Pap. 17-01, Off. Financ. Res.

Olberg R, Worthington A, Venator K. 2000. Prey pursuit and interception in dragonflies. *J. Comp. Physiol. A* 186:155–62

Page SE. 2011. *Diversity and Complexity*. Princeton, NJ: Princeton Univ. Press

Palmer RG, Arthur WB, Holland JH, LeBaron B, Tayler P. 1994. Artificial economic life: a simple model of a stock market. *Physica D* 75:264–74

Preis T, Golke S, Paul W, Schneider JJ. 2006. Multi-agent based order book model of financial markets. *Europhys. Lett.* 75:510–16

Rieck C. 1994. Evolutionary simulation of asset trading strategies. In *Many-Agent Simulation and Artificial Life*, ed. E Hillebrand, J Stender, pp. 112–36. Amsterdam: IOS Press

Romer P. 2016. *The trouble with macroeconomics*. Commons Meml. Lect., Omicron Delta Epsilon Soc., Jan. 5

Saari DG. 1995. Mathematical complexity of simple economics. *Not. Am. Math. Soc.* 42:222–30

Saari DG. 1996. The ease of generating chaotic behavior in economics. *Chaos Solut. Fractals* 7:2267–78

Scarf H. 1960. Some examples of the global instability of the competitive equilibrium. *Int. Econ. Rev.* 1:157–72

Shi J, Ren A, Chen C. 2009. Agent-based evacuation model of large public buildings under fire conditions. *Autom. Constr.* 18:338–47

Shleifer A, Vishny R. 2011. Fire sales in finance and macroeconomics. *J. Econ. Perspect.* 25:29–48

US House, Subcomm. Investig. Overs., Comm. Sci. Technol. 2010. *Building a Science of Economics for the Real World*, Hearing (Serial 111-106), 111 Congr., 2nd sess., July 10, statement of Robert M. Solow. **https://www.gpo.gov/fdsys/pkg/CHRG-111hhrg57604/pdf/CHRG-111hhrg57604.pdf**

Syll LP. 2016. *On the Use and Misuse of Theories and Models in Mainstream Economics*. London: Coll. Publ.

Thurner S, Farmer JD, Geanakoplos J. 2012. Leverage causes fat tails and clustered volatility. *Quant. Finance* 12:695–707

Tirole J. 2011. Illiquidity and all its friends. *J. Econ. Lit.* 49(2):287–325

Trichet J-C. 2010. *Reflections on the nature of monetary policy non-standard measures and finance theory*. Opening address, ECB Cent. Bank. Conf., Nov. 18, Frankfurt, Ger.

Zeeman E. 1974. On the unstable behavior of stock exchanges. *J. Math. Econ.* 1:39–49

Zheng H, Son Y-J, Chiu Y-C, Head L, Feng Y, et al. 2013. *A primer for agent-based simulation and modeling in transportation applications*. Rep. FHWA-13-054, Fed. Highway Adm.

Information Disclosure in Financial Markets

Itay Goldstein[1] and Liyan Yang[2]

[1]Department of Finance, Wharton School, University of Pennsylvania, Philadelphia, Pennsylvania 19104; email: itayg@wharton.upenn.edu

[2]Department of Finance, Joseph L. Rotman School of Management, University of Toronto, Toronto, Ontario M5S 3E6, Canada; email: liyan.yang@rotman.utoronto.ca

Annu. Rev. Financ. Econ. 2017. 9:101–25

First published as a Review in Advance on July 11, 2017

The *Annual Review of Financial Economics* is online at financial.annualreviews.org

https://doi.org/10.1146/annurev-financial-110716-032355

Copyright © 2017 by Annual Reviews.
All rights reserved

JEL codes: D82, G14, M41

Keywords

disclosure, market quality, crowding-out effect, learning from prices, real efficiency, welfare

Abstract

Information disclosure is an essential component of regulation in financial markets. In this article, we provide a cohesive analytical framework to review certain key channels through which disclosure in financial markets affects market quality, information production, efficiency of real investment decisions, and traders' welfare. We use our framework to address four main aspects. First, we demonstrate the conventional wisdom that disclosure improves market quality in an economy with exogenous information. Second, we illustrate that disclosure can crowd out the production of private information and that its overall market-quality implications are subtle and depend on the specification of information-acquisition technology. Third, we review how disclosure affects the efficiency of real investment decisions when financial markets are not just a side show, as real decision makers can learn information from them to guide their decisions. Last, we discuss how disclosure in financial markets affects investors' welfare through changing trading opportunities and through beauty-contest motives. Overall, our review suggests that information disclosure is an important factor for understanding the functioning of financial markets and that there are several trade-offs that should be considered in determining its optimal level.

1. INTRODUCTION

Disclosure of information in financial markets is at the forefront of regulatory efforts to improve financial market quality and stability. Greenstone, Oyer & Vissing-Jorgensen (2006, p. 399) write that "since the passage of the Securities Act of 1933 and the Securities Exchange Act of 1934, the federal government has actively regulated US equity markets. The centerpiece of these efforts is the mandated disclosure of financial information." Recently, these efforts have been very prominent, with the Sarbanes–Oxley Act of 2002 and the Dodd–Frank Act of 2010 emphasizing various aspects of improved disclosure. For example, the Sarbanes–Oxley Act was passed "to protect investors by improving the accuracy and reliability of corporate disclosures made pursuant to the securities laws, and for other purposes" (Pub. L. 107–204, 116 Stat. 745).

Disclosure regulation comes in different forms and affects different activities. Over time, firms have increasingly been required to disclose information about their operations and financial activities in financial reports to their investors. Similarly, investors are required to disclose information about their holdings in firms that might pertain to activism, intentions of activism, or acquisitions intentions that could ultimately affect firm value. Moreover, improved quality of public information is also achieved by increasing the reliability of credit ratings and by greater disclosure of macroeconomic and industry-related information. Recently, following the financial crisis of 2008, governments increased the amount of disclosure available about banks by conducting annual stress tests and making their results publicly available. This has led to significant public debate (Goldstein & Sapra 2013).

The academic literature is quite ambiguous about the effects of disclosure and its overall desirability. It is well understood that disclosure can potentially promote some important goals: By leveling the playing field in financial markets, it can increase market liquidity and market efficiency and can decrease the cost of capital for firms. However, much has been written about potential unintended consequences of disclosure, which occur because of the crowding out of private information production, the destruction of risk-sharing opportunities, and the promotion of destabilizing beauty-contest incentives. Given the flow of new regulations related to disclosure in recent years, researchers have been delving more and more into the topic, trying to understand the pros and cons and answering key questions, such as: What is the optimal level of disclosure in terms of promoting market quality and social welfare? What types of disclosure are most beneficial? In what circumstances is disclosure desirable?

Our goal in this review is to present the main forces that have been put forward in the discussion on the effects of disclosure in financial markets. As this is a review of theoretical literature, we use a workhorse model that has been used extensively in the literature on information and disclosure in financial markets, and we show how the main forces are manifested within this framework. We hope this will be useful to researchers who wish to build on existing theories in developing new ones, testing existing empirical implications, or understanding ongoing policy debates. We do not attempt an all-inclusive survey of the extant disclosure literature (some excellent surveys include those of Dye 2001, Verrecchia 2001, Kanodia 2006, Leuz & Wysocki 2008, and Kanodia & Sapra 2017). Instead, we aim to organize a few leading forces within a cohesive analytical framework, so that the pros and cons of disclosure can be more easily sorted out and evaluated for different environments.

The structure of this review is as follows. Section 2 presents the basic framework for studying information and disclosure in financial markets, building on the work of Grossman & Stiglitz (1980), Hellwig (1980), and Verrecchia (1982a). We show basic results demonstrating how increased precision of public information, which is achieved via enhanced disclosure, improves common measures of market quality. That is, we show that disclosure increases liquidity and market efficiency and decreases the cost of capital and return volatility. These results capture the usual intuition that guides regulators in imposing greater disclosure.

In Section 3, we extend the basic framework to endogenize the acquisition of private information by market participants, building on work by Verrecchia (1982b), Diamond (1985), and others. We demonstrate the basic argument that increased disclosure leads to crowding out of private-information acquisition. This implies that the effect of disclosure on market quality is more nuanced once private information is endogenized and that it depends on the amount of information being disclosed, on the information-acquisition technology, and on the measure of market quality being considered.

Although the analysis in Sections 2 and 3 considers measures of market quality, these measures do not translate easily into a clear objective function to tell how much disclosure is desirable. Section 4 extends the framework, reviewing papers that emphasize the role of the financial market in producing information that guides decisions on the real side of the economy. This is in the spirit of the literature on the market feedback effect, which is reviewed by Bond, Edmans & Goldstein (2012). This enables the analysis of optimal disclosure in light of its effect on the efficiency of real investment decisions (e.g., Gao & Liang 2013; Han, Tang & Yang 2016). An interesting dimension revealed by papers in this realm of work is that the type of information being disclosed is key in determining whether disclosure is desirable (Bond & Goldstein 2015, Goldstein & Yang 2016).

Finally, Section 5 considers extensions of the basic framework that allow us to study the effect of disclosure on the welfare of investors in financial markets and, as a result, to pin down optimal disclosure. Whereas the traditional view is that disclosure enhances the welfare of investors, a classic result by Hirshleifer (1971) shows that disclosure destroys risk-sharing opportunities and is thus welfare reducing. More recently, Kurlat & Veldkamp (2015) suggested a reduction in trading opportunities as another way in which disclosure's effects can be negative. Another common argument is that disclosure can be harmful because of beauty-contest incentives, leading all investors to want to do the same thing. In such a case, greater precision of public information leads investors to put too much weight on it, thus reducing welfare (Morris & Shin 2002).

2. A BASIC MODEL OF INFORMATION AND DISCLOSURE

We introduce a basic framework that enables us to discuss the various effects of disclosure in financial markets in a unified way. We rely on the noisy rational-expectations equilibrium (noisy REE) model, which is a workhorse model that has been used extensively in the literature on information and disclosure in financial markets. The model we describe in this section builds on early contributions by Grossman & Stiglitz (1980), Hellwig (1980), and Verrecchia (1982a). The model has the traditional CARA-normal feature; that is, traders have constant absolute risk aversion (CARA) preferences, and all random variables are normally distributed.

2.1. Setup

There are two dates, $t = 1$ and $t = 2$. At date 1, two assets are traded in a competitive financial market: a risk-free asset and a risky asset. The risky asset is usually thought of as equity issued by a firm, but it can also be a different asset, e.g., a corporate bond. The risk-free asset has a constant value of 1 and is in unlimited supply. The risky asset pays an uncertain cash flow at the final date $t = 2$, denoted by $\tilde{v}$. We assume that $\tilde{v}$ is normally distributed with a mean of 0 and a precision (reciprocal of variance) of τ_v—that is, $\tilde{v} \sim N(0, \tau_v^{-1})$, with $\tau_v > 0$.[1] The risky asset is traded at an endogenous price $\tilde{p}$ and has a fixed supply $Q \geq 0$.

[1]We use a tilde (˜) to signify an exogenous random variable and use τ to denote its precision; i.e., for a random variable $\tilde{z}$, we have $\tau_z = 1/\text{Var}(\tilde{z})$.

There are three types of traders in the financial market: informed traders, uninformed traders, and liquidity traders. The first two types of traders have CARA utility over their wealth at date 2 with a risk aversion coefficient of $\gamma > 0$. They can represent individuals or institutions who trade the risky asset. The total mass of the first two types of traders is 1, with a fraction $\mu \in [0, 1]$ being informed traders and a fraction $1 - \mu$ being uninformed traders. Prior to trading, informed trader i observes a private signal $\tilde{s}_i$, which contains information about the fundamental value $\tilde{v}$ of the risky asset in the following form:

$$\tilde{s}_i = \tilde{v} + \tilde{\varepsilon}_i, \quad \text{with } \tilde{\varepsilon}_i \sim N(0, \tau_\varepsilon^{-1}) \text{ and } \tau_\varepsilon > 0, \tag{1.}$$

where $(\tilde{v}, \{\tilde{\varepsilon}_i\}_{i\in[0,\mu]})$ are mutually independent. For now, we take both μ and τ_ε as exogenous. We endogenize them later.

A common way to introduce disclosure into this model is to add a public signal $\tilde{y}$ as follows:

$$\tilde{y} = \tilde{v} + \tilde{\eta}, \quad \text{with } \tilde{\eta} \sim N(0, \tau_\eta^{-1}) \text{ and } \tau_\eta \geq 0 \tag{2.}$$

(see, e.g., Diamond 1985; Verrecchia 2001; Morris & Shin 2002; Hughes, Liu & Liu 2007; Lambert, Leuz & Verrecchia 2007). For example, $\tilde{y}$ can be thought of as announcements made by the firm about its future prospects or as economic statistics published by government agencies, central banks, or other parties (e.g., credit rating agencies). The precision τ_η controls the quality of the public signal $\tilde{y}$, with a high value of τ_η signifying that $\tilde{y}$ is more informative about the asset cash flow $\tilde{v}$ (i.e., signifying more disclosure). More disclosure can be achieved by making more frequent announcements or by releasing more accurate data. (We assume that traders can costlessly interpret the public signal $\tilde{y}$. Some studies have considered settings in which traders can only extract a noisy version of $\tilde{y}$ and where their public data processing abilities can be different; see, e.g., Indjejikian 1991, Pagano & Volpin 2012, Di Maggio & Pagano 2017.) Much of our analysis is concerned with how the parameter τ_η affects market outcomes. Note that we focus on the effect of ex ante disclosure quality, in the sense of an improvement in the precommitted precision of public information. We do not address strategic ex post disclosure, where firms choose whether to disclose based on their signal, which involves a signaling effect. There is a large literature that addresses these issues (see, e.g., Grossman 1981; Milgrom 1981; Dye 1985; Jung & Kwon 1988; Acharya, DeMarzo & Kremer 2011; Guttman, Kremer & Skrzypacz 2014). Also note that public information in Equation 2 represents disclosure about fundamental information, so we do not discuss the literature on market transparency, which explores the effect of disclosing information about trading positions and prices (see, e.g., Madhavan 1995; Pagano & Röell 1996; Bloomfield & O'Hara 1999; Naik, Neuberger & Viswanathan 1999; Huddart, Hughes & Levine 2001; Easley, O'Hara & Yang 2014; for a discussion of the interactions between disclosure of fundamental information and transparency of the trading process, see Di Maggio & Pagano 2017).

Liquidity traders, also called noise traders in the literature, demand $\tilde{x}$ units of the risky asset, where $\tilde{x} \sim N(0, \tau_x^{-1})$, with $\tau_x \in (0, \infty)$, is independent of other shocks in the economy. Noise trading provides the randomness that makes the rational-expectations equilibrium partially revealing, which is crucial to sustaining trading in equilibrium. In the baseline model, we take the size τ_x^{-1} of noise trading as exogenous. We endogenize it later. Note that there are various ways to endogenize noise trading in asymmetric information models, such as endowment shocks (e.g., Diamond & Verrecchia 1981, Diamond 1985) or private investment opportunities (e.g., Wang 1994; Easley, O'Hara & Yang 2014).

2.2. Equilibrium

The equilibrium requires that (*a*) informed and uninformed traders choose investments in assets to maximize their expected utility conditional on their respective information sets, including the asset price $\tilde{p}$, the public signal $\tilde{y}$, and (for informed traders) the private signal $\tilde{s}_i$; (*b*) the markets clear so that the demand for the risky asset equals the exogenous supply Q; and (*c*) informed and uninformed traders have rational expectations in the sense that their beliefs about all random variables are consistent with the true underlying distributions and equilibrium behaviors.

Constructing a noisy REE boils down to solving a price function that depends on the public information $\tilde{y}$, informed traders' private information $\tilde{s}_i$, and noise trading $\tilde{x}$. By the law of large numbers, the noise terms $\tilde{\varepsilon}_i$ in the private signals $\tilde{s}_i$ wash out, and thus we conjecture that the price $\tilde{p}$ is a function of $(\tilde{y}, \tilde{v}, \tilde{x})$. The literature focuses on a linear price function of the form

$$\tilde{p} = p_0 + p_y\tilde{y} + p_v\tilde{v} + p_x\tilde{x}, \tag{3}$$

where the p-coefficients are endogenously determined in equilibrium. Here we restrict our attention to this form.

Informed trader i has an information set $\{\tilde{y}, \tilde{s}_i, \tilde{p}\}$. The CARA-normal setup implies that the demand function of informed trader i is

$$D_I(\tilde{y}, \tilde{s}_i, \tilde{p}) = \frac{E(\tilde{v}|\tilde{y}, \tilde{s}_i, \tilde{p}) - \tilde{p}}{\gamma \mathrm{Var}(\tilde{v}|\tilde{y}, \tilde{s}_i, \tilde{p})}.$$

For trader i, the information contained in the price is equivalent to the signal $\tilde{s}_p$:

$$\tilde{s}_p \equiv \frac{\tilde{p} - (p_0 + p_y\tilde{y})}{p_v} = \tilde{v} + \rho^{-1}\tilde{x}, \quad \text{with } \rho = \frac{p_v}{p_x}, \tag{4}$$

which is normally distributed, with mean $\tilde{v}$ and precision $\rho^2\tau_x$. Applying Bayes' rule to compute the conditional moments in the demand function, we can obtain

$$D_I(\tilde{y}, \tilde{s}_i, \tilde{p}) = \frac{\tau_\varepsilon\tilde{s}_i + \tau_\eta\tilde{y} + \rho^2\tau_x\tilde{s}_p - (\tau_v + \tau_\varepsilon + \tau_\eta + \rho^2\tau_x)\tilde{p}}{\gamma}. \tag{5}$$

Similarly, an uninformed trader has an information set $\{\tilde{y}, \tilde{p}\}$, and we can compute this trader's demand function for the risky asset as follows:

$$D_U(\tilde{y}, \tilde{p}) = \frac{E(\tilde{v}|\tilde{y}, \tilde{p}) - \tilde{p}}{\gamma \mathrm{Var}(\tilde{v}|\tilde{y}, \tilde{p})} = \frac{\tau_\eta\tilde{y} + \rho^2\tau_x\tilde{s}_p - (\tau_v + \tau_\eta + \rho^2\tau_x)\tilde{p}}{\gamma}. \tag{6}$$

The market-clearing condition is

$$\int_0^\mu D_I(\tilde{y}, \tilde{s}_i, \tilde{p})di + (1 - \mu)D_U(\tilde{y}, \tilde{p}) + \tilde{x} = Q. \tag{7}$$

To derive the equilibrium price function, we insert Equations 5 and 6 into Equation 7 to solve the price in terms of the public signal $\tilde{y}$, the fundamental $\tilde{v}$, and the noise trading $\tilde{x}$, and we then compare with the conjectured price function in Equation 3 to obtain a system defining the unknown p-coefficients.

Solving this system yields the following result: For any $\mu \in [0, 1]$ and $\tau_\varepsilon \geq 0$, there exists a unique partially revealing noisy REE, with price function of the form in Equation 3, where

$$p_0 = \frac{-\gamma Q}{\mu\tau_\varepsilon + \tau_v + \tau_\eta + \rho^2\tau_x}, \quad p_y = \frac{\tau_\eta}{\mu\tau_\varepsilon + \tau_v + \tau_\eta + \rho^2\tau_x},$$
$$p_v = \frac{\mu\tau_\varepsilon + \rho^2\tau_x}{\mu\tau_\varepsilon + \tau_v + \tau_\eta + \rho^2\tau_x}, \quad p_x = \frac{\rho\tau_x + \gamma}{\mu\tau_\varepsilon + \tau_v + \tau_\eta + \rho^2\tau_x}, \tag{8}$$

with $\rho = \mu\tau_\varepsilon/\gamma$.

2.3. Market Quality and Disclosure

The effect of disclosure is often understood by examining different measures of market quality. We now define four common measures, explain their origins, and discuss how they are affected by greater disclosure.

2.3.1. Market liquidity. Market liquidity refers to a market's ability to facilitate the purchase or sale of an asset without drastically affecting the asset's price. The literature has used the coefficient p_x in the price function (Equation 3) to inversely measure market liquidity: A smaller p_x means that liquidity trading $\tilde{x}$ has a smaller price impact, and thus the market is deeper and more liquid. Formally,

$$\text{Liquidity} \equiv \frac{1}{p_x}. \tag{9}$$

This measure of market liquidity is often referred to as Kyle's (1985) lambda.

The illiquidity measure p_x can also be linked to another often used measure, the bid-ask spread. Suppose that a liquidity trader comes to the market with a buying order $\tilde{x} = +1$. By Equation 3, this trader expects on average to fulfill this order at an ask price quoted by the market, $\text{Ask} \equiv E(\tilde{p}|\tilde{x} = +1) = p_0 + p_x$. Similarly, if the liquidity trader wants to sell an order $\tilde{x} = -1$, then, on average, the trader expects to fulfill the order at a bid price $\text{Bid} \equiv E(\tilde{p}|\tilde{x} = -1) = p_0 - p_x$. As a result, the bid-ask spread is

$$\text{Bid-ask spread} = \text{Ask} - \text{Bid} = 2p_x.$$

Thus, p_x is indeed positively associated with the bid-ask spread.

From Equation 8, we know that disclosure improves market liquidity; that is, $\partial\text{Liquidity}/\partial\tau_\eta > 0$. Intuitively, more precise public information implies that there is less uncertainty about the asset value, so rational traders trade more aggressively against liquidity traders. As a result, changes in liquidity trading are absorbed with a smaller price change.

2.3.2. Market efficiency. Market efficiency, also called price efficiency or informational efficiency, concerns how informative the prevailing market prices are about the future values of the traded assets. An underlying reason for promoting market efficiency is that it is believed to be a good proxy for real efficiency, by which more information in prices about underlying values improves real investment decisions.[2] In Section 4, we refine this statement. In the literature (e.g., Vives 2008, Peress 2010, Ozsoylev & Walden 2011), researchers measure market efficiency using the precision of the posterior about an asset fundamental conditional on its price,[3] that is,

$$\text{Market efficiency} \equiv \frac{1}{\text{Var}(\tilde{v}|\tilde{p})}. \tag{10}$$

Given that $\tilde{v}$ and $\tilde{p}$ are normally distributed, $1/\text{Var}(\tilde{v}|\tilde{p})$ is positively related to the correlation coefficient $\text{Corr}(\tilde{v}, \tilde{p})$ between $\tilde{v}$ and $\tilde{p}$, that is,

$$\frac{1}{\text{Var}(\tilde{v}|\tilde{p})} = \frac{\tau_v}{1 - [\text{Corr}(\tilde{v}, \tilde{p})]^2}.$$

[2]Fama & Miller (1972, p. 335) note that an informationally efficient market "has a very desirable feature. In particular, at any point in time market prices of securities provide accurate signals for resource allocation; that is, firms can make production-investment decisions. . . ."

[3]Equation 10 gives the most standard measure for market efficiency. In the context of learning from prices examined in Section 4, one can also measure the additional information contained in the price relative to that in the disclosure as $1/\text{Var}(\tilde{v}|\tilde{p}, \tilde{y}) - 1/\text{Var}(\tilde{v}|\tilde{y})$.

For this reason, one can also use $\text{Corr}(\tilde{v}, \tilde{p})$ to measure market efficiency (e.g., Goldstein & Yang 2014).

Using Equation 8, we can show that disclosure improves market efficiency, that is, $\partial[1/\text{Var}(\tilde{v}|\tilde{p})]/\partial\tau_\eta > 0$. Intuitively, more public information before the price is formed directly injects more fundamental information into the price through updating traders' forecasts about the asset payoff. This implies that the price tracks fundamental value more closely.

2.3.3. Cost of capital. In this one-period model, the return on the risky asset is $\tilde{v} - \tilde{p}$, as at date 2, the uncertainty is resolved and the asset price is its fundamental value $\tilde{v}$. The expected return $E(\tilde{v} - \tilde{p})$ is often interpreted as the cost of capital on the risky asset (e.g., Easley & O'Hara 2004; Hughes, Liu & Liu 2007; Lambert, Leuz & Verrecchia 2007). A lower cost of capital benefits the issuer of the security, as it enables the issuer to sell the security at a higher price.

From Equation 8, we have

$$E(\tilde{v} - \tilde{p}) = \frac{\gamma Q}{\mu\tau_\varepsilon + \tau_v + \tau_\eta + \left(\frac{\mu\tau_\varepsilon}{\gamma}\right)^2 \tau_x}. \tag{11}$$

Thus, the cost of capital $E(\tilde{v} - \tilde{p})$ is positively affected by risk aversion γ and asset supply Q in the numerator. This is because traders are willing to pay a lower price when they are more risk averse and have to hold more of the asset on average, so the risk they have to bear is higher. The expression in the denominator is equal to

$$\frac{\mu}{\text{Var}(\tilde{v}|\tilde{y}, \tilde{s}_i, \tilde{p})} + \frac{1-\mu}{\text{Var}(\tilde{v}|\tilde{y}, \tilde{p})},$$

which is inversely related to the average risk perceived by traders per unit of the security. When the perceived risk goes up, the cost of capital also increases. Disclosure affects the cost of capital only through affecting the perceived risk: A higher level of disclosure lowers the cost of capital by lowering traders' average risk; that is, $\partial E(\tilde{v} - \tilde{p})/\partial\tau_\eta < 0$.

2.3.4. Return volatility. Return volatility $\sigma(\tilde{v} - \tilde{p}) = \sqrt{\text{Var}(\tilde{v} - \tilde{p})}$ is another measure that attracts attention from academics and regulators. Using Equation 8, we can show that disclosure lowers return volatility; that is, $\partial\sigma(\tilde{v} - \tilde{p})/\partial\tau_\eta < 0$. This is because more public information improves market efficiency, which thus brings the asset price $\tilde{p}$ closer to the fundamental $\tilde{v}$.

2.3.5. Summary. To summarize the results discussed thus far, we can see that for a given fraction μ of informed traders and a given precision of their information τ_ε, disclosure improves all typical measures of market quality. It increases market liquidity and market efficiency and decreases the cost of capital and return volatility. This is the conventional wisdom that is often put forward to argue for greater disclosure with the intent of improving the functioning of the financial market. This is consistent with many academic papers (e.g., Diamond & Verrecchia 1991; Verrecchia 2001; Easley & O'Hara 2004; Hughes, Liu & Liu 2007; Lambert, Leuz & Verrecchia 2007; Gao 2008) and with the logic behind recent regulatory acts, such as the Sarbanes–Oxley Act of 2002 and the Dodd–Frank Act of 2010.[4]

[4]For example, in its final ruling on shortening the reporting deadline for insider trading to two business days, the Securities and Exchange Commission (SEC 2002) argues that "making this information available to all investors on a more timely basis should increase market transparency, which will likely enhance market efficiency and liquidity."

3. INFORMATION ACQUISITION AND CROWDING-OUT EFFECT

In Section 2, both the fraction μ of informed traders and the precision τ_ε of informed traders' private information were exogenous. In this setup, disclosure was shown to improve various measures of market quality, as it enabled more information to get into prices, improving market liquidity, market efficiency, etc. However, a natural question is: How do changes in disclosure affect private-information production, which is central to financial markets? Beginning to think about the effects of disclosure more broadly, various researchers have endogenized the variables μ and τ_ε that capture the amount of private information in the market (e.g., Verrecchia 1982b; Diamond 1985; Kim & Verrecchia 1994; Gao & Liang 2013; Colombo, Femminis & Pavan 2014). One key finding in their studies is that more public information can weaken the incentives of traders to become informed and/or to acquire more precise information. In other words, public information crowds out the production of private information. This can weaken and potentially reverse the direct effect of disclosure on some market-quality variables. In this section, we augment the baseline model in Section 2 with information acquisition to illustrate the crowding-out effect.

3.1. Setup

We add an information-acquisition date, $t = 0$, to the baseline model in Section 2. The information-acquisition technology closely follows Grossman & Stiglitz (1980) and Verrecchia (1982a). At date 0, there exists a unit mass of identical CARA traders. Trader i can become informed by paying a cost to acquire a private signal $\tilde{s}_i$ in the form of Equation 1, which has a trader-specific precision $\tau_{\varepsilon i}$. The information-acquisition cost $C(\tau_{\varepsilon i})$ has two parts[5]: a fixed cost $c_{\mathrm{F}} \geq 0$ and a variable cost $c_{\mathrm{V}}(\tau_{\varepsilon i})$, where $c_{\mathrm{V}}(\cdot)$ is an increasing, smooth, and convex function satisfying $c_{\mathrm{V}}(0) = 0$. For instance, we can think of traders as financial institutions, and their information-acquisition activities typically involve both a fixed cost (such as the overhead cost of establishing a research department) and a variable cost (such as the cost of hiring analysts to produce financial reports). In equilibrium, an endogenous fraction μ of traders decide to acquire private information, and these traders become the informed traders in the financial market at date 1. We can show that the informed traders choose the same precision level τ_ε in equilibrium, and thus the economies at dates 1 and 2 are the same as in the baseline model.

The equilibrium in this extended economy consists of an information-acquisition equilibrium at date 0 and a noisy REE at date 1. The noisy REE at date 1 is still characterized by Equations 3 and 8. The information-acquisition equilibrium at date 0 is characterized by (*a*) an intensive margin, τ_ε^*—how precise is the information that informed traders acquire?—and (*b*) an extensive margin, μ^*—how many traders decide to become informed? In the literature, researchers have either fixed $\mu^* = 1$ and considered the crowding-out effect of disclosure on τ_ε^* (e.g., Verrecchia 1982b) or fixed the value of τ_ε^* and considered the crowding-out effect on μ^* (e.g., Diamond 1985). As we show below, both settings can naturally emerge endogenously in our setup and may have different implications.

Let us consider a particular trader i. Suppose that a fraction μ of traders are informed and acquire signals with precision τ_ε. When trader i stays uninformed, we use $\mathrm{CE_U}(\tau_\varepsilon, \mu)$ to denote this trader's ex ante expected utility (certainty equivalent) at the trading stage. When trader i

[5]Although the information-acquisition cost is measured in terms of traders' wealth at date 0, it can represent both the monetary cost and the time cost. Recently, Dugast & Foucault (2017) and Kendall (2017) have explicitly modeled the time cost of information.

decides to become informed and acquire a private signal with precision $\tau_{\varepsilon i}$, we use $\mathrm{CE_I}(\tau_{\varepsilon i}; \tau_\varepsilon, \mu)$ to denote this trader's ex ante expected utility. Note that in $\mathrm{CE_I}(\tau_{\varepsilon i}; \tau_\varepsilon, \mu)$, trader i can only choose $\tau_{\varepsilon i}$ and will take (τ_ε, μ) as given. Following an argument similar to that of Grossman & Stiglitz (1980), we can compute $\mathrm{CE_U}(\tau_\varepsilon, \mu)$ and $\mathrm{CE_I}(\tau_{\varepsilon i}; \tau_\varepsilon, \mu)$ and analyze equilibrium outcomes.

Three types of information-acquisition equilibriums arise. First, when c_F, the fixed cost of information acquisition, is sufficiently small, all traders become informed, that is, $\mu^* = 1$; this case mimics the one studied by Verrecchia (1982b). Here, $\mathrm{CE_U}(\tau_\varepsilon^*, 1) \leq \mathrm{CE_I}(\tau_\varepsilon^*; \tau_\varepsilon^*, 1)$, so traders choose to become informed when all others are informed, and the precision of information τ_ε^* is pinned down by the first-order condition: $\partial \mathrm{CE_I}(\tau_\varepsilon^*; \tau_\varepsilon^*, 1)/\partial \tau_{\varepsilon i} = 0$. Second, when c_F takes an intermediate value, an intermediate proportion of traders choose to become informed: $\mu^* \in (0, 1)$. The equilibrium is pinned down by a condition that makes traders indifferent between producing the equilibrium amount of information and remaining uninformed, $\mathrm{CE_U}(\tau_\varepsilon^*, \mu^*) = \mathrm{CE_I}(\tau_\varepsilon^*; \tau_\varepsilon^*, \mu^*)$, and by a first-order condition that guarantees that the level of precision is chosen optimally, $\partial \mathrm{CE_I}(\tau_\varepsilon^*; \tau_\varepsilon^*, \mu)/\partial \tau_{\varepsilon i} = 0$. It turns out that in equilibrium, the precision of information produced τ_ε^* is independent of disclosure quality τ_η, and thus this case mimics the one studied by Diamond (1985). Finally, when c_F is sufficiently large, no trader chooses to become informed, which is guaranteed by the condition $\mathrm{CE_U}(0, 0) \geq \max_{\tau_{\varepsilon i}} \mathrm{CE_I}(\tau_{\varepsilon i}; 0, 0)$.

Figure 1 graphically illustrates these equilibrium outcomes. For this illustration, we assume that the variable cost function takes a quadratic form, $c_\mathrm{V}(\tau_{\varepsilon i}) = (k/2)\tau_{\varepsilon i}^2$, and that the parameter values are $\tau_v = \tau_x = \gamma = Q = 1$ and $k = 0.1$. The figure plots the regimes of equilibrium types in the parameter space of $(c_\mathrm{F}, \tau_\eta)$. Generally speaking, as c_F and τ_η become larger, an equilibrium with a lower μ^* is more likely to prevail. This feature is a reflection of the crowding-out effect, which we explain in more detail in Section 3.2.1.

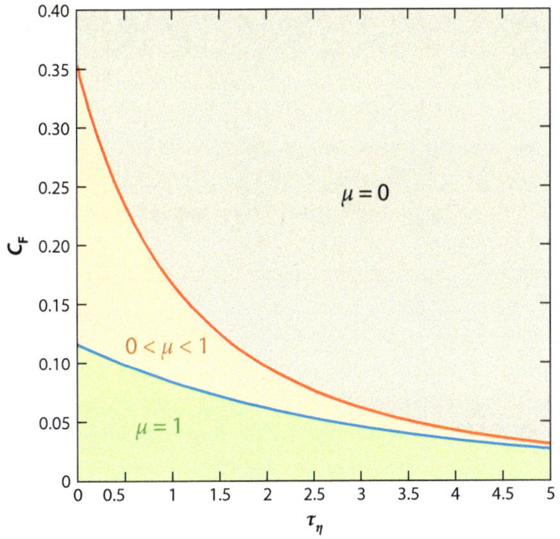

Figure 1

Equilibrium types in the economy with endogenous information acquisition. This figure plots the equilibrium types in the space of $(\tau_\eta, c_\mathrm{F})$, where parameter τ_η controls the disclosure quality and parameter c_F denotes the fixed cost of information acquisition. The variable cost of information acquisition takes a quadratic form, $c_\mathrm{V}(\tau_{\varepsilon i}) = (k/2)\tau_{\varepsilon i}^2$. The parameter values are $\tau_v = \tau_x = \gamma = Q = 1$ and $k = 0.1$.

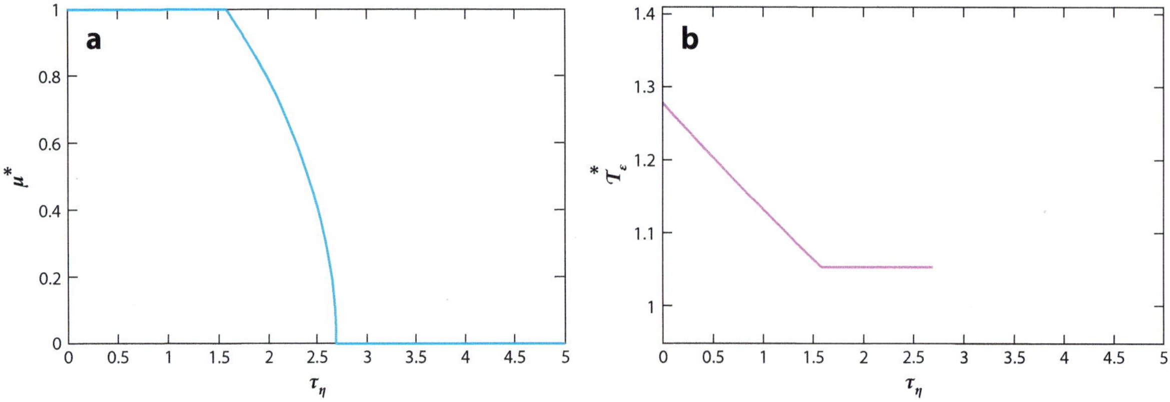

Figure 2

The crowding-out effect. This figure plots (*a*) the equilibrium fraction μ^* of informed traders and (*b*) the equilibrium precision τ_ε^* of informed traders' private information against the disclosure quality τ_η. The variable cost of information acquisition takes a quadratic form, $c_V(\tau_{\varepsilon i}) = (k/2)\tau_{\varepsilon i}^2$. The parameter values are $\tau_v = \tau_x = \gamma = Q = 1$, $c_F = 0.07$, and $k = 0.1$.

3.2. The Effect of Disclosure

We now reexamine the effect of disclosure when private information is endogenous.

3.2.1. The crowding-out effect on private information. The results below follow directly from the equilibrium analysis in Section 3.1 and demonstrate the crowding-out effect. First, when all traders are informed, so that $\mu^* = 1$, the equilibrium precision of information τ_ε^* decreases with increasing quality of public information τ_η. Second, when an intermediate fraction of traders choose to become informed, so that $\mu^* \in (0, 1)$, this fraction decreases with increasing quality of public information τ_η (in this case the precision τ_ε^* is unaffected). These two results reproduce the crowding-out effects studied by Verrecchia (1982b) and Diamond (1985), respectively. Intuitively, when both public information and private information are about the same random variable $\tilde{v}$, they are substitute, and thus additional public information motivates traders to cut back on their costly private acquisition activities either in the form of producing less-precise private information or in the form of becoming uninformed.

In **Figure 1**, we can see how an increase in disclosure makes it more likely that we should move to an equilibrium with a smaller fraction of informed traders. **Figure 2** continues this example with the same parameters, illustrating the crowding-out effect more directly. We now also set $c_F = 0.07$. We plot the equilibrium fraction μ^* of informed traders and the equilibrium precision τ_ε^* of private information as functions of the precision τ_η of public information. We see that globally, both μ^* and τ_ε^* weakly decrease with τ_η. Starting from low disclosure, all traders choose to become informed, and an increase in disclosure reduces the precision of their information. Then, at some point, the fraction of informed traders starts decreasing as disclosure continues to improve, eventually drying up all the information produced privately in the market. Hence, public disclosure clearly crowds out private information. We now examine the effect that this has on the measures of market quality studied in Section 2.3.

3.2.2. Effect on market quality. In Section 2, disclosure had an unambiguous effect on four measures of market quality—market liquidity, market efficiency, cost of capital, and return volatility—increasing the first two and decreasing the other two. However, things ought to be

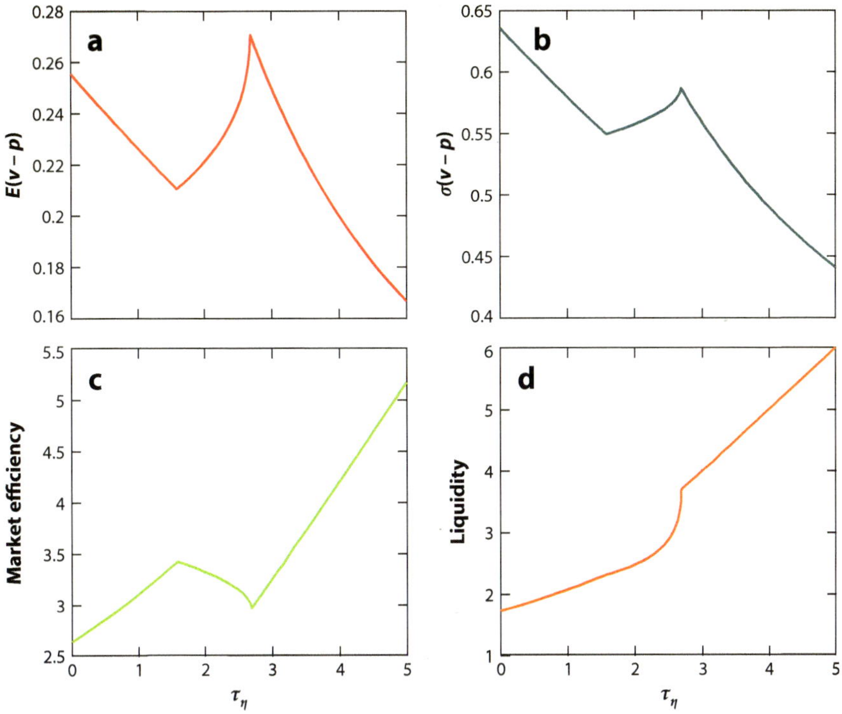

Figure 3

The effect of disclosure on an economy with endogenous information acquisition. This figure plots (*a*) the cost of capital $E(\tilde{v} - \tilde{p})$, (*b*) return volatility $\sigma(\tilde{v} - \tilde{p})$, (*c*) market efficiency $1/\text{Var}(\tilde{v}|\tilde{p})$, and (*d*) market liquidity $1/p_x$ as functions of disclosure quality τ_η. The variable cost of information acquisition takes a quadratic form, $c_V(\tau_{\varepsilon i}) = (k/2)\tau_{\varepsilon i}^2$. The parameter values are $\tau_v = \tau_x = \gamma = Q = 1$, $c_F = 0.07$, and $k = 0.1$.

more complicated once we consider the crowding-out effect on private information. We use **Figure 3** to demonstrate the overall effect of disclosure on these measures once private information adjusts endogenously on the basis of the analysis above. **Figure 3** uses the same parameter values as does **Figure 2**. It turns out that the effect of disclosure is often nonmonotonic and that the results depend on whether crowding out happens in the extensive margin (as in Diamond 1985) or the intensive margin (as in Verrecchia 1982b) and on which measure of market quality we inspect.

Let us consider the effect of disclosure τ_η on the cost of capital $E(\tilde{v} - \tilde{p})$. Recall that without considering private information to be endogenous, disclosure has a direct negative effect on the cost of capital. **Figure 3** shows that, in the presence of endogenous private information, there are three different regimes. First, when τ_η is small, $E(\tilde{v} - \tilde{p})$ decreases as τ_η increases. In this regime, μ^* is fixed at 1 and τ_ε^* decreases with increasing τ_η, which corresponds to the work of Verrecchia (1982b). Here, the crowding out of private information happens in the intensive margin. The decrease in private information following an increase in disclosure increases the risk faced by traders, pushing to an average increase in the cost of capital, but this is not strong enough to overcome the direct reducing effect that disclosure has on the cost of capital. Second, when τ_η takes intermediate values, $E(\tilde{v} - \tilde{p})$ starts to increase with τ_η. Here, $\mu^* \in (0, 1)$ decreases with τ_η and τ_ε^* is fixed, which corresponds to the work of Diamond (1985), where the crowding out happens in the extensive margin. Now the decrease in private information as a result of increased disclosure is sufficiently strong that the cost of capital increases with disclosure, in opposition to the direct effect. Hence, the indirect effect of crowding out on the extensive margin is more powerful in this regime. Third, when τ_η is high, $E(\tilde{v} - \tilde{p})$ decreases with increasing τ_η again. Here, $\mu^* = 0$, so disclosure no longer affects private information, and only the direct reducing effect of disclosure on the cost of capital is present.[6] Overall, we see that the crowding out of private information by public information implies that disclosure no longer has a uniformly negative effect on the cost of capital, so the total effect must be evaluated more carefully and depends on the exact information structure in place.

Considering the effect of disclosure on market efficiency and return volatility, we can see effects very similar to those described above for the cost of capital. The exception is the measure of liquidity, which is monotonically increasing in disclosure. Here, the crowding-out effect of private information does not interfere with the positive direct effect that disclosure has on liquidity. This is because the crowding-out effect partly benefits market liquidity, as it weakens adverse selection induced by private information.

4. DISCLOSURE AND REAL EFFICIENCY

The above analysis has shown the effect that disclosure has on four commonly mentioned variables that capture different dimensions of market quality. We first showed how disclosure unambiguously improves these measures when we consider only its direct effect, but then showed that disclosure tends to crowd out private-information production and, as a result, has a more nuanced effect on the different measures. One issue with the above analysis is that these measures do not translate easily into a clear objective function that will help us tell when disclosure is desirable and when it is not.

In this section we address this issue and extend our basic framework, reviewing papers that have attempted to pin down optimal disclosure policy with a clear objective function in mind. The papers reviewed here emphasize the role of the financial market in producing information and in guiding the decisions on the real side of the economy, e.g., investment decisions made by firm managers. This idea goes back to Hayek (1945), who argued that prices are an important source of information because they aggregate information from many market participants. There is a vast recent literature exploring the implications of this market feedback effect; a recent survey is provided by Bond, Edmans & Goldstein (2012). The papers reviewed here explore optimal disclosure policy, taking into account how disclosure affects the information provided by the market and the efficiency of the investment decisions that are guided by the market. This, of course, is related to the concept of market efficiency discussed in Section 2. However, as should be clear from the analysis here, market efficiency and real efficiency are not always aligned. The latter refers to the efficiency of the market in revealing information needed for decisions on the real side of the economy. Real efficiency is what the models here feature, based on an objective function developed from first principles. For a broader discussion, see Bond, Edmans & Goldstein (2012) and the distinction they make between forecasting price efficiency and revelatory price efficiency.

4.1. Crowding-Out Effect and Optimal Disclosure Policy

The crowding-out effect reviewed in Section 3 suggests that disclosure can reduce the amount of private information in the price. Thus, if a firm manager tries to learn information from the price,

[6]Tang (2014) uses a figure similar to **Figure 3** to explain the nonmonotonic relation between the cost of capital and disclosure, but her model follows that of Diamond (1985), so her analysis does not recognize the contrasting implications of extensive versus intensive margins.

the crowding-out effect tends to harm the manager's learning quality. However, as we reviewed in Section 2, disclosure can benefit the firm by lowering the cost of capital when information is exogenous. Gao & Liang (2013) study the resulting trade-off to examine the optimal disclosure policy of a firm. We now present an extension of our CARA-normal setup that captures their trade-off.

We extend the model in Section 3 to include another active player (the firm) and an intermediate date ($t = 1\frac{1}{2}$). We interpret the traded risky asset as the asset-in-place of a firm. The firm is endowed with information $\tilde{s}_{\mathrm{F}} = \tilde{v} + \tilde{\varepsilon}_{\mathrm{F}}$, with $\tilde{\varepsilon}_{\mathrm{F}} \sim N(0, \tau_{\mathrm{F}}^{-1})$ and $\tau_{\mathrm{F}} > 0$. At the beginning of date 0, the firm chooses a disclosure policy that commits it to disclose a noisy version of $\tilde{s}_{\mathrm{F}}$ to the financial market at date 1 in the following form:

$$\tilde{y} = \tilde{s}_{\mathrm{F}} + \tilde{\delta}, \quad \text{with } \tilde{\delta} \sim N(0, \tau_{\delta}^{-1}) \text{ and } \tau_{\delta} \in [0, \infty]. \tag{12}$$

All of the underlying random variables ($\tilde{v}, \tilde{\varepsilon}_{\mathrm{F}}, \tilde{\delta}, \{\tilde{\varepsilon}_i\}_i, \tilde{x}$) are mutually independent. We can rewrite $\tilde{y}$ in Equation 12 in the form defined in Equation 2 by defining $\tilde{\eta} \equiv \tilde{\varepsilon}_{\mathrm{F}} + \tilde{\delta}$, where $\tilde{\eta} \sim N(0, \tau_{\eta}^{-1})$ with $\tau_{\eta} = (\tau_{\mathrm{F}}^{-1} + \tau_{\delta}^{-1})^{-1} \in [0, \tau_{\mathrm{F}}]$. The parameter τ_{η} still controls the disclosure quality. In particular, when $\tau_{\eta} = 0$, the firm does not disclose any information, and when $\tau_{\eta} = \tau_{\mathrm{F}}$, the firm discloses its information $\tilde{s}_{\mathrm{F}}$ without error.

The firm also has a growth opportunity whose productivity is related to $\tilde{v}$. The firm invests in the growth opportunity at $t = 1\frac{1}{2}$, so it can look into the asset price $\tilde{p}$ to extract information about $\tilde{v}$. The growth opportunity's cash flow $\tilde{G}$ is realized at date 2, and it takes the following form:

$$\tilde{G} = \sqrt{\Phi}\tilde{v}I - \frac{I^2}{2}, \tag{13}$$

where I is the investment made by the firm at $t = 1\frac{1}{2}$ and the parameter $\Phi > 0$ captures the size of the growth option. As in the work of Subrahmanyam & Titman (1999) and Foucault & Gehrig (2008), we assume that the growth opportunity is separate from the asset-in-place and is nontradable, to keep the model tractable. In this extended economy, the firm makes two decisions: a disclosure-policy decision at $t = 0$ and a real-investment decision at $t = 1\frac{1}{2}$. We assume that the firm is risk-neutral and cares about both the asset-in-place and the growth opportunity. To simplify things relative to Section 3, we assume that private information acquisition does not incur a fixed cost and that only the variable cost function remains, for instance, $c_{\mathrm{V}}(\tau_{\varepsilon i}) = (k/2)\tau_{\varepsilon i}^2$, with $k > 0$. All the other features of the model are the same.

The noisy REE in the financial market at date 1 is still characterized as in Section 2, and the information-acquisition equilibrium at date 0 is still characterized as in Section 3. We now examine the two decisions of the firm. At $t = 1\frac{1}{2}$, the firm has an information set $\{\tilde{s}_{\mathrm{F}}, \tilde{p}, \tilde{y}\} = \{\tilde{s}_{\mathrm{F}}, \tilde{s}_p\}$, where $\tilde{s}_p$ is the market signal given by Equation 4. The firm's optimal investment policy maximizes the expected value of the growth opportunity in Equation 13 given the information available, implying that $I(\tilde{s}_{\mathrm{F}}, \tilde{s}_p) = \sqrt{\Phi}E(\tilde{v}|\tilde{s}_{\mathrm{F}}, \tilde{s}_p)$. Inserting $I(\tilde{s}_{\mathrm{F}}, \tilde{s}_p)$ back into the growth opportunity and taking the unconditional expectation yields the expected growth value:

$$E(\tilde{G}) = \frac{\Phi}{2}\left(\frac{1}{\tau_v} - \frac{1}{\tau_v + \tau_{\mathrm{F}} + (\tau_{\varepsilon}/\gamma)^2\tau_x}\right). \tag{14}$$

We can see that the expected growth value increases with the precision $(\tau_{\varepsilon}/\gamma)^2\tau_x$ of the price signal $\tilde{s}_p$. This is a result of the feedback effect. The firm benefits from having more precise information in the price about the fundamental $\tilde{v}$ because then it can make a more efficient investment decision. By the crowding-out effect, additional disclosure lowers the precision τ_{ε} of private information produced and so makes the price signal $\tilde{s}_p$ less accurate. As a result, disclosure can harm the firm by reducing the value of the growth option.

At $t = 0$, the firm chooses an optimal disclosure policy τ_η. Following Langberg & Sivaramakrishnan (2010), we assume that the firm's objective at date 0 is a weighted average of the expected price of the asset-in-place and its expected growth opportunity value, $\alpha E(\tilde{p}) + (1 - \alpha)E(\tilde{G})$, with $\alpha \in (0, 1)$. (For instance, the firm is balancing the interests of its short-term shareholders, who sell the shares at a price $\tilde{p}$, and its long-term shareholders, who care about the firm's terminal cash flows $\tilde{v} + \tilde{G}$.) Here, the expected price $E(\tilde{p})$ of the asset-in-place is derived from Equations 3 and 8, and the expected value of the growth option $E(\tilde{G})$ is given by Equation 14. Then the optimal disclosure policy τ_η^{opt} balances two forces. On the one hand, greater disclosure increases $E(\tilde{p})$ by reducing the uncertainty faced by financial-market traders, thus reducing the cost of capital they impose on the firm.[7] On the other hand, greater disclosure crowds out private information production and so deprives the firm of valuable information, thereby reducing the efficiency of its investment decision and the value of its growth option. As a result, one can show that when Φ/Q is relatively high, that is, when the firm's growth opportunity is large relative to its asset-in-place, the negative effect of disclosure dominates, and thus the firm chooses to disclose less. This model therefore implies that growth firms are endogenously more opaque than value firms.

4.2. Liquidity-Chasing Noise Trading

Another negative effect of disclosure on real efficiency is studied by Han, Tang & Yang (2016). They follow the approach of modeling discretionary liquidity traders in the market microstructure literature (e.g., Admati & Pfleiderer 1988, Foster & Viswanathan 1990) and show that greater disclosure attracts more noise trading. We now modify the model presented in Section 4.1 to illustrate this mechanism.

We shut down the information-acquisition activities of the CARA traders at date 0 and endow each of them with a private signal $\tilde{s}_i$ with precision τ_ε. There is also a large mass of discretionary liquidity traders who are risk-neutral, uninformed, and ex ante identical.[8] These traders are discretionary in the sense that at date 0, each chooses whether to participate in the market at date 1 by optimally balancing the expected loss from trading against informed CARA traders versus an exogenous liquidity benefit B of market participation. If discretionary liquidity trader l decides to trade, this trader has to trade $\tilde{u}$ units of risky asset, where $\tilde{u} \sim N(0, 1)$ and is perfectly correlated across liquidity traders. The equilibrium mass L^* of liquidity traders participating in the market determines the noise trading active in the market: $\tilde{x} \equiv L^*\tilde{u}$ and $\tau_x^{-1} = L^{*2}$. All other features of the model in Section 4.1 are unchanged.

We now characterize the market participation equilibrium of discretionary liquidity traders at date 0. At that point, discretionary liquidity trader l faces the following trade-off. First, trading generates an exogenous benefit $B > 0$, which represents the exogenous liquidity needs. Second, because liquidity traders are trading against informed CARA traders, they will incur endogenous trading losses on average. Then the expected utility of participating in the market for discretionary liquidity trader l is

$$W(L; \tau_\eta) = B + E[\tilde{u} \cdot (\tilde{v} - \tilde{p})] = \underbrace{B}_{\text{liquidity benefit}} - \underbrace{p_x(L; \tau_\eta) \times L}_{\text{trading cost}}. \qquad 15.$$

[7] Recall that, for simplicity, we assumed here that information acquisition does not have a fixed cost. Then, based on the results in the previous section, the crowding-out effect of disclosure only happens in the intensive margin, and the cost of capital decreases as the level of disclosure increases.

[8] In practice, these traders can represent institutional traders—e.g., index funds or exchange-traded funds—who need to rebalance portfolios around index recompositions or when receiving flow shocks.

Here, L is the mass of liquidity traders choosing to participate in the market and $p_x(L;\tau_\eta)$ is given by Equation 8, with $\tau_x^{-1} = L^2$. Note that, given market liquidity, expected trading losses are increasing in L because when more liquidity traders participate, they exert stronger price pressure, given that they trade in the same direction. In equilibrium, an endogenous mass L^* of liquidity traders choose to participate in the market, while the rest choose not to. Hence, L^* is determined by the indifference condition: $W(L^*;\tau_\eta) = 0$.

Equation 15 shows that discretionary liquidity traders have incentives to chase market liquidity. That is, if a change in the trading environment improves market liquidity (i.e., p_x decreases), then, other things being equal, expected trading losses decrease and discretionary liquidity traders are more likely to participate in the market. As disclosure promotes market liquidity, releasing public information induces more discretionary liquidity traders to choose to participate in the market; that is, $\partial L^*/\partial\tau_\eta > 0$.

Disclosure also affects real efficiency through affecting the firm's learning from the price. By observing the price $\tilde{p}$, the firm obtains a signal $\tilde{s}_p$ with a precision $(\tau_\varepsilon/\gamma)^2\tau_x$. Recall that in this economy, the precision of noise trading is given by $\tau_x = 1/L^{*2}$, which implies that the precision of the information in the price decreases as the level of disclosure increases: $\partial[\tau_\varepsilon/(\gamma L^*)]^2/\partial\tau_\eta < 0$. That is, more public information attracts additional liquidity trading and, as a result, the price reveals less fundamental information, thereby reducing real efficiency.

4.3. Multiple Dimensions of Disclosure

The models discussed in Sections 4.1 and 4.2 highlight the negative real-efficiency effects of disclosure. Two recent papers, by Bond & Goldstein (2015) and Goldstein & Yang (2016), point out that in the presence of multiple dimensions of information, the real-efficiency implications of disclosure might be different depending on what dimension of information is disclosed.

Bond & Goldstein (2015) show that a decision maker on the real side of the economy should disclose information about issues on which he or she knows more than the market and keep silent about issues on which he or she wants to learn from the market. Bond & Goldstein cast their idea in a trading model where the decision maker is the government, which makes an intervention decision. We now extend the baseline model in Section 2 to illustrate the mechanism. Suppose that the firm's cash flow $\tilde{v}$ at date 2 is given by $\tilde{v} = T + \tilde{v}_B$, where $\tilde{v}_B \sim N(0,\tau_B^{-1})$ with $\tau_B > 0$. The component T is the result of endogenous government intervention based on its private information and the asset price $\tilde{p}$. For example, one can think of the government bailouts of AIG and Citigroup in the recent financial crisis. Specifically, we add an additional date, $t = 1\frac{1}{2}$, at which the government chooses T to maximize

$$E\left[-\frac{(T-\tilde{v}_A)^2}{2} + cT \,\middle|\, \mathcal{I}_G\right],$$

where $\tilde{v}_A \sim N(0,\tau_A^{-1})$ (with $\tau_A > 0$), $c > 0$ is a constant, and $\mathcal{I}_G$ is the government's information set. As discussed by Bond & Goldstein (2015), this objective function qualitatively captures many government motives, such as promoting social surplus and maintaining stability in the financial sector.

Note that in this setting, the asset cash flow $\tilde{v}$ is ultimately driven by two underlying random variables, $\tilde{v}_A$ and $\tilde{v}_B$. We assume that the government wants to learn from the market more about element $\tilde{v}_A$ than about element $\tilde{v}_B$. For example, $\tilde{v}_A$ determines the benefit from intervention, as it reflects the spillover effect from an individual bank's failure, and this is something the government needs to learn about from the market. In contrast, $\tilde{v}_B$ is information about the bank's expected direct cash flows, which is information that the government has direct access to. For simplicity, suppose that the government knows $\tilde{v}_B$ perfectly and only receives a private signal $\tilde{s}_G$ on $\tilde{v}_A$, where $\tilde{s}_G = \tilde{v}_A + \tilde{\varepsilon}_G$ with $\tilde{\varepsilon}_G \sim N(0, \tau_G^{-1})$ and $\tau_G > 0$. Traders have private information on $\tilde{v}_A$ in the form of Equation 1 but know nothing about $\tilde{v}_B$. That is, trader i receives a signal $\tilde{s}_i = \tilde{v}_A + \tilde{\varepsilon}_i$ with $\tilde{\varepsilon}_i \sim N(0, \tau_\varepsilon^{-1})$ and $\tau_\varepsilon > 0$. So the asset price $\tilde{p}$ will aggregate private signals $\tilde{s}_i$ and convey information on $\tilde{v}_A$. The government can use disclosure to affect the information-aggregation process of the price. Specifically, at date 1 before the financial market opens, the government discloses two public signals, $\tilde{y}_A = \tilde{s}_G + \tilde{\eta}_A$ and $\tilde{y}_B = \tilde{v}_B + \tilde{\eta}_B$, where $\tilde{\eta}_A \sim N(0, \tau_{\eta A}^{-1})$ (with $\tau_{\eta A} \in [0, \infty]$) and $\tilde{\eta}_B \sim N(0, \tau_{\eta B}^{-1})$ (with $\tau_{\eta B} \in [0, \infty]$). All the underlying random variables $(\tilde{v}_A, \tilde{v}_B, \tilde{\varepsilon}_G, \tilde{\eta}_A, \tilde{\eta}_B, \{\tilde{\varepsilon}_i\}_i)$ are mutually independent.

The price function in the financial market at date 1 takes the form $\tilde{p} = p_0 + p_{yA}\tilde{y}_A + p_{yB}\tilde{y}_B + p_v\tilde{v}_A + p_x\tilde{x}$, where the p-coefficients are endogenous. At $t = 1\frac{1}{2}$, the government has an information set $\mathcal{I}_G = \{\tilde{s}_G, \tilde{y}_A, \tilde{y}_B, \tilde{v}_B, \tilde{p}\}$. To the government, the price is still equivalent to the signal $\tilde{s}_p$ as in Equation 4, i.e.,

$$\tilde{s}_p = \frac{\tilde{p} - p_0 - p_{yA}\tilde{y}_A - p_{yB}\tilde{y}_B}{p_v} = \tilde{v}_A + \rho^{-1}\tilde{x}, \quad \text{with } \rho = \frac{p_v}{p_x}.$$

Thus, the government's intervention policy is

$$T(\tilde{s}_G, \tilde{s}_p) = \arg\max_T E\left[-\frac{(T - \tilde{v}_A)^2}{2} + cT \,\middle|\, \tilde{s}_G, \tilde{y}_A, \tilde{y}_B, \tilde{v}_B, \tilde{p}\right]$$

$$= E(\tilde{v}_A \mid \tilde{s}_G, \tilde{s}_p) + c = \frac{\tau_G}{\tau_A + \tau_G + \rho^2\tau_x}\tilde{s}_G + \frac{\rho^2\tau_x}{\tau_A + \tau_G + \rho^2\tau_x}\tilde{s}_p + c. \quad 16.$$

The precision $\rho^2\tau_x$ of signal $\tilde{s}_p$ still captures the extra information that the government learns from the market. As in Section 4.1, in equilibrium, the government's utility increases with precision $\rho^2\tau_x$, as a higher $\rho^2\tau_x$ means that the government is making a more informed intervention decision. In this sense, $\rho^2\tau_x$ is a measure of real efficiency.

Financial trader i has an information set $\{\tilde{s}_i, \tilde{y}_A, \tilde{y}_B, \tilde{p}\}$, which is equivalent to $\{\tilde{s}_i, \tilde{y}_A, \tilde{y}_B, \tilde{s}_p\}$. The CARA-normal setup implies that trader i's demand for the risky asset is

$$D(\tilde{s}_i, \tilde{y}_A, \tilde{y}_B, \tilde{p}) = \frac{E[T(\tilde{s}_G, \tilde{s}_p) + \tilde{v}_B \mid \tilde{s}_i, \tilde{y}_A, \tilde{y}_B, \tilde{s}_p] - \tilde{p}}{\gamma \operatorname{Var}[T(\tilde{s}_G, \tilde{s}_p) + \tilde{v}_B \mid \tilde{s}_i, \tilde{y}_A, \tilde{y}_B, \tilde{s}_p]}. \quad 17.$$

Using the expression for $T(\tilde{s}_G, \tilde{s}_p)$ in Equation 16 and the market-clearing condition, $\int_0^1 D(\tilde{s}_i, \tilde{y}_A, \tilde{y}_B, \tilde{p})\mathrm{d}i + \tilde{x} = Q$, we can solve for $\tilde{p}$ in terms of $(\tilde{y}_A, \tilde{y}_B, \tilde{v}_A, \tilde{x})$. Comparing this solved price with the conjectured price function, we then form a system in terms of the p-coefficients that characterizes the noisy REE in the financial market.

The key results can be summarized as follows: Disclosing information about $\tilde{v}_A$ harms the government through impairing its learning quality from the price, whereas disclosing information about $\tilde{v}_B$ benefits the government. Intuitively, consider the extreme cases where the government fully discloses one of the signals. (For intermediate cases, the intuition is similar but more difficult to convey.) First, if the government fully discloses its signal on $\tilde{v}_A$ so that $\tilde{y}_A = \tilde{s}_G$ and $\tau_{\eta A} = \infty$, then $T(\tilde{s}_G, \tilde{s}_p)$ is perfectly known by financial traders, so they will no longer put any weight on their own private signals $\tilde{s}_i$. As a result, the price does not aggregate $\tilde{s}_i$ anymore and the government learns nothing from the price. Effectively, there is a crowding-out effect, whereby disclosing information about something the traders know makes them trade less on this information and reduces the ability of the government to learn from their information. Interestingly, this crowding out does not operate through the incentives to produce information, as we saw previously in this review, but through the ability to trade on existing information. It is captured by the numerator of traders' demand function (Equation 17), as the availability of public information reduces the speculative value of their private information and causes them to trade less aggressively. Second, suppose that the government fully discloses its information on $\tilde{v}_B$ so that $\tilde{y}_B = \tilde{v}_B$ and $\tau_{\eta B} = \infty$. Then financial traders no longer need to forecast $\tilde{v}_B$, which lowers the risk they face, making traders trade more aggressively on $\tilde{s}_i$. This effect of reducing uncertainty, originating from the fact that traders are risk averse, is reflected by the denominator of their demand function (Equation 17), as the reduction in risk incentivizes them to trade more on their information. In consequence, the price will aggregate more of traders' private information, benefiting the government's learning from the price.

The mechanism in the work of Goldstein & Yang (2016) is different and does not rely on risk aversion, as they study an environment in which all players are risk neutral. In their model, what matters for determining which information will be reflected by prices is the relative intensity at which agents trade on different pieces of information. Assuming again two dimensions of information, which in the context of a regular firm could represent the demand for the firm's products and the quality of its production technology, and assuming that agents have access to signals on both, Goldstein & Yang show that revealing more precise information on the dimension about which the firm already knows will cause traders to trade more aggressively on the dimension about which the firm wants to learn and will enable the firm to learn more from the price. The opposite will be true if more precise public information is revealed on what the firm is trying to learn; this will crowd out valuable private information from being incorporated into the price, reducing the firm's ability to learn from the price.

There is another important distinction in the work of Goldstein & Yang (2016) relative to the literature. In most models discussed above, such as those of Gao & Liang (2013) and Bond & Goldstein (2016), public information is disclosed by the real decision maker, so the decision maker does not directly learn from the disclosed information. In some scenarios, this may not be the case. For example, a firm manager can benefit directly from public information disclosed by the government or by other agencies. In these scenarios, disclosure has both a direct effect of providing new information to the decision maker and an indirect effect of affecting price informativeness. The analysis of Goldstein & Yang (2016) considers both effects. Paradoxically, for the reason discussed above, more disclosure about the variable that the real decision maker wants to learn can backfire, as it interferes with the ability of the market to reveal this type of information, attenuating the positive direct effect of better disclosure. In cases where the market is very effective at processing information, the indirect effect can be stronger than the direct effect, implying that better disclosure can reduce the overall quality of information available to the decision maker and can harm real efficiency, even though the decision maker directly learns from the public information.[9]

The analysis of multiple dimensions of information can be linked to the debate on the optimal disclosure of stress-test results (for a survey, see Goldstein & Sapra 2013). Stress-test results are useful for regulators to make intervention decisions and for creditors to determine whether to roll over their debt or extend more credit to financial institutions. However, one must keep in mind that disclosure of these results will crowd out information from the financial market. Based on the papers described here, disclosure is undoubtedly beneficial when the stress-test result is about issues in which the regulator or creditors have a relative informational advantage over the financial

[9]Amador & Weill (2010) construct a monetary model and show that disclosure about monetary and productivity shocks can lower welfare through reducing the informational efficiency of the good-price system. This effect is similar to the indirect price informativeness effect discussed by Goldstein & Yang (2016), although Amador & Weill (2010) do not explore the different implications of different types of disclosure.

market. However, when the stress-test result is about something that the regulator or creditors know relatively less than the financial market, disclosing such information makes market prices less informative, which can lead to negative efficiency outcomes.

5. INVESTORS' WELFARE

The previous section described the various effects of disclosure on the efficiency of real investment decisions. Another important issue that has to be considered in evaluating the effects of disclosure is the implications for the welfare of traders in the financial market. As mentioned in Section 2, the usual argument invoked in favor of disclosure is that it improves market quality, which is perceived to have positive effects for investors in financial markets. However, as we discuss in this section, several models in the literature have shown that disclosure can have negative effects on investors' welfare. Hence, it is not always warranted to implement "investor protection" regulations that improve disclosure. In the next two subsections, we discuss two families of models that develop ideas along these lines.

5.1. Destruction of Trading Opportunities

The well-known Hirshleifer (1971) effect is a powerful argument against public disclosure of information. The idea is that when traders face idiosyncratic risks arising from, say, heterogeneous endowment shocks, public disclosure decreases welfare by reducing the risk-sharing opportunities available to traders. More recently, Kurlat & Veldkamp (2015) studied a related channel through which disclosure harms investors. In their setting, investors benefit when they have access to assets with a higher risk and a higher return, and these opportunities are eliminated by public disclosure of information. The common theme of both channels is that disclosure harms investors through destroying trading opportunities. We now extend the baseline model in Section 2 to illustrate these channels.

For the Hirshleifer effect to arise, we assume that traders trade to share risks rather than to speculate on private information. Specifically, we assume that at date 2, trader i receives an endowment of labor income, $\tilde{q}_i \tilde{v}$, where $\tilde{q}_i \sim N(0, \sigma_q^2)$ with $\sigma_q \geq 0$, and $\tilde{q}_i$ is independent of $\tilde{v}$ and also independent across traders. When trading at date 1, trader i knows his or her exposure $\tilde{q}_i$ to the risky asset but has no private information about the asset value $\tilde{v}$. To simplify things further, we assume that there are no noise traders in the model. The other features of the model are unchanged, and, in particular, the public signal $\tilde{y}$ is still given by Equation 2. In this economy, trader i's demand for the risky asset is

$$D_i(\tilde{y}, \tilde{p}) = \frac{E(\tilde{v}|\tilde{y}, \tilde{p}) - \tilde{p}}{\gamma \operatorname{Var}(\tilde{v}|\tilde{y}, \tilde{p})} - \tilde{q}_i. \qquad 18.$$

In Equation 18, the first term is the demand of a CARA trader without endowment shocks, who is attempting to make a profit on the deviations of prices from the expected fundamental value, and the second term is the hedging term capturing trader i's attempt to reduce the endowment risk. Combining Equation 18 with the market-clearing condition, we can compute the asset price $\tilde{p}$ as

$$\tilde{p} = E(\tilde{v}|\tilde{y}) - \gamma \operatorname{Var}(\tilde{v}|\tilde{y}) Q. \qquad 19.$$

As there is no private information or noise trading, the price depends only on the public signal $\tilde{y}$.

Inserting Equation 18 into trader i's objective function yields the indirect utility at the trading stage as follows:

$$U_i(\tilde{y}, \tilde{p}, \tilde{q}_i) = -\exp\left(-\underbrace{\frac{[E(\tilde{v}|\tilde{y}) - \tilde{p}]^2}{2\text{Var}(\tilde{v}|\tilde{y})}}_{\text{trading gains}} - \gamma \underbrace{\tilde{p}\tilde{q}_i}_{\text{wealth}}\right). \quad 20.$$

In Equation 20, the term $\tilde{p}\tilde{q}_i$ captures the fact that each unit of labor income increases trader i's wealth by the price $\tilde{p}$ of the risky asset, as it has the same cash flow as the risky asset. The term $[E(\tilde{v}|\tilde{y}) - \tilde{p}]^2/[2\text{Var}(\tilde{v}|\tilde{y})]$ represents the benefit from trading the risky asset given the trading behavior in Equation 18. This term essentially captures the effect highlighted by Kurlat & Veldkamp (2015).

We can use the certainty equivalent $\text{CE} \equiv -(1/\gamma)\log(-E[U_i(\tilde{y}, \tilde{p}, \tilde{q}_i)])$ to study the ex ante utility of trader i. To formally see the effect shown by Kurlat & Veldkamp (2015), let us turn off the Hirshleifer effect by dropping traders' idiosyncratic endowments and assuming that they simply trade the quantity put on the market by the issuer, that is, $\sigma_q = 0$ and $Q > 0$. Using Equation 19, the first term in the utility function in Equation 20 can be expressed as

$$\frac{[E(\tilde{v}|\tilde{y}) - \tilde{p}]^2}{2\text{Var}(\tilde{v}|\tilde{y})} = \frac{\gamma^2 Q^2}{2}\text{Var}(\tilde{v}|\tilde{y}) = \frac{\gamma^2 Q^2}{2}\frac{1}{\tau_v + \tau_\eta}. \quad 21.$$

Then

$$\text{CE} = \frac{\gamma Q^2}{2}\frac{1}{\tau_v + \tau_\eta},$$

which decreases as disclosure quality τ_η increases. The intuition is as follows: Greater disclosure brings the asset price closer to its fundamental, so traders cannot enjoy the benefit of trading a risky asset. In the limit, if $\tilde{y}$ perfectly reveals $\tilde{v}$, then the risky asset becomes riskless, and traders lose all access to risk in their portfolio. The argument is very simple: If traders trade the risky asset in equilibrium, then we can infer that they derive utility from it, and this utility is lost if we shut down risk by revealing the information publicly. Note that this model takes the perspective of the investors by pointing out that they could be made worse off by greater disclosure quality. One should remember that the issuer could be made better off by disclosure, for several reasons. For example, if the issuer is risk neutral and cares about the average selling price of the security, then, as discussed in Section 2.3.3, disclosure leads to a lower cost of capital, which in turn benefits the issuer. As the model is not a zero-sum game, in general the welfare loss of the investors and the welfare gain of the issuer do not cancel out.

Now let us turn off the effect of Kurlat & Veldkamp (2015) and demonstrate the Hirshleifer effect; that is, suppose that $\sigma_q > 0$ and $Q = 0$. In this case, the asset is no longer provided by the issuer and traders trade among themselves to hedge against their endowment shocks. We can compute

$$\text{CE} = \frac{1}{2\gamma}\log\left(1 - \gamma^2\sigma_q^2\frac{\tau_\eta}{\tau_v(\tau_v + \tau_\eta)}\right),$$

which again decreases with increasing τ_η. Intuitively, as traders are risk averse, they benefit from trading risk-sharing contracts that insure against their exposure to idiosyncratic shocks. Disclosure reduces risk-sharing opportunities, as once the asset value is known, it is no longer possible to insure against its realization.

The Hirshleifer effect suggests that disclosure is unambiguously bad. This is true when there is enough capital in risk-sharing markets to allow them to work. However, this is not always the case.

Consider, for example, the interbank market, which is used to share risk among banks. During the recent financial crisis, when aggregate conditions were bleak, this market was not able to function, as too many banks suffered shortages. This arguably led to market breakdown. Goldstein & Leitner (2015) study a model to consider a trade-off between the negative Hirshleifer effect and a positive effect of disclosure to prevent market breakdown. They find that, in good times, disclosure is undesirable because of the Hirshleifer effect. In bad times, however, some disclosure is necessary to get the risk-sharing market to work. They characterize optimal disclosure schemes in the spirit of the Bayesian persuasion literature following Kamenica & Gentzkow (2011). Importantly, full disclosure is not desirable, and optimal disclosure is just enough to restart the risk-sharing market by separating traders into different groups and excluding some of them from risk-sharing arrangements.

5.2. Coordination and Beauty Contests

Keynes (1936) argues that stock markets share the essence of a beauty contest because the actions of traders are governed not only by their expectations about the true value of traded assets, but also by their expectations about what other traders believe. There are many other environments, such as currency attacks or bank runs, in which agents have not only fundamental concerns but also strategic concerns. In these contexts, public disclosure provides more than just information about fundamentals, as it plays a coordination role of informing agents of what other agents know and so helping each agent to predict the actions of others. This coordination role can be detrimental to efficiency and welfare in the sense that agents place too much weight on the public signal relative to weights that would be used by a social planner. In an example described by Scharfstein & Stein (1990), investors' coordination motive originates from a reputation concern—they want to appear smart by following the same information that others are following—but ends up harming the quality of investment and monitoring decisions.

The coordination mechanism and its general implications are best demonstrated by Morris & Shin (2002). We now review their model. To keep consistency, we adopt similar notations as in our baseline model in Section 2. The underlying state is given by $\tilde{v}$, which is drawn from an improper uniform prior over the real line (i.e., $\tau_v = 0$). There is a continuum $[0, 1]$ of agents. Agent i chooses action D_i, and we use $\mathbf{D}$ to denote the action profile over all agents. Agent i has access to both a private signal $\tilde{s}_i$ and a public signal $\tilde{y}$, given by Equations 1 and 2, respectively.

In the work of Morris & Shin (2002), the beauty-contest motive is directly built into agents' preferences. Specifically, the utility for agent i is given by

$$u_i(\tilde{v}, \mathbf{D}) = -(1-b)(D_i - \tilde{v})^2 - b(L_i - \bar{L}), \qquad 22.$$

where $b \in (0, 1)$ is a constant, $L_i = \int_0^1 (D_j - D_i)^2 \mathrm{d}j$, and $\bar{L} = \int_0^1 L_j \mathrm{d}j$. Hence, the agent has an incentive (with weight $1 - b$) to take an action close to the fundamentals (e.g., buy more of the asset when the fundamentals are high) and an incentive (with weight b) to take an action close to others' actions (e.g., buy when others are buying). Then the action taken by agent i is given by

$$D(\tilde{s}_i, \tilde{y}) = \arg\max_{D_i} E[u_i(\tilde{v}, \mathbf{D}) \,|\, \tilde{s}_i, \tilde{y}] = (1-b)E(\tilde{v}|\tilde{y}, \tilde{s}_i) + bE(\bar{D}|\tilde{y}, \tilde{s}_i), \qquad 23.$$

where $\bar{D}$ is the average action in the population, i.e., $\bar{D} = \int_0^1 D(\tilde{s}_i, \tilde{y})\mathrm{d}i$. Hence, the agent makes a decision based on the expected level of the fundamental $\tilde{v}$ and the expectation of what other agents will do. Parameter b controls the intensity of the beauty-contest motive.

We consider an equilibrium in which each agent follows a linear strategy of the form $D(\tilde{s}_i, \tilde{y}) = \kappa_s \tilde{s}_i + \kappa_y \tilde{y}$, where κ_s and κ_y are endogenous coefficients. Inserting this conjectured strategy into

Equation 23, we can find the expression for $D(\tilde{s}_i, \tilde{y})$. We then compare coefficients in this computed expression with those in the conjectured linear strategy to compute κ_s and κ_y as follows:

$$\kappa_s = \frac{\tau_\varepsilon(1-b)}{\tau_\varepsilon(1-b)+\tau_\eta} \quad \text{and} \quad \kappa_y = \frac{\tau_\eta}{\tau_\varepsilon(1-b)+\tau_\eta}. \tag{24}$$

When there is no beauty-contest motive (i.e., when $b = 0$), the weight κ_y that is put on the public signal is based on the precision of the two signals, as in Bayesian updating. When the beauty-contest motive arises and strengthens (i.e., when $b > 0$ and increases), the weight κ_y on the public signal increases. The reason is that whereas both signals provide information about the fundamental, the public signal carries additional weight, given that it also provides information about what other agents know, and hence it helps in predicting their actions.

In the work of Morris & Shin (2002), the excessive weight on the public signal harms social welfare, which is defined as the (normalized) average of individual utilities. By Equation 22, social welfare is

$$W(\tilde{v}, \mathbf{D}) \equiv \frac{1}{1-b}\int_0^1 u_i(\tilde{v}, \mathbf{D})\mathrm{d}i = -\int_0^1 (D_i - \tilde{v})^2 \mathrm{d}i. \tag{25}$$

A social planner would seek to keep all agents' actions close to $\tilde{v}$. This is because the beauty-contest motive cancels out across individuals and so does not affect social welfare. Thus, if the social planner can specify the weight that each agent puts on the public signal $\tilde{y}$, that weight would be $\kappa_y^{\text{opt}} = \tau_\eta/(\tau_\varepsilon + \tau_\eta)$, which is lower than the equilibrium weight κ_y on $\tilde{y}$. Thus, the coordination role of public information is welfare reducing.

The implication is that greater disclosure might harm agents' welfare. Formally, using Equations 24 and 25, we can compute the expected welfare in equilibrium as

$$E[W(\tilde{v}, \mathbf{D})|\tilde{v}] = -\frac{\tau_\eta + \tau_\varepsilon(1-b)^2}{[\tau_\eta + \tau_\varepsilon(1-b)]^2}.$$

Direct computation shows that $E[W(\tilde{v}, \mathbf{D})|\tilde{v}]$ is U-shaped in the precision τ_η of public information. Intuitively, releasing public information has two effects on welfare. The positive effect stems from the informational role; that is, more public information helps agents to predict the state $\tilde{v}$ more accurately. The negative effect stems from the coordination role; that is, agents put too much weight on public information, and this is exacerbated when the public information is more precise. The overall result is that when the public information is sufficiently coarse, the negative effect dominates, whereas when the public information is sufficiently accurate, the positive effect dominates. Hence, increasing the precision of disclosure is desirable when disclosure is already quite precise.

We point out that the negative welfare effect of coordination is not general. It follows here because the beauty-contest element in individual utility is of zero-sum nature. Angeletos & Pavan (2007) show that, in other settings, coordination is socially valuable, so welfare necessarily increases with the precision of public information. One such example is investment complementarity, in which the production of one firm positively depends on the aggregate production of all firms in the same industry. Colombo, Femminis & Pavan (2014) extend the work of Angeletos & Pavan (2007) to allow for endogenous acquisition of private information.

Although Morris & Shin (2002) take the beauty-contest motive as given, it is important to ask where this motive might come from. After all, most traditional models of financial markets, built from first principles, do not necessarily predict that traders would like to do what other traders do. Allen, Morris & Shin (2006) and Cespa & Vives (2015) endogenize the beauty-contest motive using short horizons of financial traders. A short-horizon trader has to close his or her investment positions in an asset before its fundamental value is realized, so this trader's payoff depends on how much other traders would like to pay, rather than on how much he or she expects the fundamental value of the asset will be. As in the work of Morris & Shin (2002), public information again plays two roles in affecting trading: an informational role, because it conveys information about the unknown fundamental value, and a coordination role, because it is common to the information sets of all traders and helps a short-horizon trader to predict the future liquidation value when he or she closes positions.

Gao (2008) uses the setting of Allen, Morris & Shin (2006) to examine the implications of disclosure for market efficiency. The setting is an extension of our baseline model in Section 2, with one more date ($t = 0$) and hence with two trading periods ($t = 0$ and $t = 1$). The risky asset still pays off $\tilde{v}$ at date 2. Traders' short horizons are characterized by an overlapping-generations assumption. Gao (2008) focuses his analysis on the implication of disclosure for market efficiency at date 0. He shows that greater disclosure always drives stock prices closer to the fundamental value and hence improves market efficiency. The reason lies in an endogenous link between the two roles of public information in affecting the trading of date-0 traders. The coordination role occurs because short-horizon traders correctly believe in the first place that future traders will use public information because of its information value. When the information value becomes less, traders at date 0 overuse it less because they (again, correctly) believe that others will be using it less. Thus, the coordination role is always secondary to the informational role in terms of market efficiency in the setting of Gao (2008). Note that this result does not directly speak to traders' welfare because, as we discuss in Section 5.1, a more informative price may actually harm traders.

Goldstein, Ozdenoren & Yuan (2011) endogenize the beauty-contest motive using a model in which the aggregate trading of currency speculators reveals new information to a central bank and affects its policy decision. The beauty-contest motive arises in their setting because speculators know that a large speculative currency attack has the potential to convince the central bank that the fundamentals are weak, so each speculator would like to second-guess other speculators' actions to better coordinate. As a result, speculators put excessive weight on signals that are correlated with other speculators' information. In this setting, the central bank may inadvertently strengthen the coordination motive by releasing more information that becomes common to speculators, which backfires by reducing the informational content that the central bank learns from the attack, leading the bank to make more policy mistakes.

6. CONCLUSION

The analysis provided in this article demonstrates key insights from the literature on how information disclosure in financial markets affects market quality, information production, real efficiency, and traders' welfare. As the analysis shows, there are many aspects to consider when evaluating the effects of disclosure and the optimal regulation of the level and form of disclosure. We have showed here how many of these effects can be manifested in a cohesive analytical framework that has proven useful in understanding trading and information in financial markets. As disclosure is being used more and more as a tool by regulators to increase market quality, it is important to consider its different implications. We hope that our review will be useful for researchers interested in advancing the theoretical and empirical work in the area and for policy analysis as regulations of market disclosure continue to evolve.

DISCLOSURE STATEMENT

The authors are not aware of any affiliations, memberships, funding, or financial holdings that might be perceived as affecting the objectivity of this review.

ACKNOWLEDGMENTS

We thank Patrick Bolton, Thierry Foucault, Pierre Jinghong Liang, Marco Pagano, Haresh Sapra, Joel Shapiro, and Zhuo Zhong for comments and suggestions. L.Y. thanks the Social Sciences and Humanities Research Council of Canada for financial support.

LITERATURE CITED

Acharya VV, DeMarzo P, Kremer I. 2011. Endogenous information flows and the clustering of announcements. *Am. Econ. Rev.* 101:2955–79

Admati A, Pfleiderer P. 1988. A theory of intraday patterns: volume and price variability. *Rev. Financ. Stud.* 1:3–40

Allen F, Morris S, Shin HS. 2006. Beauty contests and iterated expectations in asset markets. *Rev. Financ. Stud.* 19:719–52

Amador M, Weill PO. 2010. Learning from prices: public communication and welfare. *J. Polit. Econ.* 118:866–907

Angeletos GM, Pavan A. 2007. Efficient use of information and social value of information. *Econometrica* 75:1103–42

Bloomfield R, O'Hara M. 1999. Market transparency: Who wins and who loses? *Rev. Financ. Stud.* 12:5–35

Bond P, Edmans A, Goldstein I. 2012. The real effects of financial markets. *Annu. Rev. Financ. Econ.* 4:339–60

Bond P, Goldstein I. 2015. Government intervention and information aggregation by prices. *J. Finance* 70:2777–811

Cespa G, Vives X. 2015. The beauty contest and short-term trading. *J. Finance* 70:2099–154

Colombo L, Femminis G, Pavan A. 2014. Information acquisition and welfare. *Rev. Econ. Stud.* 81:1438–83

Diamond DW. 1985. Optimal release of information by firms. *J. Finance* 40:1071–94

Diamond DW, Verrecchia R. 1981. Information aggregation in a noisy rational expectations economy. *J. Financ. Econ.* 9:221–35

Diamond DW, Verrecchia R. 1991. Disclosure, liquidity, and the cost of capital. *J. Finance* 46:1325–59

Di Maggio M, Pagano M. 2017. Financial disclosure and market transparency with costly information processing. *Rev. Finance.* In press. doi: 10.1093/rof/rfx009

Dugast J, Foucault T. 2017. *Data abundance and asset price informativeness.* Work. Pap, HEC Paris

Dye RA. 1985. Disclosure of nonproprietary information. *J. Account. Res.* 23:123–45

Dye RA. 2001. An evaluation of essays on disclosure and the disclosure literature in accounting. *J. Account. Econ.* 32:181–235

Easley D, O'Hara M. 2004. Information and the cost of capital. *J. Finance* 59:1553–83

Easley D, O'Hara M, Yang L. 2014. Opaque trading, disclosure, and asset prices: implications for hedge fund regulation. *Rev. Financ. Stud.* 27:1190–237

Fama EF, Miller M. 1972. *The Theory of Finance.* New York: Holt, Rinehart & Winston

Foster FD, Viswanathan S. 1990. A theory of the interday variations in volume, variance, and trading costs in securities markets. *Rev. Financ. Stud.* 3:593–624

Foucault T, Gehrig T. 2008. Stock price informativeness, cross-listings, and investment decisions. *J. Financ. Econ.* 88:146–68

Gao P. 2008. Keynesian beauty contest, accounting disclosure, and market efficiency. *J. Account. Res.* 46:785–807

Gao P, Liang P. 2013. Informational feedback effect, adverse selection, and the optimal disclosure policy. *J. Account. Res.* 51:1133–58

Goldstein I, Leitner Y. 2015. *Stress tests and information disclosure.* Work. Pap., Wharton Sch., Univ. Pa.

Goldstein I, Ozdenoren E, Yuan K. 2011. Learning and complementarities in speculative attacks. *Rev. Econ. Stud.* 78:263–92

Goldstein I, Sapra H. 2013. Should banks' stress test results be disclosed? An analysis of the costs and benefits. *Found. Trends Finance* 8:1–54

Goldstein I, Yang L. 2014. *Market efficiency and real efficiency: the connect and disconnect via feedback effects.* Work. Pap., Wharton Sch., Univ. Pa.

Goldstein I, Yang L. 2016. *Good disclosure, bad disclosure*. Work. Pap., Wharton Sch., Univ. Pa.
Greenstone M, Oyer P, Vissing-Jorgensen A. 2006. Mandated disclosure, stock returns, and the 1964 Securities Acts Amendments. *Q. J. Econ.* 121:399–460
Grossman, S. 1981. The informational role of warranties and private disclosure about product quality. *J. Law Econ.* 24:461–83
Grossman S, Stiglitz J. 1980. On the impossibility of informationally efficient markets. *Am. Econ. Rev.* 70:393–408
Guttman I, Kremer I, Skrzypacz A. 2014. Not only what but also when: a theory of dynamic voluntary disclosure. *Am. Econ. Rev.* 104:2400–20
Han B, Tang Y, Yang L. 2016. Public information and uninformed trading: implications for market liquidity and price efficiency. *J. Econ. Theory* 163:604–43
Hayek FA. 1945. The use of knowledge in society. *Am. Econ. Rev.* 35:519–30
Hellwig M. 1980. On the aggregation of information in competitive markets. *J. Econ. Theory* 22:477–98
Hirshleifer J. 1971. The private and social value of information and the reward to inventive activity. *Am. Econ. Rev.* 61:561–74
Huddart S, Hughes JS, Levine CB. 2001. Public disclosure and dissimulation of insider trades. *Econometrica* 69:665–81
Hughes JS, Liu J, Liu J. 2007. Information asymmetry, diversification, and cost of capital. *Account. Rev.* 82:705–29
Indjejikian R. 1991. The impact of costly information interpretation on firm disclosure decisions. *J. Account. Res.* 29:277–301
Jung W-O, Kwon YK. 1988. Disclosure when the market is unsure of information endowment of managers. *J. Account. Res.* 26:146–53
Kamenica E, Gentzkow M. 2011. Bayesian persuasion. *Am. Econ. Rev.* 101:2590–615
Kanodia C. 2006. Accounting disclosure and real effects. *Found. Trends Account.* 1:167–258
Kanodia C, Sapra H. 2017. A real effects perspective to accounting measurement and disclosure: implications and insights for future research. *J. Account. Res.*
Kendall C. 2017. *The time cost of information in financial markets*. Work. Pap., Univ. South. Calif.
Keynes JM. 1936. *The General Theory of Employment, Interest, and Money*. London: Macmillan
Kim O, Verrecchia RE. 1994. Market liquidity and volume around earnings announcements. *J. Account. Econ.* 17:41–67
Kurlat P, Veldkamp L. 2015. Should we regulate financial information? *J. Econ. Theory* 158:697–720
Kyle A. 1985. Continuous auctions and insider trading. *Econometrica* 53:1315–35
Lambert R, Leuz C, Verrecchia RE. 2007. Accounting information, disclosure, and the cost of capital. *J. Account. Res.* 45:385–420
Langberg N, Sivaramakrishnan K. 2010. Voluntary disclosures and analyst feedback. *J. Account. Res.* 48:603–45
Leuz C, Wysocki P. 2008. *Economic consequences of financial reporting and disclosure regulation: a review and suggestions for future research*. Work. Pap., Univ. Chic.
Madhavan A. 1995. Consolidation, fragmentation, and the disclosure of trading information. *Rev. Financ. Stud.* 8:579–603
Milgrom PR. 1981. Good news and bad news: representation theorems and applications. *Bell J. Econ.* 12:380–91
Morris S, Shin HS. 2002. The social value of public information. *Am. Econ. Rev.* 92:1521–34
Naik N, Neuberger A, Viswanathan S. 1999. Disclosure regulation in markets with negotiated trades. *Rev. Financ. Stud.* 12:873–900
Ozsoylev H, Walden J. 2011. Asset pricing in large information networks. *J. Econ. Theory* 146:2252–80
Pagano M, Röell A. 1996. Transparency and liquidity: a comparison of auction and dealer markets with informed trading. *J. Finance* 51:579–611
Pagano M, Volpin P. 2012. Securitization, transparency, and liquidity. *Rev. Financ. Stud.* 25:2417–53
Peress J. 2010. Product market competition, insider trading, and stock market efficiency. *J. Finance* 65:1–43
Scharfstein D, Stein J. 1990. Herd behavior and investment. *Am. Econ. Rev.* 80:465–79
SEC (Secur. Exch. Comm.). 2002. *Final rule: ownership reports and trading by officers, directors, and principal security holders.* Release Nos. 34-46421, 35-27563, IC-25720, File No. S7-32-01, SEC, Washington, DC. **https://www.sec.gov/rules/final/34-46421.htm**

Subrahmanyam A, Titman S. 1999. The going-public decision and the development of financial markets. *J. Finance* 54:1045–82

Tang Y. 2014. Information disclosure and price discovery. *J. Financ. Markets* 19:39–61

Verrecchia RE. 1982a. Information acquisition in a noisy rational expectations economy. *Econometrica* 50:1415–30

Verrecchia RE. 1982b. The use of mathematical models in financial accounting. *J. Account. Res.* 20:1–42

Verrecchia RE. 2001. Essays on disclosure. *J. Account. Econ.* 32:97–180

Vives X. 2008. *Information and Learning in Markets: The Impact of Market Microstructure*. Princeton, NJ: Princeton Univ. Press

Wang J. 1994. A model of competitive stock trading volume. *J. Polit. Econ.* 102:127–68

What Shapes Consumer Choice and Financial Products? A Review

Sumit Agarwal,[1] Souphala Chomsisengphet,[2] and Cheryl Lim[3]

[1]McDonough School of Business, Georgetown University, Washington, DC 20057; email: ushakri@yahoo.com

[2]Office of the Comptroller of the Currency, Washington, DC 20219

[3]EDHEC Business School, Singapore 049145

Annu. Rev. Financ. Econ. 2017. 9:127–46

First published as a Review in Advance on September 20, 2017

The *Annual Review of Financial Economics* is online at financial.annualreviews.org

https://doi.org/10.1146/annurev-financial-110716-032417

Copyright © 2017 by Annual Reviews. All rights reserved

JEL codes: D11, D12, D14, D18

Keywords

consumer finance, consumer behavior, consumer bias, consumer credit, choice inefficiencies, cognitive ability, consumer financial regulation, mortgage debt, personal investments, financial products

Abstract

Central to the field of consumer finance is that consumers make financial decisions that do not always coincide with the financial decisions ideally depicted in optimal economic models. In this review, we discuss developments in the field of household finance, focusing on how consumers make suboptimal financial decisions across different types of settings and factors that affect their decisions. Rather than conducting a comprehensive survey, we focus specifically on consumer choice in the context of research on credit card borrowing, housing and mortgage debts, investment and savings decisions, and spending and consumption. We also discuss financial product design and marketing, as well as the regulatory landscape of lenders of consumer financial products. We present five future research directions and considerations for researchers and policymakers.

1. INTRODUCTION

Only in the past decade has the field of consumer finance gained much attention. One notable impetus was John Campbell's presidential address to the American Finance Association in 2006. Campbell (2006) contended that a well-functioning financial market depends on households' effective financial decisions and behaviors in the market, and he offered powerful motivations to further develop research in the field of household finance. Shortly thereafter, the housing meltdown and financial crisis in 2008 generated contentious debate about the role of consumer financial decisions and the role of intermediaries of consumer financial products in causing both the crisis and suboptimal consumer welfare outcomes in general. In response to market failures, policymakers implemented policies [e.g., the Home Affordable Modification Program in 2009, the Credit Card Accountability Responsibility and Disclosure (CARD) Act in 2009, and the Dodd–Frank Act in 2010] to protect consumers and regulate lenders, providing applied microeconomists with natural experiments to study the impact of policies related to the consumer credit market on lender and household behavior. Technological advancements that allow for more efficient collection, storage, and processing of large amounts of consumer credit data now allow applied microeconomists to develop more rigorous empirical analyses. As a result, there has been a growing body of empirical research to better understand consumer and lender choice and behavior, as well as the levers that drive them.

Central to the field of consumer finance is that consumers make financial decisions that do not always coincide with the financial decisions ideally depicted in neoclassical economic models of optimal consumer choice or behavior (Campbell 2006). Researchers are uncovering the challenges that a household faces when making financial decisions and managing its finances, the limitations in cognitive ability and behavioral biases that hinder optimal decision-making, the impact of financial service providers' business models and business decisions, and the extent to which regulators can influence and safeguard consumer behavior. Small deviations from optimal decision-making at the consumer level can have potentially important aggregate implications (e.g., Gabaix & Laibson 2006; for a similar result on firms, see Akerlof & Yellen 1985), especially given that the value at stake is high (as of Q1 2016, US households owed about $12.25 trillion in debt; see FRBNY 2016) and that these financial decisions affect most households (Zinman 2014). Moreover, Agarwal et al. (2009) show that consumers make mistakes across many domains of financial products, and such mistakes are likely to be correlated. Thus, together they can add up to be economically costly to consumers.

In this review, we discuss developments in the field of household finance, focusing on how consumers make suboptimal financial decisions across different types of settings and factors that affect these suboptimal decisions. Rather than conducting a comprehensive survey, we focus specifically on consumer choice in the context of research on credit card borrowing, housing and mortgage debts, investment and savings decisions, and spending and consumption. We also discuss financial product design and marketing, as well as the regulatory landscape of lenders of consumer financial products. We review major contributions and identify open research questions.

2. CONSUMER CHOICE INEFFICIENCIES AND SUBOPTIMAL FINANCIAL BEHAVIOR

Following Shefrin & Thaler (1988), who provide a behaviorally realistic treatment of household financial saving and consumption saving decisions, there has been continuous growth in academic research studying factors that affect consumer financial decision-making and related behavioral biases in household finance. Whereas Shefrin & Thaler (1988) present a theory of the role of costly self-control, mental accounting, and framing, many researchers are documenting specific evidence of how consumer financial decisions are inefficient and the factors that affect these suboptimal choices in various important settings. Below we survey the literature on consumer decisions to borrow in the credit card and mortgage markets, to invest and save for retirement, and to spend and consume.

2.1. Credit Card Contract Choice and Borrowing

Shui & Ausubel (2004) study credit card contract choice using a 1995 large-scale randomized experiment with 600,000 consumers facing the choice between six different credit card offers with different introductory interest rates and durations. The authors document two important behaviors: (*a*) Consumers prefer an introductory offer with a lower interest rate and a shorter duration to one with a higher interest rate and a longer duration, even though they would benefit more from choosing the latter; and (*b*) consumers are reluctant to switch and many consumers who have switched before fail to switch again. Shui & Ausubel (2004) argue that this behavior is puzzling because consumers would actually pay lower interest rate costs, ex post, under the longer introductory offer. [In related research, DellaVigna & Malmendier (2004) find that consumers systematically choose suboptimal membership plans at health clubs. Miravete (2003) finds consumers' choices of telephone billing plans to be closer to optimal.] One limitation of the study of Shui & Ausubel is the use of aggregate credit and saving outcomes, which makes the link between borrowing and present bias indirect and does not allow for evaluation of individual behavior.

Meier & Sprenger (2010) overcome the limitation of aggregate data by combining directly elicited time preference measures with administrative data on credit card borrowing. They measure individual discount factors using an incentivized-choice experiment with a sample of about 600 low-to-moderate-income individuals at two Volunteer Income Tax Assistance centers in Boston over the period 2006–2007. Their results show that present-biased individuals are 15% more likely to have credit card debts. Conditional on borrowing, they borrow 25% more (measured by outstanding balances on revolving accounts from the credit reports) than dynamically consistent individuals. The correlation is robust after controlling for income, credit constraints, and sociodemographic characteristics. The study faces some concerns about external validity, given that the data cover a small sample of low-income consumers in Boston.

Also overcoming the aggregate data limitation, Agarwal et al. (2015b) document consumer mistakes in choosing a credit card contract using individual-level data from a unique experiment in which a bank offers consumers in the United States a choice between two credit card contracts (one with an annual fee but a lower interest rate and one with no annual fee but a higher interest rate). Whereas, on average, consumers choose a credit card contract that minimizes their net costs, the authors document that about 40% of consumers choose the ex post suboptimal credit card contract, with some households incurring hundreds of dollars of avoidable interest charges. The probability of choosing the suboptimal contract, however, declines with the dollar magnitude of the potential error, and consumers with larger errors are more likely to subsequently switch to the optimal contract. Using a merged dataset of payday loan borrowing and credit card history at the individual level, Agarwal, Skiba & Tobacman (2009) find that most consumers borrowed on payday loans despite having substantial unused liquidity on their credit cards. This is highly inefficient, given that the cost of payday loan borrowing is substantially larger relative to the cost of credit card borrowing; the annual percentage rate on a payday loan is usually more than 100%.

With respect to credit card borrowing, Ausubel (1991) documents that consumers are overly sensitive to promotional teaser interest rates generally offered by credit card lenders, but are insensitive to the go-to, post-teaser interest rates, which result in credit card interest rates being sticky. Ausubel (1991) further finds that consumers are overly sensitive to such rates possibly because consumers underestimate their future credit card borrowing at the higher, post-teaser interest rates. Gross & Souleles (2002b) are also among the first researchers to document another credit card debt puzzle: US households tend to hold significant credit card debt and sizable liquid assets simultaneously, which is irrational or suboptimal according to the traditional economic model, as returns on liquid assets are typically lower than the interest charged on credit card debt. Bertaut, Haliassos & Reiter (2009) use data from the Survey of Consumer Finance to confirm that the credit card debt puzzle is a persistent behavioral phenomenon. In a similar spirit, Zinman (2009) concludes that credit card debt revolvers borrow high and lend low. He estimates that 27–30% of US households with credit cards lose $10 per month by not using demand deposits to pay down credit card debt. In a more recent study, Stango & Zinman (2016) find that there is a huge dispersion in borrowing costs in the United States across individuals and that this is caused by two factors: Annual percentage rate (APR) offers vary widely across lenders, and borrowers vary in shopping intensity. Stango & Zinman show that the difference in APRs paid by shoppers versus nonshoppers could be as large as the difference in APRs paid by borrowers in the best versus worst credit score deciles.

US households owe about $712 billion in credit card debt as of Q1 2016 (FRBNY 2016). Wang & Keys (2014) document that 29% of credit card account holders' monthly repayments are at or near the required minimum payment. In terms of repaying credit card debt, Kuchler (2015) uses daily balances and transactions of bank accounts and credit cards of consumers who signed up online with a financial management service to study how consumers stick to their plan to reduce their debt balance each month. For each committed/planned dollar of debt paydown, consumers reduced their debt by only 25–30 cents on average. Agarwal et al. (2015d) study the effect of a nudging disclosure requirement in the CARD Act of 2009, which requires credit card lenders to disclose information about the interest savings that could be achieved if the credit card holders were to pay off balances in 36 months rather than making minimum payments. They detect only a 0.4-percentage-point increase in the share of accounts making the 36-month payment value and no evidence of a change in overall payments. Similarly, Wang & Keys (2014) find that fewer than 1% of credit card account holders adopt the 36-month repayment plan amount disclosed in the CARD Act.

Using panel data of credit card account repayment behavior, Gross & Souleles (2002a) document an increase in credit card borrowers' willingness to default on their debt because of a reduction in the costs of defaulting, which include social, informational, and legal costs. Andersson et al. (2013) also document changes in the pecking order of consumer default behavior. Specifically, consumers were eight times more likely to prioritize payments on mortgage debt over credit card payments before the 2008 financial crisis. In contrast, the same consumers were just as likely to default on mortgage debt as on credit card debt during the crisis. One of the main factors contributing to the change in pecking order behavior could be strategic default behavior resulting from large levels of negative equity during the housing meltdown (see, for example, Campbell & Cocco 2015).

2.2. Mortgage Finance

In the area of mortgage financing, forward-looking behavior and cost minimization have been offered as possible explanations for consumers' choice of mortgage form. The decision between a fixed-rate mortgage (FRM) and an adjustable-rate mortgage (ARM) depends on expected future costs and is related to the borrower's expectation about whether these are likely to be higher or lower in the future. For example, if borrowers expect that future inflation is likely to be high, they are more likely to choose an FRM. Kuchler & Zafar (2015) also provide evidence of how personal experience shapes expectations in housing and labor markets. Individuals who have experienced more volatile price changes are likely to perceive future house price changes to be more uncertain, and individuals experiencing unemployment are likely to be more pessimistic about nationwide unemployment.

Campbell & Cocco (2003, 2015) model household mortgage choice and mortgage default decision under borrowing constraints and find that households care more about the current interest costs than about the lifetime costs of the loan. This suggests that the spread between FRM and ARM rates should be the primary determinant of the choice between an FRM versus an ARM product. Using a nine-country panel and instrumental variables methods to examine how near-term one-year rational expectations of future movements in ARM rates affect mortgage choice, Badarinza, Campbell & Ramadorai (2017) find that the current spread between FRM and ARM rates as well as near-term rational expectations of ARM rates affect mortgage choice, whereas longer-term three-year rational forecasts have a weaker effect. This suggests that households are concerned with current interest costs as well as interest costs over the life of the loan.

One important feature of the US mortgage market is the fact that mortgage borrowers can generally refinance their mortgage in order to reduce the mortgage balance, extract the equity in their home, and/or reduce their interest rate. Agarwal & Mazumder (2013) derive a closed-form optimal refinance solution and find that the interest rate differential for an optimal refinance typically ranges from 100 to 200 basis points. Researchers have also documented inefficiencies in making this refinancing decision with respect to rate and timing. For example, Agarwal, Rosen & Yao (2016) find that about 59% of borrowers refinance suboptimally. More specifically, they estimate that about 52% of borrowers choose a suboptimal rate, 17% of borrowers wait too long to refinance, and about 10% make both rate and timing mistakes. Keys, Pope & Pope (2016) quantify the cost of this inefficiency. In their random sample of outstanding US mortgages in December 2010, about 20% of financially unconstrained households for whom refinancing was optimal had not done so. This is equivalent to forgone savings of about $160 per month over the remaining life of each loan, or a total discounted present value of $11,500 in forgone savings per borrower.

During the housing meltdown of 2008, households experienced large levels of negative equity. The literature on mortgage default emphasizes the important role of home equity in inducing a homeowner to default on a mortgage (e.g., Deng, Quigley & Van Order 2000; Elul et al. 2010; Campbell & Cocco 2015). Whereas many argue that negative equity in houses induced strategic default behavior during the crisis of 2008, Bhutta, Dokko & Shan (2010) document that, of the households that purchased their home at the peak of the housing bubble in 2006, about 80% default on their mortgage because of a combination of income shocks and negative equity. In addition, the authors find that many of these households, despite having little financial incentive to keep paying their mortgage, as they bought their homes during the height of the bubble and put little money toward their down payments, keep paying their mortgage. The median borrower stops paying mortgage when housing equity falls to −62%.

2.3. Investment and Retirement Decisions

In investment decisions, Korniotis & Kumar (2013) show that the apparent inefficiencies are concentrated portfolios, excessive trading, and preference for local stocks. They point out, though, that all three instances of portfolio distortions could arise either from an informational advantage, which means the investor is smart, or from psychological biases. By contrast, Malmendier & Nagel (2016) as well as Botsch & Malmendier (2015) show empirically that lifetime experiences are a determinant of differences in expectations and affect financial decision-making. Households that experienced good stock returns during their lifetimes invest more of their wealth in stocks, whereas households that experienced good bond returns during their lifetimes invest more in bonds.

In retirement decisions, the inefficiency is in failing to maximize benefit from retirement plans and accounts. Choi, Laibson & Madrian (2011) analyze the 401(k) investment choices of employees at seven companies and find that employees older than 59½ were contributing less than the employer matching contribution threshold despite being vested in their match and being able to make penalty-free 401(k) withdrawals for any reason. This means that, on average, 36% of match-eligible employees over the age of 59½ forgo arbitrage profits that average 1.6% of their annual pay, or $507. More interestingly, Choi, Laibson & Madrian find that a survey educating employees about the free lunch they are forgoing raised contribution rates by only a statistically insignificant 0.67% of income among those completing the survey. The tax inefficiency of asset allocations of households investing in taxable and tax-deferred accounts (TDAs) is another puzzle. Whereas theory, for example in the work of Dammon, Spatt & Zhang (2004) and Shoven & Sialm (2004), suggests that savers should locate higher-tax assets such as bonds in their TDAs while keeping low-tax assets (equities) in taxable accounts, observed portfolios show otherwise and are not tax efficient. Amromin (2003) explains this puzzle with precautionary portfolio choice; i.e., borrowing-constrained households forgo tax efficiency for allocations that provide more liquidity in bad income states. His empirical analysis suggests that the choice between holding a tax-efficient portfolio and accepting a degree of portfolio tax inefficiency is related to the presence and intensity of precautionary motives.

The extent to which individuals optimize their savings to take advantage of tax-deferred accounts is also actively researched. Researchers in the United States are empirically assessing the extent to which tax-preferred savings individual retirement accounts (IRAs) such as 401(k) and Roth 401(k) can increase the amount of private saving. They investigate the causal relationship by exploiting the variation in (*a*) initiation of topping up in tax-subsidized savings accounts (Attanasio & DeLeire 1994), (*b*) policy on eligibility (Gale & Scholz 1994), (*c*) balance of tax-subsidized savings accounts (Venti & Wise 1987, 1988), and (*d*) eligibility (Benjamin 2003, Gelber 2011) to see whether there is significant change in taxable savings or total wealth.[1] Recent developments in behavioral economics show that automatic enrollment significantly increases saving within retirement accounts (Choi et al. 2001, Madrian & Shea 2001, Thaler & Benartzi 2004). Recent work by Beshears et al. (2017) analyzes administrative data from 11 US firms that introduced a Roth IRA retirement plan between 2006 and 2010. They find no significant reduction in total 401(k) contribution rates following the introduction of the Roth IRA (deferred tax benefit), which implies that take-home pay declines and total retirement saving increases following the introduction of the Roth IRA. The authors analyze additional survey data and attribute their finding to employee confusion or inattention to the tax properties of the Roth IRA and behavior bias of partition dependence, rather than employees making an active, calculated decision. Arnberg & Barslund (2014) study the crowding-out effect of Danish mandatory pension schemes for renters. They find that for every euro paid to mandatory pension accounts there is a reduction of 0–30 cents in other private savings depending on age. They attribute the low crowding-out effect on private savings to liquidity constraints. By contrast, Chetty et al. (2014), using rich panel data on all private savings, find that retirement savings policy in Denmark does not effectively increase

[1] Conclusions from these empirical studies are mixed, as they are based on different econometrical assumptions. There are two major concerns. The first is low-quality and infrequent data, and the second is the unobserved heterogeneity in the disposition to save between the treatment and control groups, which can bias the estimated effects on private saving.

private saving, given that 85% of individuals are passive savers who are unresponsive to subsidies, whereas the other 15% of individuals are active savers who respond to tax subsidies by shifting assets across accounts. The authors conclude that there are substantial crowding-out effects and that automatic contributions are more effective in increasing saving rates than tax-subsidized savings policy.

2.4. Spending and Consumption Decisions

Researchers are focusing efforts to better understand factors that stimulate household consumption. The secular decline in the US personal savings rate, which began in the 1980s, coincides roughly with a secular increase in the dissemination and use of credit cards. One conjecture is that increased access to and use of credit cards have stimulated consumer spending. Several early studies (Hirschman 1979, Feinberg 1986, Prelec & Simester 2001), using surveys and experiments, provide support for this conjecture. Similarly, in the area of mortgage debt, access to better loan terms appears to stimulate consumption. Brady, Canner & Maki (2000), Canner, Dynan & Passmore (2002), and Greenspan & Kennedy (2008) find that homeowners who refinanced their mortgages on more favorable terms, supported by rising home values in the 1990s to mid-2000s, spent more. Greenspan & Kennedy (2008) estimate the sources and uses of equity extracted from homes and find that the amount of equity extracted that was used for personal consumption expenditure rose from \$26.3 billion in 1991 to \$182.7 billion in 2005, or from about 10% of free cash resulting from equity extraction to about 13%.

Some studies take a completely different direction and look at the behavioral effects of payment mechanisms and the action of paying per se. Soman (2001) argues that certain mediums of payment, such as cash and check, affect consumers' future spending behaviors through two mechanisms: (*a*) rehearsal, which causes consumers to more accurately recall past expenses, and (*b*) immediacy (an immediate depletion of wealth). Both mechanisms make consumers more averse to spending. The use of credit cards, however, does not bring such a negative impact on spending and therefore leads to a greater propensity to spend. In a subsequent field study, Soman (2003) collected receipts from shoppers at the exit of a large supermarket and found that the positive effect of credit card use on spending was mainly on the purchase of flexible items (an expense that may vary depending on price and quantity available), but not on inflexible goods (which are needed irrespective of changes in price and other factors). Another explanation is the payment transparency hypothesis; i.e., credit cards and other payment tools are different in the transparency or vividness with which individuals can feel the outflow of money, with cash being the most transparent mode of payment; the more transparent the payment outflow, the greater the aversion to spending or the higher the pain of paying (Prelec & Loewenstein 1998). Similarly, Raghubir & Srivastava (2008) find the same effect in an experimental study in which they asked participants to estimate the budget for a hypothetical Thanksgiving party, where the specified payment medium was cash or credit card. They find that when credit card was the payment medium, participants' estimates of the total costs for the party were significantly higher. Interestingly, when participants were instructed to consider the costs of each item individually and add them up, there was no difference between costs using cash and credit card.

Taking a different approach, behavioral economists exploit natural experiments to understand whether income shocks and other stimuli affect consumption spending and in what ways. Agarwal, Liu & Souleles (2007) estimate how consumers responded to federal income tax rebates in 2001 in terms of monthly responses of credit card payments, spending, and debt. They find that consumers initially increased their credit card payments, i.e., paid down debt, but soon afterward increased their spending. Spending increased most for consumers who were most likely to be liquidity constrained, whereas debt declined most for unconstrained consumers. In a more recent study, Agarwal & Qian (2014) study consumption behavior after an exogenous unanticipated income shock: a one-time cash payment to Singaporeans announced in February 2011 and paid out at the end of April 2011. Estimating the announcement and disbursement effects, they find that consumption rose significantly after the fiscal policy announcement, with consumers spending SGD0.80 on average for every SGD1 received during the subsequent 10 months. They also find a strong announcement effect, i.e., 19% of the response occurred via credit cards within the first 2 months of the announcement. Interestingly, consumers switched to using debit cards after disbursement before finally increasing spending on credit cards in later months. Consumers with low liquid assets or with low credit card limits experienced stronger consumption responses.

Whereas unexpected income shocks from national policy are one good source of natural experiments, another set of studies draw on changes in day-to-day living to understand how predictable income streams that households expect affect their spending behavior. Empirical evidence shows that even anticipated income shocks cause changes in household spending behavior. Parker (2015) estimates the propensity of households to spend in response to the arrival of predictable, lump-sum payments, using households in the Nielsen Consumer Panel, which received $25 million in federal stimulus payments that were distributed randomly across weeks. He finds the propensity to spend to be a persistent household trait. It is unrelated to expectation errors, almost unrelated to crude measures of procrastination and self-control, moderately related to sophistication and planning, and highly related to impatience. By contrast, Stephens (2008) estimates the consumption response to predictable increases in discretionary income following the final payment of a vehicle loan and finds that a 10% increase in discretionary income leads to a 2–3% increase in non-durable consumption. This may be a result of borrowing constraints. In an earlier paper, Stephens (2006) examines consumption in response to paycheck arrival. Contrary to the basic rational expectations life-cycle/permanent income hypothesis, which predicts that household consumption should not respond to anticipated paycheck arrival because a regular paycheck does not provide new information, he finds household consumption to be excessively sensitive to paycheck receipt. The finding cannot be explained by any underlying monthly expenditure fluctuations common to all households, whereas liquidity constraints measured by wealth and age can account for the excess sensitivity.

3. FACTORS THAT AFFECT CONSUMER SUBOPTIMAL FINANCIAL CHOICE AND BEHAVIOR

Poor financial decisions have a material impact on households' lifetime welfare, and some households clearly make better decisions than others. Small deviations from optimal decision-making at the consumer level might still potentially have important aggregate implications (e.g., Gabaix & Laibson 2006). Therefore, understanding why consumers behave suboptimally has important policy implications, as suboptimal choices and biases can dampen economic growth and increase the costs for social security systems. The main drivers explaining consumer choice inefficiencies are cognitive limitations, lack of financial literacy, time preference, self-control and incentives, psychological biases, and social networks.

3.1. Cognitive Limitations and Financial Literacy

One strand of the literature on suboptimal consumer financial decision focuses on the role of cognitive limitations, either from innate characteristics (Agarwal & Mazumder 2013) or aging (Agarwal et al. 2009). Agarwal & Mazumder (2013) explicitly link cognitive abilities to financial mistakes.

Specifically, they study the effect of cognitive abilities on two consumer financial decisions where suboptimal behavior is well defined: (*a*) the optimal use of credit cards for convenience transactions when transactions are fully paid for within the grace period, and after a balance transfer from an existing account to a new card, and (*b*) a financial mistake that involves recognizing the APR for the value of their home during a home equity loan application. Agarwal & Mazumder use a direct measure of cognitive abilities—the Armed Forces Qualifying Test—to show that consumers with higher math scores are substantially less likely to make financial mistakes. Other studies by Agarwal et al. (2009) and Korniotis & Kumar (2011) explore the effects of aging and experience on financial decision-making and find that the adverse effects of aging dominate the positive effects of experience. To understand the effect of aging on financial decision-making, Agarwal et al. (2009) study life-cycle patterns in financial mistakes using a proprietary database that measures 10 different types of credit behavior. These mistakes include the suboptimal use of credit card balance transfer offers, the misestimation of the value of one's home, and excess interest rates and fee payments. They find that middle-aged adults make fewer financial mistakes than younger or older adults, which implies a U-shaped pattern with the cost-minimizing age occurring around age 53. Korniotis & Kumar (2011) document that whereas older and more experienced investors have greater knowledge about investment, they do not effectively apply their knowledge and skills as a result of cognitive deterioration.

Attention and a bias to action is another explanation for better financial decision-making. Andersen et al. (2015) studied inattention and inertia in Danish households and found that younger, better-educated, and higher-income households have less inertia and less inattention. Financial wealth and housing wealth appear to have opposite effects—there is least inertia and inattention among households whose housing wealth is high relative to their financial wealth. In the authors' mixture model of household refinancing types, household characteristics affect both inattention (a low proportion of rational refinancers) and residual inertia (a low probability that fully inattentive households refinance). They found that the two attributes are positively correlated, with cross-sectional correlation of 0.62.

Another explanation for why consumers make financial mistakes is that they lack sufficient knowledge about financial concepts and instruments to make informed financial decisions (Agarwal et al. 2010). Gerardi, Goette & Meier (2013) find a robust relationship between numerical ability and mortgage default, after controlling for a broad set of sociodemographic variables that are not driven by other aspects of cognitive ability. They find that whereas numerical ability does not impact the choice of mortgage contract, but affects the incidence of mortgage default, individuals with limited numerical ability default on their mortgage as a result of behavior unrelated to the initial choice of mortgage. The good news is that there is some evidence showing that financial decision-making does improve with experience. For example, Agarwal, Rosen & Yao (2016) show evidence that borrowers learn from their refinancing experiences and make fewer mistakes on their second refinancing.

Other research shows that many consumers are ill prepared to meet their financial goals (Agarwal et al. 2010); take out payday loans at astronomical interest rates when cheaper forms of credit are available (Agarwal, Skiba & Tobacman 2009); choose suboptimal credit contracts (Agarwal et al. 2015b); fail to optimally refinance mortgages (Agarwal, Driscoll & Laibson 2013); and fail to plan for retirement, reaching it with little or no savings (Lusardi, Mitchell & Curto 2009).

Some research focuses on the importance of improving consumers' financial literacy. Hilgert, Hogarth & Beverly (2003) explore the connection between financial knowledge and behavior using consumer survey data. They find that those who have more financial knowledge are more likely to engage in recommended financial practices. They conclude that financial education, when combined with skill-building and audience-targeted motivational strategies, may help drive desired behavioral changes in the way that consumers manage their finances. Agarwal et al. (2010) also find substantially lower default rates among graduates of a long-term voluntary counseling program targeting low- to moderate-income households. They attribute the results to two factors. First, the program requires prospective borrowers to acquire budgeting and credit management skills. Second, aggressive post-purchase counseling is targeted at early delinquency—counselors identify and target households on the basis of soft information picked up during the program. Moreover, Fernandes, Lynch & Netemeyer (2014) conduct a meta-analysis of the relationship of financial literacy and of financial education to financial behaviors in 168 papers covering 201 prior studies, and find that interventions to improve financial literacy explain only 0.1% of the variance in financial behaviors studied, and their effects decay over time. Even large interventions with many hours of instruction have negligible effects 20 months after the time of intervention, and the partial effects of financial literacy diminish dramatically with controls for psychological traits omitted in prior studies. They suggest that just-in-time financial education tied to specific behaviors it intends to help would be more effective than financial education that is not elaborated or acted upon soon afterward.

3.2. Time Preferences, Self-Control, and Incentives

A second strand of research tries to explain inefficient consumer choices in relation to time preferences, self-control, and incentives. Present bias, in which a decision-maker places more emphasis on the present than the future, has been documented in the literature. Present-biased preferences can be seen as a result of the interplay between two separate decision-making systems: the affective system, which values immediate gratification and sharply discounts all future periods, and the deliberative system, which makes long-term plans and displays higher discount factors. Laibson (1997) develops a theoretical framework showing how present bias can drive credit card borrowing and can constrain future choices. Laibson, Repetto & Tobacman (2003) present a model of hyperbolic discounting to explain the coexistence of credit card debt and accumulation of assets for retirement. The accumulation of illiquid assets coexists with revolving credit card debts because hyperbolic consumers act patiently with respect to long-term objectives and impatiently with short-term objectives. On this basis, they propose that credit card borrowing is intended for short-term consumption smoothing, whereas accumulation of illiquid assets is an instrument of self-control.

Empirical support of present bias includes the work of Shui & Ausubel (2004), who, as stated earlier, find that consumers prefer an introductory offer with a lower interest rate and a shorter duration to one with a higher interest rate and a longer duration, even though they would benefit more from choosing the latter, and that consumers are reluctant to switch and many consumers who have switched before fail to switch again. These findings suggest time inconsistency in consumer behavior, which can be explained with hyperbolic preferences. By means of a unique field study using an incentivized choice experiment and administrative credit card borrowing data, Meier & Sprenger (2010) find that present-biased individuals are more likely to hold credit card debt. Findings by Kuchler (2015), which indicate that a consumer's decision to pay down debt is affected by his or her level of impatience, highlight the importance of present bias in consumer decisions.

Other papers, such as those of Bertaut, Haliassos & Reiter (2009) and Telyukova (2013), identify a set of motives related to self-control. Bertaut, Haliassos & Reiter (2009) show the coexistence of credit card debt with substantial accumulation of assets for retirement in the context of a self-checking motive using the "accountant shopper" model, in which an individual or household has two separate selves, an "accountant" and a "shopper," who act contemporaneously to handle different decisions. The accountant handles bill payment and long-term financial planning, whereas the shopper determines consumption expenditures based on the credit available. When the shopper exhibits self-control problems, the accountant intervenes to control the shopper by limiting the unused credit available. This explanation, however, has limitations; it is idealistic to think that the accountant would consistently act to check the shopper in a rational manner. The household puzzle itself is a reflection of this limitation; it has been shown that households lose an average of $374 per year, or 1.5% of total annual after-tax income. Telyukova (2013) offers a precautionary motive and highlights the importance of liquidity: Households are not using money in the bank to pay off accumulated credit card debt because they anticipate needing that money in situations where credit cards cannot be used. As a result, households consume both cash goods and credit card goods concurrently.

In their study, Agarwal et al. (2015b) find that the probability of choosing a suboptimal contract declines with the dollar magnitude of the potential error, and consumers with larger errors were more incentivized to subsequently switch to the optimal contract. Lehnert & Maki (2007) offer strategic default as another motive. They study consumer bankruptcy behavior and find that states with higher levels of statutory exemptions—below which debtors are permitted to keep their assets while debts are forgiven—face higher consumer bankruptcy rates and contain households that are more likely to simultaneously hold low-return liquid assets and owe high-cost unsecured debt. They also find that the credit card debt puzzle is more prevalent in the United States where exemption levels are higher, and this supports their hypothesis. This, however, provides a plausible motive for only a limited group of consumers, as most people are unlikely to file for bankruptcy.

3.3. Psychological Bias

A third strand of literature identifies and assesses the role of psychological biases—among others, perceived control (Perry & Morris 2005), optimism (Puri & Robinson 2007), disposition (Odean 1998), narrow framing (Kumar & Lim 2008), and propensity to gamble (Kumar 2009)—as well as the extent to which smartness is a determinant of psychological biases (Korniotis & Kumar 2013).

One key factor that influences propensity to save, to budget, and to control spending is perceived control. Perry & Morris (2005) examine the relationship between consumer financial knowledge, income, and locus of control on financial behavior. They find that consumers who perceive that they have higher levels of control over outcomes, as well as better knowledge and financial resources, are more likely to save, budget, and control spending. Optimism, which is correlated with positive beliefs about future economic conditions and related to numerous work and life choices, is also a key influencing factor, with a moderate amount of optimism being beneficial. Puri & Robinson (2007) develop a novel measure of optimism by comparing self-reported life expectancy in the Survey of Consumer Finance with that implied by statistics. They find that moderate optimists display reasonable financial behavior, whereas extreme optimists display financial behavior that is generally not considered prudent.

Kumar (2009) identifies the propensity to gamble, finding that greater expenditure in lotteries is associated with greater investment in lottery-type stocks. Similarly, state lotteries and lottery-type stocks are also likely to attract very similar socioeconomic clienteles.

Although we know that psychological biases exist to varying extents in different people, it is also important to understand what drives this variation. Korniotis & Kumar (2013) develop an empirical model of smartness that can identify skilled investors ex ante using only their demographic characteristics. They then investigate the role of psychological mechanisms and information allocation on some commonly known stock market puzzles, namely portfolio concentration, excessive trading, and preference for local stocks. They find that smartness is a determinant of various psychological biases, i.e., smart investors have fewer psychological biases, and therefore perform better. But what factors determine smartness? Korniotis & Kumar (2013) find that superior information is the key factor behind the performance of smart investors, even when their decisions are contrary to standard economic reasoning. Zhang (2006) also showed that higher information uncertainty, resulting from poor information and high volatility of a firm's fundamentals, increases behavioral biases and investors' underreaction to new public information.

3.4. Social Networks

The literature on information accessed and transmitted highlights the role of social networks and peer pressure on financial decision-making. Hong, Kubik & Stein (2004) investigate how social interaction influences stock market participation and conclude that more social consumers, for example those who have reported interacting with neighbors and attending church, are more likely to invest. Hong, Kubik & Stein (2005) also find that a mutual fund manager is more likely to buy or sell a particular stock if other managers in the same city are buying or selling the same stock, even after controlling for local preferences. They explain this effect using an epidemic model in which investors spread information to one another by word of mouth.

Similarly, Bailey et al. (2016) use data from Facebook to show that social interactions with friends can influence housing market expectations and investment behavior. Specifically, they show that individuals whose geographically distant friends experienced larger recent house price gains are more optimistic about property investments in their own local housing markets and are actually more likely to invest in the housing market. Duflo & Saez (2003) conduct a field experiment and find not only that individuals who received a financial incentive to participate in a fair providing information on TDA retirement plans were more likely to enroll in the plan, but also that their colleagues were more likely to enroll; this is evidence of spill-over effects based on social interactions. Yet when Grinblatt & Keloharju (2001) analyze the relationship between stockholding and spatial proximity, language, and culture, they find that the influence of distance, language, and culture is less prominent among the most investment-savvy investors than among households and less savvy investors.

4. FINANCIAL PRODUCT DESIGN AND MARKETING

The design of financial products and the way they are marketed are also important factors that influence consumer choice; the behavioral literature has ample studies on the effects of frames on choice (Tversky & Kahneman 1986). Shefrin & Statman (1993) also suggest that some investors prefer one financial product over another because of the way identical cash flows are framed. They study the role of prospect theory, hedonic framing, behavioral life-cycle theory, and cognitive errors in the design of financial products and suggest that a behavioral framework can offer insights into many other features of security design such as designation of mutual funds as "growth" and "income" funds, design of lotteries to have a particular combination of prices, and design of stocks to have prices within a trading range. Gabaix & Laibson (2006) study information shrouding in an economy with some myopic (or less informed) consumers. They find that, in equilibrium, optimizing firms exploit myopic consumers by shrouding costly add-ons, whereas sophisticated customers are able to exploit these marketing schemes. Gabaix & Laibson also show that the practice continues because it is not possible to profitably drive away the business of the sophisticated or the myopic.

There is also evidence that the way mortgages are marketed to consumers has important implications. Using a controlled experiment in a large US commercial bank when loan officers were incentivized to prospect for loans, Agarwal & Ben-David (2014) find that loan sizes, volume, and defaults increased despite the fact that there was no change to the bank's credit standards. They find that loan officers placed greater weight on hard information and approved many applications that would otherwise have been rejected, preferring to convince existing applicants to borrow larger amounts than source new applications. This resulted in a higher default rate and the loss of predictive power of the bank's credit model. Gurun, Matvos & Seru (2016) study the relationship between advertising subprime lenders and the nature of mortgages obtained by consumers, measuring the relative expensiveness of a given mortgage, i.e., the excess rate after accounting for a broad set of borrower, contract, and regional characteristics. They find a strong positive relationship between the intensity of local advertising and the expensiveness of mortgages extended by lenders in a given region, with the strongest relationship applying to advertising through newspapers, the most heavily used advertising channel. They also found that advertising is most effective when targeted at groups that are likely to be less informed about mortgages such as the poor, the less educated, and minorities. Their findings support the persuasive view, i.e., that advertising in the subprime mortgage market was used to steer consumers into expensive choices, rather than the informative view, i.e., that advertising helps consumers to find cheaper products.

In addition, consumers face a number of challenges: the complexity of financial products, information asymmetry, and, perhaps, less-than-scrupulous practices on the part of providers. Examples include excessive fees, high interest rates, prepayment penalties, and clauses barring borrowers from seeking judicial redress for predatory behavior by lenders (Engel & McCoy 2001). Bostic et al. (2012) find evidence that antipredatory lending laws, holding all else constant, changed the type of mortgage products that lenders offered in the market. Specifically, the introduction of state antipredatory lending laws induced lenders to substitute between mortgage products; in locations where such laws were introduced, they reduced mortgage products that have prepayment penalties, adjustable-rate and hybrid-rate mortgages, balloon payments, interest-only loans, and low- and no-documentation loans, and at the same time increased teaser rates, which extend the period during which borrowers have low monthly mortgage payments. Agarwal, Driscoll & Laibson (2013) provide explicit evidence of systematic mortgage lending abuse, in which customers with good credit quality are steered toward more expensive, predatory subprime mortgage terms. Moreover, Agarwal et al. (2014) present evidence that predatory lending practices contributed to the higher mortgage default rates among subprime borrowers, raising them by about a third and aggravating the subprime crisis. Although it is hard to disagree that mortgages with abusive terms are costly to borrowers and taxpayers, the extent of these practices is hard to quantify.

In addition, Agarwal & Ben-David (2014) present evidence that when a large US commercial bank incentivized loan officers to prospect for new business, the unintended consequences were a dramatic loss of critical soft information, larger loans, poorer credit quality, and higher default rates; i.e., the change in the bank's business model unintentionally led to riskier lending at consumers' expense. In the area of credit cards, complexity stems from the great variety of rates and fees that cater to diverse consumer risk profiles and preferences. The innovations that gave less credit-worthy consumers access to credit cards have also made it more difficult for them to fully understand the true cost of credit, therefore making it more challenging for them to select credit cards and manage their use (Canner & Elliehausen 2013).

How, then, can we design financial products for the benefit of consumers? Specifically on the topic of mortgage debt, Campbell (2013) studies cross-country variation in mortgage market structure and draws insights from urban economics, asset pricing, behavioral finance, financial intermediation, and macroeconomics to improve on mortgage market design, especially in the United States. Campbell finds that three types of behavioral heterogeneity impact mortgage lenders' incentives and mortgage innovations: moving propensity, financial sophistication, and present-biased preferences. Campbell also concluded that although it may be possible for economists to recommend an ideal mortgage system by solving the dynamic contracting problem, the design of mortgage markets must proceed in a more ad hoc and flexible way, learning from international experience and integrating insights from different fields.

5. REGULATION

Although the financial crisis has triggered a surge of interest in regulating consumer financial products, researchers are still debating both sides of the regulatory coin, for example, in the studies of Campbell et al. (2011) and Posner & Weyl (2013). Proponents of regulation argue that consumer financial markets have become increasingly unfair. Firms take advantage of consumers' behavioral biases—such as myopia, present bias, and inattention—to earn large profits, especially from unsophisticated and poor consumers (Agarwal et al. 2015c). Such proponents suggest that regulation and additional information can protect less sophisticated consumers and reduce aggregate borrowing costs. Banks also have the least incentive to lend to consumers who are most in need of credit (Agarwal et al. 2015c). Critics, however, are skeptical about the effectiveness of consumer financial regulations. Whereas limits on hidden fees, for example, can shift surplus from more sophisticated to less sophisticated consumers (Gabaix & Laibson 2006), there is less evidence that regulators can bring about an across-the-board reduction in consumer costs. Such critics suggest that regulators may just be playing a game of regulatory whack-a-mole, where efforts to limit certain fees will simply lead firms to offset reduced revenue with higher prices on other product dimensions, as well as to restrict the supply of credit. Even proponents of regulating late fees, such as Barr, Mullainathan & Shafir (2009, p. 50), are worried that "the reduced revenue stream to lenders from these fees would mean that other rates and fees would be adjusted to compensate."

Campbell (2016) frames the regulation discussion in the context of tension between laissez-faire advocates and interventionists. Household finance is the focus of interventionist attention for several reasons: (*a*) Individuals have to make increasingly difficult financial decisions with bigger consequences; (*b*) higher education is becoming more expensive and posing a challenge in countries where it is not publicly provided; (*c*) rising home prices are stressing traditional systems for financing homeownership; (*d*) improving information technology is facilitating the development of more complex and confusing products; and (*e*) behavioral economics has opened the eyes of academics to financial behaviors that were not carefully examined before, showing that many households are not up to the challenge of managing their finances. Also, household mistakes may not be purely idiosyncratic and can be correlated across households; this creates endogenous risk and is therefore a factor that needs to be managed by the financial system.

The vital questions are as follows: How effective has regulation been so far? What types of regulations work? How do we improve upon the way we regulate to balance the needs of consumers and other stakeholders? How do we make use of behavioral elements to make regulation more effective? Agarwal et al. (2015c) analyze the effectiveness of consumer financial regulation by considering the CARD Act of 2009. They estimate that regulatory limits on credit card fees reduced overall borrowing costs by an annualized 1.6% of average daily balances, with savings of more than 5.3% for consumers with FICO scores below 660, and no evidence of an offsetting increase in interest charges or a reduction in the volume of credit. This means that the CARD Act saved consumers an estimated $11.9 billion per year. Agarwal et al. (2015d) further provide a framework to help regulators understand the implications of regulating hidden fees by estimating firms' pass-through of cost shocks and the salience of the regulated hidden fee. They show that the framework predicts the degree of offset from the CARD Act in an ex ante analysis. In terms of interventions, Agarwal et al. (2015d) also analyze a nudge that disclosed the interest savings from paying off balances in 36 months rather than making minimum payments and detected a small increase in the share of accounts making the 36-month payment value, but no evidence of a change in overall payments.

The results of another study show the nature and degree of substitutability between debit and credit, which have implications for antitrust regulators. Zinman (2009) models consumer choice at the point of sales and finds that consumers who revolve debt or face a binding credit limit constraint are substantially less likely to incur credit card charges and substantially more likely to use a debit card, conditional on several proxies for transaction demand and tastes. Zinman also finds that debit use increases with credit limit constraints and decreases with credit card possession, and that debit is becoming a stronger substitute for credit over time. Heidhues & Kőszegi (2010) study how requiring credit contracts to have a linear structure and prohibiting large penalties for deferring small amounts of repayment can raise welfare. They analyze contract choices, loan repayment behavior, and welfare in a model of a competitive credit market when borrowers have a taste for immediate gratification. This is consistent with many credit cards and subprime mortgages, where terms are such that most nonsophisticated borrowers overborrow and pay penalties to back-load repayment, causing welfare loss.

More generally, Agarwal et al. (2009) analyze nine regulatory strategies with a view to helping individuals avoid financial mistakes, especially those resulting from cognitive decline: laissez-faire, disclosure, nudges, financial "drivers' licenses," advance directives, fiduciaries, asset safe harbors, and ex post and ex ante regulatory oversight. They also ask what the appropriate regulatory response should be. They argue that if the market for third-party advice and fiduciary services functioned well, the market equilibrium would have three phases. (*a*) Early in life, each individual would write a plan for his or her future consumption and investment, contingent on major events (including cognitive decline beyond a specified threshold). (*b*) In the second phase, cognitive testing and observation would monitor the individual for the onset of significant cognitive decline. (*c*) Finally, when the prespecified threshold is crossed, the individual's plan would be enforced by a fiduciary, or the individual's assets would be placed in a financial instrument with a state-contingent payout scheme. The market already provides financial products with this feature, for example annuities that eliminate complex asset deaccumulation decisions. The authors argue, however, that an unregulated market solution may not work well and that government intervention is probably needed. The ideal form of intervention is yet unclear, and more empirical analyses and field experiments are needed to identify the regulatory response that best balances the marginal costs against the potential benefits. Campbell et al. (2011) argue that regulation must be tailored to specific problems to be beneficial and must be accompanied by research to measure the effectiveness of the interventions. This is especially the case for consumer financial regulation on market failure and limited consumer rationality in financial decision-making. They illustrate the need for, and the limits of, regulation through three case studies: mortgage markets, payday lending, and financial retirement consumption.

Yet another strand of literature explores the ability of government to induce change and finds this avenue to be limited. Agarwal et al. (2015a) examine the ability of the government to influence debt renegotiation by evaluating the effects of the 2009 Home Affordable Modification Program, which provided intermediaries with sizable financial incentives to renegotiate mortgages. They find that the program generated an increase in renegotiation intensity within the program while adversely affecting negotiations performed outside the program. The overall impact of the program is likely to be limited—it was estimated to reach just one-third of the targeted 3–4 million households—with a few large servicers responding at half the rate of others. This is likely because of servicer-specific factors, for example pre-existing organizational capabilities. These findings suggest that the government's ability to quickly induce changes in servicer behavior through financial incentives is limited and highlight significant barriers to the effectiveness of such policies.

What, then, is the main challenge for economists in the area of consumer financial regulation? Campbell (2016, p. 25) succinctly states that "beyond the easy cases where behaviorally biased households can be 'nudged' to avoid mistakes with minimal effects on rational households, financial regulators face a difficult trade-off between the benefits of regulation to households that make mistakes, and the costs of regulation to other financial market participants. The task for economists is to confront this trade-off explicitly, bringing to bear the highest quality evidence that modern applied microeconomics can make available."

6. CONCLUSION

In this article, we reviewed the developments in research on factors that influence consumer choice and financial products within the field of household finance. Specifically, we looked at consumer behavior and biases, financial literacy and education, and financial product design and marketing, and we outlined the key research questions to explore further. Here we highlight five future research directions and considerations for policymakers.

First, how widespread and important are losses resulting from poor financial decision-making? What fraction of aggregate wealth, and of the wealth of older adults, is lost because of poor choices? What are the costs? We believe that the studies so far have examined only the tip of the iceberg; the bulk of mistakes that are being made probably lie elsewhere, including decisions regarding annuities, structured financial products, real estate investment pools, and other complex and/or retirement-related concerns.

Second, although we have found that there are many consumer behaviors and biases, both rational and irrational, their relative effects are still unclear. In particular, do we know which effects are dominant? Is it possible to come up with a general model of consumer financial behavior? Can this be a useful reference to guide financial product design and regulation, much like how Apple shapes our smartphone usage habits and Starbucks shapes our coffee drinking culture?

Third, policy research so far has focused on interventions and their effects on consumer welfare, as well as on how to improve consumer financial literacy. Perhaps attention should also be given to studying the incentives of financial services providers. Rather than rely on a "stick" approach, can we create conditions for a sustainable win-win for consumer and provider?

Fourth, policy researchers also face fascinating challenges in deriving optimal contracts, policy responses, and enforcement (Zinman 2014) because of inherent behavioral complexity, information asymmetry, and enforcement idiosyncrasy. What new methodologies and further research do we need to improve on current consumer financial policies?

Finally, as adoption of financial technology (fintech) grows in consumer finance, consumers will decide how to use these new technologies, and regulators will need to decide how to react to these new developments. As these technologies become entrenched and coexist with traditional financial services, how will consumer behavior and market dynamics change? There will be the need to re-examine how each of the levers—consumer behavior and biases, financial literacy and education, financial product design, and marketing and regulation—has adapted or needs to be adapted.

DISCLOSURE STATEMENT

The authors are not aware of any affiliations, memberships, funding, or financial holdings that might be perceived as affecting the objectivity of this review.

LITERATURE CITED

Agarwal S, Amromin G, Ben-David I, Chomsisengphet S, Evanoff DD. 2010. Learning to cope: voluntary financial education and loan performance during a housing crisis. *Am. Econ. Rev.* 100(2):495–500

Agarwal S, Amromin G, Ben-David I, Chomsisengphet S, Evanoff DD. 2014. Predatory lending and the subprime crisis. *J. Financ. Econ.* 113(1):29–52

Agarwal S, Amromin G, Ben-David I, Chomsisengphet S, Piskorski T, Seru A. 2015a. Policy intervention in debt renegotiation: evidence from the Home Affordable Modification Program. *J. Polit. Econ.* 125:654–712

Agarwal S, Ben-David I. 2014. *Loan prospecting and the loss of soft information.* NBER Work. Pap. 19945, Cambridge, MA

Agarwal S, Chomsisengphet S, Liu C, Souleles NS. 2015b. Do consumers choose the right credit contracts? *Rev. Corp. Finance Stud.* 4(2):239–57

Agarwal S, Chomsisengphet S, Mahoney N, Stroebel J. 2015c. *Do banks pass through credit expansions to consumers who want to borrow?* NBER Work. Pap. 21567, Cambridge, MA

Agarwal S, Chomsisengphet S, Mahoney N, Stroebel J. 2015d. Regulating consumer financial products: evidence from credit cards. *Q. J. Econ.* 130(1):111–64

Agarwal S, Driscoll JC, Gabaix X, Laibson D. 2009. The age of reason: financial decisions over the life cycle and implications for regulation. *Brookings Pap. Econ. Act.* 40(2):51–117

Agarwal S, Driscoll JC, Laibson D. 2013. Optimal mortgage refinancing: a closed-form solution. *J. Money Credit Bank.* 45(4):591–622

Agarwal S, Liu C, Souleles NS. 2007. The reaction of consumer spending and debt to tax rebates—evidence from consumer credit data. *J. Polit. Econ.* 115(6):986–1019

Agarwal S, Mazumder B. 2013. Cognitive abilities and household financial decision making. *Am. Econ. J. Appl. Econ.* 5(1):193–207

Agarwal S, Qian W. 2014. Consumption and debt response to unanticipated income shocks: evidence from a natural experiment in Singapore. *Am. Econ. Rev.* 104(12):4205–30

Agarwal S, Rosen RJ, Yao V. 2016. Why do borrowers make mortgage refinancing mistakes? *Manag. Sci.* 62(12):3494–509

Agarwal S, Skiba PM, Tobacman J. 2009. Payday loans and credit cards: new liquidity and credit scoring puzzles? *Am. Econ. Rev.* 99(2):412–17

Akerlof GA, Yellen JL. 1985. A near-rational model of the business cycle, with wage and price inertia. *Q. J. Econ.* 100(Suppl.):823–38

Amromin G. 2003. Household portfolio choices in taxable and tax-deferred accounts: another puzzle? *Eur. Finance Rev.* 7(3):547–82

Andersen S, Campbell JY, Nielsen KM, Ramadorai T. 2015. *Inattention and inertia in household finance: evidence from the Danish mortgage market.* NBER Work. Pap. 21386, Cambridge, MA

Andersson F, Chomsisengphet S, Glennon D, Li F. 2013. The changing pecking order of consumer defaults. *J. Money Credit Bank.* 45(23):251–75

Arnberg S, Barslund M. 2014. *The crowding-out effect of mandatory labour market pension schemes on private savings: evidence from renters in Denmark.* Work. Doc. 390, Cent. Eur. Policy Stud., Brussels

Attanasio OP, DeLeire TC. 1994. *IRAs and household saving revisited: some new evidence.* NBER Work. Pap. 4900, Cambridge, MA

Ausubel LM. 1991. The failure of competition in the credit card market. *Am. Econ. Rev.* 81(1):50–81

Badarinza C, Campbell JY, Ramadorai T. 2017. What calls to arms? International evidence on interest rates and the choice of adjustable-rate mortgages. *Manag. Sci.* In press

Bailey M, Cao R, Kuchler T, Stroebel J. 2016. *Social networks and housing markets.* NBER Work. Pap. 22258, Cambridge, MA

Barr M, Mullainathan S, Shafir E. 2009. The case for behaviorally informed regulation. In *New Perspectives on Regulation*, ed. D Moss, J Cisternino, pp. 25–62. Cambridge, MA: Tobin Proj.

Benjamin DJ. 2003. Does 401(k) eligibility increase saving?: evidence from propensity score subclassification. *J. Public Econ.* 87(5–6):1259–90

Bertaut CC, Haliassos M, Reiter M. 2009. Credit card debt puzzles and debt revolvers for self-control. *Rev. Finance* 13(4):657–92

Beshears J, Choi JJ, Laibson D, Madrian BC. 2017. Does front-loading taxation increase savings? Evidence from Roth 401(k) introductions. *J. Public Econ.* 151:84–95

Bhutta N, Dokko JK, Shan H. 2010. *The depth of negative equity and mortgage default decisions.* Work. Pap. 2010–35, Finance Econ. Discuss. Ser., Fed. Reserve Board, Washington, DC

Bostic R, Chomsisengphet S, Engel K, McCoy P, Pennington-Cross A, Wachter S. 2012. Mortgage product substitution and state anti-predatory lending laws: better loans and better borrowers? *Atl. Econ. J.* 40(3):273–94

Botsch M, Malmendier U. 2015. *Inflation experiences and contract choice—evidence from residential mortgages.* Work Pap., Bowdoin Coll.

Brady PJ, Canner GB, Maki DM. 2000. The effects of recent mortgage refinancing. *Fed. Reserve Bull.* 2000:441–50

Campbell JY. 2006. Household finance. *J. Finance* 61(4):1553–604

Campbell JY. 2013. Mortgage market design. *Rev. Finance* 17(1):1–33

Campbell JY. 2016. Restoring rational choice: the challenge of consumer financial regulation. *Am. Econ. Rev. Pap. Proc.* 106(5):1–30

Campbell JY, Cocco JF. 2003. Household risk management and optimal mortgage choice. *Q. J. Econ.* 118(4):1449–94

Campbell JY, Cocco JF. 2015. A model of mortgage default. *J. Finance* 70(4):1495–554

Campbell JY, Jackson HE, Madrian BC, Tufano P. 2011. Consumer financial protection. *J. Econ. Perspect.* 25(1):91–114

Canner GB, Dynan KE, Passmore W. 2002. Mortgage refinancing in 2001 and early 2002. *Fed. Reserve Bull.* 2002:469–81

Canner GB, Elliehausen GE. 2013. Consumer experiences with credit cards. *Fed. Reserve Bull.* 2013:1–36

Chetty R, Friedman JN, Leth-Petersen S, Nielsen TH, Olsen T. 2014. Active versus passive decisions and crowd-out in retirement savings accounts: evidence from Denmark. *Q. J. Econ.* 129(3):1141–219

Choi JJ, Laibson D, Madrian BC. 2011. $100 bills on the sidewalk: suboptimal investment in 401(k) plans. *Rev. Econ. Stat.* 93(3):748–63

Choi JJ, Laibson D, Madrian BC, Metrick A. 2001. *Defined contribution pensions: plan rules, participant decisions, and the path of least resistance.* NBER Work. Pap. 8655, Cambridge, MA

Dammon RM, Spatt CS, Zhang HH. 2004. Optimal asset location and allocation with taxable and tax-deferred investing. *J. Finance* 59(3):999–1037

DellaVigna S, Malmendier U. 2004. Contract design and self-control: theory and evidence. *Q. J. Econ.* 119(2):353–402

Deng Y, Quigley JM, Van Order R. 2000. Mortgage terminations, heterogeneity and the exercise of mortgage options. *Econometrica* 68(2):275–307

Duflo E, Saez E. 2003. The role of information and social interactions in retirement plan decisions: evidence from a randomized experiment. *Q. J. Econ.* 118(3):815–42

Elul R, Souleles NS, Chomsisengphet S, Glennon D, Hunt R. 2010. What "triggers" mortgage default? *Am. Econ. Rev.* 100(2):490–94

Engel KC, McCoy PA. 2001. A tale of three markets: the law and economics of predatory lending. *Tex. L. Rev.* 80:1255–381

Feinberg RA. 1986. Credit cards as spending facilitating stimuli: a conditioning interpretation. *J. Consumer Res.* 13(3):348–56

Fernandes D, Lynch JG, Netemeyer RG. 2014. Financial literacy, financial education, and downstream financial behaviors. *Manag. Sci.* 60(8):1861–83

FRBNY (Fed. Reserve Bank N.Y.). 2016. *Quarterly report on household debt and credit, May 2016.* Res. Stat. Group, FRBNY, New York

Gabaix X, Laibson D. 2006. Shrouded attributes, consumer myopia, and information suppression in competitive markets. *Q. J. Econ.* 121(2):505–40

Gale WG, Scholz JK. 1994. Intergenerational transfers and the accumulation of wealth. *J. Econ. Perspect.* 8(4):145–60

Gelber AM. 2011. How do 401(k)s affect saving? Evidence from changes in 401(k) eligibility. *Am. Econ. J. Econ. Policy* 3(4):103–22

Gerardi K, Goette L, Meier S. 2013. Numerical ability predicts mortgage default. 110(28):11267–71

Greenspan A, Kennedy J. 2008. Sources and uses of equity extracted from homes. *Oxf. Rev. Econ. Policy* 24(1):120–44

Grinblatt M, Keloharju M. 2001. How distance, language, and culture influence stockholdings and trades. *J. Finance* 56(3):1053–73

Gross DB, Souleles NS. 2002a. An empirical analysis of personal bankruptcy and delinquency. *Rev. Financ. Stud.* 15(1):319–47

Gross DB, Souleles NS. 2002b. Do liquidity constraints and interest rates matter for consumer behavior? Evidence from credit card data. *Q. J. Econ.* 117(1):149–85

Gurun UG, Matvos G, Seru A. 2016. Advertising expensive mortgages. *J. Finance* 71(5):2371–416

Heidhues P, Kőszegi B. 2010. Exploiting naïvete about self-control in the credit market. *Am. Econ. Rev.* 100(5):2279–303

Hilgert MA, Hogarth JM, Beverly SG. 2003. Household financial management: the connection between knowledge and behavior. *Fed. Reserve Bull.* 2003:309–22

Hirschman EC. 1979. Differences in consumer purchase behavior by credit card payment system. *J. Consumer Res.* 6(1):58–66

Hong H, Kubik JD, Stein JC. 2004. Social interaction and stock market participation. *J. Finance* 59(1):137–63

Hong H, Kubik JD, Stein JC. 2005. Thy neighbor's portfolio: word-of-mouth effects in the holdings and trades of money managers. *J. Finance* 60(6):2801–24

Keys BJ, Pope DG, Pope JC. 2016. Failure to refinance. *J. Financ. Econ.* 122(3):482–99

Korniotis GM, Kumar A. 2011. Do older investors make better investment decisions? *Rev. Econ. Stat.* 93(1):244–65

Korniotis GM, Kumar A. 2013. Do portfolio distortions reflect superior information or psychological biases? *J. Financ. Quant. Anal.* 48(1):1–45

Kuchler T. 2015. *Sticking to your plan: empirical evidence on the role of present bias for credit card debt paydown*. Work. Pap., Stern Sch. Bus., N.Y. Univ.

Kuchler T, Zafar B. 2015. *Personal experiences and expectations about aggregate outcomes*. Staff Rep. 748, Fed. Reserve Bank N.Y., New York

Kumar A. 2009. Who gambles in the stock market? *J. Finance* 64(4):1889–933

Kumar A, Lim SS. 2008. How do decision frames influence the stock investment choices of individual investors? *Manag. Sci.* 54(6):1052–64

Laibson D. 1997. Golden eggs and hyperbolic discounting. *Q. J. Econ.* 112(2):443–78

Laibson D, Repetto A, Tobacman J. 2003. A debt puzzle. In *Knowledge, Information, and Expectations in Modern Macroeconomics*, ed. P Aghion, R Frydman, J Stiglitz, M Woodford, pp. 228–66. Princeton, NJ: Princeton Univ. Press

Lehnert A, Maki D. 2007. Consumption, debt, and portfolio choice: testing the effects of bankruptcy law. In *Household Credit Usage*, ed. S Agarwal, BW Ambrose, pp. 55–76. New York: Palgrave Macmillan

Lusardi A, Mitchell OS, Curto V. 2009. *Financial literacy among the young: evidence and implications for consumer policy*. Work. Pap. 91, Cent. Res. Pensions Welf. Policies, Turin, Italy

Madrian B, Shea DF. 2001. The power of suggestion: inertia in 401(k) participation and savings behavior. *Q. J. Econ.* 116(4):1149–87

Malmendier U, Nagel S. 2016. Learning from inflation experiences. *Q. J. Econ.* 131(1):53–87

Meier S, Sprenger C. 2010. Present-biased preferences and credit card borrowing. *Am. Econ. J. Appl. Econ.* 2(1):193–210

Miravete EJ. 2003. Choosing the wrong calling plan? Ignorance and learning. *Am. Econ. Rev.* 93(1):297–310

Odean T. 1998. Volume, volatility, price, and profit when all traders are above average. *J. Finance* 53(6):1887–934

Parker J. 2015. *Why don't households smooth consumption? Evidence from a 25 million dollar experiment*. NBER Work. Pap. 21369, Cambridge, MA

Perry VG, Morris MD. 2005. Who is in control? The role of self-perception, knowledge, and income in explaining consumer financial behavior. *J. Consumer Aff.* 39(2):299–313

Posner E, Weyl EG. 2013. Benefit-cost analysis for financial regulation. *Am. Econ. Rev.* 103(3):393–97

Prelec D, Loewenstein G. 1998. The red and the black: mental accounting of savings and debt. *Mark. Sci.* 17(1):4–28

Prelec D, Simester D. 2001. Always leave home without it: a further investigation of the credit-card effect on willingness to pay. *Mark. Lett.* 12(1):5–12

Puri M, Robinson DT. 2007. Optimism and economic choice. *J. Financ. Econ.* 86(1):71–99

Raghubir P, Srivastava J. 2008. Monopoly money: the effect of payment coupling and form on spending behavior. *J. Exp. Psychol. Appl.* 14(3):213–25

Shefrin HM, Statman M. 1993. Behavioral aspects of the design and marketing of financial products. *Financ. Manag.* 22(2):123–34

Shefrin HM, Thaler RH. 1988. The behavioural life-cycle hypothesis. *Econ. Inq.* 26(4):609–43

Shoven JB, Sialm C. 2004. Asset location in tax-deferred and conventional savings accounts. *J. Public Econ.* 88(1–2):23–38

Shui H, Ausubel LM. 2004. *Time inconsistency in the credit card market*. Presented at Annu. Utah Winter Finance Conf., 14th, June 7

Soman D. 2001. Effects of payment mechanism on spending behavior: the role of rehearsal and immediacy of payments. *J. Consumer Res.* 27(4):460–74

Soman D. 2003. The effect of payment transparency on consumption: quasiexperiments from the field. *Mark. Lett.* 14(3):173–83

Stango V, Zinman J. 2016. Borrowing high versus borrowing higher: price dispersion and shopping behavior in the U.S. credit card market. *Rev. Financ. Stud.* 29(4):979–1006

Stephens M. 2006. Paycheque receipt and the timing of consumption. *Econ. J.* 116(513):680–701

Stephens M. 2008. The consumption response to predictable changes in discretionary income: evidence from the repayment of vehicle loans. *Rev. Econ. Stat.* 90(2):241–52

Telyukova IA. 2013. Household need for liquidity and the credit card debt puzzle. *Rev. Econ. Stud.* 80(3):1148–77

Thaler RH, Benartzi S. 2004. Save More Tomorrow™: using behavioral economics to increase employee saving. *J. Polit. Econ.* 112(S1):S164–87

Tversky A, Kahneman D. 1986. Rational choice and the framing of decisions. *J. Bus.* 59(4):S251–78

Venti SF, Wise DA. 1987. IRAs and saving. In *The Effects of Taxation on Capital Accumulation*, ed. M Feldstein, pp. 7–52. Chicago: NBER/Univ. Chicago Press

Venti SF, Wise DA. 1988. The determinants of IRA contributions and the effect of limit changes. In *Pensions in the U.S. Economy*, ed. Z Bodie, JB Shoven, DA Wise, pp. 9–52. Chicago: NBER/Univ. Chicago Press

Wang J, Keys B. 2014. *Perverse nudges: minimum payments and debt paydown in consumer credit cards*. Meet. Pap. 323, Soc. Econ. Dyn., Stony Brook, NY

Zhang XF. 2006. Information uncertainty and stock returns. *J. Finance* 61(1):105–37

Zinman J. 2009. Debit or credit? *J. Bank. Finance* 33(2):358–66

Zinman J. 2014. *Household debt: facts, puzzles, theories, and policies*. NBER Work. Pap. 20496, Cambridge, MA

Mutual Funds in Equilibrium

Jonathan B. Berk[1,2] and Jules H. van Binsbergen[2,3]

[1]Graduate School of Business, Stanford University, Stanford, California 94305; email: jbberk@stanford.edu

[2]National Bureau of Economic Research, Cambridge, Massachusetts 02138

[3]Wharton School, University of Pennsylvania, Philadelphia, Pennsylvania 19104; email: julesv@wharton.upenn.edu

Annu. Rev. Financ. Econ. 2017. 9:147–67

First published as a Review in Advance on September 15, 2017

The *Annual Review of Financial Economics* is online at financial.annualreviews.org

https://doi.org/10.1146/annurev-financial-110716-032454

Copyright © 2017 by Annual Reviews.
All rights reserved

JEL codes: G11, G20, G23, J24, J31

Keywords

skill, value added, alpha, rational expectations, returns to scale

Abstract

Historically, the literature on money management has inconsistently applied the rational expectations equilibrium concept. We explain why and summarize developments in the money management literature that do apply this concept correctly. We demonstrate that the rational expectations equilibrium approximates the observed equilibrium in the money management space at least as well as it does in the stock market. Recent work reveals that there is little support for the common conclusion that, as a group, investors in the money management space are naive and that mutual fund managers are charlatans. Even today, equilibrium thinking is not nearly as prevalent in mutual fund research as it is in the rest of asset pricing. This state of play provides a multitude of opportunities for future research in the area.

1. INTRODUCTION

The introduction of the rational expectations equilibrium framework was one of the key intellectual insights that has defined modern financial economics. The idea that the price of a stock adjusts to ensure that the expected excess return of the stock (i.e., the expected return in excess of the risk-free rate) is solely a function of its risk dominates how the field teaches and thinks about stock prices and returns. Often termed the efficient market hypothesis, this idea is commonplace in the finance literature today. In fact, one would be hard-pressed to find a financial economist who does not appreciate the implication of the rational expectations assumption on the behavior of stock prices.

In this article, we evaluate the state of the investment management literature by assessing to what degree the same equilibrium thinking has penetrated that literature. What we show is that, until recently, the penetration was slight. Not correctly applying the rational expectations paradigm has been costly. For years this literature has been caught in a quagmire of seemingly contradictory results. Much of this confusion persists even today.

Until recently, many financial economists maintained a rather schizophrenic view of investors. When investors invest directly in stocks, the widely accepted view is that the rational expectations equilibrium so closely approximates the actual equilibrium that changes in stock prices in reaction to news can be used as evidence in a court of law as a measure of the value of that news. However, when investors invest indirectly in stocks through mutual funds, the generally accepted view was that, in this market, investors are naive. Consequently, according to this view, they choose to invest almost exclusively in investments with negative net present value (NPV) (Malkiel 1995, Carhart 1997, Fama & French 2010). Furthermore, investor naiveté is so dominant that the market does not equilibrate, so returns reflect things other than risk; in particular, returns reflect managerial skill (or lack thereof). Moreover, because fund flows into mutual funds are known to be highly predictable on the basis of past performance, but past performance has little or no predictability for future performance, researchers concluded that mutual fund investors acted on information that was worthless, which the literature has named return chasing. What is particularly perplexing about this dichotomous view of investors is that there is substantial overlap in the investors in both markets.

In the past 10 years, many of these apparent puzzles in the money management literature have been resolved by applying the rational expectations equilibrium concept consistently in the two markets (Berk & Green 2004, Berk & van Binsbergen 2015). In this article, we review these developments and show that the rational expectations equilibrium approximates the observed equilibrium in the money management space at least as well as it does in the stock market. Moreover, we show that the prior conclusions—that investors in the money management space are entirely naive and that mutual fund managers are all charlatans—are incorrect and result from inconsistently applying the rational expectations equilibrium concept. When the concept is applied correctly, empirical tests reveal that there is in fact little support for either conclusion.

2. BACKGROUND

Ironically, there is a close relationship between how the rational expectations paradigm came to dominate the way financial economists think about stock returns and how they thought about money management returns. For this reason, we begin by briefly reviewing the history of how the paradigm developed.

Although the equilibrium concept was first proposed by John Muth (1961), it was popularized in financial economics in a series of articles by Eugene Fama (1965, 1970, 1976) and became known as the efficient market hypothesis. An important, and much emphasized, implication of the rational expectations equilibrium is that, in such an equilibrium, the quality of a firm's actions and decisions cannot be measured by the expected return subsequent to the action or decision. Because investors compete with each other for attractive investment opportunities, the price of the attractive stocks (and bonds) is bid up to reflect the successfulness of the firm. That is, investors reward a successful firm with a high market capitalization, not a high expected return going forward.

Instead of debating the theoretical point, the literature quickly shifted to empirically testing whether it is possible to find deviations in the data from the rational expectations equilibrium. Whereas there is little consensus in the literature as to whether prices reflect all (publicly) available information, there is widespread agreement that, at a minimum, prices reveal a substantial fraction of the information, making the cross-sectional distribution of firm size (as measured by market capitalization) a much better measure of firms' success than the cross-sectional distribution of subsequent returns. The extent to which this idea has become widely accepted can be gauged by the fact that the change in value of a company upon the release of public information is admissible in a court of law as evidence of the value of the information itself. Put differently, it is widely accepted today that the main implication of the rational expectations paradigm is that the impact of information on a firm is measured by the change in value that results instantaneously when the information is released and not by the expected returns going forward after the information is released.

Although the rational expectations paradigm came to dominate the pricing of financial assets, it had little influence on the pricing of a closely related financial product, the mutual fund. In that literature, exactly the opposite paradigm prevailed. In analyzing the behavior of mutual funds, researchers ignored the total size of the fund and instead used the future realized return as the measure of the quality of the fund. The two paradigms have radically different predictions, so the conclusions of the literatures about the value of information were radically different. Stock price reactions were viewed as highly informative, whereas changes in mutual fund sizes were deemed random and uninformative. Because mutual fund investors caused these random changes by responding to returns, they were deemed naive return chasers. In addition, researchers found that, on average, mutual funds did not deliver extra returns to their investors; i.e., there was no outperformance, which was interpreted as implying that there was no information in mutual fund returns, leading to the widely accepted perception that mutual fund managers lacked skill.

Before we examine the implications of consistently applying the rational expectations paradigm to both kinds of financial products, it is worthwhile to consider why financial economists schizophrenically applied different concepts to two closely related investment products. We believe the answer lies in the original work that argued for using the rational expectations equilibrium concept to price stocks (Fama 1965, Malkiel 1995). In arguing for the rational expectations paradigm, researchers took the position that stock prices impound all information. Under this assumption, no agent should be able to predict future performance, so no agent should be able to make money picking stocks. To demonstrate the empirical validity of this position, they used the performance of mutual funds. They argued that because mutual funds did not deliver positive net alpha to their investors, mutual fund managers lacked stock-picking skill. The implication they drew from this evidence was that if even the professionals who claimed to have the ability to pick stocks could not, stock prices must indeed impound all information. However, this argument inconsistently uses the rational expectations paradigm. By assuming that the rational expectations equilibrium described stock markets but not the equilibrium in money management, these researchers used the net alpha to measure stock-picking ability and thus incorrectly concluded that there was no value to additional information other than what was already impounded in prices. Once this inconsistency was put in place, it persisted, resulting in financial economists inconsistently applying the paradigm in the two literatures.

Just as in stock markets, in mutual funds, investors also compete for attractive investment opportunities. In this case, the attractive investment opportunities are skilled fund managers (rather than skilled firm managers) and the information of relevance is the degree to which mutual fund managers can successfully pick stocks. There is, however, an important difference between the two markets. Unlike stock markets, in the money management market, the price is fixed. That is, regardless of how skilled the manager who manages the fund is, when an investor invests in a mutual fund, the price the investor pays for the fund is always the market value of the fund's underlying assets. What this implies is that the market does not equilibrate through prices, but rather it equilibrates in quantities (i.e., fund size). Other than that difference, the rational expectations equilibrium has identical implications across the two markets. The size of the fund measures the quality of the manager, and the expected return of the fund measures its risk.

To understand how the mutual fund market equilibrates, take a manager that delivers positive average risk-adjusted returns (net alphas) to investors. Investors soon find out about this manager and compete for that extra return by showering the manager with additional money. The size of the fund thus increases, and, because the manager's investment ideas are finite, eventually the additional money cannot be put to productive use. This lowers the return the manager makes until investors no longer receive an extra return (i.e., the net alpha falls to zero). At this point the flows stop because investors no longer face an attractive investment opportunity.

In the rational expectations equilibrium, competition between investors ensures that the expected risk-adjusted excess return to investors (the net alpha) is zero, implying that it no more measures the quality of a mutual fund manager than the expected return of a stock measures the quality of a firm manager. For stocks, the equilibrium is reached by bidding up the price of a successful firm, thereby lowering the expected return to its equilibrium level, whereas for mutual funds, the equilibrium is reached by increasing the size of the fund. As is the case for stocks, the cross-sectional distribution of mutual fund success is predominantly reflected in the cross-sectional distribution of fund size as opposed to the distribution of risk-adjusted excess returns to investors (net alpha). Just as with stocks, more skilled managers manage larger funds, less skilled managers manage (very) small funds, and they all make comparable net alphas close to zero.

In stock markets, the rational expectations paradigm is often tested by assessing the extent to which future returns are predictable given a news announcement. This predictability provides evidence of the competitiveness of stock markets and the rationality of investors. Nobody argues that it is informative about the quality of firm management. The same logic applies in the mutual fund space. If net alphas are not zero, we learn something about the rational expectations of investors and the competition they face.

Theoretical models in economics are particularly useful if they can match moments in the data that they were not designed to explain. Rational expectations models in mutual funds have performed remarkably well in this regard, producing several predictions that the baseline model (Berk & Green 2004) was not calibrated to. For example, the equilibrium arguments of Berk & Green (2004) can be successfully employed to explain the behavior of closed-end funds (Berk & Stanton 2007) and to understand the role of firms in the mutual fund space (Berk, van Binsbergen & Liu 2017). Finally, the insight has been successfully applied to infer which risk model investors are using. Berk & van Binsbergen (2016) and Barber, Huang & Odean (2016) find, using mutual fund data, that the capital asset pricing model (CAPM) best explains investor behavior, and Blocher & Molyboga (2017) confirm these findings using hedge fund data.

3. THE RATIONAL EXPECTATIONS EQUILIBRIUM

Consider the following simple model of mutual fund management (Berk & Green 2004). Let us start with a mutual fund manager who can generate a gross alpha (the alpha before fees have been taken out) that depends on the amount of invested capital, q, equal to

$$\alpha^g(q) = a - bq. \tag{1}$$

In words, the manager extracts from financial markets an extra amount a on the first cent managed. Because the manager has a finite supply of investment ideas and invests his or her best ideas first, the extra amount decreases at a rate b for every additional dollar the manager invests.[1] The total dollar amount this manager extracts from financial markets, which we term the value added, is the product of the gross alpha and assets under management (AUM):

$$V(q) \equiv q\alpha^g(q) = q(a - bq). \tag{2}$$

If we assume that the manager's objective is to maximize value added, then the optimal amount to invest maximizes this quadratic function. Taking first-order conditions with respect to q and setting this equal to zero gives

$$q^* = \frac{a}{2b}, \tag{3}$$

implying that gross alpha at the optimum is

$$\alpha^g(q^*) = \frac{a}{2}. \tag{4}$$

The value added at the maximum is given by

$$V^* = \frac{a^2}{4b}. \tag{5}$$

Figure 1 plots the value added (V) and gross alpha (α^g) as a function of q. **Figure 1** also shows the value added and gross alpha at the optimal amount of money. Before we consider the investor's problem, it is worth comparing this manager to a manager of lower quality. Consider manager 2. Manager 2 runs out of good ideas more quickly than manager 1. That is, whereas manager 2 makes the same extra return on the first cent (equal to a), the rate at which the return deteriorates is twice as large and is equal to $2b$ instead of b. In **Figure 2**, we plot the gross alpha of both managers, as well as their value added. The optimal investment amount for manager 2 is twice as small as that for manager 1 and is equal to $a/4b$. Because the gross alpha at the optimum is independent of the parameter b, both managers have the same gross alpha, equal to $a/2$ at the optimum. Hence, gross alpha is not correlated with skill. If we were to use gross alpha as a measure of skill, we would come to the (wrong) conclusion that both managers are equally skilled. This result follows only from the fact that, if there are decreasing returns to scale, returns are not a good measure of (or proxy for) value, and no assumptions related to rational expectations are required.

We now turn to investors and assume that they have rational expectations. A rational investor will chase any investment opportunity with positive NPV. This implies that all assets earn an expected return commensurate with the risk of the asset. As a consequence, all funds must have net alphas of zero:

$$\alpha^n(q) = \alpha^g(q) - f = a - bq - f. \tag{6}$$

If manager 1 picks his or her fee, f, equal to

$$f = \frac{a}{2},$$

[1] For ease of exposition, we assume that the gross alpha is a linear function of fund size q, but the arguments presented do not rely on this linearity.

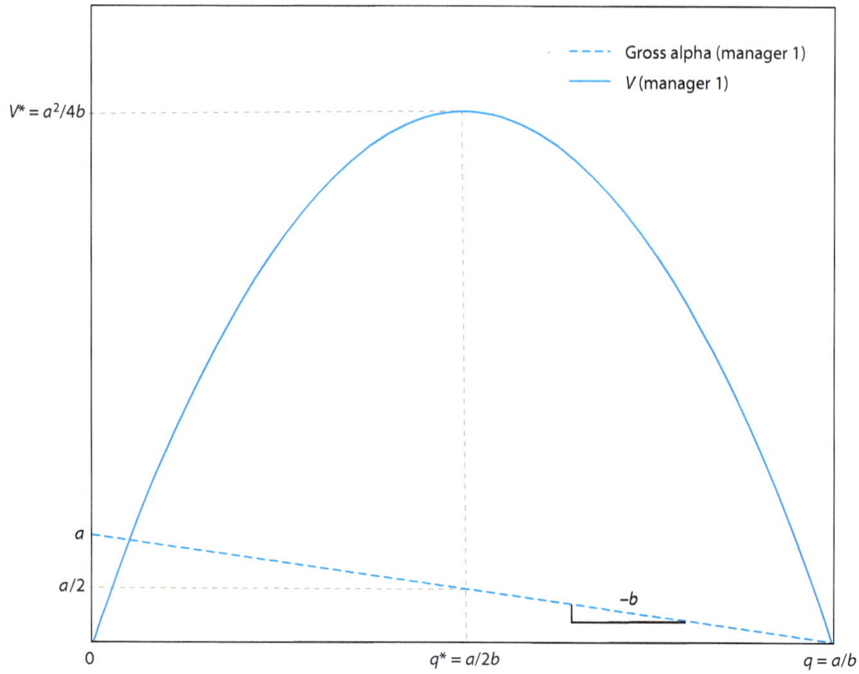

Figure 1

Size, value added, and gross alpha. The graph shows the relationship between size and value added/gross alpha.

investors will choose to invest $q^* = a/2b$ in the fund. As a consequence, the fund's net alpha will be zero and the market will be in equilibrium. If manager 2 picks the same fee, in this case the equilibrium investment is $a/4b$. That is, although both managers have the same gross (and net) alpha, manager 1 has twice as much money in equilibrium as manager 2. The total amount of money manager 1 extracts from markets is $V^* = \alpha^g(q^*)q^* = (a/2) \times (a/2b) = a^2/4b$, which is twice the amount that manager 2 extracts, $(a/2) \times (a/4b) = a^2/8b$, reflecting the fact that manager 1 is twice as skilled.

Before we turn to the dynamics, it is worth emphasizing the essential characteristics of this equilibrium. Note that net alphas are always zero, so net alphas are not informative of managerial ability. Similarly, the gross alpha is also uninformative. These return measures fail to measure skill for the same reason that we teach our students to use present-value measures in place of internal rate of return (IRR) measures when making an investment decision. These days, nearly all textbooks in finance point out that IRR measures are flawed because they do not properly take into account the scale of the project. As we have already seen, the scale of a mutual fund is an endogenous quantity that is determined in equilibrium. Therefore, just as the IRR does not help us rank investment projects (we need the present value for that), the alpha does not help us rank managers. A necessary (but not sufficient) condition under which return measures can be used to make an investment decision is that the investment opportunity under consideration be infinitely scalable. Although such an assumption might be a reasonable approximation when considering a very small investor in a large market, one would be hard-pressed to argue that mutual fund managers fit this description.

Although most financial economists would likely agree that it is unnecessary to test the hypothesis that opportunities with positive NPV are in infinite supply in the economy as a whole,

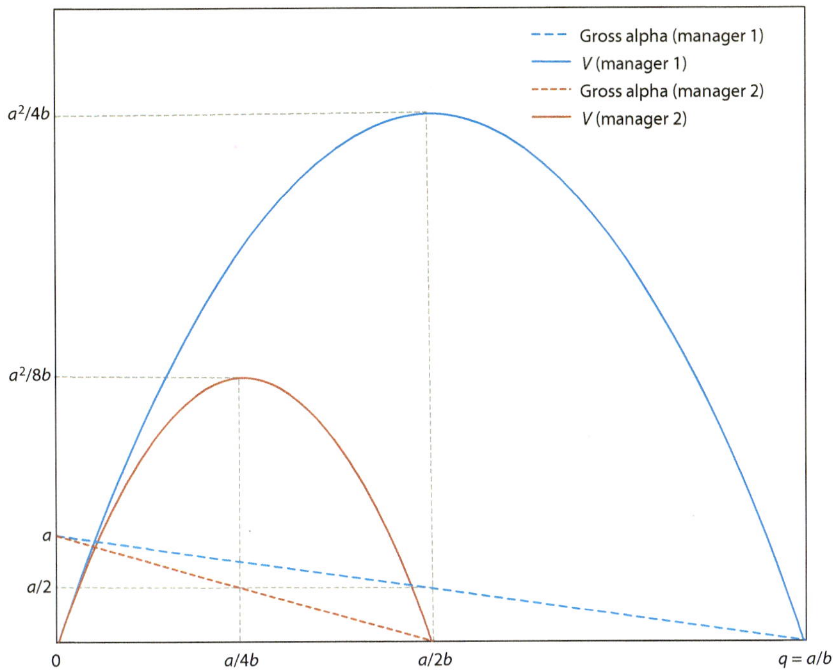

Figure 2

Size, value added, and gross alpha. The graph shows the relationship between size and value added/gross alpha for two managers. Manager 1 is more skilled than manager 2, although both make the same gross alpha on the first cent they invest. Manager 1 has an investment strategy that is more scalable than that of manager 2. That is, the parameter b representing decreasing returns to scale is higher for manager 2 than for manager 1.

the mutual fund literature has nevertheless spent considerable effort testing this hypothesis in the mutual fund space. Not surprisingly, the literature has come to the conclusion that it is unrealistic to assume that mutual funds face constant returns to scale. There is now mounting evidence that, all else equal, the return performance of a fund deteriorates with fund size (Pastor, Stambaugh & Taylor 2014, 2015).

Thus far, the model we have derived is restrictive because we have assumed that both managers and investors know the skill level (production function) of the manager. In reality, neither a nor b is likely to be known to either investors or managers. For simplicity, assume that managers and investors are symmetrically informed about the production function, and let $a_t = E_t[a]$ and $b_t = E_t[b]$ denote the conditional expectations of the parameters in the production function. Clearly, both a_t and b_t will change over time as the participants learn. Consequently, the optimal amount of capital changes, which, in the above equilibrium, would require managers to continuously change their fees to ensure that investors would be willing to invest the optimal amount of capital. This equilibrium dynamic is counterfactual. Fees do not respond to information; fund size does.

The key to understanding how managers maximize the value they extract without continuously adjusting their fees is to consider the manager's problem. Notice that from the manager's perspective, it is always suboptimal to invest anything other than q^* in active management. Consequently, the manager will continue to invest this amount, regardless of the fee, either by borrowing money if possible (when investors choose to invest less than q^* because the fee is too high) or by indexing the excess money (when investors choose to invest more than q^* because the fee is too low).

Let us explicitly consider the second case. Suppose that the fund size at time t, q_t, is larger than $q_t^* = a_t/2b_t$ because $f < a_t/2$. The optimal strategy for the manager is to put q_t^* into active management and index the difference, $q_t - q_t^*$. By definition, the indexed money earns no alpha, so the equilibrium gross alpha on the whole fund is given by

$$\left(\frac{q_t^*}{q_t}\right)\frac{a_t}{2} + \left(\frac{q_t - q^*}{q_t}\right)0 = \frac{a_t^2}{4q_t b_t}. \qquad 7.$$

In equilibrium, the net alpha of the fund must be zero. Imposing this restriction gives

$$\frac{a_t^2}{4q_t b_t} - f = 0. \qquad 8.$$

The equilibrium size of the fund is thus

$$q_t = \frac{a_t^2}{4fb_t}. \qquad 9.$$

Notice that this dynamic equilibrium, in which fees are fixed, shares an important characteristic with the static equilibrium: In both cases, the gross alpha equals the fee charged and therefore is not a reliable measure of managerial skill. Given that the size of the fund adjusts to ensure that the gross alpha and the fee are equal, it is not appropriate to think about gross alpha and fund size as two independent entities. Because they are related in equilibrium, the size of the fund and the gross alpha (i.e., the fee) are not separately identified by the parameters that determine managerial skill. Their product, however, is uniquely identified by those two parameters: Regardless of the fee the manager chooses, the product of the size of the fund (q) and the equilibrium gross alpha (the fee) equals

$$V_t^* = \frac{a_t^2}{4fb_t} f = \frac{a_t^2}{4q_t b_t} q_t = \frac{a_t^2}{4b_t}. \qquad 10.$$

This product is what we call the value added of the fund. It is the correct way to measure managerial skill because it measures the manager's value added and is a function of only the skill of the manager.

In summary, with indexing and fixed fees, fund size adjusts to ensure that the gross alpha is sufficiently high to cover the manager's fees. There is a wide range of fees that all allow the manager to fully exploit his or her skill and extract the optimal amount of money from financial markets. What this implies is that the fee charged is irrelevant: Managers can choose to charge a high fee and manage a small fund, or charge a low fee and manage a large fund. In both cases, the amount the manager makes and the return the investors earn are the same. Because gross alpha must equal the fee in equilibrium, it too is irrelevant. These insights also shed light on recent developments in the mutual fund market. One common argument is that the large growth in AUM of low-fee mutual funds is a testament to the success of that part of the industry relative to their high-fee counterparts. What the arguments above make clear is that we should expect low-fee funds to be larger even if there is no difference between the skill level of the managers and no difference in the returns that investors earn (i.e., a zero net alpha).

This simple dynamic rational expectations equilibrium is able to explain the important empirical regularities documented in the mutual fund literature, as well as resolve the most important puzzles. Specifically, the fact that the future return performance of a fund is unpredictable follows directly from the rational expectations equilibrium requirement that net alpha always be zero. Fund size, in this equilibrium, continuously adjusts in response to information. One source of information is past returns, so the equilibrium predicts that the flow of funds will respond to past performance. This relation between flow and performance is not evidence of investor suboptimality—quite the contrary. It is evidence of the competitiveness with which investors chase investment opportunities with positive NPV. As we have already mentioned, the model also has new predictions about empirical moments (e.g., value added) that were not identified at the time the model was derived. We review the empirical performance of the model using these moments in Section 6.

Finally, the equilibrium described above teaches another important lesson. Some have argued that investment managers should be more generous to their investors by lowering their fees, thereby giving up a larger part of their performance to their investors. What the equilibrium shows is that it is not the manager's choice of fees that sets the return to investors equal to zero. It is competition between investors for good investment opportunities. The fee is irrelevant to this discussion. The only way a manager can be more generous to his or her investors is if the manager stops accepting money from new investors, thereby favoring old investors over new investors.

4. MEASURING MUTUAL FUND PERFORMANCE

Now that we have explained how the rational expectations equilibrium works in mutual funds, we can turn to a central question in that literature: How is fund performance measured? The answer to this question depends on what we mean by fund performance. Often, what financial economists mean is the performance of investors in the fund: How much better off would the marginal investor be by investing an additional dollar in that fund? In this case, the measure of performance is the fund's net alpha. If, however, the objective is to measure how skilled the fund manager is, then, as we have seen, alpha measures are uninformative. To answer the skill question, we must use the correct measure of fund performance: value added. The unfortunate fact is that, until recently, financial economists have used alpha measures almost exclusively to measure managerial skill, and in doing so have reached the incorrect conclusion that managers are unskilled. As we demonstrate in Section 6, when the correct measure is used, a different picture emerges.

Value added always measures the amount of money extracted from markets regardless of whether the rational expectations paradigm holds. To understand why, notice that

$$V_t = q_t \alpha_t^{\mathrm{g}}(q_t) = q_t \alpha_t^{\mathrm{n}}(q_t) + q_t f,$$

where $\alpha_t^{\mathrm{n}}(q_t)$ is the net alpha of the fund as a function of fund size. The first term in this equation is the amount of money the manager either gives to or takes from investors. The second term is the amount of money the manager takes in compensation. Notice that there is no other source of funds. What this observation implies is that the money the manager takes in compensation can come from one of only two places: It can come either from skill (through stock picking) or from investors (by underperforming). So the sum of what the manager takes in compensation and what the manager either gives or takes from investors must equal the amount of money the manager makes from stock picks. This observation relies only on this budget constraint. It requires no other auxiliary assumptions.

The fact that both the measure of investor performance (net alpha) and the measure of value extracted from financial markets do not depend on any further assumptions implies that they are independent of whatever null hypothesis is assumed. For example, a very common null in the mutual fund literature is that managers have no skill. To reject this null, one must show that value added is positive. Another interesting null is that the rational expectations equilibrium describes the behavior of mutual funds. To reject this null, one would need to show that the net alpha of the fund is nonzero. Finally, one could also test the null that the mutual fund market is perfectly competitive, so all investment opportunities with positive NPV are competed away. To reject this null, one would need to show that the net alpha is positive. In summary, then, the net alpha is informative about investor rationality and the degree of competition in markets. Value added is informative about the skill level of fund managers.

5. BENCHMARKS

The Achilles' heel of the mutual fund literature is how to construct a manager's counterfactual performance absent any skill. Generally, two methods have been applied. The standard practice in financial economics is not to construct the alternative investment opportunity itself, but rather to simply adjust for risk using a risk model. In recent years, the extent to which risk models accurately correct for risk has been subject to extensive debate. In response to this, mutual fund researchers have opted to directly construct the alternative investment opportunity. Although in principle this approach is a sensible way to address the issue of not knowing the correct model of risk, the way this approach is typically implemented in practice replaces one shortcoming with another. What researchers have typically done is assume that investors' next best investment opportunities are spanned by the factor-mimicking portfolios in the Fama–French–Carhart factor specification (Fama & French 1996, Carhart 1997). That is, they have interpreted the factor-mimicking portfolios in these factor specifications as investment opportunities available to investors, rather than risk factors.

There are two reasons why these factor portfolios are not investable opportunities. The first is straightforward. These portfolios do not include transaction costs. In essence, you cannot compare the performance of a fund that incurs transaction costs to a fund that does not. The second issue is more subtle. The factors that are typically used were identified in the late 1980s and 1990s and were popularized by Fama & French (1996) and Carhart (1997). However, most studies include data that begin at least 20 years before those factors were identified. In those earlier years, investors would not have known about these portfolios and obviously could not have invested in them. By using these portfolios to benchmark managers, researchers are effectively evaluating managers in 1970 using 1990s technology. Any manager who, in 1970, knew about the investment opportunities afforded by these portfolios should be given credit for this knowledge and the subsequent outperformance.

By benchmarking managers against noninvestable benchmarks, researchers are effectively handicapping managers. To estimate the size of this handicap, we can evaluate the performance of these noninvestable factor portfolios against a set of passive and investable benchmarks. The most obvious set to use is the set of index funds offered by the Vanguard company. The advantage of using these funds is that they are constructed for the purpose of giving investors the least costly method to diversification. This explicit objective is not shared by alternative benchmarks constructed by companies such as Morningstar. Moreover, Vanguard is not only the market leader offering this service, but also the pioneer in the space. For example, the 11 funds listed in **Table 1** span the set of all index funds offered by the firm. In each case, the Vanguard fund was the first index fund to offer that particular strategy. That means that these funds are natural indicators to use to determine when a strategy becomes widely known to all investors.

It is not uncommon in the mutual fund literature to use style benchmarks that are identified either by the fund itself or by external organizations such as Morningstar. The problem with using these benchmarks is that many funds regularly deviate from the style objectives they report and advertise. By simply projecting each fund's excess return on the excess returns on all available Vanguard index funds, such potential misclassifications are avoided.

Table 2 shows the results of evaluating the performance of each factor-mimicking portfolio using the set of passively managed index funds offered by Vanguard (for details of how the benchmarks are constructed, see Berk & van Binsbergen 2015). Only the market portfolio does

Table 1 Benchmark Vanguard index funds

Fund	Ticker	Asset class	Inception date
S&P 500 index	VFINX	Large-cap blend	August 31, 1976
Extended market index	VEXMX	Mid-cap blend	December 21, 1987
Small-cap index	NAESX	Small-cap blend	January 1, 1990[a]
European stock index	VEURX	International	June 18, 1990
Pacific stock index	VPACX	International	June 18, 1990
Value index	VVIAX	Large-cap value	November 2, 1992
Balanced index	VBINX	Balanced	November 2, 1992
Emerging markets stock index	VEIEX	International	May 4, 1994
Mid-cap index	VIMSX	Mid-cap blend	May 21, 1998
Small-cap growth index	VISGX	Small-cap growth	May 21, 1998
Small-cap value index	VISVX	Small-cap value	May 21, 1998

This table lists the set of Vanguard index funds used to calculate the Vanguard benchmark. The listed ticker is for Investor-class shares, which we use until Vanguard introduced an Admiral class for the fund, and thereafter we use the return on Admiral-class shares (Admiral-class shares have lower fees but require a higher minimum investment).
[a]NAESX was introduced earlier but was originally not an index fund. It was converted to an index fund in late 1989, so the date in the table reflects the first date we included the fund in the benchmark set.

not have a statistically significant positive alpha. The other portfolios returned economically large abnormal returns, from 22 basis points (bp)/month to as much as 70 bp/month for the momentum portfolio. As this portfolio incurs the most transaction costs, it is not surprising that it exhibits the largest outperformance. What **Table 2** shows is that the factor-mimicking portfolios were much better investment opportunities than what was actually available to investors at the time. Given the flaws inherent in using the factor portfolios as benchmarks, we advocate using the Vanguard portfolios instead. We suggest that, to evaluate mutual fund performance, one should construct a fund's benchmark by finding the closest portfolio in the set of Vanguard index funds. That is, if R_t^j is the excess return (over the risk-free rate) earned by investors in the j-th Vanguard index fund at time t, then the benchmark return for fund i is given by

$$R_{it}^{\mathrm{B}} = \sum_{j=1}^{n(t)} \beta_i^j R_t^j, \qquad 11.$$

where $n(t)$ is the total number of index funds offered by Vanguard at time t and β_i^j is obtained from the appropriate linear projection of the i-th active mutual fund onto the set of Vanguard index funds. Using Vanguard index funds as the benchmark recognizes the industrial organization

Table 2 Net alpha of FFC portfolios

	MKT	SMB	HML	UMD
Alpha (bp/month)	2	22	35	70
t-Statistic	0.83	2.80	3.37	3.38
Adjusted R^2	99%	74%	52%	15%

We regress each FFC factor portfolio on the Vanguard benchmark portfolios. This table lists the estimate and t-statistic of the constant term (alpha) of each regression as well as the R^2 of each regression. Table adapted from Berk & van Binsbergen (2015). Abbreviation: bp, basis point.

of the mutual fund industry. The dynamic evolution of active strategies is therefore automatically accounted for. Thus, one can be certain that investors had the opportunity to invest in the funds at the time. In addition, the returns of these funds necessarily include transaction costs. Notice, also, that if we were to use this benchmark to evaluate a Vanguard index fund itself, we would conclude that that fund adds value equal to the dollar value of the fees it charges. Vanguard funds add value because they provide investors with the lowest-cost means to diversification. Consequently, when we use net returns on Vanguard index funds as the benchmark, we are explicitly accounting for the value added of diversification services. Because active funds also provide diversification services, our measure credits them with this value added. Using the gross return on Vanguard index funds as the benchmark measures the value added over and above diversification services; see Berk & van Binsbergen (2015).

Using this benchmark, we can now construct an empirical estimate of net alpha and value added. To construct an estimate of value added, first subtract the realized return of the benchmark from the (gross) realized return of the fund, $R_{it}^{\mathrm{g}} - R_{it}^{\mathrm{B}}$. This quantity is then multiplied by the real size of the fund (AUM adjusted by inflation) at the end of the previous period, $q_{i,t-1}$, to obtain the realized value added between times $t-1$ and t:

$$V_{it} \equiv q_{i,t-1}\left(R_{it}^{\mathrm{g}} - R_{it}^{\mathrm{B}}\right). \tag{12}$$

The time series average of V_{it} measures a fund's value added. Similarly, if R_{it}^{n} is the net return investors in the fund earn (i.e., the return after all fees are taken out), then define

$$\varepsilon_{it} \equiv R_{it}^{\mathrm{n}} - R_{it}^{\mathrm{B}}. \tag{13}$$

The time series average of ε_{it} is an estimate of the fund's net alpha.

6. MANAGERIAL SKILL

We begin describing the results reported by Berk & van Binsbergen (2015). The authors measure the average value added of mutual fund managers over the period 1977–2011 in January 1, 2000, dollars.[2] The results are reported in **Table 3**. The authors find that mutual fund managers are skilled. The average fund adds an economically significant \$140,000/month. There is also large variation across funds. On average, the fund at the 99th percentile generated \$7.82 million/month, and the fund at the 90th percentile generated \$750,000/month. The median fund lost an average of \$20,000/month, and only 43% of funds had positive estimated value added. The main insight is that most managers destroyed value, but, because most of the capital is controlled by skilled managers, as a group, active mutual funds added considerable value.

Successful funds are more likely to survive than unsuccessful funds. Consequently, one can think about the average value added of all mutual funds as an estimate of the ex ante distribution of talent. We can also compute the average V_{it} in the data set without first averaging by funds. Because surviving funds are overrepresented in this mean, we obtain an estimate of the ex post distribution of talent, that is, the average skill of the set of funds actually managing money. Not surprisingly, this estimate is higher. The average fund added \$270,000/month.

Berk & van Binsbergen (2015) also show that managerial skill is persistent. This is demonstrated by first sorting funds into deciles using the skill ratio: the estimated value of a fund's value added divided by its standard error. The skill ratio at any point in time is essentially the t-statistic of the value added estimate measured over the entire history of the fund until that time. Funds in the

[2] Data are available from 1962, but the analysis begins in 1977 because that is the year Vanguard offered its first index fund.

Table 3 Value added ($\hat{S}_i$)

Cross-sectional mean	0.14
Standard error of the cross-sectional mean	0.03
t-Statistic (cross-sectional)	4.57
1st Percentile	−3.60
5th Percentile	−1.15
10th Percentile	−0.59
50th Percentile	−0.02
90th Percentile	0.75
95th Percentile	1.80
99th Percentile	7.82
Percent with less than zero	57.01%
Overall mean	0.27
Standard error of the overall mean	0.05
t-Statistic (overall)	5.74
Number of funds	5,974

For every fund in our database, we estimate the monthly value added, $\hat{S}_i$. The cross-sectional mean, standard error, t-statistic, and percentiles are statistical properties of this distribution. The percent with less than zero is the fraction of the distribution that has value added estimates less than zero. The overall mean, standard error, and t-statistic are computed by computing the average value added in the data set. Means, standard errors, and percentiles are reported as millions of year-2000 dollars/month. Table adapted from Berk & van Binsbergen (2015).

10th (top) decile are funds where we have the most confidence that the actual value added over the sorting period is positive. Similarly, funds in the 1st (bottom) decile are funds where we have the most confidence that the actual value added in the sorting period is negative. The authors then calculate the average value added for the funds in each decile over a specified future horizon. At the end of the horizon, the procedure is repeated until the end of the data set. The procedure is run for time horizons of 3–10 years.

Figure 3 plots the mean as well as the two standard error bounds for each decile for each time horizon. From **Figure 3**, it appears that there is evidence of persistence as far out as 10 years. The point estimate of the average value added of 10th-decile managers is positive at every horizon, and this is always the best-performing decile. The value added estimates are economically large. Although the data are clearly noisy, the average 10th-decile manager adds about $2 million/month.

Figure 4 reports perhaps the most surprising result of Berk & van Binsbergen (2015). It repeats the above analysis, except that, rather than ranking funds by the skill ratio, it ranks funds by managerial compensation at time t: the current size of the fund multiplied by the fee charged. By comparing **Figure 4** to **Figure 3**, one can see that sorting by compensation better predicts future performance. Although the skill ratio does a good job of identifying the highest-skilled managers, it does less well at differentiating mediocre managers. Current compensation is better able to differentiate all managers. Because investors determine compensation (by determining the size of the fund), these results indicate that investors reward managers who are more skilled (on the basis of future performance) with higher compensation today. This means that investors are able to identify better managers ex ante. Indeed, investors appear to use more information to make this decision than what is contained in the skill ratio. Other recent examples of research that documents the rationality of mutual investors include the work of Choi, Kahraman & Mukherjee (2014) and Franzoni & Schmalz (2017).

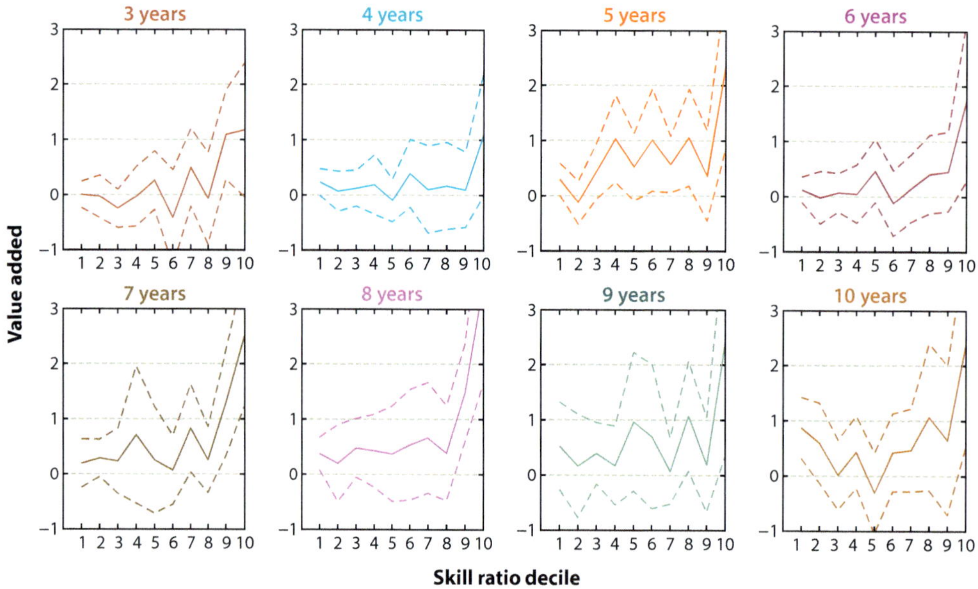

Figure 3

Out-of-sample value added. Each graph displays the average out-of-sample value added, $\hat{S}_i$ (in millions of year-2000 dollars/month), of funds sorted into deciles according to skill ratio over the future horizon indicated. The solid lines indicate the performance of each decile and the dashed lines indicate the two standard error bounds. Figure adapted from Berk & van Binsbergen (2015).

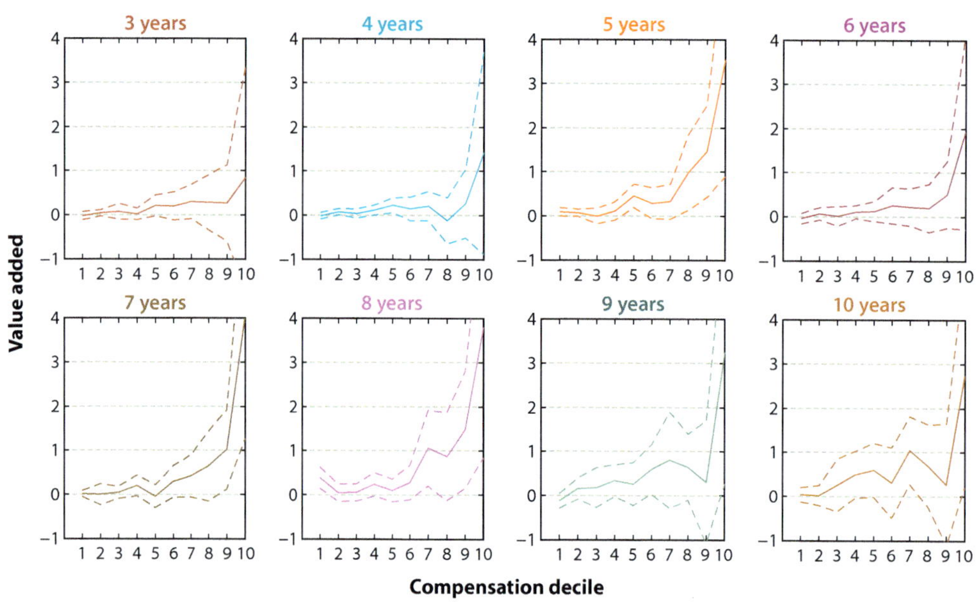

Figure 4

Value added, sorted by compensation. Each graph displays average out-of-sample value added, $\hat{S}_i$ (in millions of year-2000 dollars/month), of funds sorted into deciles on the basis of total compensation (fees × assets under management). The solid lines indicate the performance of each decile and the dashed lines indicate 95% confidence bands (two standard errors from the estimate). Figure adapted from Berk & van Binsbergen (2015).

Table 4 Net alpha (bp/month)

	Full data set		US equity only	
	Vanguard benchmark	FFC factor portfolios	Vanguard benchmark	FFC factor portfolios
Equally weighted	2.74	−3.88	−0.72	−6.70
t-Statistic (equal weighting)	0.73	−1.40	−0.20	−2.66
Value weighted	−0.95	−5.88	−4.68	−8.34
t-Statistic (value weighting)	−0.31	−2.35	−1.58	−3.70
Number of funds	5,974	6,054	2,731	2,811

The table reports the net alpha of two investment strategies: investing \$1 every month by equally weighting over all existing funds and investing \$1 every month by value weighting (on the basis of assets under management) over all existing funds. Abbreviation: bp, basis point.

7. INVESTOR PERFORMANCE REVISITED

Perhaps the most widely cited empirical observation in the mutual fund literature is that investors in active mutual funds earn a negative alpha. The evidence of Berk & van Binsbergen (2015) demonstrates that this observation is an artifact of two implementation choices made in almost all research that studies this question. The first and more important is the one we identified in Section 5: Researchers artificially handicapped funds by benchmarking them to noninvestable strategies. The second is a data snooping bias. Almost all prior research documenting this underperformance dropped more than half of the observations by restricting attention to funds that only invest in US stocks and starting the time series in the early 1980s. We can think of no reason for this data selection procedure.

We begin by estimating the average net alpha by calculating the average ε_{it} across all funds by equally weighting and value weighting the funds. As **Table 4** shows, over this time period, estimated net alpha is not statistically distinguishable from zero. For comparison purposes, the table recalculates these estimates under the two implementation choices made by the literature. Because the factor portfolios can be constructed in 1962, in this case we begin the analysis in 1962. As one would expect, when funds are handicapped by requiring them to outperform a noninvestable benchmark, the net alpha estimate drops. If one then also drops funds that hold international stocks, the net alpha drops again. With both implementation choices, the net alpha estimate is indeed negative and statistically significantly different from zero.

The evidence in **Table 4** is consistent with the rational expectations equilibrium. Importantly, however, that equilibrium imposes further restrictions. It requires that any realized return in excess of the benchmark be unpredictable. **Figure 5** repeats the persistence analysis in the previous section but, instead of reporting value added, it reports net alpha. That is, at the beginning of each horizon, funds are sorted into deciles using the skill ratio and then the weighted average ε_{it} of the decile over the horizon is calculated. From **Figure 5** it is clear that, although value added is highly predictable, net alpha is not predictable. Highly skilled managers are no more likely to deliver a positive net alpha to their investors than less skilled managers.

The overall conclusion is that the evidence is remarkably consistent with the rational expectations equilibrium paradigm. Markets appear to be highly competitive, so that investors do not earn excess returns. By the same token, funds do not underperform on average, so investors appear to rationally allocate the right amount of capital to active management. Skilled managers do exist, but there is large heterogeneity of skill. Investors recognize skill and thus direct capital toward the most skilled managers. Consequently, the most skilled managers manage the largest funds, and

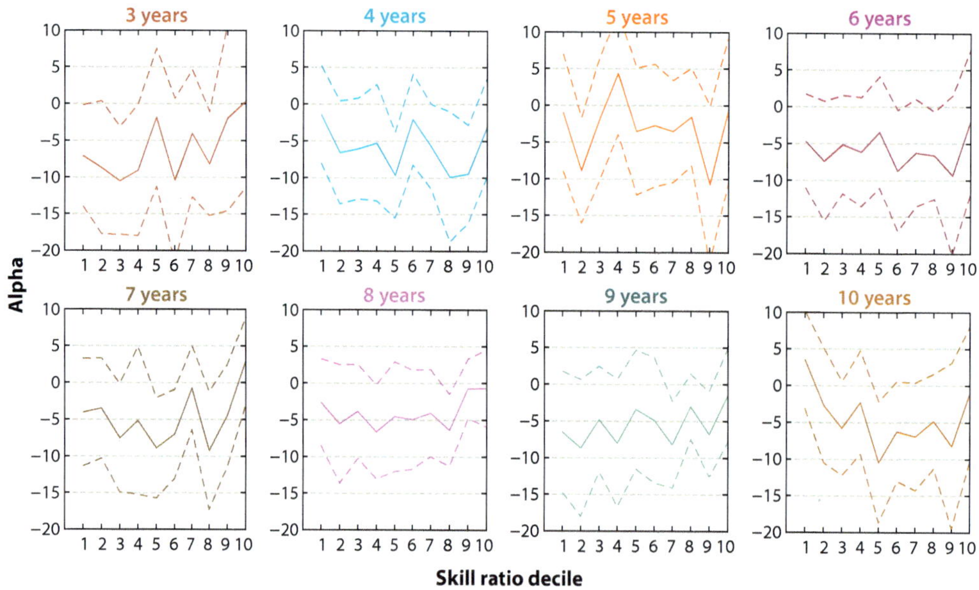

Figure 5

Out-of-sample net alpha. Each graph displays the out-of-sample performance (in bp/month) of funds sorted into deciles according to skill ratio over the future horizon indicated. The solid lines indicate the performance of each decile and the dashed lines indicate 95% confidence bands (two standard errors from the estimate). Figure adapted from Berk & van Binsbergen (2015). Abbreviation: bp, basis point.

manager compensation, which is primarily determined by fund size, predicts future managerial dollar performance.

8. THE STATE OF THE LITERATURE

Given the success of the rational expectations paradigm in explaining the observed equilibrium in mutual funds, a natural question is: How often do financial economists doing research in this area inconsistently apply the paradigm? To get a sense of this, we analyzed how often researchers used alpha measures, rather than value added, to measure skill. We plot, in **Figure 6**, the total number of publications by year in the three leading finance journals (*Journal of Financial Economics*, *Journal of Finance*, and *Review of Financial Studies*) that use alpha measures (usually net alpha and sometimes also gross alpha) to assess managerial skill. The total number since 1995 is 59 papers. Only a handful of very recent papers use value added measures in their study. Several other papers are explicitly interested in research questions related to returns to investors. For those research questions, the net alpha is of course the right measure to use.

9. IMPLICATIONS

The implication of the evidence presented in Sections 6 and 7 is that the same paradigm explains the behavior of stock market investors and mutual fund investors. This insight opens the opportunity for researchers to investigate questions that traditionally have been restricted to stock markets in mutual fund markets. In this section we illustrate the potential gain to knowledge of following this approach by reviewing two articles that test important economic questions using the mutual fund database.

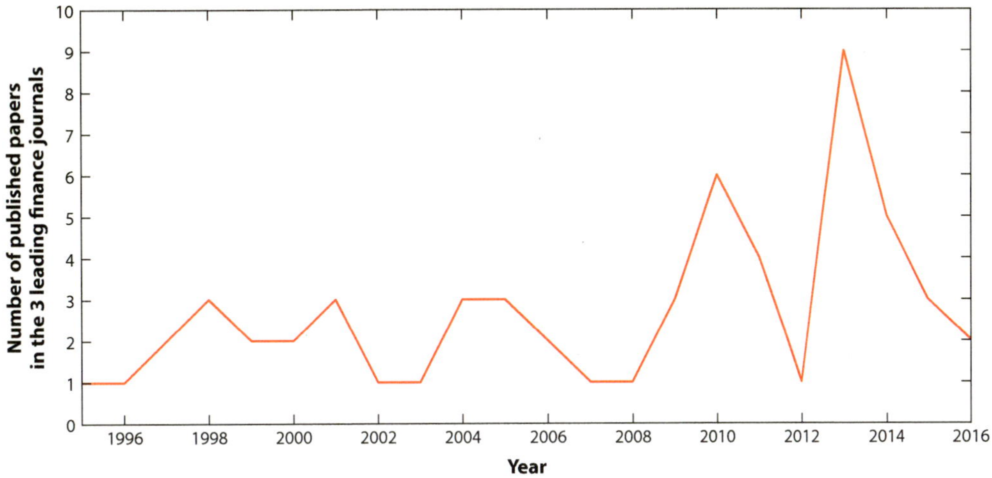

Figure 6

This graph shows the total number of publications by year in the three leading finance journals (*Journal of Financial Economics*, *Journal of Finance*, and *Review of Financial Studies*) that use alpha (usually net alpha and sometimes also gross alpha) to assess managerial skill.

9.1. The Importance of Firms

A central question in corporate finance is why firms exist. The mutual fund industry is an ideal place to study this question for several reasons. First, it is one of the few sectors in the economy where employee productivity is observable. Thus, one can observe the change in employee productivity that results from firm decisions. Second, in a world with perfectly rational players, no information asymmetries, and no other frictions, the role of a mutual fund firm would be irrelevant because investors themselves would efficiently allocate their own capital among managers. That is, for regular firms, outside investors allocate money to the firm as a whole, and only the firm itself allocates that capital within its boundaries. For mutual funds, however, investors can also allocate money within the firm by allocating capital to particular funds. As a consequence, any allocation decision by the firm can in principle be undone by the investors themselves. This helps us define a very clear counterfactual. By observing the change in value added following a personnel decision, we can estimate the value of the decisions and thus provide a lower bound on how much value firm decisions add.

Berk, van Binsbergen & Liu (2017) find that a decision to increase a portfolio manager's AUM leads to an increase in the manager's productivity as measured by value added. Similarly, they find that decisions to reduce managers' responsibilities by taking away assets also lead to increases in subsequent value added. They find that the decision to reallocate capital to a manager adds at least $474,000 per manager per month. By comparing this lower bound to the total value added in the industry, they find that the firm is responsible for at least 30% of the total value added of the average manager. Mutual fund firms appear to add substantial value by intermediating between investors and managers and thereby efficiently matching capital to skill.

The findings of Berk, van Binsbergen & Liu (2017) suggest that mutual fund firms have private information about their managers that investors do not have. Firms use that private information to improve upon investors' capital allocations. Interestingly, the authors find that the value added of managers goes up after a demotion, suggesting that mutual fund executives have a better knowledge of their manager's ability than the managers themselves. This finding is consistent with our assumption in Section 3 that managers do not know their own ability. Finally, firms' private information might also explain the finding, described in Section 6, that compensation better predicts future performance than the skill ratio. By intermediating between investors and managers, firms are able to use their private information to improve capital allocation. Investors, recognizing this skill, invest more money in the firm's funds (something that is also documented by the authors), thereby making fund size (and thus dollar fees) a better predictor of future performance than the information in past returns.

9.2. Evaluation of Risk

Despite half a century of research on the topic, the field of financial economics is far from reaching a consensus on how to adjust for risk. The capital asset pricing model (CAPM), originally derived by Sharpe (1964), Lintner (1965), and Mossin (1966), remains controversial largely because beta does not appear to explain the cross section of asset returns. As a result, in the years since the model was first proposed, financial economists have derived numerous extensions in an attempt to bring the model's predictions in line with the historical evidence. The results of this research have been mixed. Although the extensions appear to perform better than the original model, to a large extent one would not expect otherwise. Like the epicycles that were added to the Ptolemaic planetary system, many of the extensions were derived to explain the observed shortcomings of the original model. To properly evaluate these models, an independent test is required, that is, the extensions to the CAPM need to be confronted with empirical facts that they were not designed to explain. The mutual fund database is an ideal environment to conduct such a test.

As argued before, neoclassical asset pricing models for stock markets all assume that investors have rational expectations and asset markets are perfectly competitive. Consequently, investors compete fiercely with one another to find investment opportunities with positive NPV and, in doing so, eliminate them. Thus, a key prediction of any capital asset pricing model is that, when an investment opportunity with nonzero NPV presents itself in capital markets (that is, an asset is mispriced relative to the model), investors must react by submitting buy or sell orders until the opportunity no longer exists (the mispricing is removed). As we have discussed previously, the prices of actively managed mutual funds are fixed, and therefore markets can only eliminate positive-NPV opportunities through capital flows into and out of the funds. These flows therefore reveal which asset pricing model investors are actually using.

An important advantage of using capital flows to test asset pricing models is that there is no reason why a model that has been constructed to fit price (return) data should also fit flow data unless it is a model of risk. That is, the importance of additional risk factors that were added in response to the poor performance of the CAPM can be independently assessed by examining the flow of capital into investment opportunities that have positive alpha under the original model, but zero alpha under the extension. To reject the original model in favor of the extension, one must also observe no capital flows into such opportunities. Once we consistently apply the rational expectations model to mutual funds, fund flow data provide an independent test of whether it makes sense to replace the original model with one of the extensions.

Berk & van Binsbergen (2016) undertake this test. They consider a wide range of models: the CAPM originally derived by Sharpe (1964), Lintner (1965), Mossin (1966), and Treynor (1961); the reduced form factor models specified by Fama & French (1993) and Carhart (1997) that were motivated by Ross (1976); and the dynamic equilibrium models derived by Merton (1973), Breeden (1979), Campbell & Cochrane (1999), Kreps & Porteus (1978), Epstein & Zin (1991), and Bansal & Yaron (2004). Their results reveal that investors are using the CAPM to make investment decisions. Perhaps more surprising is that there is very little evidence that they are using any other model. Investors do not seem to be using the risk factors identified by Fama & French (1993) and Carhart (1997). Importantly, the CAPM better explains flows than no model at all, indicating that investors do price risk. Most surprisingly, the CAPM also outperforms a naive model in which investors ignore beta and simply chase any outperformance relative to the market portfolio. Investors' capital allocation decisions reveal that they use the CAPM beta. The fact that the factor models better explain the cross section of stock returns than the CAPM appears to be an artifact of the fact that those models are designed to that end. When confronted by data that the models were not designed to fit, they perform poorly.

The result that investors appear to be using the CAPM to make their investment decisions is very surprising in light of the well-documented failure of the CAPM to adequately explain the cross-sectional variation in expected stock returns. In addition, much of the flows in and out of mutual funds remain unexplained. To that end the paper leaves as an unanswered question whether the unexplained part of flows results because investors use a superior, yet undiscovered, risk model, or whether investors use other, non-risk-based criteria to make investment decisions.

10. CONCLUSION

Whereas the field of finance has consistently applied the lessons from the rational expectations framework to the pricing of stocks, it has struggled to apply those same principles to mutual funds. Although price adjustments in stocks are seen as an equilibrium response to new information, adjustments in fund size were seen as uninformed actions (and characterized as return chasing) by naive investors. This way of thinking has led that literature astray. Measuring the skill of mutual fund managers using alpha measures is only appropriate under all-else-equal arguments that ignore equilibrium effects. Just as the successfulness of a firm is predominantly reflected in the market capitalization of that firm (and not in the expected return on the firm's stock going forward), the cross-sectional distribution of fund manager skill is predominantly reflected in fund size as opposed to alpha. Net alpha measures are still useful, but not for inferring managerial skill. Instead, they tell us something about the rationality of investors and the competitiveness of financial markets.

Because so many papers have erroneously used net alpha as a measure of managerial skill, many of the conclusions of the literature should be revisited. For example, many studies find that net alpha measures can be predicted by various managerial characteristics, such as their age, their education, their socioeconomic background, etc. Interpreting those studies as teaching us something about managerial skill, as the authors of those studies do, is a mistake. In fact, those studies teach us something about investors. If older managers have lower net alphas than younger managers, that does not imply that older managers are less skilled than younger ones. Instead, it simply shows that investors invest too much money with older managers and too little with younger ones, suggesting that, like some prices, investment flows might also be sticky. The relationship between managerial characteristics and managerial skill can be assessed only by using value added as the left-hand-side variable.

Several researchers have argued that it is possible to find subgroups of funds and/or specific time periods over which the average return to investors (net alpha) is statistically significantly negative. Provided such findings are not driven by data mining, these papers can teach us important lessons regarding the validity of the rational expectations hypothesis. If researchers were to conclude that the rational expectations paradigm fails in the investment management space, to be consistent, they would need to question the validity of the same paradigm in stocks. After all, there is considerable overlap in investors in the two markets. Given the rapid changes in the investment management space with the continued growth of strategies available through index investing and/or exchange-traded funds, the industry provides a wealth of data that can help us better understand financial markets and their participants.

DISCLOSURE STATEMENT

The authors are not aware of any affiliations, memberships, funding, or financial holdings that might be perceived as affecting the objectivity of this review.

ACKNOWLEDGMENTS

This article is not intended to be an impartial review of the mutual fund literature. Instead, it reflects our view of recent advances in that literature. For discussions over the years, we thank Anat Admati, Peter DeMarzo, Darrell Duffie, Vincent Glode, Marco Grotteria, Binying Liu, Christian Opp, Lubos Pastor, Paul Pfleiderer, Rob Stambaugh, Richard Stanton, and, of course, Rick Green, who left us too early and to whom we dedicate this article.

LITERATURE CITED

Bansal R, Yaron A. 2004. Risks for the long run: a potential resolution of asset pricing puzzles. *J. Finance* 59(4):1481–50

Barber BM, Huang X, Odean T. 2016. What risk factors matter to investors? Evidence from mutual fund flows. *Rev. Financ. Stud.* 29:2600–42

Berk JB, Green RC. 2004. Mutual fund flows and performance in rational markets. *J. Political Econ.* 112(6):1269–95

Berk JB, Stanton RH. 2007. Managerial ability, compensation, and the closed-end fund discount. *J. Finance* 62(2):529–56

Berk JB, van Binsbergen JH. 2015. Measuring skill in the mutual fund industry. *J. Financ. Econ.* 118(1):1–20

Berk JB, van Binsbergen JH. 2016. Assessing asset pricing models using revealed preference. *J. Financ. Econ.* 119(1):1–23

Berk JB, van Binsbergen JH, Liu B. 2017. Matching capital and labor. *J. Finance*. In press. **http://onlinelibrary.wiley.com/doi/10.1111/jofi.12542/abstract**

Blocher J, Molyboga M. 2017. The revealed preference of sophisticated investors. *Eur. Financ. Manag.* In press

Breeden DT. 1979. An intertemporal asset pricing model with stochastic consumption and investment opportunities. *J. Financ. Econ.* 7(3):265–96

Campbell JY, Cochrane JH. 1999. By force of habit: a consumption-based explanation of aggregate stock market behavior. *J. Political Econ.* 107:205–51

Carhart MM. 1997. On persistence in mutual fund performance. *J. Finance* 52:57–82

Choi D, Kahraman B, Mukherjee A. 2014. *Performance-chasing behavior and mutual funds: new evidence from multi-fund managers*. Presented at Am. Finance Assoc. Annu. Meet., Jan. 3–5, Philadelphia

Epstein LG, Zin SE. 1991. Substitution, risk aversion, and the temporal behavior of consumption and asset returns: an empirical analysis. *J. Political Econ.* 99:263–86

Fama EF. 1965. The behavior of stock market prices. *J. Bus.* 38(1):34–105

Fama EF. 1970. Efficient capital markets: a review of theory and empirical work. *J. Finance* 25(2):383–417

Fama EF. 1976. Efficient capital markets: reply. *J. Finance* 31(1):143–45

Fama EF, French KR. 1993. Common risk factors in the returns on stocks and bonds. *J. Financ. Econ.* 33(1):3–56

Fama EF, French KR. 1996. Multifactor explanations of asset pricing anomalies. *J. Finance* 51:55–87

Fama EF, French KR. 2010. Luck versus skill in the cross section of mutual fund returns. *J. Finance* 65(5):1915–47

Franzoni FA, Schmalz MC. 2017. Fund flows and market states. *Rev. Financ. Stud.* 30(8):2621–73

Kreps DM, Porteus EL. 1978. Temporal resolution of uncertainty and dynamic choice theory. *Econometrica* 46(1):185–200

Lintner J. 1965. The valuation of risk assets and the selection of risky investments in stock portfolios and capital budgets. *Rev. Econ. Stat.* 47(1):13–37

Malkiel BG. 1995. Returns from investing in equity mutual funds 1971 to 1991. *J. Finance* 50(2):549–72

Merton RC. 1973. Optimum consumption and portfolio rules in a continuous-time model. *J. Econ. Theory* 3:373–413

Mossin J. 1966. Equilibrium in a capital asset market. *Econometrica* 34(4):768–83

Muth JF. 1961. Rational expectations and the theory of price movements. *Econometrica* 29(3):315–35

Pastor L, Stambaugh RF, Taylor LA. 2014. *Do funds make more when they trade more?* NBER Work. Pap. 20700

Pastor L, Stambaugh RF, Taylor LA. 2015. Scale and skill in active management. *J. Financ. Econ.* 116:23–45

Ross SA. 1976. The arbitrage theory of capital asset pricing. *J. Econ. Theory* 13(3):341–60

Sharpe WF. 1964. Capital asset prices: a theory of market equilibrium under conditions of risk. *J. Finance* 19(3):425–42

Treynor J. 1961. *Toward a theory of the market value of risky assets*. Unpublished manuscript

Exchange-Traded Funds

Itzhak Ben-David,[1,2] Francesco Franzoni,[3,4] and Rabih Moussawi[5]

[1]Fisher College of Business, The Ohio State University, Columbus, Ohio 43210

[2]National Bureau of Economic Research, Cambridge, Massachusetts 02138

[3]Università della Svizzera Italiana, 8900 Lugano, Switzerland

[4]Swiss Finance Institute, CH-8006 Zurich, Switzerland

[5]Villanova School of Business, Villanova University, Villanova, Pennsylvania 19085

Annu. Rev. Financ. Econ. 2017. 9:169–89

First published as a Review in Advance on August 11, 2017

The *Annual Review of Financial Economics* is online at financial.annualreviews.org

https://doi.org/10.1146/annurev-financial-110716-032538

Copyright © 2017 by Annual Reviews.
All rights reserved

JEL codes: G12, G14, G15

Keywords

ETFs, mutual funds, investment managers, volatility, arbitrage, fund flows

Abstract

Over nearly a quarter of a century, exchange-traded funds (ETFs) have become one of the most popular passive investment vehicles among retail and professional investors because of their low transaction costs and high liquidity. By the end of 2016, the market share of ETFs exceeded 10% of the total market capitalization traded on US exchanges, representing more than 30% of overall trading volume. ETFs revolutionized the asset management industry by taking market share from traditional investment vehicles such as mutual funds and index futures. Because ETFs rely on arbitrage activity to synchronize their prices with the prices of the underlying portfolio, trading activity at the ETF level translates to trading of the underlying securities. Researchers have found that although ETFs enhance price discovery, they also inject nonfundamental volatility into market prices and affect the correlation structure of returns. Furthermore, ETFs impact the liquidity of the underlying portfolios, especially during events of market stress.

1. INTRODUCTION

Since the mid-1990s, exchange-traded funds (ETFs) have become a popular investment vehicle because of their low transaction costs and intraday liquidity. ETF sponsors issue securities that are traded on the major stock exchanges, and, for the most part, these instruments aim to replicate the performance of an index. ETFs have shown spectacular growth. By the end of 2016, they represented over 10% of the market capitalization of securities traded on US stock exchanges, more than 30% of the overall daily trading volume, and about 20% of the aggregate short interest.

This article synthesizes the academic literature on ETFs with a focus on trading and markets. First, we provide a brief overview of the mechanics of ETFs. Second, we analyze the research that explores the popularity of passive asset management in general and ETFs in particular. Third, we survey the literature that discusses the effects of ETFs on the quality of financial markets.

In the first part of this article, we describe how ETFs work and what distinguishes them from other pooled investment vehicles. ETFs either hold a basket of securities passively (physical replication) or enter into derivative contracts delivering the performance of an index (synthetic replication), or they do a mixture of the two. They issue securities that are claims on the underlying pool of securities.[1] ETF shares are traded on stock exchanges, and investors can take either long or short positions. Two mechanisms keep ETF prices in line with those of the basket that they aim to track: primary and secondary market arbitrage. The first mechanism involves the creation and redemption of ETF shares by special intermediaries called authorized participants (APs). When ETF prices and the prices of the underlying securities diverge, APs typically buy the less expensive asset (ETF shares or a basket of the underlying securities) and exchange it for the more expensive asset, leading to the creation or redemption of ETF shares. The second mechanism is arbitraging ETFs and their underlying portfolios (through long and short positions) by market participants in an attempt to benefit from the closing of price discrepancies between the two assets. The price pressure from the trades leads to convergence of the prices. Because such trading involves the risk that, in any finite time horizon, prices will not converge, it is an arbitrage only in a loose sense.

The second part of this article describes the rise of passive investment and the role of ETFs in the passive asset management space. Passive asset management has expanded in recent decades, raising questions about what is driving this phenomenon and about its implications for financial markets and investors. Whereas some researchers view this trend as evidence that financial markets are becoming more efficient, others warn that passive investments may have adverse effects on price efficiency and welfare. Several studies document that ETFs capture market share that was previously taken by traditional passive investment vehicles such as index mutual funds, closed-end funds, and index futures.

The third part of this article focuses on how ETFs impact financial markets. In general, researchers disagree about the effects of ETFs on the securities market. In principle, the positive and negative effects of ETFs are not necessarily mutually exclusive. Some researchers argue that ETFs have little adverse effect on financial markets and even present some evidence of improved price efficiency, whereas others present evidence that ETFs lead to negative consequences to markets by increasing nonfundamental return volatility, altering correlation patterns, and reducing the

[1]Exchange-traded pooled investment vehicles are collectively designated as exchange-traded products (ETPs). These include ETFs; exchange-traded notes (ETNs), which are senior debt notes and do not invest in a portfolio of securities or a portfolio of derivatives on those securities; and exchange-traded commodities (ETCs), which provide investors exposure to individual commodities or baskets and can be structured as funds or notes. In this review, we restrict our attention to ETFs, which have been the main focus of the literature, given that they represent 95% of the ETP value in the United States.

liquidity of securities. In particular, scholars have raised the concern that the mechanical basket arbitrage trading that characterizes ETFs can propagate liquidity shocks across markets and thus deteriorate the quality of prices. This concern is especially acute given that ETFs are traded by high-turnover investors, who potentially create liquidity shocks that impound prices at high frequencies. Also, ETF ownership appears to induce excessive correlation of the securities in the ETFs' baskets. Finally, recent episodes of extreme market turbulence (e.g., the Flash Crash on May 6, 2010, and the market selloff of August 24, 2015) have revealed that the liquidity provision in ETFs is subject to sudden dry-ups.

Overall, ETFs have transformed the asset management world by introducing low-cost investment vehicles that are traded continuously. The academic literature acknowledges this financial innovation but also points to some potential weaknesses that appear to be sufficiently important to draw regulatory scrutiny.

2. THE MECHANICS OF EXCHANGE-TRADED FUNDS

ETFs are investment entities that issue securities that trade continuously on public exchanges. Most ETFs are legally structured as open-end investment companies,[2] and the majority aim to track a securities index. Unlike mutual funds, which allow investors to acquire or redeem shares only at the end of the trading day, ETFs enable investors to trade their shares continuously throughout the trading day.

ETFs combine features of both open- and closed-end funds. Like open-end mutual funds, ETFs allow the creation and redemption of shares in the fund. Like closed-end funds, the shares of ETFs are traded on exchanges. However, the open-end property creates a much greater opportunity for effective arbitrage in ETFs than in closed-end funds, which explains the significantly smaller deviations of ETF prices from the net asset value (NAV) than occurs with closed-end funds (Lee, Shleifer & Thaler 1991; Pontiff 1996).

There are two major types of ETFs, which differ in how they replicate the underlying index: physical ETFs and synthetic ETFs. Physical ETFs attempt to closely follow the return of their benchmark index by holding all or a representative sample of the index stocks in their portfolios, with weights to closely mimic those in the index. In contrast, synthetic ETFs track an index by entering into derivative contracts, such as total return swaps on the benchmark index. The creation of ETF shares occurs most often in kind for physical ETFs and in cash for synthetic ETFs. Synthetic ETFs are more popular in Europe than in the United States.

The two types of ETFs are subject to different sources of counterparty risk. Physical ETFs engage in security lending (see, e.g., Blocher & Whaley 2016), which exposes the fund to the risk of default of the security borrower. Synthetic ETFs are exposed to the risk of default of the counterparty in the derivative contract. Of course, both types of agreements require collateral.

The popularity of ETFs has skyrocketed in recent years. ETF daily trading volume exceeded 36% of overall stock market trading volume in the first half of 2016, despite the fact that ETFs' capitalization is only about 10% of the market (see **Figures 1** and **2**). ETFs are also popular instruments for short-selling purposes (hedging or directional bearish bets), with about 20% of the overall short interest on US exchanges being in ETF shares (see **Figure 3**).[3]

[2]Some ETFs are classified as unit investment trusts (such as the SPY, the ETF on the S&P 500 sponsored by State Street). Unit investment trusts may not engage in security lending of their portfolio securities, which is one the main differences with other ETFs organized as open-end investment companies.

[3]SPY is considered the most traded security in the world, with an average daily volume of more than 115 million shares in 2017.

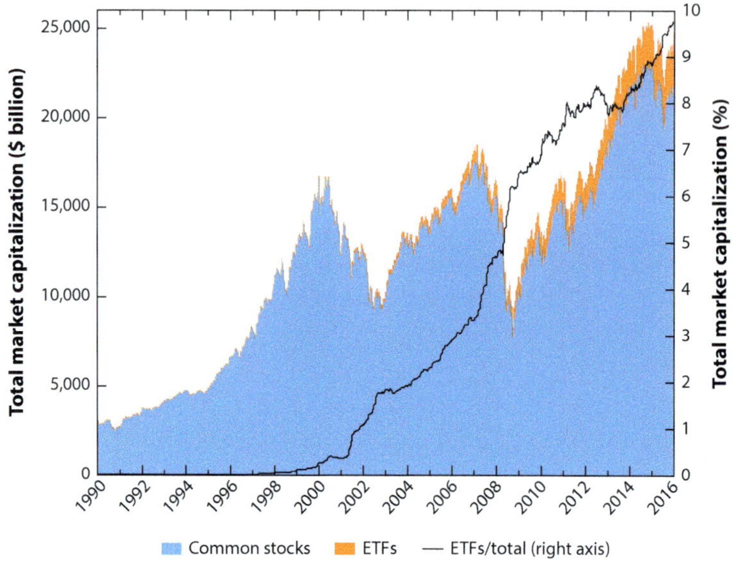

Figure 1

Time series of the total market capitalization and the assets under management of ETFs.

The market price of ETF shares often diverges from the NAV of the underlying basket because of asynchronous trading of the ETF and the underlying assets. This fact can generate an opportunity for arbitrage between the ETF shares and the underlying basket of securities when the

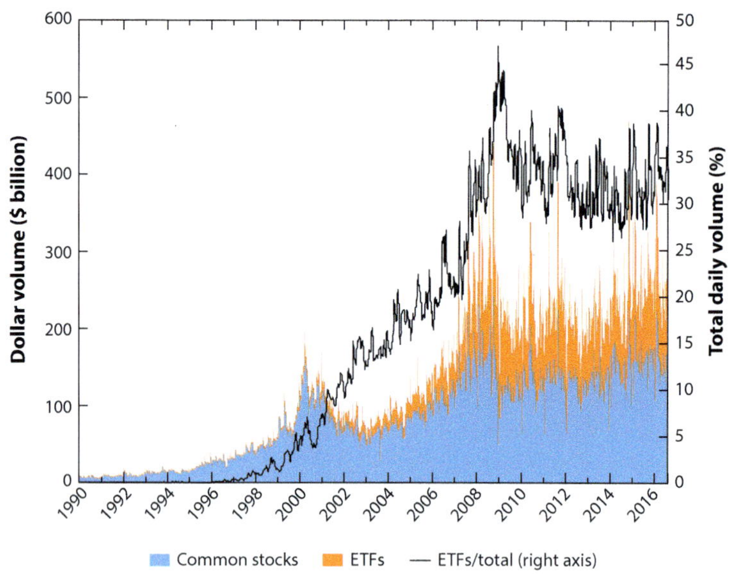

Figure 2

Time series of daily trading volume.

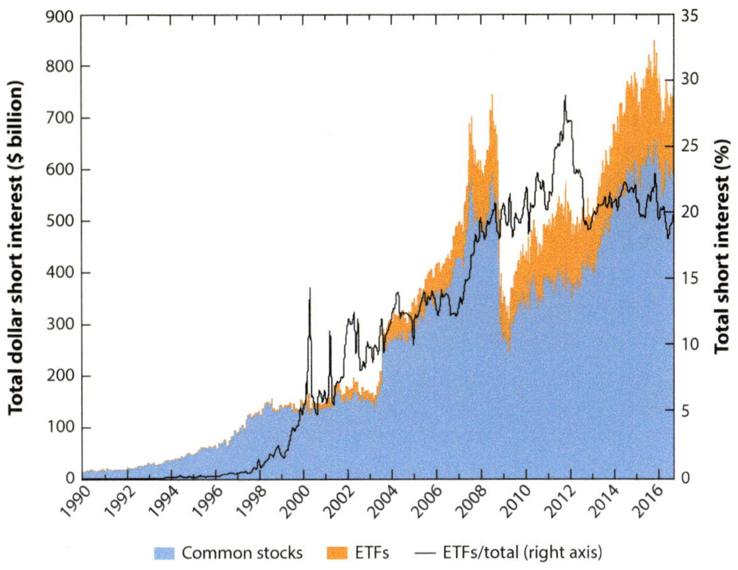

Figure 3

Time series of short interest.

discrepancy exceeds the transaction costs. Two types of market participants are poised to benefit from such differences in prices: APs and secondary market arbitrageurs.[4]

APs are a small group of institutions that are allowed to trade directly with the ETF sponsor in the primary market. These transactions typically take place in kind, with securities being exchanged for ETF shares. The APs help to eliminate price discrepancies by purchasing the cheaper asset on the market and selling the more expensive one. When the ETF price is lower than the NAV, the APs purchase ETF shares and redeem them for the underlying securities. When the ETF price is higher than the NAV, the APs purchase the underlying securities and exchange them for newly issued ETF shares. Finally, the APs turn back to the market and sell either the underlying securities that they received or the newly issued ETF notes. These trades apply downward pressure on the prices of the expensive asset and upward pressure on the price of the less expensive asset, so price discrepancy is kept under narrow bounds.[5] Arbitrageurs can monitor the ETF price as well as the intraday indicative net asset value (IIV or INAV) of the ETF basket during the day on most financial platforms. ETF INAVs are computed using the intraday dollar values of the ETF creation baskets and are published every 15 seconds for underlying baskets that trade continuously in US markets.

The primary market transactions to create or redeem ETF shares occur in large blocks called creation units. Although more than 70% of the ETFs traded in the United States have creation units with blocks of 50,000 ETF shares, a few ETFs have larger creation units, equivalent to more than 100,000 shares. A daily creation basket provides the specific names and quantities of securities or other assets designed to track the performance of the portfolio as a whole, and which the APs

[4]These could be market makers or other investors such as hedge funds and proprietary trading desks.

[5]Broman (2016a) estimates the distribution of the extent of the discrepancy between ETF prices and the NAV values based on ETF mid-point quotes at the end of the day over the 2006–2012 period. He documents that the standard deviation of the discrepancy is about 0.10% for large ETFs and 0.15% for small ETFs; see also Petajisto (2017).

need to deposit in exchange for an ETF creation unit.[6] The AP generally pays all of the trading costs associated with the operation along with an additional creation/redemption fee paid to the ETF sponsor. This fee averages $1,047 per creation unit, with a median fee of $500 per creation unit (less than 1 basis point for most ETFs). According to Antoniewicz & Heinrichs (2014), there are, on average, 34 APs per ETF. Some AP firms also function as ETF market markers by providing continuous quotes and liquidity for an ETF's shares in the secondary market. In the process of creating and redeeming ETF shares with domestic underlying securities, APs are generally not required to post collateral up front unless they fail to clear these transactions within a T + 3[7] settlement date.[8] In some cases, certain APs have three additional days to settle trades (a total of T + 6) if their failure to deliver is the result of bona fide market making. Further details about the mechanics and operation of ETFs are provided by Antoniewicz & Heinrichs (2014), Hill et al. (2015), and Hill (2016).

The second mechanism through which ETF and NAV prices are arbitraged is the trading activity of market participants. Specifically, secondary market arbitrageurs are market makers or traders who take a position (long or short) in the ETF and an opposite position in the main components of the index or a closely related instrument (e.g., another ETF or futures contract), hoping that the discrepancy in prices will eventually disappear. This, of course, is not pure textbook arbitrage because it entails the risk of widening price discrepancy between the ETF and the underlying securities, and the horizon over which convergence will occur is uncertain (Shleifer & Vishny 1997). In today's markets, such trading activity is often performed by hedge funds through automatic algorithmic trading or by some of the same firms that make markets for ETFs.

3. THE RISE OF PASSIVE INVESTING

Investment managers in the asset management industry can be broadly classified as engaging in either active or passive investing. Active managers engage in stock-picking securities and market timing to beat a benchmark or to generate an absolute return. In contrast, passive managers construct a portfolio that aims to replicate the performance of an index, such as the S&P 500. Whereas the performance of active investors is typically measured as absolute returns or index-adjusted returns (alpha), the performance of passive investors is measured by their ability to minimize the tracking error with respect to the index. ETFs are passive investment vehicles in nature; they own a basket of securities that mimics an index. Active ETFs, a recent innovation in the ETF space, try to beat their benchmark much like active mutual funds. To date, however, they represent only 1.8% of the assets under management (AUM) in the US equity ETF market (see **Table 1**).

ETFs began trading widely in the mid-1990s [the first ETF in the US market was the Standard and Poor's Depository Receipt (SPDR), identified by the ticker SPY, which began trading in 1993], and their popularity has expanded rapidly ever since. **Table 1** presents time-series statistics about US and foreign stock ownership by active mutual funds, passive mutual funds, and ETFs, in addition to ownership by fixed-income funds. In mid-2016, ETFs directly owned about $1.35 trillion of the US common stock market, compared with the approximately $6.8 trillion

[6]In certain cases (e.g., some fixed income ETFs), the creation or redemption basket might contain different combinations of securities and/or cash relative to the overall ETF portfolio. In other cases, actively managed ETFs, for example, are required to publish their complete portfolio holdings in addition to their creation and redemption baskets. For further information, see Shreck & Antoniewicz (2012).

[7]The Securities and Exchange Commission (SEC) adopted a T + 2 settlement cycle effective in September 2017 (SEC 2017).

[8]Creation and redemption orders are processed by the National Securities Clearing Corporation (NSCC), a subsidiary of the Depository Trust and Clearing Corporation (DTCC). The creation and redemption baskets are maintained at the DTCC on a daily basis by the ETF sponsor.

Table 1 Time series of assets under management

	US equity funds				Foreign equity funds				Fixed-income funds			
	ETFs		Mutual funds		ETFs		Mutual funds		ETFs		Mutual funds	
Year	**Index**	**Active**	**Index**	**Active**	**Index**	**Active**	**Index**	**Active**	**Index**	**Active**	**Index**	**Active**
1999	31.2	0.0	334.9	2,632.6	2.0	0.0	19.1	504.3	0.0	0.0	20.0	2,181.3
2000	63.0	0.1	327.1	2,586.2	2.0	0.0	19.2	457.5	0.0	0.0	23.9	2,403.0
2001	78.7	0.0	308.3	2,231.8	2.9	0.0	17.7	364.5	0.0	0.0	33.5	2,890.1
2002	91.8	0.0	255.3	1,708.5	5.3	0.0	18.3	310.4	3.9	0.0	42.6	3,007.6
2003	131.0	0.0	365.1	2,325.1	13.9	0.0	31.5	448.5	4.7	0.0	46.1	2,887.2
2004	183.6	0.1	443.6	2,687.7	33.1	0.0	51.1	601.7	8.5	0.0	54.3	2,803.5
2005	219.9	0.0	486.3	2,918.1	64.0	0.0	79.1	791.4	15.0	0.0	63.6	2,953.1
2006	282.5	0.5	592.0	3,299.1	107.7	0.0	125.9	1,105.3	20.5	0.0	75.9	3,364.7
2007	384.3	2.4	665.5	3,532.0	169.7	0.0	177.7	1,396.4	34.3	0.0	109.5	4,242.7
2008	289.9	11.3	479.2	2,323.7	104.2	0.1	102.4	845.5	55.6	0.0	134.3	5,001.6
2009	435.5	10.5	660.0	2,998.9	199.1	0.3	130.0	1,185.1	100.1	0.0	185.8	4,986.8
2010	565.8	11.6	823.5	3,496.8	260.0	0.8	184.1	1,383.6	132.3	1.5	233.9	4,910.5
2011	612.2	11.7	856.9	3,349.6	223.0	0.0	179.8	1,190.3	183.1	3.8	276.1	4,913.6
2012	755.7	11.3	1,024.5	3,662.9	305.0	0.0	234.6	1,424.3	235.7	9.7	319.8	5,292.1
2013	1,012.7	13.2	1,432.8	4,774.0	378.1	0.0	306.1	1,799.4	227.7	10.9	324.2	5,127.9
2014	1,233.1	19.5	1,706.2	5,065.8	396.7	1.2	357.5	1,778.9	280.5	9.8	397.5	5,282.8
2015	1,235.3	22.5	1,688.7	4,975.7	455.3	0.8	319.5	1,953.4	324.9	12.8	427.9	5,266.5
2016	1,329.4	24.0	1,805.6	5,044.1	434.5	0.9	349.2	1,958.9	381.6	15.5	481.1	5,458.8

The table presents the time series of assets under management in billions of US dollars. Index funds include both traditional index funds and smart-beta index funds. Source: authors' calculations and the Center for Research in Securities Prices. Abbreviation: ETF, exchange-traded fund.

owned by mutual funds.[9] **Table 1** shows that the growth rate of AUM is dramatically different across fund types. From 1999 to 2016, US equity index mutual funds grew from \$0.3 trillion to \$1.8 trillion, and actively managed US equity mutual funds grew from \$2.6 trillion to \$5.0 trillion. In contrast, US equity ETFs grew from \$0.03 trillion to \$1.3 trillion. Trends are similar for foreign equity funds and fixed-income funds.

3.1. Migration from Active to Passive Investment

In recent decades, index investing has become popular among both individual investors and institutions. This change has prompted researchers to attempt to explain trends in the asset management space and explore their implications for market quality (French 2008, Stambaugh 2014).

There could be multiple reasons for the migration from active to passive investments. Investors could have realized that the market is more efficient than previously thought, meaning that low-cost passive investments produce comparable or even superior performance (e.g., Sharpe ratio) to after-fees active funds. Also, index funds provide a cost-efficient way to expose investors to certain common risk factors (Cong & Xu 2016). Stambaugh (2014) reports a sharp drop in the share of active funds over the past three decades and analyzes an equilibrium model in which active

[9]Authors' calculation. These figures show ownership by ETFs and mutual funds that are traded in the United States. In other words, they exclude commodities, futures-based instruments, fixed income, global equities, leveraged ETFs, and short bias.

and passive management coexist. Active management benefits from exploiting the noise in prices that retail traders create. In equilibrium, the remainder of capital is invested in passive funds. The increase in passive investment means that arbitrage opportunities disappear, indicating that the market is becoming more efficient. Not all researchers share the view that the rise of passive asset management is an indication of improved market efficiency. Bond & García (2016) present a model in which indexing reduces investors' welfare. The rationale is that the cash flows of some stocks have high exposure to economic shocks and therefore command relatively low stock prices. Given their small relative weight in the index, an indexing investor will have low exposure to these stocks. However, if an investor is not exposed to the same economic shocks, he or she will be better off having greater exposure to these stocks. Thus, indexing may lead to suboptimal portfolio composition for some investors. Wurgler (2011) warns against the adverse effects of rising indexation. He argues that indexing can create distortion in securities' valuations and provides examples such as inclusion and deletion effects (see, e.g., Shleifer 1986; Kaul, Mehrotra & Morck 2002; Wurgler & Zhuravskaya 2002; Greenwood 2005), comovement of the stock with the index (see, e.g., Greenwood & Sosner 2007; Basak & Pavlova 2013, 2016; Da & Shive 2014), and higher sensitivity to crashes (because many market participants change their index exposure on the basis of past performance). Baltussen, Da & van Bekkum (2016) conduct a cross-country study and find that the degree of presence of indexing vehicles (futures, ETFs, and index mutual funds) in the stock market is associated with stronger negative serial correlation of the underlying indices.

A parallel trend in the marketplace over the past few decades has been an increase in concentration in the asset management space. A likely explanation is the economies of scale that passive asset managers enjoy, which makes consolidation attractive. This trend is discussed by Ben-David et al. (2015). The researchers find that the top 10 institutional investors owned about 5% of the US stock market in 1980, and that this share had increased to over 23% by the end of 2014. The authors hypothesize that large institutional investors cause an increase in the volatility of the securities held in their underlying portfolios. The idea is that units (e.g., funds) within large institutional investors share common resources such as marketing, research, and risk management departments. As a result, fund flows are correlated across units, and investment decisions by unit managers are similar. Both factors cause units to engage in large trades, compared to what a collection of independent units would engage in. These large trades ultimately increase the volatility of the traded securities. The authors present evidence for the correlation induced by central resources: They document that mutual funds that are part of the same family have fund flows that are more correlated and their stock holdings are more similar than for independent funds. To establish causality, the authors compare the volatility of stocks before and after mergers of large institutional investors (as institutions tend to consolidate some of their central functions following mergers). Indeed, the authors find that stocks owned by the merged entity have higher volatility than they did pre-merger.

The rise in passive investment also has implications for corporate policies as the nature and composition of institutional investors change. Bradley & Litan (2011a,b) argue that ETFs and index funds are poor at corporate governance. Consequently, private firms are reluctant to list on stock exchanges because passive investors, and primarily ETFs, slow down price discovery and eventually jam value signals to managers. Empirical studies have generally found results contradicting this claim. Boone & White (2015) use the change in the ownership of institutional investors following index reconstitution to test the information production of firms. When a stock moves from being at the bottom of the Russell 1000 index to the top of the Russell 2000 index, there is a sharp increase in institutional ownership, primarily among passive indexers. They find that as ownership by index funds increases, firms become more transparent in their reporting. Appel, Gormley & Keim (2016) use a similar natural experiment to measure the effects of ownership by passive investors on corporate governance. They show that, in fact, passive investors actively promote strong corporate governance. Ownership by passive investors has a positive causal effect on a host of issues in corporate governance, such as the removal of poison pills, restrictions on shareholders' ability to call special meetings, fewer dual-class share structures, and more independent directors.

3.2. Can Exchange-Traded Funds Coexist with Traditional Investment Vehicles?

Empirical studies find that ETFs gained market share at the expense of traditional indexing products. Agapova (2011) studies mutual funds and ETFs in the 2000–2004 period and finds evidence for both substitution and clientele effects. Although ETFs and mutual funds provide similar investment index exposure and thus are substitutes, the products may appeal to different types of investors. ETFs may be more tax efficient and therefore may appeal to tax-sensitive investors. Furthermore, mutual funds may appeal to short-term investors because of the absence of commission fees, whereas ETFs may appeal to long-term investors because of lower management fees. Ben-David, Franzoni & Moussawi (2013) test these propositions and find opposite results: Investors in ETFs have significantly shorter horizons. Barnhart & Rosenstein (2010) present evidence that, as ETFs gained market share in the United States, the discounts of closed-end funds widened and their trading volume declined. Market participants argue that ETFs are aggressively competing with futures to win big investors, with many ETFs having lower fees than the futures roll costs.[10]

Several researchers argue that ETFs and mutual funds have distinct features and therefore appeal to different audiences. Guedj & Huang (2009) propose a model that explores whether ETFs and open-end mutual funds can coexist in equilibrium. In their model, ETFs are more efficient indexers but are exposed to liquidity shocks resulting from continuous trading. In contrast, mutual funds are less sensitive to liquidity shocks and are therefore valued by investors who are averse to such exposure. In equilibrium, ETFs offer a cheaper investment option for investors who are willing to bear the liquidity shock risk, and mutual funds provide implicit insurance against such shocks. Madhavan et al. (2014) argue that ETFs are a superior investment alternative for fully funded investors over index futures because ETFs provide low transaction costs and avoid the mispricing that often occurs around the futures rolling dates.

Sponsors of ETFs also compete with traditional asset managers for fees. In addition to the management fees that are charged to the ETF fund, sponsors of ETFs benefit from fees generated from lending the securities owned by the fund. Blocher & Whaley (2016) report that lending fees are as important as management fees and that, when managers of stock ETFs have discretion, they tilt their portfolio holdings toward stocks with higher lending fees. This practice raises the concern that ETFs are exposed to collateral risk, which could occur when borrowers of shares fail to deliver promised shares at the same time that the ETF is required to redeem its own shares (Mackintosh & Lin 2011). Evans et al. (2017) report evidence that recent increases in ETF settlement failures are mainly related to the creation/redemption process when APs/market makers delay the creation and delivery settlement of ETF creation units for several days after supplying the ETF shares in the secondary market, a phenomenon called operational shorting. The authors find that high levels of ETF operational shorting and settlement failures are associated with subsequent increases in financial stress. Hurlin et al. (2014) investigate this claim among European ETFs during 6 months

[10]Because futures contracts have an expiration date, one must renew the position every time the futures expires, an action that involves a cost (see Rennison 2016, Toplensky 2016).

in 2012 and find no evidence of this buildup in risk during the studied period. It is important to note, however, that the universe that they study is limited in both time and scope; thus, their results do not necessarily extend to other economic situations, such as market stress.

The substitution of traditional investment vehicles with ETFs has additional implications for investors. Bhattacharya et al. (2017) report that retail traders who invest in ETFs perform worse than retail traders who stick with traditional funds. They argue that the ease of ETF trading leads retail investors to attempt to time the market. Because retail investors are bad traders in general (Barber & Odean 2000, Frazzini & Lamont 2008), this behavior results in poor performance. In the same vein, Goetzmann & Massa (2003) find that index mutual fund investors appear to chase returns: Flows are stronger following positive past returns. These flows do not have predictive power about future returns. Clifford, Fulkerson & Jordan (2014) and Broman (2016c) conduct similar analyses using more recent ETF data and find essentially similar patterns. Whereas the phenomenon of chasing returns by investors is known from active mutual funds (Berk & Green 2004), where it is often attributed to responding to news about managerial skill, it appears irrational for investors to chase the returns of a passive index.

4. DO EXCHANGE-TRADED FUNDS IMPACT ASSET PRICES? THEORY AND EMPIRICAL EVIDENCE

Through the continuous arbitrage between ETFs and the underlying securities, ETFs create an additional layer of liquidity on top of the underlying assets. This design could cause two apparently opposite effects. The additional liquidity that ETFs add can enhance price discovery in the underlying securities, hence making them more informationally efficient. At the same time, nonfundamental trades at the ETF could propagate to the underlying securities, leading to mispricing. It is entirely plausible that these two effects coexist.

4.1. Price Discovery and Liquidity

Because of their low costs and high liquidity, many investors may view ETFs as their preferred investment vehicle for taking directional bets on the index (Stratmann & Welborn 2012, Broman & Shum 2016), therefore introducing index-related information into ETF prices. In turn, APs and arbitrageurs ensure that the prices of the underlying securities do not diverge from those of the ETF. The result is that this trading activity helps transmit systematic information from the ETF to the underlying securities and provides liquidity to the underlying securities. Thus, ETFs could potentially improve price discovery at the index level and enhance liquidity at the level of the underlying securities.

Lettau & Madhavan (2016), Madhavan (2016), and Madhavan & Sobczyk (2016) advance the view that ETFs enhance the functioning of financial markets. The researchers argue that because ETFs provide a cost-effective tool for investors who wish to make directional bets on the index, they will reflect the new information before the underlying securities. These researchers claim that, as long as arbitrage is frictionless, ETFs do not propagate shocks into securities, but rather expedite price discovery. In other words, the price discovery at the ETF level leads to price discovery at the underlying securities level.

Several studies confirm empirically that ETFs enhance price discovery. Richie, Daigler & Gleason (2008) compare the comovement of S&P 500 futures, the main ETF on this index (SPY), and the underlying portfolio. They conclude that prices deviate little between the futures contract and ETFs but that there are larger deviations from the underlying portfolio. Glosten, Nallareddy & Zou (2016) find that stocks incorporate information more quickly once they are in ETF portfolios. They argue that some of the increased comovement of stocks with indices that has been documented by other researchers (see below) can be explained by better incorporation of systematic information into stock prices. Wermers & Xue (2015), in a study sponsored by Lyxor Asset Management, also report enhanced price discovery at the ETF level. Their goal is to separate informed trading from noise trading in ETFs. Their identifying assumption is that informed investors trade the ETF or futures. Therefore, on days when ETFs lead the underlying securities portfolio, informed trading dominates. In contrast, on days when ETFs lag the index, the ETF is primarily traded by noise traders. Using this identification strategy, they find that price movements driven by informed traders dominate and are permanent. Price movements driven by noise traders reverse on average. Also, Marshall, Nguyen & Visaltanachoti (2013) find that ETFs move ahead of the underlying portfolio, especially when the liquidity of the underlying securities is low. Li & Zhu (2016) present another mechanism through which ETFs may enhance price efficiency. They argue that arbitrageurs use ETFs to circumvent short-sale constraints at the stock level. The authors use data on short interest of ETFs to compute the indirect short interest that is applied to each individual stock through ETFs that hold it. They document that this measure of stock-level short interest predicts stock returns and conclude that ETFs help improve market efficiency through this channel.

Other researchers present evidence suggesting that ETFs degrade informational efficiency of the securities in their baskets. Da & Shive (2014) document increased comovement in returns in the stocks that are part of an index. They argue that when investors trade on news related to the index, they trade the ETF more actively. The mechanical basket trading of the underlying securities tied to the ETF through arbitrage exhibits higher return comovement with the index and a lower degree of idiosyncratic volatility. Therefore, individual stock response is expected to be less timely and less sensitive to idiosyncratic earnings news. An implication of this result is that the lagged response to idiosyncratic shocks may exacerbate certain anomalies (e.g., postearnings announcement drift). Israeli, Lee & Sridharan (2017) show that stocks owned by ETFs have higher trading costs; have higher comovement with the index; exhibit lower informational efficiency, measured as lower future earnings response coefficients; and receive less analyst coverage. Bradley & Litan (2011a,b) argue that private firms are reluctant to list on stock exchanges because passive investors, primarily ETFs, slow down price discovery. Broman (2016a) and Brown, Davies & Ringgenberg (2016) document that the degree and direction of mispricing between ETFs and their underlying securities comove across ETFs. Both groups conclude that ETFs attract short-horizon noise traders with correlated demand across investment styles. Broman (2016b) provides further evidence that ETFs attract sentiment-driven noise traders. He examines ETFs that trade on multiple countries and documents that country-specific ETF mispricings are correlated with the country-specific stock market.

Another strand of empirical studies finds that ETFs have conflicting effects on liquidity provision to the underlying securities. In one direction, as argued above, ownership by ETFs can increase liquidity in the underlying securities. This happens through the arbitrage trades that take place between the ETF and the underlying securities. Marshall, Nguyen & Visaltanachoti (2015) document patterns that illustrate the activity of arbitrageurs. They find that the liquidity of ETFs is correlated with the liquidity of the underlying stocks. The more liquid the underlying stocks are, the greater the ability of arbitrageurs to engage in arbitrage trades, making the ETF liquid as well. Agarwal et al. (2016) document that the liquidity of ETFs comoves with the liquidity of the assets in the ETF baskets. The authors show that higher ETF ownership is associated with higher comovement of liquidity among large and small stocks alike.[11] They further document that this

[11]This study is related to two previous papers. Coughenour & Saad (2004) test whether liquidity provision is correlated across stocks that are assigned to the same New York Stock Exchange (NYSE) specialists. The idea is that capital constraints are

comovement of liquidity has increased in recent years and that it is greater during crisis versus noncrisis periods. In the mutual funds market, Schultz & Shive (2016) show that ownership by mutual funds increases the liquidity of the underlying bonds through flows to and from the mutual funds, which induce trading.

Conversely, some argue that ETFs can decrease the liquidity of the underlying securities. Specifically, because ETFs provide an inexpensive way to trade, they can crowd out traders from the underlying assets and decrease liquidity. Petajisto (2017) finds a significant deviation of ETF prices from those of the underlying assets, especially for illiquid assets. Piccotti (2014) documents that in some ETFs, the deviation from the value of the underlying assets is permanent, which he argues may be the result of market segmentation. Investors may be willing to pay a premium for access to assets with greater liquidity. Dannhauser (2017) finds that the introduction of corporate bond ETFs leads to a decrease in the liquidity of the underlying bonds, suggesting a crowding-out effect. Pan & Zeng (2016) propose a complementary effect: Because APs have a dual role in financial markets—APs and market makers—they may occasionally consume more liquidity than they provide. This may happen when there is selling pressure by investors during times of market stress. APs may not be willing to engage in arbitrage when the underlying securities are illiquid. The authors present evidence that APs' trading volume declines when market volatility (captured by the VIX) is high, suggesting that APs operate like arbitrageurs who have limited capital, withdrawing from the market when volatility is high (Ben-David, Franzoni & Moussawi 2012; Nagel 2012).

4.2. Propagation of Demand Shocks to Underlying Securities

The additional layer of liquidity that ETFs provide may also serve as a transmission mechanism for nonfundamental shocks from ETFs to the underlying securities. Malamud (2015) develops a model for ETFs in which APs create and redeem ETF shares. He shows that the creation/redemption mechanism propagates temporary liquidity shocks into the underlying securities. The model also indicates that, as the liquidity of the underlying securities increases, the degree of shock propagation increases.

A key component in the proposed mechanism for noise transmission is the existence of demand shocks at the ETF level. In recent years, ETFs have seen high share turnover (see **Figure 2**) and are traded by traders with short horizons (Ben-David, Franzoni & Moussawi 2013). Many of these investors tend to make directional bets and hold the securities for a short period of time. As such, they may use ETFs as low-cost investment conduits for these bets. Stratmann & Welborn (2012) and Broman & Shum (2016) find evidence to support this conjecture. They document that investors use ETFs as a way to take short-term directional bets on the market. Previous literature on short-term investors shows the adverse effects of investors with a short horizon. Stein (1987) argues that the entry of short-term speculators lowers the informational efficiency of prices, deterring long-term investors from participating in the market. Cella, Ellul & Giannetti (2013) find that the presence of short-horizon institutional investors during market turmoil exacerbates price drops because these investors exit the market. This evidence is consistent with findings of Ben-David, Franzoni & Moussawi (2012), who show that hedge funds, which on average have higher turnover than other investors, exited the stock market during the financial crash of 2008–2009.

Some studies have tested whether ETF ownership causes higher volatility in the underlying securities. Ben-David, Franzoni & Moussawi (2013) propose that a demand shock can move the

common per specialist. Koch, Ruenzi & Starks (2016) provide evidence that stock-level liquidity is correlated across stocks with common ownership.

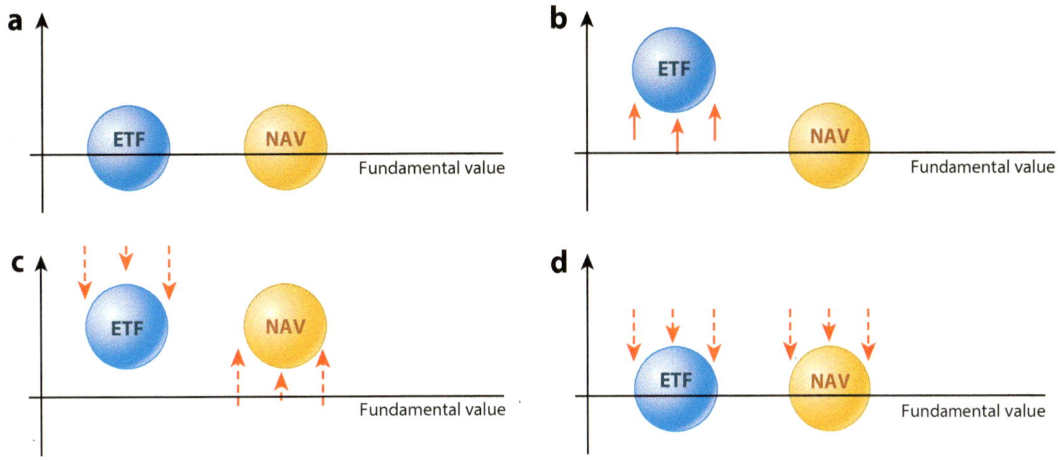

Figure 4

Illustration of the propagation of liquidity shocks via arbitrage. (*a*) Initial equilibrium. (*b*) Liquidity shock to ETF. (*c*) Initial outcome of arbitrage: The shock is propagated to the NAV and the ETF price starts reverting to the fundamental value. (*d*) Equilibrium reestablished: After some time, both the ETF price and the NAV revert to the fundamental value.

ETF price away from the fundamental value (**Figure 4*a*,*b***). If there is limited liquidity in the underlying securities' market, the underlying securities' prices are temporarily pushed away from the fundamental value (**Figure 4*c***). In the long run, liquidity flows back into the market, and both the ETF price and the underlying securities' prices revert back to their fundamental value (**Figure 4*d***). The repeated arrival of demand shocks in the ETF market, through a mechanism like the one just described, can create a link between ETF ownership of stocks and return volatility. Ben-David, Franzoni & Moussawi (2013) identify a causal effect of ETF ownership on stock volatility using an exogenous shift in ETF ownership that occurs annually through the Russell 1000/2000 reconstitution. Stocks that switch indices experience a sharp change in ETF ownership. The Russell 1000 and Russell 2000 indices are based on stock market capitalization: The Russell 1000 includes the largest 1,000 traded stocks in the United States, and the Russell 2000 tracks the performance of the next 2,000 smaller stocks. Once per year, Russell reconstitutes the indices, and some stocks switch membership according to a mechanical rule. Some stocks in the Russell 2000 that have experienced an increase in their market capitalization switch to the Russell 1000, and those whose market capitalization has decreased switch from the Russell 1000 to the Russell 2000. The researchers use an identification strategy based on the idea that ETF ownership is higher for the top stocks in the Russell 2000 than for the bottom stocks at the Russell 1000, despite the fact that members in the latter group have larger market capitalization than those in the former group. The authors control for changes in other types of institutional ownership and document that the effect of ETF ownership is statistically and economically significant. Using this identification strategy, the authors conclude that stock volatility increases substantially following this exogenous increase in ETF ownership. Furthermore, the authors show that ETF flows correlate with price movements in the same direction as the flows. This price movement partially reverts over the next few days, consistent with the initial shock being liquidity motivated. These findings suggest that the increased volatility is, at least in part, nonfundamental. Krause, Ehsani & Lien (2014) also find that stocks owned by ETFs have higher volatility and higher volume. Their setting, however, lacks a strategy to identify exogenous variation in ETF ownership. Thus, the higher volatility may be a result of a selection process in which ETFs end up holding more liquid—and thus more volatile—stocks.

Other researchers argue that price reversals at the underlying securities level could be evidence of ETF flows putting temporary price pressure on the underlying stocks, which ultimately revert. Staer (2014) finds that ETF flows are contemporaneous with index returns and that these price effects partly revert after a few days. Baltussen, Da & van Bekkum (2016) find that the serial correlation of stock markets became more negative following indexation. They interpret this result as evidence that index products impound nonfundamental shocks (which then revert) into the underlying security prices.

The same mechanism of propagation of nonfundamental shocks from ETFs to the underlying securities should also apply to other investment vehicles and to derivatives. Indeed, most studies in this area have found confirming evidence. Coval & Stafford (2007), for instance, find that mutual funds that experience strong outflows engage in fire sales, which have a significant and long-lasting price impact on the underlying securities. In the futures market, MacKinlay & Ramaswamy (1988) report that the volatility of index futures is higher than that of the corresponding index itself. In addition, they find that the idiosyncratic component of futures' returns tends to be autocorrelated, suggesting that it is driven by temporary mispricing. Chang, Cheng & Pinegar (1999) document that the introduction of futures trading increased the volatility of stocks in the Nikkei index. Roll, Schwartz & Subrahmanyam (2007) present evidence of Granger causality between prices in the futures and equity markets. In contrast, Bessembinder & Seguin (1992) determine that only the unexpected trading activity of stock futures is correlated with stock volatility. They conclude that these patterns are consistent with the idea that futures trading enhances the liquidity of the underlying securities without adding significant noise.

Another approach to testing for market inefficiency relates to the correlation of securities with the index, once the securities are owned by ETFs. The conjecture is that ETF prices are set by investor demand for the index, as opposed to demand for the individual securities. Therefore, ETF prices primarily reflect systematic shocks, and because of the arbitrage mechanism, the underlying securities will display greater comovement with the index. Basak & Pavlova (2013, 2016) propose a similar mechanism in the context of institutional investment. In their model, when institutional investors measure their performance relative to an index, they overweight assets that are included in the index, leading to an increase in asset prices, price volatility, and correlation with other indices.

Empirical studies have found evidence supporting this mechanism. Da & Shive (2014) show that stocks that are part of an index tend to comove with the index and thus lose their idiosyncratic volatility. The effect is stronger for illiquid stocks and at times of market turbulence. They instrument ETF ownership by the inception and closure of ETF funds. Sullivan & Xiong (2012) and Israeli, Lee & Sridharan (2017) find similar evidence in an empirical setting in which ETF ownership is endogenous. Chinco & Fos (2016) develop a model in which many ETFs need to rebalance their portfolios. They show that small changes in stock prices can trigger large rebalancing cascades that affect the prices of all the securities within the same ETF. They conclude that there is a feedback effect in which the rebalancing activity exacerbates the original price shock that prompted the rebalancing.

It is important to note that the apparently conflicting evidence about improved price discovery in the presence of ETFs and the evidence for greater inefficiencies are not necessarily contradictory or mutually exclusive. It is possible that prices more quickly reflect certain pieces of information, and, at the same time, also are more impacted by liquidity shocks. Bhattacharya & O'Hara (2016) propose a model in which ETFs hold assets that are less liquid than the ETF itself. Therefore, some of the price discovery happens at the ETF level. Market makers try to extract relevant information from the ETF about the underlying securities. However, market makers extract a noisy signal, which causes them to propagate noise when they trade the underlying securities.

4.3. Leveraged ETFs

Leveraged ETFs have attracted substantial attention from academics, regulators, and market commentators because these ETFs need to actively rebalance their portfolios on an ongoing and predictable basis toward the end of the trading day. Leveraged ETFs strive to achieve returns that are a multiple of the underlying index (e.g., ×2, ×3), or the inverse return on the index (often called bear ETFs), as in a short strategy. To achieve their desired return patterns, these funds rely on leverage or derivatives and need to rebalance their portfolios following price movements of the underlying index. The concern expressed by several parties is that these rebalancing actions have a significant impact on the market. For example, leveraged ETFs were blamed in the 1% run-up in the last 18 minutes of trade of the S&P 500 on October 10, 2011, despite the absence of any news (Sorkin 2011). According to Cheng & Madhavan (2009), the dynamics of leveraged ETFs lead to same-direction rebalancing (even for bear funds), akin to portfolio insurance. They also argue that short-term speculators are attracted to these products because they allow traders to make short-term, highly leveraged bets. Jiang & Yan (2016) explore the nature of flows to regular and leveraged ETFs and show that regular ETF flows can be characterized as momentum traders, whereas leveraged ETF flows are contrarians.

Several studies have attempted to test the claim that leveraged ETFs create a price impact when rebalancing their portfolios. Bai, Bond & Hatch (2015) focus on the real estate sector and find that rebalancing by leveraged ETFs increases the volatility of the underlying stocks and contributes to price momentum. Tuzun (2014) calls leveraged ETFs "the new portfolio insurers" because their rebalancing reinforces the original price movement and thus increases market volatility. His estimation shows that leveraged ETFs contributed significantly to market volatility during the financial crisis of 2008–2009. Shum et al. (2016) present evidence that stock-level end-of-day volatilities are higher following the rebalancing of leveraged ETFs. In contrast, Ivanov & Lenkey (2016) argue that claims about the impact of leveraged ETFs are exaggerated. They show that flows into ETFs counterbalance the hedging demand of ETFs, mitigating their effects on the underlying securities. Despite this compelling argument, the effects documented by Bai, Bond & Hatch (2015) and Shum et al. (2016) use net rebalancing, i.e., after flows in the opposite direction are taken into account.

ETFs that track volatility indices have properties similar to leveraged ETFs. Volatility indices do not reflect the returns of a constant basket of traded assets, but rather are calculated based on prices of derivatives with weights that change daily, according to the expiration date of the derivatives (e.g., the VIX in the United States). Thus, the ETFs that track the index need to rebalance their portfolios daily in order to match the returns of the index. This setting is ideal to test whether rebalancing affects the prices of the underlying derivatives. Dong (2016) reports that the introduction of VIX ETFs, which hold VIX futures, created strong predicted demand because of rebalancing on the VIX futures and caused a predictable price impact.

4.4. Exchange-Traded Funds During Episodes of Market Turmoil

ETFs received much attention during several episodes when markets tumbled and ETF prices appeared to deviate from the prices of the portfolios of the underlying securities. These incidents prompted regulators to be concerned about the possibility that ETFs serve as a transmission conduit for liquidity shocks (Office of Financial Research 2013). In particular, the concern is that during market turbulence, market makers and arbitrageurs cease intermediation activity because they do not have reliable pricing information. As a result, their absence can lead to illiquidity in the underlying securities, amplification of the shock, and transmission to other assets.

During several episodes in recent years, ETFs have displayed a high level of illiquidity during times of market turbulence, which has led regulators and academics to investigate whether ETFs exacerbate liquidity shocks. Perhaps the most well-known example of a market breakdown in recent years was the Flash Crash of May 6, 2010. On that day, the market was volatile because news about the Greek debt crisis was anticipated. The breakdown in market activity started with an unusual trading volume in S&P 500 e-mini futures contracts, which spread to the equity market and caused the S&P 500 to decline by about 9% within 20 minutes. Hundreds of stocks experienced sharp declines in prices. Borkovec et al. (2010) report that the liquidity of ETFs declined dramatically during the crash: Spreads widened significantly, and the limit order book dried up. They interpret this finding as evidence that market participants exited the market once signs of extreme volatility and illiquidity appeared. As a result of the exodus of liquidity providers, price discovery no longer took place at ETFs and there was a disconnect between the returns of ETFs and the returns of the underlying securities. Madhavan (2012) reviews the academic literature discussing the causes of the Flash Crash and agrees that liquidity providers exited the market. He argues that the departure of ETF prices from those of the underlying securities was rooted in the fragmentation of markets. Madhavan claims that stocks are more sensitive to liquidity shocks when markets are fragmented. He finds evidence suggesting that these stocks lost much liquidity during the Flash Crash event and that ETFs linked to these stocks experienced the heaviest volume of canceled orders and price deviations.

Peterffy (2010), who owns and heads one of the largest stock broker houses in the United States, testified that because of bad news from Europe, institutions sold ETF shares. Arbitrageurs bought ETF shares and sold short the underlying stocks. Because of sparse liquidity in some exchanges, some of the arbitrage programs diagnosed unreliable price data and withdrew from the market, leading to a positive feedback loop. As a result, the dry-up of arbitrage capital caused the mispricing between ETFs and the underlying stocks to widen. This mechanism is similar to the model of Pan & Zeng (2016), which attempts to explain the behavior of arbitrageurs. At times of market stress, when the securities underlying an ETF are illiquid, APs may abstain from engaging in arbitrage activity. It is important to note that prior literature has documented that arbitrageurs exit the market at times of market stress, potentially exacerbating market turbulence (e.g., Aragon & Strahan 2012; Ben-David, Franzoni & Moussawi 2012). There are also similarities to the model by Cespa & Foucault (2014). In their theory, market participants rely on information contained in the prices of one asset to price another, e.g., ETFs and the index constituents. However, when one asset becomes temporarily less liquid and its price becomes noisier, market participants are more cautious in trading the second asset, leading to lower liquidity. Thus, liquidity shocks travel across assets because they are informationally connected.

Following the Flash Crash, several regulators and market commentators voiced concerns about ETFs. Ramaswamy (2011) generalizes the findings from events of market turbulence and argues that some ETFs may pose a risk to the financial system. In particular, he argues that synthetic and exotic ETFs (e.g., leveraged ETFs, bear ETFs) use leverage, swaps, and derivatives to track the index. He says that past experience shows that assets with a long chain of intermediaries and counterparties may cause or exacerbate financial shocks via risk exposure along the chain of financial intermediaries.

After the Flash Crash of 2010, the Securities and Exchange Commission (SEC) adopted rules to halt trading in individual securities, including ETFs, that exhibit extreme volatility swings. Subsequently, on August 24, 2015, extreme price movements triggered trading halts of 5 minutes or longer for more than 300 ETFs; 11 ETFs were halted 10 times or more (Driebusch, Vaishampayan & Josephs 2015). Following steep declines in the futures market prior to the stock market opening, there was a big run on ETF prices immediately after 9:30 AM, which caused several ETFs to trade at sharp discounts relative to their NAV. ETF market makers and APs arguably withdrew from the market after a trading pause in the futures market, which they used to hedge their exposure in volatile trading sessions (Dieterich 2015). On August 24, 42% of the overall volume in US equity markets was ETF trading, despite a big fraction of the trading halts being attributed to US-listed ETFs. The shock that hit ETF prices was eventually transmitted to several large underlying stocks without an apparent fundamental reason (SEC 2015).[12] This event could very well be an example of the liquidity and arbitrage model proposed by Pan & Zeng (2016), in which arbitrageurs stay on the sidelines during market stress because of concerns that the mispricing may widen; eventually this behavior becomes self-fulfilling, as the absence of arbitrage by itself leads to greater mispricing. Agarwal et al. (2016) use the August 24 event to test whether ETFs pose a liquidity risk in times of market stress. They find improvements in underlying stock liquidity during the period when trading in the ETFs with wild price swings was halted that day. Their results suggest that ETFs create an additional layer of commonality in the liquidity of underlying securities that comes into play in times of market stress. In other words, when the price of an ETF diverges from the price of the underlying portfolio, APs and arbitrageurs trade in an attempt to correct the mispricing. This mechanical trading activity provides liquidity at the stock level; however, the direction of the liquidity (buy or sell) is correlated across the different securities that compose the ETF basket, usually a sample of the underlying index.

June 20, 2013, is another instance when the prices of ETFs plummeted because of a lack of countering arbitrage forces. On that day, the prices of stocks in many emerging markets declined sharply. The ETFs that track the indices of these emerging markets and that are traded in the United States experienced sharp price declines as well. However, because the foreign markets were closed during the operating hours of the US markets, APs and arbitrageurs appear to have abstained from the market, letting ETF prices collapse under the selling pressure of US investors (Condon & Kaske 2013).

These events show that across several market occasions, the prices of ETFs have diverged from the prices of the underlying portfolios because of a lack of arbitrage between the two assets. The model of Pan & Zeng (2016) appears to explain the withdrawal of arbitrage capital from the market. Their model suggests that at times, APs have little incentive to engage in arbitrage, for example, because of an accumulation of inventory. In these cases, they may abstain from the market, leading to greater mispricing.

5. CONCLUSION AND DIRECTIONS FOR FUTURE RESEARCH

ETFs are perhaps the greatest game-changer in the asset management industry in the first decades of the twenty-first century. These investment vehicles offer a combination of features that have not been available to investors before: low-cost transactions, intraday liquidity, and passive index tracking. The rise of ETFs is part of a wider process that has taken place in the asset management industry over the past three decades: Passive management has expanded, while at the same time the asset management landscape has become more concentrated. Although some of the implications of these trends have been studied (e.g., Ben-David et al. 2015), some important research questions remain open. In particular, do the low transaction costs of ETFs enable short-term trading, creating a new breed of short-term speculators that did not exist before? In other words, do ETFs attract speculators who traded other investment vehicles before the introduction of ETFs (e.g.,

[12]For example, DVY's decline of 35% caused significant price pressure on large underlying basket stocks, such as GE, which dropped by as much as 21% before reverting back to prior values after the DVY's price stabilized during the day.

closed-end funds), or did they start speculating once ETFs were available? Do these traders have a significant impact on the quality of prices?

The literature presents mixed evidence about the effects of ETFs on the informational efficiency of the underlying securities. On the one hand, researchers have found that ETFs allow information to be more efficiently impounded into security prices. On the other hand, evidence indicates that securities prices have become noisier since the introduction of ETFs. It is possible that both phenomena are taking place in parallel: Security prices impound information more efficiently once they are included in ETFs' baskets and, at the same time, become more volatile for nonfundamental reasons. Missing to date is a welfare analysis exploring the net effect of ETFs on market participants. Do ETFs increase informational efficiency overall? Are there corners of the financial markets where the informational gains are particularly large, and others where they are negative? Are there times in which ETFs increase price efficiency and market quality and others in which they detract along those dimensions?

The ability of ETF prices to truly reflect the value of the underlying securities depends on the presence of agents who facilitate arbitrage: high-frequency arbitrageurs, hedge funds, and APs. The concerns raised by academics and regulators about the risks that these classes of investors may create during events of market turbulence deserve additional investigation. Specifically, there is a concern that ETFs provide a false sense of liquidity: that they are liquid in a normal trading environment, but during turbulent times, liquidity dries up because APs and arbitrageurs stay out of the market. The effect could be exacerbated if the presence of ETFs crowds out (i.e., withdraws) liquidity from the underlying assets (e.g., corporate bonds, as in Dannhauser 2017). It is important that financial economists continue to explore the integrity of financial markets and warn against potential market breakdowns that could negatively impact the real economy and be potentially harmful for society at large.

Understanding the effects of ETFs on liquidity and efficiency as well as their mechanism is important not only from an academic standpoint, but also from a regulatory perspective. As a result of the financial crisis of 2008, and also because of a few later episodes when the ETF arbitrage mechanism has broken down, both investors and policymakers have raised concerns about the fragility of the ETF market (Rennison & Hale 2016; Wigglesworth, Bullock & Rennison 2016); for example, the former head of the SEC, Mary Jo White, recently hinted at a large-scale review of the ETF landscape by the US financial market regulator (White 2016). Our hope is that the academic research about ETFs is useful in quantifying the systemic risks that these investment vehicles pose and that it can potentially help address them.

DISCLOSURE STATEMENT

The authors are not aware of any affiliations, memberships, funding, or financial holdings that might be perceived as affecting the objectivity of this review.

LITERATURE CITED

Agapova A. 2011. Conventional mutual index funds versus exchange-traded funds. *J. Financ. Markets* 14:323–43

Agarwal V, Hanouna P, Moussawi R, Stahel C. 2016. *Do ETFs increase the commonality in liquidity of underlying stocks?* Work. Pap., Villanova Univ.

Antoniewicz R, Heinrichs J. 2014. Understanding exchange-traded funds: how ETFs work. *ICI Res. Perspect.* 20(5):1–39

Appel IR, Gormley TA, Keim DB. 2016. Passive investors, not passive owners. *J. Financ. Econ.* 121(1):111–41

Aragon GO, Strahan PE. 2012. Hedge funds as liquidity providers: evidence from the Lehman bankruptcy. *J. Financ. Econ.* 103(3):570–87

Bai Q, Bond SA, Hatch B. 2015. The impact of leveraged and inverse ETFs on underlying real estate returns. *Real Estate Econ.* 43(1):37–66

Baltussen G, Da Z, van Bekkum S. 2016. *Indexing and stock market serial dependence around the world.* Work. Pap., Notre Dame Univ.

Barber BM, Odean T. 2000. Trading is hazardous to your wealth: the common stock investment performance of individual investors. *J. Finance* 55(2):773–806

Barnhart SW, Rosenstein S. 2010. Exchange-traded fund introductions and closed-end fund discounts and volume. *Financ. Rev.* 45(4):973–94

Basak S, Pavlova A. 2013. Asset prices and institutional investors. *Am. Econ. Rev.* 103(5):1728–58

Basak S, Pavlova A. 2016. A model of financialization of commodities. *J. Finance* 71(4):1511–55

Ben-David I, Franzoni F, Moussawi R. 2012. Hedge funds stock trading during the financial crisis of 2007–2009. *Rev. Financ. Stud.* 25(1):1–54

Ben-David I, Franzoni F, Moussawi R. 2013. *Do ETFs increase stock volatility?* Work. Pap., Ohio State Univ.

Ben-David I, Franzoni F, Moussawi R, Sedunov J. 2015. *Mammoth institutional investors (previously circulated as The granular nature of large institutional investors).* Work. Pap., Ohio State Univ.

Berk JB, Green RC. 2004. Mutual fund flows and performance in rational markets. *J. Political Econ.* 112(6):1269–95

Bessembinder H, Seguin PJ. 1992. Futures-trading activity and stock price volatility. *J. Finance* 47:2015–34

Bhattacharya A, O'Hara M. 2016. *Can ETFs increase market fragility? Effect of information linkages in ETF markets.* Work. Pap., Cornell Univ.

Bhattacharya U, Loos B, Meyer S, Hackethal A. 2017. Abusing ETFs. *Rev. Finance* 21(3):1217–50

Blocher J, Whaley RE. 2016. *Two-sided markets in asset management: exchange-traded funds and securities lending.* Work. Pap., Vanderbilt Univ.

Bond P, García D. 2016. *The equilibrium consequences of indexing.* Work. Pap., Univ. Washington

Boone AL, White JT. 2015. The effect of institutional ownership on firm transparency and information production. *J. Financ. Econ.* 117(3):508–33

Borkovec M, Domowitz I, Serbin V, Yegerman H. 2010. Liquidity and price discovery in exchange-traded funds. *J. Index Invest.* 1(2):24–42

Bradley H, Litan RE. 2011a. *Choking the recovery: why new growth companies aren't going public and unrecognized risks of future market disruptions.* Work. Pap., Kaufman Found., Kansas City, MO

Bradley H, Litan RE. 2011b. *ETFs and the present danger to capital formation.* Work. Pap., Kaufman Found., Kansas City, MO

Broman MS. 2016a. Liquidity, style investing and excess comovement of exchange-traded fund returns. *J. Financ. Markets* 30:27–53

Broman MS. 2016b. *Local demand, preferred habitats and excess comovement.* Work. Pap., Syracuse Univ.

Broman MS. 2016c. *Why do investors chase passive returns?* Work. Pap., Syracuse Univ.

Broman MS, Shum P. 2016. *Does liquidity encourage short-term trading? Evidence from exchange-traded funds.* Work. Pap., Syracuse Univ.

Brown DC, Davies SW, Ringgenberg MC. 2016. *ETF arbitrage and return predictability.* Work. Pap., Univ. Ariz.

Cella C, Ellul A, Giannetti M. 2013. Investors' horizons and the amplification of market shocks. *Rev. Financ. Stud.* 26(7):1607–48

Cespa G, Foucault T. 2014. Illiquidity contagion and liquidity crashes. *Rev. Financ. Stud.* 27(6):1615–60

Chang EC, Cheng JW, Pinegar Y. 1999. Short-sales constraints and price discovery: evidence from the Hong Kong market. *J. Finance* 62(5):2097–121

Cheng M, Madhavan A. 2009. The dynamics of leveraged and inverse exchange-traded funds. *J. Invest. Manag.* 7(4):43–62

Chinco A, Fos V. 2016. *The sound of many funds rebalancing.* Work. Pap., Univ. Ill., Urbana-Champagne, IL

Clifford CP, Fulkerson JA, Jordan BD. 2014. What drives ETF flows? *Financ. Rev.* 49(3):619–42

Condon C, Kaske M. 2013. ETF tracking errors in rout shows access comes with risks. *Bloomberg*, June 23

Cong LW, Xu D. 2016. *Rise of factor investing: asset prices, informational efficiency, and security design.* Work. Pap., Univ. Chic.

Coughenour JF, Saad MM. 2004. Common market makers and commonality in liquidity. *J. Financ. Econ.* 73:37–69

Coval J, Stafford E. 2007. Asset fire sales (and purchases) in equity markets. *J. Financ. Econ.* 86(2):479–512

Da Z, Shive S. 2014. *Exchange traded funds and asset return correlations.* Work. Pap., Notre Dame Univ.

Dannhauser CD. 2017. The impact of innovation: evidence from corporate bond exchange-traded funds (ETFs). *J. Financ. Econ.* In press

Dieterich C. 2015. The great ETF debacle explained. *Barron's*, Sep. 5. **http://www.barrons.com/articles/the-great-etf-debacle-explained-1441434195**

Dong XS. 2016. *Price impact of ETP demand on underliers.* Work. Pap., Princeton Univ.

Driebusch C, Vaishampayan S, Josephs L. 2015. Wild trading exposed flaws in ETFs. *Wall Street Journal*, Sep. 13. **http://www.wsj.com/articles/wild-trading-exposed-flaws-in-etfs-1442174925**

Evans R, Moussawi R, Pagano MS, Sedunov J. 2017. *ETF failures-to-deliver: naked short-selling or operational shorting?* Work. Pap., Villanova Univ.

Frazzini A, Lamont OA. 2008. Dumb money: mutual fund flows and the cross-section of stock returns. *J. Financ. Econ.* 88:299–322

French KR. 2008. The cost of active investing. *J. Finance* 63(4):1537–73

Glosten L, Nallareddy S, Zou Y. 2016. *ETF trading and informational efficiency of underlying securities.* Work. Pap., Duke Univ.

Goetzmann WN, Massa M. 2003. Index funds and stock market growth. *J. Bus.* 76(1):1–28

Greenwood R. 2005. Short- and long-term demand curves for stocks: theory and evidence on the dynamics of arbitrage. *J. Financ. Econ.* 75(3):607–49

Greenwood R, Sosner N. 2007. Trading patterns and excess comovement of stock returns. *Financ. Anal. J.* 63:69–81

Guedj I, Huang J. 2009. *Are ETFs replacing index mutual funds?* Work. Pap., Univ. Tex.

Hill JM. 2016. The evolution and success of index strategies in ETFs. *Financ. Analysts J.* 72(5):8–13

Hill JM, Nadig D, Hougan M, Fuhr D. 2015. *A comprehensive guide to exchange-traded funds (ETFs).* Work. Pap., CFA Inst. Res. Found.

Hurlin C, Iseli G, Pérignon C, Yeung SCH. 2014. *The collateral risk of ETFs.* Work. Pap., HEC Paris

Israeli D, Lee CMC, Sridharan S. 2017. Is there a dark side to exchange traded funds (ETFs)? An information perspective. *Rev. Account. Stud.* 22:1048–83

Ivanov IT, Lenkey SL. 2016. *Are concerns about leveraged ETFs overblown?* Work. Pap. 2014-106, Finance Econ. Discuss. Ser., Fed. Reserve Board, Washington, DC

Jiang W, Yan H. 2016. *Financial innovation, investor behavior, and arbitrage: evidence from the ETF market.* Work. Pap., Chin. Univ. Hong Kong

Kaul A, Mehrotra V, Morck R. 2002. Demand curves for stocks do slope down: new evidence from an index weights adjustment. *J. Finance* 55:893–912

Koch A, Ruenzi S, Starks L. 2016. Commonality in liquidity: a demand-side explanation. *Rev. Financ. Stud.* 29(8):1943–74

Krause T, Ehsani S, Lien D. 2014. Exchange-traded funds, liquidity and volatility. *Appl. Financ. Econ.* 24(24):1617–30

Lee C, Shleifer A, Thaler RH. 1991. Investor sentiment and the closed-end fund puzzle. *J. Finance* 46(1):75–109

Lettau M, Madhavan A. 2016. *ETF 101 for economists.* Work. Pap., Univ. Calif., Berkeley

Li FW, Zhu Q. 2016. *Synthetic shorting with ETFs.* Work Pap., Univ. Tex., Austin

MacKinlay AC, Ramaswamy K. 1988. Index-futures arbitrage and the behavior of stock index futures prices. *Rev. Financ. Stud.* 1(2):138–58

Mackintosh P, Lin V. 2011. *ETF trade strategy: triple trouble.* Work. Pap., Credit Suisse

Madhavan AN. 2012. Exchange-traded funds, market structure, and the Flash Crash. *Financ. Anal. J.* 68(4):20–35

Madhavan AN. 2016. *Exchange-Traded Funds and the New Dynamics of Investing.* Oxford, UK: Oxford Univ. Press

Madhavan AN, Marchioni U, Li W, Du DY. 2014. Equity ETFs versus index futures: a comparison for fully funded investors. *J. Index Invest.* 5(2):66–75

Madhavan AN, Sobczyk A. 2016. Price dynamics and liquidity of exchange-traded funds. *J. Invest. Manag.* 14(2):1–17
Malamud S. 2015. *A dynamic equilibrium model of ETFs*. Work. Pap., Swiss Finance Inst., Zurich
Marshall BR, Nguyen NH, Visaltanachoti N. 2013. ETF arbitrage: intraday evidence. *J. Bank. Finance* 37(9):3486–98
Marshall BR, Nguyen NH, Visaltanachoti N. 2015. *ETF liquidity*. Work. Pap., Massey Univ.
Nagel S. 2012. Evaporating liquidity. *Rev. Financ. Stud.* 25(7):2005–39
Off. Financ. Res. 2013. *Asset Management and Financial Stability*. Washington, DC: Off. Financ. Res.
Pan K, Zeng Y. 2016. *ETF arbitrage under liquidity mismatch*. Work. Pap., Harvard Univ.
Petajisto A. 2017. Inefficiencies in the pricing of exchange-traded funds. *Financ. Anal. J.* 73(1):24–54
Peterffy T. 2010. *Comments*. Joint CFTC-SEC Advis. Comm. Emerg. Regul. Issues Meet., June 22. **https://www.interactivebrokers.com/download/CFTC-SEC_Adv_Comittee_Speech.pdf**
Piccotti LR. 2014. *An ETF premium puzzle and a market segmentation explanation*. Work. Pap., Rutgers Univ.
Pontiff J. 1996. Costly arbitrage: evidence from closed-end funds. *Q. J. Econ.* 111(4):1135–51
Ramaswamy S. 2011. *Market structures and systemic risks of exchange-traded funds*. Work. Pap., Bank Int. Settl., Basel, Switz.
Rennison J. 2016. Low-cost ETF challengers eat into derivatives market. *Financial Times*, Sept. 11
Rennisonn J, Hale T. 2016. Explosive growth of bond ETFs stirs fears of impending crisis. *Financial Times*, Oct. 19.
Richie N, Daigler RT, Gleason KC. 2008. The limits to stock index arbitrage: examining S&P 500 futures and SPDRs. *J. Futures Markets* 28(12):1182–205
Roll R, Schwartz E, Subrahmanyam A. 2007. Liquidity and the law of one price: the case of the futures-cash basis. *J. Finance* 62(5):2201–34
Schultz P, Shive S. 2016. *Mutual funds and bond liquidity*. Work. Pap., Notre Dame Univ.
SEC (Secur. Exch. Comm.). 2015. *Equity market volatility*. Res. Note, Div. Trading Markets, SEC, Washington, DC. **https://www.sec.gov/marketstructure/research/equity_market_volatility.pdf**
SEC (Secur. Exch. Comm.). 2017. *SEC adopts T + 2 settlement cycle for securities transactions*. News Release, March 22. **https://www.sec.gov/news/press-release/2017-68-0**
Shleifer A. 1986. Do demand curves for stocks slope down? *J. Finance* 41(3):579–90
Shleifer A, Vishny RW. 1997. The limits of arbitrage. *J. Finance* 52(1):35–55
Shreck M, Antoniewicz S. 2012. ETF basics: the creation and redemption process and why it matters. *ICI Viewpoints*, Jan. 19. **https://www.ici.org/viewpoints/view_12_etfbasics_creation**
Shum P, Hejazi W, Haryanto E, Rodier A. 2016. Intraday share price volatility and leveraged ETF rebalancing. *Rev. Finance* 20(6):2379–409
Sorkin AR. 2011. Volatility, thy name is E.T.F. *New York Times*, Oct. 1
Staer A. 2014. *Fund flows and underlying returns: the case of ETFs*. Work. Pap., Univ. Calif., Irvine
Stambaugh RF. 2014. Investment noise and trends. *J. Finance* 69(4):1415–53
Stein JC. 1987. Informational externalities and welfare-reducing speculation. *J. Political Econ.* 95(6):1123–45
Stratmann T, Welborn JW. 2012. *Exchange-traded funds, fails-to-deliver, and market volatility*. Work. Pap., George Mason Univ.
Sullivan RN, Xiong JX. 2012. How index trading increases market vulnerability. *Financ. Anal. J.* 68(2):70–84
Toplensky R. 2016. Investors replace futures with ETFs. *Financial Times*, March 23
Tuzun T. 2014. *Are leveraged and inverse ETFs the new portfolio insurers?* Work. Pap., Board Gov., Fed. Reserve Syst.
Wermers R, Xue J. 2015. *Intraday ETF trading and the volatility of the underlying*. Work. Pap., Univ. Md.
White MJ. 2016. *The future of investment company regulation*. Keynote address at Invest. Co. Inst. Gen. Meet., May 20, Washington, DC. **https://www.sec.gov/news/speech/white-speech-keynote-address-ici-052016.html**
Wigglesworth R, Bullock N, Rennison J. 2016. SEC gears up for major review of exchange traded funds. *Financial Times*, Oct. 20
Wurgler J. 2011. On the economic consequences of index-linked investing. In *Challenges to Business in the Twenty-First Century*, ed. G Rosenfeld, JW Lorsch, R Khurana, pp. 20–34. Cambridge, MA: Am. Acad. Arts Sci.
Wurgler J, Zhuravskaya E. 2002. Does arbitrage flatten demand curves for stocks? *J. Bus.* 75(4):583–608

An Overview of China's Financial System

Franklin Allen,[1] Jun "QJ" Qian,[2] and Xian Gu[3]

[1]Imperial College London, London SW7 2AZ, United Kingdom; email: f.allen@imperial.ac.uk

[2]Fanhai International School of Finance, Fudan University, Shanghai 200433, China

[3]School of Finance, Central University of Finance and Economics, Beijing 100081, China

Annu. Rev. Financ. Econ. 2017. 9:191–231

First published as a Review in Advance on September 13, 2017

The *Annual Review of Financial Economics* is online at financial.annualreviews.org

https://doi.org/10.1146/annurev-financial-112116-025652

Copyright © 2017 by Annual Reviews. All rights reserved

JEL codes: O5, K0, G2

Keywords

banks, nonperforming loans, markets, alternative finance, hybrid sector, financial crisis

Abstract

We provide a review of China's financial system and consider the challenges it faces and future reforms. The formal sectors of the financial system, which include a fast-growing stock market and are dominated by a banking sector with large state-owned banks, have played a critical role in financing the state sectors and the investment-driven economic growth model. However, the formal sectors have not served the needs of the private sectors or of households; these dynamic sectors have been financed by alternative finance sectors operating largely outside the markets and formal institutions. Going forward, financial markets need to be further developed to provide more support for the private sectors, including technology and services industries; the formal and alternative sectors should work together to improve the efficiency of resource allocation to better support the new model of consumption- and innovation-driven growth. Finally, the financial system needs to reduce the likelihood of damaging financial crises, which have included a real estate crisis, a banking crisis triggered by defaults on corporate and local government debt, and a twin crisis in the currency market and the banking sector.

1. INTRODUCTION

One of the enduring puzzles surrounding China's rapid economic growth during the past few decades is how it was achieved with an underdeveloped financial system. Despite more than 30 years of reforms, the development of the financial sector is lagging behind that of the overall economy. Prior research finds that the relationship between the structure of financial systems and economic growth in the real economy differs significantly across countries. We provide a comprehensive review of China's financial system and compare it with financial systems in other countries in terms of its role in supporting economic growth.[1] We examine the formal sectors of the financial system, including a large intermediation sector with many state-owned banks and other institutions in addition to a stock market that has been growing fast since its inception in 1990. We also examine an alternative finance sector, which largely operates outside the markets and formal institutions and consists of alternative financing channels (all nonmarket, nonbank sources), governance mechanisms, and institutions. In addition, we consider challenges facing the Chinese financial system and discuss further reforms to help prevent financial crises that could disrupt the transition and further growth of the economy.

We draw four main conclusions. First, compared with other developed and emerging economies, China's financial system has been dominated by a large banking system. All of the Big Five banks (see Section 2.2) and other large institutions have already been publicly listed in recent years, including being cross-listed in developed markets such as Hong Kong and the United States, with the government still being the largest shareholder and remaining in control. These state-owned banks have played a critical role in funding state-owned enterprises (SOEs) and large government projects, including infrastructure, and in supporting the investment-driven growth model. The ownership structure and listing status have served these banks well in terms of avoiding the crises encountered by major financial institutions in developed countries that were at the center of the 2007–2009 global financial crisis. However, high levels of corporate and local government debt, along with risks accumulated both on and off the balance sheets of these banks, pose threats to the stability of the banking sector. Given that a large portion of nonperforming loans (NPLs) result from poor decisions made by state-owned banks to lend to the state sectors, we regard this part of the banking sector problem as a fiscal issue that the government can resolve, as the government did during the first half of the 2000s decade, when NPLs of the banking sector reached 20% of GDP.

Our second conclusion concerns China's financial markets. The stock market now has more than 3,000 firms listed and traded in the Shanghai and Shenzhen exchanges, and the domestic A-share market is the second largest in the world in terms of total market capitalization, trailing only the US equity markets. The bond market has also been growing fast in recent years, dominated by the issuance and trading of government bonds and corporate bonds issued by large SOEs and other large and highly rated firms. Markets have also supported the state sectors by allowing SOEs and other government entities to raise funds through the issuance of stocks and bonds. In a recent paper, Allen et al. (2017c) point out that the key structural problem for the A-share stock market is its underrepresentation of firms from nonstate sectors, which results from deficiencies in IPO listing and delisting procedures. These institutional problems lead to poor performance of the stock market relative to markets in both developed and emerging economies and relative to Chinese firms listed overseas, including in Hong Kong, Singapore, and the United States. Further

[1] China's economic growth rate remains high relative to other countries after the global financial crisis. Based on the report of the World Bank (2015) for the International Comparison Program, China overtook the United States in terms of GDP PPP (purchasing power parities) during the year 2014.

development of the Chinese stock market remains a key task for the Chinese financial system, so that it can provide more support for the private sectors and deliver stable and higher returns to households as compared to the bond market.

Third, the alternative financial sector has played an important role in supporting the growth of the most dynamic sector of the economy. In an earlier paper, Allen, Qian & Qian (2005) argue that the most successful part of the financial system, in terms of supporting the growth of the overall economy, is not the formal financial sector (banks and markets), but rather a sector of alternative financing channels, such as informal financial intermediaries; internal financing and trade credits; and coalitions of various forms among firms, investors, and local governments. This alternative financial sector has supported the growth of a hybrid sector with various types of ownership structures, which has been growing much faster than both the state sector (all the SOEs) and the listed sector (all the firms listed in the A-share market).[2] Going forward, this sector and the formal financial sector should coexist and provide more support for the private sectors and for households and should improve the efficiency of resource allocation in the entire economy.

Fourth, a significant challenge for China's financial system is to avoid damaging financial crises that could severely disrupt economic growth and stability. These crises could include traditional financial crises, e.g., a banking sector crisis stemming from an accumulation of NPLs and a sudden drop in banks' profits, or a crisis/crash resulting from speculative asset bubbles in the real estate market (or in the stock market, if bubbles similar to that formed during the first half of 2015 appear again). Since China's entrance into the World Trade Organization (WTO) in 2001, the integration of China's financial system and overall economy with the rest of the world has significantly sped up, but large-scale and sudden capital flows and foreign speculation increase the likelihood of a currency crisis or a twin crisis (simultaneous foreign exchange and banking crises), depending on how the government and central bank respond. Given the recent addition of the renminbi (RMB) into the IMF's special drawing rights (SDR) basket, China should continue to improve the status of the RMB as a true global currency and not retreat from the process of capital account liberalization. At the current time, an imminent threat to the stability of the financial system is a significant drop in housing prices in multiple regions of the country, accompanied by widespread defaults and bankruptcies of highly levered firms and local government agencies. We discuss further reforms in the real estate and local government sectors to prevent such crises.

In summary, the formal sectors of the financial system have played a critical role in financing the state sectors and the old, investment-driven economic growth model, but have not met the financing and investment needs of the private sectors and of households. These dynamic sectors—the key engine behind China's long-term growth—have been financed by alternative finance sectors operating largely outside the markets and formal institutions. Going forward, financial markets need to be further developed to provide more support for the private sectors, including technology and services industries. The formal and alternative sectors should work together to improve the efficiency of resource allocation to better support the new model of consumption and innovation-driven growth. Finally, further reforms are needed to reduce the likelihood of damaging financial crises. The remaining sections of this article are organized as follows. In Section 2, we briefly review the history of China's financial system's development and present aggregate evidence on China's financial system. In Section 3, we examine China's banking and nonbanking financial intermediaries over time and the recent developments in the shadow banking system. In Section 4, we briefly examine the growth and irregularities of financial markets, including the stock market,

[2]Our definition of the hybrid sector includes all nonstate, nonlisted firms, including privately or individually owned firms, and firms that are partially owned by local governments (e.g., Township and Village Enterprises).

bond market, real estate market, and listed firms, and consider the effects of several initiatives to develop new markets and further develop existing markets, as well as changes in corporate governance among listed firms. In Section 5, we examine the shadow financial sector, including alternative financial channels and governance mechanisms. In Section 6, we examine different types of financial crises and their potential effects on China's financial system in the near future. Finally, Section 7 concludes.

In terms of converting RMB into US dollars, we use an exchange rate of US$1 = RMB 8.28 (yuan) for transactions and events occurring before 2005, and the spot rate at the end of each year for activities during and after 2005.

2. OVERVIEW OF CHINA'S FINANCIAL SYSTEM

2.1. The Finance-Growth Nexus

The main reason that financial development and real growth are connected is that financial systems allow households and firms to intertemporally smooth expenditures and share risks. Through acquiring information and allocating capital, financial systems can improve the ex ante assessment of investment opportunities and enhance growth by spurring technological innovation (Allen & Gale 1999). Another important role of financial systems is to achieve an optimal allocation of risk, especially diversifiable risks. For instance, financial markets ease risk diversification by inducing a portfolio shift toward projects with higher expected returns (Greenwood & Jovanovic 1990, Obstfeld 1994). Better risk diversification in international financial markets enhances economic growth by exploiting the benefits of international trade (Helpman & Razin 1978).

Many empirical studies have demonstrated the positive association between financial development and economic growth (e.g., Goldsmith 1969, King & Levine 1993, Levine & Zervos 1998). For example, Rajan & Zingales (1998) confirm the finance-growth nexus at a microeconomic level using 36 industries in 42 countries and show that industrial sectors that are more dependent on external finance develop disproportionately faster in countries with more developed financial markets. At the end of the 1990s, economists also suggested the influence of institutions—legal, political, social, or cultural—on countries' long-term economic growth (Robinson, Acemoglu & Johnson 2004). For example, La Porta et al. (1997, 1998) essentially document that legal origin is important in explaining cross-country differences in financial development (see also Beck et al. 2001; Beck, Demirgüç-Kunt & Maksimovic 2005). Furthermore, La Porta et al. (2002) study the performance of government involvement with the financial sector, showing that higher degrees of public ownership are associated with lower levels of bank development and slower economic growth.

There are also numerous empirical studies on the association between financial structure and economic structure, as banks and stock markets play different financial roles. However, the literature is not fully conclusive on this. Beck et al. (2001) document that countries do not show faster growth with either market-based or bank-based financial systems. What matters more is the overall development of the financial sector and the efficiency of the relevant legal system. Tadesse (2002) finds that the association between the financial sector and real growth depends on the overall development of the financial sector and real economy, indicating that, whereas market-based systems perform better in countries with more developed financial systems, bank-based systems fare better in countries with less developed financial systems. Levine & Zervos (1998) also find that both the initial level of turnover ratio in stock markets and banking development enter the growth regression significantly; however, they emphasize that the mere size of a stock market is not significant and that what matters is the level of activity in the market.

However, as Allen, Qian & Qian (2005) document, China is an important counterexample to the findings in the finance-growth nexus literature. Without a well-developed legal or financial system, it has been one of the fastest-growing economies around the globe. In recent years, the shadow banking system has been growing dramatically in China and has complemented the standard financial sector by providing funding to the real sector and supporting growth (see, e.g., Acharya et al. 2016, Allen et al. 2016). Although China's real growth has been slowing down slightly to a so-called new normal status in the past 2–3 years, its success may provide us with new insights into the finance-nexus literature.

2.2. A Brief Review of the History of China's Financial System

Before 1949, China's financial system was well developed, with many rapidly growing private banks.[3] However, all pre-1949 capitalist companies and institutions were nationalized after the foundation of the People's Republic of China in 1949. Between 1950 and 1978, China's financial system consisted of a single bank: the People's Bank of China (PBOC), which was owned and controlled by the central government under the Ministry of Finance and which served as both the central bank and a commercial bank, controlling about 93% of the total financial assets of the country and handling almost all financial transactions.

The first main structural change began in 1978 and ended in 1987. In 1977, the PBOC was separated from the Ministry of Finance as a top-tier unit of the State Council, and some of its former commercial banking businesses were taken over by the largest three state-owned banks in China: The Bank of China (BOC)[4] was given the mandate to specialize in transactions related to foreign trade and investment; the People's Construction Bank of China (PCBC), originally formed in 1954, was set up to handle transactions related to fixed investment (especially in manufacturing); the Agricultural Bank of China (ABC) was set up in 1979 to deal with all banking business in rural areas; and the PBOC was formally established as China's central bank and a two-tier banking system was formed. The fourth state-owned commercial bank, the Industrial and Commercial Bank of China (ICBC), was formed in 1984, and took over the rest of the commercial transactions of the PBOC. Finally, the fifth state-owned commercial bank, the Bank of Communications (BComm), was reestablished in 1987. For most of the 1980s, the development of the financial system can be characterized by the fast growth of financial intermediaries outside of the Big Five banks (ABC, BComm, BOC, ICBC, and PCBC). Regional banks, rural credit cooperatives (RCCs), urban credit cooperatives (UCCs), and other nonbank financial intermediaries, such as trust and investment corporations (TICs), emerged and proliferated in this period.

The inception of China's stock market, including the two domestic stock markets, is the most significant event for China's financial system in the 1990s. Both markets, one in Shanghai [the Shanghai Stock Exchange (SSE)] and the other in Shenzhen [the Shenzhen Stock Exchange (SZSE)], were established in December 1990 and grew fast in the 1990s and 2000s. In parallel with the development of the stock market, the real estate market also went from nonexistence in the early 1990s to a size comparable with that of the stock market by 2007.[5] Both the stock and real

[3] For a description of the pre-1949 history of China's financial system, see Allen, Qian & Qian (2008) and Allen et al. (2012c); for anecdotal evidence on China's financial system in the same period, see, for example, Lee (1993) and Kirby (1995).

[4] BOC was originally established in 1912 as a private bank in Shanghai and is among the oldest Chinese banks. During 1912–1928, BOC was responsible for some functions of the central bank, such as managing the Treasury and issuing notes. After 1949, BOC started to specialize in transactions related to foreign currency.

[5] At the end of 2007, the total market capitalization of the two domestic exchanges (SSE and SZSE) was about $4.5 trillion and total investment in the real estate market was around $3.12 trillion.

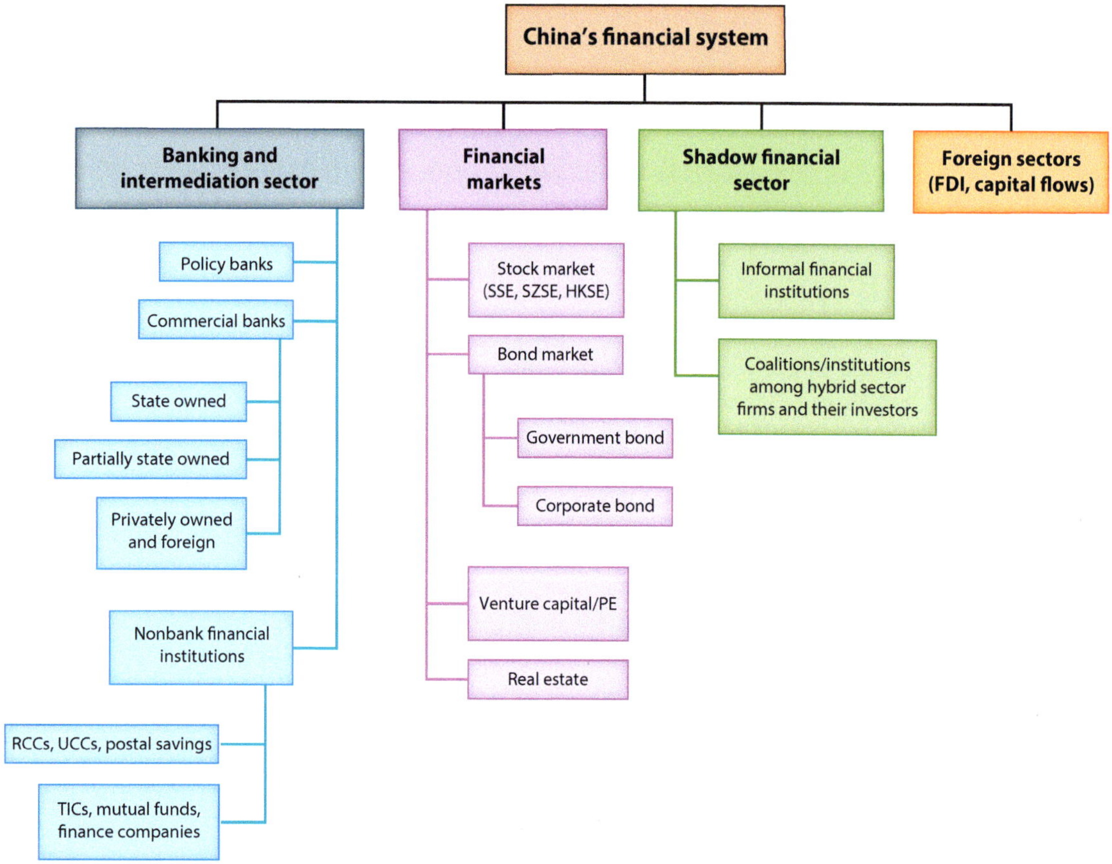

Figure 1

Overview of China's financial system. Abbreviations: FDI, foreign direct investment; HKSE, Hong Kong Stock Exchange; PE, private equity; RCC, rural credit cooperative; SSE, Shanghai Stock Exchange; SZSE, Shenzhen Stock Exchange; TIC, trust and investment corporation; UCC, urban credit cooperative.

estate markets are characterized by high volatilities and speculative short-term behavior by many investors, which in part result from the fact that the development of a supportive legal framework and institutions has been lagging behind that of other sectors. We provide a brief analysis of the status and problems of the financial markets in Section 4.

Following the Asian Financial Crisis in 1997, financial sector reform focused on state-owned banks and especially the problem of NPLs; the China Banking Regulation Committee (CBRC) was also established to oversee the banking industry. We further discuss the banking sector and related issues in Section 3. After China joined the WTO in 2001 and after the exchange rate reform in mid-2005, China began to face increasing competition from foreign financial institutions and larger-scale capital inflows and outflows. We discuss these issues in Section 6.

Figure 1 depicts the current structure of the entire financial system. In the following sections, we describe and examine each of the major sectors of the financial system. In addition to the standard sectors of banking and nonbanking intermediation and financial markets, we document the importance of the shadow financial sector in contributing to the high growth of the real economy. Other literature also discusses China's foreign sectors, which we do not cover in this article. For discussions on the history and the role of these sectors in supporting the growth of the economy, see, for example, Prasad & Wei (2007).

3. THE BANKING AND NONBANK INTERMEDIATION SECTOR

In this section we examine China's banking and nonbank intermediation sector. We first review aggregate evidence on the banking sector. The high level of NPLs relative to assets had been the most severe issue in China's banking sector, but was mainly solved in the early 2000s before the crisis of 2007–2009, and after that it has again become one of the difficult issues in the sector. We review evidence on the development of nonstate banks and other financial intermediaries, as well as the recent development of shadow banking.

3.1. Aggregate Evidence on the Banking Sector

China's household savings rates have been high in the past decades, similarly to those in other Asian economies. The main causes of this fact lie in the fast growth of the economy and the sharp increase in personal income with limited investment opportunities.

In **Table 1** we break down China's bank loans by maturity, loan purpose, and borrower type during the period 1994–2013.[6] We find that bank loans have been one of the important financing sources for hybrid sector firms. However, according to the PBOC, at the end of 2010, outstanding bank loans in local currency amounted to RMB 30.29 trillion, with 52.2% flowing to the state-owned sector. This number had declined slightly to 47.6% at the end of 2014 but still stays at a higher level compared to the 8.0% flowing to collectively owned companies and the 44.4% flowing to privately owned companies (**Table 2**).[7] From **Table 1** we can see that the size of loans to the hybrid sector, in terms of loans to Township and Village Enterprises, privately and collectively owned firms, and joint ventures, is also much smaller than that of loans to SOEs in manufacturing industries (industrial loans and commercial loans). The government supports the state-owned sectors much more than the hybrid sectors through granting larger-scale bank loans via state-owned banks (e.g., Brandt & Zhu 2000).

3.2. An Analysis of Nonperforming Loans and Further Reform in the Banking Sector

China's banking sector is dominated by large state-owned banks, namely, the Big Five banks (ABC, BComm, BOC, ICBC, and PCBC). The dominance of the Big Five banks also implies that the degree of competition within the banking sector has been low.[8] As of the end of 2015, the Big Five banks accounted for 40.5% of the banking industry in terms of total assets (**Table 3**). The

[6]As the PBOC changed the breakdown method of bank loans in terms of loan purposes and borrower types in 2010, we cannot obtain continuous data under the old classification since then.

[7]The percentage of loans that have flowed to different sectors (state-owned, collectively owned, and privately owned sectors) is calculated on the basis of the Annual Statistics Reports on Bank Loans of Financial Institutions by the PBOC.

[8]China's concentration ratio in the banking sector has been falling sharply in the past decade with the entrance of many nonstate banks and intermediaries. Demirgüç-Kunt & Levine (2001) compare the bank concentration measured by the share of the assets of the Big Five banks to total assets in the banking sector and find that China's rank is among the highest in the world, with a ratio of 91% at the end of 1997. However, with the rapid development of the banking sector in recent decades (e.g., the establishment of different city commercial banks and even private banks in recent years), the banking sector has been much less concentrated.

Table 1 Breakdown of bank loans (end-of-year figures in billions of RMB)

Year	Total loans	Short-term loans	Industrial loans	Commercial loans	Infrastructure construction loans	Agricultural loans	Loans to Township and Village Enterprises (TVEs)	Privately owned firms	Joint ventures and cooperative firms
1994	3,997.60	2,694.87	994.83	1,050.98	61.72	114.39	200.24	15.59	79.23
1995	5,054.41	3,337.20	1,177.47	1,283.71	79.93	154.48	251.49	19.62	99.91
1996	6,115.66	4,021.00	1,421.33	1,533.26	97.38	191.91	282.19	27.98	134.63
1997	7,491.41	5,541.83	1,652.66	1,835.66	159.11	331.46	503.58	38.67	189.10
1998	8,652.41	6,061.32	1,782.15	1,975.24	162.87	444.42	558.00	47.16	248.75
1999	9,373.43	6,388.76	1,794.89	1,989.09	147.69	479.24	616.13	57.91	298.58
2000	9,937.11	6,574.81	1,701.93	1,786.85	161.71	488.90	606.08	65.46	304.98
2001	11,231.47	6,732.72	1,863.67	1,856.34	209.96	571.15	641.30	91.80	326.35
2002	13,129.39	7,424.79	2,019.05	1,797.31	274.80	688.46	681.23	105.88	269.74
2003	15,899.62	8,366.12	2,275.60	1,799.44	300.21	841.14	766.16	146.16	256.94
2004	17,819.78	8,684.06	2,389.66	1,707.41	278.01	984.31	806.92	208.16	219.84
2005	19,469.04	8,744.92	2,251.67	1,644.76	298.37	1,152.99	790.18	218.08	197.53
2006	22,534.72	9,853.44	2,865.40	1,667.15	361.26	1,320.82	622.20	266.76	183.27
2007	26,169.09	11,447.79	3,362.33	1,783.33	374.19	1,542.93	711.26	350.77	206.91
2008	30,339.46	12,518.17	3,614.29	1,773.22	368.46	1,762.88	745.40	422.38	227.08
2009	39,968.48	14,661.13	3,876.92	1,948.33	364.68	2,162.25	902.90	712.10	218.03
2010	47,919.56	16,623.34	NA	NA	NA	NA	NA	NA	NA
2011	54,794.67	20,313.26	NA	NA	NA	NA	NA	NA	NA
2012	62,990.96	24,827.28	NA	NA	NA	NA	NA	NA	NA
2013	71,896.15	29,023.78	NA	NA	NA	NA	NA	NA	NA

Source: Statistical Yearbooks of China, CEIC database (1985–2013). Abbreviation: NA, not available.

Table 2 Bank loans to state-owned versus private sectors

	State-owned	Collectively owned	Privately owned	Total
Outstanding loan amount (billions of RMB)				
2010	15,823.50	2,843.84	11,624.15	30,291.49
2011	17,094.66	3,497.98	14,424.30	35,016.94
2012	18,689.85	3,638.98	16,954.17	39,282.99
2013	20,465.74	3,648.51	19,904.98	44,019.22
2014	24,830.06	4,185.14	23,147.23	52,162.42
Percentage of loan amount				
2010	52.24	9.39	38.37	100.00
2011	48.82	9.99	41.19	100.00
2012	47.58	9.26	43.16	100.00
2013	46.49	8.29	45.22	100.00
2014	47.60	8.02	44.38	100.00

Source: Annual Statistics Reports on Loans by Financial Institutions (2011–2015) by the People's Bank of China.

CBRC approved the establishment of the first five private banks in China in 2014[9]; however, most of the commercial banks are majority owned by the central or local governments, or with the government as the ultimate controller. In the past decade, the most severe problem for China's banking sector and even for the entire financial system has been the high level of NPLs, and, in particular, NPLs among the Big Five banks after the global financial crisis resulting from the large number of investment projects undertaken to stimulate the economy. Reducing the amount of NPLs to normal levels was a high priority for China's financial system before the recent fast rise of shadow banking.

3.2.1. Comparing NPLs and recent growth. We compare NPLs in China, other major Asian economies, and the United States during 1997–2013 on the basis of the official figures in Panel A of **Table 4**. We measure NPLs by their size (in US$ billion) and also as a percentage of GDP in the same year. Cross-country comparison since 1998, when Asian countries recovered from a financial crisis, suggests that China's NPLs were the highest in the group in 2000–2007, and as high as 20–20.5% in 2000–2001. However, the level of NPLs (over GDP) in China has shown a clear downward trend since the peak in 2000–2001, with the total amount of NPLs also falling during 2004–2011 (for further discussion on China's NPLs, see Allen et al. 2012c). In fact, compared with other developed countries that were hit by the global financial crisis, China's banking system did well from 2008 to 2010, with NPL to GDP ratios lower than 2.0%. However, after the "four trillion" fiscal stimulus package in 2009, the ratio of NPLs over GDP has once again shown an upward trend. As bad as some of the NPL numbers in the early years in Panel A of **Table 4** appear, they may still significantly underestimate the amount of NPLs within China's banking system, according to some critics.[10]

[9]As of April 2017, there are in total only six approved private banks. A full list of the names of commercial banks in China can be found at the website of the CBRC: **http://www.cbrc.gov.cn/chinese/jrjg/index.html**.

[10]For more details, see Allen, Qian & Gu (2015). Consistent with their point of view, Lardy (1998) argues that most of Chinese state-owned banks would have gone bankrupt if we use the international standard on NPLs.

Table 3 Bank total assets by different types of banks (billions of RMB)

Year	State-owned banks	Shareholding banks	City commercial banks	Rural cooperative banks	Rural commercial banks	Rural credit cooperatives	Foreign banks	New rural financial institutions/postal saving banks	Policy banks
2003	16,051.17	2,959.86	1,462.17	0.00	38.48	2,650.93	415.97	898.44	2,124.70
2004	17,981.67	3,647.60	1,705.63	0.00	56.54	3,077.10	582.29	1,084.96	2,412.25
2005	21,005.00	4,465.49	2,036.69	275.04	302.89	3,142.70	715.45	1,378.68	2,928.32
2006	24,236.35	5,444.59	2,593.79	465.36	503.81	3,450.28	927.87	1,612.20	3,473.23
2007	28,500.00	7,274.20	3,340.50	646.00	609.70	4,343.40	1,252.50	1,768.70	4,278.10
2008	32,575.10	8,833.70	4,132.00	1,003.30	929.10	5,211.30	1,344.80	2,216.30	5,645.40
2009	40,799.80	11,818.10	5,680.00	1,279.10	1,866.10	5,494.50	1,349.20	2,704.50	6,945.60
2010	46,894.30	14,903.70	7,852.60	1,500.20	2,767.00	6,391.10	1,742.30	3,510.10	7,652.10
2011	53,633.60	18,379.40	9,984.50	1,402.50	4,252.70	7,204.70	2,153.50	4,353.60	9,313.30
2012	60,040.10	23,527.10	12,346.90	1,283.50	6,275.10	7,953.50	2,380.40	5,351.10	11,217.40
2013	65,600.50	26,936.10	15,177.80	1,232.20	8,521.80	8,595.10	2,562.80	6,210.00	12,527.80
2014	71,014.10	31,380.10	18,084.20	957.00	11,527.30	8,831.20	2,792.10	7,098.10	15,614.00
2015	78,163.00	36,988.00	22,680.20	762.50	15,234.20	8,654.10	2,680.80	8,302.40	19,284.70

Source: China Banking Regulatory Commission.

As a large fraction of the NPLs among state-owned banks, and, in particular, the Big Five banks, resulted from poor lending decisions made for SOEs, some of which stemmed from political or other noneconomic reasons, it can be argued that the natural party to bear the burden of reducing the NPLs is the government. As discussed above, most commercial banks in China are state-owned, and historically the state-owned banks served the purpose of funding SOEs and government projects, which support the old model of economic growth. According to statistics from the CBRC, 33.8% of the total amount of NPLs are from the manufacturing industry, followed by 31.4% from the wholesale and retail industry. On the basis of NPL data by industry released by the CBRC and the proportion of the state sector by industry for the listed companies, we estimate that NPLs to the state-owned sector accounted for approximately 61.3% of all NPLs in 2008, decreasing to 56.8% in 2015.[11] If we treat the NPL issue as a fiscal problem for China, then the ultimate way to solve it would be sustained high economic growth.[12] In other words, if economic growth slows down significantly, it can be difficult for government to roll over debt, which can further trigger systemic risk for the banking system. In this regard, Panel B of **Table 4** compares total outstanding government debt. Depending on data availability, total government debt is measured either by the sum of all types of domestic and foreign debt (in the United States, Japan, and India) or by the level of outstanding government bonds (in all other countries) in a given year.

China's local government debt has been growing rapidly in recent years, mainly because of the large amount of fixed-asset investment in infrastructure to stimulate economic growth after the 2007–2009 financial crisis. By the end of June 2013, the total local government debt amounted to RMB 17.89 trillion, RMB 10.89 trillion of which was debt that the government had the responsibility to repay. According to the audit report released in 2011, the total local government debt amounted to RMB 10.72 trillion as of 2010.[13] Thus, the average annual growth rate of the total local government debt from 2011 to 2013 was about 22.7%. The main funding sources of the local government are bank loans, trust and leasing financing, and bond issuing. In terms of the usage of the debts, most of the funds are used in municipal construction, communication and transportation, and land overhaul and preservation.

If we aggregate the NPLs and total government debt, China's total government burden puts it in the middle of the pack: lower than those of Japan, the United States, and India, comparable with those of Taiwan and Korea, and higher only than that of Indonesia. On the basis of these crude comparisons, it seems that, going forward, NPLs should not be an arduous burden for the Chinese government (or the banking sector), whereas the same cannot be said for Japan or the United States. Caution is needed for this conclusion: First, given the massive fiscal stimulus plan launched in 2009 and debt roll-over pressure, the new NPLs in China may grow faster than in other countries; and second, China's economy is in the middle of a transition from the old mode to the consumption- or innovation-driven mode, and growth has been slowing down in recent years. However, if the government still relies heavily on infrastructure or manufacturing sectors with overcapacity to maintain growth momentum, government debt may still be on the rise in the near future.

[11]However, given that the listed companies (even if they are non-SOEs) are more likely to get loans from banks than unlisted (and smaller) companies, these results may underestimate the ratio of NPLs flowing from the state-owned sector.

[12]See, for example, Perkins & Rawski (2008) for a review and projections on the prospects of long-run economic growth and statistics in China.

[13]The Audit Report on local government debt in 2011 was released by the National Audit Office: **http://www.audit.gov.cn/n5/n25/c63566/content.html**.

Table 4 A comparison of nonperforming loans (NPLs) and government debt by country

Panel A: Size of NPLs in billions of US dollars (and as percentage of GDP in the same year)							
Year	**China**	**United States**	**Japan**	**South Korea**	**India**	**Indonesia**	**Taiwan**
1997	NA	66.9 (0.8%)	217.4 (5.1%)	16.2 (3.1%)	NA	0.2 (0.1%)	19.6 (6.5%)
1998	20.5 (2.0%)	71.3 (0.8%)	489.7 (12.7%)	23.2 (6.7%)	12.7 (3.1%)	5.5 (5.2%)	21.8 (7.9%)
1999	105.1 (9.7%)	72.2 (0.8%)	547.6 (12.6%)	54.4 (12.2%)	14.0 (3.2%)	3.2 (3.8%)	27.2 (9.1%)
2000	269.3 (22.5%)	90.1 (0.9%)	515.4 (11.1%)	35.5 (6.9%)	12.9 (2.8%)	6.3 (2.7%)	33.2 (10.3%)
2001	265.3 (20.0%)	108.4 (1.1%)	640.1 (15.6%)	12.2 (2.5%)	13.2 (2.8%)	4.3 (1.7%)	37.9 (13.0%)
2002	188.4 (13.0%)	107.8 (1.0%)	552.5 (14.1%)	9.9 (1.8%)	14.8 (3.0%)	3.3 (2.0%)	30.7 (10.4%)
2003	181.2 (11.0%)	95.9 (1.0%)	480.1 (11.3%)	11.7 (1.9%)	14.6 (2.5%)	4.7 (1.5%)	23.1 (7.7%)
2004	207.4 (10.7%)	81.3 (0.9%)	334.8 (7.3%)	10.0 (1.5%)	14.4 (2.2%)	3.8 (2.1%)	26.4 (5.1%)
2005	164.2 (7.3%)	84.6 (0.7%)	183.3 (4.0%)	7.6 (1.0%)	13.4 (1.7%)	6.0 (1.5%)	11.2 (3.2%)
2006	157.4 (5.9%)	103.8 (0.8%)	157.8 (3.6%)	8.2 (0.9%)	11.2 (1.3%)	5.2 (1.4%)	11.3 (3.1%)
2007	166.8 (5.1%)	168.1 (1.2%)	148.6 (3.4%)	8.3 (0.8%)	13.6 (1.2%)	4.5 (1.0%)	10.0 (2.6%)
2008	80.6 (1.9%)	328.7 (2.3%)	190.8 (3.7%)	13.0 (1.4%)	15.4 (1.3%)	4.3 (0.8%)	9.0 (2.3%)
2009	72.6 (1.5%)	477.5 (3.3%)	188.4 (3.63%)	13.9 (1.5%)	18.2 (1.3%)	4.6 (1.0%)	6.7 (1.8%)
2010	68.1 (1.1%)	423.4 (2.9%)	208.7 (3.82%)	26.8 (2.6%)	20.7 (1.2%)	4.3 (0.6%)	3.8 (0.9%)
2011	67.9 (0.9%)	359.0 (2.4%)	213.0 (3.6%)	13.4 (1.2%)	22.4 (1.2%)	5.4 (0.6%)	3.1 (0.7%)
2012	79.1 (1.0%)	351.6 (2.2%)	219.5 (3.7%)	14.6 (1.3%)	29.4 (1.6%)	5.4 (0.6%)	3.2 (0.7%)
2013	96.3 (1.0%)	260.0 (1.5%)	180.9 (3.7%)	15.8 (1.2%)	31.4 (1.6%)	5.6 (0.6%)	3.0 (0.6%)

(Continued)

Table 4 *(Continued)*

Panel B: Outstanding government debt in billions of US dollars							
Year	Outstanding government bonds (China)	Total government debt (United States)	Total government debt (Japan)	Outstanding Treasury bonds (South Korea)	Total public debt (India)	Outstanding government bonds (Indonesia)	Outstanding government bonds (Taiwan)
1997	66.5	5,802.8	4,254.0	5.3	NA	NA	NA
1998	93.8	5,788.8	4,858.0	14.4	178.4	NA	NA
1999	127.3	5,822.7	6,053.1	28.5	260.2	34.1	36.6
2000	165.1	5,612.7	6,209.8	32.7	232.4	45.1	45.1
2001	188.6	5,734.4	6,036.0	39.8	225.4	43.5	52.4
2002	233.5	6,169.4	6,321.3	45.2	250.2	42.1	61.5
2003	273.0	6,789.7	6,852.9	67.9	259.7	48.0	72.8
2004	311.3	7,335.6	7,446.6	107.0	299.6	44.7	81.8
2005	350.0	7,809.5	8,299.5	165.5	347.1	39.9	93.7
2006	364.6	8,451.4	7,587.1	216.7	375.2	45.7	99.7
2007	599.8	8,950.7	7,707.7	245.0	472.0	51.8	103.8
2008	701.6	9,985.8	8,966.2	217.8	496.4	52.8	114.5
2009	753.6	12,867.5	9,466.8	290.9	556.6	52.5	116.0
2010	805.3	14,551.8	11,284.9	329.4	643.6	68.4	133.0
2011	1,128.5	15,248.0	12,334.5	349.7	640.9	72.2	153.4
2012	1,220.2	16,458.0	11,521.9	397.1	742.1	75.9	161.6
2013	1,406.7	17,376.5	9,667.1	439.7	748.0	71.7	170.5

Sources are as follows. China: Statistical Bureau of China, People's Bank of China, Chinese Banking Regulatory Commission. United States: Board of Governors of the Federal Reserve Bank, Statistical Abstracts of the United States. Japan: Statistical Bureau of Japan. South Korea: Ministry of Strategy and Finance, Bank of Korea, Korean Statistical Information Service, International Monetary Fund, World Bank. India: Ministry of Finance. Indonesia: Bank Indonesia. Taiwan: National Statistical Bureau of Taiwan, Bloomberg, Chinabond, Financial Supervisory Commission. Abbreviation: NA, not available.

Recognizing the importance of NPLs and its responsibility to reduce them, the Chinese government took several measures, including the injection of large amounts of foreign currency reserves into the Big Five banks to prepare them for going public, as well as the establishment of four state-owned asset management companies (AMCs) and local AMCs to assume the NPLs accumulated in BOC, PCBC, ABC, and ICBC and liquidate them. (For more details on the process of the Big Five banks going public, see Allen et al. 2012b; Allen, Qian & Gu 2015). As a result of these measures, NPLs had been considerably reduced before the global financial crisis, but they have increased again since the crisis. The high level of NPLs has again become one of the most severe issues in the banking sector. It is likely that the government will set up more local AMCs to clear up the NPLs. However, if the economy maintains its current pace of growth, the Chinese government could write off a large fraction of remaining and newly accumulated NPLs to avert any serious problems. By contrast, if the growth of the economy significantly slows down while the accumulation of NPLs continues, problems in the banking sector could lead to a financial crisis. This could spill over into other sectors of the economy and cause a slowdown in growth or a recession.

3.2.2. The improvement of efficiency in the state-owned banks. The authorities in the banking sector in China put forward a series of measures to improve its efficiency in the past decades. As discussed above, the size of NPLs in the banking sector critically depends on the efficiency of banks. For instance, state-owned banks have diversified and improved their loan structure by increasing consumer-related loans while being more active in risk management and monitoring of loans made to SOEs.[14] In the 1990s, the authorities also reformed the organization structure of banks to provide more incentives to banks and their employees.[15] After China's entrance into the WTO in 2001, many state-owned banks started implementing new lending processes that grant more authority to individuals to make loan decisions and monitor loan performance and also require banks' senior managers to be responsible for final approval of loan contracts (see, e.g., Qian et al. 2015).

One of the most important steps to improve the efficiency of the banking sector is the privatization process, which mainly includes the listing of state-owned banks. The IPOs of the large state-owned banks were successful in terms of total proceeds raised, and they all attracted significant foreign ownership at the IPO date as well (for more details on the success of the IPOs of China's state-owned banks, see Allen et al. 2012b). However, there are two pressing issues with the privatization process. The first is whether more competition (e.g., the entrance of more foreign banks or the introduction of private banks in recent years) is good for improving the efficiency of China's banking sector with the government still being the largest owner. The experiences of other countries seem to suggest a positive link between bank competition and efficiency.[16] The second issue is that the government plays dual roles as both the regulator and the majority owner of the banking sector. The recent global financial crisis suggests that government ownership/guarantees can improve financial stability and reduce the likelihood of crises under some

[14]For example, according to China Quarterly Monetary Policy Reports of the PBOC, the ratio of consumer lending to total loans outstanding made from all banks increased from 1% in 1998 to 17% in 2013; by September 2014, RMB 14.75 trillion (or $2,397.2 billion) of outstanding bank loans had been extended to consumers.

[15]For example, reforms taking place in the mid-1990s provided local banks with more autonomous power and, after the 1994 reforms, approved credit volume for specialized banks was based on a maximum ratio between loans and deposits instead of administrative quotas, which provided those banks with greater flexibility to use within-bank transfers to adjust fund allocation.

[16]For example, with a sample of both state-owned and non-state-owned banks, Berger et al. (2009) show that the addition of foreign ownership stakes into banks' ownership structure is associated with a significant improvement of bank efficiency.

circumstances, whereas this could also reduce efficiency or induce financial institutions to take excessive risk and further exacerbate the issue of moral hazard. Hence, applying these ideas to China, there could be potential conflict between the government's dual roles in both regulation and majority ownership. That is, the majority control by the government could enhance banking regulation and help to prevent crises but could also lead to poor risk management in the large state-owned banks.

One problem that hinders banks' efforts to improve efficiency is poor and inconsistent enforcement of bankruptcy laws and creditor protection. China's first bankruptcy law, passed in 1986, governed only SOEs and had little impact in practice. The latest bankruptcy law, which was enacted in August 2006 and became effective on June 1, 2007, applies to all enterprises except partnerships and sole proprietorships. In many aspects, the new law resembles bankruptcy laws in developed countries. For example, an independent bankruptcy administrator who manages the debtor's frozen assets after the court accepts the bankruptcy filing has been introduced. The law highlights that administrators should be professionals independent from the filing company. However, enforcement of the law still remains weak and inconsistent compared to that in developed countries, and few distressed and insolvent firms have been delisted after filing for bankruptcy.[17]

3.2.3. Interest rate liberalization reforms. Since the liberalization of the interbank offered rate on June 1, 1996, several steps of interest rate liberalization have been implemented. From 1996 to 2004, the PBOC liberalized, in succession, the interest rate in the monetary market and bond market, the bank deposit and loan rate in foreign currency, and the RMB agreement deposit rates. After that, the pace of interest rate liberalization slowed down, but it has picked up again since 2011, partly because of the fast development of the corporate bond market and banks' wealth management products. In July 2013, the PBOC removed the lower limit on lending rates, which had been set at 70% of its fixed benchmark, and announced that loan interest rates should be set "on the basis of market supply and demand," taking account of credit risk. On May 1, 2015, the deposit insurance system, which guarantees 99.7% of deposits, was launched. On October 23, 2015, the PBOC removed the upper limit on the deposit rate, which has been regarded as one of the most important steps in liberalizing interest rates.

3.3. Growth of Nonstate Financial Intermediaries

Recent years have seen the fast development of nonstate banks and other (state and nonstate) financial institutions in China. The development of these sectors has provided funding to support the growth of the hybrid sector and will also allow China to have a stable and functioning banking system in the future.

3.3.1. Development of other nonstate banks. During the period 2001–2013, although the Big Five banks dominated in every aspect of the banking sector, the role of other banks in the banking sector cannot be ignored. As of 2013, other banks (including foreign banks) and credit cooperatives'

[17]According to the National Development and Reform Commission, 67,000 small and midsized enterprises were shut down in the first half of 2008, but only 2,955 bankruptcy cases were filed nationwide for the same year. The firms that were shut down but that did not file for bankruptcy have been called zombie enterprises in China. However, because of the difficult and costly process of IPOs, the shells of these zombie firms are highly valuable. Hence, when a listed firm is in distress (with the ST flag), typically other (nonlisted) firms will invest in and restructure the ST firm to avoid delisting. For more details on the weak enforcement of bankruptcy law, see Garnaut et al. (2004) and Fan et al. (2008). The situation has changed significantly in recent years, with the number of the bankruptcy cases rising dramatically from 2012 to 2016.

total assets constituted more than 70% of those of the Big Five banks (the actual fraction is likely to be higher because of incomplete information on all types of deposit-taking institutions); similar comparisons can be made for total deposits and outstanding loans. In addition, these banks and institutions appear to have fewer NPLs than the largest state-owned banks. **Table 5** provides evidence on the growth of nonbank intermediaries. Overall, nonbank intermediaries have been growing remarkably since the late 1990s, with the non–Big Five shareholding commercial banks, RCCs, and TICs being the largest institutions in terms of total assets within the nonbank financial sector. As a step to boost lending to the private sector and improve competition in the banking system, the CBRC granted private capital the same entry standards to the banking industry as other capital in May 2012, meaning that private companies could now buy into banks through private stock placements, new share subscription, equity transfers, and mergers and acquisitions (M&As). Further, private investment is also welcomed in trust, financial leasing, and auto-financing companies. Along these lines, after the Third Plenum of the 18th Communist Party of China Central Committee in November 2013, the government also allowed private investors that meet certain requirements to set up small and medium-sized banks and other financial institutions. Finally, our coverage of nonbank financial institutions excludes various forms of informal financial intermediaries, some of which are deemed illegal but which overall provide a considerable amount of financing to firms in the hybrid sector.

3.3.2. Recent development of other financial institutions. The strong demand for capital by the real economy and the limited loan quota of the traditional banking system have led to the fast growth of other financial institutions and of shadow banking, especially the trust industry and other small-scale lending companies, since 2009. Allen et al. (2017b) show that the trust industry has overtaken the insurance industry as the largest nonbanking financial sector since 2012, with total assets amounting to RMB 16.7 trillion and its ratio of outstanding total trust assets to GDP being 23.7% at the end of 2015. **Table 5** breaks down China's total social financing from 2002 to 2013.[18] From 2006 to 2013, trust loans and entrusted loans ranked as the top two types of social financing in terms of average annual growth, with rates of 55.8% and 37.8%, respectively. At the end of 2013, new trust loans and entrusted loans accounted for only 10.6% and 14.7% of social financing, respectively, but were still trending upward. In addition, loans made by small-scale companies have been growing rapidly since 2010. By September 2014, the amount of outstanding loans made by small-scale lending companies was RMB 907.9 billion,[19] with an average quarter-on-quarter growth rate of 13.2% from 2010 to 2014. Other (alternative) financing channels, such as relationship lending or lending from private (unofficial) credit agencies but not standard financial institutions, are also regarded as a part of shadow banking, on which we elaborate in Section 5.

There have been a few studies on China's rising shadow banking in recent years (e.g., Allen et al. 2016; Dang, Wang & Yao 2016; Chen, He & Liu 2017). Overall, the high growth of credit by nonbank financial institutions and shadow banking is driven by the following factors. First, historically, because both lending and deposit interest rates were regulated, the lending interest rate was lower than the growth rate of output, leading to high demand for financing. The regulatory

[18]The term total social financing is defined by the PBOC as the total funds the real economy obtained from the financial system over a certain period of time. It measures money offered by domestic suppliers, including financial institutions, Chinese households, and nonfinancial entities. Thus, it is a liquidity measurement that covers loans in local currency, loans in foreign currency, entrusted loans, trust loans, bank acceptance bills, net corporate bond financing, and nonfinancial enterprise equity financing. For discussion of the statistics, details, and meaning of this term, see PBOC (2011).

[19]Because of the fast growth of small-scale lending companies, the PBOC has released a quarterly report on small-scale lending companies since the fourth quarter of 2010.

Table 5 Breakdown of total social financing in China (billions of RMB)

Year	Total amount of social financing	Loan in local currency	Loan in foreign currency	Entrusted loan	Trust loan	Bank acceptance bill	Net corporate bond financing	Nonfinancial enterprise equity financing
2002	2,011.2	1,847.5	73.1	17.5	NA	69.5	36.7	62.8
2003	3,411.3	2,765.2	228.5	60.1	NA	201.1	49.9	55.9
2004	2,862.9	2,267.3	138.1	311.8	NA	29.0	46.7	67.3
2005	3,000.8	2,354.4	141.5	196.1	NA	2.4	201.0	33.9
2006	4,269.6	3,152.3	145.9	269.5	82.5	150.0	231.0	153.6
2007	5,966.3	3,632.3	386.4	337.1	170.2	670.1	228.4	433.3
2008	6,980.2	4,904.1	194.7	426.2	314.4	106.4	552.3	332.4
2009	13,910.0	9,594.2	926.5	678.0	436.4	460.6	1,236.7	335.0
2010	14,019.0	7,945.1	485.5	874.8	386.5	2,334.6	1,106.3	578.6
2011	12,829.0	7,471.5	571.2	1,296.2	203.4	1,027.1	1,365.8	437.7
2012	15,763.0	8,203.8	916.3	1,283.8	1,284.5	1,049.9	2,255.1	250.8
2013	17,316.8	8,891.7	584.9	2,546.6	1,840.3	775.6	1,811.2	221.9

Source: Aggregate Statistics from the People's Bank of China and CEIC (2002–2013). Abbreviation: NA, not available.

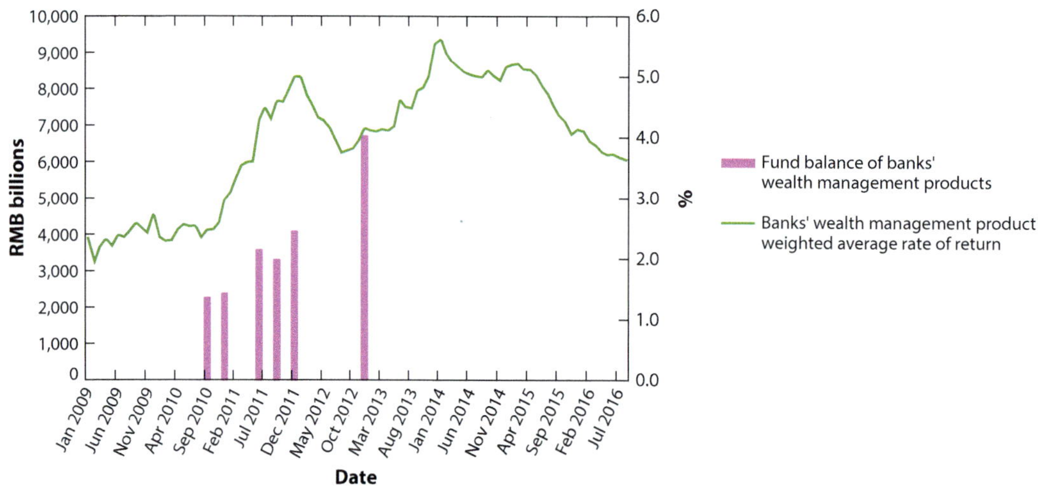

Figure 2

Recent growth of banks' wealth management products, 2009–2016. Source: CEIC database (**https://www.ceicdata.com**).

trigger for shadow banking in China was strict enforcement of a 75% cap on bank loan-to-deposit (LTD) ratios in an environment with deposit rate ceilings (see, e.g., Acharya et al. 2016, Hachem & Song 2016). Second, the central bank of China, the PBOC, imposes loan quotas in some restrictive areas (e.g., the real estate industry and industries with overcapacity) through window guidance to commercial banks (see also Allen et al. 2017a). Because of strict regulation on lending to the real estate industry and to local government financing platforms, there has been a large gap between the demand for financing and bank loans in these areas. As a result, many real estate companies can get financing only through trust loans or other sources. Third, the growth rate of bank deposits was much lower than that of bank loans for a long period starting from 1979, except for the years 1984–1986, 1988, and 1997, whereas, since 2009, the opposite has been the case. This is partly because of the restricted deposit interest rate and a relatively higher return of financial assets required by Chinese households, and partly because of a drop in trade surplus and capital inflows after 2009. Therefore, deposits derived from foreign exchange settlement started to decline. In order to meet the required LTD ratio, banks have to raise funds by issuing wealth management products. From the end of 2010 to 2013, the fund balance of banks' wealth management products grew from RMB 2,265 billion to RMB 9,500 billion (**Figure 2**), with the average return rate ranging between 2.5% and 5.5%.[20]

4. FINANCIAL MARKETS

In this section we examine China's financial markets, including the stock market, the bond market, the real estate markets, and the asset management industry. After the global crisis, the bond market and the asset management industry experienced rapid growth, with the performance of

[20]The average return rate of banks' wealth management products is published by the Institute of Finance and Banking of the Chinese Academy of Social Science. The average return rate for 1-year products soared to about 7.0% when monetary conditions were tight during the credit crunch in the summer of 2013. The average return for those products issued by shareholding banks was even higher during the time period when the PBOC suspended repo transactions in the summer of 2013. For more details on the pricing of wealth management products, see Acharya et al. (2016) and Hachem & Song (2016).

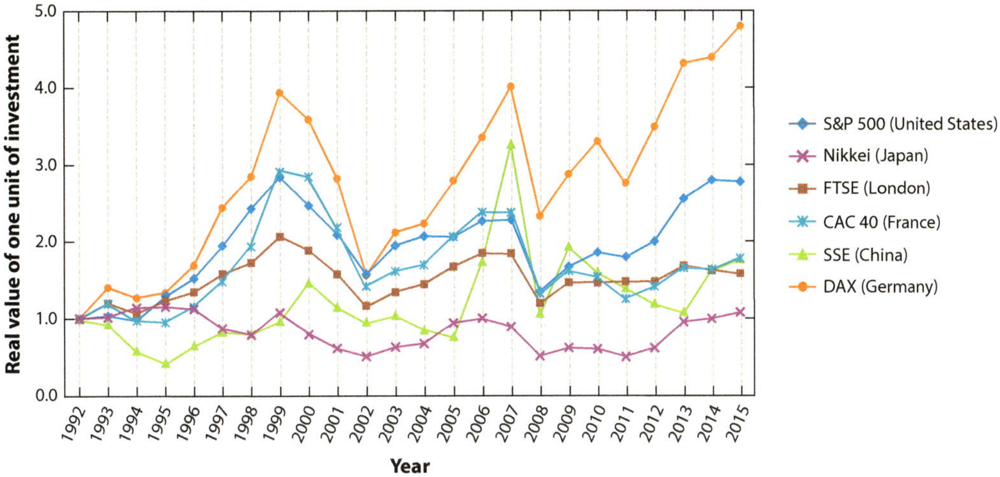

Figure 3

A comparison of the performance of major stock indexes between December 1992 and December 2015 (buy-and-hold returns of one unit of investment, adjusted for inflation). Source: CEIC database (**https://www.ceicdata.com**).

the equity market being quite mixed. Then we briefly review publicly traded companies' financing and investment decisions. Finally, we discuss the further development of financial markets as well as corporate governance and the performance of listed firms.

4.1. Overview of Stock Markets

After less than three decades of development, China's stock market has become one of the largest ones in the world in terms of market capitalization. However, growth in the stock market has been volatile in the past decades. High growth rates prevailed throughout most of the 1990s, and the market reached a peak by the end of 2000. As shown in **Figure 3**, the market, indicated by the SSE index, reversed during the next 5 years, dropping from 2,103 in the beginning of 2001 to 1,079 in December 2005, and then recovered in 2006 and rose to a high of 5,954 by the end of October 2007. However, after a string of negative news worldwide (culminating with the global crisis initiated by subprime loans) and domestically (including high levels of inflation), the market lost three-quarters of its value by the end of 2008. During rebounding economic growth, China's stock market bounced back in 2013 and soared in the first half of 2015. In summer 2015, the stock market crashed. However, the drop did not erase all of the gains the market made in 2015.

Figure 3 compares the performance of some of the major stock exchanges around the world as measured by the buy-and-hold return in the period from December 1992 to December 2015 (gross return at December 2015 with 1 unit of currency invested in each of the valued-weighted stock indexes at the end of 1992). We plot inflation-adjusted real returns. Over this period, the performance of the value-weighted SSE index (the calculation for the SZSE is very similar) was below those of the DAX (Germany) and the S&P 500 (United States), about the same as those of the FTSE (United Kingdom) and the CAC (France), and above that of the Nikkei (Japan), the worst among the group. According to the World Federation of Exchanges, at the end of 2013, the SSE was ranked the seventh largest market in the world in terms of market capitalization, and the SZSE was ranked the eleventh. The Hong Kong Stock Exchange (HKSE), where selected firms from mainland China have been listed and traded, was ranked the sixth largest in the world. Needless to say, Chinese financial markets will play an increasingly important role in world financial markets.

Besides the two main stock exchanges in Shanghai and Shenzhen, there are two complementary markets, the Second-Tier Market (*er ban shi chang*, similar to the NASDAQ) for small and medium enterprises (SMEs) and the Third-Tier Market (*san ban shi chang*). The Third-Tier Market was established in July 2001 to provide a share transferring platform for delisted firms and other over-the-counter (OTC) transactions. Opened in June 2004, the Second-Tier Market was designed to lower the entry barrier for SME firms, especially new start-ups in high-tech industries. Also, in 2006, a market (*xin san ban shi chang*, or New Third-Tier Market) was established to deal with the equity transactions of nonlisted shareholding companies in a high-tech zone (*zhong guan cun*) in Beijing. On October 23, 2009, China launched the NASDAQ-style Growth Enterprise Market (GEM; *chuang ye ban*), mainly to provide financing for private SMEs, especially high-tech and electronics firms. The companies on the New Third-Tier Market can be transferred to the GEM or to a small and medium-sized plate if approved by the CSRC. In June and August 2010, the SZSE started to release the indexes of GEM: ChiNext and ChiNext Composite, respectively. Since 2012, the development of China's stock market has accelerated. On July 8, 2012, the State Council approved the expansion of the New Third-Tier Market into the National Equities Exchange and Quotations (NEEQ), a nationwide market in Beijing, Tianjin, Shanghai, and Wuhan. On December 14, 2013, the State Council decided to enlarge the volume of the NEEQ, allowing all kinds of SMEs to perform equity transactions on this market. The NEEQ has been seen as an incubator for the GEM and for SMEs in the SZSE. Other recent developments in the stock markets include the pilot launch of preference shares and the possibility of transforming the approval-based system for IPOs into a registration-based system.

Despite the recent rapid development in China's stock market, there is abundant evidence that the market is still not efficient in that prices and investors' behavior are not necessarily driven by fundamental values of listed firms. For example, in an important paper, Morck, Yeung & Yu (2000) found that due to poor protection of minority investors and imperfect regulation, stock prices are more synchronous in emerging markets, including China, than in developed countries. The degree of manipulation and insider trading in China is greater than in the United States. Moreover, given that each IPO must go through a process of approval by the CSRC, more politically connected firms are more likely to be listed. Once listed, firms are rarely delisted in China. Hence, the problematic IPO and delisting processes may further increase the inefficiency of the Chinese stock market (for more details, see, e.g., Allen, Qian & Qian 2008).

4.2. Overview of Bond Markets and Their Recent Rapid Growth

Table 6 provides information on China's bond markets. The government bond market had an annual growth rate of 22.3% during the period 1990–2013 in terms of newly issued bonds, and total outstanding bonds reached RMB 9,547.1 billion (or $1,565.1 billion) at the end of 2013.[21] The second largest component of the bond market is called policy financial bonds, with a total outstanding amount of RMB 6,501.9 billion (or $1,027.2 billion) at the end of 2011. These bonds are issued by policy banks, which operate under the supervision of the Ministry of Finance,

[21] On July 26, 2007, Moody's raised the rating of China's government bonds to A1 from A2. These ratings are better than or comparable to Moody's ratings of government bonds from most emerging economies. However, due to accumulated local government debt, continuous capital outflows, and increasing growth risks in recent years, Moody's went on to downgrade China's government bonds. For example, in March 2016, Moody's changed the outlook on China's government credit ratings from stable to negative (Moody's 2016).

Table 6 China's bond markets, 1995–2013 (billions of RMB)

Year	Treasury bonds			Policy financial bonds			Corporate bonds		
	Amount issued	Redemption amount	Balance	Amount issued	Redemption amount	Balance	Amount issued	Redemption amount	Balance
1995	151.09	49.70	330.03	NA	NA	170.85	30.08	33.63	64.66
1996	184.78	78.66	436.14	105.56	25.45	250.96	26.89	31.78	59.77
1997	241.18	126.43	550.89	143.15	31.23	362.88	25.52	21.98	52.10
1998	380.88	206.09	776.57	195.02	32.04	512.11	15.00	10.53	67.69
1999	401.50	123.87	1,054.20	180.09	47.32	644.75	15.82	5.65	77.86
2000	465.70	152.50	1,367.40	164.50	70.92	738.33	8.30	0.00	86.16
2001	488.40	228.60	1,561.80	259.00	143.88	853.45	14.70	0.00	100.86
2002	593.43	226.12	1,933.60	307.50	155.57	1,005.41	32.50	0.00	133.36
2003	628.01	275.58	2,260.36	456.14	250.53	1,165.00	35.80	0.00	169.16
2004	692.39	374.99	2,577.76	414.80	177.87	1,401.93	32.70	0.00	201.86
2005	704.20	404.55	2,877.40	585.17	205.30	1,781.80	204.65	3.70	401.81
2006	888.33	620.86	3144.87	898.00	379.0	2,300.80	393.83	167.24	553.29
2007	2313.91	584.68	4874.10	1109.02	413.36	2992.68	505.85	288.09	768.33
2008	855.82	753.14	4976.78	1082.30	406.38	3668.6	843.54	327.78	1285.06
2009	1792.70	707.15	5795.00	1167.80	374.53	4481.88	1662.90	440.00	2440.59
2010	1977.83	1004.34	6768.49	1319.27	564.84	5236.32	1549.15	509.92	3467.18
2011	1710.01	1095.85	7382.65	1997.27	731.70	6501.88	2354.80	1021.56	4645.68
2012	1615.42	1798.71	7199.36	2141.50	NA	NA	3736.55	NA	7771.00
2013	2023.00	899.60	9547.10	1981.10	NA	NA	3679.17	NA	9324.20
Yearly growth	22.30%	23.05%	22.54%	28.28%	26.79%	37.20%	28.08%	26.18%	30.76%

This table presents the development of China's bond markets. Policy financial bonds are issued by policy banks, which belong to the Treasury Department, and the proceeds of bond issuance are invested in government-run projects and industries such as infrastructure construction (similar to municipal bonds in the United States). Source: Aggregate Statistics from the People's Bank of China (2000–2013) and the Statistical Yearbook of China 2000. Abbreviation: NA, not available.

and the proceeds of bond issuance are invested in government-run projects and industries such as infrastructure construction (similar to municipal bonds in the United States). Compared to government-issued bonds, the size of the corporate bond market was relatively small before the global financial crisis. However, it has been growing dramatically in recent years. In terms of newly issued volume, since 2011 the corporate bond market has been larger than the Treasury bond market. Since May 2012, unlisted and small and medium-sized companies have been allowed to issue corporate bonds in the stock exchanges. Further, in January 2015, the CSRC announced a new reform in the corporate bond market that removed both the sponsorship and the screening systems for bond issuance. Since then, the corporate bond issuance system has been very close to a registering system. The volume of corporate bond issuance increased sevenfold.[22] By the end of July 2016, China's domestic bond market capitalization was RMB 41.63 trillion ($6.28 trillion), a total very close to that of the domestic equity market (including both the SSE and SZSE), which was RMB 46.32 trillion ($6.99 trillion).

The relatively slow growth of the bond markets in China and other parts of Asia in the past years stems from two main reasons (see, e.g., Herring & Chatusripitak 2000). First, a lack of sound accounting and auditing systems and high-quality bond rating agencies has been a factor.[23] Given the low creditor protection and court inefficiency in China and most other emerging economies, the recovery rates for bondholders during default are low, which in turn leads to underinvestment in the market by domestic and foreign investors. Second, the lack of a well-constructed yield curve has also been a factor in China in the past, given the small size of the publicly traded Treasury bond market and a lack of historical prices. However, the situation has improved very fast in the past 5 years, and the terms of China's Treasury bonds now range from 1 month to 30 years. Third, regulation fragmentation has also partly led to the slow development of the bond markets in China. China's bond markets have been segmented, with one interbank bond market established in 1996 and regulated by the PBOC and NDRC, and a corporate bond market established in 2007 and regulated by the CSRC and the two stock exchanges. The multiple regulators make bond issuance a long and difficult process.

4.3. Evidence on the Listed Sector

In this section we briefly examine the listed sector in China. Because of weak enforcement of standards and processes in this sector, in practice the accessibility of equity markets for firms in the hybrid sector has been much lower than for former SOEs. Allen, Qian & Qian (2005) find that 80% of their sample of more than 1,100 listed firms had been converted from former SOEs. In recent years, the government has attempted to change the composition of listed firms by relaxing regulations toward hybrid sector firms, including by the establishment of the recently opened GEM.

Listed firms in China issued both tradable and nontradable shares until the share reform in 2005–2007 (discussed in Section 4.6.2). Nontradable shares were held either by the government or

[22] According to statistics from the SSE and SZSE, the volume of total corporate bond issuance (excluding enterprise bonds and midterm notes issued in the interbank market) in 2014 was about RMB 145 billion and in 2015 was about RMB 1,031 billion.

[23] Dagong Global Credit Ratings, approved by the PBOC and established in 1994, is a leading rating agency in China. In 2010, Dagong Global released its first sovereign ratings report, in which the Chinese and German sovereign debt received higher ratings (AA+ and a stable outlook) than those of the United States, United Kingdom, and Japan (AA or lower ratings and a negative outlook) (China Daily 2010). However, by the end of 2016, only a small number of bonds traded in the interbank bond market or exchange markets had been rated by leading global rating agencies such as Standard & Poor's.

by other state-owned legal entities (i.e., other listed or nonlisted firms or organizations). In 2009, nontradable shares constituted about 53% of all shares, according to statistics from the CSRC, but this proportion fell rapidly from 2010 to 2012. At the end of 2012, nontradable shares constituted about 24% of all shares, and the majority of tradable shares were A shares. Among tradable shares, Class A and B shares are listed and traded on either the SSE or the SZSE; Class A shares are issued to and traded by Chinese investors, and Class B shares are issued to and traded by foreign investors, including those from Taiwan and Hong Kong as well as qualified foreign institutional investors (QFIIs). Whereas the two share classes issued by the same firm are identical in terms of shareholder rights (e.g., voting and dividend rights), B shares were formerly traded at a significant discount relative to A shares and are traded less frequently than A shares.[24] The B-share discount has been reduced significantly since the CSRC allowed Chinese citizens to invest in and trade B shares (with foreign currency accounts) in 2001. In addition, Class H shares, issued by companies registered in mainland China and approved by the CSRC to be listed in Hong Kong, are traded on the HKSE. Finally, there are N shares and S shares, for firms listed in the United States and in Singapore, respectively, but operating in China; we omit discussions on these shares, as they are not listed on the domestic exchanges. After the share reforms discussed in Section 4.6, government shares became G shares and became tradable.

Generally, internal and external governance for the listed sector is weak, for several reasons. First, according to the 2005 revision of the Company Law, listed firms in China have a two-tiered board structure: a Board of Directors (5–19 members) and a Board of Supervisors (at least 3 members), with supervisors ranking above directors. The main duty of the Board of Supervisors is to monitor firms' operations as well as top managers and directors, whereas the Board of Directors fulfills duties similar to those of its counterparts in the United States, including appointing and firing CEOs (for more details on the structure of these boards, see Allen, Qian & Qian 2005). However, it is very likely that some board members are nominated and appointed by firms' parent companies, as the Company Law in 2005 did not specify that each member of the board must be elected by shareholders through general shareholder meetings. On the basis of firm-level compensation data (available since 1998 because of disclosure requirements), Fung, Firth & Rui (2003) and Kato & Long (2006) find that no listed firms grant stock options to CEOs or board members. The situation is somewhat different now. Among SOEs listed overseas, the barriers to exercising stock options have been overcome, and some senior executives have been granted stock options.[25] However, the cash-based compensation level of CEOs is still much lower than that of their counterparts in developed countries, and the consumption of perks, such as company cars, is prevalent.

Second, value-increasing M&As in China are difficult, which can be attributed to an ownership structure characterized by a large number of nontradable shares, including cross-holdings of shares among listed firms and institutions. According to China Venture (2011), in 2010 there were 2,656 M&A deals involving listed firms, totaling $169.6 billion, a small fraction of the total market capitalization. In many deals, a hybrid sector (nonlisted) firm acquires a listed firm that was converted from an SOE, and the large amount of nontradable shares held by the state remains

[24]Explanations of the B-share discount include: (*a*) Foreign investors face higher information asymmetry than domestic investors; (*b*) lower B-share prices compensate for the lack of liquidity (resulting from low trading volume); and (*c*) the A-share premium reflects a speculative bubble component among domestic investors; for more details, see, e.g., Chan, Menkveld & Yang (2008) and Mei, Scheinkman & Xiong (2009).

[25]Examples include the former chairman of the China National Offshore Oil Corporation, Wei Liucheng, and the former chairman of Bank of China (Hong Kong), Liu Mingkang, who have received substantial rewards.

intact after the transaction. Such an acquisition can be a means by which low-quality, nonlisted companies bypass listing standards and gain access to financial markets (see, e.g., Du et al. 2008).

Third, a factor contributing to the occurrence of corporate scandals is the lack of institutional investors (including nondepository financial intermediaries), as these are a very recent addition to the set of financial institutions in China. Professional investors would perhaps not be so easily taken in by simple deceptions. Another factor is that the enforcement of laws is questionable because of the lack of legal professionals and institutions.

Fourth, the government plays a dual role for many listed firms, being both regulator and blockholder. The main role of the CSRC (the counterpart of the Securities and Exchange Commission in the United States) is to monitor and regulate stock exchanges and listed companies. The government exercises its shareholder control rights in listed firms through the Bureau of National Assets Management, which holds large fractions of nontradable shares or other SOEs (with their holdings of nontradable shares). However, as the senior managers of the Bureau are government officials, it is possible that they might not have strong incentives to diligently pursue their fiduciary role, as their compensation may not be tied to performance. Moreover, as documented above, the dual roles of the government as both a regulator and a shareholder might lead to conflicting goals, which could further weaken the effectiveness of each role. (For a description of the complicated relationships between the various regulatory agencies and central government branches, and of how these relationships affect the decision making process surrounding regulations and enforcement, see Pistor 2010.) On the basis of a sample of 625 firms, with 28% of the CEOs being former or current government bureaucrats, Fan, Wong & Zhang (2007) find that the 3-year post-IPO average stock returns of the sample underperform the market by 20% and that the underperformance of firms with such politically connected CEOs exceeds the underperformance of those without politically connected CEOs by almost 30%.

4.4. Real Estate Market

Like China's other economic sectors, the real estate market has long been operating under the dual tracks of both central planning and market-oriented systems. Prior to 1998, government control was dominant and mortgages were not designated for retail customers and households. Chinese citizens working for the government and for government-owned companies and organizations could purchase properties at prices significantly below market prices, with subsidies coming from their employers. Reform policies introduced in 1998 aimed to end the distribution of properties by employers and to establish new housing finance and market systems. Since then, the development of the real estate sector has been stimulated by the residential housing reform and by the growth of individual mortgages, along with rising household income and demand for quality housing. **Figure 4** shows total real estate investments and their funding sources over time. Total investment increased from RMB 321 billion in 1996, 12% of national fixed-assets investment, to RMB 8.6 trillion in 2013, 19% of national fixed-assets investment. Most of the investment funds have come from domestic sources. Not surprisingly, bank loans are the most important source of real estate financing. China's continuing economic growth (especially in private sectors), urbanization and industrialization, limited land supply, and increasing foreign direct investments and institutional investments will further enhance the liquidity and long-term prospects of China's real estate assets.

Real estate prices in major cities have risen sharply in recent years, and whether these fast growing prices are bubbles and how to cool down the markets are among the most closely watched and hotly debated issues in China. We provide some simple analysis here; for a more thorough analysis, see, e.g., Deng, Gyourko & Wu (2012a) and Fang et al. (2015). In **Figure 5**, we plot and

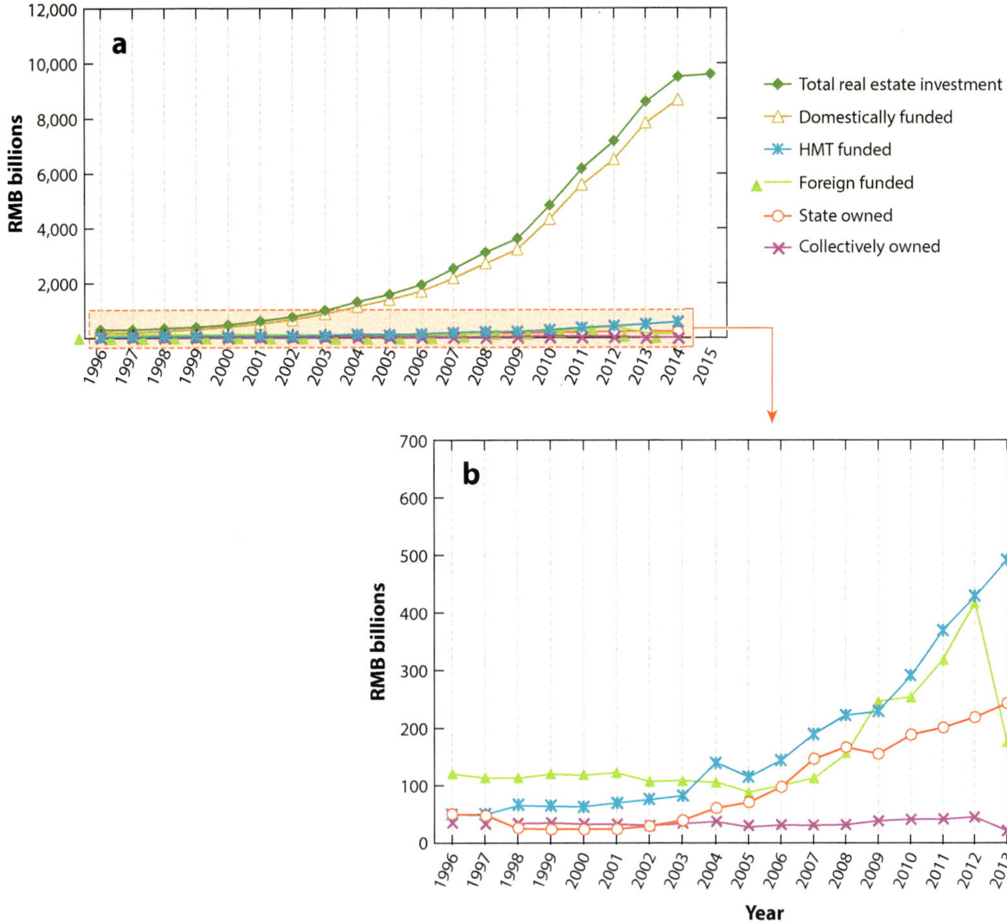

Figure 4

(*a*) Funding sources of real estate investment, 1996–2015. (*b*) Enlargement of red shaded area in panel *a*. Source: CEIC database (**https://www.ceicdata.com**).

compare growth rates of national average housing prices and disposable household income over the period 2002–2015. Actual housing prices (RMB per square meter) and disposable income are normalized so that all charts begin at 100 in 2002; hence, the vertical axes measure growth rates, and all values for prices and income are adjusted for inflation. If housing prices grow significantly faster than disposable income, there may exist bubbles in the housing markets. On the basis of **Figure 5**, it appears that at the national level there are no signs of bubbles. However, the situation is different for a few first-tier cities, such as Beijing, Shanghai, and Shenzhen (see also Fang et al. 2015). The gap between disposable income per capita and housing prices in Beijing and Shanghai was large from 2008 to 2012 but has tended to shrink since 2012, whereas in Shenzhen the gap is still getting larger, indicating possible bubbles in some first-tier cities.

Since 2004, the government has been taking aggressive measures to curb the rapid growth of housing prices. For example, one of the most frequently used policies is increasing the PBOC's required reserve deposit ratio. From 2010 to 2013, facing rapidly rising housing prices in main cities, especially in the first-tier cities, the government employed interventions such as increased

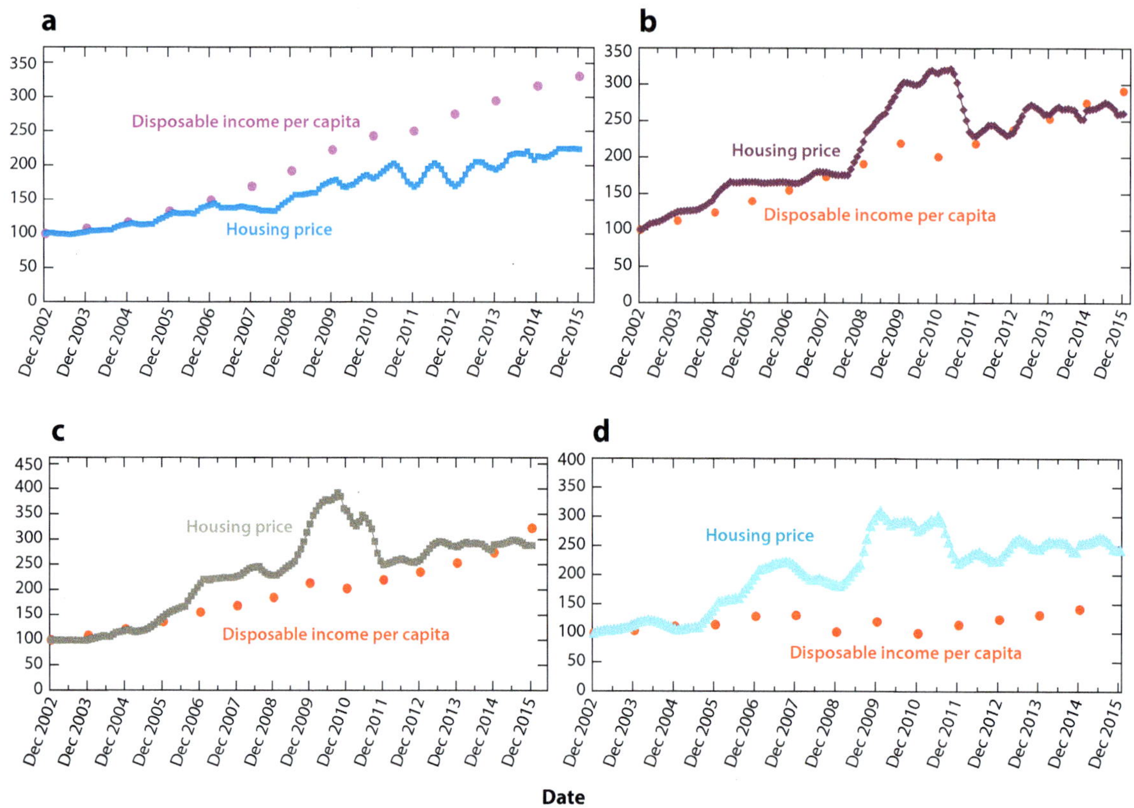

Figure 5

Comparison of the growth of housing prices and disposable household income for (*a*) the whole nation, (*b*) Shanghai, (*c*) Beijing, and (*d*) Shenzhen. Source: CEIC database (**https://www.ceicdata.com**).

equity down payment shares (from 20% to 30%) for first homes more than 90 m^2 in size; increased equity down payment shares (from 40% to 60–70%)[26] for second homes; strict enforcement of a 20% individual capital gains income tax rate for second-hand property transactions, based on the difference between purchase price and sale price of property; and direct administrative orders on how much land and how many building units may be developed (for more details, see State Council 2009, 2010; Deng, Gyourko & Wu 2012a). However, the impact of these measures on the housing markets seems to be limited. One reason, as postulated by many observers, is that because various government agencies and officials have played a major role in developing commercial properties, it is not in their best interest to see market corrections. The evidence of Deng, Gyourko & Wu (2012a) provides some support for this view. They find that much of the increase in housing prices is occurring in land values. Using land auctions data from Beijing, they also find that SOEs controlled by the central government paid 27% more than other bidders for otherwise equivalent

[26]Equity down payment shares for second homes are different across the country. After the release of the Five New Measures in early March 2013, in the cities of Beijing, Shanghai, Guangzhou, and Hangzhou, the required share was increased to 70%. In the city of Shenyang, the required share is 65%. In other cities, including Shenzhen, Nanjing, and Wuhan, the required share is 60% (for further discussion on the measures taken by China's government to control housing prices, see Allen et al. 2012c).

land parcels. It is argued that, as many vested government officials also invested in the property market, the measures that have effectively controlled housing prices in advanced economies, such as collecting property taxes, will not be enforced in China. This could also partly explain the continuously rising housing prices in the recent decade.

Our results on housing prices are based on simple measures; however, the analyses of Deng, Gyourko & Wu (2012a), who use more sophisticated metrics and regressions controlling for other factors that may affect housing prices, yield the result that there may well be bubbles in some first-tier cities, such as Beijing, Shanghai, and Shenzhen. There is some evidence that speculative foreign capital (hot money) flowing into China is partially responsible for the accelerated rise in real estate markets (see, e.g., Chu & Sing 2004, Guo & Huang 2010). However, some studies suggest that despite the enormous price appreciation, the Chinese housing boom is different in nature from the housing bubbles in the United States and Japan. For example, from the demand side, Fang et al. (2015) use a comprehensive data set of mortgage loans issued by a major Chinese commercial bank from 2003 to 2013 and construct a set of housing price indexes for 120 major cities in China, showing that, because banks in China imposed down payments of more than 30% on all mortgage loans, they are protected from borrowers' default risk even in the event of a sizable meltdown in the housing market. Moreover, there is also much less securitization, and hence the issuing banks are the ones monitoring and collecting payments. From the supply side, Deng, Gyourko & Wu (2016) show that although there has been high inventory in some lower-tier cities, the situation in the first- and second-tier cities is much better. A drop in housing prices in some areas could lead to a drop in many households' wealth (Deng, Gyourko & Wu 2012b).

4.5. Asset Management

The development of the mutual fund industry in China started in 1992, when the first fund (ZiBo) was established. In 1997, the first version of mutual fund regulation was drafted and passed by the CSRC. **Figure 6** shows the development of the mutual fund industry in China. After having only a handful of funds in 1998, China has 65 fund companies managing 1,621 different funds as of the fourth quarter of 2013. The total net asset value increased from RMB 11 billion (or \$1.3 billion) in 1998 to about RMB 4.74 trillion (\$775.7 billion) in the first quarter of 2014. The growth of open-ended funds contributed to most of the growth in the industry. As of the first quarter of 2013, 1,621 funds were open-ended and 136 were closed-ended, with 94.5% of the total fund value managed by open-ended funds. The most popular investment style is actively managed (domestic) equity, with only a few index funds and exchange-traded funds. Many mutual fund companies are owned by securities and other financial services companies.

The first fund managed by a QFII was set up in 2002 after the announcement of the QFII Act. The State Administration of Foreign Exchange (SAFE), a government agency affiliated with the PBOC, is the regulator of QFII funds. The introduction of QFII funds that allow qualified foreign investors to invest in Chinese securities markets was intended to improve market efficiency and corporate governance in the listed sector. In August 2006, the CSRC revised the QFII rules to promote more participation from foreign investors. Under the new rules, there has been a significant increase in applications from foreign investors for QFII quotas. As of November 2013, there were a total of 251 approved QFIIs operating in China. The approved investment quotas reached \$49.1 billion. With the partial opening up of the capital account, the RQFII (RMB qualified foreign institutional investors) program was approved by the State Council in August 2011, allowing foreign institutional investors to invest in the domestic securities market within an approved quota. The initial quota was RMB 20 billion in January 2012 and was increased to RMB 144.6 billion in November 2013.

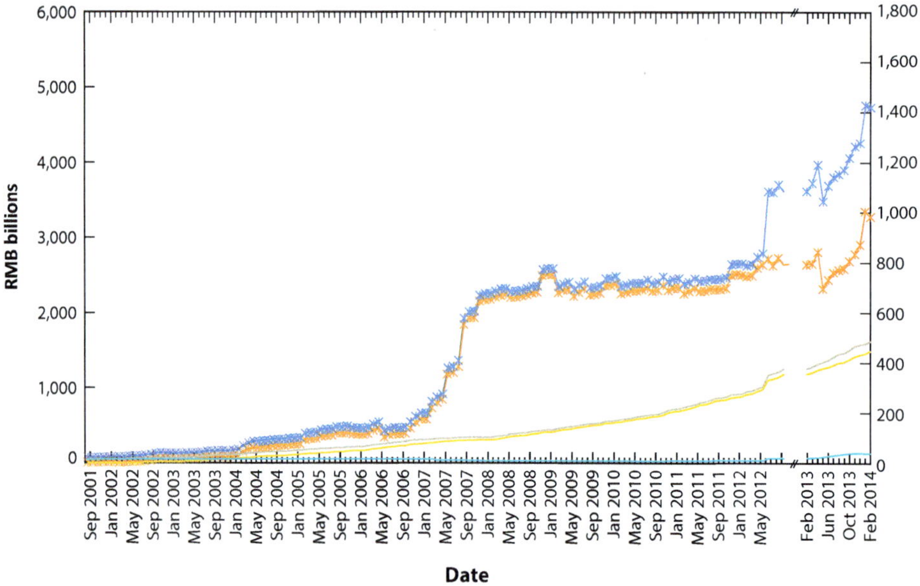

Figure 6

Growth in China's mutual fund industry (2001–2014). Source: CEIC database (**https://www.ceicdata.com**).

The approval for qualified domestic institutional investors (QDIIs) to invest in overseas markets also came after the QFII Act, in July 2006. QDII funds are invested in stocks, bonds, real estate investment trusts, and other mainstream financial products in markets such as New York, London, Tokyo, and Hong Kong. Similar to the QFII scheme, this is a transitional arrangement that provides limited opportunities for domestic investors to have access to foreign markets at a stage in which a country or territory's currency is not freely convertible and capital flows are restricted. By November 2013, QDIIs had approved investment quotas of $81.4 billion. As a result of the recent turmoil in the global financial markets, the performance of QDII funds has been poor. With the future opening up of the domestic market to foreign investors, China's asset management industry is expected to continue its fast growth in the future. The further growth of the economy and continuing reform of the pension system will generate both demand for and supply of capital for the industry.

4.6. Regulations and Further Changes in Financial Markets

Although the financial markets are developing fast, the financial system is still dominated by a large banking system. It is expected that in the future the financial markets will develop more as a result of ongoing financial reforms by the central government. Newly introduced financial products and more developed markets can enhance the risk management capabilities of China's financial institutions and firms. Deep and efficient markets can also provide alternatives to banks that wish to raise large amounts of capital. As we have documented, the performance of the stock market has been very volatile. The poor performance of this market, especially since the recent global financial crisis to 2014, relative to developed economies (the United States) and large emerging economies (Brazil, Russia, India, and South Africa) has been striking, given the robust performance of China's real economy (Allen et al. 2017c). We attribute this to several factors, which include limited self-regulation and formal regulation, the large overhang of shares owned by government entities, the lack of listed firms in the hybrid sector, the lack of institutional investors relative to individual investors, and relatively limited financial markets and products. Efforts are currently being made to overcome these weaknesses, but solutions will take some time to implement.

4.6.1. Regulations. There are two ways in which markets are regulated in practice, each having advantages and disadvantages: (*a*) market forces and self-regulation and (*b*) government regulation.

A good example of regulation through market forces and self-regulation is provided by the capital markets in the United Kingdom in the nineteenth and early twentieth centuries (Michie 1987). The markets performed extremely well, with London being the financial center of the world, although the government seldom intervened. Reputation and trust were important factors in the smooth operation of these markets (see, e.g., Franks, Mayer & Rossi 2009).

We argue below that China's hybrid sector is another example of a situation where market forces are effective. Formal regulation and legal protections do not play a major role, yet financing and governance mechanisms are quite effective. In this case, as we shall see, it appears that competition, in addition to reputation and trust, works well.

In contrast, discussions on fraud, insider trading, and manipulation in financial markets suggest that, in China's formal markets, these alternative mechanisms do not work well. However, government regulation in the financial sector, along the lines of the government interventions after the Great Depression in the 1930s and the subprime financial crisis in 2008 in the United States, may allow China's markets to function better (see, e.g., La Porta, Lopez-de-Silanes & Shleifer 2006).

4.6.2. Sale of government shares in listed firms. One of the major problems that Chinese stock markets have faced in recent years has been caused by the large amount of shares in listed companies owned by the government and government entities. The Chinese government attempted sales of state shares of selected firms in 1999 and 2001, but halted the process both times after share prices plunged and investors grew panicky about the value of the entire market.

In 2005, the government announced a plan of fully floating state shares. Under this plan, the remaining state shares among listed firms were converted to G shares. The CSRC outlined the format for compensating existing shareholders and also imposed lockups and restrictions on the amount of G shares that could be sold immediately after they became tradable. Moreover, the plan specified that G shares were not allowed to be traded or transferred within 12 months of the implementation of the share structure reform. Shareholders who own more than 5% of the original nontradable shares can trade no more than 5% of the outstanding shares within 1 year and no more than 10% within 2 years of the implementation of the reform. These restrictions on G-share sales were intended to reduce the downward pressure on the stock price, maintain market stability, and protect the interests of public investors. The details of the fully floating plan for a firm, including the number of G shares to be granted to each Class A shareholder and the time window (e.g., 1–3 years) of G shares to become fully floating, had to be approved by two-thirds of Class A shareholders of the firm.

A pilot program of share reform started in April 2005. By the end of 2006, 96% of all listed companies at that time had completed share reforms. The success of share reform also partly contributed to the rise of the stock market in 2006–2007.[27]

[27]Hwang, Zhang & Zhu (2006) document that share reform increases turnover, especially for firms with low liquidity prior to the reform, and reduces speculative trading. Although share prices drop significantly on the day of share supply increases, shareholder wealth increases by 15% overall. Bortolotti, Beltratti & Caccavaio (2011) document an 8% abnormal return

4.6.3. A greater range of financial products and recent developments in securitization.

A greater range of financial products allows investors to form diversified portfolios with more than just stocks. As discussed above, corporate bond markets, along with better enforcement of bankruptcy laws and bond rating agencies, provide an alternative class of assets to stocks. The introduction of more derivative securities, such as forwards, futures, and options on commodities (already in place and trading) as well as on other securities, enlarges the risk management toolbox of investors and firms. On April 16, 2010, China launched an index future tracking the Shanghai-based Hushen 300, the index of 300 Shanghai- and Shenzhen-listed Class A shares. On the first day, four contracts were traded. Of the 2,200 index future accounts opened as of May 4, 2010, 95% were individuals and the rest were institutional investors. The launch of this long-awaited index future was a major step in the reform of capital markets in China and introduced a new tool for risk management. Along with this index future, margin trading and short selling of shares were also permitted.

In addition, the insurance industry has expanded remarkably through issuing insurance investment products (e.g., in property and auto insurance as well as life and medical insurance). The trust industry has overtaken the insurance industry since 2012 as the largest sector within the nonbank financial industry, as a large number of structured wealth management products have been issued after 2009 to support the growth of real estate and infrastructure. In March 2005, the State Council approved the pilot implementation of asset securitization, including credit asset securitization in China's interbank market and corporate asset securitization by securities companies. In August 2013, the State Council released a statement to scale up the pilot of securitization of good-quality bank loans in the interbank market as a part of a financial market liberalization project. Given that banks' balance sheets have expanded tremendously since the global financial crisis of 2007–2009, this is a step forward to diversify credit risk outside the Chinese banking system and a way to clear space on bank balance sheets for new lending.

5. THE SHADOW FINANCIAL SECTOR AND EVIDENCE ON HYBRID SECTOR FIRMS

5.1. Comparison of the Hybrid Sector Versus the State and Listed Sectors

Survey and anecdotal evidence shows that the hybrid sector is more productive than the state and listed sectors.[28] The output from the hybrid sector increased from 1998 to 2012 and exceeded that of the other two sectors in 1998 (**Figure 7*a***). The total output in 2011 was almost $11,444 billion for the hybrid sector, whereas it was about $4,812 billion for the state and listed sectors combined.[29] Over the period from 1998 to 2011, the hybrid sector grew at an annual rate of more than 30%, whereas the state and listed sectors combined grew at about 20% during the same

around the date of the share reform announcement. Liao & Liu (2008) show that market reactions to share reforms are positively associated with the quality of the listed firms (as measured by firm disclosure), providing evidence of improved market efficiency (for further discussion on the share reforms of 2005–2007, see Allen et al. 2012c).

[28]All firms, including hybrid sector firms, must disclose accounting and financial information to the local Bureau of Commerce and Industry, and most of the reports are audited. However, these data are then aggregated into Statistical Yearbooks without any firm-level publications.

[29]Because of data limitations, our calculations underestimate the output of the state and listed sectors, as we consider only those firms with at least 50% state ownership, excluding those not majority owned by the state. We calculate the output of the hybrid sector using the difference between the total output and the total for the other two sectors. However, as only 20% of listed firms are not majority owned by the state, our calculations should not have a large bias.

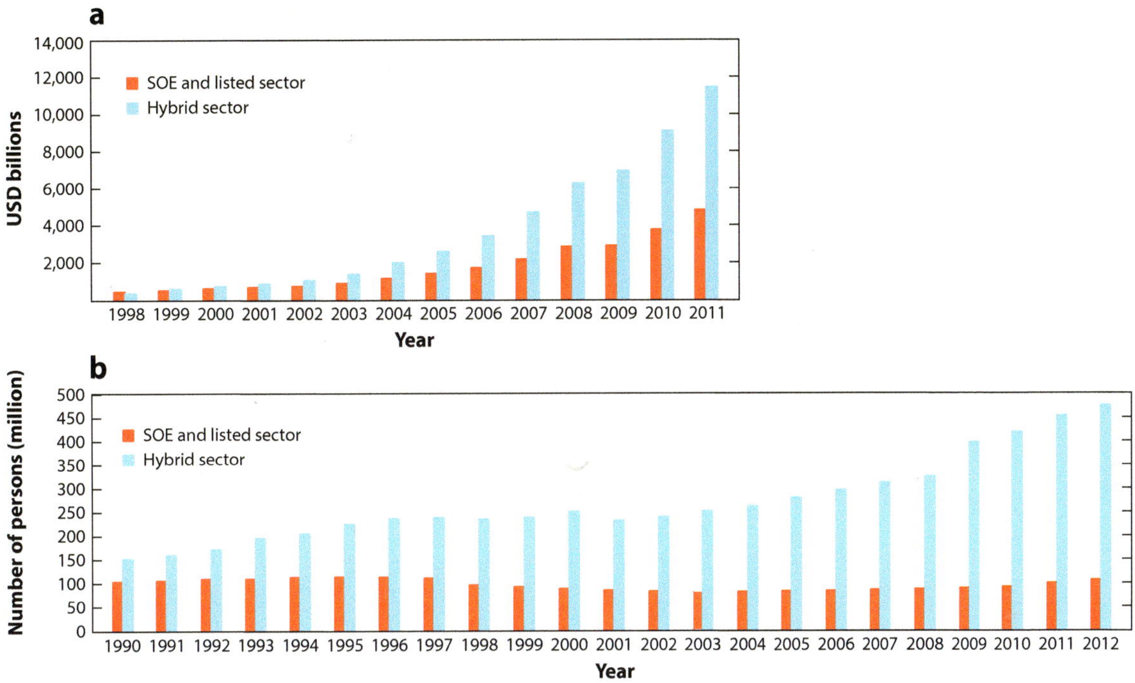

Figure 7

(*a*) Comparison of sectors by industrial output. Total industrial output for the state sector [state-owned enterprises (SOEs)] and listed sector (publicly listed and traded firms) combined and for the hybrid sector (all other firms) during 1998–2011. (*b*) Comparison of sectors by employment. Total number of workers employed by the state and listed sectors combined and by the hybrid sector during 1990–2012. Source: CEIC database (**https://www.ceicdata.com**).

period.[30] There has been a fundamental change in the state, listed, and hybrid sectors in terms of their contribution to the entire economy: The state sector contributed more than two-thirds of China's GDP in 1980, and the contributions of (nonagricultural) privately owned firms, a type of hybrid sector firm, were negligible (Nat. Bur. Stat. China 1998), but in 2011 the state sector contributed only 15% of GDP (Nat. Bur. Stat. China 2012). In fact, with large samples of firms (from different sources) with various ownership structures, Dollar & Wei (2007) and Liu & Siu (2011) alike find that the return on capital is much higher in nonstate sectors than in the state sector and that a capital reallocation from state to private sectors would generate more growth in the economy. Fan, Rui & Zhao (2008) and Li, Yue & Zhao (2009) document that state-owned firms in China have much easier access to the debt market and, accordingly, higher leverage than nonstate firms. Given their government protection, these firms also have easier access to bank loans, especially credit extended by state-owned banks, and their costs for bankruptcy and financial distress are much lower.

[30]There is an ongoing process of privatizing SOEs. This may potentially bias the growth rate of the hybrid sector upward, as firms shift from the state sector to the hybrid sector. However, the overwhelming majority of SOEs became listed sector firms (the main channel through which SOEs were partially privatized prior to 2004), and thus this process is unlikely to change the validity of the results above.

5.2. Discussion on How the Shadow Financial Sector Works

There are two main aspects to alternative financing channels in the hybrid sector: the way in which investment is financed and corporate governance (for further discussion on how these alternative mechanisms work, see Allen et al. 2012c).

First, once a firm is established and doing well, internal finance can provide the funds necessary for growth. Allen, Qian & Qian (2005) find that about 60% of the funds raised by the hybrid sector are generated internally, including funds from family and friends and loans from private (unofficial) credit agencies (see also Tsai 2002). Some of the seed money could also come from illegal channels such as bribery, insider trading, or speculation during the early stages of the development of both financial markets and the property market.

Second, perhaps the most significant corporate governance mechanism is competition in product and input markets, which has worked well in both developed and developing countries (see, e.g., McMillan 1995, 1997; Allen & Gale 2000c). The success of hybrid sector firms in Wenzhou and of other firms described by Allen, Qian & Qian (2005) suggests that it is only those firms that have the strongest comparative advantage in an industry (in a given area) that have survived and prospered. A relevant factor for competition in an industry is entry barriers for new firms, as lower entry barriers foster competition. Djankov et al. (2002) examine entry barriers across 85 countries and find that countries with heavier regulation of entry have higher government corruption and larger unofficial economies and that those with lighter regulation of entry have more democratic and limited governments. With much lower barriers to entry compared to other countries with similar (low) GDP per capita, China is an outlier in the sample of Djankov et al., given that it is one of the least democratic countries and that such countries tend to have high barriers to entry. Survey evidence from Allen, Qian & Qian (2005) reveals that there exist shadow methods to remove entry barriers in China, which can reconcile these seemingly contradictory facts.

Another mechanism is reputation, trust, and relationships. Greif (1989, 1993) suggests that reputation, implicit contractual relations, and coalitions can complement the formal legal and contract enforcement and solve the problems of asymmetric information. Certain aspects of the growth of these institutions resemble what worked to promote commerce and the financial system in China prior to 1949 (see, e.g., Kirby 1995) and the operation of the nonstandard financial sector today (Allen, Qian & Qian 2005), in terms of how firms raise funds and contract with investors and business partners. In addition, Greif (1993) and Stulz & Williamson (2003) point out the importance of cultural and religious beliefs for the development of institutions, legal origins, and investor protections.

There are other effective corporate governance mechanisms. First, in countries with weak protection of shareholder rights, family-run firms tend to be common, whereas, in countries with strong shareholder protection, institutional ownership appears to perform more effectively (Burkart et al. 2011). Survey evidence on the hybrid sector presented by Allen, Qian & Qian (2005) and empirical results on the listed sector, along with evidence from Claessens, Djankov & Lang (2000), Claessens et al. (2002), and Allen et al. (2012a), suggest that family firms are the norm in China and other Asian countries and that these firms have performed well. If cooperation among different suppliers of inputs is necessary and all suppliers benefit from a firm doing well, then a good equilibrium with no external governance is possible, as internal, mutual monitoring can ensure the optimal outcome (Allen & Gale 2000b). Allen, Qian & Qian (2005) and Allen et al. (2012a) present evidence on the importance of trade credits as a form of financing for firms in the hybrid sector. Cooperation and mutual monitoring can ensure payments (as long as funds are available) among business partners despite the lack of external monitoring and contract enforcement. The importance of trade credits is also found in other emerging economies (for India, see, e.g., Allen et al. 2012a) as well as in developed countries (for the United States, see Burkart et al. 2011).

6. FINANCIAL CRISES

In this section, we consider financial crises in China. In general, financial crises often accompany the development of a financial system. Conventional wisdom says that financial crises are bad. Often they disrupt production and lower social welfare, as did the Great Depression in the United States. However, Ranciere, Tornell & Westermann (2003) report an empirical observation that countries that have experienced occasional crises have grown on average faster than countries without crises. (For a review of the growth and crisis literature, see Allen & Oura 2004; for a demonstration that crises can be optimal, see Allen & Gale 2004b; for reviews of the crisis literature, see Allen & Gale 2007, Benoit et al. 2017.) Given China's current situation, with high NPL levels in the banking sector, high real estate prices, and an accelerated process of capital account liberalization, any crisis that occurs is likely to be a classic banking or currency crisis or a twin crisis. It is perhaps more likely to be of the damaging type that disrupts the economy and social stability than of the more benign type that aids growth. Thus, in considering financial reforms, the desirability of preventing crises needs to be taken into account.

6.1. Banking Crises and Market Crashes

Among traditional financial crises, banking panics, arising from banks' lack of liquid assets to meet total withdrawal demands, whether anticipated or unanticipated, have often been particularly disruptive. In recent years, banking crises have often been preceded by abnormal price rises (bubbles) in real estate and/or stock markets. When the bubble bursts or asset markets collapse, banks or other financial institutions that have excessive exposure to equity and real estate markets might encounter liquidity or even solvency issues. Allen & Gale (2000a) provide a theory of bubbles and crises based on the existence of an agency problem. A crucial determinant for asset prices is the amount of credit that is provided for speculative investment. Financial liberalization, by expanding the volume of credit, can interact with the agency problem and lead to a bubble in asset prices.

In China, there are several factors that could trigger a banking crisis. First, as discussed in previous sections, if NPLs continue to accumulate or if economic growth slows down significantly, it is possible that withdrawal of funds from banks will occur, which might cause a banking crisis. Second, besides the high level of NPLs, the close nexus between banks and the real estate sector may also cause problems. When property prices rise, more speculative money, taking the form of bank loans, would flow into the housing market. The agency problem in real estate lending and investment could make the issue even worse. As suggested by the recent global financial crisis, if real estate prices fall suddenly and unexpectedly, defaults on bank loans could increase enough to trigger a banking panic and crisis. Given the strong relationship between the government sector and the banking sector, the government could help to control the risk-taking behaviors of banks by regulation and direct intervention as a shareholder. In fact, the Chinese banking sector and financial markets were not much affected by the 2007–2009 global financial crisis. As for the issue of NPLs in the banking sector, it is expected that the government will set up more local asset management firms to tackle this. Although we recognize above that the government's dual role as a regulator and as a majority owner can be problematic, it can also be beneficial in terms of both preventing and coping with crises.

6.2. Capital Account Liberalization, Twin Crises, and Contagion

History has shown that financial liberalization can cause problems in emerging market economies. Kaminsky & Reinhart (1999) find that the advent of financial liberalization in many economies in the 1980s, in which free capital in- and outflows and competition from foreign investors and financial institutions follow in the home country, has often led to twin banking and currency crises. In an emerging market, this is often then accompanied by an exchange rate crisis as the government chooses between lowering interest rates to ease the banking crisis and raising them to defend the home currency. Finally, a significant fall in output occurs, and the economy enters a recession.

In recent years, authorities have sought to make the Chinese currency more widely used internationally and to accelerate capital account opening. In July 2010, for instance, the PBOC and the Hong Kong Monetary Authority jointly announced that RMB would be deliverable in Hong Kong, creating the CNH market, a new offshore market in RMB. In late September 2013, the Chinese government launched the pilot of the Shanghai Free Trade Zone, with an emphasis on exploring ways to facilitate investment and financing remittance, promoting the convertibility of the capital account as well as the cross-border use of RMB to allow enterprises and individuals in the pilot zone to use RMB to carry out cross-border trade in a more flexible way. On August 11, 2015, the PBOC announced that it would improve the RMB to US dollar central parity rate formation mechanism, a change that is called the 8.11 Exchange Rate Reform.[31] Since the reform, market supply and demand have played a more decisive role in determining the central parity exchange rate. On the same day, the RMB central parity rate rose by 200 basis points, indicating that the PBOC was trying to listen to the market price, although it claimed that it would closely monitor the exchange market and stabilize the market expectation. On October 1, 2016, the RMB was officially added to the IMF's SDR basket, joining the US dollar, the euro, the yen, and the British pound, an action that is regarded as recognition and reinforcement of China's continuing reform progress.

Prior to the financial crisis of 2007–09, Chinese exports grew consistently and strongly for decades, which led to an accumulation of foreign assets. However, with capital outflow and the RMB exchange rate becoming more flexible, authorities had to sell US dollars and purchase RMB to maintain the domestic currency's value when necessary, leading to a negative flow of foreign reserves as well as a rapid decline in foreign reserves from RMB 3.99 trillion in June 2014 to RMB 2.99 trillion in January 2017 (**Figure 8**). After the PBOC's tightening of capital outflow in recent months, the flow of foreign reserves has come back to positive numbers since February 2017.[32] Capital account liberalization can attract more foreign capital; however, large-scale and sudden capital flows and foreign speculation significantly increase the likelihood of a twin crisis. A key question is, when and to what extent should a country liberalize its capital account and let the

[31]The daily quotes of the central parity that market makers report to the China Foreign Exchange Trade System before the market opens should refer to the closing rate of the interbank foreign exchange market on the previous business day, and the demand and supply conditions in the foreign exchange market and the exchange rate movements of the major currencies should also be considered comprehensively. For further information, see Allen et al. (2017a).

[32]However, given that the RMB is in the SDR basket and President Xi stated in his January 17, 2017, speech in Davos that China will protect and lead global trade and integration (Lan 2017), the capital account liberalization process will not stop once the flows are stabilized.

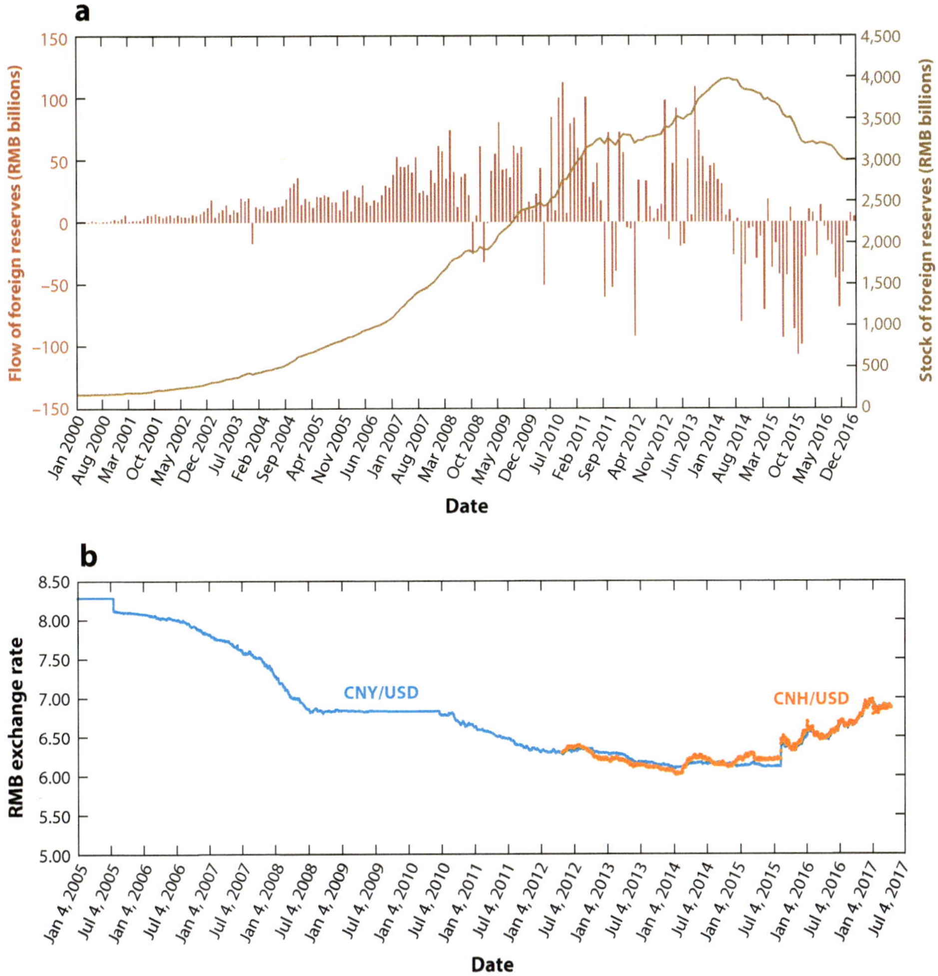

Figure 8

Foreign reserves and foreign exchange rate. (*a*) Flow and stock of foreign reserves. Source: People's Bank of China. (*b*) RMB exchange rate. Sources: People's Bank of China, ICAP.

exchange rate float? Chang, Liu & Spiegel (2015) employ a dynamic stochastic general equilibrium model calibrated to Chinese and global data to show that a regime combining a partially liberalized capital account and a floating exchange rate performs best, although liberalizing either capital controls or exchange rate targets leads to gains in macroeconomic stability and welfare. Alessandria & Qian (2005) use a model of endogenous financial intermediation to demonstrate that an efficient financial sector prior to liberalization is neither necessary nor sufficient for a successful financial liberalization. Applying these ideas to China, even though the overall efficiency of China's banking sector is still low compared to international standards, banks can have a stronger incentive to limit the moral hazard concerning borrowers' choices of investment projects through monitoring and design of loan contracts (e.g., adjusting interest rates and/or maturities) after a capital account liberalization. This would improve the efficiency of the banking sector; therefore, financial liberalization, which allows foreign financial institutions to enter China's lending markets, can improve welfare, as competition provides stronger incentives for banks to discourage moral hazard in investment.

Given the rapid growth and recent decline in foreign exchange reserves and the high volume of speculative capital inflows and outflows in anticipation of an RMB revaluation in the past decade, a currency crisis that may trigger a banking crisis is a possibility. What happens then will depend on how the government and central bank respond. Floating rates can prevent continuous capital outflows so that the government would not use up its exchange reserves. If the exchange rate movement is limited to a narrow band, then there may be a classic currency crisis. This, in turn, may trigger a banking crisis if there are large withdrawals from banks as a result. Quickly adopting a full float can help to avoid a twin crisis and thus reduce the overall economic cost of a currency crisis.[33]

Another phenomenon that has been present in many recent crises (e.g., the 1997 Asian Financial Crisis) is contagion of financial crises. A small shock that initially affects only a particular region or sector can spread by contagion within the banking system or asset markets to the rest of the financial sector, and then to the entire economy and possibly to other economies (see, e.g., Allen & Gale 2000d, 2004a).

Given China's current financial system, what is the likelihood of financial contagion caused by contractual interlinkages (as in the interbank market) or by a meltdown in asset prices in the event of forced sales? China's interbank market has grown very quickly since its inception in 1981, and the government and the PBOC have correspondingly increased regulation by limiting participation of nonbank financial institutions and by imposing restrictions on interest rate movements. In 1996, a nationwide interbank market, the National Interbank Funding Center, was set up. In 2006, the Shanghai Head Office of the PBOC started to take on the responsibility of managing entries, quotas, and information disclosures of the center. By November 2016, the number of members of the center had increased to 1,602. Such increasing interlinkages can potentially create contagion if a crisis develops in one area or sector. For instance, a credit crunch in the interbank market occurred in June 2013 when 7-day interbank repo rates soared to 11.62%, which was the highest daily fixing since 2003. The PBOC stepped in by injecting capital and rebuilding confidence in the interbank market, largely resolving the market confusion. The credit crunch was ended by the PBOC's introduction of liquidity tools such as the Short-Term Liquidity Operation (SLO) and Standing Lending Facility (SLF) (see, e.g., Allen et al. 2017a). Regarding a meltdown of asset prices, this can happen because of a limited supply of liquidity if there is a rapid liquidation of assets, which is what occurred in the recent stock market crash in the summer of 2015. The Chinese stock market was bearish after the global financial crisis of 2007–2009, until mid-2014. The CSI 300 index, which represents the broad Chinese A-share market, rose from 2,050 to a high of 5,178, then collapsed and lost 34% in 20 days, with 1,000 points of the index erased in 1 week alone. This crash was also ended by a series of interventions by different authorities, including the PBOC, the CSRC, and China Securities Finance. Allen et al. (2017a) give a detailed review of the activities of these authorities during the episode and conclude that their rescue plans helped stabilize the market during the crash, albeit at the cost of more uncertainty and volatility because of their trial-and-error approach in implementing these policies. A more serious threat is

[33]Chang & Velasco (2001) develop a model of twin crises based on the model of bank runs of Diamond & Dybvig (1983). They assume that the ratio of currency to consumption is controlled by the central bank. In their model, there exist both a good and a bad equilibrium. In some situations, consumers receive profits from short- or long-term investments (a good equilibrium), and in other situations everyone believes that a crisis will occur, so a twin crisis is a self-fulfilling outcome (a bad equilibrium).

the real estate market, particularly if there is a significant drop in housing prices accompanied by bankruptcies and forced selling. This could potentially interact with bank interlinkages and cause a systemic problem. As mentioned above, a crash in real estate could be the cause of a financial crisis in China if it occurs without proper government interventions.

7. CONCLUDING REMARKS

In this article, we examined the development of China's financial system and the linkage between the financial sector and the real economy in China. Compared with the financial markets, the large banking system dominated by state-owned banks has played a critical role in financing the growth of different types of firms in the past decades. We have also stressed the positive role of informal finance and the shadow banking system in China. The shadow financial sector relies on alternative financing channels including internal finance, and on alternative governance mechanisms, such as those based on trust, reputation and relationships. However, much theoretical and empirical research is needed to understand the advantages and disadvantages of these alternative institutions compared to Western-style legal institutions in supporting a fast-growing economy such as China's. Moreover, the government has implemented a number of reforms in the financial system. An important area of research is to find out which reforms are successful and which are unsuccessful. It will be interesting to investigate, both theoretically and empirically, the effects that opening up the Chinese financial system to the rest of the world will have both on China and on the rest of the world. Finally, China's financial system still faces the risk of instability in the future, especially during the period of reforms. More research is needed to understand the vulnerabilities in China's financial system.

DISCLOSURE STATEMENT

The authors are not aware of any affiliations, memberships, funding, or financial holdings that might be perceived as affecting the objectivity of this review.

ACKNOWLEDGMENTS

We thank the reviewer for very helpful comments that substantially improved this article.

LITERATURE CITED

Acharya V, Qian J, Yang Z. 2016. *In the shadow of banks: wealth management products and issuing banks' risks in China*. Work. Pap., N.Y. Univ.

Alessandria G, Qian J. 2005. Endogenous financial intermediation and real effects of capital account liberalization. *J. Int. Econ.* 67:97–128

Allen F, Chakrabarti R, De S, Qian J, Qian M. 2012a. Financing firms in India. *J. Financ. Intermed.* 21:409–45

Allen F, Gale D. 1999. Diversity of opinion and financing of new technologies. *J. Financ. Intermed.* 8:68–89

Allen F, Gale D. 2000a. Bubbles and crises. *Econ. J.* 110:236–55

Allen F, Gale D. 2000b. *Comparing Financial Systems*. Cambridge, MA: MIT Press

Allen F, Gale D. 2000c. Corporate governance and competition. In *Corporate Governance: Theoretical and Empirical Perspectives*, ed. X Vives, pp. 23–94. London: Cambridge Univ. Press

Allen F, Gale D. 2000d. Financial contagion. *J. Political Econ.* 108:1–33

Allen F, Gale D. 2004a. Financial fragility, liquidity and asset prices. *J. Eur. Econ. Assoc.* 2:1015–48

Allen F, Gale D. 2004b. Financial intermediaries and markets. *Econometrica* 72:1023–61

Allen F, Gale D. 2007. *Understanding Financial Crises*. New York: Oxford Univ. Press

Allen F, Gu X, Kuang H, Qian J. 2017a. *The People's Bank of China: from 1948 to 2016*. Work. Pap., Imp. Coll. London

Allen F, Gu X, Qian J, Qian Y. 2017b. *Implicit guarantee and shadow banking: the case of trust products*. Work. Pap., Imp. Coll. London

Allen F, Oura H. 2004. Sustained economic growth and the financial system. *Monet. Econ. Stud. Bank Jpn.* 22(S-1):95–119

Allen F, Qian J, Gu X. 2015. China's financial system: growth and risk. *Found. Trends Finance* 9(3–4):197–319

Allen F, Qian J, Qian M. 2005. Law, finance, and economic growth in China. *J. Financ. Econ.* 77:57–116

Allen F, Qian J, Qian M. 2008. China's financial system: past, present, and future. In *China's Great Economic Transformation*, ed. L Brandt, T Rawski, pp. 506–68. Cambridge, UK: Cambridge Univ. Press

Allen F, Qian J, Shan C, Zhao M. 2012b. The IPO of Industrial and Commercial Bank of China and the "Chinese model" of privatizing large financial institutions. *Eur. J. Finance* 20:599–624

Allen F, Qian J, Shan C, Zhu L. 2017c. *Dissecting the long-term performance of the Chinese stock market*. Work. Pap., Imp. Coll. London

Allen F, Qian J, Zhang C, Zhao M. 2012c. China's financial system: opportunities and challenges. In *Capitalizing China*, ed. J Fan, R Morck, pp. 63–148. Chicago: Univ. Chic. Press

Allen F, Qian Y, Tu G, Yu F. 2016. *Entrusted loans: a closer look at China's shadow banking system*. Work. Pap., Imp. Coll. London

Anderlini J. 2010. Chinese banks face state loans turmoil. *Financial Times*, July 26. **https://www.ft.com/content/73c71f2e-988a-11df-a0b7-00144feab49a**

Beck T, Demirgüç-Kunt A, Levine R, Maksimovic V. 2001. Financial structure and economic development: firm, industry and country evidence. In *Financial Structure and Economic Growth: A Cross Country Comparison of Banks, Markets and Development*, ed. A Demirgüç-Kunt, R Levine, pp. 189–242. Cambridge, MA: MIT Press

Beck T, Demirgüç-Kunt A, Maksimovic V. 2005. Financial and legal constraints to growth: Does firm size matter? *J. Finance* 60:137–77

Benoit S, Colliard J-E, Hurlin C, Pérignon C. 2017. Where the risks lie: a survey on systemic risk. *Rev. Finance* 21:109–52

Berger A, Hasan I, Zhou M. 2009. Bank ownership and efficiency in China: What will happen in the world's largest nation? *J. Bank. Finance* 33:113–30

Bortolotti B, Beltratti A, Caccavaio M. 2011. *The stock market reaction to the non-tradable share reform in China*. Work. Pap. 1339, Eur. Cent. Bank, Frankfurt, Ger.

Brandt L, Zhu X. 2000. Redistribution in a decentralized economy: growth and inflation in China under reform. *J. Political Econ.* 108:422–39

Burkart M, Elligensen T, Giannetti M. 2011. What you sell is what you lend? Explaining trade credits contracts. *Rev. Financ. Stud.* 24:1261–98

Chan K, Menkveld A, Yang Z. 2008. Information asymmetry and asset prices: evidence from the China foreign share discount. *J. Finance* 63:159–96

Chang C, Liu Z, Spiegel MM. 2015. Capital controls and optimal Chinese monetary policy. *J. Monet. Econ.* 74:1–15

Chang R, Velasco A. 2001. A model of financial crises in emerging markets. *Q. J. Econ.* 116:489–518

Chen Z, He Z, Liu C. 2017. *The financing of local government in China: stimulus loan wanes and shadow banking waxes*. Work. Pap., Booth Sch. Bus., Univ. Chic.

China Daily. 2010. China unveils first sovereign credit rating report. *ChinaDaily*, July 12. **http://www.chinadaily.com.cn/china/2010-07/12/content_10092373.htm**

China Venture. 2011. *China M&A Market Statistics & Analysis 2010*. Beijing: China Venture Invest. Consult.

Chu Y, Sing TF. 2004. Inflation hedging characteristics of the Chinese real estate market. *J. Real Estate Portf. Manag.* 10:145–54

Claessens S, Djankov S, Fan J, Lang L. 2002. Expropriation of minority shareholders in East Asia. *J. Finance* 57:2741–71

Claessens S, Djankov S, Lang L. 2000. The separation of ownership and control in East Asian corporations. *J. Financ. Econ.* 58:81–112

Dang TV, Wang H, Yao A. 2016. *Chinese shadow banking: bank-centric misperceptions*. Work. Pap., Columbia Bus. Sch.

Demirgüç-Kunt A, Levine R. 2001. *Financial Structure and Economic Growth: Cross-Country Comparisons of Banks, Markets, and Development*. Cambridge, MA: MIT Press

Deng Y, Gyourko J, Wu J. 2012a. Evaluating conditions in major Chinese housing markets. *Reg. Sci. Urban Econ.* 42:531–43

Deng Y, Gyourko J, Wu J. 2012b. *Land and house price measurement in China*. NBER Work. Pap. 18403

Deng Y, Gyourko J, Wu J. 2016. Evaluating the risk of Chinese housing markets: what we know and what we need to know. *China Econ. Rev.* 39:91–114

Diamond D, Dybvig P. 1983. Bank runs, deposit insurance, and liquidity. *J. Political Econ.* 91:401–19

Djankov S, La Porta R, Lopez-de-Silanes F, Shleifer A. 2002. The regulation of entry. *Q. J. Econ.* 117:1–37

Dollar D, Wei S-J. 2007. *Das (wasted) kapital: firm ownership and investment efficiency in China*. Work. Pap. 07/9, Int. Monet. Fund, Washington, DC

Du J, Rui O, Wong S. 2008. *Financing motivated takeovers: the case of China*. Work. Pap., Chin. Univ. Hong Kong

Fan J, Huang J, Zhu N. 2013. Institutions, ownership structures and distress resolution in China. *J. Corp. Finance* 23:71–87

Fan J, Rui O, Zhao M. 2008. Public governance and corporate finance: evidence from corruption cases. *J. Comp. Econ.* 36(3):343–64

Fan J, Wong TJ, Zhang T. 2007. Politically-connected CEOs, corporate governance and post-IPO performance of China's partially privatized firms. *J. Financ. Econ.* 84:330–57

Fang H, Gu Q, Xiong W, Zhou L-A. 2015. *Demystifying the Chinese housing boom*. NBER Work. Pap. 21112

Franks J, Mayer C, Rossi S. 2009. Ownership: evolution and regulation. *Rev. Financ. Stud.* 22(10):4009–56

Fung P, Firth M, Rui O. 2003. *Corporate governance and CEO compensation in China*. Work. Pap., Chin. Univ. Hong Kong

Garnaut R, Ligang S, Yang Y. 2004. *SOE restructuring in China*. Work. Pap. 204, Stanford Cent. Int. Dev., Stanford Univ.

Goldsmith RW. 1969. *Financial Structure and Development*. New Haven, CT: Yale Univ. Press

Greenwood J, Jovanovic B. 1990. Financial development, growth, and the distribution of income. *J. Political Econ.* 98:1076–107

Greif A. 1989. Reputation and coalitions in Medieval trade: evidence on the Maghribi traders. *J. Econ. Hist.* 49:857–82

Greif A. 1993. Contract enforceability and economic institutions in early trade: the Maghribi traders' coalition. *Am. Econ. Rev.* 83:525–48

Guo F, Huang YS. 2010. Does "hot money" drive China's real estate and stock markets? *Int. Rev. Econ. Finance* 19:452–66

Hachem K, Song ZM. 2016. *Liquidity regulation and unintended financial transformation in China*. NBER Work. Pap. 21880

Helpman E, Razin A. 1978. *A Theory of International Trade Under Uncertainty*. New York: Academic

Herring R, Chatusripitak N. 2000. *The case of the missing market: the bond market and why it matters for financial development*. Work. Pap., Wharton Financ. Inst. Cent., Univ. Pa.

Hwang C-Y, Zhang S, Zhu Y. 2006. *Float liquidity, speculation, and stock prices: evidence from the share structure reform in China*. Work. Pap., Nanyang Technol. Univ.

Kaminsky G, Reinhart C. 1999. The twin crises: the causes of banking and balance-of-payments problems. *Am. Econ. Rev.* 89:473–500

Kato T, Long C. 2006. Executive compensation, firm performance, and corporate governance in China: evidence from firms listed in the Shanghai and Shenzhen stock exchanges. *Econ. Dev. Cult. Change* 54(4):945–83

King RG, Levine R. 1993. Finance and growth: Schumpeter might be right. *Q. J. Econ.* 32:513–42

Kirby W. 1995. China unincorporated: company law and business enterprise in twentieth-century China. *J. Asian Stud.* 54:43–63

La Porta R, Lopez-de-Silanes F, Shleifer A. 2002. Government ownership of commercial banks. *J. Finance* 57:265–301

La Porta R, Lopez-de-Silanes F, Shleifer A. 2006. What works in securities laws? *J. Finance* 61:1–32

La Porta R, Lopez-de-Silanes F, Shleifer A, Vishny RW. 1997. Legal determinants of external finance. *J. Finance* 52:1131–50

La Porta R, Lopez-de-Silanes F, Shleifer A, Vishny RW. 1998. Law and finance. *J. Political Econ.* 106:1113–55

Lan H. 2017. Xi addresses Davos forum for first time to advance global growth, governance. *Xinhua*, Jan. 17. **http://news.xinhuanet.com/english/2017-01/18/c_135991766.htm**

Lardy NR. 1998. *China's Unfinished Economic Revolution*. Washington, DC: Brookings Inst. Press

Lee TV. 1993. Risky business: courts, culture, and the marketplace. *Univ. Miami Law Rev.* 47:1335–414

Levine R, Zervos S. 1998. Stock markets, banks and economic growth. *Am. Econ. Rev.* 88:537–58

Li K, Yue H, Zhao L. 2009. Ownership, institutions, and capital structure: evidence from China. *J. Comp. Econ.* 37(3):471–90

Liao Li, Liu B. 2008. *Moral hazard, information disclosure and market efficiency: evidence from China's share reform*. Work. Pap., Tsinghua Univ.

Liu Q, Siu A. 2011. Institutions, financial development, and corporate investment: evidence from an implied return on capital in China. *J. Financ. Quant. Anal.* 46(6):1831–63

McMillan J. 1995. China's nonconformist reform. In *Economic Transition in Eastern Europe and Russia: Realities of Reform*, ed. E Lazear, pp. 419–33. Stanford, CA: Hoover Inst. Press

McMillan J. 1997. Markets in transition. In *Advances in Economics and Econometrics*, Vol. 2, ed. DM Kreps, KF Wallis, pp. 210–39. Cambridge, UK: Cambridge Univ. Press

Mei J, Scheinkman J, Xiong W. 2009. *Speculative trading and stock prices: evidence from Chinese A–B share premia*. NBER Work. Pap. 11362

Michie RC. 1987. *The London and New York Stock Exchanges 1850–1914*. London: Allen & Unwin

Moody's. 2011. Scale of problem loans to Chinese local governments greater than anticipated. *Moody's*, July 5. **https://www.moodys.com/research/Moodys-Scale-of-problem-loans-to-Chinese-local-governments-greater?docid=PR_222068**

Moody's. 2016. Moody's changes outlook on China Aa3 government bond rating to negative from stable; affirms Aa3 rating. *Moody's*, March 2. **https://www.moodys.com/research/Moodys-changes-outlook-on-Chinas-Aa3-government-bond-rating-to–PR_343931**

Morck R, Yeung BY, Yu W. 2000. The information content of stock markets: why do emerging markets have synchronous stock price movement? *J. Financ. Econ.* 58:215–60

Natl. Bur. Stat. China. 1998. *China Statistical Yearbook 1998*. Beijing: China Stat. Press

Natl. Bur. Stat. China. 2012. *China Statistical Yearbook 2012*. Beijing: China Stat. Press

Obstfeld M. 1994. Risk-taking, global diversification, and growth. *Am. Econ. Rev.* 84:1310–29

PBOC (People's Bank of China). 2011. *China Monetary Policy Report, Quarter Four, 2010*. Beijing: PBOC. **http://www.pbc.gov.cn/zhengcehuobisi/125207/125227/125957/126000/2850140/index.html**

Perkins D, Rawski T. 2008. Forecasting China's economic growth to 2025. In *China's Great Economic Transformation*, ed. L Brandt, T Rawski, pp. 829–86. Cambridge, UK: Cambridge Univ. Press

Pistor K. 2010. The governance of China's finance. In *Capitalizing China*, ed. JPH Fan, R Morck, pp. 35–60. Chicago: Univ. Chic. Press

Prasad E, Wei S-J. 2007. The Chinese approach to capital flows: patterns and possible explanations. In *Capital Controls and Capital Flows in Emerging Economies*, ed. S Edwards, pp. 421–80. Chicago: Univ. Chic. Press

Qian J, Strahan P, Yang Z. 2015. The impact of incentives and communication costs on information production: evidence from bank lending. *J. Finance* 70(4):1457–93

Rajan R, Zingales L. 1998. Financial development and growth. *Am. Econ. Rev.* 88:559–86

Ranciere R, Tornell A, Westermann F. 2003. *Crises and growth: a re-evaluation*. NBER Work. Pap. 10073

Robinson J, Acemoglu D, Johnson S. 2004. Institutions, volatility and crises. In *Growth and Productivity in East Asia*, ed. T Ito, AK Rose, pp. 71–108. Chicago: Univ. Chic. Press

State Council. 2009. *Gazette of executive meeting of the State Council*. State Counc. Release, Dec. 14. **http://www.gov.cn/ldhd/2009-12/14/content_1487025.htm**

State Council. 2010. *Circular of the State Council on resolutely containing the precipitous rise of housing prices in some cities*. State Counc. Release, April 17. **http://www.gov.cn/zhuanti/2015-06/13/content_2878981.htm**

Stulz R, Williamson R. 2003. Culture, openness, and finance. *J. Financ. Econ.* 70:261–300

Tadesse S. 2002. Financial architecture and economic performance: international evidence. *J. Financ. Intermed.* 11:429–54

Tsai K. 2002. *Back-Alley Banking*. Ithaca, NY: Cornell Univ. Press

World Bank. 2015. *Purchasing Power Parities and the Real Size of World Economies: A Comprehensive Report of the 2011 International Comparison Program*. Washington, DC: World Bank. **http://siteresources.worldbank.org/ICPEXT/Resources/ICP-2011-report.pdf**

The Development of China's Stock Market and Stakes for the Global Economy

Jennifer N. Carpenter[1] and Robert F. Whitelaw[1,2]

[1]Stern School of Business, New York University, New York, NY 10012;
email: carpenter@stern.nyu.edu, rwhitela@stern.nyu.edu

[2]National Bureau of Economic Research, Cambridge, Massachusetts 02138

Annu. Rev. Financ. Econ. 2017. 9:233–57

First published as a Review in Advance on August 10, 2017

The *Annual Review of Financial Economics* is online at financial.annualreviews.org

https://doi.org/10.1146/annurev-financial-110716-032333

Copyright © 2017 by Annual Reviews.
All rights reserved

JEL codes: E44, F30, G12, G14, G15, G18, G32, G34, G38, G40, L20, O16, O53, P21, P31, P34

Keywords

capital allocation, price informativeness, listing choice, market integration, A-share premium, global investing

Abstract

The rise of China and fivefold growth of its stock market over the past decade have fueled a growing literature on this market in financial economics. On the corporate side, researchers have evaluated the progress of China's stages of privatization, analyzed biases in the selection of firms for listing, and documented massive underpricing of initial public offerings. On the asset pricing side, researchers have studied the price premium of domestic A shares over their foreign-share counterparts, analyzed the firm-specific information content of prices, provided new evidence on informational and behavioral effects in prices, and begun to identify systematic cross-sectional patterns in returns. Numerous areas are ripe for future research as China's stock market continues to grow in global influence and as ongoing reform provides new natural experiments. Challenges for the field will be to gain familiarity with China's distinctive financial system and to avoid overapplying research paradigms developed for the US setting.

1. INTRODUCTION

China's financial system evolved from a one-bank system under Mao Zedong to a four-bank system under Deng Xiaoping and is still dominated by its state-controlled bank sector, with over $30 trillion of assets. Its modern stock market opened only in 1990, primarily as a platform for privatizing state-owned enterprises (SOEs), and the selection of firms for listing has been tightly controlled by the government. Until 2005, only a third of the stock market's shares were tradable, with the nontradable remainder held by the state or by state-backed entities, and its total market capitalization did not surpass $1 trillion until 2006. During these early years, the stock market endured repeated scandals and gained a reputation as a casino manipulated by speculators. Because it was small, segmented from other global financial markets, and embedded in a financial system entirely different from that in the United States, it was regarded as a specialized topic by the academic finance community, and little research on China's stock market was included in top journals.

Several developments over the past decade have changed this picture and made China's stock market an important subject for mainstream research in financial economics. First, China's GDP has more than tripled to over $11 trillion as of 2016, making it an economic superpower on par with the United States in purchasing power. Second, its stock market has grown more than fivefold to over $7 trillion in market capitalization as of May 2017, becoming the world's second largest. The number of listings has more than doubled to over 3,200, partly as a result of the introduction of the Small and Medium Enterprise (SME) and ChiNext boards on the Shenzhen Stock Exchange (SZSE) in 2004 and 2009, which has opened capital channels to smaller and more entrepreneurial firms. These boards exist alongside the main boards of the Shanghai Stock Exchange (SSE) and the SZSE, where larger, more mature firms list. In addition, the Split-Share Structure Reform of 2005 enabled the unlocking of nontradable shares, and the tradable fraction in 2016 represents over 75% of the total. Third, China has become the world's largest investor, with $5 trillion of total fixed-asset investment in 2016, compared with $3.7 trillion in the United States and $1 trillion in Japan, making the efficiency of its capital allocation system a matter of global interest. Fourth, the explosion of debt used to finance China's postcrisis stimulus through the expansion of the banking and shadow banking sectors has raised concerns about the stability and efficiency of the financial system, making China's stock market an important alternative financing channel; it is a source of equity capital for firms, an investment opportunity for households, and an aggregator of diffuse information about corporate prospects for use in managerial decision-making.

China's stock market became a focal point for global attention during the stock market run-up and crash of spring and summer 2015, stalling the US Federal Reserve's interest rate liftoff and creating turbulence throughout global financial markets. Nevertheless, MSCI has continued negotiations with the China Securities Regulatory Commission (CSRC) over reforms necessary for full inclusion of China's stock market in its Emerging Markets Index, a major step toward integration of China's stock market with international financial markets. This highlights the interest of foreign investors and has increased pressure for reforms designed to increase liquidity and lift constraints on the free flow of capital. Meanwhile, top finance journals have increasingly opened up to China-focused research, fueling a growing body of literature. In a survey of empirical research on China's stock market, Lu & Fu (2014) find that the average number of articles on this topic published in seven top finance journals rose from one per year during 2000–2007 to over five per year during 2008–2013.

On the corporate side of the stock market, researchers have focused primarily on the effects of the various stages of privatization on firm performance, the determinants of initial public offering (IPO) underpricing, and the selection of firms for listing, marking the progress of reforms but highlighting the continued importance of firms' political connections. A challenge in financial economics research on China is that because the setting there is so different from that in most other finance studies, there is a risk of overapplying existing paradigms and oversimplifying conclusions. This risk is especially great in corporate finance, where maximization of individual firm value is ingrained as firms' primary objective, whereas other objectives may be more important for many firms in China. As Lin, Cai & Li (1998) emphasize, SOEs in China are charged with social, economic, and strategic objectives. They are a significant piece of the social safety net and the principal building blocks of China's planned economy. SOE reform remains one of the most important corporate finance issues in China; calls for the restructuring of firms in industries plagued by overcapacity are countered by the desire to preserve employment and social stability as well as by resistance from vested interests. Future research that seeks to evaluate the successes and failures of SOE reform might do well to view its objectives more broadly than is customary. Other areas ripe for further research include selection biases created by the IPO approval process and the broader question of Chinese corporate listing choice among alternative domestic and international exchanges.

On the asset pricing side, the literature has addressed several interesting issues. The premium in the prices of A shares, accessible to domestic investors, over the prices of their B-share counterparts, accessible to foreign investors, has been attributed to discount rate differentials associated with differential information and investment opportunity sets. B-share issuance has died out since the Qualified Foreign Institutional Investor (QFII) program was established in 2002. However, the premium in A-share prices over the H-share prices of their Hong Kong–listed counterparts persists despite the 2014 and 2016 openings of the Shanghai- and Shenzhen–Hong Kong Stock Connect programs, which have enabled cross-market trading, and remains a puzzle. Another strand of asset pricing research uses distinctive aspects of the stock market to construct new tests of information and behavioral effects in asset prices, such as location, status, and trust effects. A different focal point has been the firm-specific information content of A-share prices and its cross-sectional variation. Yet a further line of research studies the cross section of A-share returns, with increasing power to discern pricing patterns as the sample period grows. Again, although numerous special features of China's markets present new research opportunities, they also require adaptation of existing paradigms and methodologies. These features include 1-day minimum holding periods, 10% daily price move limits, short-sale restrictions, trading suspensions, IPO suspensions, direct government interventions, and special treatment status for distressed stocks, as well as nontradable shares, market segmentation, and limited institutional participation.

Research on China's nascent equity mutual fund and derivatives markets is also becoming possible and looks likely to be fruitful. The institutional interface between the stock market and household investors is still underdeveloped, leaving most household savers to choose between investing in bank products and trading individual stocks. The growth of China's managed equity industry should provide researchers with a world of new evidence on the economics of asset management and on the role of institutional investors in corporate governance, stock price informativeness, and household portfolio choice and welfare. The development of equity derivatives markets in China may also shed new light on the potential of derivatives to quantify tail risks and help complete markets. The potential for increased market participation by global institutional investors and the possibility of an offshore derivatives market in domestic Chinese stock indexes may also illuminate the possibly distinct roles of domestic versus foreign investors in stock market development and efficiency.

China's increasing presence in global financial markets and ongoing financial reforms continue to supply researchers with a wealth of important new developments and natural experiments to study. A challenge for the field will be to gain familiarity with a financial system unlike that in the United States: It is centrally controlled, bank-dominated, and uniquely relationship-driven, as

Allen, Qian & Qian (2005) show, rather than being based primarily on securities markets and legal contracts. Such familiarity will be essential for framing the best questions and drawing correct inferences.

2. PRIVATIZATION, INITIAL PUBLIC OFFERINGS, AND LISTING CHOICE

China's modern stock market opened in Shanghai and Shenzhen in 1990 during the final years of the leadership of Deng Xiaoping. One of the primary goals of this stock market experiment was to create a platform for the partial privatization of China's SOEs, a major step in their ongoing reform. This objective significantly shaped the stock market's initial form and development (Allen & Shen 2011). The selection of firms for listing, the initial pricing, and the subsequent ownership structure were tightly controlled and monitored by the government. The original split-share ownership structure defined five classes of shares; about two-thirds of shares were nontradable (state shares, legal person shares, and employee shares) and one-third were tradable [A shares priced in renminbi (RMB) and held by domestic Chinese investors and also foreign shares, including both B shares priced in USD or Hong Kong dollars (HKD) and traded in Shanghai or Shenzhen, respectively, and H shares priced in HKD and traded in Hong Kong].

Figure 1 shows the time series of the number of listed firms and the composition of market capitalization by ownership class since 1991. Nontradable state shares, owned by the central or local government, averaged almost half of total shares during the first 15 years of the market's operation. Nontradable legal person shares, typically owned by institutions or business agencies that supported the start-up of the firm, often with local government backing but potentially with more profit-oriented interest than state-share owners, typically constituted another 20% of total shares. The Split-Share Structure Reform of 2005 unlocked a significant number of nontradable shares through a mechanism that compensated holders of tradable shares for potential adverse price effects, but almost 25% of total shares remain nontradable today. Similarly, listing registration is still tightly restricted by the CSRC, with almost 500 firms in line for approval as of May 2017.

2.1. Privatization

One of the first strands of the academic literature on China's stock market studies the effects of these stages of privatization on listed firms. Sun & Tong (2003) evaluate the success of China's share issue privatization (SIP) on firm performance in SOEs listed during 1994–1998. China's privatization process took place during a wave of privatization around the world, ranging from the privatization of nationalized firms in the United States and United Kingdom on seasoned stock exchanges to mass voucher privatization programs in Russia and Eastern Europe, as studied in a literature surveyed by Megginson & Netter (2001). Following the methodology of this literature, Sun & Tong (2003) find that SIP increases SOE earnings, sales, and workers' productivity, but not profitability. Wei, Xie & Zhang (2005) analyze the relation between Tobin's Q and ownership structure in partially privatized SOEs during 1991–2001 and find negative effects from state and institutional ownership and positive effects from foreign ownership. In contrast, Calomiris, Fisman & Wang (2010) study B-share stock returns after the announcements of proposed sales of government shares and find a negative effect, concluding that efficiency costs of government ownership might be outweighed by benefits of political connections. China's SIP was itself part of a longer-term reform of SOEs begun when Deng Xiaoping took power in 1978. Li (1997) finds a marked improvement in total factor productivity in SOEs in China between 1980 and 1989, raising the question of disentangling the effects of SIP from the effects of other ongoing SOE reforms.

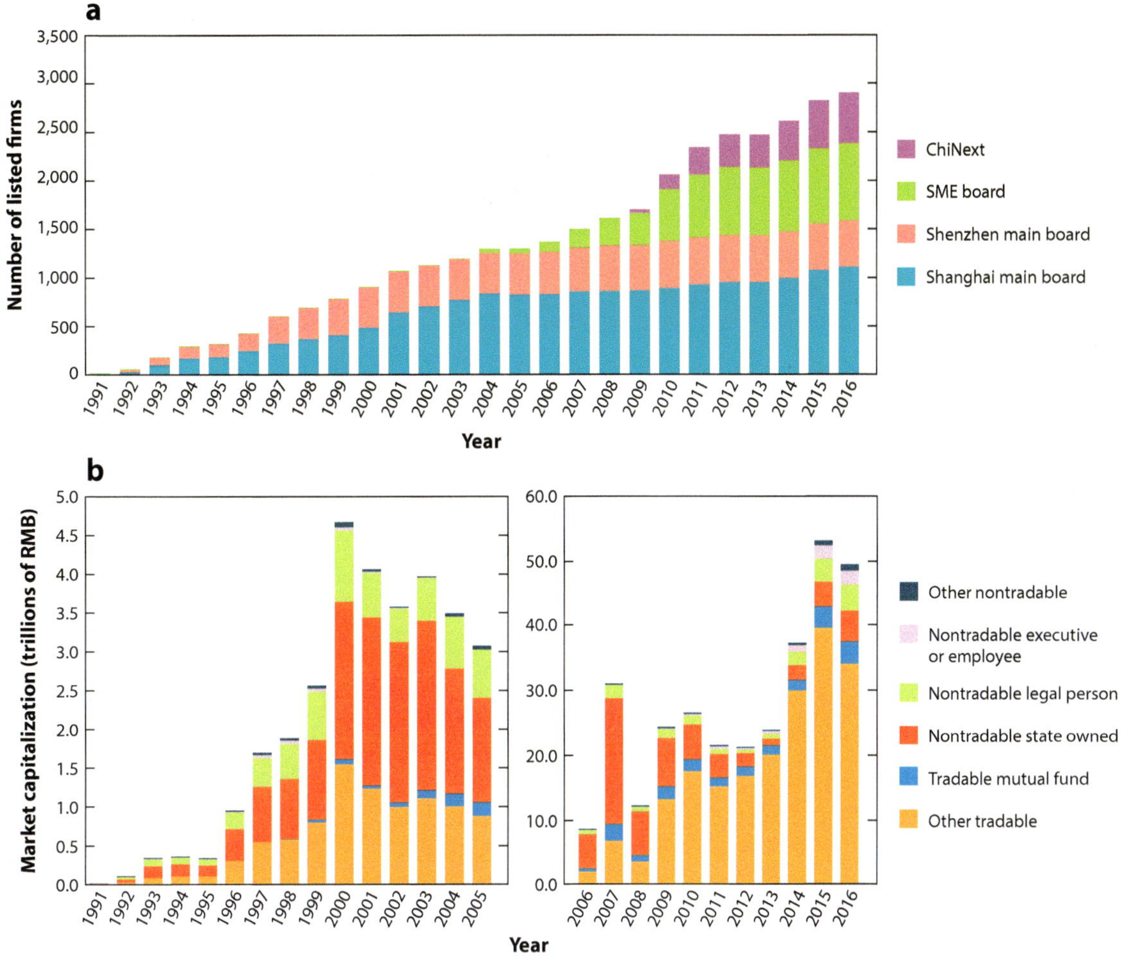

Figure 1

(*a*) Number of firms and (*b*) market capitalization of firms listed on China's stock market, 1991–2016. (*b*) The time series of market capitalization is split at the year 2006 to accommodate a significant increase in scale. Figure adapted from Carpenter, Lu & Whitelaw (2017). Abbreviations: RMB, renminbi; SME, Small and Medium Enterprise.

The Split-Share Structure Reform of 2005 ushered in a second stage of privatization in China. As Li et al. (2011) and Liao, Liu & Wang (2014) explain, regulators and investors had become increasingly aware of problems created by the split-share ownership structure, which weakened minority shareholder protection and stifled the market for corporate control. After a number of unsuccessful attempts to unlock nontradable shares, the CSRC devised a market mechanism to compensate holders of tradable shares for potential adverse price impacts. Holders of nontradable shares in each firm would have to negotiate compensation to holders of tradable shares sufficient to secure their approval of the unlocking, which in turn would take place gradually over a period of 1 year or longer. Most firms completed the reform by the end of 2007.

Liao, Liu & Wang (2014) use this reform as a natural experiment to measure the effect of privatization on firm performance. They find that the expectation of privatization boosted SOE output, profits, and employment but did not improve operating efficiency or corporate governance. In contrast to studies of privatization in other transition economies, such as the study of Barberis et al. (1996), who find that new management is most important for the success of privatization, Liao, Liu & Wang (2014) conclude that stimulating incumbent managers' incentives with the prospect of privatization also has positive effects. Chen et al. (2012) find that Chinese firms, especially those with weak governance, reduced cash holdings after the 2005 reform, suggesting that the reform led to better alignment between controlling and minority shareholders and relaxed financial constraints.

Li et al. (2011) and Firth, Lin & Zou (2010) study the cross-sectional determinants of the compensation ratio, or compensation paid to holders of tradable shares as a fraction of the value of their shares. Portfolio theory and evidence from Silber (1991) suggest that holders of nontradable shares stand to gain from the ability to diversify after the unlocking. In contrast, holders of tradable shares stand to lose from adverse price impacts. Li et al. (2011) find empirically that the compensation ratio is increasing in firm idiosyncratic risk and the fraction of nontradable shares, highlighting the stock market's traditional role in efficiently allocating risk. Firth, Lin & Zou (2010) consider a different angle and show that the compensation ratio is increasing in state ownership and decreasing in mutual fund ownership. They conclude that firms with higher state ownership were keener to comply with CSRC objectives and complete the reform quickly, whereas firms with higher fund ownership could be more easily pressured to accept terms because senior fund managers serve at the approval of the CSRC. This highlights the influence of the state in corporate transactions.

Abnormal stock returns in short windows around the key announcements during this process were arguably consistent with market efficiency, considering the effects on the supply of shares and liquidity, as argued by Beltratti, Bortolotti & Caccavaio (2016). However, after a successful unlocking negotiation, formerly nontradable shares were restricted from sale for periods of 1 year or longer, depending on ownership levels. Liao, Liu & Wang (2011) study stock returns around the lock-up expirations and find average abnormal returns of −14%, representing declines even larger than those documented by Ofek & Richardson (2000) around the unlocking of IPO shares in the United States. Lou, Wang & Yuan (2014) show that transfer prices of nonfloating shares reflect less earnings information than market prices of floating shares, but reflect more information after the 2005 reform than before.

Despite significant progress in privatization, state ownership and the dichotomy between state-controlled and privately owned firms remain defining characteristics of China's corporate sector. In a study of internal capital markets in state-controlled and privately owned business groups over the period 2004–2013, D. Chen et al. (2015) find that privately owned groups allocate capital to units with better investment opportunities, whereas state-controlled groups do the opposite. They find that promotion in state-controlled groups depends on avoiding layoffs, and when the chairman is near promotion, capital is allocated to large, struggling employers.

Whited & Zhao (2015) go beyond maximization of individual firm value to the question of the total value of China's corporate sector and find that capital structure misallocation is even more severe across firms than within firms. They find that if China's debt and equity markets were as developed as in the United States, China would gain 70–100% in firm value. Liu & Siu (2012) report the related result that discount rates used for investment decisions appear to vary across otherwise similar firms on the basis of their ownership, suggesting that not all firms can be value-maximizing. Interestingly, the discount rates of state firms tend to increase toward those of private firms after partial privatization. These results are consistent with those of Hsieh & Klenow (2009), who estimate that a hypothetical reallocation of capital and labor in China to the levels of efficiency seen in the United States would increase total factor productivity by 30–50%.

If possible, it would also be useful to evaluate the progress of China's corporate sector with respect to socialist objectives. Central planners might argue that compromises in value are outweighed by gains in enhanced social welfare or GDP growth. Skeptics would counter that central planners' primary objective is political control. The field of corporate finance may be well positioned to shed more light on this issue. Given the rapid growth of China's corporate sector, its progress and objectives are of broad relevance.

2.2. Initial Public Offerings

Another early strand of literature studies IPOs in China. A large literature on IPOs in the United States focuses on their underpricing and long-run performance, and the literature on IPOs in China follows this lead. The review articles of Jenkinson & Ljungqvist (2001) and Ritter & Welch (2002) lay out the theories of underpricing and evidence from the United States. According to these, underpricing compensates uninformed bidders for the winner's curse, compensates investors for uncertainty about firm value, compensates informed investors for information revelation, addresses reputation concerns of underwriters, and serves as a signal of favorable prospects to be recouped in subsequent offerings.

IPO underpricing in China is an order of magnitude greater than in the United States, with average A-share IPO returns of 100–900% in studies surveyed by Yu & Tse (2006), compared with 20% in the United States according to Ritter & Welch (2002). Several papers examine the cross-sectional determinants of A-share IPO underpricing in China during the 1990s. For example, Chinese investors face a long and unpredictable lag between IPO subscription and listing dates, as regulators put firms through a more extended administrative process than in other countries. Mok & Hui (1998) and Chan, Wang & Wei (2004) find that deeper underpricing is associated with longer time lags between offering and listing, with conflicting results on the effects of state ownership. Su & Fleisher (1999) find evidence in support of the signaling hypothesis, in which firms that underprice recoup losses in their seasoned equity offerings (SEOs). Chen, Firth & Kim (2004) also find underpricing is associated with listing lag, government ownership, and SEO activity. Yu & Tse (2006) find evidence from online fixed-price offerings in support of the winner's curse hypothesis.

A concern with these studies is that the setting in China is so different from that in the United States that it is not clear how much the United States–based theories apply. First, it seems unlikely that these theories could explain IPO returns of the magnitudes seen in China. Mok & Hui (1998) describe how over half a million people flocked to Shenzhen in 1992 to queue for lottery forms to buy shares from a handful of issues with little or no information about the companies they might buy. Such large excess demand suggests the presence of deliberate government subsidies to investors in IPO pricing. It would be useful to understand the political logic behind these subsidies. Moreover, cross-sectional variation in such subsidies could confound tests for the elements of investor compensation and issuer signaling that are evident in US underpricing. Furthermore, theories based on US underwriting mechanisms may not apply well in China. Yu & Tse (2006) report that during 1996–2002, the most common offering method was online fixed-price offering, in which the offer price was set to earnings times a price-to-earnings ratio consistent with that of the firm's industry peers, subject to a cap by the CSRC.

Although underpricing has been large, it may not be the best conceptual starting point. As various authors explain, the central government sets an annual quota for new issues and allocates it across provinces and industries according to regional development goals. The first question would then seem to be: What determines which firms get selected? Not only is this issue of importance in its own right, but it also likely alters the model of IPO underpricing. A more recent literature bears on this selection issue. Fan, Wong & Zhang (2007) show that 3-year post-IPO stock returns at firms with politically connected CEOs underperform those at other firms by 18%, and these firms also have poorer operating performance and are more likely to appoint other bureaucrats to their boards. Fan, Wong & Zhang also find lower IPO returns when CEOs are politically connected. In contrast, Bao, Johan & Kutsuna (2016) find better post-IPO performance for politically connected firms in a later sample covering 2009–2012, although these connections do increase the probability of IPO approval. Piotroski & Zhang (2014) also document the politicization of the IPO selection process. They find that incentives for capital market development induce incumbent politicians to accelerate IPOs, and that firms with connections to incumbents rush to complete IPOs before turnover, leading to lower-quality offerings around promotion events.

Allen et al. (2017) shine additional light on the selection issue by comparing the financial and accounting performance of listed firms to that of matched nonlisted firms. They find that selection is problematic in that listed firms are poorer performers than nonlisted firms both ex ante and ex post. One of the selection criteria is that firms must show at least 3 years of positive earnings in order to gain approval, and Allen et al. (2017) argue that this can lead to value-destroying short-termism. Jia, Pownall & Zhao (2014) interpret red chips and P chips, which are, respectively, state-owned and private Chinese firms incorporated outside China and listed in Hong Kong, as firms that would have been rejected for mainland listing and use them as controls for approved firms. They find that SOEs listed on the mainland exchanges are better politically connected than red chips and that private firms listed on the mainland exchanges are more profitable than P chips. Cong, Howell & Zhang (2017) study the effects of China's four IPO suspensions between 2004 and 2015 and find that the resulting delay in the listing of approved firms stunts these firms' standardization processes, with adverse consequences for patent applications, underwriting syndicate structure, and executive compensation and hiring.

The implications of the listing selection process are potentially far-reaching. As Allen et al. (2017) argue, this selection process alters the composition of the listed corporate sector, with potentially serious consequences for growth. It also hinders the development of the market for private equity, where IPOs are a key exit strategy. However, the potential availability of matched samples of successful and rejected applicants creates a rich new laboratory for the study of the causal effects of public listing. Whereas, in the United States, firms have been delisting in recent years, thousands of firms in China may seek public listing in the coming decades.

2.3. Corporate Listing Choice

Chinese firms actually have a range of potential incorporation and listing choices, making China a uniquely rich setting for research on the determinants and consequences of corporate listing choice. Chinese firms incorporated in mainland China can apply to list A shares and B shares on the SSE or SZSE, or H shares on the Stock Exchange of Hong Kong (SEHK). The SSE and SZSE each have main boards, where larger, more mature companies (including most SOEs) list, and the SZSE also has the SME and ChiNext boards, with more relaxed listing standards, which are designed to accommodate smaller and more entrepreneurial firms. Similarly, the SEHK has a main board and a Growth Enterprise Market. Chinese firms can also avoid the need for CSRC approval by incorporating outside of China, typically in the Cayman Islands, the British Virgin Islands, Bermuda, or Hong Kong. From there, they have a choice of listing on the SEHK as red chips or P chips, on the New York Stock Exchange (NYSE) or NASDAQ as N shares, or, in rarer cases, on the London Stock Exchange (LSE) as L shares or the Singapore Exchange (SGX) as S shares. Pan & Brooker (2014) report that over 1,000 Chinese firms had listed overseas by 2011 and tabulate the geography and time series of these listings.

Table 1 Potential listing venues for Chinese firms

	SSE	SZSE	SEHK	NYSE	NASDAQ
Legal costs	Low	Low	Medium	High	High
Dual class permitted	No	No	No	Yes	Yes
Earnings/size requirement	Strict positive earnings threshold for 3 consecutive years	Strict positive earnings threshold for 3 consecutive years for main board, softer thresholds for SME and ChiNext boards	Softer 3-year earnings threshold	Softer 3-year earnings or size threshold	Even softer earnings or size threshold
Selection mechanism	IB sponsorship and CSRC approval	IB sponsorship and CSRC approval	IB sponsorship	Registration based	Registration based
Average processing time	10 months	10 months	6 months	4 months	4 months
Total market capitalization, August 2016 (trillions of dollars)	4.0	3.2	3.2	19.3	9.1
Parent company	CSRC	CSRC	HK Exchanges and Clearing Limited	Intercontinental Exchange	The Nasdaq OMX Group
Year founded	1990	1990	1891	1792	1971
Number of listed companies, August 2016	1,114	1,796	1,925	3,176	3,170

Abbreviations: CSRC, China Securities Regulatory Commission; IB, investment bank; NYSE, New York Stock Exchange; SEHK, Stock Exchange of Hong Kong; SME, Small and Medium Enterprise; SSE, Shanghai Stock Exchange; SZSE, Shenzhen Stock Exchange.

Table 1 summarizes the listing requirements, legal costs, processing time, and number and size of Chinese firms for mainland, Hong Kong, and US exchanges. Whereas listing in China is least expensive, incorporating overseas is generally most expensive because it requires foreign legal counsel, particularly when the firm uses a complex variable interest entity structure to bypass Chinese restrictions on foreign direct investment in strategic industries. Therefore, foreign incorporation is generally an option only for larger firms. Requirements on prelisting net income also vary across exchanges. The SSE is strictest, requiring 3-year cumulative net profits in excess of RMB 30 million, whereas the NASDAQ is the most tolerant, allowing negative earnings for firms that meet other criteria. Finally, governance requirements also vary across exchanges. The US exchanges allow dual-class structures with differential voting rights, whereas the Hong Kong and Chinese exchanges do not.

In addition to differential listing requirements, Chinese firms may also consider longer-term effects of listing choice. Evidence from the literature on cross-listing on US exchanges provides some insights: Compared to firms that do not cross-list, firms that cross-list exhibit lower voting premia and thus better minority shareholder protection; are more likely to terminate poorly performing CEOs; and have higher Tobin's Q, lower cost of capital, and larger stock return and trading volume reactions to earnings announcements (Doidge 2004; Doidge, Karolyi & Stulz 2004; Bailey, Karolyi & Salva 2006; Lel & Miller 2008; Hail & Leuz 2009).

In the Chinese setting, Carpenter, Lu & Whitelaw (2017) show that A-share price informativeness about future profits of firms with H shares dual-listed on the SEHK is lower than A-share price informativeness of firms that are not dual-listed. Conversely, Loh (2016) finds that H-share price informativeness of firms with A shares dual-listed on the mainland exchanges is lower than H-share price informativeness of firms that are not dual-listed. Similarly, Kot & Tam (2016) find that H-share prices contain less firm-specific information after Hong Kong–listed Chinese firms dual-list A shares in the mainland, although Li, Brockman & Zurbruegg (2015) argue that H shares contain more firm-specific information than A shares, and Hu et al. (2016) find that investment is more sensitive to H-share prices. Foucault & Gehrig (2008) show theoretically that cross-listing should increase stock price informativeness and improve investment decision-making. Empirically, however, Fernandes & Ferreira (2008) find that whereas cross-listing on US exchanges improves price informativeness for firms from developed markets, it reduces it for firms from emerging markets. Perhaps, when listing across segmented markets, gains from broadening the investor base are offset by adverse effects of discount rate shocks from the foreign market leaking into local prices and scrambling signals about future earnings.

In a preliminary study of the listing choices of Chinese firms on the SSE, SEHK, NYSE, and NASDAQ, Shen (2016) finds that industrial firms tend to list in China, whereas firms in the technology, media, and telecommunications sector tend to list in the United States. The issue of listing choice is likely to become increasingly important as large numbers of Chinese firms seek to go public in the coming decades, particularly if overseas listing remains popular. The stakes will be especially high if different listing choices lead to significant differences in corporate outcomes.

3. EQUITY PRICING

On the asset pricing side, researchers have studied several interesting issues, including differential pricing across segmented markets, the firm-specific information content of prices, and cross-sectional pricing patterns in China. More generally, the literature has exploited unique features of China's stock market to provide new evidence on issues of broad interest.

3.1. The A-Share Premium Puzzle

The early literature on the pricing of Chinese equities focuses on the premium in A-share prices relative to B-share prices. Firms can issue two classes of tradable shares in the domestic Chinese stock market with identical cash flow and voting rights: A shares and B shares. Prior to 2001, domestic Chinese investors could hold only A shares, whereas foreign investors could hold only B shares, and numerous studies report that B shares typically traded at discounts of 60–80% relative to their A-share counterparts during this period. This large domestic share premium is in contrast to the foreign share premium found in other markets, such as in Finland (Hietala 1989), Thailand (Bailey & Jagtiani 1994), Switzerland (Stulz & Wasserfallen 1995), and Mexico (Domowitz, Glen & Madhavan 1997).

The literature offers several explanations for the A-share premium. Chakravarty, Sarkar & Wu (1998) argue that domestic investors are better informed about firms' prospects and therefore face lower conditional variance and require lower returns. Chen, Lee & Rui (2001) find that B-share discounts are primarily a result of lower liquidity in the B-share market. Fernald & Rogers (2002) attribute A-share premia to the limited investment opportunity set available to domestic investors. However, Ma (1996) finds no evidence that A-share premia are correlated with differences in real interest rates in China and the United States. Chan & Kwok (2005) find that A-share premia are negatively correlated with the relative supply of A shares and positively correlated with the supply of B shares. Chan, Menkveld & Yang (2008) provide an explanation based on information asymmetry within the A-share market and find that traditional measures of information asymmetry help to explain the cross section of A-share premia.

Mei, Scheinkman & Xiong (2009) use the dual-class structure to test the theory that speculative trading in the presence of short-sales constraints can lead to overvaluation (Miller 1977; Harrison & Kreps 1978; Chen, Hong & Stein 2002; Scheinkman & Xiong 2003). They view B-share prices as controls for stock fundamentals and find that A-share premia are cross-sectionally correlated with turnover rates and idiosyncratic return volatility, proxies for speculative motives in trading. In 2001, the CSRC allowed domestic Chinese investors to hold B shares, which brought B-share discounts down to 40%, according to Karolyi, Li & Liao (2009). They find that the firms with the greatest declines in B-share discounts were those with the lowest state ownership and conclude that political risk is an important determinant of the price differential.

With the introduction of the QFII program in 2002, which allows qualified foreign institutional investors to directly hold A shares, B-share issuance and trading has largely died out. However, A-share premia over corresponding H shares with identical cash flow and voting rights are still prevalent for firms that are dual-listed in mainland China and Hong Kong. **Figure 2** shows the time series of the median A-H premium, i.e., A-share price divided by H-share price, for the full sample of dual-listed firms, as well as for firms in the lower half of this sample as ranked by market capitalization (i.e., smaller firms) and for firms in the financial and manufacturing sectors, since 2006. The full-sample median has been about 1.5 or 2 in recent years, but was over 3 in 2009 and peaked in the 10–15 range in the late 1990s and early 2000s. The median A-H premium for smaller firms is consistently higher than for larger firms, possibly reflecting the shell value of a listing on the domestic Chinese stock market that could potentially be acquired by a firm seeking to circumvent the usual listing process for A shares. A-H premia are consistently higher for firms

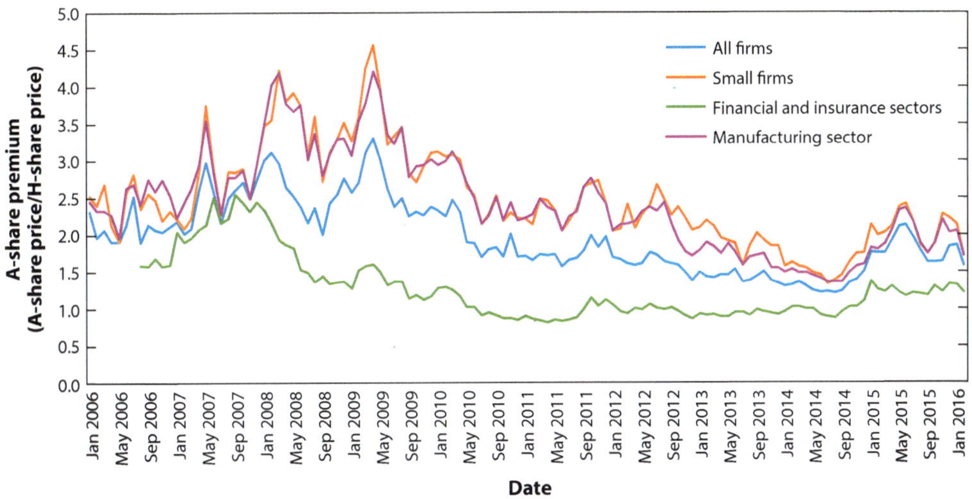

Figure 2

Median A-share premium, i.e., A-share price divided by H-share price, 2006–2016. Shown are the full sample of firms with dual listings of A shares in Shanghai or Shenzhen and H shares in Hong Kong (*blue*); the half of this sample containing smaller firms (*orange*); firms in the financial and insurance sectors (*green*); and firms in the manufacturing sector (*purple*).

in the manufacturing sector and lower for firms in the financial sector, where the median premium fell below 1 during 2010 and 2011.

The premium of A-share prices over their dual-listed H-share twins has persisted despite the 2007 introduction of the Qualified Domestic Institutional Investor (QDII) program, which allows qualified domestic Chinese investors to invest limited amounts outside China, as well as the 2014 and 2016 openings of the Shanghai– and Shenzhen–Hong Kong Stock Connect programs, which allow cross-market trading in a selection of stocks, including all dual-listed stocks. This violation of the law of one price does not represent an arbitrage opportunity because the significant degree of segmentation remaining between the two markets means that convergence trades expose would-be arbitrageurs to the risk of large short-term losses. Chung, Hui & Li (2013) attribute this price disparity to differential parameter uncertainty faced by investors in the two markets, whereas Guo, Tang & Yang (2013) emphasize variation in corporate governance characteristics that may proxy for the possibility of wealth expropriation by controlling shareholders or corporate insiders. However, neither explanation is fully consistent with the substantial cross-sectional and time-series variation evident in **Figure 2**, and thus the A-share premium remains a puzzle. Nonetheless, the existence of multiple claims on identical cash flows, or at least claims on cash flows subject to similar shocks, traded in different venues by different groups of investors, presents the intriguing possibility of gaining additional insight into the determination of discount rates.

3.2. Information Asymmetry and Behavioral Effects

Several papers take advantage of distinctive features of China's stock market to construct new tests of asset pricing theories, particularly with respect to information asymmetry and behavioral effects. In addition to market segmentation for dual-listed stocks, restrictions on investor trading location and the dominance of retail investors—who hold 58% of the market, according to Jia, Wang & Xiong (2015), and account for 80% of trading volume, according to the CSRC—help to make China's stock market a rich new laboratory for the study of asset pricing.

Feng & Seasholes (2004) use account-level data to study correlation in trading across groups of individuals in different locations, exploiting the restriction that individuals in China are allowed to open only one account and must place all trades through the branch office where the account was opened. Consistent with the logic of Brennan & Cao (1997) that nearby investors are better informed than those farther away, and will thus react less to information and will execute trades of opposite sign, they find that trades of investors across branches within a given region are positively correlated and that trades across regions are negatively correlated. Jia, Wang & Xiong (2015) study the reactions of A- and H-share prices of dual-listed stocks to analysts' revisions of earnings forecasts and find that A-share prices react more strongly to revisions from local, mainland-based analysts, whereas H-share prices react more strongly to revisions from foreign analysts. They attribute this result to investors' greater trust in analysts from their home region, associated with social and cultural factors such as those studied by Guiso, Sapienza & Zingales (2008, 2009). Jia, Wang & Xiong (2015) distinguish this trust effect from the information asymmetry effect of Brennan & Cao (1997) by contrasting price reactions to analysts' revisions with price reactions to earnings announcements. They acknowledge that limited investor attention and information immobility effects, as in the work of Peng & Xiong (2006) and Van Nieuwerburgh & Veldkamp (2009), could also play a role and amplify the effects of social trust.

Andrade, Bian & Burch (2013) identify China's stock market as a natural setting for the study of asset price bubbles generated by dispersion in investor beliefs because of its short-sale constraints and the dominance of retail investors. Focusing on the 2007 stock price bubble, they find that stocks with greater analyst coverage had smaller bubbles, attributing this to analysts' coordinating beliefs across investors. Chang et al. (2015) provide evidence on the origins of investor disagreement by studying the relation between linguistic diversity and diversity of investor opinion across provinces in China. They show that, in provinces where a greater number of unique languages are spoken, investors express greater disagreement, as observed both in opinions posted on stock message boards and through measures of household trading activity.

Hong et al. (2014) exploit the uneven rise in household wealth and the growth of the middle class across Chinese regions over the period 1998–2012 to test for evidence of keeping-up-with-the-Joneses preferences and trading for status concerns. They use a province or city's GDP per capita as a proxy for status concerns and use the difference between small and large stock turnover as a proxy for local stock turnover. They show that investors in regions that became richer faster traded more actively in small local stocks. Chen, Jiang & Tong (2016) use economic policy uncertainty as a proxy for belief dispersion in the time series to provide evidence in support of the theory of overvaluation in the presence of short-sale restrictions. Bian, Su & Wang (2015) study the effects of the prohibition of intraday round-trip stock trades and show that illiquidity discounts in prices decay over the course of the trading day.

These studies illustrate the power of employing unique features of China's markets to address questions of broad interest. As more and better data become available and researchers become more familiar with these data, such analyses will likely yield a range of new insights. Moreover, the ongoing development of the stock market in China and the parallel evolution of regulations promise a wealth of new natural experiments to study.

3.3. Stock Price Informativeness

Another strand of the literature studies the quantity of firm-specific information in China's stock prices. The macroeconomic stakes are high. A large literature, surveyed by Bond, Edmans & Goldstein (2012), emphasizes the stock market's special role in aggregating diffuse information across heterogeneous agents, generating useful signals for managers, and allocating capital accordingly (Grossman & Stiglitz 1980; Roll 1984; Glosten & Milgrom 1985; Kyle 1985; Dow & Gorton 1997; Wurgler 2000; Durnev, Morck & Yeung 2004; Luo 2005; Markovitch, Steckel & Yeung 2005; Chen, Goldstein & Jiang 2007; Chari & Henry 2008; Bakke & Whited 2010).

Roll (1988) first used time series regressions of individual stock returns on market and industry returns to distinguish variation attributable to common factors from variation attributable to firm-specific information. Morck, Yeung & Yu (2000) formalize the use of a stock's market model R^2 as an inverse measure of the firm-specific information content in the stock price and study average R^2 of stocks over time and across countries. They show that stock synchronicity is negatively correlated with GDP per capita in a sample of 40 countries, holding out China as an example with especially high synchronicity. They document a negative correlation between stock synchronicity and the strength of property rights across countries. In a sample of US firms, Durnev et al. (2003) provide support for R^2 as an inverse measure of stock price informativeness by showing that firms with lower R^2 have more information about future earnings in their current stock returns.

Jin & Myers (2006) show theoretically that it is a firm's lack of transparency, rather than weak property rights per se, that boosts its R^2, and find empirically that average R^2 is positively correlated with country-level measures of opacity in a sample of 40 countries. However, in a sample of firms from 25 developing countries, Chan & Hameed (2006) show that stocks with greater analyst coverage have higher stock price synchronicity. In a sample of 48 countries, Fernandes & Ferreira (2009) find that enforcement of insider trading laws increases firm-specific stock return variation, although the effect is stronger among developed markets than among emerging markets. In a sample of Chinese-listed firms, Gul, Kim & Qiu (2010) study cross-sectional variation in stock synchronicity and find that synchronicity is a hump-shaped function of ownership concentration and that it is greater when the largest shareholder is connected to the government. They also find that synchronicity decreases with audit quality and foreign ownership.

As Morck, Yeung & Yu (2013) acknowledge, cross-country comparisons of stock price informativeness based on stocks' average market model R^2 are confounded by cross-country variation in market-level volatility, which mechanically boosts individual R^2 for a given level of idiosyncratic volatility. Therefore, to quantify stock price informativeness in China and compare it to that in the United States, Carpenter, Lu & Whitelaw (2017) follow the methodology of Bai, Philippon & Savov (2016). They measure stock price informativeness as the predicted variation in a cross-sectional regression of future earnings on the logarithm of past market valuations, scaled by book assets, together with other controls. They show that stock price informativeness in China varies over the period 1995–2011, with a low in 2001 when the casino theory of the stock market was proposed, but is rarely statistically significantly lower than that in the United States, and often even exceeds that in the United States. This result is surprising, given the dominance of retail traders, and is in striking contrast to the view that China's stock market is inefficient or disconnected from stock fundamentals. It suggests that China's stock market has an important informational role to play in generating useful signals for managers and investors and in improving the efficiency of capital allocation and corporate investment decisions in China.

However, China's frequent regulatory experiments and interventions can undermine price informativeness and the link between firm-specific fundamentals and prices, as Brunnermeier, Sockin & Xiong (2017) show theoretically. Minor adjustments such as changes in the stamp duty on stock transactions seem to have had little effect on prices (Peng, Tang & Wang 2014); however, dramatic revisions in restrictions on margin financing during 2014 and 2015 appear to have fueled large stock market gyrations (Qian 2016). Moreover, government interventions to support prices during this period increased stock synchronicity (Lou 2016). Whereas regulatory reforms are a necessary and welcome part of the development of the market, a permanent policy of heavy-handed intervention seems counterproductive (Smith 2016).

3.4. Cross-Sectional Patterns in Returns

The cross-sectional pricing of Chinese stocks has also attracted the attention of researchers. The A-share market was legally segmented for many years and is still dominated by Chinese investors, so China is the only large-scale laboratory for investigating such pricing effects in a setting independent of the more integrated markets that have been the subject of most of the literature. In this context, the natural question is whether Chinese investors price the same factors as those priced elsewhere. In addition, the unique features of China's stock market and its economy more generally suggest that China-specific factors might play an important role.

With regard to cross-sectional pricing phenomena that have been found in other markets, Chen et al. (2010) provide both a survey of the earlier literature and an examination of a comprehensive set of 18 variables. The results from this earlier literature are mixed, probably for two reasons. First, there is only a short history of stock returns, so the power to detect any effects is limited. Second, as Chen et al. (2010) note, there is probably less cross-sectional heterogeneity across traded firms in China in the early part of the sample period than in the later part. The initial public listings constituted a set of large SOEs from a limited number of industries. The more recent, rapid expansion of the SME and ChiNext boards of the SZSE, which brought smaller, younger, and fundamentally different firms into the market, may be important for identifying interesting effects.

Papers using these richer data report results that are quite consistent with those documented in other markets (Fama & French 1992; Jegadeesh & Titman 1993; Amihud 2002; Ang et al. 2006; Bali, Cakici & Whitelaw 2011). Size (e.g., C. Chen et al. 2015), illiquidity (e.g., Chen et al. 2010), volatility (e.g., Cakici, Chan & Topyan 2011), and extreme returns (e.g., Nartea, Kong & Wu 2017) appear to be statistically and economically significant predictors of returns in the cross section. There is less consensus about the robustness of the ability of scaled prices, e.g., book-to-market or earnings-to-price ratios, to forecast returns. C. Chen et al. (2015) argue that this predictive power is confined to the 1995–1996 period, whereas Carpenter, Lu & Whitelaw (2017) document a more persistent value effect. Interestingly, momentum, which one might conjecture would be a strong effect in a retail-driven market such as China, is weak or nonexistent, except when one controls for a host of other factors (Carpenter, Lu & Whitelaw 2017). One reason for the mixed results may be that methodology matters more in China than in other markets (Xu & Zhang 2014). For example, value weighting, float weighting, and equal weighting can give very different portfolio returns in China, where nontradable shares dominated the market for much of the sample, where a significant number of large firms have shares cross-listed in other markets (such as Hong Kong), and where there are many large SOEs.

Whereas the majority of studies employ variables previously used in other markets, some researchers either use China-specific variables or interpret the results in the context of China's unique setting. Motivated by the unique regulatory environment in China, which arguably creates more information asymmetry across investors, Choi, Jin & Yan (2016) find that stocks with higher information asymmetry, as proxied by the aggressiveness of institutional investor trading, exhibit higher future returns. Chen, Demirer & Jategaonkar (2015) document that stocks with greater sensitivity to cross-sectional return dispersion also exhibit higher returns, interpreting dispersion as a measure of uncertainty associated with economic transitions, which is particularly high in a fast-growing developing economy such as China. Hilliard & Zhang (2015), while examining traditional size and book-to-market effects, condition the magnitudes of the associated premia on measures of monetary policy and herding, the former being a possible proxy for the willingness of the government to intervene to prop up firms and the latter being a potentially important phenomenon in the retail-driven Chinese market. Finally, Carpenter, Lu & Whitelaw (2017) use the fraction of state ownership and the fraction of nontradable shares as potential measures of the extent to which firms are subject to either state support or policy risk, and Liu, Shu & Wei (2017) provide evidence of priced political risk in the context of the Bo Xilai political scandal.

As a whole, these papers on cross-sectional predictability suggest a market that is functioning in much the same way as the markets of other developed and emerging economies, at least in terms of priced factors, but there is clearly more to be done, as the cross section of firms will continue to expand in size and scope. One important point is that these composition effects suggest that a generalized least squares approach in a Fama–Macbeth regression context, weighting the coefficients from each cross-sectional regression by the amount of information that they contain, could conceivably use the information more efficiently (Carpenter, Lu & Whitelaw 2017).

4. EQUITY MUTUAL FUNDS AND DERIVATIVES

Markets for equity mutual funds and derivatives support stock markets by providing opportunities for equity risk management, generating incremental information, increasing liquidity, and improving corporate governance. Although China's stock market has grown to over $7 trillion, of which over 75% is tradable, its markets for equity mutual funds and derivatives are still very small and new. The equity mutual fund market began in 1998 but still has only $500 billion under management. By contrast, the Investment Company Institute (ICI) (2016) reports that US domestic equity mutual funds have over $7 trillion under management, representing over 30% of US stock market capitalization. Derivatives markets are at an even earlier stage of development. The market for stock index futures opened in 2010, and index options began trading in 2015.

4.1. Equity Mutual Funds

The market for managed equity available to Chinese household investors remains surprisingly small relative to the size of the stock market, despite efforts by the CSRC to encourage the development of the equity mutual fund market. Yao (2012) highlights significant agency problems between investors and fund managers that might deter investors. Although the market for active management might require time for managers to develop expertise, track records, and reputation, it would seem that low-fee index funds should be straightforward to set up and should offer much in terms of diversification and cost savings to retail investors who are directly holding and trading small numbers of stocks. One impediment is the underdevelopment of platforms to market these products to households.

The academic literature on mutual funds in China is just beginning. Yuan, Xiao & Zou (2008) examine whether mutual fund ownership in China improves corporate performance, as suggested by Admati, Pfleiderer & Zechner (1994). Although the evidence on the impact of institutional ownership from developed countries is mixed (Smith 1996, Wahal 1996, Morck & Nakamura 1999, Allen 2001, Woidtke 2002, Cornett et al. 2007), Yuan, Xiao & Zou (2008) find that mutual fund ownership increases a firm's Tobin's Q and other measures of firm performance. Tang, Wang & Xu (2012) study the relationship between mutual fund size and performance in China. In contrast to Chen et al. (2004), who show that fund returns decline with lagged fund size in the United States, Tang, Wang & Xu (2012) find a hump-shaped relation between fund performance and size, resulting from conflicting effects of economies of scale and liquidity.

4.2. Equity Futures and Options

Whereas the mutual fund market provides risk management to retail investors and can increase incentives for information generation and corporate monitoring, derivatives markets allow institutional investors to trade risks wholesale and can provide additional information about the distributions of returns on underlying assets (Breeden & Litzenberger 1978, Chiras & Manaster 1978, Manaster & Rendleman 1982, Figlewski & Webb 1993, Pan & Poteshman 2006). Commodity, currency, and bond futures have traded on exchanges in China since the early 1990s, but stock index futures did not trade until 2010, when the China Financial Futures Exchange (CFFEX) introduced futures on the CSI 300 index, the index of the 300 largest and most active stocks listed on the SSE and SZSE. In April 2015, the CFFEX also introduced futures on the CSI 500 index, consisting of smaller stocks, and on the SSE50 index of large stocks. In February 2015, the SSE introduced options on the SSE50 exchange-traded fund (ETF), which itself had begun trading in 2005.

In the tradition of earlier literature on futures markets (Stein 1987; Harris 1989; Chan, Chan & Karolyi 1991; Bessembinder & Seguin 1992; Chan 1992), preliminary research on stock index futures in China focuses on volatility transmission between the spot and futures markets and on price discovery, with mixed results (Yang, Yang & Zhou 2012; Chen et al. 2013; Xie & Mo 2014). Most recently, Han & Liang (2017) find that severe restrictions on trading of CSI 300 and CSI 500 futures, introduced in September 2015, reduced the quality of the spot market in terms of bid-ask spreads, liquidity, and volume.

Research on equity options is also in an early stage, but China provides a compelling example of the importance of options in incomplete markets and in settings where volatility risk is high. Xiong & Yu (2011) study the Chinese warrants bubble of 2005–2008 and find evidence in support of the theory that belief dispersion and short-sale restrictions led to overvaluation. However, Wang, Zhou & Zhu (2016) counter that many of the observed warrant prices can be reconciled with a model of option pricing in incomplete markets. In preliminary research, we find that deviations from put-call parity were close to zero in the early months of SSE50 ETF option trading but spiked up after the ban on short selling of the SSE50 ETF in July 2015 and futures market restrictions in September 2015, with puts becoming expensive relative to their synthetic counterparts. This finding is consistent with the work of Ofek, Richardson & Whitelaw (2004). Clearly, equity derivatives are a substitute channel for margin trading and short selling, so restrictions on their trading can have deleterious effects on the quality of stock prices, similar to restrictions on trading in the underlying spot market.

5. THE ROLE OF GLOBAL INVESTORS

Whereas much of the development of China's stock markets over their almost 30-year history has been driven by domestic concerns, global investors are now becoming increasingly influential. As China has made initial steps toward relaxing capital controls and Chinese investors have viewed international investments as increasingly attractive, in part because of fear of depreciation of China's currency, capital outflows have become an increasing concern. One remedy for these outflows would be to replace them with offsetting inflows from global investors, with the stock market being a natural destination. The presence of sophisticated international institutional investors might also increase the informativeness of prices and reduce the cost of capital, as argued by Carpenter, Lu & Whitelaw (2017). For example, Huang & Zhu (2015) and Li, Brockman & Zurbruegg (2015) offer evidence that QFII investors improve corporate governance and increase the amount of firm-specific information in stock prices. In addition, it is natural that global investors have begun to appreciate the diversification benefits and investment opportunities associated with getting access to China's market, as documented by Carpenter, Lu & Whitelaw (2017).

The QFII and Renminbi Qualified Institutional Investor (RQFII) programs that have existed since 2002 and 2011 are not ideal for accessing these investment opportunities because of licensing requirements, quotas, and repatriation restrictions. Thus, it is not surprising that many global investors have eschewed exposure to A shares, instead getting exposure to China through Chinese companies traded in more accessible markets such as Hong Kong and the United States. **Table 2** illustrates this phenomenon in the context of the US ETF market, providing details on the 10 largest China-focused ETFs. Both the largest and oldest ETFs hold equities traded outside of China, tracking primarily float-weighted, large-cap indexes. However, these internationally traded shares are not a substitute for shares traded domestically, given the time-varying pricing differentials between domestic and foreign-listed shares discussed in Section 3.1 and the associated relatively low correlations. It is only since 2010 that ETFs tracking broader A-share indexes have been introduced, and they have not yet gained significant traction within the international investment community.

This lack of traction is partly a result of the fact that, historically, major index providers did not include A shares in their flagship indexes or else included them at weights much lower than the size of the market would imply. For example, MSCI has for the past 3 years been considering including A shares in their Emerging Markets Index, to which over $1.5 trillion of assets are benchmarked. In June 2017, MSCI announced plans to include at least 222 A shares at a total

Table 2 Top 10 US exchange-traded funds (ETFs) investing in Chinese firms

Ticker	Name	Assets under management (millions of dollars)	Index	Composition	Number of holdings	Inception date
FXI	iShares China Large-Cap ETF	3,146	FTSE China 50	Hong Kong–traded (e.g., H shares, P chips)	50	October 5, 2014
MCHI	iShares MSCI China ETF	2,407	MSCI China	Non-China-traded (e.g., H shares, N shares)	150	March 29, 2011
GXC	SPDR S&P China ETF	870	S&P China BMI	Non-China-traded (e.g., H shares, N shares)	350	March 19, 2007
KWEB	KraneShares CSI China Internet ETF	454	CSI China Overseas Internet	Non-China-traded (e.g., H shares, N shares) Internet companies	33	July 31, 2013
ASHR	Deutsche X-Trackers Harvest CSI 300 China A-Shares ETF	353	CSI 300	China-traded (A shares)	300	November 6, 2013
PGJ	PowerShares Golden Dragon China Portfolio ETF	174	NASDAQ Golden Dragon China	US-traded (N shares)	62	December 9, 2004
YINN	Direxion Daily FTSE China Bull 3× Shares ETF	154	FTSE China 50	Levered 3×, e.g., using total return swaps	NA	December 3, 2009
KBA	KraneShares Bosera MSCI China A ETF	110	MSCI China A	China-traded (A shares)	413	March 4, 2014
CHAD	Direxion Daily CSI 300 China A Share Bear 1× Shares ETF	94	CSI 300	Inverse −1×, e.g., using total return swaps	NA	June 17, 2015
CQQQ	Guggenheim China Technology ETF	94	AlphaShares China Technology	Non-China-traded (e.g., H shares, N shares) information technology companies	73	December 8, 2009

The 10 largest US ETFs investing in Chinese firms, ranked by assets under management as of May 25, 2017. Source: etfdb.com.

weight of less than 1%, with future increases in the number of shares and weighting dependent on the success of negotiations between MSCI and the CSRC over reforms necessary to ensure market accessibility. Increased representation in MSCI indexes would boost global demand for A shares, an outcome that the CSRC clearly desires; Burnham, Gakidis & Wurgler (2017) find that inclusion in the MSCI Emerging Markets Index increases the fraction of a stock's shares held by benchmarked portfolios to 45% of their total market capitalization. Thus, MSCI has significant power to accelerate regulatory reform. The Shanghai– and Shenzhen–Hong Kong Stock Connect programs now appear to be the focal point of these negotiations, and MSCI is apparently pushing for two key concessions: a reduction in the number and duration of voluntary trading halts and the right to freely construct derivative contracts that rely on A-share prices. It is possible that global investors will have increasing influence over additional aspects of stock market regulation in China, and development of the derivatives markets discussed in Section 4 may actually occur outside of China. More generally, there is a vast literature on the effects of market integration on all manner of financial and economic outcomes. Henry (2000a,b) documents positive impacts on investment, wages, equity prices, and economic growth. More recently, Rey (2015) finds evidence of negative effects created by the volatility of foreign capital flows, but there is some question about whether concerns based on the experiences of smaller emerging markets are applicable to an economy and financial market as large as China's.

6. CONCLUSION

The rise of China and the fivefold growth of its stock market over the past decade have fueled a growing literature in financial economics. As China's stock market continues to grow in global influence, numerous areas are ripe for future research. More extensive research on the progress of China's SOE reform and the effects of equity capital infusion and privatization on corporate governance, profitability, and social impact would be of broad relevance. Additional evidence on the selection of firms for listing would also clarify numerous issues. Conversely, the range of listing alternatives available to Chinese firms creates a rich laboratory for studying the determinants and consequences of corporate listing choice. On the asset pricing side, ongoing reforms are likely to present opportunities for new tests and experiments, including the opening of new Stock Connect programs between China and international exchanges, the inclusion of China in international equity indexes, ad hoc government interventions, and continued reforms to improve liquidity, price discovery, and freer capital flow. In addition, segmented markets for dual-listed stocks can yield new evidence on differential discount rates. More broadly, the expanding panel of data will support deeper analysis of cross-sectional and market-level asset pricing in China.

One challenge for researchers will be to gain familiarity with China's distinctive financial system and avoid overapplying research paradigms developed for the US setting. A more pragmatic concern is the issue of the availability and accessibility of high-quality data. The China Stock Market and Accounting Research (CSMAR) database is now widely available and easily accessible on Wharton Research Data Services (WRDS), and it provides data on publicly traded Chinese equities similar to the data on US firms provided by the Center for Research in Security Prices (CRSP) and Compustat, in addition to providing a comprehensive mutual fund database. To a large extent, however, the data are limited to A and B shares, with extremely limited coverage of Chinese firms listed in other markets. Services such as Datastream and Bloomberg, which are oriented toward practitioners, have data across the full universe of trading locations, but in our experience the historical data are not fully adequate for academic research. Perhaps the most reliable and comprehensive data are available through the Wind Datafeed Service, which provides historical data for stocks, bonds, derivatives, and funds, as well as economic data and access to the underlying primary documents and filings. However, Wind is not easily accessible to much of the research community. In addition, a wealth of data has been collected by Chinese government agencies and regulators, but for the most part these data are also not easily accessible. One way to stimulate more valuable and interesting research would be to facilitate greater access to these resources.

Finally, although there are a host of interesting and unanswered research questions about China's developing stock market, the key issue from a domestic and global economic perspective is the role of this market in sustaining China's future economic growth. China is at a pivotal point in its development as it attempts to transition from a state-controlled, investment-driven economy to one that is more market-oriented and consumption-driven. It is also at a critical point in its path to integration in global financial markets, as highlighted by the debate over the inclusion of Chinese A shares in MSCI indexes. The development of the financial system in general and the stock market in particular will likely play an instrumental role in both of these transitions. There are two important questions. First, can the stock market improve the efficiency of capital allocation and support broader financial stability? Second, can the stock market serve as a platform for greater global diversification, thus improving risk sharing and potentially lowering the cost of capital for Chinese companies? Research that speaks to these questions is of primary importance.

DISCLOSURE STATEMENT

The authors are not aware of any affiliations, memberships, funding, or financial holdings that might be perceived as affecting the objectivity of this review.

ACKNOWLEDGMENTS

We thank Menachem Brenner, Steve Figlewski, Harrison Hong, Sabrina Howell, Kose John, Roy Smith, Bruce Tuckman, Jeff Wurgler, and Hong Yan for helpful comments. We also thank Olivia Domba, Fangzhou Lu, and Dongchen Zou for excellent research assistance.

LITERATURE CITED

Admati AR, Pfleiderer P, Zechner J. 1994. Large shareholder activism, risk sharing, and financial market equilibrium. *J. Political Econ.* 102:1097–130

Allen F. 2001. Do financial institutions matter? *J. Finance* 56:1165–75

Allen F, Qian J, Qian M. 2005. Law, finance, and economic growth in China. *J. Financ. Econ.* 77:57–116

Allen F, Qian J, Shan SC, Zhu JL. 2017. *Dissecting the long-term performance of the Chinese stock market*. Work. Pap., Shanghai Adv. Inst. Finance

Allen WT, Shen H. 2011. *Assessing China's top-down securities markets*. NBER Work. Pap. 16713

Amihud Y. 2002. Illiquidity and stock returns: cross-section and time-series effects. *J. Financ. Markets* 5:31–56

Andrade SC, Bian J, Burch TR. 2013. Analyst coverage, information, and bubbles. *J. Financ. Quant. Anal.* 48:1573–605

Ang A, Hodrick RJ, Xing Y, Zhang X. 2006. The cross-section of volatility and expected returns. *J. Finance* 61:259–99

Bai J, Philippon T, Savov A. 2016. Have financial markets become more informative? *J. Financ. Econ.* 122:625–54

Bailey W, Jagtiani J. 1994. Foreign ownership restrictions and stock prices in the Thai capital market. *J. Financ. Econ.* 36:57–87

Bailey W, Karolyi GA, Salva C. 2006. The economic consequences of increased disclosure: evidence from international cross-listings. *J. Financ. Econ.* 81:175–213

Bakke T-E, Whited TM. 2010. Which firms follow the market? An analysis of corporate investment decisions. *Rev. Financ. Stud.* 23:1941–80

Bali TG, Cakici N, Whitelaw RF. 2011. Maxing out: stocks as lotteries and the cross-section of expected returns. *J. Financ. Econ.* 99:427–46

Bao X, Johan S, Kutsuna K. 2016. Do political connections matter in accessing capital markets? Evidence from China. *Emerg. Markets Rev.* 29:24–41

Barberis N, Boycko M, Shleifer A, Tsukanova N. 1996. How does privatization work? Evidence from the Russian shops. *J. Political Econ.* 104:764–90

Beltratti A, Bortolotti B, Caccavaio M. 2016. Stock market efficiency in China: evidence from the split-share reform. *Q. Rev. Econ. Finance* 60:125–37

Bessembinder H, Seguin PJ. 1992. Futures-trading activity and stock price volatility. *J. Finance* 47:2015–34

Bian J, Su T, Wang J. 2015. *Non-marketability and one-day selling lockup*. Presented at Asian Finance Assoc. Conf., June 30, Changsha, China

Bond P, Edmans A, Goldstein I. 2012. The real effects of financial markets. *Annu. Rev. Financ. Econ.* 4:339–60

Breeden DT, Litzenberger RH. 1978. Prices of state-contingent claims implicit in option prices. *J. Bus.* 51:621–51

Brennan MJ, Cao HH. 1997. International portfolio investment flows. *J. Finance* 52:1851–80

Brunnermeier MK, Sockin M, Xiong W. 2017. *China's model of managing the financial system*. Work. Pap., Princeton Univ.

Burnham TC, Gakidis H, Wurgler J. 2017. *Investing in the presence of massive flows: the case of MSCI country reclassifications*. Work. Pap., Stern Sch. Bus., N.Y. Univ.

Cakici N, Chan K, Topyan K. 2011. *Cross-sectional stock return predictability in China*. Work. Pap., Fordham Univ.

Calomiris CW, Fisman R, Wang Y. 2010. Profiting from government stakes in a command economy: evidence from Chinese asset sales. *J. Financ. Econ.* 96:399–412

Carpenter JN, Lu F, Whitelaw RF. 2017. *The real value of China's stock market*. Work. Pap., Stern Sch. Bus., N.Y. Univ.

Chakravarty S, Sarkar A, Wu L. 1998. Information asymmetry, market segmentation and the pricing of cross-listed shares: theory and evidence from Chinese A and B shares. *J. Int. Financ. Markets Inst. Money* 8:325–56

Chan K. 1992. A further analysis of the lead–lag relationship between the cash market and stock index futures market. *Rev. Financ. Stud.* 5:123–52

Chan K, Chan KC, Karolyi GA. 1991. Intraday volatility in the stock index and stock index futures markets. *Rev. Financ. Stud.* 4:657–84

Chan K, Hameed A. 2006. Stock price synchronicity and analyst coverage in emerging markets. *J. Financ. Econ.* 80:115–47

Chan K, Kwok JKH. 2005. Market segmentation and share price premium evidence from Chinese stock markets. *J. Emerg. Market Finance* 4:43–61

Chan K, Menkveld AJ, Yang Z. 2008. Information asymmetry and asset prices: evidence from the China foreign share discount. *J. Finance* 63:159–96

Chan K, Wang J, Wei KCJ. 2004. Underpricing and long-term performance of IPOs in China. *J. Corp. Finance* 10:409–30

Chang Y-C, Hong HG, Tiedens L, Wang N, Zhao B. 2015. *Does diversity lead to diverse opinions? Evidence from languages and stock markets*. Work. Pap. 134, Rock Cent. Corp. Gov, Stanford Univ.

Chari A, Henry PB. 2008. Firm-specific information and the efficiency of investment. *J. Financ. Econ.* 87:636–55

Chen C, Hu X, Shao Y, Wang J. 2015. *Fama–French in China: size and value factors in Chinese stock returns*. Work. Pap., Univ. Hong Kong

Chen C-D, Demirer R, Jategaonkar SP. 2015. Risk and return in the Chinese stock market: Does equity return dispersion proxy risk? *Pac. Basin Finance J.* 33:23–37

Chen D, Jiang D, Ljungqvist A, Lu H, Zhou M. 2015. *State capitalism versus private enterprise*. NBER Work. Pap. 20930

Chen G, Firth M, Kim J-B. 2004. IPO underpricing in China's new stock markets. *J. Multinatl. Financ. Manag.* 14:283–302

Chen G-M, Lee B-S, Rui O. 2001. Foreign ownership restrictions and market segmentation in China's stock markets. *J. Financ. Res.* 24:133–55

Chen H, Han Q, Li Y, Wu K. 2013. Does index futures trading reduce volatility in the Chinese stock market? A panel data evaluation approach. *J. Futures Markets* 33:1167–90

Chen J, Hong H, Huang M, Kubik JD. 2004. Does fund size erode mutual fund performance? The role of liquidity and organization. *Am. Econ. Rev.* 94:1276–302

Chen J, Hong H, Stein JC. 2002. Breadth of ownership and stock returns. *J. Financ. Econ.* 66:171–205

Chen J, Jiang F, Tong G. 2016. *Economic policy uncertainty in China and stock market expected returns*. Work. Pap., Xiamen Univ.

Chen Q, Chen X, Schipper K, Xu Y, Xue J. 2012. The sensitivity of corporate cash holdings to corporate governance. *Rev. Financ. Stud.* 25:3610–44

Chen Q, Goldstein I, Jiang W. 2007. Price informativeness and investment sensitivity to stock price. *Rev. Financ. Stud.* 20:619–50

Chen X, Kim KA, Yao T, Yu T. 2010. On the predictability of Chinese stock returns. *Pac. Basin Finance J.* 18:403–25

Chiras DP, Manaster S. 1978. The information content of option prices and a test of market efficiency. *J. Financ. Econ.* 6:213–34

Choi JJ, Jin L, Yan H. 2016. *Informed trading and expected returns*. Work. Pap., Yale Univ.

Chung T-K, Hui C-H, Li K-F. 2013. Explaining share price disparity with parameter uncertainty: evidence from Chinese A- and H-shares. *J. Bank. Finance* 37:1073–83

Cong W, Howell ST, Zhang R. 2017. How public markets foster firm standardization: evidence from Chinese IPOs. Work. Pap., Stern Sch. Bus., N.Y. Univ.

Cornett MM, Marcus AJ, Saunders A, Tehranian H. 2007. The impact of institutional ownership on corporate operating performance. *J. Bank. Finance* 31:1771–94

Doidge C. 2004. US cross-listings and the private benefits of control: evidence from dual-class firms. *J. Financ. Econ.* 72:519–53

Doidge C, Karolyi GA, Stulz RM. 2004. Why are foreign firms listed in the US worth more? *J. Financ. Econ.* 71:205–38

Domowitz I, Glen J, Madhavan A. 1997. Market segmentation and stock prices: evidence from an emerging market. *J. Finance* 52:1059–85

Dow J, Gorton G. 1997. Stock market efficiency and economic efficiency: is there a connection? *J. Finance* 52:1087–129

Durnev A, Morck R, Yeung B. 2004. Value-enhancing capital budgeting and firm-specific stock return variation. *J. Finance* 59:65–105

Durnev A, Morck R, Yeung B, Zarowin P. 2003. Does greater firm-specific return variation mean more or less informed stock pricing? *J. Account. Res.* 41:797–836

Fama EF, French KR. 1992. The cross-section of expected stock returns. *J. Finance* 47:427–65

Fan JPH, Wong TJ, Zhang T. 2007. Politically connected CEOs, corporate governance, and post-IPO performance of China's newly partially privatized firms. *J. Financ. Econ.* 84:330–57

Feng L, Seasholes MS. 2004. Correlated trading and location. *J. Finance* 59:2117–44

Fernald J, Rogers JH. 2002. Puzzles in the Chinese stock market. *Rev. Econ. Stat.* 84:416–32

Fernandes N, Ferreira MA. 2008. Does international cross-listing improve the information environment. *J. Financ. Econ.* 88:216–44

Fernandes N, Ferreira MA. 2009. Insider trading laws and stock price informativeness. *Rev. Financ. Stud.* 22:1845–87

Figlewski S, Webb GP. 1993. Options, short sales, and market completeness. *J. Finance* 48:761–77

Firth M, Lin C, Zou H. 2010. Friend or foe? The role of state and mutual fund ownership in the split share structure reform in China. *J. Financ. Quant. Anal.* 45:685–706

Foucault T, Gehrig T. 2008. Stock price informativeness, cross-listings, and investment decisions. *J. Financ. Econ.* 88:146–68

Glosten LR, Milgrom PR. 1985. Bid, ask and transaction prices in a specialist market with heterogeneously informed traders. *J. Financ. Econ.* 14:71–100

Grossman SJ, Stiglitz JE. 1980. On the impossibility of informationally efficient markets. *Am. Econ. Rev.* 70:393–408

Guiso L, Sapienza P, Zingales L. 2008. Trusting the stock market. *J. Finance* 63:2557–600

Guiso L, Sapienza P, Zingales L. 2009. Cultural biases in economic exchange? *Q. J. Econ.* 124:1095–131

Gul FA, Kim J-B, Qiu AA. 2010. Ownership concentration, foreign shareholding, audit quality, and stock price synchronicity: evidence from China. *J. Financ. Econ.* 95:425–42

Guo L, Tang L, Yang SX. 2013. Corporate governance and market segmentation: evidence from the price difference between Chinese A and H shares. *Rev. Quant. Finance Account.* 41:385–416

Hail L, Leuz C. 2009. Cost of capital effects and changes in growth expectations around US cross-listings. *J. Financ. Econ.* 93:428–54

Han Q, Liang J. 2017. Index futures trading restrictions and spot market quality: evidence from the recent Chinese stock market crash. *J. Futures Markets* 37:411–28

Harris L. 1989. S&P 500 cash stock price volatilities. *J. Finance* 44:1155–75

Harrison JM, Kreps DM. 1978. Speculative investor behavior in a stock market with heterogeneous expectations. *Q. J. Econ.* 92:323–36

Henry PB. 2000a. Do stock market liberalizations cause investment booms? *J. Financ. Econ.* 58:301–34

Henry PB. 2000b. Stock market liberalization, economic reform, and emerging market equity prices. *J. Finance* 55:529–64

Hietala PT. 1989. Asset pricing in partially segmented markets: evidence from the Finnish market. *J. Finance* 44:697–718

Hilliard J, Zhang H. 2015. Size and price-to-book effects: evidence from the Chinese stock markets. *Pac. Basin Finance J.* 32:40–55

Hong H, Jiang W, Wang N, Zhao B. 2014. Trading for status. *Rev. Financ. Stud.* 27:3171–212

Hsieh C-T, Klenow PJ. 2009. Misallocation and manufacturing TFP in China and India. *Q. J. Econ.* 124:1403–48

Hu G, Huang S, Xiao JZ, Zou H. 2016. *Which price to learn from? Evidence from cross listings with market segmentation.* Work. Pap., Tianjin Univ. Finance Econ.

Huang W, Zhu T. 2015. Foreign institutional investors and corporate governance in emerging markets: evidence of a split-share structure reform in China. *J. Corp. Finance* 32:312–26

ICI (Invest. Co. Inst.). 2016. *2016 Investment Company Factbook.* Washington, DC: ICI

Jegadeesh N, Titman S. 1993. Returns to buying winners and selling losers: implications for stock market efficiency. *J. Finance* 48:65–91

Jenkinson T, Ljungqvist A. 2001. *Going Public: The Theory and Evidence on How Companies Raise Equity Finance.* Oxford, UK: Oxford Univ. Press

Jia C, Wang Y, Xiong W. 2015. *Social trust and differential reactions of local and foreign investors to public news.* NBER Work. Pap. 21075

Jia W, Pownall G, Zhao J. 2014. *Does the Chinese government value good firms? Evidence from P-chips and Red-chips listed in Hong Kong.* Work. Pap., Emory Univ.

Jin L, Myers SC. 2006. R^2 around the world: new theory and new tests. *J. Financ. Econ.* 79:257–92

Karolyi GA, Li L, Liao R. 2009. A (partial) resolution of the Chinese discount puzzle: the 2001 deregulation of the B-share market. *J. Financ. Econ. Policy* 1:80–106

Kot HW, Tam LHK. 2016. Are stock price more informative after dual-listing in emerging markets? Evidence from Hong Kong-listed Chinese companies. *Pac. Basin Finance J.* 36:31–45

Kyle AS. 1985. Continuous auctions and insider trading. *Econometrica* 53:1315–35

Lel U, Miller DP. 2008. International cross-listing, firm performance, and top management turnover: a test of the bonding hypothesis. *J. Finance* 63:1897–937

Li K, Wang T, Cheung Y-L, Jiang P. 2011. Privatization and risk sharing: evidence from the split share structure reform in China. *Rev. Financ. Stud.* 24:2499–525

Li S, Brockman P, Zurbruegg R. 2015. Cross-listing, firm-specific information, and corporate governance: evidence from Chinese A-shares and H-shares. *J. Corp. Finance* 32:347–62

Li W. 1997. The impact of economic reform on the performance of Chinese state enterprises, 1980–1989. *J. Political Econ.* 105:1080–106

Liao L, Liu B, Wang H. 2011. Information discovery in share lockups: evidence from the split-share structure reform in China. *Financ. Manag.* 40:1001–27

Liao L, Liu B, Wang H. 2014. China's secondary privatization: perspectives from the split-share structure reform. *J. Financ. Econ.* 113:500–18

Lin JY, Cai F, Li Z. 1998. Competition, policy burdens, and state-owned enterprise reform. *Am. Econ. Rev.* 88:422–27

Liu LX, Shu H, Wei KCJ. 2017. The impacts of political uncertainty on asset prices: evidence from the Bo scandal in China. *J. Financ. Econ.* 125:286–310
Liu Q, Siu A. 2012. Institutions and corporate investment: evidence from investment-implied return on capital in China. *J. Financ. Quant. Anal.* 46:1831–63
Loh J. 2016. *Information in Hong Kong H-share prices*. BS Honors Thesis, Stern Sch. Bus., N.Y. Univ.
Lou F, Wang J, Yuan H. 2014. Stock liquidity and the pricing of earnings: a comparison of China's floating and nonfloating shares. *Emerg. Markets Finance Trade* 50:140–57
Lou S. 2016. *The effect of government intervention on stock synchronicity in China*. BS Honors Thesis, Stern Sch. Bus., N.Y. Univ.
Lu H, Fu J. 2014. Structural changes in Chinese stock market: a review of empirical research. *China Account. Finance Rev.* 16:39–65
Luo Y. 2005. Do insiders learn from outsiders? Evidence from mergers and acquisitions. *J. Finance* 60:1951–82
Ma X. 1996. Capital controls, market segmentation and stock prices: evidence from the Chinese stock market. *Pac. Basin Finance J.* 4:219–39
Manaster S, Rendleman RJ. 1982. Option prices as predictors of equilibrium stock prices. *J. Finance* 37:1043–57
Markovitch DG, Steckel JH, Yeung B. 2005. Using capital markets as market intelligence: evidence from the pharmaceutical industry. *Manag. Sci.* 51:1467–80
Megginson WL, Netter JM. 2001. From state to market: a survey of empirical studies on privatization. *J. Econ. Lit.* 39:321–89
Mei J, Scheinkman JA, Xiong W. 2009. Speculative trading and stock prices: evidence from Chinese AB share premia. *Ann. Econ. Finance* 10:225–55
Miller EM. 1977. Risk, uncertainty, and divergence of opinion. *J. Finance* 32:1151–68
Mok HMK, Hui YV. 1998. Underpricing and aftermarket performance of IPOs in Shanghai, China. *Pac. Basin Finance J.* 6:453–74
Morck R, Nakamura M. 1999. Banks and corporate control in Japan. *J. Finance* 54:319–39
Morck R, Yeung B, Yu W. 2000. The information content of stock markets: Why do emerging markets have synchronous stock price movements? *J. Financ. Econ.* 58:215–60
Morck R, Yeung B, Yu W. 2013. *R-squared and the economy*. NBER Work. Pap. 19017
Nartea GV, Kong D, Wu JG. 2017. Do extreme returns matter in emerging markets? Evidence from the Chinese stock market. *J. Bank. Finance* 76:189–97
Ofek E, Richardson M. 2000. *The IPO lock-up period: implications for market efficiency and downward sloping demand curves*. Work. Pap., Stern Sch. Bus., N.Y. Univ.
Ofek E, Richardson M, Whitelaw RF. 2004. Limited arbitrage and short sales restrictions: evidence from the options markets. *J. Financ. Econ.* 74:305–42
Pan F, Brooker D. 2014. Going global? Examining the geography of Chinese firms' overseas listings on international stock exchanges. *Geoforum* 52:1–11
Pan J, Poteshman AM. 2006. The information in option volume for future stock prices. *Rev. Financ. Stud.* 19:871–908
Peng L, Xiong W. 2006. Investor attention, overconfidence and category learning. *J. Financ. Econ.* 80:563–602
Peng Z, Tang Q, Wang K. 2014. Adjustment of the stamp duty on stock transactions and its effect on the Chinese stock market. *Emerg. Markets Finance Trade* 50:183–96
Piotroski JD, Zhang T. 2014. Politicians and the IPO decision: the impact of impending political promotions on IPO activity in China. *J. Financ. Econ.* 111:111–36
Qian J. 2016. *The 2015 stock panic of China: a narrative*. Work. Pap., Shanghai Jiao Tong Univ.
Rey H. 2015. *Dilemma not trilemma: the global financial cycle and monetary policy independence*. NBER Work. Pap. 21162
Ritter JR, Welch I. 2002. A review of IPO activity, pricing, and allocations. *J. Finance* 57:1795–828
Roll R. 1984. Orange juice and weather. *Am. Econ. Rev.* 74:861–80
Roll R. 1988. R^2. *J. Finance* 43:541–66
Scheinkman JA, Xiong W. 2003. Overconfidence and speculative bubbles. *J. Political Econ.* 111:1183–220
Shen J. 2016. *A study on the listing choices of Chinese companies*. BS Honors Thesis, Stern Sch. Bus., N.Y. Univ.
Silber WL. 1991. Discounts on restricted stock: the impact of illiquidity on stock prices. *Financ. Anal. J.* 47:60–64

Smith MP. 1996. Shareholder activism by institutional investors: evidence from CalPERS. *J. Finance* 51:227–52

Smith RC. 2016. Is China the next Japan? *Indep. Rev.* 21:275–298

Stein JC. 1987. Informational externalities and welfare-reducing speculation. *J. Political Econ.* 95:1123–45

Stulz RM, Wasserfallen W. 1995. Foreign equity investment restrictions, capital flight, and shareholder wealth maximization: theory and evidence. *Rev. Financ. Stud.* 8:1019–57

Su D, Fleisher BM. 1999. An empirical investigation of underpricing in Chinese IPOs. *Pac. Basin Finance J.* 7:173–202

Sun Q, Tong WHS. 2003. China share issue privatization: the extent of its success. *J. Financ. Econ.* 70:183–222

Tang K, Wang W, Xu R. 2012. Size and performance of Chinese mutual funds: the role of economy of scale and liquidity. *Pac. Basin Finance J.* 20:228–46

Van Nieuwerburgh S, Veldkamp L. 2009. Information immobility and the home bias puzzle. *J. Finance* 64:1187–215

Wahal S. 1996. Pension fund activism and firm performance. *J. Financ. Quant. Anal.* 31:1–23

Wang Y, Zhou G, Zhu Y. 2016. *The Chinese warrant bubble: a fundamental analysis*. Work. Pap., Tsinghua Univ.

Wei Z, Xie F, Zhang S. 2005. Ownership structure and firm value in China's privatized firms: 1991–2001. *J. Financ. Quant. Anal.* 40:87–108

Whited TM, Zhao J. 2015. *Capital structure misallocation*. Work. Pap., Univ. Mich.

Woidtke T. 2002. Agents watching agents? Evidence from pension fund ownership and firm value. *J. Financ. Econ.* 63:99–131

Wurgler J. 2000. Financial markets and the allocation of capital. *J. Financ. Econ.* 58:187–214

Xie S, Mo T. 2014. Index futures trading and stock market volatility in China: a difference-in-difference approach. *J. Futures Markets* 34:282–97

Xiong W, Yu J. 2011. The Chinese warrants bubble. *Am. Econ. Rev.* 101:2723–53

Xu J, Zhang S. 2014. The Fama–French three factors in the Chinese stock market. *China Account. Finance Rev.* 16:210–27

Yang J, Yang Z, Zhou Y. 2012. Intraday price discovery and volatility transmission in stock index and stock index futures markets: evidence from China. *J. Futures Markets* 32:99–121

Yao Y. 2012. The core issues of open-ended funds in China: conflicts of interest and ownership structure. *Int. J. Acad. Res. Bus. Soc. Sci.* 2:443–79

Yu T, Tse YK. 2006. An empirical examination of IPO underpricing in the Chinese A-share market. *China Econ. Rev.* 17:363–82

Yuan R, Xiao JZ, Zou H. 2008. Mutual funds? Ownership and firm performance: evidence from China. *J. Bank. Finance* 32:1552–65

A Firm's Cost of Capital

Ravi Jagannathan,[1,2,3] José Liberti,[1,4] Binying Liu,[5] and Iwan Meier[6]

[1]Kellogg School of Management, Northwestern University, Evanston, Illinois 60208; email: rjaganna@kellogg.northwestern.edu

[2]National Bureau of Economic Research, Cambridge, Massachusetts 02138

[3]Shanghai Advanced Institute of Finance, Shanghai Jiao Tong University, Shanghai 200030, China

[4]Department of Finance, Kellstadt Graduate School of Business, DePaul University, Chicago, Illinois 60622

[5]Department of Finance, Hong Kong University of Science and Technology, Hong Kong

[6]Department of Finance, HEC Montréal, Montréal, Québec H3T 2A7, Canada

Annu. Rev. Financ. Econ. 2017. 9:259–82

The *Annual Review of Financial Economics* is online at financial.annualreviews.org

https://doi.org/10.1146/annurev-financial-110716-032429

Copyright © 2017 by Annual Reviews. All rights reserved

JEL codes: G31, G32

Keywords

cost of capital, capital structure, cost of debt, cost of equity, weighted average cost of capital, divisional cost of capital

Abstract

To create value, a firm must invest in projects that provide a return greater than the cost of capital. The cost of capital is not observed and its estimation requires assumptions on investors' consumption, savings, and portfolio decisions. We review the academic literature on firms' cost of financial capital and the estimation of the different components: cost of equity, cost of debt, and their relative weights. We also review various approaches to estimating the cost of capital and the assumptions justifying these approaches.

1. INTRODUCTION

Managers of modern corporations often undertake projects requiring substantial capital expenditures. Capital expenditure decisions are typically irreversible, and mistakes can be costly to the firm's security holders and to society as a whole.[1] The textbook approach to ensuring that capital expenditure decisions are in the interest of firms' security holders is to undertake projects that have a positive net present value; i.e., the return on invested capital exceeds the cost of capital. A key input for computing the net present value is the cost of financial capital. A small change in the cost of capital, and thus the discount rate, can result in a large change in the present value of the expected future cash flows from the project under consideration.

Managers of firms are not the only ones who make use of the cost of capital. Financial intermediaries such as investment bankers regularly estimate firm values to advise their clients on potential acquisitions, divestitures, and decisions to go public. The cost of capital is a key input in their valuation models.

Various definitions of the cost of capital have been proposed in the academic literature and in popular corporate finance textbooks. Despite broad agreement that the cost of capital represents investors' required expected rate of return on investment, which represents the best available expected return on a comparable investment offered in the market (for alternative definitions of the cost of capital, see Pratt & Grabowski 2008), computing the cost of capital is not straightforward. Difficulties arise from the fact that firms use a variety of financing methods, and payments made to investors who hold securities are not all treated the same way for purposes of corporate and personal income tax. Further, the differential treatment of cash flows for income tax purposes changes over time.[2]

The choice of securities used by a firm to finance its activities affects its managers' incentives and thereby the characteristics of future cash flows. Hence, the choice of capital structure can affect a firm's cost of capital and make some methods of financing more attractive while at the same time imposing additional costs. Furthermore, a firm's projects under consideration can be exposed to different types of risks than existing operations (which leads one to consider not merely the companywide cost of capital, but also the project-specific cost of capital; for discussion, see Damodaran 2001, Grinblatt & Titman 2001, Ross et al. 2015). For firm valuation, the cost of capital depends on a firm's current and expected future capital structure and reflects the risks of its cash flows from current and expected future operations. For capital budgeting decisions, the cost of capital must reflect the risk of a firm's planned projects and the associated capital structures.

The rest of this article is organized as follows. In Section 2, we discuss the cost of capital and its dependence on capital structure. We discuss the cost of equity capital in Section 3 and the cost of debt and other types of capital in Section 4. In Section 5, we discuss how a firm obtains the weighted average cost of capital (WACC) and explain its use in capital budgeting decisions. We conclude in Section 6.

[1]Corporate capital expenditures represent a large fraction of the economy. In 2015, US nonfinancial businesses spent $1,927 billion on fixed investments, which was 8.8% of the market value of equities of those firms and 10.7% of US GDP (Fed. Reserve Syst. 2015, tables F.102 and L.223; see also the discussion by Jagannathan & McGrattan 1995).

[2]Four reform proposals with similar objectives have been made in the past 6 years (Morgan Stanley Res. 2016). The President's Framework for Business Tax Reform of 2016 reduces the tax preference for debt-financing investment. The House Republican Blueprint for Tax Reform of 2016 allows interest expense tax deductions on interest income only. The Bipartisan Tax Fairness and Simplification Act of 2011 limits the deductibility of corporate interest to its noninflationary (real) component. The proposed American Business Competitiveness Act provides a 10-year phase-out of the interest deduction.

2. THE ROLE OF CAPITAL STRUCTURE

When evaluating a capital investment project, a firm needs to decide on the optimal mix of securities that will be used to finance it, typically debt and equity. A natural question that arises is whether the relative weights of different types of securities, i.e., the capital structure, will affect the (weighted average) cost of capital or, equivalently, the value of the project when the capital structure does not affect the expected cash flows from the project.[3] Modigliani & Miller (1958) show that in a frictionless market, the value of a firm does not depend on the firm's capital structure. In this case, the cost of capital is also independent of the capital structure.

Corporate income tax, an important source of friction, introduces the government as a third claimant to a firm's cash flows. Because interest expenses are tax deductible, the use of debt reduces the taxes paid to the government by the firm, thereby increasing the cash flows allocated to the firm's equity holders and debtholders. Consequently, the value of the project increases and the after-tax WACC declines with the increased use of debt in the capital structure, relative to the otherwise similar no-tax scenario. Tax in this framework is considered a negative cost, or a subsidy from the government for the use of debt. Jensen (1986) argues that the use of debt has other benefits because it reduces the agency conflict between managers and shareholders resulting from the classic free cash flow problem (for a survey of the literature, see Harris & Raviv 1990). Therefore, capital structure can affect firms' expected cash flows and risks for reasons other than taxes.[4] Although the use of debt has benefits and reduces the after-tax WACC, the direct and indirect costs of financial distress increase with the use of debt. This in turn reduces the expected future cash flows of the firm, which, all else being equal, reduces firm value.[5] Miller (1977) argues that personal income taxes must also be taken into account, which attenuates the impact of the tax benefits from the use of debt on the after-tax WACC.[6] Graham, Leary & Roberts (2015) find that although firms have increased their financial leverage over the past century, it is difficult to explain the increase only on the basis of the tax advantage of debt.

We expect firms to choose the capital structure that is best for them in light of these costs and benefits of debt in the capital structure. However, as managerial actions are not directly observable, firm managers may act in their own interest, deviating from the capital structure that is best for the firm (Israel 1992, Zwiebel 1996, Morellec 2004). Capital structure also changes over time because of fluctuations in the market value of the firm's equity. However, when direct and indirect costs associated with issuing and repurchasing equity are significant, firms whose shares are fairly priced may be reluctant to issue or repurchase equity to adjust their capital structure to the desired

[3] There are other securities that have received attention in corporate finance textbooks: preferred shares, convertible debt, options, etc. They are important, but their magnitudes are relatively small in the aggregate, although they may be preferred in particular situations. We do not consider these securities in this review.

[4] Dasgupta & Sengupta (1993), Perotti & Spier (1993), and Hennessy & Livdan (2009) discuss the beneficial role of debt in negotiations. Berk, Stanton & Zechner (2010) argue that firms refrain from issuing debt to facilitate longer-term labor contracts, which may favorably affect the firm's cash flows. Bolton & Scharfstein (1990) and Chevalier (1995) discuss the competitive disadvantage that may arise from the use of debt. For a comprehensive discussion of agency issues, see Berk & DeMarzo (2017).

[5] For a discussion of the significance of bankruptcy and agency costs in the theory of capital structure, see Haugen & Senbet (1988). Titman (1984) argues that indirect costs can be significant. Opler & Titman (1994) find that sales growth of highly levered firms is 18% lower in economic downturns than for otherwise similar firms in R&D-intensive industries. Almeida & Philippon (2007) find that for a BBB-rated firm, the cost of financial distress can be as high as 4.5% of its predistress value.

[6] Graham (2000) finds that the capitalized tax benefit of debt is reduced from 9.7% to 4.3% of firm value when personal taxes are taken into account. As we cannot identify the marginal taxpayer, we do not treat personal taxes in this review.

level (Leland & Pyle 1977; Ross 1977; Myers & Majluf 1984; Masulis & Korwar 1986; Mikkelson & Partch 1986; Korajczyk, Lucas & McDonald 1991; Hu, Saa-Requejo & Santa-Clara 2010). The indirect costs arise because the firm's managers have more information than stock market participants, resulting in adverse selection. The firm's managers are likely to issue equity when they view the market price to be high and are likely to repurchase when they view the market price to be low, and the market will take this into account when setting prices. This is consistent with the work of Strebulaev (2007), who finds that changes in the capital structure of firms are more likely to result from changes in stock prices than from managerial design (see also Kester 1986, Baskin 1989, and Titman & Wessels 1988, who find negative correlations between leverage and past profitability across firms; for a survey of the trade-off theory of capital structure and the pecking order theory of security issuance, see Frank & Goyal 2008).

To summarize, a firm's cost of capital and its cash flows depend on the firm's capital structure. In this article, however, we do not examine the determinants of a firm's capital structure. We take it as given and review the literature on the cost of equity and debt, two of the most important components of the cost of capital, before proceeding to examine the firm's weighted cost of capital.

3. COST OF EQUITY

When expected returns remain constant over time and investors have rational expectations, the historical average stock return provides a consistent estimate of what investors expect to get from investing in a firm's equity. This estimate can be noisy, however: Individual firms' stock returns are highly volatile, and few firms have a sufficiently long time series of observations on returns to provide precise estimates of expected returns.[7] Furthermore, a firm's exposure to risks and the return that investors expect to earn are likely to change over time, and historical averages do not necessarily reflect what return investors will expect for investing in the firm's stocks at a given point in time. For these reasons, we need an asset pricing model, one that will help us more precisely assess the investors' expected return for providing equity capital to a firm.

The first general equilibrium asset pricing model was the capital asset pricing model (CAPM) of Sharpe (1964) and Lintner (1965):

$$E_t[R_{i,t+1}] - R^F_{t+1} = \beta_t \left(E_t\left[R^M_{t+1}\right] - R^F_{t+1}\right), \qquad 1.$$

where $R_{i,t+1}$ is the return of an individual security during period $t+1$; R^M_{t+1} is the return on the aggregate wealth (market) portfolio; R^F_{t+1} is the risk-free return; $\beta_t = \mathrm{Cov}_t(R^M_{t+1}, R_{i,t+1})/\mathrm{Var}_t(R^M_{t+1})$; and $E_t[\cdot]$, $\mathrm{Cov}_t(\cdot)$, and $\mathrm{Var}_t(\cdot)$ denote the expectation, covariance, and variance operators, respectively, conditional on information available at time t. The model assumes that markets are perfect and frictionless and also that investors have homogenous beliefs, are myopic with a one-period horizon, and choose mean variance efficient portfolios. Merton (1973) considers a more general environment where investors are time-separable expected utility maximizers who care about the mean and variance as well as the other moments of the returns on the portfolio of assets that they hold. Furthermore, investors are long-lived and continuously revise their consumption and investment plans. He obtains a multifactor version of the CAPM where the return

[7] Suppose that returns are independent and identically normally distributed with a standard deviation of 40% per year. In this case, the average annual return computed using 25 years of data will have a standard deviation of 8% per year, and the 95% confidence region will be the sample mean $\pm 16\%$.

on the market portfolio is the dominant factor, and the other factors help investors hedge the risks resulting from changes in investment opportunities that occur over time. Ross (1976) introduces a multifactor asset pricing model based on the assumption that security returns have a strictly linear, finite-dimensional factor structure. In other words, well-diversified portfolios of securities are subject only to factor-related risks; investors who determine prices in financial markets have rational expectations and can trade securities without transactions costs; and there are no arbitrage opportunities in financial markets, i.e., strictly positive payoffs have strictly positive prices.

The theoretical factor models discussed above predict the expected return on a security given its exposure to systematic risk factors, the risk premium on those factors, and the risk-free return. Subsequent developments in the asset pricing literature examine the nature of the relation between macroeconomic fundamentals, the risk-free rate, and factor risk premia (see, for example, Lucas 1978, Breeden 1979, Campbell & Cochrane 1999, Bansal & Yaron 2004, Jagannathan & Wang 2007, Kogan & Papanikolaou 2014).

In empirical studies of asset pricing models, the value-weighted stock index portfolio of all exchange-traded stocks is commonly used to represent the market portfolio. Multifactor asset pricing models have received wide attention in the empirical finance literature. Prominent among them is the one by Fama & French (1993), who provide evidence that two additional factors, the spread in expected returns between small and large firm stocks and the spread in expected returns between firm stocks with high and low book-to-market ratios, explain a significant part of the cross section of expected stock returns not explained by the market factor. Jagannathan & Wang (1996) provide a more detailed analysis of the results of Fama & French (1993). This line of research has led to numerous multifactor models. We refer to McLean & Pontiff (2015) for a detailed list of these factors. Further, a common concern forcefully conveyed by Harvey, Liu & Zhu (2015) is that it is often difficult to distinguish whether these empirical factors capture real drivers of the cross-section of stock returns or whether they are the product of statistical coincidences in the data.

The fundamental concern over the validity of numerous factors discovered over the past decades has motivated another line of research that directly asks market participants what kinds of models they use to price different securities. The logic here is simple but insightful: In a sophisticated market, a factor model cannot possibly be right if the vast majority of investors do not use that model in making their investment decisions. Graham & Harvey (2001) survey 392 chief financial officers (CFOs) throughout the United States and Canada and find that most corporate managers, in making their investment decisions, use the CAPM over any other factor model. Also, a concern that is often overlooked is the self-fulfilling role of finance education in determining the asset pricing models that market participants adopt and use in pricing the systematic risk of securities. Fernández (2009) reviews 100 textbooks published between 1979 and 2008 and reports that 89 explicitly recommend the use of the CAPM. Berk & van Binsbergen (2015) provide additional insights into this question by investigating the kinds of risks to which mutual fund investors respond. Their findings confirm that investors are sensitive to systematic risk, but do not respond to other proposed risk factors such as the factors of Fama & French (1993) or the momentum factor.

Several consumption-based asset pricing models, starting with those of Lucas (1978) and Breeden (1979) (we refer to these models as the standard consumption-based CAPM), have been proposed in the literature to provide the theoretical framework that relates the market discount rate to fundamentals of the economy, such as consumption and dividend dynamics. However, although the standard consumption-based CAPM's importance in providing the foundation for subsequent asset pricing studies cannot be overstated, it is not without many shortcomings. The most widely acknowledged failure of the standard consumption-based CAPM is that it cannot explain why the equity risk premium is so high while simultaneously the risk-free rate is so low with very little variability.

Subsequent theoretical asset pricing models, such as those of Campbell & Cochrane (1999) and Bansal & Yaron (2004), seek to address these shortcomings of the standard consumption-based CAPM. Campbell & Cochrane (1999) replace constant relative risk aversion preferences with external habit formation preferences, by which investors are averse to risks that would drop consumption close to a subsistence level. As a consequence, as consumption falls closer to this subsistence level, investors' marginal utility of consuming today increases relative to future periods, and, therefore, the risk premium rises. The long-run risk model of Bansal & Yaron (2004) makes two modifications to the canonical CAPM. First, it replaces the time-additive preferences of the canonical CAPM with investor preferences for the early resolution of uncertainty through the work of Epstein & Zin (1989). Second, it allows for high persistence and stochastic volatility in the consumption dynamics of the representative investor.

Despite the rich literature on consumption-based asset pricing models, these models have not been widely used in practice for estimating the cost of capital of individual firms. To a large extent this is because consumption data is measured with error and is available only with low frequencies, making it difficult to accurately estimate a firm's exposure to consumption risk. Campbell (1993) and Jagannathan & Marakani (2015) show that dynamic consumption-based asset pricing models have an equivalent intertemporal CAPM representation given in Merton (1976), where the factors are returns on particular portfolios of traded assets that resemble the empirical multifactor models that are widely used in the empirical asset pricing literature.

Given this background, here we adopt the Sharpe–Lintner CAPM as the default model for expositional purposes and for illustrating the issues involved in assessing a firm's cost of capital. The CAPM is a one-period model, but firms typically use the estimated cost of capital based on the CAPM for evaluating investment projects that have a longer life. The implicit assumption is that CAPM-based estimates of investors' required expected returns provide a reasonable starting point that can be further refined based on additional firm-specific information.

On the basis of the CAPM, the expected return on the securities of a firm is a function of three variables: the market risk premium, the risk-free rate, and the firm's beta (i.e., the sensitivity of the firm's equity return to the market portfolio's return). We proceed to discuss the common approaches to estimating these three variables. Our discussion can be readily extended for generating the inputs for multifactor models.

3.1. Market Risk Premium

The value-weighted portfolio of exchange-traded stocks in the United States (stock index portfolio) is commonly used as a proxy for the market portfolio in the CAPM. The market risk premium is the extra return over the risk-free return that investors expect to receive from investing in the market portfolio. A common approach has been to estimate the risk premium as the historical average market return minus the risk-free return. Another method, used by Graham & Harvey (2001), is to directly ask CFOs what discount rates they use in their investment decisions. However, it is important to note that the view of a collection of CFOs does not necessarily reflect the view of the marginal market participant.

A different alternative is to estimate the expected return on the stock index portfolio on the basis of the present-value relationship between the value of the stock index portfolio, its long-run expected return, and the long-run expected growth rates of its dividends. An estimate of the market risk premium is obtained by subtracting the prevailing interest rate. Assuming that the expected dividend growth rates are constant, this relationship is given by the Gordon growth model:

$$\frac{P_t}{D_t} = \frac{1+\bar{G}}{\bar{R}-\bar{G}} \Leftrightarrow \bar{R} = \left(1+\bar{G}\right)\frac{D_t}{P_t} + \bar{G}, \qquad 2.$$

where P_t/D_t is the price-to-dividend ratio of the market portfolio at time t, $\bar{G}$ is the constant growth rate of dividends, and $\bar{R}$ is the long-run expected return (stock yield, which is analogous to bond yield) of the stock index portfolio. Although information about dividends can be noisy at the individual stock level, dividends behave better at the aggregate level. Fama & French (2002) compare market risk premium estimates based on the Gordon growth model with those based on historical averages. They find the former to be more stable across different sample periods.[8]

The Gordon growth model assumes both expected market return and expected dividend growth rates to be constant. However, this assumption is not supported by the data. As Cochrane (2008) points out, because price-to-dividend ratios vary over time, either market returns or dividend growth rates (or both) have to be predictable over time. Subsequent research has documented evidence supporting the predictability of market returns and dividends. Although market risk premium estimates based on models in the earlier literature may not be better than historical averages (Goyal & Welch 2008), more recent models appear to perform better (for some of the more recent models for estimating the market risk premium, see van Binsbergen & Koijen 2010; Kelly & Pruitt 2013; Li, Ng & Swaminathan 2013; Jagannathan & Liu 2016).

To allow for time-varying market risk premia and dividend growth rates, one approach in the literature is to use Campbell & Shiller's (1988) dynamic version of the Gordon growth model. Equations 3 and 4 follow from the log-linearized present-value relation that links the stock index portfolio's log price-to-dividend ratio, its expected stream of future log changes in dividends, and the sequence of its expected future return:

$$p_t - d_t = \frac{\kappa_0}{1-\kappa_1} + \sum_{s=0}^{\infty}\kappa_1^s\left(E_t\left[\Delta d_{t+s+1}\right] - E_t\left[r_{t+s+1}\right]\right), \qquad 3.$$

where lowercase variables represent the natural logarithm of corresponding uppercase variables and κ_0 and κ_1 are log linearization constants that are functions of steady-state values of the variables. So the expected long-run return of the market portfolio, defined as the weighted average of the expected market returns across different time horizons, is given by

$$\bar{r}_t = (1-\kappa_1)\sum_{s=0}^{\infty}\kappa_1^s E_t\left[r_{t+s+1}\right] = \kappa_0 - (1-\kappa_1)(p_t - d_t) + (1-\kappa_1)\sum_{s=0}^{\infty}\kappa_1^s E_t\left[\Delta d_{t+s+1}\right]. \qquad 4.$$

Expected dividend growth rates can then be estimated using one of the time-series models for dividends.

[8]For the period 1990–2002, the payout ratio for S&P 500 firms was 86%, and repurchases were 74% of dividends. For the period 2003–2015, the payout ratio increased to 93%, and repurchases were 148% of dividends. We may expect the increased payout to decrease the future growth rate of dividends. In contrast, the increased repurchases may increase the future growth rate of dividends. Personal tax rates may also shift over time. Such structural shifts mean that we cannot only rely on historical averages to measure what we should expect going forward; for discussion, see Jagannathan, McGrattan & Scherbina (2001).

Li, Ng & Swaminathan (2013) use another variation of the dynamic Gordon growth model, known as the implied cost of capital model. Their approach uses sell-side analysts' earnings forecasts to estimate the long-run expected return on the stock index portfolio and does not rely on a log-linear approximation (see also Madden 1998; Claus & Thomas 2001; Gebhardt, Lee & Swaminathan 2001; Easton 2004; a 20-year moving average of past earnings growth rates instead of growth rates based on analysts' earnings forecasts is used by Ferreira & Santa-Clara 2011).

In what follows, we assume that the term structure of market risk premia is flat. Empirically, van Binsbergen, Brandt & Koijen (2012) construct synthetic dividend strips of the market index and show that the term structure of risk premia is downward sloping during recessions. That is, on an annualized basis, investors need a higher risk premium for near-term cash flows than for far-term cash flows during recessions. Explaining why we observe this phenomenon is still an ongoing research topic.

3.2. Risk-Free Rate

Estimating the risk-free rate is a much easier task than estimating the risk premium. The conventional wisdom is to use Treasury bills and bonds as a proxy for the risk-free asset. It is important to note that the maturity of the Treasury bills and bonds used should correspond to the time horizon of the project. For example, if one were to use the CAPM to estimate the required rate of return of a 10-year project, then the 10-year bond yield should be used as the proxy for the risk-free rate. By contrast, if one were to use the CAPM to estimate the required rate of return for a security in perpetuity, then one should use the longest bond maturity that is liquid. The market risk premium used should also correspond to the maturity of the risk-free return that is used.

3.3. Market Beta

The basic approach to estimating beta is to use rolling-window regressions. The approach of using a 5-year window of monthly data, as initially proposed by Black, Jensen & Scholes (1972) and Fama & MacBeth (1973), is still widespread in practice. A shorter time window generates betas based on more recent information that likely better represents the current risk of the firm and allows for more time variation, as beta is assumed to be constant over the time window. However, statistical power suffers unless data frequency is increased. Using daily data improves the accuracy of covariance estimation, as in Merton (1980). However, in increasing the frequency to daily one needs to address market microstructure effects, especially for thinly traded stocks, which otherwise lead to a downward bias of beta estimates. A frequently used method, illustrated by Dimson (1979), is to include n lagged and leading values for the market return, R^M, in the index mode regression and to take the sum of these coefficients[9]:

$$R_{i,t} = \sum_{k=-n}^{n} \beta_k R_t^M + \varepsilon_{i,t}. \quad 5.$$

[9]Scholes & Williams (1977) take the sum of the coefficients b_k from three separate regressions of the stock return on the lagged, contemporaneous, and leading market returns. This sum beta is then adjusted in the following way:

$$\frac{\sum_{k=-1}^{1} b_k}{1+2\rho},$$

where ρ is the autocorrelation of the market return.

Beta estimates using historical data are often noisy, and outliers can lead to extreme beta estimates (regarding the use of higher-frequency data to obtain more precise estimates of betas, see Andersen et al. 2006; Bollerslev, Li & Todorov 2016).

Vasicek (1973) proposes a Bayesian estimate of beta, where the sample beta is adjusted toward the prior estimate, with the degree of adjustment being proportionate to the precision of the beta and prior estimates.

$$\hat{\beta}_{i,t}^{\text{Vasicek}} = \frac{\bar{b}_{i,t}^{*}/\sigma_{b_{i,t}^{*}}^{2} + b_{i,t}/s_{b_{i,t}}^{2}}{1/\sigma_{b_{i,t}^{*}}^{2} + 1/s_{b_{i,t}}^{2}}, \qquad 6.$$

where $\bar{b}_{i,t}^{*}$ and $\sigma_{b_{i,t}^{*}}^{2}$ denote the prior mean and variance, $b_{i,t}$ denotes the sample estimate of $\beta_{i,t}$, and $s_{b_{i,t}}^{2}$ denotes the sampling variance of $b_{i,t}$. The most basic prior density is a normal distribution with mean and variance of beta estimated from the cross section of stocks of interest, such as a major stock index or all stocks recorded in CRSP. The mean of the prior is approximately one. In Vasicek's (1973) procedure, the posterior distribution is the sum of the precision of the sample beta and that of the prior distribution.

Karolyi (1992) proposes using more informative priors than simple cross-sectional average and variance. He groups stocks into portfolios based on firm characteristics such as size and industry. The one-year rolling sample estimate of beta is then shrunk toward the one-year rolling portfolio beta (for more recent results on Karolyi's shrinkage beta, see Cosemans et al. 2016; they group firms by the 48-industry portfolio classification of Fama & French 1997). Shrinkage estimators use priors to improve the accuracy of the rolling beta estimate. The simplest prior is that the average beta of all stocks equals one. This is the basis for the Bloomberg adjusted beta, where the weights are two-thirds on the rolling window estimate and one-third on the prior of one.[10] These weights are selected heuristically. Damodaran (2002) argues that fixed weights are questionable, as they do not allow for variation of the speed of convergence across companies. For example, betas of diversified firms are expected to converge faster than those of firms that focus on one business sector. Vasicek (1973) points out that such a procedure overadjusts more accurate estimates and underadjusts less accurate ones.[11]

4. COST OF DEBT

At first glance it may appear that calculating the cost of debt is straightforward because we observe the interest payments on debt. On closer examination, several issues arise. The interest rate a firm pays on its debt may not be representative of its current borrowing costs, as interest rates may have changed because of changes in general economic conditions or changes in the firm's characteristics. When there is no active market for the firm's debt, we need to rely on a model for estimating the cost of debt. Further, debt imposes constraints on the firm's operations through covenants, and not meeting debt obligations imposes costs of financial distress. These costs, both direct and indirect, are borne not only by debtholders but also by other stakeholders, including equity holders. The indirect costs imposed on equity holders are particularly difficult to measure (Mello & Parsons 1992).

[10]Fixed weights have a long tradition. Vasicek (1973) reports that, at the time, this weighting scheme was employed by Merrill Lynch, Pierce, and Fenner & Smith, Inc.

[11]Levi & Welch (2016) recommend a variation of Vasicek's (1973) approach using 1–4 years of daily return data for estimating betas.

A commonly used measure of the pre-corporate-tax cost of a corporate bond (i.e., the expected holding period return on a firm's bond) is its yield to maturity adjusted for the expected loss because of potential default based on the bond's credit rating and the prevailing economic conditions. As the risk-free interest rate and the credit spread generally depend on the time horizon, it is necessary to use bonds that match the term structure of cash flows from the capital budgeting project under consideration.

When the firm's bond is not traded in a liquid market, an estimate of the promised yield can be obtained as the average of the yields on similar bonds in the same credit rating class. (For a discussion on using the average of the yield spread over Treasury bonds on several comparable bonds in the same rating class to minimize the effect of thin trading and market microstructure effects, see Damodaran 2012.) The spread between the promised yield on a firm's debt and the prevailing risk-free interest rate on Treasury securities of similar maturity depends on the firm's bond credit rating and other firm- and bond-specific characteristics. When there are no credit ratings available for the firm's bond, it may be feasible to assign a synthetic rating to the firm based on a model of credit rating as in Blume, Lim & MacKinlay (1998) and Jorion, Shi & Zhang (2009). The canonical model is that of Merton (1974); for a survey of credit risk models, see Duffie & Singleton (2012).

Elton et al. (2001) find that, for actively traded bonds for which dealer quotes were available, the expected default accounts for a surprisingly small fraction of the credit spread on corporate bonds. A large part of the spread results from state taxes and a risk premium associated with exposure to systematic economy-wide risk factors affecting equities.[12] Huang & Huang (2012) find that credit risk accounts for only a small fraction of yield spreads for investment-grade bonds but, as expected, for a much higher fraction of yield spreads for high-yield bonds, and the conclusions are robust across a wide class of structural models. These findings provide a justification for assessing the pre-corporate-tax expected risk premium on debt using linear factor models such as the three-factor model of Fama & French (1993), which can be combined with the expected return on Treasury bonds to get an estimate of the pre-corporate-tax cost of debt.[13]

Corporate debt securities may have embedded options. For example, they may be convertible into equity of the firm under certain conditions and may be callable by the firm or puttable by the investor. Valuing convertible bonds and computing their expected returns requires a valuation model if the convertibility option is not deep out of the money (Brennan & Schwartz 1977; Ingersoll 1977; Kang & Lee 1996; Ayache, Forsyth & Vetzal 2003; Barone-Adesi, Bermúdez & Hatgioannides 2003).

To arrive at the after-tax cost of debt, it is necessary to estimate the marginal tax rate of the firm over the life of the capital budgeting project under consideration, which may be different from the firm's statutory tax rate. For example, if the firm expects to make losses, or has a substantial tax-loss carry forward, the tax benefits from the tax deductibility of interest expenses may occur in the years following the date when the expense is incurred.

---

[12] Campello, Chen & Zhang (2008) construct a proxy for the expected return on the stock of a firm on the basis of the credit spread of its bonds. They find that the cross section of this measure of expected stock return across firms can be explained by the three-factor model of Fama & French (1993). This lends support to the view that credit spreads are affected by economy-wide risk factors that also affect equity returns.

[13] In cases where the expected loss from potential default is high, as in the case of non-investment-grade high-yield debt, it may be necessary to use a dynamic model of the term structure of credit spreads, as in the work of Leland & Toft (1996), or some variation that builds on the work of Merton (1976) (see also Brennan & Schwartz 1978; Altman 1991; Longstaff & Schwartz 1995; Anderson & Sundaresan 1996; Jarrow, Lando & Turnbull 1997; Duffee 1999; Duffie & Singleton 1999; Collin-Dufresne, Goldstein & Martin 2001).

Preferred shares have agreed-upon dividends and in this respect resemble bonds. Preferred dividends have priority over ordinary dividends and may have voting rights. When preferred dividends are not paid in a year, the dividend obligations are typically carried over to the next year, with priority over other dividends. Preferred shares often have an embedded option to convert into common equity and may be callable by the firm at prespecified dates (for a model of preferred stock value, see Emanuel 1983). Although only a small percentage of exchange-listed firms use preferred stock for financing, it is often used to fund new ventures (Gilson & Schizer 2003).

5. THE USE OF THE COST OF CAPITAL IN CAPITAL BUDGETING

5.1. A Firm's Weighted Average Cost of Capital

Earlier, we defined the cost of capital as an opportunity cost that corresponds to the expected return an investor can earn elsewhere in the market for a comparable investment with similar systematic risk. Because a firm uses a mix of securities to fund its operations, the firm's cost of capital is a weighted average of the costs of the different types of capital the firm uses. The costs of the different types of capital, and hence the WACC, depend on how the funds are used. For example, when the proceeds are used to acquire another firm, the acquiring firm may have to change the capital structure of the target firm to reflect the risks and costs/benefits involved.

For expositional convenience, we consider only two types of funding: straight debt and common stock.[14] In this section, we assume that interest payments on debt are not allowed as expenses for computing corporate income taxes and that there are no financial-distress or agency-related costs. In this case, capital structure is irrelevant. The cash flow available for distribution to the equity holders and debtholders of the firm, which is often referred to as the unlevered free cash flow (FCF), is given by

$$\text{FCF} = \text{EBIT}\,(1 - T_C) - \text{NINV}, \tag{7.}$$

where EBIT represents earnings before interest and taxes, and NINV represents net investment (capital expenditures minus depreciation plus change in net working capital). Define the pretax WACC (unlevered cost of capital), R_U, as

$$\text{WACC}_{\text{pretax}} = R_U = R_D \frac{D}{D+S} + R_S \frac{S}{D+S}, \tag{8.}$$

where D and S represent the market values of debt and equity, and R_D and R_S the corresponding expected returns; we omit the time subscript t to simplify notation. Discounting unlevered free cash flows by the unlevered cost of capital gives the value of the hypothetical all-equity (unlevered) firm, V_U.

[14]Operating leases, the most common off-balance-sheet financing method, require special mention. If the value of operating leases is substantial and is not included in the working capital, it is desirable to capitalize and include it as a liability in the capital structure of the firm.

5.2. A Firm's Cost of Capital with Debt Tax Shield

We now describe three main methods that are generally used to account for the value of debt tax shields[15]: the WACC approach, the levered cash flow to total capital [or capital cash flow (CCF)] approach, and the adjusted present value (APV) approach.

Define WACC as

$$\mathrm{WACC} = R_D(1 - T_C)\frac{D}{D+S} + R_S\frac{S}{D+S}. \qquad 9.$$

WACC represents a tax-adjusted discount rate (Miles & Ezzell 1980). Discounting the unlevered free cash flow at WACC yields the value of the levered firm, V_L, i.e., the value of the debt and equity of the firm. Surveys conducted over the past 25 years find that 74–93% of firms surveyed use WACC calculations to evaluate projects (Bierman 1993, Bruner et al. 1998, Gitman & Vandenberg 2000, Jagannathan et al. 2016).[16]

In the CCF approach, which is due to Kaplan & Ruback (1995) and Ruback (2002) and is also known as compressed APV, the present value of capital cash flows (defined as FCF plus the interest tax shield, $R_D T_C$) is computed using the unlevered cost of capital, R_U, which gives the value of the levered firm, V_L.

In the APV approach, introduced by Myers (1974), the present value of the tax shield is computed separately and added to the unlevered value of the firm, i.e., $V_L = V_U + V_{TS}$, where V_{TS} is the present value of the interest tax shield.

We now use the stochastic discount factor approach (Hansen & Richard 1987) to derive the value of the tax shield under various assumptions. The discussion using the stochastic discount factor relies on the work of Arzac & Glosten (2005). Following Arzac & Glosten, we can write the value of the hypothetical unlevered all-equity firm as

$$V_{U,0} = \sum_{t=1}^{\infty} E\left[M_t \mathrm{FCF}_t\right], \qquad 10.$$

where M_t is the time-t stochastic discount factor[17] and FCF_t is the time-t free cash flow. The stochastic discount factor represents the time-zero price of a dollar received at time t if a particular set of market conditions prevail, divided by the probability of such conditions prevailing at time t. As we assumed that the firm is financed only by common equity and straight debt, the time-zero value of the levered firm is given by

$$V_{L,0} = S_0 + D_0, \qquad 11.$$

where S_0 and D_0 are the time-zero value of equity and debt, respectively. Then the value of the tax shield is given by

$$V_{TS,0} = V_{L,0} - V_{U,0}. \qquad 12.$$

For interested readers, we now provide a derivation based on the stochastic discount factor representation, following Arzac & Glosten (2005). To those not familiar with this framework

[15] Graham (2000) estimates that interest tax shields account for 9.7% of firm value (before personal taxes). Cooper & Nyborg (2007) illustrate this point with the example of a company with a 30% debt-to-total capital ratio and a 40% corporate tax rate. In this case, and under some assumptions that we discuss later, the debt tax shield accounts for 12% of the total firm value.

[16] Mukhlynina & Nyborg (2016) survey consultants, investment bankers, private equity professionals, and asset managers, predominantly based in Western Europe, and report that 82% of the respondents "almost always" or "always" use WACC. Of respondents to their survey, 41.5% are consultants, 26.5% investment bankers, 21.3% private equity professionals, and 10.7% asset managers.

[17] When the CAPM holds, $M_t = a + bR_t^M$, where a and b are constants and R_t^M is the time-t return on the market index portfolio; for an extensive discussion of the stochastic discount factor framework, see Cochrane (2005).

Table 1 Tax shields, cost of unlevered equity, and formulas for unlevering equity betas under different leverage assumptions

	Constant debt level	Constant market leverage ratio: Discrete	Constant market leverage ratio: Continuous
Value of tax savings	$V_{TS} = T_C D$ (Modigliani & Miller 1963, equation 3)	$V_{TS} = \left(\frac{T_C R_D D}{R_U - g}\right)\left(\frac{1+R_U}{1+R_D}\right)$ (Miles & Ezzell 1985, equation 21, for $g = 0$; Arzac & Glosten 2005, table 1)	$V_{TS} = \frac{T_C R_D D}{R_U - \gamma}$ (Harris & Pringle 1985, p. 240, for $\gamma = 0$; Arzac & Glosten 2005, table 1)
Cost of equity	$R_S = R_U + \frac{D}{S}(1 - T_C)(R_U - R_D)$ (Modigliani & Miller 1963, equation 12.c)	$R_S = R_U + \left[(R_U - R_D)\left(1 - \frac{T_C R_D}{1+R_D}\right)\right]\frac{D}{S}$ (Taggart 1991, exhibit 2, equation 2B.4)	$R_S = R_U + \frac{D}{S}(R_U - R_D)$ (Taggart 1991, exhibit 2, equation 2C.4)
Tax-adjusted discount rate	$W_L = \left(1 - T_C \frac{D}{S+D}\right) R_U$ (Miller & Modigliani 1966, equation 9)	$W_L = R_U - T_C R_D \left(\frac{D}{D+S}\right)\left(\frac{1+R_U}{1+R_D}\right)$ (Miles & Ezzell 1980, equation 20)	$W_L = R_U - \frac{T_C R_D D}{S+D}$ (Harris & Pringle 1985, p. 239, for $\gamma = 0$; Arzac & Glosten 2005, table 1)
Levered beta	$\beta_S = [1 + (1 - T_C)\frac{D}{S}]\beta_U$ (Hamada 1972, equations 4a and 5)	$\beta_S = \left[1 + \left(1 - \frac{T_C R_D}{1+R_D}\right)\frac{D}{S}\right]\beta_U - \left(1 - \frac{T_C R_D}{1+R_D}\right)\frac{D}{S}\beta_D$ (Miles & Ezzell 1985, equation 27, for $\beta_D = 0$; Arzac & Glosten 2005, table 1)	$\beta_S = \left(1 + \frac{D}{S}\right)\beta_U - \left(\frac{D}{S}\right)\beta_D$ (Harris & Pringle 1985; Miles & Ezzell 1985; Sick 1990; Taggart 1991; Ruback 2002; Arzac & Glosten 2005, p. 458)

The value of the levered firm is the sum of the market value of debt and equity, $V_L = D + S$. The value of the tax shield is $V_{TS} = V_L - V_U$, where V_L is the value of the levered firm and V_U is the value of the unlevered firm. A firm's perpetual growth rate is denoted by g. We consider only corporate taxes.

and to practitioners in general, we recommend skipping the rest of this section and moving on to Section 5.3, and we refer to **Table 1**. **Table 1** provides formulas for tax shields, for the cost of unlevered equity, and for unlevering equity betas under different capital structure scenarios.

Assuming that the market value of the outstanding debt changes only because of new issues or principal payments and that these are undertaken to maintain a constant market leverage ratio, Arzac & Glosten (2005, p. 454) show that the value of tax shields is given by

$$V_{TS,0} = T_C D_0 + T_C \frac{D_0}{S_0} \sum_{t=1}^{\infty} E\left[M_t (S_t - S_{t-1})\right]. \qquad 13.$$

Suppose $\text{FCF}_t = \text{FCF} + \varepsilon_t$, where $E_t(\varepsilon_{t+1}) = 0$. In this case, it can be verified that equity value is a constant independent of time, i.e., $S_t = S$ (we omit the time subscript 0 for notational convenience). The second term in Equation 13 becomes zero, giving the well-known result of Modigliani & Miller (1963), $V_{TS} = T_C D$. Equation 13 also assumes firms to be profitable enough to pay the full corporate tax rate every year in perpetuity (Cooper & Nyborg 2007).

When $\text{FCF}_{t+1} = \text{FCF}_t(1 + \varepsilon_{t+1})$ and $E_t[M_{t+1}\varepsilon_{t+1}] = 0$, we also get $V_{TS} = T_C D$. Another case is when $E_t[M_{t+1}\varepsilon_{t+1}] < 0$. This arises when the CAPM holds and $S_t - S_{t-1}$ is positively correlated with the market portfolio and negatively correlated with the stochastic discount factor. In this case, changes in debt levels are also negatively correlated with the stochastic discount factor. Hence, $V_{TS} < T_C D$.

WACC assumes that the firm's market leverage ratio remains constant; if the firm's market value changes, the capital structure is rebalanced. When the future value of the firm is uncertain, a constant leverage ratio means that the debt level and the corresponding tax shields are also uncertain. Miles & Ezzell (1980) observe that at time $t-1$, the levered firm value, $V_{L,t-1}$, is known with certainty, and thus the tax shield at time t has no systematic risk. At time $t-2$, however, the tax shield at time t is uncertain because the value of the firm at time $t-1$ is a random variable from the perspective of time $t-2$. Therefore, we discount the tax shield in the first year at the debt rate, R_D, and the tax shields in the following periods at the unlevered cost of equity, R_U. When cash flows are expected to grow in perpetuity at a constant rate g per period, the level of debt is also expected to increase at the same rate, as is the value of future tax shields. Arzac & Glosten (2005) show that the value of the tax shield is given by

$$V_{TS,0} = \left(\frac{T_C R_D D_0}{R_U - g}\right)\left(\frac{1+R_U}{1+R_D}\right) \qquad 14.$$

[this result is derived by Miles & Ezzell (1980) using backward iteration]. Cooper & Nyborg (2008) argue that we should use the debt's yield as the cost of debt rather than its expected rate of return because interest payments are tax deductible. **Table 1** also includes the expression for the value of tax shields when market leverage is adjusted continuously.

In contrast to the WACC approach, APV accounts for the present value of tax shields from debt separately and, therefore, can allow for arbitrary time series patterns in leverage. Even when the leverage ratio remains constant, the interest tax shield will vary over time, depending on the future value of the firm. Therefore, with a constant market leverage ratio, the tax shield is as risky as the assets of the firm (Harris & Pringle 1985, Miles & Ezzell 1985). The stochastic discount factor approach to valuation used by Arzac & Glosten (2005) clarifies the issues involved in the debate that followed the work of Fernández (2004).[18]

5.3. Divisional/Project Cost of Capital

The risk of a project within a firm typically differs from the firm's overall risk. The same holds for the cost of capital. Because a division or a project is not traded as a separate entity, the systematic risk (beta, as we assume that the CAPM holds) of the project cannot be estimated using standard methods.

The common practice is to use information about comparable firms to infer the asset beta of the industry to which a project belongs. Most textbooks discuss the pure play approach, introduced by Fuller & Kerr (1981), to estimate divisional cost of capital. A pure play is a firm that operates in only one line of business. In evaluating a project, one would only select firms focusing on one line of business, which should be the same as that of the project. The main drawback of this approach is the lack of availability of pure plays; it is difficult to find a sufficient number of comparable firms, given that multidivisional firms are not eligible peers. Further, pure

[18] Assuming that debt grows at rate g, according to Fernández (2004), the present value of tax savings becomes $V_{TS} = (T_D R_D D)/(R_U - g)$. Arzac & Glosten (2005) and Cooper & Nyborg (2006) show that this is a result of using $V_{TS} = DT_C$ (from Modigliani & Miller 1963) for a constant market leverage policy, which is incorrect. Arzac & Glosten (2005) show that this would hold if one ignores that D_{t-1} has no systematic risk at time 1 and discounts the principal payments at the cost of unlevered equity. The result does not hold under continuous rebalancing of leverage, as shown by Arzac & Glosten (2005), or under other assumptions (Cooper & Nyborg 2006).

plays are likely smaller firms, whose expected return is measured with more error. To remedy this problem, Ehrhardt & Bhagwat (1991) propose the full-information approach, where both pure play and multidivisional firms are candidate comparable firms. A firm is a portfolio of all its projects, and the risk of the firm is its weighted average. If we know the market values of the divisions, we can compute the divisional weights, and estimates of the betas can be obtained from a cross-sectional regression of the multidivisional firm beta on these weights (Ehrhardt & Bhagwat 1991, Krueger & Linke 1994, Kaplan & Peterson 1998). Chua, Chang & Wu (2006) observe that the original full-information approach for estimating divisional betas assumes that multidivisional firms finance all of their divisions in the same way. However, the pure play approach can be combined with the full-information approach to get better estimates of project betas.

Once we have determined the set of comparable firms, we need to remove the effect of capital structure on the equity betas of comparable firms. Under Modigliani & Miller's (1963) assumptions of constant debt level and risk-free debt, the levered beta, β_S, and unlevered beta, β_U, are related as follows (Hamada 1972):

$$\beta_S = \left[1 + (1 - T_C)\frac{D}{S}\right]\beta_U. \tag{15}$$

This formula is consistent with the value of the tax shields being proportional to the market value of debt. Therefore, the tax shields are as risky as the debt. When comparable firms keep a constant market leverage ratio, β_S and β_U are related as follows (Harris & Pringle 1985):

$$\beta_S = \beta_U + \left(\frac{D}{S}\right)(\beta_U - \beta_D). \tag{16}$$

In this case, tax shields are as risky as the assets of the firm.

Miles & Ezzell (1980) consider more general leverage ratio dynamics and assume that tax shields are as risky as debt during the first period and as risky as the firm's assets in the following periods. In this case,

$$\beta_S = \beta_U + \left(\frac{D}{S}\right)(\beta_U - \beta_D)\left(1 - \frac{T_C R_D}{(1 + R_D)}\right). \tag{17}$$

In selecting the set of comparable firms, we need to address at least three questions. First, how should we select comparable firms: Should we use industry affiliation, size, growth, or a combination of other firm characteristics? Second, if industry affiliation helps to identify accurate comparable firms, what is the preferred industry classification system? Third, what is the optimal number of comparable firms to be used? There is a vast literature addressing these questions. For selection criteria, see Bhojraj & Lee (2002) and Ecker et al. (2013); for issues relating to industry classification, see Bhojraj & Lee (2002) and Bhojraj, Lee & Oler (2003); for a discussion on the optimal number of comparable firms to be used, see Eberhart (2001).

We calculate the expected return on equity and the WACC between the years 2000 and 2016. The summary statistics and variable definitions used in the analysis are reported in **Table 2**. The average WACC for this period is 8.33%, with a median of 7.96%. After several filters are applied to the data, the sample contains 6,680 firm-year observations over 17 years, or 4,277 days. **Table 2** describes the construction of our final sample.

The year-end common variables for 2016 corresponding to **Table 2** are 2.45% for the 10-year Treasury bond yield; 9% for the expected market return; and 3.98%, 4.03%, 4.20%, and 4.73% for Moody's corporate bond ratings AAA, AA, A, and BAA, respectively. These common variables

Table 2 Summary statistics

Variable	Average	Standard deviation	Median	Number of observations
Common to firms				
Moody's rating A	5.601	1.182	5.770	17
Moody's rating AA	5.304	1.120	5.490	17
Moody's rating AAA	5.042	1.022	5.260	17
Moody's rating BAA	6.210	1.133	6.210	17
$E[R^M]$	10.030	1.154	9.750	17
10-year Treasury bond yield	3.451	1.138	3.830	17
Annualized value-weighted R^M	9.360	23.710	25.560	4,277
R^F	2.160	0.152	1.080	4,277
Specific to each firm				
β_S	0.923	0.456	0.900	6,680
T_C (%)	32.660	11.500	34.790	6,680
$E[R_S]$	9.655	3.164	9.247	6,680
$E[R_D]$	5.970	1.144	5.980	6,680
$D/(D+S)$	0.243	0.161	0.209	6,680
$S/(D+S)$	0.757	0.161	0.791	6,680
WACC	8.333	2.593	7.959	6,680

This table reports the summary statistics of the variables used in the calculation of the expected return on equity and the calculation of the weighted average cost of capital (WACC) between 2000 and 2016. The variables are classified as either common to all firms in the sample or specific to each firm in the sample. Returns and yields are annualized. Moody's bond indices are from Bloomberg; $E[R^M]$ is the expected market rate of return computed using data from Li, Ng & Swaminathan (2013), provided by B. Swaminathan; and the 10-year Treasury bond yield is the 10-year US Treasury constant maturity rate. We use the year-end value of these variables to report the statistics. Annualized value-weighted R^M is the annualized average daily value-weighted total (i.e., including distributions) market return from CRSP. R^F is the annualized average daily risk-free rate from Kenneth French's website: **http://mba.tuck.dartmouth.edu/pages/faculty/ken.french/data_library.html**. β_S is the Dimson beta calculated from 1 year of daily stock returns. The regression is of the form

$$R_{i,t} - R_t^F = \alpha_i + \beta_{i,0}\left(R_t^M - R_t^F\right) + \beta_{i,1}\left(R_{t-1}^M - R_{t-1}^F\right) + \beta_{i,2}\left(R_{t-2}^M - R_{t-2}^F\right) + \epsilon_{i,t},$$

where R_t^F is the day-t risk-free rate from Kenneth French's website, R_t^M is the day-t value-weighted market average returns including distribution from CRSP, and $R_{i,t}$ is the day-t return on stock of firm i from CRSP. Equity beta for each firm i is the sum of the coefficient estimates for $\beta_{i,0}$, $\beta_{i,1}$, and $\beta_{i,2}$. When a firm has multiple classes of stocks, beta equity for that firm is chosen as the beta of the primary stock of that firm identified by the Compustat-CRSP link-table on WRDS. We require 220 days of returns data for betas, and we winsorize betas at -3 and 5 as in the work of Levi & Welch (2016). Further, T_C is the effective corporate tax rate, calculated as $T_C = 1 - $ (net income)/(pretax income). For firms with negative pretax income or negative net income, we use the statutory tax rate of 35%. The expected return on equity, $E[R_S]$, is calculated using Equation 1. $E[R_S] < 0$ are dropped from the calculations. WACC is calculated using Equation 9. $E[R_D]$ is the average bond yield corresponding to the rating of the firm. In **Table 3**, we show the relation between ratings and bond yields. D is the book value of debt, defined as debt in current liabilities plus total long-term debt (dlc + dltt in Compustat mnemonics). S is the market value of equity, computed using data from CRSP. For firms with multiple classes, we calculate the market capitalization as the sum of market capitalization of all classes of common shares.

are used to construct the cost of capital for the year 2016, reported in **Table 3**. The average WACC in 2016 is 7.84%. In **Table 4** we report the relation between ratings and bond yields in order to construct the expected return on debt. The average bond yields correspond to the rating of the firm.

In **Table 5** we report the WACC across the 10 Fama–French industries for the year 2016. **Figure 1** plots the minimum and maximum value-weighted WACC for the 10 Fama–French industries.

Table 3 **Weighted average cost of capital (WACC) in 2016**

Variables	Average	Standard deviation	Median	Number of observations
β_S	1.038	0.557	0.988	400
T_C (%)	29.560	11.530	32.480	400
$E[R_S]$	9.249	3.651	8.924	400
$E[R_D]$	4.570	0.256	4.730	400
$D/(D+S)$	0.228	0.131	0.205	400
$S/(D+S)$	0.772	0.131	0.795	400
WACC	7.840	2.710	7.711	400

This table reports the summary statistics for WACC and its components in 2016. All variables are defined in **Table 2**.

Table 4 **Relation between issuer ratings and bond yields**

Moody's issuer rating	S&P long-term local issuer credit rating	Bond yield
Aaa	AAA, AAA*–	Moody's Bond Indices Corporate AAA
Aa1, Aa1*+, Aa1*–	AA+, AA+*+, AA+*–	Moody's Bond Indices Corporate AA
Aa2, Aa2*+, Aa2*–	AA, AA*+, AA*–	Moody's Bond Indices Corporate AA
Aa3, Aa3*+, Aa3*–	AA–, AA–*+, AA–*–	Moody's Bond Indices Corporate AA
A1, A1*+, A1*–	A+, A+*–, A+*+	Moody's Bond Indices Corporate A
A2, A2*+, A2*–	A, A*+, A*–	Moody's Bond Indices Corporate A
A3, A3*+, A3*–	A–, A–*+, A–*–, A–u	Moody's Bond Indices Corporate A
Baa1, Baa1*, Baa1*+, Baa1*–	BBB+, BBB+*, BBB+*+, BBB+*–, BBB+u	Moody's Bond Indices Corporate BAA
Baa2, Baa2*, Baa2*+, Baa2*–	BBB, BBB*, BBB*+, BBB*–, BBBu	Moody's Bond Indices Corporate BAA
Baa3, Baa3*, Baa3*+, Baa3*–	BBB–, BBB–*+, BBB–*, BBB–*–, BBB–u	Moody's Bond Indices Corporate BAA

This table reports the relation between Moody's issuer rating, S&P long-term local issuer credit rating, and bond yield. For bond yields, we use the year-end value of daily Moody's bond indices, which is the average bond yield for all the bonds that have a common rating. We use both Moody's issuer rating and the S&P long-term local issuer credit rating to identify the rating of a firm, as sometimes only one of the two ratings is available for a firm. Ratings and yields are from Bloomberg.

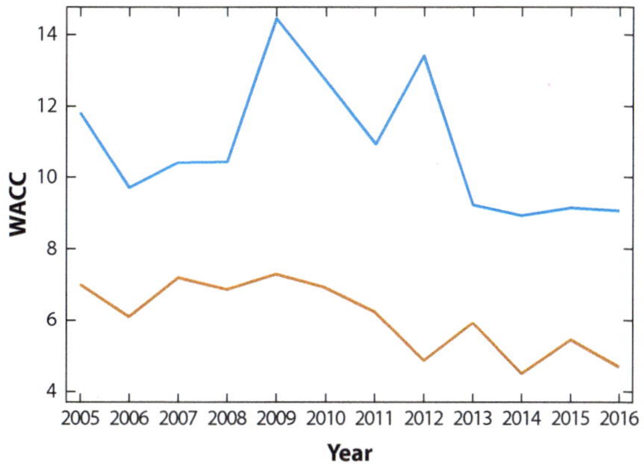

Figure 1

This figure plots the minimum (*brown*) and maximum (*blue*) value-weighted average cost of capital (WACC) for the 10 Fama–French industries between 2005 and 2016. Variables are defined in **Table 2**.

Table 5 Weighted average cost of capital (WACC) across industries in 2016

Variable	Durable	Energy	High-tech	Health	Manufacturing	Nondurable	Shops	Telecom	Utilities	Other
Market capitalization	333	1,486	4,782	2,193	2,240	1,511	2,301	1,287	999	2,271
Market capitalization for firms with rating	218	1,246	3,486	1,627	1,767	1,304	1,750	994	856	1,183
% Coverage by market capitalization	65.5%	83.8%	72.9%	74.2%	78.9%	86.3%	76.0%	77.2%	85.7%	52.1%
Number of firms	78	154	569	544	389	135	318	77	101	389
Number of firms with rating	12	26	59	23	77	34	43	10	66	50
% Coverage by number of fims	15.4%	16.9%	10.4%	4.2%	19.8%	25.2%	13.5%	13.0%	65.3%	12.9%
β_S	1.42	1.25	0.98	0.74	0.97	0.53	0.77	0.68	0.53	1.05
T_C (%)	30.71	22.35	20.60	18.35	26.60	27.77	33.84	35.69	32.32	25.37
$E[R_S]$	11.74	10.65	8.87	7.28	8.78	5.92	7.52	6.90	5.93	9.32
$E[R_D]$	4.61	4.33	4.22	4.28	4.29	4.42	4.34	4.55	4.61	4.49
$D/(D+S)$	0.44	0.18	0.12	0.15	0.16	0.18	0.14	0.27	0.41	0.23
$S/(D+S)$	0.56	0.82	0.88	0.85	0.84	0.82	0.86	0.73	0.59	0.77
WACC	8.02	9.05	8.21	6.66	7.78	5.40	6.85	5.86	4.69	7.93

This table reports summary statistics for WACC and its components across the 10 Fama–French industries in 2016. All variables are defined in **Table 2**. We compute the average of the firm-specific measures weighted by the market capitalization of each firm. In aggregating the components to compute WACC, we restrict the sample to only those firms that have a WACC calculated in **Table 2**. The definitions of the Fama–French industries can be found at Kenneth French's website: **http://mba.tuck.dartmouth.edu/pages/faculty/ken.french/Data_Library/det_10_ind_port.html**. The market capitalization of all Compustat/CRSP US incorporated nonfinancial firms is shown in billions of dollars. Market capitalization for firms with ratings represents the market capitalization of firms with bond yield data available in billions of dollars. Also shown are the total number of firms and the number of firms for which some of the WACC component data are not available (mostly bond yield data).

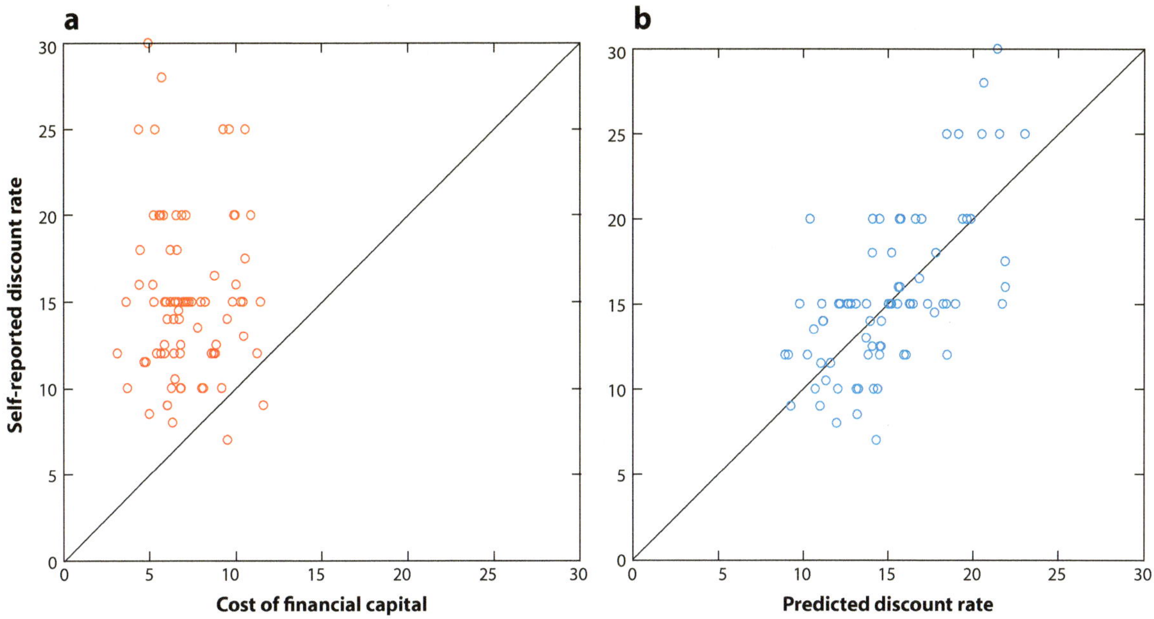

Figure 2

Self-reported discount rates versus cost of financial capital and predicted cost of capital. (*a*) Each survey firm's self-reported discount rate is plotted against its cost of financial capital. The capital asset pricing model (CAPM) is used to compute the cost of equity on the basis of the firm's beta from Barra, an equity risk premium of 3.83% (Graham & Harvey 2005), and a debt interest rate corresponding to the predicted rating computed using the model of Jorion, Shi & Zhang (2009). (*b*) Each survey firm's self-reported discount rate is plotted against the discount rate predicted by the model of Jagannathan et al. (2016). Both panels also show the 45° line. Figure adapted from Jagannathan et al. (2016) with permission.

5.4. Operational and Managerial Constraints Affect the Capital Budgeting Process

Operational and managerial constraints may lead firms to use higher discount rates, exceeding their financial cost of capital, and to forgo positive investment opportunities. Jagannathan et al. (2016) evaluate different hypotheses and conclude that operational issues can prevent firms from taking profitable opportunities. In circumstances where there is limited managerial bandwidth, firms may also be forced to forgo projects with positive net present value, suggesting that these dimensions are more important than financial constraints for many firms. **Figure 2** plots the self-reported discount rates (hurdle rates) of 86 survey respondents that provided their identity against the firm's financial cost of capital (**Figure 2*a***) and against discount-rate estimates from a model that includes operational constraints (**Figure 2*b***). The estimates from the model by Jagannathan et al. (2016) shown in **Figure 2*b*** are more closely aligned to the 45° line, i.e., these estimates better explain the discount rates firms use than financial cost of capital alone as in **Figure 2*a***.

6. CONCLUDING REMARKS

In a world with frictions, a firm's cost of capital depends on its capital structure and on taxes. We review the methods used to estimate the costs of equity and debt, the two most important components of capital structure. The Sharpe–Lintner CAPM continues to be the most widely used method for computing the cost of equity capital. We review methods to compute the expected return on debt, given the credit risk involved and the promised yield. WACC combines the costs of equity and debt, accounting for debt's tax benefits, assuming the debt-to-equity ratio is constant. We discuss other methods that account for the tax benefits of debt and that remain valid when capital structure changes over time. As Arzac & Glosten (2005) show, the stochastic discount factor approach (Hansen & Richard 1987) provides a framework for relating the different approaches used in practice.

DISCLOSURE STATEMENT

The authors are not aware of any affiliations, memberships, funding, or financial holdings that might be perceived as affecting the objectivity of this review.

ACKNOWLEDGMENTS

We thank Marco Sammon for valuable comments and Jiaheng Yu for excellent research assistance.

LITERATURE CITED

Almeida H, Philippon T. 2007. The risk-adjusted cost of financial distress. *J. Finance* 62(6):2557–86

Altman EI. 1991. Defaults and returns on high-yield bonds through the first half of 1991. *Financ. Anal. J.* 47(6):67–77

Andersen TG, Bollerslev T, Diebold FX, Wu G. 2006. Realized beta: persistence and predictability. In *Advances in Econometrics: Econometric Analysis of Economic and Financial Time Series*, Vol. B, ed. T Fomby, D Terrell, pp. 1–40. Bingley, UK: Emerald Group

Anderson RW, Sundaresan S. 1996. Design and valuation of debt contracts. *Rev. Financ. Stud.* 9(1):37–68

Arzac ER, Glosten LR. 2005. A reconsideration of tax shield valuation. *Eur. Financ. Manag.* 11(4):453–61

Ayache E, Forsyth PA, Vetzal KR. 2003. Valuation of convertible bonds with credit risk. *J. Deriv.* 11(1):9–29

Bansal R, Yaron A. 2004. Risks for the long run: a potential resolution of asset pricing puzzles. *J. Finance* 59(4):1481–509

Barone-Adesi G, Bermúdez A, Hatgioannides J. 2003. Two-factor convertible bonds valuation using the method of characteristics/finite elements. *J. Econ. Dyn. Control* 27(10):1801–31

Baskin J. 1989. Dividend policy and the volatility of common stock. *J. Portf. Manag.* 15(3):19–25

Berk JB, DeMarzo PM. 2017. *Corporate Finance*. Boston: Pearson. 4th ed.

Berk JB, Stanton R, Zechner J. 2010. Human capital, bankruptcy, and capital structure. *J. Finance* 65(3):891–926

Berk JB, van Binsbergen JH. 2015. Measuring skill in the mutual fund industry. *J. Financ. Econ.* 118(1):1–20

Bhojraj S, Lee CMC. 2002. Who is my peer? A valuation-based approach to the selection of comparable firms. *J. Account. Res.* 40(2):407–39

Bhojraj S, Lee CMC, Oler DK. 2003. What's my line? A comparison of industry classification schemes for capital market research. *J. Account. Res.* 41(5):745–74

Bierman H Jr. 1993. Capital budgeting in 1992: a survey. *Financ. Manag.* 22(3):24

Black F, Jensen MC, Scholes M. 1972. The capital asset pricing model: some empirical tests. In *Studies in the Theory of Capital Markets*, ed. M Jensen, pp. 79–121. New York: Praeger

Blume ME, Lim F, MacKinlay C. 1998. The declining credit quality of U.S. corporate debt: myth or reality? *J. Finance* 53(4):1389–413

Bollerslev T, Li SZ, Todorov V. 2016. Roughing up beta: continuous versus discontinuous betas, and the cross-section of expected stock returns. *J. Financ. Econ.* 120(3):464–90

Bolton P, Scharfstein DS. 1990. A theory of predation based on agency problems in financial contracting. *Am. Econ. Rev.* 80(1):93–106

Breeden DT. 1979. An intertemporal asset pricing model with stochastic consumption and investment opportunities. *J. Financ. Econ.* 7(3):265–96

Brennan MJ, Schwartz ES. 1977. Convertible bonds: valuation and optimal strategies for call and conversion. *J. Finance* 32(5):1699–715
Brennan MJ, Schwartz ES. 1978. Corporate income taxes, valuation, and the problem of optimal capital structure. *J. Bus.* 51(1):103–14
Bruner RF, Eades KM, Harris RS, Higgins RC. 1998. Best practices in estimating the cost of capital: survey and synthesis. *Financ. Pract. Educ.* 8(1):13–28
Campbell JY. 1993. Intertemporal asset pricing without consumption data. *Am. Econ. Rev.* 83(3):487–512
Campbell JY, Cochrane J. 1999. Force of habit: a consumption-based explanation of aggregate stock market behavior. *J. Political Econ.* 107(2):205–51
Campbell JY, Shiller RJ. 1988. The dividend-price ratio and expectations of future dividends and discount factors. *Rev. Financ. Stud.* 1(3):195–228
Campello M, Chen L, Zhang L. 2008. Expected returns, yield spreads, and asset pricing tests. *Rev. Financ. Stud.* 21(3):1297–338
Chevalier JA. 1995. Capital structure and product-market competition: empirical evidence from the supermarket industry. *Am. Econ. Rev.* 85(3):415–35
Chua J, Chang PC, Wu Z. 2006. The full-information approach for estimating divisional betas: implementation issues and tests. *J. Appl. Finance* 16(1):53–61
Claus J, Thomas J. 2001. Equity premia as low as three percent? Evidence from analysts' earnings forecasts for domestic and international stock markets. *J. Finance* 56(5):1629–66
Cochrane JH. 2005. *Asset Pricing*. Princeton, NJ: Princeton Univ. Press. Revis. ed.
Cochrane JH. 2008. The dog that did not bark: a defense of return predictability. *Rev. Financ. Stud.* 21(4):1533–75
Collin-Dufresne P, Goldstein RS, Martin JS. 2001. The determinants of credit spread changes. *J. Finance* 56(6):2177–207
Cooper IA, Nyborg KG. 2006. The value of tax shields IS equal to the present value of tax shields. *J. Financ. Econ.* 81(1):215–25
Cooper IA, Nyborg KG. 2007. Valuing the debt tax shield. *J. Appl. Corp. Finance* 19(2):50–59
Cooper IA, Nyborg KG. 2008. Tax-adjusted discount rates with investor taxes and risky debt. *Financ. Manag.* 37(2):365–79
Cosemans M, Frehen R, Schotman PC, Bauer R. 2016. Estimating security betas using prior information based on firm fundamentals. *Rev. Financ. Stud.* 29(4):1072–112
Damodaran A. 2001. *Corporate Finance: Theory and Practice*. New York: Wiley. 2nd ed.
Damodaran A. 2002. *Estimating risk parameters*. Work. Pap., Stern Sch. Bus., N.Y. Univ.
Damodaran A. 2012. *Investment Valuation: Tools and Techniques for Determining the Value of Any Asset*. Hoboken, NJ: Wiley. 3rd ed.
Dasgupta S, Sengupta K. 1993. Sunk investment, bargaining and choice of capital structure. *Int. Econ. Rev.* 34(1):203–20
Dimson E. 1979. Risk measurement when shares are subject to infrequent trading. *J. Financ. Econ.* 7(2):197–226
Duffee GR. 1999. Estimating the price of default risk. *Rev. Financ. Stud.* 12(1):197–226
Duffie D, Singleton KJ. 1999. Modeling term structures of defaultable bonds. *Rev. Financ. Stud.* 12(4):687–720
Duffie D, Singleton KJ. 2012. *Credit Risk: Pricing, Measurement, and Management*. Princeton, NJ: Princeton Univ. Press
Easton PD. 2004. PE ratios, PEG ratios, and estimating the implied expected rate of return on equity capital. *Account. Rev.* 79(1):73–95
Eberhart AC. 2001. Comparable firms and the precision of equity valuations. *J. Bank. Finance* 25(7):1367–400
Ecker F, Francis J, Olsson P, Schipper K. 2013. Estimation sample selection for discretionary accruals models. *J. Account. Econ.* 56(2):190–211
Ehrhardt MC, Bhagwat YN. 1991. A full-information approach for estimating divisional betas. *Financ. Manag.* 20(2):60–69
Elton EJ, Gruber MJ, Agrawal D, Mann C. 2001. Explaining the rate spread on corporate bonds. *J. Finance* 56(1):247–77
Emanuel D. 1983. A theoretical model for valuing preferred stock. *J. Finance* 38(4):1133–55

Epstein LG, Zin SE. 1989. Substitution, risk aversion, and the temporal behavior of consumption and asset returns: a theoretical framework. *Econometrica* 57(4):937–69

Fama EF, French KR. 1993. Common risk factors in the returns on stocks and bonds. *J. Financ. Econ.* 33(1):3–56

Fama EF, French KR. 1997. Industry cost of equity. *J. Financ. Econ.* 43(2):152–93

Fama EF, French KR. 2002. The equity premium. *J. Finance* 67(2):637–59

Fama EF, MacBeth JD. 1973. Risk, return and equilibrium: empirical tests. *J. Political Econ.* 81(3):607–36

Fed. Reserve Syst. 2015. *Financial accounts of the United States 2015*. Stat. Release, Board Gov., Fed. Reserve Syst., Washington, DC

Fernández P. 2004. The value of tax shields is NOT equal to the present value of tax shields. *J. Financ. Econ.* 73(1):145–65

Fernández P. 2009. *The equity premium in 100 textbooks*. Work. Pap., IESE Bus. Sch., Madrid

Ferreira MA, Santa-Clara P. 2011. Forecasting stock market returns: The sum of the parts is more than the whole. *J. Financ. Econ.* 100(3):514–37

Frank MZ, Goyal VK. 2008. Trade-off and pecking order theories of debt. In *Handbook of Empirical Corporate Finance*, Vol. 2, ed. BE Eckbo, pp. 135–202. Amsterdam: Elsevier

Fuller RJ, Kerr HS. 1981. Estimating the divisional cost of capital: an analysis of the pure-play technique. *J. Finance* 36(5):997–1009

Gebhardt WR, Lee CMC, Swaminathan B. 2001. Toward an implied cost of capital. *J. Account. Res.* 39(1):135–76

Gilson RJ, Schizer DM. 2003. Understanding venture capital structure: a tax explanation for convertible preferred stock. *Harvard Law Rev.* 116(3):874–916

Gitman LJ, Vandenberg PA. 2000. Cost of capital techniques used by major US firms: 1997 vs. 1980. *Financ. Pract. Educ.* 10(2):53–68

Goyal A, Welch I. 2008. A comprehensive look at the empirical performance of equity premium prediction. *Rev. Financ. Stud.* 21(4):1455–508

Graham JR. 2000. How big are the tax benefits of debt? *J. Finance* 55(5):1901–41

Graham JR, Harvey CR. 2001. The theory and practice of corporate finance: evidence from the field. *J. Financ. Econ.* 60(2):187–243

Graham JR, Harvey CR. 2005. The long-run equity risk premium. *Finance Res. Lett.* 2:185–94

Graham JR, Leary MT, Roberts MR. 2015. A century of capital structure: the leveraging of corporate America. *J. Financ. Econ.* 118(3):658–83

Grinblatt M, Titman S. 2001. *Financial Markets and Corporate Strategy*. Boston: McGraw-Hill/Irwin. 2nd ed.

Hamada RS. 1972. The effect of the firm's capital structure on the systematic risk of common stocks. *J. Finance* 27(2):435–52

Hansen LP, Richard SF. 1987. The role of conditioning information in deducing testable restrictions implied by dynamic asset pricing models. *Econometrica* 55(3):587–613

Harris M, Raviv A. 1990. Capital structure and the informational role of debt. *J. Finance* 45(2):321–49

Harris RS, Pringle JJ. 1985. Risk-adjusted discount rates: extensions from the average risk case. *J. Financ. Res.* 8(3):237–44

Harvey CR, Liu Y, Zhu H. 2015. ...And the cross-section of expected returns. *Rev. Financ. Stud.* 29(1):5–68

Haugen RA, Senbet LW. 1988. Bankruptcy and agency costs: their significance to the theory of optimal capital structure. *J. Financ. Quant. Anal.* 23(1):27–38

Hennessy CA, Livdan D. 2009. Debt, bargaining, and credibility in firm–supplier relationships. *J. Financ. Econ.* 93(3):382–99

Hu JH, Saa-Requejo J, Santa-Clara P. 2010. A structural model of default risk. *J. Fixed Income* 19(3):77–94

Huang J-Z, Huang M. 2012. How much of the corporate–Treasury yield spread is due to credit risk? *Rev. Asset Pricing Stud.* 2(2):153–202

Ingersoll JE. 1977. A contingent claims valuation of convertible securities. *J. Financ. Econ.* 4(3):289–322

Israel R. 1992. Capital and ownership structures, and the market for corporate control. *Rev. Financ. Stud.* 5(2):181–98

Jagannathan R, Liu B. 2016. *Dividend dynamics, learning, and expected stock index returns*. NBER Work. Pap. 21557

Jagannathan R, Marakani S. 2015. Price-dividend ratio factor proxies for long-run risks. *Rev. Asset Pricing Stud.* 5(1):1–47
Jagannathan R, Matsa DA, Meier I, Tarhan V. 2016. Why do firms use high discount rates? *J. Financ. Econ.* 120(3):445–63
Jagannathan R, McGrattan ER. 1995. The CAPM debate. *Fed. Reserve Bank Minneap. Q. Rev.* 19(4):2–17
Jagannathan R, McGrattan ER, Scherbina A. 2001. The declining U.S. equity premium. *Fed. Reserve Bank Minneap. Q. Rev.* 24(4):3–19
Jagannathan R, Wang Y. 2007. Lazy investors, discretionary consumption, and the cross-section of stock returns. *J. Finance* 62(4):1623–61
Jagannathan R, Wang Z. 1996. The conditional CAPM and the cross-section of expected returns. *J. Finance* 51(1):3–53
Jarrow RA, Lando D, Turnbull SM. 1997. A Markov model for the term structure of credit risk spreads. *Rev. Financ. Stud.* 10(2):481–523
Jensen MC. 1986. Agency costs of free cash flow, corporate finance, and takeovers. *Am. Econ. Rev.* 76(2):323–29
Jorion P, Shi C, Zhang S. 2009. Tightening credit standards: the role of accounting quality. *Rev. Account. Stud.* 14(1):123–60
Kang J-K, Lee YW. 1996. The pricing of convertible debt offerings. *J. Financ. Econ.* 41(2):231–48
Kaplan PD, Peterson JD. 1998. Full-information industry betas. *Financ. Manag.* 27(2):85–93
Kaplan SN, Ruback RS. 1995. The valuation of cash flow forecasts: an empirical analysis. *J. Finance* 50(4):1059–93
Karolyi AG. 1992. Predicting risk: some new generalizations. *Manag. Sci.* 38(1):57–74
Kelly B, Pruitt S. 2013. Market expectations in the cross-section of present values. *J. Finance* 68(5):1721–56
Kester WC. 1986. Capital and ownership structure: a comparison of United States and Japanese manufacturing corporations. *Financ. Manag.* 15(1):5–16
Kogan L, Papanikolaou D. 2014. Growth opportunities, technology shocks, and asset prices. *J. Finance* 69(2):675–718
Korajczyk RA, Lucas DJ, McDonald RL. 1991. The effect of information releases on the pricing and timing of equity issues. *Rev. Financ. Stud.* 4(4):685–708
Krueger MK, Linke CM. 1994. A spanning approach for estimating divisional cost of capital. *Financ. Manag.* 23(1):64–70
Leland HE, Pyle DH. 1977. Informational asymmetries, financial structure, and financial intermediation. *J. Finance* 32(2):371–87
Leland HE, Toft KB. 1996. Optimal capital structure, endogenous bankruptcy, and the term structure of credit spreads. *J. Finance* 51(3):987–1019
Levi Y, Welch I. 2016. *Best practice for cost-of-capital estimates.* Work. Pap. 17-4, Marshall Sch. Bus., Univ. South. Calif.
Li Y, Ng DT, Swaminathan B. 2013. Predicting market returns using aggregate implied cost of capital. *J. Financ. Econ.* 110(2):419–36
Lintner J. 1965. The valuation of risk assets and the selection of risky investments in stock portfolios and capital budgets. *Rev. Econ. Stat.* 47(1):13–37
Longstaff FA, Schwartz ES. 1995. A simple approach to valuing risky fixed and floating rate debt. *J. Finance* 50(3):789–819
Lucas RE. 1978. Asset prices in an exchange economy. *Econometrica* 46(6):1429–45
Madden BJ. 1998. *CFROI Valuation: A Total System Approach to Valuing the Firm.* Chicago: Holt Value Assoc.
Masulis RW, Korwar AN. 1986. Seasoned equity offerings: an empirical investigation. *J. Financ. Econ.* 15(1–2):91–118
McLean RD, Pontiff J. 2015. Does academic research destroy stock return predictability? *J. Finance* 71(1):5–32
Mello AS, Parsons JE. 1992. Measuring the agency cost of debt. *J. Finance* 47(5):1887–904
Merton RC. 1973. An intertemporal capital asset pricing model. *Econometrica* 41(5):867–87
Merton RC. 1974. On the pricing of corporate debt: the risk structure of interest rates. *J. Finance* 29:449–70
Merton RC. 1976. Option pricing when underlying stock returns are discontinuous. *J. Financ. Econ.* 3(1–2):125–44

Merton RC. 1980. On estimating the expected return on the market: an exploratory investigation. *J. Financ. Econ.* 8(4):323–61

Mikkelson WH, Partch MM. 1986. Valuation effects of security offerings and the issuance process. *J. Financ. Econ.* 15(1–2):31–60

Miles JA, Ezzell JR. 1980. The weighted average cost of capital, perfect capital markets, and project life: a clarification. *J. Financ. Quant. Anal.* 15(3):719–30

Miles JA, Ezzell JR. 1985. Reformulation tax shield valuation: a note. *J. Finance* 40(5):1485–92

Miller MH. 1977. Debt and taxes. *J. Finance* 32(2):261–75

Miller MH, Modigliani F. 1966. Some estimates of the cost of capital to the electric utility industry, 1954–57. *Am. Econ. Rev.* 56:333–91

Modigliani F, Miller MH. 1958. The cost of capital, corporation finance and the theory of investment. *Am. Econ. Rev.* 48(3):261–97

Modigliani F, Miller MH. 1963. Corporate income taxes and the cost of capital: a correction. *Am. Econ. Rev.* 53(3):433–43

Morellec E. 2004. Can managerial discretion explain observed leverage ratios? *Rev. Financ. Stud.* 17(1):257–94

Morgan Stanley Res. 2016. *US elections 2016: losing interest*. Res. Rep., Oct. 4

Mukhlynina L, Nyborg KG. 2016. *The choice of valuation techniques in practice: education versus profession*. Res. Pap. 16-36, Swiss Finance Inst., Zurich

Myers SC. 1974. Interactions in corporate financing and investment decisions: implications for capital budgeting. *J. Finance* 29(1):1–25

Myers SC, Majluf NS. 1984. Corporate financing and investment decisions when firms have information that investors do not have. *J. Financ. Econ.* 13(2):187–221

Opler TC, Titman S. 1994. Financial distress and corporate performance. *J. Finance* 49(3):1015–40

Perotti EC, Spier KE. 1993. Capital structure as a bargaining tool: the role of leverage in contract renegotiation. *Am. Econ. Rev.* 83(5):1131–41

Pratt SP, Grabowski R. 2008. *Cost of Capital: Applications and Examples*. New York: Wiley

Ross SA. 1976. The arbitrage theory of capital asset pricing. *J. Econ. Theory* 13(3):341–60

Ross SA. 1977. The determination of financial structure: the incentive-signaling approach. *Bell J. Econ.* 8(1):23–40

Ross SA, Westerfield RW, Jaffe JF, Jordan BD. 2015. *Corporate Finance*. Boston: McGraw-Hill/Irwin. 11th ed.

Ruback RS. 2002. Capital cash flows: a simple approach to valuing risky cash flows. *Financ. Manag.* 31(2):85–103

Scholes M, Williams J. 1977. Estimating betas from nonsynchronous data. *J. Financ. Econ.* 5(3):309–27

Sharpe WF. 1964. Capital asset prices: a theory of market equilibrium under conditions of risk. *J. Finance* 19(3):425–42

Sick GA. 1990. Tax-adjusted discount rates. *Manag. Sci.* 36:1432–50

Strebulaev IA. 2007. Do tests of capital structure theory mean what they say? *J. Finance* 62(4):1747–87

Taggart RA Jr. 1991. Consistent valuation and the cost of capital expressions with corporate and personal taxes. *Financ. Manag.* 20:8–20

Titman S. 1984. The effect of capital structure on a firm's liquidation decision. *J. Financ. Econ.* 13(1):137–51

Titman S, Wessels R. 1988. The determinants of capital structure choice. *J. Finance* 43(1):1–19

van Binsbergen JH, Brandt M, Koijen R. 2012. On the timing and pricing of dividends. *Am. Econ. Rev.* 102(4):1596–618

van Binsbergen JH, Koijen R. 2010. Predictive regressions: a present-value approach. *J. Finance* 65(4):1439–71

Vasicek OA. 1973. A note on using cross-sectional information in Bayesian estimation of security betas. *J. Finance* 28(5):1233–39

Zwiebel J. 1996. Dynamic capital structure under managerial entrenchment. *Am. Econ. Rev.* 86(5):1197–215

The Fundamentals Underlying Oil and Natural Gas Derivative Markets

John E. Parsons

Sloan School of Management, Massachusetts Institute of Technology, Cambridge, Massachusetts 02142; email: jparsons@mit.edu

Annu. Rev. Financ. Econ. 2017. 9:283–300

First published as a Review in Advance on August 11, 2017

The *Annual Review of Financial Economics* is online at financial.annualreviews.org

https://doi.org/10.1146/annurev-financial-110716-032610

Copyright © 2017 by Annual Reviews. All rights reserved

JEL codes: D40, G10, G13, L22

Keywords

commodity futures, commodity derivatives, price discovery, industry structure

Abstract

What determines the range and boundaries of energy derivative markets? Why is the oil futures trade dominated by contracts on two grades and locations when the global trade encompasses many grades and locations? Should we expect change in the near future? We review research on the establishment and performance of energy derivative markets, focusing on the two major energy commodities: oil and natural gas. For both commodities, trade in derivatives arose at the conclusion of a historical process in which production along the value chain that had been coordinated by vertically integrated companies or similar institutional structures switched to being coordinated through markets. Consequently, much of the research reviewed here is about the structural changes that made it possible for markets to assume this role. This review encompasses research into the price discovery function, which determines how many successful futures contracts are needed for each commodity.

1. INTRODUCTION

What determines the range and boundaries of energy derivative markets? Why is the oil futures trade dominated by contracts on two grades and locations, when the global trade encompasses many different grades of oil shipped from, through, and to many other locations? One of the two benchmark futures grades is West Texas Intermediate (WTI), delivered into Cushing, Oklahoma, a confluence of pipelines in the US interior. The other is Brent crude, produced from the North Sea and traded as tanker cargoes out of that region. Although there exist a select few derivative contracts associated with other locations and grades, including a blend from the Persian Gulf, trade in these is small. Countries in the Asia Pacific region now account for 35% of global oil consumption (BP 2016). Nevertheless, there is no significant derivative linked to a delivery point in the region. Although Russia is a major oil exporter, efforts to develop a futures contract linked to the country's Urals blend have, so far, not met with success. Why? Should we expect this situation to change in the near future?

We review here research on the establishment and performance of energy derivative markets, focusing on the two major energy commodities: oil and natural gas. For both oil and natural gas, trade in derivatives arose at the conclusion of a historical process in which production along a value chain that had been coordinated by vertically integrated companies or similar institutional structures switched to being coordinated through markets in the physical commodities. Consequently, much of the research reviewed here is about the structural changes that made it possible for markets to assume this role. In both cases, once markets in the physical commodity gained their central role, markets in derivatives quickly arose and became the preferred location for price discovery. This review encompasses research into this price discovery function, which is pertinent to answering the question of how many successful futures contracts are needed for each industry.

This review complements earlier reviews of commodity derivative markets by, e.g., Rouwenhorst & Tang (2012), who discuss these markets from the perspective of the investor, Cheng & Xiong (2014), who discuss how financial investors in commodities affect risk sharing and price discovery, and Parsons (2013b), who covers the corporate use of derivatives to hedge oil price risk. Here the focus is instead on the link between the industrial structure of a given energy market and the role of futures trading. Whereas the literature reviewed by Cheng & Xiong (2014) discusses how financial investors perturb price discovery in futures markets, the literature reviewed here discusses the fundamentals underlying that price discovery role.

The term "derivatives" encompasses exchange-traded futures and options as well as the over-the-counter (OTC) market in swaps and many other instruments. Exchange-traded futures have generally played a leading role in energy markets of all kinds, which is a contrast to some other sectors of the derivatives world, such as interest rates and credit, where OTC trade has dominated. Consequently, this review focuses largely on the development of trade in futures. However, it gives attention to OTC markets where that is essential to appreciating the proper place of the trade in futures.

Section 2 covers the oil market and Section 3 covers the natural gas market. Both sections begin with a discussion of the historical industry restructuring that shifted coordination along the value chain to markets in the physical commodity, provide details on the historical rise of futures markets, and conclude with discussion on the potential evolution in futures markets.

2. OIL

2.1. Industry Restructuring

An active spot market in crude oil is a prerequisite for futures trade, and this prerequisite was lacking at the start of the 1970s. At that time, global flows in crude oil were controlled by the so-called Seven Sisters: Exxon, Mobil, Texaco, SoCal (Chevron), Gulf, Royal Dutch/Shell, and British Petroleum (BP). Much of their control was based on concessionary access to resources in oil-producing countries, including those organized into the Organization of Petroleum Exporting Countries (OPEC). Economically, concessionary access is comparable to direct ownership. As Adelman (1972) documents, this oligopoly was able to exercise market power, which, along with the favorable terms of the concessions, assured the companies high margins. The value chain, from production through transportation, refining, and marketing, was controlled as a vertically integrated operation. Where independents operated downstream—for example as refiners—their dealings with the suppliers were managed through long-term contracts or arrangements.

A global market in oil developed during the 1970s and 1980s out of a transformation of the global industry, as detailed by Mohnfeld (1984) and Verleger (1987, 1988). Between 1973 and 1982, through a number of actions involving nationalizations and renegotiations of concession terms, the producing countries took control of their resources and radically reversed the pricing relationship with the Seven Sisters. This included the two dramatic price hikes associated with the 1973–1974 oil embargo and the 1979–1980 oil crisis. The total amount of global oil controlled by these seven companies fell from 30.0 million barrels per day (mbd) in 1973 to 15.2 mbd in 1982, a drop of 14.8 mbd. This translated into a drop in their share of the production outside the Communist bloc from 62% to 37%. In 1972, 85% of the oil they controlled was so-called equity oil, which earned them the highest margins. By 1982 this had fallen to 43% of the now smaller total, or 6.7 mbd. Per Verleger (1987, p. 168), "The majors had been replaced by a large number of medium sized oil companies, producing-country oil companies, consuming-country oil companies, and traders."

This disruption to the old industry structures dramatically changed patterns of competition and trade, enabling the development of active spot market trading. Where previously the Seven Sisters had carefully managed production and their own refinery capacity, the uneven pattern of nationalizations and renegotiation created imbalances in crude production and refinery capacities. In addition, the shift of pricing control to the producing countries undermined the profitability of the long-term relationships through which the Seven Sisters had previously supplied other refiners with crude. Finally, the pricing power newly exercised by OPEC became a spur to develop new, non-OPEC sources of production in the North Sea, Mexico, Alaska, Malaysia, and elsewhere. OPEC's share of production outside the Communist bloc and North America declined from 84% in 1969 to 59% in 1983. The Seven Sisters now competed with other companies for these new resources, creating a much more liquid market along the supply chain. Altogether, the decade produced a dramatic rupture in the vertical integration along the value chain and an increased role for spot market trading in crude and products globally. Mohnfeld (1984) reports that the volume of spot crude supplies increased from a level of 1–3% in 1979 to an estimated one-third of crude oil traded in 1983. At the same time, the price of crude oil became much more volatile, as documented by Verleger (1987) and Dvir & Rogoff (2009). This increased the potential need for well-functioning spot and futures markets.

In parallel with these changes to global trade, the 1970s and 1980s saw a reshaping of the dynamics within the US industry that also promoted a shift to an active spot market, as described by Yergin (1991) and Dvir & Rogoff (2009). Throughout the mid-century, US domestic production and prices had been subject to both federal and state regulation, and imports had been managed through a complex and changing system of quotas. This stemmed from the 1930 discovery of the giant East Texas Oil Field and the sudden availability of a cheap supply that dramatically depressed the price in the midst of the Great Depression. As it happened, the excess supply had largely dissipated by the start of the 1970s. For the first time since World War II, the Texas Railroad Commission allowed production at 100% of capacity in 1971. This new domestic situation intersected with the new global context. Once the OPEC nations seized control of their resources and managed their capacity to maintain a high global price, North America became one of the many sources of competitive supply outside of OPEC. In January 1981, the United States decontrolled all prices in crude oil and products. The changing market structure and changing dynamics in supply and demand brought changes in marketing practices. Verleger (1987, 1988) documents the shift from a system of posted prices to regularly updated quotations of spot prices in various markets and for various products. The growth of spot market trading manifested itself in a sudden explosion of alternative sources for price data and intensive competition among these sources to deliver more data feeds on an ever faster basis. From refineries to final customers, such as airlines and gas stations, the room for independent operators and the scope of competition expanded suddenly. The vertically integrated companies started treating each of their business units as distinct profit centers.

Another particularly important development in the changing global context is the creation of the Brent market associated with the North Sea oil fields. Although the presence of oil had been documented decades earlier, and although certain key discoveries had been made in the 1960s, the oil price hike of 1973–74 suddenly made it profitable to accelerate development. Production from the UK shelf multiplied more than sixfold between 1976 and 1982, as related by Atkinson, Brooks & Hall (1983). The process continued in later years and elsewhere in the North Sea. This produced another important stream of crude oil feeding into the global marketplace, which competed with OPEC production. As described by Weiner (1989), an informal market in tanker cargoes out of the region developed, known as the Brent market, complete with standardized terms and trading conventions, and prices in this market quickly became a well-monitored benchmark for the industry.

2.2. Crude Oil Derivatives

Modern futures markets in crude oil and refined products began to appear in the 1970s, as recounted by Dale (1991) and Simkins & Jia (2016).[1] The New York Cotton Exchange established a propane contract in 1971. Although it was not remarkably successful at first, the contract survived and was later sold to the New York Mercantile Exchange (NYMEX), which is now owned by the CME. This was followed by a failed attempt at a futures contract for delivery of Oklahoma crude and another failed attempt at a futures contract for delivery of crude into Rotterdam. Success finally came with NYMEX's 1978 introduction of a futures contract on heating oil delivered into New York Harbor. Remarking on this success in 2002, the US Energy Information Administration (EIA) (2002, pp. 23–24) reported that "trading volume in a successful contract can climb dramatically. For example, the annual trading volumes of the No. 2 heating oil contract grew from 25,910 in 1978 to more than 932,000 in 1980, to 5.7 million in 1989, and to a record 9.6 million in 2000." This was followed by NYMEX's 1983 introduction of the WTI crude oil futures contract. Dominguez (1989) notes that, at its launch, volume in the WTI futures contracts averaged less than 1,000 contracts daily (less than 1,000,000 barrels), but by the end of 1987, volume exceeded 18,000 contracts daily. In 2015, average daily volume totaled nearly 600,000 contracts. In 1985, NYMEX added futures contracts in gasoline. In 1994, NYMEX added a residual fuel oil contract as well as a crack spread contract. In later years, as the portfolio of traded physical products shifted, available futures contracts shifted, too, now including biofuels and petrochemicals.

[1]Weiner (2003) documents that the nineteenth-century United States boasted at least 20 exchanges where crude oil was traded before the extreme consolidation of the industry by the Standard Oil Trust eliminated them.

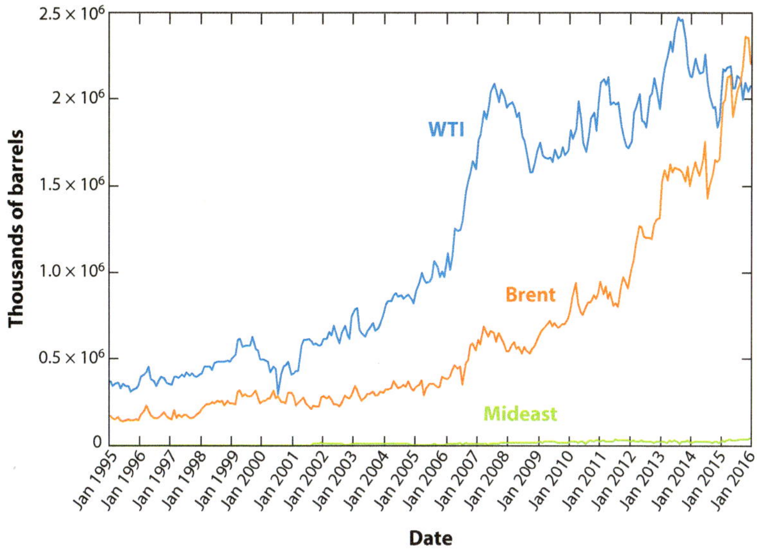

Figure 1

Total open interest across all futures contracts in three types of crude oil. WTI (*blue*) aggregates open interest on NYMEX's WTI contract and open interest on ICE's copycat WTI contract. Brent (*orange*) aggregates open interest on ICE's Brent contract and open interest on NYMEX's copycat Brent contract. Mideast (*green*) aggregates open interest on the Dubai Mercantile Exchange's Oman contract and TOCOM's Middle East Crude Oil contract. Figure data are from Bloomberg. Abbreviations: ICE, Intercontinental Exchange; NYMEX, New York Mercantile Exchange; TOCOM, Tokyo Commodity Exchange; WTI, West Texas Intermediate.

Since the successful establishment of futures contracts on crude oil and oil products in the 1980s and 1990s, the markets have continued to grow. **Figure 1** shows that total open interest in the WTI more than quadrupled from 1995 through 2015.

The UK's Brent market also evolved its own derivatives in the 1980s and 1990s. These were initially extrapolated from the forward physical market, in which the industry developed tools for financial settlement of physical delivery obligations. These obligations included a process for canceling offsetting transactions that developed in the so-called daisy chain of forward shipments owed between different companies. In 1988, the International Petroleum Exchange (IPE), located in London, took this a step further and established a futures contract in Brent, complete with all of the usual institutional features, including marking to market, margining, and central clearing. The contract is now owned by the Intercontinental Exchange (ICE), and the scale of trading in the Brent futures contract has recently overtaken that of the WTI contract. As seen in **Figure 1**, the open interest is also comparable across the two crudes.

Derivative trade in crude oil is overwhelmingly dominated by contracts on WTI and Brent. In fact, the exchanges that pioneered each of the contracts (NYMEX for WTI and ICE for Brent) now each offer a copycat contract on the other product: ICE offers a WTI contract tied to the price on NYMEX, and NYMEX offers a Brent contract tied to the price on the ICE exchange. The next most important set of contracts are those linked to the price of crude oil exported from the Persian Gulf, much of which is destined for East Asian markets. The Tokyo Commodity Exchange (TOCOM) has listed one of these contracts, priced in yen, since 2001. The Dubai Mercantile Exchange has listed another, priced in US dollars, since 2007. Nevertheless, the futures trade in these Mideast crudes remains very limited, as seen in **Figure 1**. Total open interest in these contracts has grown to only about 2% of trade in WTI.

Other derivative contracts are less significant still. For example, exchanges currently offer futures and basis contracts on a few other North American benchmark prices—such as Louisiana Light Sweet and Canadian Heavy—but with very limited trade. Since 2005, the Multi Commodity Exchange of India Ltd. has listed a crude oil futures contract that is a mirror of NYMEX's WTI contract. It is priced in rupees and is supposedly deliverable in Mumbai, but in reality it provides an opportunity for Indian investors to speculate on the WTI price. Since 2000, as Chinese demand for oil has grown dramatically, interest has been expressed in developing a local China-based crude oil futures contract. A fuel oil futures contract has been trading on the Shanghai Futures Exchange since 2004, and there are regular announcements about coming crude oil futures contracts.[2] However, the opening of actual trading has been regularly postponed. The St. Petersburg International Mercantile Exchange (SPIMEX) is in the process of launching a futures contract on Russian Urals-grade oil.

In addition to exchange-traded futures and options on crude and refined products, there is a large OTC derivative market. Unfortunately, prior to the 2007–2008 financial crisis, little information was publicly available about this segment of derivative trade. With the passage of the Dodd–Frank Act in the United States and related legislation in other countries, many transactions must now be reported to data repositories and to national regulatory authorities such as the US Commodity Futures Trading Commission (CFTC). This new stream of data is not yet comprehensive, and what is available exhibits many quality problems. Nevertheless, it promises new insight about the size and structure of the financial market beyond the traditional exchange-traded futures and options contracts. For example, a recent report from economists at the CFTC (Mixon, Onur & Riggs 2016) shows that open interest in WTI-linked OTC derivatives in the United States is roughly 80% of the open interest in the WTI exchange-traded futures and options market in the United States. Therefore, incorporating the OTC market into the picture nearly doubles the open interest. (This includes some double counting, as a portion of OTC dealers' exposures are brought to the futures market in order to hedge the dealers' books.) The data show that the two portions of the market exhibit some important similarities and differences. Commercial end-users (including producers, processors, merchants, and customers) hold net short positions in both portions of the market. Financial end-users (including investment funds and hedge funds but not derivative dealers) hold net long positions in both. The maturity structure of the open interest is roughly the same across the two. However, the open interest of commercial end-users is more heavily weighted to the OTC market, whereas the open interest of financial end-users is more heavily weighted to the futures and options market. The data are limited to US swaps on WTI. Derivatives on Brent and many smaller markets can also be traded in the OTC market, but we still have almost no data on these.

With the establishment of liquid trade in futures, price discovery quickly moved from the spot market to the futures market, i.e., from the market in the physical product to the financial market, as documented by Schwarz & Szakmary (1994). Bekiros & Diks (2008) and Shrestha (2014) find evidence for price discovery in both the futures and spot markets. Just as importantly, the futures market provides price discovery all along the term structure. A long literature describes how the term structure in commodities reflects the supply and demand for intertemporal shifts in production, most obviously through storage, but also through changes in production. The literature dates

[2]Tang & Zhu (2016) show how capital controls in China create a demand for using commodities as collateral, which affects pricing, convenience yield, and inventories; the Shanghai fuel oil futures contract is one of the contracts analyzed.

back to Kaldor (1939), Working (1949), Telser (1958), and Brennan (1958). Among the many recent contributions are those of Williams & Wright (1991); Litzenberger & Rabinowitz (1995); Routledge, Seppi & Spatts (2000); Kogan, Livdan & Yaron (2005); Carlson, Khoker & Titman (2007); and Gorton, Hayashi & Rouwerhorst (2013). This theory has been integrated with the hedging pressure theory, which dates back to Keynes (1930), in work reviewed by Acharya, Lochstoer & Ramadorai (2013). Storage and production models emphasize the equilibrium mean-reverting process component of commodity prices, which is impounded into the term structure of futures prices.

Simple statistical models of crude oil prices, such as those of Schwartz & Smith (2000) and Cortazar & Schwartz (2003), put the half-life of these mean-reverting shocks at less than 1 year. This makes sense of the concentration of futures trading in the shorter-maturity contracts, as these are the contracts that reflect temporary variations in supply and demand that are critical to adapting inventories, transport, and short-term production plans. Initially, this meant 1-, 2-, and 3-month contracts with virtually no trade in later months. Today, although contracts are available 9 years forward, approximately 78% of the open interest is concentrated in maturities of less than 1 year. Another 16% of the open interest is in maturities of 1–2 years, 4% in maturities of 2–3 years, and the remaining 2% in maturities longer than 3 years (Mixon, Onur & Riggs 2016). It should be noted that because the scale of trade is much greater now than in the early years of trading, even contracts with maturity out to 4 years have more open interest and liquidity than did the most liquid 1-, 2-, and 3-month contracts as recently as 2000.

2.3. Further Development

We now return to the question that opened this review: What determines the range and boundaries of energy derivative markets? In particular, how many crude oil futures contracts should we expect the market to produce? With the growth of East Asia as a destination for global crude oil deliveries, is a futures contract linked to East Asia necessary?

Regarding the last question, the answer from the literature is, in my opinion, no. In order for an East Asia futures contract to be successful, two conditions would need to be met. First, an active local spot trade is a precondition for any local futures contract. Second, the local price would have to be an important contribution to the global price discovery process. Neither condition is yet met.

In the 1980s and 1990s, the lack of any futures contract linked to a local spot price reflected, in part, the readiness of Japan, as the major importing country, to do business through long-term contracts with its Middle East suppliers, foreclosing the creation of an active spot market in East Asian deliveries. China, too, has chosen to manage its own production and imports through vertical arrangements that have foreclosed a major role for spot trade, with some modest exceptions. There are some signs that both countries are considering changes, but until a vibrant spot market is developed, there is no possibility for a meaningful futures trade.

The second condition is likely to be a more permanent obstacle to the success of an East Asian futures contract. The answer to the question, "How many crude oil futures contracts are needed?" appears to be "one", or at least "one main one". This answer comes out of an old debate about the structure of global trade in oil. Adelman (1984, p. 5) staked out one side of the debate, asserting that "the world oil market, like the world ocean, is one great pool." This is the rallying cry of those who believe in the law of one global price for crude oil, with variations arising across locations because of transportation costs and variations arising across grades of oil because of processing costs. Weiner (1991) staked out a competing view, arguing for a high degree of regionalization in prices and price adjustments. The two positions are sometimes presented as mutually exclusive, with the ensuing literature supporting one or the other. For example, Bentzen (2007) uses cointegration tests and error correction model estimation to support the one great pool viewpoint, and Dai et al. (2015) provide an updated statistical analysis in favor of some regionalization. In fact, the two viewpoints are not mutually exclusive. The varying crude oil prices at different locations and for different grades may be driven by a single primary factor that reflects an evolving global supply and demand balance, while simultaneously being driven by a set of secondary factors reflecting local perturbations around that balance that cannot be immediately arbitraged but that also are not lasting. Fattouh (2010) presents an analysis of price differentials at various locations, including both spot and futures prices, consistent with this integrated view.

This is pertinent to the structure of futures markets because it speaks to how many different regional futures contracts are needed. Insofar as there is an identifiable global supply and demand balance, a single futures contract could conceivably be sufficient for providing the necessary price discovery and hedging services. If markets are fully regionalized, then it may be necessary to have multiple contracts. Or, if markets are globalized in the long run, but there are temporary, localized price perturbations, then one contract may be the focal point for discovery and hedging of the global factors, with local contracts being necessary only to provide discovery and hedging of the basis differentials. In that structure, the global benchmark would have liquidity out to longer maturities, whereas liquidity for the local contracts would be limited to short maturities.

Thus, the two lead contracts, WTI and Brent, are battling to be the single global benchmark. Kao & Wan (2012) show that throughout much of its history, the WTI contract was the point of global price discovery in the sense of Hasbrouck's (1995) information shares model. In recent years, however, transportation bottlenecks in North America have isolated the delivery point in Cushing, Oklahoma from the global market, reversing the usual basis and, more importantly, disrupting the price change correlations, as studies by Fattouh (2010), Buyuksahin et al. (2013), and Liu, Schultz & Swieringa (2015) have documented. According to many in the industry, this has made WTI a broken benchmark. Gilje & Taillard (2016) demonstrate how this has impaired the financial choices and performance of even Canadian oil producers that have relied on using the WTI contract as a hedge. Kao & Wan (2012) find that WTI has lost much of its price discovery role as a result of these changes, although this is disputed by Elder, Miao & Ramchander (2014).

Other futures contracts defined on other locations can only supplement the global price discovery role filled by one of the dominant contracts. Research by Kaufmann & Ullman (2009) uses the WTI and Dubai contracts to illustrate the two-factor structure: They find that the far-month trading of WTI reveals one factor and the short-month trading in Dubai reveals another factor. In this two-factor structure, one contract is the primary vehicle for price discovery and the other supplements it. Only a small amount of trade in the second contract is needed, as evidenced by the small open interest in the Dubai and related contracts, at approximately 2% of the WTI contract. Many failed efforts have been made over the years to establish supplemental contracts. Indeed, as the WTI contract began to lose hedging effectiveness for Canadian producers, in 2013 the NYMEX launched a futures contract defined on Canadian crude oil production, but it failed. If an East Asian futures contract were to be established, it would most likely play a subsidiary role, as does the Dubai contract. It is not clear there is a need for another subsidiary contract. The answer to this depends upon the uniqueness of price innovations in Asian benchmark prices.

3. NATURAL GAS

3.1. Industry Restructuring

The development of an active spot market in natural gas has been a purposeful objective of regulatory restructuring. This happened first in both the United States and the United Kingdom. More recently, it has been spreading, fitfully, throughout continental Europe.

The history of US regulation preceding the eventual establishment of a well-regulated spot market is described by MacAvoy (2000) and Joskow (2013). A good starting point is the Natural Gas Act of 1938, under which the United States regulated the natural gas market using a cost-of-service model. Subsequent decades saw the expanded use of natural gas and the correspondingly gradual expansion of the US network of pipelines. However, significant stresses appeared in the 1970s and 1980s. The low regulated prices were already producing shortages when the oil price shocks of 1973–1974 and 1979–1980 suddenly incentivized even more customers to demand natural gas, creating large shortages. Then, just as the regulatory system was adapted to encourage additional production under the protection of long-term purchase contracts, oil prices started their dramatic fall in 1981–1986, creating a surplus of gas supply known as the take-or-pay contract bubble. More regulatory adjustments ensued. The key resolution came in a series of orders from the Federal Energy Regulatory Commission (FERC) together with the Natural Gas Wellhead Decontrol Act of 1989, which pushed for open access to the pipelines, including an unbundling of transportation and gas purchases as well as other pipeline services, and the right to resell gas. The FERC also specifically encouraged the creation of pipeline trading centers. Among these was the Henry Hub, created in 1988 and located in the state of Louisiana, along the Gulf Coast producing area and connecting more than a dozen pipelines delivering natural gas to markets up the East Coast and in the Midwest of the United States. This gave the Henry Hub access to a diversity of suppliers and buyers, which helped to assure a competitive spot market in the physical product.

This regulatory restructuring quickly produced changes in commercial practice and market prices. Previously, US natural gas markets had been regionally segmented. Under the old regulatory rules, the different regional histories of contracting translated into different prices. After the reform, companies sought to arbitrage price differentials across regions, and local spot prices began to reflect short-run supply as well as short-run demand factors such as seasonality. De Vany & Walls (1994, p. 78) document that in the 5 years from 1985 to 1989, the number of locations reporting spot prices "grew from a handful to more than 50." Price differentials between regions declined and the correlation between the prices in different regions increased, reflecting the creation of a national market with locational variation defined by shipping costs. Doane & Spulber (1994) document the shift in purchasing to unbundled gas and transport services, as well as the increasing share of spot deliveries, which went from approximately 0% in 1982 to more than 55% in 1987. They document increasing correlations between price changes in different regions along with other evidence of an increasingly national market. Under the new system, regional differences primarily arise where transport capacity becomes constrained. Marmer, Shapiro & MacAvoy (2007) and Brown & Yucel (2009) document some returning segmentation during the 1990s as increases in consumption pressed against pipeline capacity constraints in certain locations. More recently, as gas production shifts from the traditional producing regions to new regions with shale gas resources, we may see some bottlenecks loosened and new bottlenecks created, as suggested in modeling by Kleit et al. (2015).

The United Kingdom's transition is described by Juris (1998), McDaniel & Neuhoff (2004), Price (2005), and Heather (2010). Since 1949, the gas industry had been operated as a national monopoly, British Gas. The 1982 Oil and Gas Act took a first small step toward enabling industrial customers to obtain gas from competing suppliers. In 1986, British Gas was privatized, and all large industrial customers were granted the right to contract with independent suppliers and use the national pipeline network to receive their gas. However, this did not prove very effective in creating actual competition in supply. Over the ensuing years, the government took several more incremental steps toward opening up supply to competition, ultimately leading to the Gas Act of 1995 and the 1997 breakup of British Gas into a gas production and supply company on the one hand and a gas transport company on the other. This facilitated competitor access to pipelines and accelerated the growth of competition in supply. British Gas's share of supply fell from 80% in 1992 to 33% by the end of 1996. The Gas Act of 1995 established a process for the daily balancing of supply by shippers across the entire National Transmission System. In addition, it created the National Balancing Point (NBP), which is a pricing convention for trading offsetting quantities into and out of the system at various locations; this is also known as a virtual hub. This evolved into the benchmark spot market in physical gas, and the NBP price for such trades is the benchmark price.

Continental Europe, too, has recently been moving to reduce the role of long-term vertical relationships in the natural gas industry and to promote the role of spot market trading. However, this is still a work in progress, and much remains to be done. Belgium and the Netherlands, which moved forward relatively quickly, now host vital spot markets at, respectively, the port of Zeebrugge and the Title Transfer Facility (TTF), another virtual hub. In 1998, the Interconnector pipeline opened, connecting Zeebrugge to the United Kingdom, and these two spot markets now play a strong role in arbitraging between the continent and the United Kingdom. Other continental European countries, including France, Germany, Italy, and Eastern European countries, have moved less quickly. Heather (2012) describes the opening of new trading hubs in France at the Point d'Échange de Gaz (PEG) Nord and Sud and in Germany at Gaspool and NetConnect Germany (NCG), although these are much less liquid than Zeebrugge and TTF. A large portion of European supply continues to be governed by long-term contracts between major suppliers such as Gazprom and local distribution utilities that bundle supply to pipeline transportation and that restrict resale. European competition authorities and gas regulators are working to eliminate such restrictions and to assure open access and unbundled supply. Prices in these long-term contracts are usually linked to oil, although, as the spot trade at natural gas hubs becomes more significant, contracts can begin to link to spot natural gas prices at local hubs. According to Stern (2014, p. 45), in 2011–2012, "45% of the gas sold in Europe was based on hub, rather than oil-linked prices," and this percentage is increasing significantly.

In contrast, the East Asia region has not developed any active spot market in natural gas. A study into the potential for a natural gas trading hub in Asia by the International Energy Agency (IEA) (2013) points out that the region is physically fragmented and has no highly interconnected high-pressure pipelines like those in North America and Europe.

In previous decades, the largest consumer of natural gas was Japan, where all of the supply arrived as shipments of liquified natural gas (LNG). These shipments were made under rigid long-term contracts negotiated with producer countries. The local gas and power utilities that have been the buyers of most of the gas and that control the gas transport and distribution system have operated under a regulatory regime that made little room for a competitive spot trade. Although there are many gas-consuming companies within Japan that could provide a competitive foundation for a wholesale market, the country has encouraged them to negotiate collectively with supplier countries in order to get better pricing. For example, in 2010, four utilities operated as the middlemen for nearly 71% of total LNG deliveries. Moreover, once supply is landed at an LNG terminal, there are no rights of open access. Natural gas distribution and sales are run by vertically integrated utilities. In addition, the domestic pipeline infrastructure is not adequately interconnected to enable significant arbitrage.

Recently, China has overtaken Japan as the largest consumer, but it, too, has not utilized a competitive spot market. The domestic market has been dominated by three state-owned companies, and one company owns 80% of the pipeline network. There has been no right of third-party access or ability to resell gas. Prices have been firmly regulated. However, as noted by Shi & Variam (2015), China has recently taken steps toward a functioning wholesale market. A process of privatization is underway, together with mandates for unbundling transport from supply and for third-party access to the pipeline network and other assets. Domestic natural gas price regulations are being gradually reformed to reflect more accurately the current cost of imports (Paltsev & Zhang 2015). However, whether these de jure steps produce de facto third-party access is an open question. The right of access has been made provisional on there being spare capacity, and currently there is a severe shortage of capacity. With use increasing quickly and pipeline infrastructure lagging, it is not clear when spare capacity will exist unless further policy changes are pursued.

Some proponents of active spot trading in East Asia have directed attention away from individual domestic markets and toward the growing international trade in LNG shipments. Historically, LNG trade had been managed through rigid long-term contracts. This practice dates back to the first shipments to Japan in the 1960s. This trade requires substantial capital investments: liquefaction facilities at the source point, the train of LNG tankers, and regasification facilities at the destination. Therefore, the earliest investments in these facilities also demanded long-term contractual commitments between buyers and sellers. In addition, in the early years, the designs of these facilities were often customized from source to destination, so that shipments could not be easily repurposed to other destinations. In addition, sellers, especially in OPEC, imposed destination clauses that helped them exercise their market power and that limited the development of spot trade. Until recently, buyers, too, have been comfortable with trade structured through long-term contracts.

Several of these limits on wholesale LNG trade have been weakened over recent years. The expanded scale of LNG trade, which has multiplied the number of buyers and sellers, has also been accompanied by a larger fraction of shipments available on a spot basis (for an analysis of this factor in determining the viability of spot trade, see Parsons 1989). Japan's Fukushima disaster radically restructured its energy picture and increased its needs for natural gas above what had previously been planned for and contracted, which has been a powerful demonstration of the value of a flexible supply. The surprising availability of cheap supplies in the United States and the move to develop export facilities in the United States have also demonstrated the value of flexibility; Stern (2014, p. 47) writes that "a consequence of the US gas surplus was the conclusion, in 2012, of the first LNG export contracts from the Sabine Pass project priced on a Henry-Hub-plus basis." Taking note of this increase in spot LNG cargoes, in 2009, the energy news and information provider Platts developed its Japan Korea Marker (JKM), a price index calculated from a survey of spot cargoes into Japan and Korea.

China, too, has identified some possible value in encouraging spot trade in LNG shipments. Stern (2014) reports that China has announced plans to create a hub in Shanghai that would enable wholesale transactions at the point of import among a few key consuming provinces, importers, and storage facilities. There already exists a small amount of spot trade there, but it remains to be seen whether this will produce a robust wholesale market.

In parallel with this growing LNG trade, the IEA (2013) describes a developing network of pipelines interconnecting Malaysia, Thailand, Indonesia, Vietnam, and the city-state of Singapore. As these nations are also involved in the LNG trade, whether as suppliers or consumers, this improves the flexibility of the overall system. Indeed, the government of Singapore is actively pursuing the goal of becoming a hub for trade in LNG. The country has long been a regional hub for crude oil cargoes as well as oil products, so it is looking to extend its regional role to natural gas. Starting with the Gas Act of 2001, the Singaporean domestic market had already been liberalized, complete with unbundling of transport from supply and open access. The IEA (2013) notes that Singapore has expanded its terminal facilities and made them able to receive ships of various sizes, as well as adding additional storage capacity. Shi & Variam (2016) note that Singapore launched a spot price index in 2015.

3.2. Natural Gas Derivatives

As far back as 1984, NYMEX attempted to extend its success from the oil market into natural gas, but its proposal was dismissed by the CFTC on the basis that the underlying physical market at that time was not yet assuredly competitive enough at the necessary scale (Doane & Spulber 1994). By 1990, when NYMEX made its new proposal for a futures contract, the CFTC had become convinced that "the supply of gas deliverable to the designated interchange Henry Hub, Louisiana, was sufficiently large in both peak and demand periods to minimize the possibility of price manipulation or congestion" (Doane & Spulber 1994, p. 487). Brinkmann & Rabinovitch (1995) report that the new contract had the fastest takeoff of a contract in the history of NYMEX. It quickly became the benchmark price throughout the North American natural gas industry. Statistical work by Nicolau, Palomba & Traini (2013) and Shrestha (2014) demonstrates that price discovery happens through the futures market as opposed to the spot market.

In the 1990s, OTC derivative trading also became an important element of the US natural gas market. Enron was a major force for this, and several other trading companies operated in this terrain. However, financial trading in natural gas was briefly disrupted by several coincident events. These included Enron's bankruptcy and the related California electricity crisis. These also included revelations of significant manipulation of natural gas and electricity markets, including wash trades and churning designed to create the illusion of liquidity at key hubs, as documented by the FERC (2003). Parsons (2013a) relates how these events combined to create financial difficulties for several leading trading companies, which drove them to exit the trading business. The impact has not proved lasting. The lack of public data on the OTC market makes it impossible to have a clear picture of the relative size of the futures and OTC portions of the market. The limited preliminary data reported by Mixon, Onur & Riggs (2016) suggest that currently the OTC market dwarfs the futures market in natural gas. It would be natural to think that the OTC market has an important role in price discovery, but there are no studies on this, probably because of the lack of available data.

The development of derivative trading in the United Kingdom is described by Bossley (1999) and Heather (2010, 2012). A small OTC market in forward contracts developed around transactions into the National Transmission System using the NBP. This was followed in 1997 by establishment of a futures contract based on the NBP and traded on the IPE (now the ICE). The futures contract quickly established itself alongside the OTC market, although the OTC trade continued to have higher volumes. The UK OTC market, too, was briefly hurt by the Enron bankruptcy and related events, but like the US market it quickly recovered. In recent years, the share of the futures market has grown, but the OTC market remains larger.

In continental Europe, derivatives linked to prices on the emerging liquid spot markets are now available, with Zeebrugge and TTF being the most relevant. However, according to Heather (2012), much of the trade is OTC and it is not yet clear that there is much liquidity.

Until recently, there had been no meaningful natural gas derivatives traded in East Asia. The IEA (2013) takes note that in 2012, the Japanese government announced a consultation between the Ministry of Economy, Trade, and Industry and 18 companies (including power and gas utilities, trading companies, and financials) with the objective of creating a natural gas futures market. At the time, they had set a start date target of April 2014, but the launch has been repeatedly postponed and now stands at late 2017. It is difficult to see how this new target can be met. Without an underlying change in the organization of the physical trade in natural gas, it is impossible to imagine a successful futures market. In the past, there have been proclamations about the value of establishing an active wholesale market, as well as efforts at reform, but follow-through has been lacking. Many interests favor the current structure. It is possible that real changes will come about, as the energy policy situation in Japan is in significant flux after the Fukushima disaster. However, until those changes materialize, any talk of an active futures market is an example of putting the cart before the horse.

China has declared its intention to develop a natural gas futures contract, although this is properly anticipated as a later stage of a reform that first establishes an effective spot trade in physical gas, so it is reasonable to imagine this is a far-off prospect.

In 2012, the ICE exchange launched a swap contract (later converted to futures) linked to the JKM LNG price index mentioned above. To date, this remains very illiquid, according to Leach (2016).

Singapore launched a futures contract in early 2016, building on its domestic spot market and its efforts to become a hub for LNG trade. However, Singapore's domestic market is extremely small relative to the regional LNG trade, and it remains to be seen whether this will prove a successful new derivative market.

3.3. Further Development

How many natural gas futures contracts should we expect the market to produce? What will be the relationship among them? North America has a large array of natural gas spot price hubs and citygate spot prices, but futures trading is dominated by the Henry Hub contract. In the United Kingdom and in northwest Europe, the NBP contract dominates derivative trade. Is this structure stable? Should we expect additional European contracts to establish parity with the NBP? Are the Henry Hub and NBP contacts in competition with one another, or do they serve different markets? What about an East Asian natural gas futures contract?

For the European region, future developments probably depend upon how well integrated the different parts of the continent are and on whether Europe succeeds in creating a single continent-wide market. For example, because the NBP and Zeebrugge spot prices are tightly linked, derivative trade may remain concentrated in the NBP as it currently is, accompanied by a small parallel trade in the Zeebrugge contract. Schultz & Swieringa (2013) present evidence that the NBP futures contract provides important price discovery for any lasting innovations at either Zeebrugge or TTF, although there is some spot volatility in each of those locations that is distinct from the NBP market. Fracturing liquidity across multiple contracts is costly, so there is a natural pressure to reduce the number of contracts to the minimum required. This pressure is not always determinant—as we have seen in the case of oil, there have long been two contracts competing to be the global benchmark—but it is significant. Therefore, unless the spot prices at other locations reflect other, distinct drivers of supply and demand that cannot be reflected in the NBP price, it is likely that the NBP futures contract will serve as the main benchmark for the continent as well. Indeed, the European Union's regulatory objective is to create an integrated market, and insofar as that means that major supply and demand shocks impact prices similarly across the continent, it would seem natural that one futures location could be sufficient for this purpose. However, if the European marketplace develops so that there are important differences in price formation between large segments of the continent, derivative trading might become more fractured. It is unclear what impact Brexit may have on the integration between the natural gas markets in the United Kingdom and the northwest of continental Europe.

What about the global marketplace? Could we see the establishment of a single global benchmark? In order to answer this, it makes sense to start by considering the degree to which there is a global natural gas market—one great pool—or several distinct regional markets, and how this may evolve going forward. Historically, natural gas markets have always been regional. The expanse of the pipeline network defined the expanse of the market. Although shipments of LNG offer the theoretical potential for linking regional markets, the scale of trade in LNG has only recently begun to transform that potential to reality. By 2008, the LNG share of world gas trade was about 28%, but regasified LNG still made up only 7.5% of world gas consumption. Brown & Yucel (2009) find that the US Henry Hub and the UK NBP spot prices affected one another during the years 1997–2008. Neumann (2009) presents mixed evidence and Li, Joyeux & Ripple (2014) argue otherwise. Kao & Wan (2009) extend the analysis to include futures prices as well as spot prices in both countries, and find a single stochastic factor for the four price series; they also find that information arrives through the two futures markets in equal measure.

In the time period for these studies, both regions were importers of natural gas, and the case for integration hinged on the possibilities for Atlantic cargoes to switch their destination to whichever continent had the higher price. Since then, the massive development of cheap shale gas in North America has eliminated virtually any imports to that continent. Without any terminals for exporting LNG, the price in North America has fallen dramatically below the price in Europe and in Asia: For the year between April 2012 and March 2013, Stern (2014, p. 47) documents approximate prices as \$2–4/MMBtu (Henry Hub), \$10–11/MBtu (UK NBP, "with oil-linked long term contract prices \$2–3 above that level"), and \$15–17/MMBtu (Japanese LNG imports). The United States is now developing export terminals—Cheniere's Sabine Pass began shipments in February 2016—but it takes time to develop the infrastructure. Consequently, the segmentation of the regional markets is clear. Even as the overall scale of LNG trade expands, Ritz (2014) argues that the concentration of suppliers and their attempt to exercise market power naturally lead to segmentation in pricing, so that the market segmentation may be lasting.

The conclusion therefore seems to be that natural gas markets are currently still segmented into regions. Consequently, there remains a need for distinct benchmark futures contracts, with the Henry Hub contract serving that role for North America and the NBP contract serving that role for the United Kingdom and Europe. Should spot trade in East Asian LNG become liquid enough, it is very likely that a futures contract on East Asian deliveries would develop that would define a third regional natural gas market.

4. CONCLUSION

The two premier crude oil futures contracts traded today—NYMEX's WTI and ICE's Brent—were established in 1983 and 1988. They compete head to head for the role as the sole global benchmark contract. They are complemented by a set of futures contracts in refined products, most of which were established in the same general time period, as well as by minor contracts for other crudes at other locations. The two premier natural gas futures contracts traded today—NYMEX's Henry Hub and ICE's NBP—were established in 1990 and 1997. They exist side by side as regional benchmarks for the US and northwest Europe, respectively. They are complemented by a set of minor contracts for delivery at other locations.

Underlying the establishment of derivative markets in each of these two industries was a preceding change in organizational structure. In the oil industry, this occurred in the 1970s, when producing nations took control of pricing power and disrupted the vertical integration established earlier by the Seven Sisters. This gave impetus to the establishment of localized spot markets that were linked together into a single global oil market. In the natural gas industry, this occurred in the 1980s and 1990s in the United States, in the 1990s in the United Kingdom, and is an ongoing process in continental Europe. In each case, natural gas supply had previously been bundled together with transportation services under a vertically integrated structure. In each case, supply was or is being unbundled from transport, so that regional spot markets have arisen or are now developing.

On the foundation of this active spot trade, the futures market quickly established itself in each industry as the preferred location for price discovery. It plays an essential role in shaping intertemporal production, storage, and transport decisions.

Although the global market in crude oil involves many different grades and locations, the derivative market is dominated by two major futures contracts, accompanied by a very few other, less liquid contracts. This reflects the limited factor structure of the crude oil price. The global crude oil market is one great pool, and a single futures contract is sufficient to capture the major shifts in supply and demand driving the global price level. Concentrating trade in one contract improves liquidity and price discovery. Nevertheless, the WTI contract and the Brent contract have operated side by side as contestants for the role of the global benchmark. Minor contracts can incorporate localized innovations that shape the term structure at the short end.

The physical trade in natural gas has always had a stronger regional character because of the role of pipeline networks and the expense of shipping LNG between continents. Consequently, the Henry Hub futures contract operates as the benchmark for North American trade, whereas the NBP futures contract operates as the benchmark for the United Kingdom and northwestern Europe. In each region, contracts on other locations play a subsidiary role.

To date, there are no significant futures contracts specific to East Asia either for crude oil or for natural gas. This is because the organizational structure of the oil and gas trade in East Asia continues to be dominated by long-term vertically integrated structures. That may be changing, which could give rise to spot markets located in East Asia. Nevertheless, the prospects for East Asian derivative markets differ across the two industries. Because of the nature of the global oil market, a specifically East Asian crude oil futures contract may make only a marginal contribution to price discovery and may therefore have limited success. In contrast, a specifically East Asian natural gas futures contract may provide an important price discovery role for the region, and therefore could have a greater likelihood of success.

DISCLOSURE STATEMENT

The author is not aware of any affiliations, memberships, funding, or financial holdings that might be perceived as affecting the objectivity of this review.

LITERATURE CITED

Acharya VV, Lochstoer LA, Ramadorai T. 2013. Limits to arbitrage and hedging: evidence from commodity markets. *J. Financ. Econ.* 109(2):441–65

Adelman MA. 1972. *World Petroleum Market.* Baltimore, MD: Johns Hopkins Univ. Press

Adelman MA. 1984. International oil agreements. *Energy J.* 5(3):1–9

Atkinson FJ, Brooks SJ, Hall SGF. 1983. The economic effects of North Sea oil. *Natl. Inst. Econ. Rev.* 38–44

Bekiros S, Diks C. 2008. The relationship between crude oil spot and futures prices: cointegration, linear and nonlinear causality. *Energy Econ.* 30:2673–85

Bentzen J. 2007. Does OPEC influence crude oil prices? Testing for co-movements and causality between regional crude oil prices. *Appl. Econ.* 39(11):1375–85

Bossley L. 1999. *Trading Natural Gas in the UK.* Oxford, UK: Oxford Inst. Energy Stud.

BP (Br. Pet.). 2016. *BP Statistical Review of World Energy, June 2016.* London: BP

Brennan MJ. 1958. The supply of storage. *Am. Econ. Rev.* 48(1):50–72

Brinkmann EJ, Rabinovitch R. 1995. Regional limitations on the hedging effectiveness of natural gas futures. *Energy J.* 16(3):113–24

Brown S, Yücel M. 2009. Market arbitrage: European and North American natural gas prices. *Energy J.* 30(Special Issue):167–85

Buyuksahin B, Lee TK, Moser JT, Robe MA. 2013. Physical markets, paper markets and the WTI–Brent spread. *Energy J.* 34(3):129–52

Carlson M, Khokher Z, Titman S. 2007. Equilibrium exhaustible resource price dynamics. *J. Finance* 62(4):1663–703

Cheng IH, Xiong W. 2014. Financialization of commodity markets. *Annu. Rev. Financ. Econ.* 6(1):419–41

Cortazar G, Schwartz ES. 2003. Implementing a stochastic model for oil futures prices. *Energy Econ.* 25(3):215–38

Dai YH, Xie WJ, Jiang ZQ, Jiang GJ, Zhou WX. 2015. Correlation structure and principal components in the global crude oil market. *Empir. Econ.* 51(4):1501–19

Dale C. 1991. *Economics of energy futures markets.* MPRA Pap. 47447

De Vany AS, Walls WD. 1994. Open access and the emergence of a competitive natural gas market. *Contemp. Econ. Policy* 12(2):77–96

Doane MJ, Spulber DF. 1994. Open access and the evolution of the US spot market for natural gas. *J. Law Econ.* 37(2):477–517

Dominguez KM. 1989. The volatility and efficiency of crude oil futures contracts. In *Oil and Money: Coping with Price Risk Through Financial Markets*, ed. KM Dominguez, JS Strong, RJ Weiner, pp. 48–97. Cambridge, MA: Energy Environ. Policy Cent.

Dvir E, Rogoff KS. 2009. *Three epochs of oil.* NBER Work. Pap. 14927

EIA (Energy Inf. Admin.). 2002. *Derivatives and Risk Management in the Petroleum, Natural Gas, and Electricity Industries.* Washington, DC: EIA

Elder J, Miao H, Ramchander S. 2014. Price discovery in crude oil futures. *Energy Econ.* 46:S18–27

Fattouh B. 2010. The dynamics of crude oil price differentials. *Energy Econ.* 32(2):334–42

FERC (Fed. Energy Regul. Commis.). 2003. *Final report on price manipulation in Western markets: fact-finding investigation of potential manipulation of electric and natural gas prices.* Docket PA02-2-000, FERC, Washington, DC

Gilje E, Taillard J. 2016. *Does hedging affect firm value? Evidence from a natural experiment.* Work. Pap., Wharton Sch., Univ. Pa.

Gorton GB, Hayashi F, Rouwenhorst KG. 2013. The fundamentals of commodity futures returns. *Rev. Finance* 17(1):35–105

Hasbrouck J. 1995. One security, many markets: determining the contributions to price discovery. *J. Finance* 50(4):1175–99

Heather P. 2010. *The evolution and functioning of the traded gas market in Britain.* Work. Pap. NG 44, Oxford Inst. Energy Stud., Univ. Oxford

Heather P. 2012. *Continental European gas hubs: Are they fit for purpose?* Work. Pap. NG 63, Oxford Inst. Energy Stud., Univ. Oxford

IEA (Int. Energy Agency). 2013. *Developing a Natural Gas Trading Hub in Asia: Obstacles and Opportunities.* Paris: IEA

Joskow PL. 2013. Natural gas: from shortages to abundance in the United States. *Am. Econ. Rev.* 103(3):338–43

Juris A. 1998. *Natural gas markets in the UK: competition, industry structure, and market power of the incumbent.* Note 138, World Bank, Washington, DC

Kaldor N. 1939. Speculation and economic stability. *Rev. Econ. Stud.* 7(1):1–27

Kao CW, Wan JY. 2009. Information transmission and market interactions across the Atlantic—an empirical study on the natural gas market. *Energy Econ.* 31(1):152–61

Kao CW, Wan JY. 2012. Price discount, inventories and the distortion of WTI benchmark. *Energy Econ.* 34(1):117–24

Kaufmann RK, Ullman B. 2009. Oil prices, speculation, and fundamentals: interpreting causal relations among spot and futures prices. *Energy Econ.* 31(4):550–58

Keynes JM. 1930. *Treatise on Money.* London: Macmillan

Kleit AN, Lo Prete C, Blumsack S, Guo N. 2015. *Weather or not? Welfare impacts of natural gas pipeline expansion in the northeastern US.* Work. Pap., Pa. State Univ.

Kogan L, Livdan D, Yaron A. 2009. Oil futures prices in a production economy with investment constraints. *J. Finance* 64(3):1345–75

Leach B. 2016. *Natural gas hub development and the Asian LNG market*. Presented at IAEE Asian Conf., 5th, Feb. 15, Perth, Aust.

Li R, Joyeux R, Ripple RD. 2014. International natural gas market integration. *Energy J.* 35(4):159–79

Litzenberger RH, Rabinowitz N. 1995. Backwardation in oil futures markets: theory and empirical evidence. *J. Finance* 50(5):1517–45

Liu WM, Schultz E, Swieringa J. 2015. Price dynamics in global crude oil markets. *J. Futures Markets* 35(2):148–62

MacAvoy PW. 2000. *The Natural Gas Market: Sixty Years of Regulation and Deregulation*. New Haven, CT: Yale Univ. Press

Marmer V, Shapiro D, MacAvoy P. 2007. Bottlenecks in regional markets for natural gas transmission services. *Energy Econ.* 29:37–45

McDaniel T, Neuhoff K. 2004. Auctions of gas transmission access: the British experience. In *Auctioning Public Assets: Analysis and Alternatives*, ed. MCW Janssen, pp. 197–229. Cambridge, UK: Cambridge Univ. Press

Mixon S, Onur E, Riggs L. 2016. *Exploring commodity trading activity: an integrated analysis of swaps and futures*. Presented at NCCC-134 Conf. Appl. Commod. Price Anal. Forecast. Market Risk Manag., April 18–19, St. Louis, MO

Mohnfeld JH. 1984. The trend of structural change in the international oil industry in the 1980s. *Annu. Rev. Energy* 9(1):155–77

Neumann A. 2009. Linking natural gas markets: Is LNG doing its job? *Energy J.* 30:187–99

Nicolau M, Palomba G, Traini I. 2013. *Are futures prices influenced by spot prices or vice-versa? An analysis of crude oil, natural gas and gold markets*. Work. Pap. 394, Dip. Sci. Econ. Soc., Univ. Politec. Marche

Paltsev S, Zhang D. 2015. Natural gas pricing reform in China: getting closer to a market system? *Energy Policy* 86:43–56

Parsons JE. 1989. Estimating the strategic value of long-term forward purchase contracts using auction models. *J. Finance* 44(4):981–1010

Parsons JE. 2013a. Do trading and power operations mix? *J. Appl. Corp. Finance* 25(4):30–36

Parsons JE. 2013b. *Mapping and measuring the channels of oil price exposure in the economy and the role of oil derivatives in reshaping them*. Work. Pap. 2013-013, Cent. Energy Environ. Policy Res., MIT

Price CW. 2005. The effect of liberalizing UK retail energy markets on consumers. *Oxford Rev. Econ. Policy* 21(1):128–44

Ritz RA. 2014. Price discrimination and limits to arbitrage: an analysis of global LNG markets. *Energy Econ.* 45:324–32

Routledge BR, Seppi DJ, Spatt CS. 2000. Equilibrium forward curves for commodities. *J. Finance* 55(3):1297–338

Rouwenhorst K, Tang K. 2012. Commodity investing. *Annu. Rev. Financ. Econ.* 4(1):447–67

Schultz E, Swieringa J. 2013. Price discovery in European natural gas markets. *Energy Policy* 61:628–34

Schwartz E, Smith JE. 2000. Short-term variations and long-term dynamics in commodity prices. *Manag. Sci.* 46(7):893–911

Schwarz TV, Szakmary AC. 1994. Price discovery in petroleum markets: arbitrage, cointegration, and the time interval of analysis. *J. Futures Markets* 14(2):147–67

Shi X, Variam HMP. 2015. China's gas market liberalisation: the impact on China–Australia gas trade. In *China's Domestic Transition in a Global Context*, ed. L Song, R Garnaut, C Fang, L Johnston, pp. 137–74. Acton, Aust.: ANU Press

Shi X, Variam HMP. 2016. Gas and LNG trading hubs, hub indexation and destination flexibility in East Asia. *Energy Policy* 96:587–96

Shrestha K. 2014. Price discovery in energy markets. *Energy Econ.* 45:229–33

Simkins B, Jia Y. 2016. Energy futures markets. In *The World Scientific Handbook of Futures Markets*, ed. AG Malliaris, WT Ziemba, pp. 407–34. Singapore: World Sci.

Stern J. 2014. International gas pricing in Europe and Asia: a crisis of fundamentals. *Energy Policy* 64:43–48

Tang K, Zhu H. 2016. Commodities as collateral. *Rev. Financ. Stud.* 29:2110–60

Telser LG. 1958. Futures trading and the storage of cotton and wheat. *J. Political Econ.* 66(3):233–55

Verleger PK. 1987. The evolution of oil as a commodity. In *Energy: Markets and Regulation*, ed. RL Gordon, HD Jacoby, MB Zimmerman, pp. 161–86. Cambridge, MA: MIT Press

Verleger PK. 1988. The role and impact of commodity market institutions in the determination of oil prices. *Annu. Rev. Energy* 13(1):359–82

Weiner RJ. 1989. The WTI futures market and the Brent forward market: a comparative analysis. *Oil and Money: Coping with Price Risk Through Financial Markets*, ed. KM Dominguez, JS Strong, RJ Weiner, pp. 7–47. Cambridge, MA: Energy Environ. Policy Cent.

Weiner RJ. 1991. Is the world oil market "one great pool"? *Energy J.* 12:95–107

Weiner RJ. 2003. *Financial innovation in an emerging market: petroleum derivatives trading in the 19th century*. Work. Pap. 98-64, Sch. Bus. Public Manag, George Washington Univ.

Williams JC, Wright BD. 1991. *Storage and Commodity Markets*. Cambridge, UK: Cambridge Univ. Press

Working H. 1949. The theory of price of storage. *Am. Econ. Rev.* 39(6):1254–62

Yergin D. 1991. *The Prize: The Epic Quest for Oil, Money, and Power*. New York: Simon & Schuster

A Primer on Portfolio Choice with Small Transaction Costs

Johannes Muhle-Karbe,[1] Max Reppen,[2] and H. Mete Soner[2]

[1]Department of Mathematics, University of Michigan, Ann Arbor, Michigan 48109; email: johanmk@umich.edu

[2]Department of Mathematics, ETH Zürich, 8092 Zürich, Switzerland; email: max.reppen@math.ethz.ch, mete.soner@math.ethz.ch

Annu. Rev. Financ. Econ. 2017. 9:301–31

First published as a Review in Advance on August 14, 2017

The *Annual Review of Financial Economics* is online at financial.annualreviews.org

https://doi.org/10.1146/annurev-financial-110716-032445

Copyright © 2017 by Annual Reviews. All rights reserved

JEL code: G11

Keywords

transaction costs, optimal investment and consumption, asymptotic expansions, viscosity solutions

Abstract

This review is an introduction to asymptotic methods for portfolio choice problems with small transaction costs. We outline how to derive the corresponding dynamic programming equations and how to simplify them in the small-cost limit. This allows one to obtain explicit solutions in a wide range of settings, which we illustrate for a model with mean-reverting expected returns and proportional transaction costs. For more complex models, we present a policy iteration scheme that allows one to numerically compute the solution.

1. INTRODUCTION

Starting with the work of Magill & Constantinides (1976), Constantinides (1986), Davis & Norman (1990), Dumas & Luciano (1991), and Shreve & Soner (1994), models with transaction costs have been the subject of intensive research. For example, much effort has been devoted to understanding liquidity premia in asset pricing (Constantinides 1986, Jang et al. 2007, Lynch & Tan 2011, Dai et al. 2016) and how transaction costs shape the trading volume in financial markets (Scheinkman & Xiong 2003; Lo, Mamaysky & Wang 2004; Gerhold et al. 2014). On a more practical level, transaction costs play a crucial role in the design and implementation of trading strategies in the asset management industry (see, e.g., Grinold 2006, Martin & Schöneborn 2011, De Lataillade et al. 2012, Martin 2014).

However, the quantitative analysis of models with trading costs is difficult. Unlike in frictionless models, the position in each asset becomes a state variable because it can no longer be adjusted immediately and for free. As a consequence, explicit solutions are no longer available even in the simplest models with constant market and preference parameters and an infinite planning horizon (Taksar, Klass & Assaf 1988; Davis & Norman 1990; Dumas & Luciano 1991). The difficulty is compounded in more complex models with random and time-varying investment opportunities. However, transaction costs become crucially important in precisely such settings where, for example, prices exhibit momentum or mean reversion (Martin & Schöneborn 2011; Collin-Dufresne et al. 2012; De Lataillade et al. 2012; Garleanu & Pedersen 2013, 2016; Martin 2014), there is switching between different regimes (Jang et al. 2007), or investors are exposed to idiosyncratic endowment shocks (Lo, Mamaysky & Wang 2004; Lynch & Tan 2011). In such settings, investors can no longer "accommodate large transaction costs by drastically reducing the frequency and volume of trade" (Constantinides 1986, p. 859), as in simple models where portfolio rebalancing is the only motive to trade. Instead, striking the right balance between adjustments to optimize performance and the induced implementation costs then becomes a central issue.

To obtain tractable results in complex models with transaction costs, it is often useful to take an asymptotic perspective and view transaction costs as small perturbations of a frictionless benchmark model. The goal is to obtain explicit asymptotic formulas for optimal trading policies and for the associated welfare effects of small transaction costs. Results of this kind were first obtained in simple concrete models that can be solved explicitly in the frictionless case (Dixit 1991; Shreve & Soner 1994; Whalley & Wilmott 1997; Janeček & Shreve 2004; Lo, Mamaysky & Wang 2004; Bichuch 2012; Bichuch & Shreve 2013; Gerhold et al. 2014). In the past few years, much progress has been made in extending these sensitivity analyses to more general settings (Soner & Touzi 2013; Bichuch 2014; Martin 2014; Rosenbaum & Tankov 2014; Ahrens 2015; Altarovici, Muhle-Karbe & Soner 2015; Kallsen & Muhle-Karbe 2015a,b; Possamaï, Soner & Touzi 2015; Bouchard, Moreau & Soner 2016; Cai, Rosenbaum & Tankov 2017a,b; Feodoria 2016; Moreau, Muhle-Karbe & Soner 2017). These results have been obtained using a range of different methods, from analytic studies of the dynamic programming equation (Soner & Touzi 2013; Martin 2014; Altarovici, Muhle-Karbe & Soner 2015; Possamaï, Soner & Touzi 2015; Moreau, Muhle-Karbe & Soner 2017) to convex duality arguments (Ahrens 2015) and weak-convergence techniques (Cai, Rosenbaum & Tankov 2017a,b).

In this survey, we review the homogenization approach put forward by Soner & Touzi (2013) for models with proportional transaction costs. This approach, based on partial differential equations, is very flexible and can be readily adapted to many variations of the model, e.g., different cost structures (Altarovici, Muhle-Karbe & Soner 2015; Altarovici, Reppen & Soner 2016; Moreau, Muhle-Karbe & Soner 2017) or preferences (Bouchard, Moreau & Soner 2016;

Melnyk, Muhle-Karbe & Seifried 2017). Hence, like the classical dynamic approach to frictionless control problems (for an overview, see, e.g., Fleming & Soner 2006), this method has the potential to be a key tool for the analysis of a wide range of complex models.[1] This review is written as a user's guide to the application of this method. We explain in detail both the basic, underlying ideas and each step of their application to a concrete problem. The goal is to provide a blueprint that will allow the reader to apply the approach to a wide range of related problems.

To illustrate the effects of transaction costs on active investment in a concrete example, we also provide a detailed discussion of a model with mean-reverting returns. Starting from the frictionless solution of Kim & Omberg (1996), we show how both the leading-order optimal trading policy and the corresponding performance loss due to the trading friction can be computed explicitly. We show that—as is true for models with constant investment opportunities (Constantinides 1986)—this leads to wide no-trade regions and a severe reduction in trading volume. However, the corresponding welfare losses are greatly amplified—the opportunity cost of not being able to "time the market" is substantial. This underlines the importance of correcting the performance of active investment strategies for trading costs (see Bajgrowicz & Scaillet 2012 and the references therein), for which the tractable asymptotic formulas reviewed here provide a convenient analytical tool.

This review is organized as follows. We introduce our continuous-time model without and with transaction costs in Section 2. We then derive the corresponding frictionless and frictional dynamic programming equations in Section 3. These partial differential equations for the value functions of the problems at hand are the starting point of the subsequent analysis. In Section 4, we outline the homogenization approach and discuss in detail how to apply it to models with proportional transaction costs. This method allows one to reduce the complexity of the problem by reducing the number of state variables, simplifying the underlying state dynamics, and postponing finite time horizons to infinity. In Section 5, we explain how this allows one to obtain explicit solutions in the model of Kim & Omberg (1996), where asset prices exhibit momentum. Section 6 provides references to several extensions of the homogenization results to more general asset dynamics, preferences, and cost structures. Finally, in Section 7, we discuss a scheme that permits the numerical computation of the solution to the simpler homogenized problem using a policy iteration algorithm. So that we can focus on the main ideas and computational issues, mathematical formalism is treated liberally throughout this survey. Rigorous verification theorems for the results presented here can be found in the work of Soner & Touzi (2013); Rosenbaum & Tankov (2014); Ahrens (2015); Altarovici, Muhle-Karbe & Soner (2015); Possamaï, Soner & Touzi (2015); Cai, Rosenbaum & Tankov (2017a,b); Feodoria (2016); Moreau, Muhle-Karbe & Soner (2017); and Melnyk & Seifried (2017).

We close this introduction by explaining some notation used in this article. Write $D_x\varphi(t,x,y,f)$, $D_{xf}\varphi(t,x,y,f)$, etc. for the partial derivatives of a multivariate function $\varphi(t,x,y,f)$. When there is no confusion, we use the more compact notation φ_x, φ_{xf}, etc. As is customary in asymptotic analysis, $\mathcal{O}(\delta)$ denotes any function satisfying $|\mathcal{O}(\delta)| \leq C\delta$ for a constant $C > 0$ and all $\delta \in [0,1]$. For any integrable random variable ξ and a time point $t \geq 0$, $E_t[\xi]$ denotes the expectation of ξ conditional on the information up to time t.

[1]Martingale methods based on the duality theory introduced by Cvitanić & Karatzas (1996) allow one to go beyond the Markovian paradigm (Ahrens 2015; Kallsen & Muhle-Karbe 2015a,b). However, they are more difficult to adapt to new models and are not applicable if the problem at hand is not convex, e.g., because of the presence of fixed trading costs.

2. MODEL

2.1. Financial Market

We consider a financial market with one safe and one risky asset with dynamics modulated by a general factor process. More precisely, the safe asset follows

$$\frac{dB_s}{B_s} = r(F_s)ds,$$

and the risky dynamics are

$$\frac{dS_s}{S_s} = [r(F_s) + \mu_S(F_s)]ds + \sigma_S(F_s)dW_s^S. \qquad 1.$$

Here, $(W_s^S)_{s\in[0,T]}$ is a standard Brownian motion; the safe rate $r(f)$, the expected excess return $\mu(f)$, and the volatility $\sigma(f)$ are sufficiently smooth deterministic functions of the factor process $(F_s)_{s\in[0,T]}$. The factor process follows an autonomous diffusion:

$$dF_s = \mu_F(F_s)ds + \sigma_F(F_s)dW_s^F. \qquad 2.$$

Here, $(W_s^F)_{s\in[0,T]}$ is another standard Brownian motion that has constant correlation $\rho \in [-1, 1]$ with the Brownian motion $(W_s^S)_{s\in[0,T]}$ driving the risky returns. Both $\mu_F(f)$ and $\sigma_F(f)$ are sufficiently regular deterministic functions.

All tractable models from the literature fit into this framework. Examples include:

1. The Black–Scholes model: The standard example for the asset dynamics is the Black–Scholes model, where the safe rate, the expected risky return, and the volatility are all constants: $r(f) \equiv r$, $\mu_S(f) \equiv \mu_S$, and $\sigma_S(f) \equiv \sigma_S$.
2. The Kim–Omberg model: To study the effects of transaction costs in a model where investment opportunities vary randomly over time, we consider the model of Kim & Omberg (1996).[2] This means that the safe rate and volatility remain constant [$r(f) \equiv r, \sigma_S(f) \equiv \sigma_S$], but the expected excess returns follow an Ornstein–Uhlenbeck process[3]: $\mu_S(f) = f$ and

$$dF_s = \kappa(\bar{F} - F_s)ds + \sigma_F dW_s^F, \qquad 3.$$

for constants κ, $\bar{F}$, and σ_F describing the mean-reversion speed, the mean-reversion level, and the volatility of the expected excess return.
3. Heston-type models: In this widely used class of models, the volatility is assumed to be a mean-reverting process. For example, Heston (1993) proposes a constant interest rate r and excess return μ_S, as well as a stochastic volatility $\sigma_S(f) = \sqrt{f}$, where the factor F is a square root process. Liu (2007) instead sets $\mu_S(f) = \alpha f$ for some constant α, retaining the other specifications of Heston. Chacko & Viceira (2005) keep Heston's constant r and μ_S, but their volatility is $\sigma_S(f) = \sqrt{1/f}$.

[2]This is a standard model for the predictability of asset returns, which has been discussed extensively in the empirical literature (Welch & Goyal 2008, Cochrane 2008). The importance of transaction costs in environments that require one to time the market is evident and is discussed by, for example, Martin & Schöneborn (2011); Collin-Dufresne et al. (2012); De Lataillade et al. (2012); Garleanu & Pedersen (2013, 2016); Martin (2014); and Moreau, Muhle-Karbe & Soner (2017).

[3]The framework of Kim & Omberg (1996) also allows other choices of μ^S and σ^S for which the Sharpe ratio μ^S/σ^S remains an Ornstein–Uhlenbeck process; this is because all of these models span the same frictionless payoff spaces. As this invariance breaks down with transaction costs, we focus on the present specification here.

2.2. Trading and Optimization

We now turn to trading and optimization in the above financial market. For concreteness, we focus on a specific portfolio choice problem where consumption takes place only at the terminal time. Extensions to more general settings do not pose any essential difficulties and are discussed in Section 6. We first briefly recall the frictionless case and then turn to models with transaction costs.

2.2.1. Frictionless case. Starting with an initial endowment of x_0 dollars in the safe account and a risky position worth y_0 dollars, an agent can trade the safe and the risky asset continuously on $[0, T]$. Without trading costs, positions can be changed freely over time, so the amount of money Y_t invested in the risky asset is therefore a suitable control variable. The wealth dynamics generated by such a strategy are obtained by simply weighting the safe and risky returns according to the corresponding investments:

$$\begin{aligned} \mathrm{d}Z_s^{t,z,f} &= Y_s\left(\left[r(F_s^{t,f}) + \mu_S(F_s^{t,f})\right]\mathrm{d}s + \sigma_S(F_s^{t,f})\mathrm{d}W_s^S\right) + (Z_s^{Y,x_0+y_0} - Y_s)r(F_s^{t,f})\mathrm{d}s, \\ s &\geq t, \quad F_t^{t,f} = f, \quad Z_t^{t,z,f} = z = x_0 + y_0, \end{aligned} \qquad 4.$$

where the superscripts in our notation refer to the initial conditions $Z_t^{t,z,f} = z$ and $F_t^{t,f} = f$.

Without trading costs, the wealth z is the only state variable we need to keep track of, apart from the factor f. In contrast, the decomposition of z into the risky position y and the safe position $x = z - y$ is irrelevant because it can be changed instantly and without cost by updating the control. If agents choose their trading strategies to maximize expected utility from terminal wealth at time T for some utility function U, we therefore expect the value function to be a deterministic function of the current time t, the current wealth z, and the current value f of the factor only:

$$v(t, z, f) = \sup_{(Y_s)_{s\in[t,T]}} E_t\left[U(Z_T^{t,z,f})\right]. \qquad 5.$$

2.2.2. Proportional transaction costs. Now suppose that trades incur a cost λ proportional to the value traded. The decomposition of the total wealth then matters, as this ratio can no longer be adjusted for free. As a consequence, we need to keep track of the evolution of the safe and risky positions separately. These quantities now both become state variables that can be adjusted only gradually. To wit, agents now choose nondecreasing adapted processes L and M that describe the cumulative transfers from the safe to the risky account and vice versa. The corresponding dynamics of the safe account are[4]

$$\begin{aligned} \mathrm{d}X_s^{t,x,y,f} &= r(F_s^{t,f})X_s^{t,x,y,f}\mathrm{d}s - (1+\lambda)\mathrm{d}L_s + (1-\lambda)\mathrm{d}M_s, \quad s \geq t, \\ X_t^{t,x,y,f} &= x. \end{aligned} \qquad 6.$$

The dynamics of the risky account are

$$\begin{aligned} \mathrm{d}Y_s^{t,x,y,f} &= Y_s^{t,x,y,f}\left(\left[r(F_s^{t,f}) + \mu_S(F_s^{t,f})\right]\mathrm{d}s + \sigma_S(F_s^{t,f})\mathrm{d}W_s^S\right) + \mathrm{d}L_s - \mathrm{d}M_s, \quad s \geq t, \\ Y_t^{t,x,y,f} &= y. \end{aligned} \qquad 7.$$

[4]This means that transaction costs are always deducted from the safe account, for both purchases and sales of the risky asset.

If agents maximize expected utility from terminal paper wealth,[5] the corresponding frictional value function will in turn depend on the current values of the safe and risky account in addition to time and the current value of the factor process:

$$v^\lambda(t,x,y,f) = \sup_{(L_s,M_s)_{s\in[t,T]}} E_t\Big[U(X_T^{t,x,y,f} + Y_T^{t,x,y,f})\Big]. \tag{8}$$

2.2.3. Fixed and proportional transaction costs. In this survey, we focus on the above model with proportional transaction costs in order to most clearly describe the main ideas of the homogenization approach for small transaction costs. However, the methods outlined here can be readily adapted to more general settings (Altarovici, Muhle-Karbe & Soner 2015; Altarovici, Reppen & Soner 2016; Moreau, Muhle-Karbe & Soner 2017). For example, in a model with proportional costs λ_p and additional fixed costs λ_f per trade, the cash dynamics in Equation 6 change to

$$X_s^{t,x,y,f} = x + \int_t^s r(F_\tau^{t,f})X_\tau^{t,x,y,f}\mathrm{d}\tau - L_s + M_s - \lambda_p(L_s + M_s) - \lambda_f J_s(L,M), \quad s \geq t,$$

where $J_s(L,M)$ is the total number of jumps of L and M up to time s. Because one pays a fixed, nonzero amount for each jump, $J_s(L,M)$ must be finite for any admissible strategy, unlike for proportional costs. Nevertheless, the value function depends on the same variables as in Equation 8.

3. DYNAMIC PROGRAMMING

The key concept for studying the value functions in Equations 5 and 8 and the corresponding optimal trading strategies is to describe them in terms of a partial differential equation derived from the dynamic programming principle of stochastic optimal control. Loosely speaking, this states that if we have already determined the optimal policy on $[t+\mathrm{d}t, T]$, then fixing this policy and optimizing over the choice at time t leads to the same solution as optimizing over the entire interval $[t,T]$. In discrete time, this means that the optimal policy can be computed by backward induction; in the continuous-time limit, a partial differential equation is obtained.[6]

3.1. Frictionless Case

Let us illustrate this idea by first briefly recalling the frictionless case. The dynamic programming principle suggests that

$$v(t,z,f) = \sup_{Y_t} E_t\Big[v\Big(t+\mathrm{d}t, z+\mathrm{d}Z_t^{t,z,f}, f+\mathrm{d}F_t^{t,f}\Big)\Big].$$

Now apply Itô's formula, insert the state dynamics (Equations 1 and 2), and cancel the stochastic integrals (because they are martingales and therefore have zero expectation if the integrands are sufficiently integrable). Finally, divide by $\mathrm{d}t$ and send $\mathrm{d}t$ to zero. Dropping the arguments to ease notation, this leads to the following equation:

$$0 = v_t + \mu_F v_f + \frac{1}{2}\sigma_F^2 v_{ff} + \sup_{Y_t}\Big(\Big[Y_t(r+\mu_S) + (z-Y_t)r\Big]v_z + \frac{1}{2}Y_t^2\sigma_S^2 v_{zz} + Y_t\rho\sigma_S\sigma_F v_{zf}\Big). \tag{9}$$

[5] One could also consider expected utility from liquidation wealth $X_T^{t,x,y,f} + (1-\lambda)Y_T^{t,x,y,f}$, but this does not affect the asymptotic results at the leading order.

[6] Here we provide only a heuristic derivation of the dynamic programming equations. For a mathematically rigorous treatment, we refer the reader to the monograph by Fleming & Soner (2006); for more recent results, see Bouchard & Touzi (2011); Bouchard & Nutz (2012); El Karoui & Tan (2013); Altarovici, Muhle-Karbe & Soner (2015); and Altarovici, Reppen & Soner (2016).

This equation incorporates the evolution of the system through the value function. Hence, the problem at time t is reduced to a simple optimization over instantaneous controls. In this particular case, we obtain a pointwise quadratic problem in Y_t whose solution is given by

$$Y_t = \theta(t, z, f) := -\frac{\mu_S(f)}{\sigma_S^2(f)} \frac{v_z(t, z, f)}{v_{zz}(t, z, f)} - \frac{\rho\sigma_F(f)}{\sigma_S(f)} \frac{v_{zf}(t, z, f)}{v_{zz}(t, z, f)}. \qquad 10.$$

Plugging this expression back into the dynamic programming equation 9 yields

$$\mathcal{A}v := v_t + \mu_F v_f + \frac{1}{2}\sigma_F^2 v_{ff} + rzv_z + \mu_S \theta v_z + \frac{1}{2}\sigma_S^2 \theta^2 v_{zz} + \theta\sigma_S\sigma_F\rho v_{zf} = 0. \qquad 11.$$

This is the dynamic programming equation for the value function v. As the optimal portfolio in Equation 10 depends on v and its derivatives, this partial differential equation is fully nonlinear. Nevertheless, it can be solved in closed form for standard utility functions of power or exponential form and for a number of particular asset dynamics (Merton 1971, Kim & Omberg 1996, Chacko & Viceira 2005, Liu 2007). This, in turn, leads to explicit expressions for the optimal trading policy in Equation 10. This is illustrated in Section 5 for the model with mean-reverting returns first studied by Kim & Omberg (1996); the closed-form solution for the corresponding dynamic programming equation 11 is provided in Section 8.

3.2. Dynamic Programming with Proportional Transaction Costs

Let us now pass to the value function (Equation 8) with proportional transaction costs. In this case, the value function depends not only on the total wealth z but rather on the full portfolio decomposition (x, y), where x is the cash position and y is the dollar amount invested in the risky asset. The dynamic programming principle then takes the following form:

$$v^\lambda(t, x, y, f) = \sup_{dM_t, dL_t} E_t\left[v^\lambda\left(t + dt,\ x + dX_t^{t,x,y,f},\ y + dY_t^{t,x,y,f},\ f + dF_t^{t,f}\right)\right].$$

As in the frictionless case, apply Itô's formula, insert the state dynamics (Equations 2, 6, and 7), cancel the stochastic integrals (because they are martingales and therefore have zero expectation if the integrands are sufficiently integrable), divide by dt, and send dt to zero. This leads to

$$\begin{aligned} 0 = v_t^\lambda + \mu_F v_f^\lambda + y(r + \mu_S)v_y^\lambda + xrv_x^\lambda + \frac{\sigma_F^2}{2} v_{ff}^\lambda + \frac{\sigma_S^2 y^2}{2} v_{yy}^\lambda + \rho\sigma_S\sigma_F y v_{yf}^\lambda \\ + \sup_{dM_t, dL_t}\left\{\left[v_y^\lambda - (1+\lambda)v_x^\lambda\right]\frac{dL_t}{dt} + \left[(1-\lambda)v_x^\lambda - v_y^\lambda\right]\frac{dM_t}{dt}\right\}. \end{aligned} \qquad 12.$$

Hence, if the marginal utility of increasing the risky position is neither too high nor too low at a point (t, x, y, f),

$$(1+\lambda)v_x^\lambda(t, x, y, f) > v_y^\lambda(t, x, y, f) > (1-\lambda)v_x^\lambda(t, x, y, f),$$

then it is not optimal to transact at all ($dM_t = dL_t = 0$). We call the set of all such positions (t, x, y, f) the no-trade region. In view of the dynamic programming equation 12, it follows that the following standard linear partial differential equation is satisfied inside it:

$$0 = v_t + \mu_F v_f + y(r + \mu_S)v_y + xrv_x^\lambda + \frac{\sigma_F^2}{2} v_{ff} + \frac{\sigma_S^2 y^2}{2} v_{yy} + \rho\sigma_S\sigma_F y v_{yf}. \qquad 13.$$

Outside the no-trade region, Equation 12 shows that the right side of this equation is less than or equal to zero, as one can always let the portfolio evolve uncontrolled. Moreover, if the marginal utility of increasing the risky position is high enough, $v_y \geq (1+\lambda)v_x$, then the optimal control is to buy

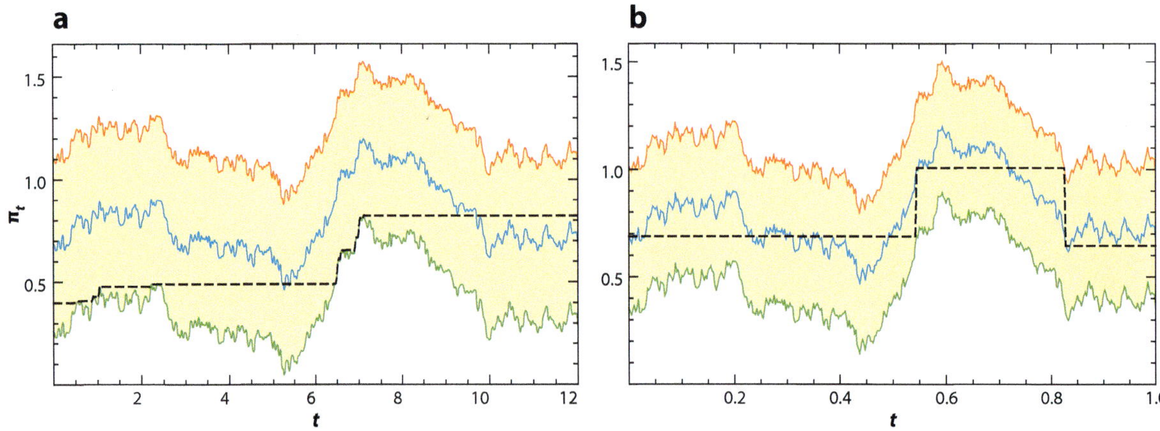

Figure 1

Simulation of the frictionless portfolio weight $\pi_t = Y_t/(X_t + Y_t)$ and the boundaries of the corresponding (asymptotic) no-trade regions in the Kim–Omberg model (*solid lines*). Dashed lines depict the paths of optimal frictional portfolios for (*a*) proportional transaction costs of 1% and (*b*) fixed costs of \$1 for an investor with an initial wealth of \$5,000. The parameters are $\gamma = 3$, $r = 0.0168$, $\sigma_S = 0.151$, $\kappa = 0.271$, $\bar{F} = 0.041$, and $\sigma_F = 0.0343$.

risky shares at an infinite rate ($\mathrm{d}L_t/\mathrm{d}t = \infty$). Conversely, it is optimal to sell risky shares at an infinite rate ($\mathrm{d}M_t/\mathrm{d}t = \infty$) whenever this marginal utility is low enough, $v_y \leq (1-\lambda)v_x$. This means that it is optimal to perform the minimal amount of trading that keeps the portfolio within the no-trade region; for an illustration of this, see **Figure 1*a***. Moreover, it follows that in order to satisfy the dynamic programming equation 12 with equality, we must have $v_y = (1+\lambda)v_x$ in the buying region and $v_y = (1-\lambda)v_x$ in the selling region. Together with Equation 13, this leads to the following variational inequality for the value function (Equation 8):

$$0 = \max\Bigg[v_t^\lambda + \mu_F v_f^\lambda + y(r+\mu_S)v_y^\lambda + xrv_x^\lambda + \frac{\sigma_F^2}{2}v_{ff}^\lambda + \frac{\sigma_S^2 y^2}{2}v_{yy}^\lambda + \rho\sigma_S\sigma_F y v_{yf}^\lambda; \quad (1+\lambda)v_x^\lambda - v_y^\lambda;\ v_y^\lambda - (1-\lambda)v_x^\lambda \Bigg]. \qquad 14.$$

Explicit solutions for this equation are not available even in the simplest models. The key difficulty is that the transaction costs increase the number of state variables by one and introduce a free boundary—the no-trade region is unknown and needs to be determined as part of the solution. In the Black–Scholes model, this requires us to solve for a time-dependent smooth curve (Dai & Yi 2009).[7] In the Kim–Omberg model, the tractability issue is further compounded, as the trading boundaries additionally depend on the mean-reverting expected return process. This lack of analytical tractability can be overcome by passing to the small-cost limit, which we discuss in Section 4.

[7]In the most tractable infinite-horizon models, the trading boundaries are constant and can be characterized by a scalar nonlinear equation (Taksar, Klass & Assaf 1988; Dumas & Luciano 1991; Gerhold, Muhle-Karbe & Schachermayer 2013; Gerhold et al. 2014); for a survey of this literature, see Guasoni & Muhle-Karbe (2013).

3.3. Dynamic Programming with Fixed Costs

Before turning to small-cost asymptotics, we briefly sketch how to adapt the above derivations for models with additional fixed costs. As only finitely many trades $\Delta L_t > 0$ or $\Delta M_t > 0$ are possible, we have

$$v^\lambda(t, x, y, f) \geq v^\lambda\Big[t,\ x - \Delta L_t + \Delta M_t - \lambda_p(\Delta L_t + \Delta M_t) - \lambda_f,\ y + \Delta L_t - \Delta M_t,\ f\Big].$$

With

$$H\Big[t, x, y, v^\lambda(t, \cdot, \cdot, f)\Big] := \sup_{\ell, m \geq 0} \Big[v^\lambda(t,\ x - \ell + m - \lambda_p(\ell + m) - \lambda_f,\ y + \ell - m,\ f)\Big],$$

it follows that the frictional value function v^λ satisfies the inequality

$$v^\lambda(t, x, y, f) \geq H\Big[t, x, y, v^\lambda(t, \cdot, \cdot, f)\Big].$$

The states for which $v^\lambda > H$ again form a no-trade region, where the same argument as in Section 3.2 shows that the frictional value function solves the linear partial differential equation 13. Combining this with the nonlinear constraint $v^\lambda = H$, which is binding outside the no-trade region, we obtain the following variational inequality for the frictional value function:

$$0 = \max\Bigg[v_t^\lambda + \mu_F v_f^\lambda + y(r + \mu_S)v_y^\lambda + xrv_x^\lambda + \frac{\sigma_F^2}{2}v_{ff}^\lambda + \frac{\sigma_S^2 y^2}{2}v_{yy}^\lambda + \rho\sigma_S\sigma_F y v_{yf}^\lambda;$$
$$H\Big[t, x, y, v^\lambda(t, \cdot, \cdot, f)\Big] - v^\lambda(t, x, y, f)\Bigg].$$

With only fixed costs ($\lambda_p = 0$), all trades are penalized equally, so the corresponding optimal policy rebalances all the way back to the frictionless target, as shown in **Figure 1*b***. Models with both fixed and proportional costs are intermediate between this regime and that of proportional costs from Section 3.2 in the sense that the optimal policy is to trade to a point in between the boundary of the no-trade region and the frictionless target portfolio (for a detailed description, see Korn 1998; Altarovici, Reppen & Soner 2016).

4. HOMOGENIZATION

We now turn to the asymptotic analysis of models with small transaction costs. To simplify the exposition, we focus on a single risky asset traded with purely proportional costs. A multi-asset model with proportional costs is discussed by Possamaï, Soner & Touzi (2015); fixed and proportional costs are treated by Altarovici, Muhle-Karbe & Soner (2015) and Altarovici, Reppen & Soner (2016); and a study of quadratic trading costs is performed by Moreau, Muhle-Karbe & Soner (2017).

As pointed out above, explicit solutions for portfolio choice problems with transaction costs are not available even in those settings that can be solved in closed form in the frictionless case. To overcome this lack of tractability, it is natural to study small transaction costs as a perturbation of the frictionless benchmark. The goal is for our setting to "reveal the salient features of the problem while remaining a good approximation to the full but more complicated model" (Whalley & Wilmott 1997, p. 308).

The method developed by Soner & Touzi (2013), which we present here, has its roots in the homogenization literature (Kozlov 1979, Papanicolaou & Varadhan 1981). This class of problems contains an ergodic fast variable, and the theory studies the limit problem as this variable oscillates more and more quickly. This leads to a homogenized equation. Interestingly, this homogenized equation is not simply the ergodic average of the original equation. Instead, it is obtained by a nontrivial coupling with a so-called corrector equation (sometimes also called the cell equation). Models with small transaction costs are only loosely in analogy with these problems, as the dependence on the portfolio composition disappears in the limit and does not immediately offer a fast variable. However, Soner & Touzi (2013) observe that, after a suitable rescaling, the deviation of the portfolio from the target position (ξ in Equation 15 below) plays the same role as the fast variable. This observation allows one to employ formal calculations similar to those in homogenization theory to characterize the asymptotic solution. Moreover, the powerful perturbed test function method of Evans (1992, 1989) can be modified to obtain rigorous convergence results (Soner & Touzi 2013; Possamaï, Soner & Touzi 2015; Altarovici, Muhle-Karbe & Soner 2015; Altarovici, Reppen & Soner 2016; Bouchard, Moreau & Soner 2016; Moreau, Muhle-Karbe & Soner 2017).

4.1. Identifying the Correct Scalings

The starting point for the asymptotic analysis is an appropriate ansatz for the value function v^λ with small transaction costs λ. To this end, a key observation of Janeček & Shreve (2004) and Rogers (2004) is that two competing effects need to be balanced. On the one hand, a narrower no-trade region leads to more frequent trading and thus also higher direct transaction costs. On the other hand, a wider no-trade region leads to larger oscillations around the frictionless target portfolio and thus higher indirect losses resulting from displacement from the optimal risk-return trade-off.

With proportional transaction costs, the amount of trading required to remain inside a small no-trade region with width Δ scales with the inverse of Δ (this is a property of reflected Brownian motion and the local time it accumulates at the boundaries). Locally around the frictionless optimum, the first-order condition implies that the value function is quadratic, so the displacement loss should scale with the squared width Δ^2 of the no-trade region. In summary, this suggests that Δ needs to minimize a total loss of the form

$$C_1\Delta^2 + \frac{C_2\lambda}{\Delta}.$$

As a consequence, the optimal no-trade region should be of order $\mathcal{O}(\lambda^{1/3})$, with a corresponding minimal utility loss of order $\mathcal{O}(\lambda^{2/3})$.[8]

4.2. Ansatz for the Asymptotic Frictional Value Function

As discussed in Section 3.2, the frictional value function v^λ depends on time t, the current value f of the factor process, and the current safe and risky positions x and y. As the transaction cost λ tends to zero, both the risky and safe positions converge to their frictionless counterparts. In order to obtain nontrivial limiting quantities for the asymptotic analysis, we therefore reparametrize the model by switching from x and y to the frictionless state variable

$$z = x + y$$

[8]For fixed costs, the argument is similar: A trade is initiated whenever the portfolio reaches the boundary of the no-trade region. At such a point, the portfolio is rebalanced to the frictionless portfolio. The time it takes Brownian motion to reach the boundary of the no-trade region is proportional to Δ^2, so the number of trades per unit of time is proportional to $1/\Delta^2$. The corresponding utility loss should therefore be of the form $C_1\Delta^2 + C_2\lambda/\Delta^2$, which has a minimizer of order $\mathcal{O}(\lambda^{1/4})$ and a minimal value of order $\mathcal{O}(\lambda^{1/2})$; for more details, see Altarovici, Muhle-Karbe & Soner (2015).

and the normalized deviation

$$\xi = \frac{y - \theta(t, z, f)}{\lambda^{1/3}} \tag{15}$$

of the risky position from its frictionless target (Equation 10).[9] In view of the discussion in Section 4.1, we then expect Equation 15 to converge to a finite limit as $\lambda \to 0$. To avoid fractional powers in the calculations below, set

$$\epsilon = \lambda^{1/3}.$$

With this notation and the above change of variables, the frictional value function can be written as

$$v^{\lambda}(t, x, y, f) =: v^{\epsilon}(t, z, \xi, f).$$

The considerations in Section 4.1 suggest that the leading-order term in the asymptotic expansion of the value function is of order $\mathcal{O}(\epsilon^2)$. Because the impact of a single trade is of higher order $\mathcal{O}(\epsilon^3)$, this term should not depend on the deviation (Equation 15) and should thus be a function $\epsilon^2 u(t, z, f)$ of only the frictionless state variables. However, the deviation of the frictionless optimizer (i.e., the position in the no-trade region) plays a key role in determining the optimal trading policy (i.e., when to start trading). To take this into account, motivated by the homogenization literature, we introduce a second term $\epsilon^4 w(t, z, \xi, f)$ in the asymptotic expansion. It is negligible at the leading order in the value expansion, but via Equation 15 its derivatives play a crucial role in determining the optimal trading policy from the variational inequality 14.

In summary, our ansatz for the asymptotic value function reads as follows:

$$v^{\epsilon}(t, z, \xi, f) = v(t, z, f) - \epsilon^2 u(t, z, f) - \epsilon^4 w(t, z, \xi, f) + \mathcal{O}(\epsilon^3). \tag{16}$$

The goal now is to determine u and w by plugging this expansion into the dynamic programming equation 14 and matching terms sorted in powers of the asymptotic parameter $\lambda = \epsilon^3$.

4.3. Asymptotic Dynamic Programming and Corrector Equations

In order to recast the variational inequality 14 in terms of the new variables z and ξ instead of x and y, we need to rewrite the corresponding differential operators. For an arbitrary function Ψ of (t, x, y, f) or, equivalently, (t, z, ξ, f), we have

$$D_x \Psi(t, x, y, f) = D_z \Psi(t, z, \xi, f) - \frac{\theta_z(t, z, f)}{\epsilon} D_\xi \Psi(t, z, \xi, f),$$
$$D_y \Psi(t, x, y, f) = D_z \Psi(t, z, \xi, f) + \frac{1 - \theta_z(t, z, f)}{\epsilon} D_\xi \Psi(t, z, \xi, f),$$

and, in turn,

$$D_{yy} \Psi(t, x, y, f) = D_z \left(D_z \Psi(t, z, \xi, f) + \frac{1 - \theta_z(t, z, f)}{\epsilon} D_\xi \Psi(t, z, \xi, f) \right)$$
$$+ \frac{1 - \theta_z(t, z, f)}{\epsilon} D_\xi \left(D_z \Psi(t, z, \xi, f) + \frac{1 - \theta_z(t, z, f)}{\epsilon} D_\xi \Psi(t, z, \xi, f) \right).$$

[9]The definition of this fast variable depends on the scaling appropriate for the problem at hand. For example, for problems with fixed rather than proportional costs, one needs to divide by $\lambda^{1/4}$ (Altarovici, Muhle-Karbe & Soner 2015).

Likewise,

$$D_f\Psi(t,x,y,f) = D_f\Psi(t,z,\xi,f) - \frac{\theta_f}{\epsilon}D_\xi\Psi(t,z,\xi,f),$$

$$D_{ff}\Psi(t,x,y,f) = D_f\left(D_f\Psi(t,z,\xi,f) - \frac{\theta_f(t,z,f)}{\epsilon}D_\xi\Psi(t,z,\xi,f)\right)$$
$$-\frac{\theta_f(t,z,f)}{\epsilon}D_\xi\left(D_f\Psi(t,z,\xi,f) - \frac{\theta_f(t,z,f)}{\epsilon}D_\xi\Psi(t,z,\xi,f)\right),$$

$$D_{yf}\Psi(t,x,y,f) = D_z\left(D_f\Psi(t,z,\xi,f) - \frac{\theta_f(t,z,f)}{\epsilon}D_\xi\Psi(t,z,\xi,f)\right)$$
$$+\frac{1-\theta_z(t,z,f)}{\epsilon}D_\xi\left(D_f\Psi(t,z,\xi,f) - \frac{\theta_f(t,z,f)}{\epsilon}D_\xi\Psi(t,z,\xi,f)\right).$$

Note the terms of order $\mathcal{O}(\epsilon^{-2})$ arising in some of these expressions. These are the reason $\epsilon^4 w(t,z,\xi,f)$ cannot be absorbed in $\mathcal{O}(\epsilon^3)$ in Equation 16 but needs to be treated separately.

With the above expressions, our ansatz (Equation 16) implies

$$\begin{aligned}
D_x v^\epsilon &= D_z v - \epsilon^2 D_z u + \epsilon^3\theta_z w_\xi + \mathcal{O}(\epsilon^4) = D_z v - \epsilon^2 D_z u + \mathcal{O}(\epsilon^3),\\
D_y v^\epsilon &= D_z v - \epsilon^2 D_z u - \epsilon^3(1-\theta_z)w_\xi + \mathcal{O}(\epsilon^4) = D_z v - \epsilon^2 D_z u + \mathcal{O}(\epsilon^3),\\
D_{yy} v^\epsilon &= D_{zz} v - \epsilon^2[D_z z u + (1-\theta_z)^2 D_{\xi\xi} w] + \mathcal{O}(\epsilon^3),\\
D_f v^\epsilon &= D_f v - \epsilon^2 D_f u + \mathcal{O}(\epsilon^3),\\
D_{ff} v^\epsilon &= D_{ff} v - \epsilon^2(D_{ff} u + \theta_f^2 D_{\xi\xi} w) + \mathcal{O}(\epsilon^3),\\
D_{yf} v^\epsilon &= D_{zf} v - \epsilon^2[u - (1-\theta_z)\theta_f D_{\xi\xi} w] + \mathcal{O}(\epsilon^3).
\end{aligned} \qquad 17.$$

We want to use these expressions to expand the frictional dynamic programming equation 14. To this end, recall its frictionless counterpart, Equation 11,

$$\mathcal{A}v := v_t + \mu_F v_f + \frac{1}{2}\sigma_F^2 v_{ff} + rzv_z + \mu_S\theta v_z + \frac{1}{2}\sigma_S^2\theta^2 v_{zz} + \theta\sigma_S\sigma_F\rho v_{zf} = 0,$$

where the corresponding optimal risky position is

$$\theta = \frac{\mu_S v_z + \rho\sigma_S\sigma_F v_{fz}}{-\sigma_S^2 v_{zz}}. \qquad 18.$$

Together with Equation 17, using $y = \theta + \epsilon\xi = \theta + \mathcal{O}(\epsilon)$ to replace $\epsilon^2 y$ with $\epsilon^2\theta + \mathcal{O}(\epsilon^3)$, the partial differential equation 13 in the no-trade region can now be expanded as follows:

$$\begin{aligned}
\mathcal{L}v^\epsilon &:= v_t^\epsilon + \mu_F v_f^\epsilon + y\left[v_y^\epsilon(\mu_S + r) - v_x^\epsilon r\right] + rzv_x^\epsilon + \frac{1}{2}\sigma_S^2 y^2 v_{yy}^\epsilon + \sigma_S y\sigma_F\rho v_{fy}^\epsilon + \frac{1}{2}\sigma_F^2 v_{ff}^\epsilon\\
&= \underbrace{\mathcal{A}v}_{\text{Eq. 11}=0} + \underbrace{(y-\theta)\mu_S v_z + \frac{1}{2}\sigma_S^2(y^2-\theta^2)v_{zz} + \sigma_S(y-\theta)\sigma_F\rho v_{zf}}_{\text{I}}\\
&\quad \underbrace{-\epsilon^2\left(u_t + rzu_z + \mu_S y u_z + \mu_F u_f + \frac{1}{2}\sigma_F^2 u_{ff} + \frac{1}{2}\sigma_S^2 y^2 u_{zz} + \sigma_S y\sigma_F\rho u_{zf}\right)}_{\text{II}}\\
&\quad - \epsilon^2 w_{\xi\xi}\underbrace{\frac{1}{2}\left[\sigma_S^2\theta^2(1-\theta_z)^2 - 2\sigma_S\sigma_F\rho\theta(1-\theta_z)\theta_f + \sigma_F^2\theta_f^2\right]}_{\alpha^2} + \mathcal{O}(\epsilon^3).
\end{aligned} \qquad 19.$$

By Equation 18,

$$\mathrm{I} = \left(\mu_S v_z + \sigma_S \sigma_F \rho v_{fz}\right)(y-\theta) + \frac{1}{2}\sigma_S^2(y^2-\theta^2) = -\sigma_S^2 v_{zz}\theta(y-\theta) + \frac{1}{2}\sigma_S^2(y^2-\theta^2)$$
$$= \frac{1}{2}\sigma_S^2 v_{zz}(y-\theta)^2 = \frac{1}{2}\sigma_S^2 v_{zz}\epsilon^2\xi^2.$$

Next, note that $y = \theta + \epsilon\xi = \theta + \mathcal{O}(\epsilon)$ implies[10]

$$\mathrm{II} = \mathcal{A}u + \mathcal{O}(\epsilon).$$

In summary, Equation 19 simplifies to the following asymptotic expansion of the dynamic programming equation in the no-trade region:

$$\mathcal{L}v^\epsilon = -\epsilon^2\left(-\frac{1}{2}\sigma_S^2\xi^2 v_{zz} + \mathcal{A}u + \frac{1}{2}\alpha^2 w_{\xi\xi}\right) + \mathcal{O}(\epsilon^3).$$

It remains to derive expansions in the buy and sell regions. To this end, we rewrite the gradient constraint from Equation 14,

$$v_x^\epsilon - (1-\epsilon^3)v_y^\epsilon,$$

using the expressions from Equation 17, obtaining

$$v_x^\epsilon - (1-\epsilon^3)v_y^\epsilon = \epsilon^3 v_y + \underbrace{(v_x - v_y)}_{\epsilon^3 w_\xi + \mathcal{O}(\epsilon^4)} = \epsilon^3(v_z + w_\xi) + \mathcal{O}(\epsilon^4).$$

Analogously, the second gradient constraint in Equation 14 can be expanded as follows:

$$v_y^\epsilon - (1-\epsilon^3)v_x^\epsilon = \epsilon^3(v_z - w_\xi) + \mathcal{O}(\epsilon^4).$$

Altogether, the asymptotic dynamic programming equation is

$$\min\left\{\epsilon^2\left(-\frac{1}{2}\sigma_S^2\xi^2 v_{zz} + \mathcal{A}u + \frac{1}{2}\alpha^2 w_{\xi\xi}\right);\ \epsilon^3(v_z + w_\xi);\ \epsilon^3(v_z - w_\xi)\right\} = 0.$$

Because factoring out ϵ^2 and ϵ^3 does not change this equation, it is equivalent to

$$\min\left\{-\frac{1}{2}\sigma_S^2\xi^2 v_{zz} + \mathcal{A}u + \frac{1}{2}\alpha^2 w_{\xi\xi};\ v_z + w_\xi; v_z - w_\xi\right\} = 0. \qquad 20.$$

The variational inequality 20, with two unknowns, w and u, turns out to effectively consist of two separate equations. To see why, write

$$a(t,z,f) := \mathcal{A}u(t,z,f).$$

Then Equation 20 can be rewritten as an equation for w and a:

$$\min\left\{-\frac{1}{2}\sigma_S^2\xi^2 v_{zz} + a + \frac{1}{2}\alpha^2 w_{\xi\xi};\ v_z + w_\xi;\ v_z - w_\xi\right\} = 0, \qquad 21.$$

where

$$\alpha^2 := \sigma_S^2\theta^2(1-\theta_z)^2 - 2\sigma_S\sigma_F\rho\theta(1-\theta_z)\theta_f + \sigma_F^2\theta_f^2 \qquad 22.$$

[10]Recall that $\mathcal{A}$ is a nonlinear operator in the frictionless dynamic programming equation 11, as the frictionless control θ depends on the solution v of the equation. In contrast, θ is already determined in terms of v here, so $\mathcal{A}$ acts as a linear operator on u.

is determined by the model parameters and the frictionless optimizer. For each value of t, z, and f, Equation 21 has a solution $\xi \mapsto w(t,z,\xi,f)$ for precisely one value of $a = a(t,z,f)$. Thus, by finding the solution (w,a) to this equation, we have obtained a unique function $a(t,z,f)$, from which we can in turn determine u as the solution of a linear partial differential equation:

$$\mathcal{A}u = a.$$

The key to this separation is the uniqueness of the solution (w,a) to Equation 21.[11] Any other choice of function u' would give another value $a' = \mathcal{A}u'$, for which, by uniqueness of (w,a), there would not exist a solution w'.

In summary, the asymptotic expansion 16 of the frictional value function is determined by the following equations:

Definition 4.1 (First corrector equation). For any (t,z,f), the first corrector equation for the pair $[w(t,z,\cdot,f), a(t,z,f)]$ is

$$\min\Bigg\{\underbrace{-\frac{1}{2}\sigma_S^2\xi^2 v_{zz} + a + \frac{1}{2}\alpha^2 w_{\xi\xi}}_{\text{no-trade region}};\ \underbrace{v_z + w_\xi;\ v_z - w_\xi}_{\text{trade regions}}\Bigg\} = 0. \qquad 23.$$

Because any constant can be added to a solution w to obtain another solution, we impose the normalization $w(t,z,0,f) = 0$, which affects neither the value expansion nor the optimal policy at the leading asymptotic order.

Definition 4.2 (Second corrector equation). Given a solution (w,a) of the first corrector equation, the second corrector equation for $u(\cdot,\cdot,\cdot)$ is

$$\mathcal{A}u(t,z,f) = a(t,z,f), \qquad u(T,z,f) = 0,$$

where $\mathcal{A}$ is the generator of the frictionless optimal wealth process, appearing in Equation 11.

The intuition for this separation into two equations is the following. In the first corrector equation, only the deviation ξ of the portfolio from its frictionless target is a variable. In contrast, the frictionless state variables (t,z,f) are treated as constants because they vary much more slowly than ξ for small transaction costs. Conversely, the fast variable ξ is averaged out in the second corrector equation determining the leading order utility loss u, in that it does not enter directly but only through the function $a(t,z,f)$ computed from the first corrector equation.

4.4. Explicit Solutions

In the present setting, the first corrector equation can be solved explicitly. This allows us to understand the comparative statics of the asymptotically optimal no-trade region and the corresponding leading-order welfare effect of small transaction costs. As a byproduct, the calculations below also explain why there is only a single value of a for which the first corrector equation has a solution.

[11] For any solution (w,a), $(w+C,a)$ is also a solution for any constant C, so the uniqueness only concerns a. However, for a given choice of normalization, e.g., $w(z,0)=0$, w is also uniquely determined. The choice of normalization affects neither the equation for u nor the policy generated from w. A precise formulation of the uniqueness result is presented by Possamaï, Soner & Touzi (2015, theorem 3.1). Similar uniqueness results are proven by Hynd (2012) and Menaldi & Robin (2013).

To find the solution, fix (t, z, f) and make the following ansatz: (*a*) The no-trade region is a symmetric interval $(-\Delta\xi, \Delta\xi)$ around the frictionless optimizer ($\xi = 0$), and (*b*) the asymptotic value function is of the following form[12]:

$$w(\xi) = w(t,z,\xi,f) = \begin{cases} c_4\xi^4 + c_2\xi^2 & \text{if } |\xi| \le \Delta\xi, \\ w(\Delta\xi) + (\xi - \Delta\xi) & \text{if } \xi \ge \Delta\xi, \\ w(\Delta\xi) - (\xi - \Delta\xi) & \text{if } \xi \le \Delta\xi. \end{cases}$$

Here, c_4 and c_2 are parameters to be determined along with a and $\Delta\xi$. In the no-trade region, plugging this ansatz into Equation 23 leads to

$$a = \frac{1}{2}\sigma_S^2\xi^2 v_{zz} - \alpha^2(6c_4\xi^2 + c_2) = \left(\frac{1}{2}\sigma_S^2 v_{zz} - 6\alpha^2 c_4\right) - \alpha^2 c_2.$$

Because this needs to hold for any value $\xi \in (-\Delta\xi, \Delta\xi)$, comparison of the coefficients of ξ^2 and 1 yields

$$c_4 = \frac{\sigma_S^2 v_{zz}}{12\alpha^2} \quad \text{and} \quad \mathrm{c}_2 = -\frac{\mathrm{a}}{\alpha^2}. \qquad 24.$$

To pin down a and $\Delta\xi$, we impose the requirement that the value function be not only continuous but also twice continuously differentiable across the trading boundaries $\pm\Delta\xi$ (these are the smooth pasting conditions of Beneš, Shepp & Witsenhausen 1980; Dumas 1991). By symmetry, this leads to the following two additional conditions:

$$0 = 12c_4(\Delta\xi)^2 + 2c_2,$$
$$v_z = 4c_4(\Delta\xi)^3 + 2c_2\Delta\xi.$$

These equations readily yield

$$a = \frac{\sigma_S^2 v_{zz}}{2}\Delta\xi^2, \qquad 25.$$

with

$$\Delta\xi = \Delta\xi(t,z,f) = \left(\frac{-v_z}{v_{zz}}\frac{3\alpha^2}{2\sigma_S^2}\right)^{1/3}. \qquad 26.$$

Together with Equation 24, this leads to a closed-form solution of the first corrector equation 23 in terms of model parameters and inputs from the frictionless optimization problem.

4.5. Asymptotically Optimal Policy

Recalling that $\lambda = \epsilon^3$, we find that the asymptotically optimal no-trade region corresponding to the leading-order variational inequality 20 is

$$\mathrm{NT}_\lambda \approx \left\{(t,x,y,f) : |y - \theta(t, x+y, f)| \le \lambda^{1/3}\Delta\xi(t,z,f)\right\}. \qquad 27.$$

In view of Equation 26 and the representation for α^2 (Equation 22), this asymptotic no-trade region is determined by (*a*) the diffusion coefficients σ_S, σ_F of the risky asset and the factor process, (*b*) the frictionless optimal portfolio θ and its derivatives θ_z, θ_f, and (*c*) the risk tolerance $-v_z/v_{zz}$ of the frictionless value function. The comparative statics of this formula for general utilities

[12]This is the lowest-order symmetric polynomial in the deviation ξ with enough degrees of freedom to ensure value matching and smooth pasting at the trading boundaries $\pm\Delta\xi$.

are discussed by Kallsen & Muhle-Karbe (2015b). Here, we focus on the case most relevant for applications: power utilities with constant relative risk aversion.

As is well known (see, e.g., Zariphopoulou 2001), power utilities $U(x) = x^{1-\gamma}/(1-\gamma)$ imply that the optimal fraction of wealth invested in a risky asset, $\pi(t,f) := \theta(t,z,f)/z$, is independent of the wealth level. Moreover, the value function inherits the homotheticity $v(t,z,f) = z^{1-\gamma}v(t,1,f)$, so $-(v_{zz}/v_z)(t,z,f) = \gamma/z$. In view of Equations 26 and 22, the asymptotic no-trade region can therefore be written in terms of risky weights (in contrast to monetary amounts) as

$$\mathrm{NT}_\lambda \approx \left\{(t,x,y,f) : \left|\frac{y}{x+y} - \pi(t,f)\right| \leq \lambda^{1/3}\Delta\pi(t,f)\right\}, \tag{28.}$$

where

$$\Delta\pi = \left[\frac{3}{2\gamma}\left(\pi^2(1-\pi)^2 - 2\pi(1-\pi)\pi_f\frac{\sigma_F}{\sigma_S} + \pi_f^2\frac{\sigma_F^2}{\sigma_S^2}\right)\right]^{1/3}. \tag{29.}$$

Hence, in this case, the half-width of the asymptotically optimal no-trade region is fully determined by the volatilities σ_S, σ_F, the risk aversion γ, and the frictionless portfolio weight π and sensitivity π_f with respect to the state variable f.

4.6. Welfare Loss

With the explicit solution of the first corrector equation from Section 4.4, we can also say more about the leading-order term $\epsilon^2 u(t,z,f)$ in the expansion of the frictional value function (Equation 16). To this end, recall that $\mathcal{A}u = a$, where a is given by Equation 25 and the differential operator $\mathcal{A}$ is defined in Equation 11. Note that $\mathcal{A}$ is the infinitesimal generator of the frictionless optimal wealth process Z_t. Hence, the Feynman–Kac formula and Equation 25 show that

$$\begin{aligned} u(t,z,f) &= E_t\left[\int_t^T -a(s,Z_s,F_s)\mathrm{d}s\right] \\ &= v_z(t,z,f)E_t^Q\left[\int_t^T -\frac{v_{zz}(s,Z_s,F_s)}{v_z(s,Z_s,F_s)}\frac{\sigma_S(F_s)^2}{2}\Delta\xi(s,Z_s,F_s)^2\mathrm{d}s\right], \end{aligned} \tag{30.}$$

where Q is the frictionless investor's marginal pricing measure, whose density process is proportional to the marginal indirect utility v_z by the first-order condition of convex duality (Karatzas & Kou 1996, Davis 1997). (In complete markets, Q is simply the unique equivalent martingale measure. In any case, the corresponding density process is known explicitly if the value function of the problem at hand can be computed in closed form.)

With the representation in Equation 30 for u, Taylor's theorem allows us to rewrite the expansion 16 as

$$v^\lambda(t,z,f) = v\Big[t, z - \mathrm{CEL}^\lambda(t,x,f), f\Big] + \mathcal{O}(\lambda). \tag{31.}$$

Here,

$$\mathrm{CEL}^\lambda(t,z,f) = \lambda^{2/3}E_t^Q\left[\int_t^T -\frac{v_{zz}(s,Z_s,F_s)}{v_z(s,Z_s,F_s)}\frac{\sigma_S(F_s)^2}{2}\Delta\xi(s,Z_s,F_s)^2\mathrm{d}s\right] \tag{32.}$$

is the certainty equivalent loss resulting from small transaction costs, i.e., the amount of initial endowment an investor would forgo in order to trade the risky asset without transaction costs. Like the asymptotic no-trade region, this measure for the welfare effect of the trading costs is determined by (*a*) the diffusion coefficients of the risky asset and the factor process, (*b*) the frictionless optimal policy and its sensitivities, and (*c*) the risk tolerance of the frictionless value function. As all of these quantities are generally random and time dependent, they are averaged with respect to both time and states.

4.6.1. Constant relative risk aversion. For power utilities with constant relative risk aversion $\gamma > 0$, Equation 32 can be simplified:

$$\mathrm{CEL}^{\lambda}(t,z,f) = z\lambda^{2/3} E_t^{\tilde{P}}\left[\int_t^T \frac{\gamma}{2}\sigma_S(F_s)^2 \Delta\pi(s,F_s)^2 \mathrm{d}s\right], \qquad 33.$$

where the expectation is computed under the measure $\tilde{P}$ whose density process is proportional to the value function $v(s, Z_s, F_s)$ evaluated along the frictionless optimal wealth process (this measure also plays an important role in the asymptotic analysis of small unhedgeable risks; see Kramkov & Sirbu 2006). By scaling out the current wealth z, this leads to the relative certainty equivalent loss, an appealing scale-invariant measure for the welfare effect of transaction costs that is also used in, for example, the numerical work of Balduzzi & Lynch (1999). Here, its small-cost approximation is obtained by averaging the frictionless optimizer, its sensitivities, and the volatilities of the risky asset and the factor process in a suitable way. These are all functions of the factor process F. To find the dynamics of F under the measure $\tilde{P}$, use Itô's formula to compute the dynamics of the density process:

$$\frac{\mathrm{d}v(s,Z_s,F_s)}{v(s,Z_s,F_s)} = \frac{\mathcal{A}v(s,Z_s,F_s)}{v(s,Z_s,F_s)}\mathrm{d}s + \frac{v_z(s,Z_s,F_s)}{v(s,Z_s,F_s)}\mathrm{d}Z_s + \frac{v_f(s,Z_s,F_s)}{v(s,Z_s,F_s)}\mathrm{d}F_s =: \mathrm{d}L_t. \qquad 34.$$

The $\mathrm{d}s$ term vanishes by the frictionless dynamic programming equation 11. It follows that the density process of $\tilde{P}$ is a stochastic exponential $\mathcal{E}(L)_t = \exp(L_t - \frac{1}{2}\langle L\rangle_t)$, and the $\tilde{P}$ dynamics of F can be readily computed using Girsanov's theorem. If the frictionless value function is known in closed form, the corresponding change of drift is once more fully explicit.

4.6.2. Long investment horizons. The relative certainty equivalent loss (Equation 33) is a function of only time and the state variable. If the planning horizon T is long, the time variable averages out and even more tractable formulas obtain. For large T, the frictionless policy $\pi(t,f)$ typically converges quickly to a steady-state value $\bar{\pi}(f)$ that depends only on the state variable (but not the current time), and the frictionless value function approximately scales as follows (Guasoni & Robertson 2012):

$$v(t,z,f) \approx \frac{z^{1-\gamma}}{1-\gamma} e^{(1-\gamma)(T-t)\mathrm{ESR}}. \qquad 35.$$

Here, the equivalent safe rate ESR is a fictitious interest rate that, in the long run, yields the same growth rate of utility as trading in the original market. With small transaction costs, Equations 31, 33, and 35 show that the corresponding leading-order expression is[13]

$$v^{\lambda}(t,x,y) \approx \frac{z^{1-\gamma}}{1-\gamma} e^{(1-\gamma)(T-t)(\mathrm{ESR}-\Delta\mathrm{ESR}_t^{\lambda})}.$$

Here, the equivalent safe rate loss resulting from small transaction costs is

$$\Delta\mathrm{ESR}_t^{\lambda} = \lambda^{2/3}\frac{\gamma}{2}\frac{1}{(T-t)} E_t^{\tilde{P}}\left[\int_t^T \Delta\pi(s,F_s)^2\sigma_S(F_s)^2\mathrm{d}s\right].$$

[13]This requires that the effect of transaction costs be small even when compounded over a long horizon. To make this argument precise, one can directly consider the infinite-horizon problem as in the work of Gerhold et al. (2014), Kallsen & Muhle-Karbe (2015b), and Melnyk & Seifried (2017).

On any finite time horizon T, this quantity is a function of time t and the value f of the state variable. However, as the horizon grows, the ergodic theorem implies that if the state variable F has a stationary distribution $\nu_F^{\tilde{P}}(\mathrm{d}f)$ under the measure $\tilde{P}$, then the equivalent safe rate loss converges to a constant, like the frictionless equivalent safe rate[14]:

$$\Delta \mathrm{ESR}^{\lambda} \approx \lambda^{2/3} \frac{\gamma}{2} \int_{-\infty}^{\infty} \Delta\bar{\pi}(f)^2 \sigma(f)^2 \nu_F^{\tilde{P}}(\mathrm{d}f). \tag{36}$$

In summary, the welfare effect in infinite-horizon models with small transaction costs can be computed by performing a simple numerical quadrature.

5. EXAMPLES

We now illustrate the asymptotic results from Section 4 in two concrete examples. As a sanity check, we first consider the Black–Scholes model and verify that the formulas derived above indeed coincide with the expressions directly obtained for this simple model (cf. Janeček & Shreve 2004, Bichuch 2012, Soner & Touzi 2013, Gerhold et al. 2014). Afterward, we turn to the Kim–Omberg model and discuss how the results change with stochastic investment opportunities.

5.1. Black–Scholes Model

For an investor with constant relative risk aversion $\gamma > 0$, the value function in the Black–Scholes model is

$$v(t,z) = \frac{z^{1-\gamma}}{1-\gamma} \exp\left[(1-\gamma)\left(r + \frac{\mu^2}{2\gamma\sigma^2}\right)(T-t)\right],$$

and the corresponding risky weight is constant: $\pi_{\mathrm{BS}} = \mu/\gamma\sigma^2$. As a consequence, the half-width (Equation 29) of the asymptotic no-trade region simplifies to

$$\Delta\pi_{\mathrm{BS}} = \left(\frac{3}{2\gamma}\pi_{\mathrm{BS}}^2(1-\pi_{\mathrm{BS}})^2\right)^{1/3}.$$

The corresponding formula for the leading-order equivalent safe rate loss is

$$\Delta \mathrm{ESR}^{\lambda} = \frac{\gamma\sigma^2}{2}\left(\frac{3\lambda}{2\gamma}\pi_{\mathrm{BS}}^2(1-\pi_{\mathrm{BS}})^2\right)^{2/3}.$$

Both of these expressions vanish if zero or full investment is optimal in the frictionless model. If this is the case, the respective frictionless optimal strategies never trade, and no transaction costs need to be paid. In contrast, transaction costs play a more important role if the frictionless target weight is close to 1/2, but even then the quantitative effects are rather small (Constantinides 1986). If a leveraged portfolio is optimal ($\pi_{\mathrm{BS}} > 1$), the welfare loss can be more substantial (Gerhold et al. 2014).

5.2. Kim–Omberg Model

Let us now sketch how the above results change in the Kim–Omberg model, where the expected excess return follows an Ornstein–Uhlenbeck process with dynamics as in Equation 3. For a power

[14]We denote by $\Delta\bar{\pi}(f)$ the half-width of the stationary no-trade region obtained from the long-run portfolio $\bar{\pi}(f)$ via Equation 29.

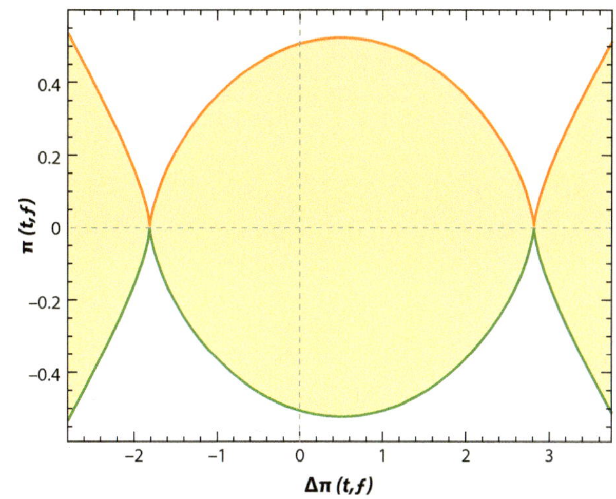

Figure 2

Half-width of the no-trade region in the Kim–Omberg model plotted against the optimal frictionless risky weight. Parameters (measured yearly) are $T = 40$, $\gamma = 3$, $r = 0.0168$, $\sigma_S = 0.151$, $\kappa = 0.271$, $\bar{F} = 0.041$, and $\sigma_F = 0.0343$ as in the study of Barberis (2000).

utility function with constant relative risk aversion $\gamma > 1$, the frictionless value function v has the following closed-form expression (Kim & Omberg 1996):

$$v(s, z, f) = \frac{z^{1-\gamma}}{1-\gamma} \exp\left(A(s) + B(s) f + \frac{1}{2} C(s) f^2 \right), \tag{37}$$

where the functions A, B, and C are explicit solutions of Riccati equations, as recalled in Section 8. The corresponding optimal risky weight is linear in the state variable:

$$\pi_{\mathrm{KO}}(s, F_s) = \frac{F_s}{\gamma \sigma_S^2} + \frac{\rho \sigma_F}{\gamma \sigma_S} [B(s) + C(s) F_s].$$

In view of Equation 29, this formula immediately yields a closed-form expression for the half-width $\Delta\pi_{\mathrm{KO}}$ of the asymptotic no-trade region with transaction costs. **Figure 1** shows a simulated sample path of the frictionless portfolio π_{KO} and the boundaries of the no-trade region $\pi_{\mathrm{KO}} \pm \Delta\pi_{\mathrm{KO}}$.

Because the frictionless risky weight is sensitive to changes in the state variable, the no-trade region no longer vanishes if the frictionless risky weight is zero or one, but instead does so at two other levels determined by the model parameters. For the parameters estimated from a long equity time series by Barberis (2000), this is illustrated in **Figure 2**, where the half-width of the no-trade region is plotted against the optimal frictionless risky weight for different values of the expected excess return.

This is complemented by **Figure 3**, which shows how the optimal frictionless portfolio and the corresponding no-trade region converge to their stationary long-run limits as the planning horizon grows. This stationary policy $\bar{\pi}_{\mathrm{KO}}$ corresponds to the stationary points $\bar{B}$ and $\bar{C}$ of the Riccati equations for $B(s)$ and $C(s)$. The corresponding no-trade region is in turn derived from Equation 29.

The long-horizon convergence of the functions $B(s)$ and $C(s)$ can also be used to simplify the computation of the leading-order relative certainty equivalent loss (Equation 36). In particular, Girsanov's theorem and the long-run convergence show that the long-term dynamics of the factor

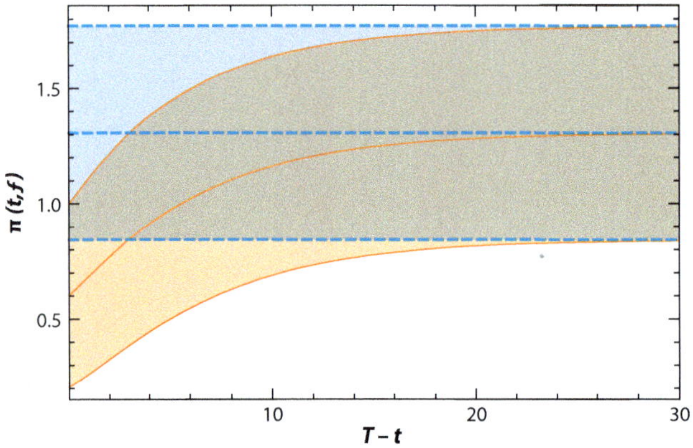

Figure 3

The frictionless position and no-trade region (*solid lines*) as a function of time (measured in years) plotted alongside infinite-horizon values (*dashed lines*). Parameters (measured yearly) are $\gamma = 3$, $r = 0.0168$, $\sigma_S = 0.151$, $\kappa = 0.271$, $\bar{F} = 0.041$, and $\sigma_F = 0.0343$ as in the study of Barberis (2000).

process F under the measure $\tilde{P}$ with density process as in Equation 34 are

$$\begin{aligned} dF_s &= \kappa(\bar{F} - F_s)ds + \sigma_F dW^F \\ &= \left\{\kappa(\bar{F} - F_s) + \sigma_F(1-\gamma)\pi_{\mathrm{KO}}(s, F_s)\sigma_S\rho + [B(s) + C(s)F_s]\sigma_F^2\right\}ds + \sigma_F d\tilde{W}^F \\ &\approx \left[\kappa(\bar{F} - F_s) + \sigma_F(1-\gamma)\bar{\pi}_{\mathrm{KO}}(F_s)\sigma_S\rho + (\bar{B} + \bar{C}F_s)\sigma_F^2\right]ds + \sigma_F d\tilde{W}^F \\ &=: \tilde{\kappa}(\tilde{F} - F_s)ds + \sigma_F d\tilde{W}^F, \end{aligned}$$

for a $\tilde{P}$-Brownian motion $\tilde{W}^F$ and suitably chosen constants $\tilde{\kappa}$ and $\tilde{F}$. Hence, for a long planning horizon, the factor process still has Ornstein–Uhlenbeck dynamics under the auxiliary measure $\tilde{P}$, and its stationary law is $\nu_F^{\tilde{P}} \sim \mathcal{N}(\tilde{F}, \sigma_F^2/2\tilde{\kappa})$. This allows computation of the relative certainty equivalent loss (Equation 36) resulting from small transaction costs as

$$\Delta \mathrm{ESR}^{\lambda}_{\mathrm{KO}} \approx \lambda^{2/3}\frac{\gamma}{\sqrt{2(\sigma_F^2/\tilde{\kappa})^2\pi}}\int_{-\infty}^{\infty}\left[\Delta\bar{\pi}_{\mathrm{KO}}(f)^2\sigma(f)^2\exp\left(-\frac{(f-\tilde{F})^2}{2(\sigma_F^2/2\tilde{\kappa})^2}\right)\right]df. \qquad 38.$$

Because the integrand is known in closed form, Equation 38 is easily evaluated by numerical quadrature. This is illustrated in **Figure 4**, which plots the relative certainty equivalence loss as a function of the proportional transaction cost. Compared to a Black–Scholes model with the same expected excess return, we observe that the welfare effect of transaction costs is indeed increased substantially by having to react to time-varying investment opportunities.

6. EXTENSIONS

So far, we have focused on the application of the homogenization approach to a portfolio choice problem with proportional transaction costs for purchases and sales of a single risky asset with Markovian dynamics. Performance has been measured in terms of expected utility from terminal wealth only, i.e., intertemporal consumption has been absent. This choice was made for concreteness and ease of exposition. In this section, we survey results from the recent literature that show that the findings outlined in Section 4 remain true much more generally.

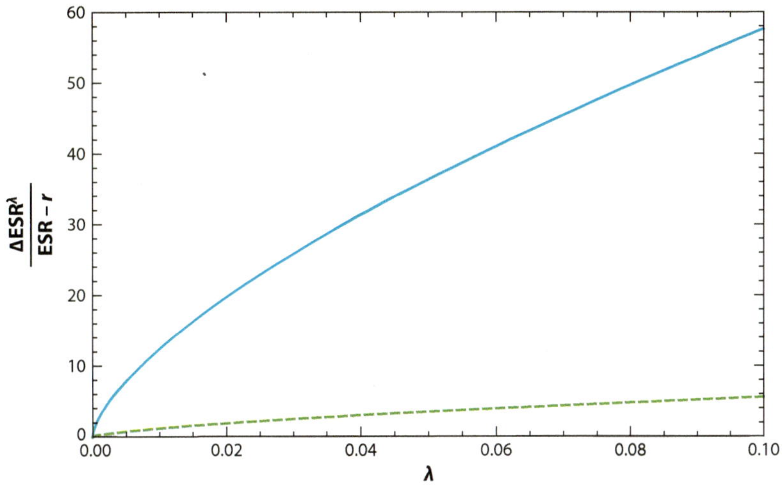

Figure 4

Relative loss in equivalent safe rate resulting from transaction costs for the Kim–Omberg model (*solid line*) and a Black–Scholes model (*dotted line*) with $\mu_S \equiv \bar{F}$, plotted against the size of the cost. Parameters (measured yearly) are $\gamma = 3$, $r = 0.0168$, $\sigma_S = 0.151$, $\kappa = 0.271$, $\bar{F} = 0.041$, and $\sigma_F = 0.0343$ as in Barberis (2000).

6.1. More General Preferences

The results of the previous sections can be readily extended to models with intermediate consumption. For example, Soner & Touzi (2013) study an infinite-horizon model with preferences of the form

$$E\left[\int_0^\infty e^{-\delta t} U(c_t)\mathrm{d}t\right] \to \max!,$$

where $\delta > 0$ is the investor's discount rate and $U(c_t)$ measures the utility from consumption rate c_t at time t. The asymptotic no-trade region for this optimization criterion turns out to be of the same form as in Equation 27—intermediate consumption is only reflected through the frictionless optimal policy. This remains true for more general additive preferences of the form

$$E\left[\int_0^T U_1(t, c_t)\mathrm{d}t + U_2(Z_T)\right] \to \max!, \qquad 39.$$

where $U_1(t, c_t)$ is the utility from intermediate consumption at time $t \in [0, T]$ and $U_2(Z_T)$ is the utility from terminal wealth Z_T at time T (for details, see Ahrens 2015, Kallsen & Muhle-Karbe 2015b). Despite this robustness result, substantial intertemporal consumption can have a nonnegligible effect if the trading costs are not small enough. The intuition is that because costs are paid from a savings account, investors are willing to accept smaller risky positions before rebalancing (Davis & Norman 1990). In infinite-horizon Black–Scholes models, this manifests itself through a downward shift of the no-trade region at the second asymptotic order $O(\lambda^{2/3})$ (Janeček & Shreve 2004; Lo, Mamaysky & Wang 2004; Gerhold, Muhle-Karbe & Schachermayer 2012). For more general models, such results are not available.

The effects of the transaction costs on optimal consumption policy are of the simplest conceivable form: It is asymptotically optimal to simply adjust the frictionless rule for the (typically lower) wealth with transaction costs (Kallsen & Muhle-Karbe 2015b). For power utility, this implies that the consumption/wealth ratio is unaffected by the trading costs (Kallsen & Muhle-Karbe 2015b, section 4).

Recently it was shown (Melnyk, Muhle-Karbe & Seifried 2017) that even the additive structure in the preferences in Equation 39 is not crucial, in that the same leading-order results also remain true for recursive preferences as in the work of Duffie & Epstein (1992) and for models with habit formation as in the work of Hindy & Huang (1993). At the leading asymptotic order, the optimal trading strategy is again completely characterized by the local curvature of agents' preferences, measured by the risk tolerance of their indirect utilities, and the consumption/wealth ratio remains unchanged. The fine structure of the preferences at hand enters only at the next-to-leading order.

6.2. More General Asset Dynamics

In previous sections, we have assumed that the joint dynamics of the asset prices (described in Equations 1 and 2) and the factor process are Markovian; i.e., all drift and diffusion coefficients are deterministic functions of the current state of the system. This assumption allows us to apply partial differential equation techniques, but is not crucial for the validity of Equations 27 and 31. Indeed, these formulas are derived by freezing the frictionless state variables for the analysis of the first corrector equation—a procedure that readily generalizes to general, not necessarily Markovian systems where drift and diffusion coefficients can be arbitrary functionals of the information flow. Even in such more general models, Equation 27 for the asymptotically optimal no-trade region and Equation 31 for the leading-order effect of small transaction costs remain valid (for details, see Kallsen & Muhle-Karbe 2015a,b; Cai, Rosenbaum & Tankov 2017a,b).

Extending the approach presented here to models with jumps leads to the analysis of nonlocal integro-differential equations. Although this appears to be a daunting task, it is shown by Rosenbaum & Tankov (2014), using probabilistic techniques, that asymptotic results similar to Equations 27 and 31 can still be obtained.

6.3. More General Transaction Costs

Although we have focused here on proportional transaction costs, this structure, too, is not crucial. At least on a formal level, fixed costs (Altarovici, Muhle-Karbe & Soner 2015), fixed and proportional costs (Altarovici, Reppen & Soner 2016), and quadratic costs (Moreau, Muhle-Karbe & Soner 2017) can be treated similarly.

In each case, the fine structure of the optimal strategy crucially depends on the transaction cost considered. With proportional costs, one performs the minimal amount of trading to remain in a no-trade interval around the frictionless target. With fixed costs, it is no longer possible to implement a strategy involving infinitely many small trades; hence, one directly trades back to a target portfolio once the boundary of the no-trade region is reached. Conversely, quadratic costs lead to smaller penalties for very small trades but make large turnover rates prohibitively expensive. Thus, optimal strategies always trade toward the target at some finite, absolutely continuous rate.

Despite these apparent differences, the coarse structures of all these models are very similar: In each case, the distance from the target is a trade-off against the specific trading cost, balanced by an appropriate control. The corresponding expected displacement and average transaction costs display the same comparative statics in each case, up to a change of asymptotic convergence rates and constants. In particular, the implications of transaction costs for welfare and average trading volume are very similar in each case (for further details, see Moreau, Muhle-Karbe & Soner 2017).

6.4. Multiple Risky Assets

The extensions sketched so far eventually lead to explicit asymptotic formulas of complexity similar to that of the benchmark model discussed in Section 4. In contrast, less is known about the case of several risky assets. In this case, the homogenization approach still reduces the dimensionality of the problem (Possamaï, Soner & Touzi 2015), but the resulting corrector equations no longer admit an explicit solution. As a consequence, numerical methods such as the policy iteration scheme in Section 7 are needed even for the asymptotic analysis. Models with quadratic costs (Garleanu & Pedersen 2013, 2016; Guasoni & Weber 2016; Moreau, Muhle-Karbe & Soner 2017) and fixed costs (Atkinson & Wilmott 1995; Altarovici, Muhle-Karbe & Soner 2015) can still be solved in closed form in the multidimensional case, but the tractability issue is exacerbated for general nonlinear costs.

7. NUMERICAL SOLUTIONS IN MULTIPLE DIMENSIONS

The corrector equations obtained by passing to the small-cost limit are considerably simpler than the original dynamic programming equation. Even in situations with multiple risky assets (Possamaï, Soner & Touzi 2015) or nonlinear costs (Altarovici, Reppen & Soner 2016), where explicit solutions are not available, this considerably simplifies the numerical analysis. In this section, we present a variant of the classical policy iteration algorithm that is tailored to the control problem at hand and that works very well in practice (alternative methods based on partial differential equation techniques can be found in the work of Muthuraman & Kumar 2006, Dai & Zhong 2010). An attractive feature of this method is that both the value function and the corresponding no-trade region are approximated simultaneously.

The main idea of policy iteration is to start with a guess for the optimal control and to compute the corresponding payoff by solving a linear equation. The result of this computation is then used to generate an improved policy by, at each point, determining the best response to this payoff. These two steps are iterated until a fixed point is found (for an overview, see, e.g., Puterman 1994).

To apply this technique in the presence of proportional transaction costs, the first step is to recognize that the first corrector equation can be interpreted as the dynamic programming equation of an ergodic control problem. Instead of using a direct policy iteration scheme as in the work of Chancelier, Messaoud & Sulem (2007), we approximate the singular controls by smooth trading rates, capped at some finite level (compare Davis & Norman 1990, section 3; Witte & Reisinger 2012), to achieve better stability (see, e.g., Azimzadeh & Forsyth 2016). The resulting control problem can then be discretized and solved by a classical scheme. Approximation by capping is a special case of the approach presented by Altarovici, Reppen & Soner (2016) for problems with proportional and fixed costs, and it can readily be generalized to other settings.

Consider a d-dimensional model with a frictionless value function v and optimal risky positions θ. To simplify the notation, all assets are traded with the same proportional transaction cost. Arguments analogous to those in Section 4 then show that the d-dimensional version of the first corrector equation 23 is

$$\min_{i=1,\dots,d} \min\left\{ -\frac{1}{2}|\sigma_S^\top \xi|^2 v_{zz} + a + \frac{1}{2}\mathrm{Tr}\left[\alpha\alpha^\top w_{\xi\xi}\right];\ v_z + w_\xi \cdot e_i;\ v_z - w_\xi \cdot e_i \right\} = 0, \qquad 40.$$

where α is a model-dependent matrix analogous to Equation 22 that depends on θ and its derivatives.

The corrector equation 40 can be interpreted as the dynamic programming equation of an infinite-horizon control problem. To wit, let L^i, M^i, and $i = 1, \dots, d$ be nondecreasing controls for

$$\Xi_s^i = \xi^i + \sum_{j=1}^{d} \alpha^{i,j}(t,z,f)W_s^j + L_s^i - M_s^i.$$

Then Equation 40 is the dynamic programming equation for the ergodic control problem

$$a(t,z,f) := \inf_{L,M} J(t,z,f;L,M), \qquad 41.$$

corresponding to the following infinite-horizon goal functional:

$$J(t,z,f;L,M) := \limsup_{s\to\infty} \frac{1}{s} E\left[\frac{1}{2}\int_0^s -v_{zz}(t,z,f)\left|\sigma_S^\top \Xi_\tau\right|^2 \mathrm{d}\tau + v_z(t,z,f)\sum_{i=1}^{d}(L_s^i + M_s^i)\right].$$

This means that the controls are chosen so as to minimize the long-run average deviations of the controlled process Ξ from zero, subject to proportional adjustment costs. Note that in this problem, the state variables (t,z,f) of the original problem are frozen, so the uncontrolled Ξ is a Brownian motion.

To solve this problem numerically, we approximate the controls L, M by absolutely continuous trading rates of the form

$$L_t^s = \int_0^s \ell^i(\Xi_\tau)\mathrm{d}\tau \quad \text{and} \quad M_s^i = \int_0^s m^i(\Xi_\tau)\mathrm{d}\tau,$$

for functions ℓ and m bounded by a finite constant K. (As the artificial constraint K tends to infinity, we then expect to approach the solution of the original problem.) With this restriction, the dynamics of the controlled process are

$$\mathrm{d}\Xi_s^i = \nu^i(\Xi;\ell,m)\mathrm{d}s + \alpha \mathrm{d}W_s,$$

where $\nu^i(\xi;\ell,m) = (\ell^i - m^i)(\xi)$. The corresponding dynamic programming equation for the restricted version of Equation 41 is

$$\min_{\substack{i=1,\ldots,d\\ \ell^i,m^i\in[0,K]}} \left[\mathcal{L}^{\ell,m}w(\xi) + f(\ell,m,\xi)\right] = -a, \quad \forall \xi \in \mathbb{R}^d,$$

where

$$\mathcal{L}^{\ell,m}w(\xi) = \nu(\xi;\ell,m)^\top \frac{\partial w}{\partial \xi}(\xi) + \frac{1}{2}\mathrm{Tr}\left[\alpha\alpha^\top \frac{\partial^2 w}{\partial(\xi^i)\partial(\xi^j)}(\xi)\right] \qquad 42.$$

and

$$f(\ell,m,\xi) = -\frac{1}{2}\left|\sigma_S^\top \xi\right|^2 v_{zz} + v_z\sum_{i=1}^{d}(\ell^i + m^i).$$

Now truncate the state space for the control problem to a large finite domain in $\mathbb{R}^d$ and consider a discretization $\mathcal{D} \subset \mathbb{R}^d$ of this set. The approximation $\mathcal{L}_{\mathcal{D}}^{\ell,m} : \mathcal{D} \mapsto \mathbb{R}$ of the operator $\mathcal{L}^{\ell,m}$ in Equation 42 outlined in Section 9 can in turn be interpreted as the transition rate matrix of a discrete control problem with dynamic programming equation

$$\min_{\substack{i=1,\ldots,d\\ \ell^i,m^i\in[0,K]}} \left(\sum_{\xi'\in\mathcal{D}} \mathcal{L}_{\mathcal{D}}^{\ell,m}(\xi,\xi')w(\xi') + f(\ell,m,\xi)\right) = -a, \quad \forall \xi \in \mathcal{D}.$$

If the truncated domain is sufficiently large, the probability of Ξ reaching its boundary is small, so the corresponding boundary conditions can be chosen arbitrarily as long as the discretized differential operator can be interpreted as the transition rate matrix of some discrete control problem. The key advantage of this scheme is that the bound K ensures that the transition probabilities are bounded away from 0, enabling us to represent the problem as a continuous-time Markov decision process for which standard policy iteration techniques apply. More specifically, this discrete problem can be solved using the following policy iteration algorithm by choosing an initial policy (ℓ_0, m_0), e.g., $\ell_0, m_0 \equiv 0$, and then iterating the following steps:

1. Compute $(w_j, a_j) \in \mathbb{R}^{|\mathcal{D}|} \times \mathbb{R}^+$ as the solution of

$$\left(\sum_{\xi' \in \mathcal{D}} \mathcal{L}_{\mathcal{D}}^{\ell_j, m_j}(\xi, \xi') w_j(\xi') + f(\ell_j, m_j, \xi) \right) = -a, \quad \forall \xi \in \mathcal{D}.$$

   Note that these are $|\mathcal{D}|$ equations for $|\mathcal{D}| + 1$ unknowns. The missing equation is obtained by normalizing w as in Section 4.

2. Find solutions ℓ_{j+1} and m_{j+1} to the $|\mathcal{D}|$ minimization problems

$$\ell_{j+1}(\xi), m_{j+1}(\xi) \in \underset{\substack{i=1,\ldots,d \\ \ell^i, m^i \in [0,K]}}{\arg\min} \left(\sum_{\xi' \in \mathcal{D}} \mathcal{L}_{\mathcal{D}}^{\ell, m}(\xi, \xi') w_j(\xi') + f(\ell, m, \xi) \right)$$

   and return to the previous step.

The iteration is terminated when the difference between a_j and a_{j-1} is small enough. It is known that this difference converges to 0 in finite time (see, e.g., Puterman 1994). Although this bound is very large for a general policy iteration scheme, it has been observed that policy iterations typically converge very quickly, often in fewer than 20 iterations (Santos & Rust 2004). The fast convergence is attained thanks to the scheme's close connections to Newton's method. (For more details on these connections, as well as the convergence rate, see Puterman & Brumelle 1979; Santos & Rust 2004; Bokanowski, Maroso & Zidani 2009.)

Solving the $|\mathcal{D}|$ optimization problems in the second step of each iteration may seem daunting at first glance. However, when trading is only conducted through the safe account but not directly between risky assets, the solution of this problem is in fact explicit. Also, in more general settings, the optimization problems are entirely independent of each other, so their solution can be fully parallelized.

For simplicity, the chosen model is a Black–Scholes market consisting of two risky assets, where an agent optimizes the power utility of consumption over an infinite horizon (with impatience parameter δ), as in Section 6.1 or in the work of Possamaï, Soner & Touzi (2015). This choice appears in the above problem only through v_{zz}, v_z, and α, and in this case

$$\alpha = (I_d - \theta_z^\top 1_d) \operatorname{diag}[\theta] \sigma_S,$$

where I_d is the d-dimensional identity matrix, $\operatorname{diag}[\theta]$ is the matrix with diagonal θ and other elements zero, and $1_d = (1, \ldots, 1)^\top \in \mathbb{R}^d$. Optimal strategies computed using this algorithm are depicted in **Figure 5**.

The policy iteration scheme presented here can readily be generalized to more complex models. For example, details and justifications for such generalizations can be found in the work of Altarovici, Reppen & Soner (2016) for a model with proportional and fixed costs, as in Section 3.3. The output of the algorithm in this setting is illustrated in **Figure 5*d*.** where the rebalancing target, to which the portfolio is readjusted once the boundaries of the no-trade region are breached, is represented visually.

8. APPENDIX: KIM–OMBERG VALUE FUNCTION

Consider a power utility function with constant relative risk aversion γ. As shown by Kim & Omberg (1996), the value function for the Kim–Omberg model (Equations 1 and 3) is then of the

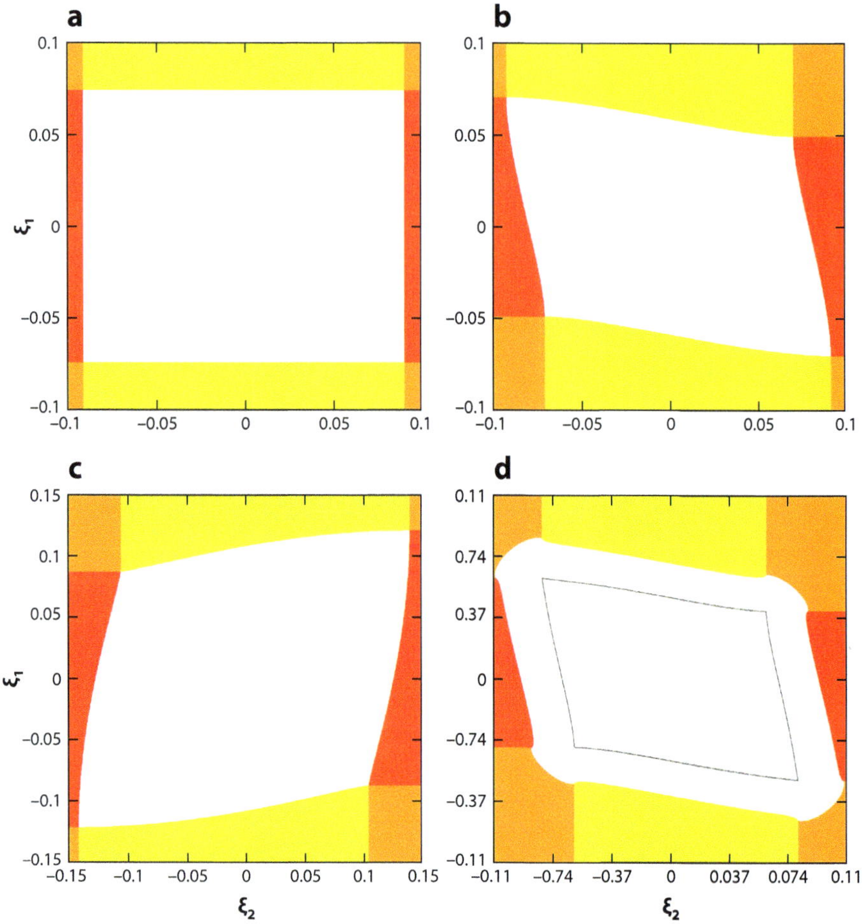

Panel	δ	γ	r	μ_1	μ_2	σ_1	σ_2	ρ	λ_f	λ_p	z
a	1	2	0.03	0.08	0.08	0.4	0.33	0.00	0	3%	$50,000
b	1	2	0.03	0.08	0.08	0.4	0.33	0.30	0	3%	$50,000
c	1	2	0.03	0.08	0.08	0.4	0.33	−0.30	0	3%	$50,000
d	1	2	0.03	0.08	0.08	0.4	0.33	0.30	$1	3%	$50,000

Figure 5

Asymptotic no-trade regions (*white*) and regions in which there is trading in the assets (*yellow*, *red*, and *orange*) are shown for different parameters (μ_i and σ_i are the expected excess return and volatility of risky assets $i = 1, 2$; ρ is the correlation between their driving Brownian motions). Each axis represents the deviation of a risky weight from its frictionless target. The interpretation of the transaction cost is as in Equation 28. Except in the corners (*orange*), trading is performed in only one asset at a time, inducing vertical or horizontal movements of the portfolio position. For example, panel *a* has a no-trade region of half-width 0.091, meaning that it is optimal to trade risky asset 2 (only) when its current weight deviates from the frictionless optimizer by 9.1% of current wealth. (*d*) The area within the no-trade region that is enclosed in a solid line is the rebalancing target, to which the portfolio is readjusted once the boundaries of the no-trade region are breached.

form

$$v(u,z,f) = \frac{z^{1-\gamma}}{1-\gamma}\exp\left(A(u) + B(u)f + \frac{1}{2}C(u)f^2\right).$$

Define

$$b = 2\left(\frac{1-\gamma}{\gamma}\frac{\sigma_F}{\sigma_S}\rho - \kappa\right), \quad \eta = \sqrt{b^2 - 4\frac{1-\gamma}{\gamma}\left(\frac{\sigma_F}{\sigma_S}\right)^2\left(1 + \frac{1-\gamma}{\gamma}\rho\right)}.$$

In the empirically relevant case when $\gamma > 1$ and $\rho < 0$, the discriminant η is positive, so A, B, and C can be identified as the normal solution of Kim & Omberg (1996):

$$C(u) = \frac{1-\gamma}{\gamma}\frac{2}{\sigma_S^2}\frac{1-\exp[-\eta(T-u)]}{2\eta - (b+\eta)\left\{1-\exp[-\eta(T-u)]\right\}},$$

$$B(u) = 4\frac{1-\gamma}{\gamma}\frac{\kappa\bar{F}}{\sigma_S^2}\frac{1-\exp\left[-\eta(T-u)/2\right]}{2\eta^2 - \eta(b+\eta)\left\{1-\exp[-\eta(T-u)]\right\}},$$

$$\begin{aligned} A(u) = {} & \frac{1-\gamma}{\gamma}\left(\gamma r + \frac{2\kappa^2\bar{F}^2}{\sigma_S^2\eta^2} + \frac{\sigma_F^2}{\sigma_S^2(\eta-b)}\right)(T-u) \\ & + \frac{1-\gamma}{\gamma}\frac{4\kappa^2\bar{F}^2}{\sigma_S^2}\frac{(2b+\eta)\exp[-\eta(T-u)] - 4b\exp[-\eta(T-u)/2] + 2b - \eta}{\eta^3\left(2\eta - (b+\eta)\left\{1-\exp[-\eta(T-u)]\right\}\right)} \\ & + \frac{1-\gamma}{\gamma}\frac{2\sigma_F^2}{\sigma_S^2}\frac{\log\left|2\eta - (b+\eta)\left\{1-\exp[-\eta(T-u)]\right\}\right|}{2\eta(\eta^2-b^2)}. \end{aligned}$$

9. APPENDIX: DISCRETIZATION SCHEME FOR POLICY ITERATION

For the numerical computations in Section 7, the differential operator of the ergodic control problem needs to be discretized. To interpret the discretized operator as the transition rate matrix of some (continuous-time) Markov decision process, the following discretization scheme is used:

$$\frac{\partial w}{\partial(\xi^i)}(\xi) \approx \begin{cases} \dfrac{w(\xi + e_i h_i) - w(\xi)}{h_i} & \text{if } \nu^i(\xi;\ell,m) > 0, \\ \dfrac{w(\xi) - w(\xi - e_i h_i)}{h_i} & \text{if } \nu^i(\xi;\ell) < 0, \end{cases}$$

$$\frac{\partial^2 w}{\partial(\xi_i)^2}(\xi) \approx \frac{w(\xi + e_i h_i) - 2w(\xi) + w(\xi - e_i h_i)}{h_i^2},$$

$$
\frac{\partial^2 w}{\partial(\xi_i)\partial(\xi_i)}(\xi) \approx \begin{cases} \dfrac{2w(\xi) + w(\xi + e_i h_i + e_j h_j) + w(\xi - e_i h_i - e_j h_j)}{2h_i h_j} \\ \quad - \dfrac{w(\xi + e_i h_i) + w(\xi - e_i h_i) + w(\xi + e_j h_j) + w(\xi - e_j h_j)}{2h_i h_j} & \text{if } A_{i,j} > 0, \\ -\dfrac{2w(\xi) + w(\xi + e_i h_i - e_j h_j) + w(\xi - e_i h_i + e_j h_j)}{2h_i h_j} \\ \quad + \dfrac{w(\xi + e_i h_i) + w(\xi - e_i h_i) + w(\xi + e_j h_j) + w(\xi - e_j h_j)}{2h_i h_j} & \text{if } A_{i,j} < 0, \end{cases}
$$

for $i, j = 1, \ldots, d$, $i \neq j$, and where h_i is the grid size in the ξ^i direction. With $A = \alpha\alpha^\top$, the approximation $\mathcal{L}^\ell_{\mathcal{D}} : \mathcal{D} \mapsto \mathbb{R}$ of the differential operator $\mathcal{L}^\ell$ is then given by

$$
\begin{aligned}
\mathcal{L}^\ell_{\mathcal{D}}(\xi, \xi) &= -\sum_{i=1}^{d} \left(\frac{A_{i,i}}{h_i^2} - \frac{1}{2} \sum_{\substack{j=1,\\ j\neq i}}^{d} \frac{|A_{i,j}|}{h_i h_j} \right) - \sum_{i=1}^{d} \frac{|\nu^i(\xi;\ell)|}{h_i}, \\
\mathcal{L}^\ell_{\mathcal{D}}(\xi, \xi + e_i h_i) &= \frac{1}{2} \left(\frac{A_{i,i}}{h_i^2} - \sum_{\substack{j=1,\\ j\neq i}}^{d} \frac{|A_{i,j}|}{h_i h_j} \right) + \sum_{i=1}^{d} \frac{\max\{0, \nu^i(\xi;\ell)\}}{h_i}, \\
\mathcal{L}^\ell_{\mathcal{D}}(\xi, \xi - e_i h_i) &= \frac{1}{2} \left(\frac{A_{i,i}}{h_i^2} - \sum_{\substack{j=1,\\ j\neq i}}^{d} \frac{|A_{i,j}|}{h_i h_j} \right) + \sum_{i=1}^{d} \frac{\max\{0, -\nu^i(\xi;\ell)\}}{h_i}, \\
\mathcal{L}^\ell_{\mathcal{D}}(\xi, \xi \pm e_i h_i \pm e_j h_j) &= \frac{\max\{0, A_{i,j}\}}{2h_i h_j}, \\
\mathcal{L}^\ell_{\mathcal{D}}(\xi, \xi \pm e_i h_i \mp e_j h_j) &= \frac{\max\{0, -A_{i,j}\}}{2h_i h_j},
\end{aligned}
$$

for $i, j = 1, \ldots, d$ and $i \neq j$. For a finite domain, we also need the condition

$$
\sum_{\xi' \in \mathcal{D}} \mathcal{L}^{\ell_j}_{\mathcal{D}}(\xi, \xi') = 0.
$$

This ensures that the Markov decision process stays within the domain at all times. As long as the domain is chosen large enough to contain the no-trade region, this is not a constraint, as the optimal strategy already ensures that the process does not exit the domain.

DISCLOSURE STATEMENT

The authors are not aware of any affiliations, memberships, funding, or financial holdings that might be perceived as affecting the objectivity of this review.

ACKNOWLEDGMENTS

M.R. and H.M.S. were partly supported by the ETH Foundation, the Swiss Finance Institute, and Swiss National Foundation grant SNF 200021_153555. Parts of this article were written while J.M.-K. was visiting the Forschungsinstitut Mathematik at ETH Zürich.

LITERATURE CITED

Ahrens L. 2015. *On using shadow prices for the asymptotic analysis of portfolio optimization under proportional transaction costs*. PhD Thesis, Univ. Kiel, Ger.

Altarovici A, Muhle-Karbe J, Soner HM. 2015. Asymptotics for fixed transaction costs. *Finance Stoch.* 19(2):363–414

Altarovici A, Reppen M, Soner HM. 2016. Optimal consumption and investment with fixed and proportional transaction costs. *SIAM J. Control Optim.* 55(3):1673–710

Atkinson C, Wilmott P. 1995. Portfolio management with transaction costs: an asymptotic analysis of the Morton and Pliska model. *Math. Finance* 5(4):357–67

Azimzadeh P, Forsyth PA. 2016. Weakly chained matrices, policy iteration, and impulse control. *SIAM J. Numer. Anal.* 54(3):1341–64

Bajgrowicz O, Scaillet O. 2012. Technical trading revisited: persistence tests, transaction costs, and false discoveries. *J. Financ. Econ.* 106(3):473–91

Balduzzi P, Lynch AW. 1999. Transaction costs and predictability: some utility cost calculations. *J. Financ. Econ.* 52(1):47–78

Barberis N. 2000. Investing for the long run when returns are predictable. *J. Finance* 55(1):225–64

Beneš VE, Shepp LA, Witsenhausen HS. 1980. Some solvable stochastic control problems. *Stochastics* 4(1):39–83

Bichuch M. 2012. Asymptotic analysis for optimal investment in finite time with transaction costs. *SIAM J. Financ. Math.* 3(1):433–58

Bichuch M. 2014. Pricing a contingent claim liability using asymptotic analysis for optimal investment in finite time with transaction costs. *Finance Stoch.* 18(3):651–94

Bichuch M, Shreve SE. 2013. Utility maximization trading two futures with transaction costs. *SIAM J. Financ. Math.* 4(1):26–85

Bokanowski O, Maroso S, Zidani H. 2009. Some convergence results for Howard's algorithm. *SIAM J. Numer. Anal.* 47(4):3001–26

Bouchard B, Moreau L, Soner HM. 2016. Hedging under an expected loss constraint with small transaction costs. *SIAM J. Financ. Math.* 7(1):508–51

Bouchard B, Nutz M. 2012. Weak dynamic programming for generalized state constraints. *SIAM J. Control Optim.* 50(6):3344–73

Bouchard B, Touzi N. 2011. Weak dynamic programming principle for viscosity solutions. *SIAM J. Control Optim.* 49(3):948–62

Cai J, Rosenbaum M, Tankov P. 2017a. Asymptotic lower bounds for optimal tracking: a linear programming approach. *Ann. Appl. Probab.* 27:2455–514

Cai J, Rosenbaum M, Tankov P. 2017b. Asymptotic optimal tracking: feedback strategies. *Stochastics*. In press

Chacko G, Viceira L. 2005. Dynamic consumption and portfolio choice with stochastic volatility in incomplete markets. *Rev. Financ. Stud.* 18(4):1369–402

Chancelier J-P, Messaoud M, Sulem A. 2007. A policy iteration algorithm for fixed point problems with nonexpansive operators. *Math. Methods Oper. Res.* 65(2):239–59

Cochrane JH. 2008. The dog that did not bark: a defense of return predictability. *Rev. Finan. Stud.* 21(4):1533–75

Collin-Dufresne P, Daniel K, Moallemi C, Saglam M. 2012. *Strategic asset allocation in the presence of transaction costs*. Work. Pap., Swiss Finance Inst., Zürich

Constantinides GM. 1986. Capital market equilibrium with transaction costs. *J. Political Econ.* 94(4):842–62

Cvitanić J, Karatzas I. 1996. Hedging and portfolio optimization under transaction costs: a martingale approach. *Math. Finance* 6(2):133–65

Dai M, Li P, Liu H, Wang Y. 2016. Portfolio choice with market closure and implications for liquidity premia. *Manag. Sci.* 62(2):368–86

Dai M, Yi F. 2009. Finite-horizon optimal investment with transaction costs: a parabolic double obstacle problem. *J. Differ. Equ.* 246(4):1445–69

Dai M, Zhong Y. 2010. Penalty methods for continuous-time portfolio selection with proportional transaction costs. *J. Comput. Finance* 13(3):1–31

Davis MHA. 1997. Option pricing in incomplete markets. In *Mathematics of Derivative Securities*, ed. MAH Dempster, SR Pliska, pp. 216–26. Cambridge, UK: Cambridge Univ. Press

Davis MHA, Norman AR. 1990. Portfolio selection with transaction costs. *Math. Oper. Res.* 15(4):676–713

De Lataillade J, Deremble C, Potters M, Bouchaud J-P. 2012. Optimal trading with linear costs. *J. Invest. Strategy* 1(3):91–115

Dixit A. 1991. Analytical approximations in models of hysteresis. *Rev. Econ. Stud.* 58(1):141–51

Duffie D, Epstein LG. 1992. Stochastic differential utility. *Econometrica* 60(2):353–94

Dumas B. 1991. Super contact and related optimality conditions. *J. Econ. Dynam. Control* 15(4):675–85

Dumas B, Luciano E. 1991. An exact solution to a dynamic portfolio choice problem under transactions costs. *J. Finance* 46(2):577–95

El Karoui N, Tan X. 2013. *Capacities, measurable selection and dynamic programming. Part II: application in stochastic control problems.* Preprint

Evans LC. 1989. The perturbed test function method for viscosity solutions of nonlinear PDE. *Proc. R. Soc. Edinburgh A* 111(3–4):359–75

Evans LC. 1992. Periodic homogenisation of certain fully nonlinear partial differential equations. *Proc. R. Soc. Edinburgh A* 120(3–4):245–65

Feodoria MR. 2016. *Optimal investment and utility indifference pricing in the presence of small fixed transaction costs.* PhD Thesis, Univ. Kiel, Ger.

Fleming WH, Soner HM. 2006. *Controlled Markov Processes and Viscosity Solutions.* New York: Springer. 2nd ed.

Garleanu N, Pedersen LH. 2013. Dynamic trading with predictable returns and transaction costs. *J. Finance* 68(6):2309–40

Garleanu N, Pedersen LH. 2016. Dynamic portfolio choice with frictions. *J. Econ. Theory* 165:487–516

Gerhold S, Guasoni P, Muhle-Karbe J, Schachermayer W. 2014. Transaction costs, trading volume, and the liquidity premium. *Finance Stoch.* 18(1):1–37

Gerhold S, Muhle-Karbe J, Schachermayer W. 2012. Asymptotics and duality for the Davis and Norman problem. *Stochastics* 84(5–6):625–41

Gerhold S, Muhle-Karbe J, Schachermayer W. 2013. The dual optimizer for the growth-optimal portfolio under transaction costs. *Finance Stoch.* 17(2):325–54

Grinold R. 2006. A dynamic model of portfolio management. *J. Invest. Manag.* 4(2):5–22

Guasoni P, Muhle-Karbe J. 2013. Portfolio choice with transaction costs: a user's guide. In *Paris–Princeton Lectures on Mathematical Finance 2013*, ed. V Henderson, R Sircar, pp. 169–201. Cham, Switz.: Springer

Guasoni P, Robertson S. 2012. Portfolios and risk premia for the long run. *Ann. Appl. Probab.* 22(1):239–84

Guasoni P, Weber M. 2016. *Optimal trading with multiple assets and cross-price impact.* Preprint

Heston SL. 1993. A closed-form solution for options with stochastic volatility with applications to bond and currency options. *Rev. Financ. Stud.* 6(2):327–43

Hindy A, Huang C-F. 1993. Optimal consumption and portfolio rules with durability and local substitution. *Econometrica* 61(1):85–121

Hynd R. 2012. The eigenvalue problem of singular ergodic control. *Commun. Pure Appl. Math.* 65(5):649–82

Janeček K, Shreve SE. 2004. Asymptotic analysis for optimal investment and consumption with transaction costs. *Fin. Stoch.* 8(2):181–206

Jang B-G, Koo HK, Liu H, Loewenstein M. 2007. Liquidity premia and transaction costs. *J. Finance* 62(5):2329–66

Kallsen J, Muhle-Karbe J. 2015a. Option pricing and hedging with small transaction costs. *Math. Finance* 25(4):702–23

Kallsen J, Muhle-Karbe J. 2015b. The general structure of optimal investment and consumption with small transaction costs. *Math. Finance.* 27:659–703

Karatzas I, Kou SG. 1996. On the pricing of contingent claims under constraints. *Ann. Appl. Probab.* 6(2):321–69

Kim T, Omberg E. 1996. Dynamic nonmyopic portfolio behavior. *Rev. Financ. Stud.* 9(1):141–61

Korn R. 1998. Portfolio optimisation with strictly positive transaction costs and impulse control. *Finance Stoch.* 2(2):85–114

Kozlov SM. 1979. The averaging of random operators. *Mat. Sb.* 109:188–202

Kramkov D, Sirbu M. 2006. Sensitivity analysis of utility-based prices and risk-tolerance wealth processes. *Ann. Appl. Probab.* 16(4):2140–94

Liu J. 2007. Portfolio selection in stochastic enviroments. *Rev. Financ. Stud.* 20(1):1–39

Lo A, Mamaysky H, Wang J. 2004. Asset prices and trading volume under fixed transactions costs. *J. Political Econ.* 112(5):1054–90

Lynch A, Tan S. 2011. Explaining the magnitude of liquidity premia: the roles of return predictability, wealth shocks, and state-dependent transaction costs. *J. Finance* 66(4):1329–68

Magill MJP, Constantinides GM. 1976. Portfolio selection with transactions costs. *J. Econ. Theory* 13(2):245–63

Martin R. 2014. Optimal trading under proportional transaction costs. *RISK* August:54–59

Martin R, Schöneborn T. 2011. Mean reversion pays, but costs. *RISK* February:96–101

Melnyk Y, Muhle-Karbe J, Seifried FT. 2017. *Lifetime investment and consumption with recursive preferences and small transaction costs*. Preprint

Melnyk Y, Seifried FT. 2017. Small-cost asymptotics for long-term growth rates in incomplete markets. *Math. Finance*. In press

Menaldi JL, Robin M. 2013. Singular ergodic control for multidimensional Gaussian-Poisson processes. *Stochastics* 85(4):682–91

Merton RC. 1971. Optimum consumption and portfolio rules in a continuous-time model. *J. Econ. Theory* 3(4):373–413

Moreau L, Muhle-Karbe J, Soner HM. 2017. Trading with small price impact. *Math. Finance* 77(2):350–400

Muthuraman K, Kumar S. 2006. Multidimensional portfolio optimization with proportional transaction costs. *Math. Finance* 16(2):301–35

Papanicolaou GC, Varadhan SRS. 1981. Boundary value problems with rapidly oscillating random coefficients. *Proc. Conf. Random Fields, 1979, Esztergom, Hung.*, pp. 835–73. Amsterdam: North-Holland

Possamaï D, Soner HM, Touzi N. 2015. Homogenization and asymptotics for small transaction costs: the multidimensional case. *Commun. Partial Differ. Equ.* 40(11):2005–46

Puterman ML. 1994. *Markov Decision Processes: Discrete Stochastic Dynamic Programming*. New York: Wiley. 1st ed.

Puterman ML, Brumelle SL. 1979. On the convergence of policy iteration in stationary dynamic programming. *Math. Oper. Res.* 4(1):60–69

Rogers LCG. 2004. Why is the effect of proportional transaction costs $O(\delta^{2/3})$? In *Mathematics of Finance*, ed. G Yin, Q Zhang, pp. 303–8. Providence, RI: Am. Math. Soc.

Rosenbaum M, Tankov P. 2014. Asymptotically optimal discretization of hedging strategies with jumps. *Ann. Appl. Probab.* 24(3):1002–48

Santos MS, Rust J. 2004. Convergence properties of policy iteration. *SIAM J. Control Optim.* 42(6):2094–115

Scheinkman JA, Xiong W. 2003. Overconfidence and speculative bubbles. *J. Political Econ.* 111(6):1183–220

Shreve SE, Soner HM. 1994. Optimal investment and consumption with transaction costs. *Ann. Appl. Probab.* 4(3):609–92

Soner HM, Touzi N. 2013. Homogenization and asymptotics for small transaction costs. *SIAM J. Control Optim.* 51(4):2893–921

Taksar M, Klass MJ, Assaf D. 1988. A diffusion model for optimal portfolio selection in the presence of brokerage fees. *Math. Oper. Res.* 13(2):277–94

Welch I, Goyal A. 2008. A comprehensive look at the empirical performance of equity premium prediction. *Rev. Financ. Stud.* 21(4):1455–508

Whalley AE, Wilmott P. 1997. An asymptotic analysis of an optimal hedging model for option pricing with transaction costs. *Math. Finance* 7(3):307–24

Witte JH, Reisinger C. 2012. Penalty methods for the solution of discrete HJB equations—continuous control and obstacle problems. *SIAM J. Numer. Anal.* 50(2):595–625

Zariphopoulou T. 2001. A solution approach to valuation with unhedgeable risks. *Finance Stoch.* 5(1):61–82

Forward-Looking Estimates of Interest-Rate Distributions

Jonathan H. Wright

Department of Economics, Johns Hopkins University, Baltimore, Maryland 21218;
email: wrightj@jhu.edu

Annu. Rev. Financ. Econ. 2017. 9:333–51

The *Annual Review of Financial Economics* is online at financial.annualreviews.org

https://doi.org/10.1146/annurev-financial-110716-032347

Copyright © 2017 by Annual Reviews.
All rights reserved

JEL codes: C53, E43, G12

Keywords

density forecasting, interest rates, options, risk premia, zero lower bound

Abstract

This article reviews methods for extracting both risk-neutral and physical density forecasts for interest rates. It presents some applications, with particular focus on issues pertaining to forward guidance and the zero lower bound. Several important applied questions in macroeconomics and monetary economics can be very directly addressed using the wealth of information in interest-rate derivative securities.

1. INTRODUCTION

Central banks, academics, and the press routinely use the yield curve to measure expectations of the future path of interest rates, although they are increasingly aware that the task is complicated by the presence of time-varying term premia (Shiller, Campbell & Schoenholtz 1983, Cochrane & Piazzesi 2005; Kim & Wright 2005; Adrian, Crump & Moench 2013). Much more can be done, however. Financial asset prices help us to measure uncertainty about future interest rates and higher moments—in fact, they can give us entire probability density functions (PDFs), although these are again complicated by risk premia. The technology for forward-looking estimates of interest-rate distributions is well established in the finance literature but is underutilized by monetary and macroeconomists. It can, in particular, be used to answer questions about the efficacy of forward guidance and the probability of being at the zero lower bound (ZLB), or of negative interest rates, at dates in the future. It can also be used to assess how the ZLB affects longer-term interest rates.

This article reviews methods for constructing forward-looking estimates of interest-rate distributions. I consider the distributions implied by the prices of options and other derivatives. These give state-price densities, i.e., distributions under the risk-neutral measure, or, more precisely, under the forward measure. Their interpretation is complicated by the presence of risk premia. I also consider methods for constructing physical density forecasts. Given the availability of actively traded interest-rate derivatives, risk-neutral PDFs for future nominal interest rates can be constructed day by day with minimal modeling assumptions and negligible measurement error. Alas, it is not so easy for physical density forecasts. These are normally constructed on the basis of historical time-series patterns of interest rates and are plagued by model and parameter uncertainty and by structural instability. In limited cases, surveys provide an alternative source of information on physical density forecasts that do not suffer from these problems.

The plan for this article is as follows. In Section 2, I review methods of constructing risk-neutral PDFs. This is a brief review of an enormous literature—far more comprehensive treatments from a finance practitioner's perspective are provided by Rebonato (2003) and Brigo & Mercurio (2006). In Section 3, I turn to physical density forecasts and discuss the pricing kernel that links the risk-neutral and physical densities. Section 4 applies the methods to Eurodollar options and other interest-rate derivatives over recent years, with particular emphasis on questions pertaining to the ZLB. This section is intended to highlight the potential uses of the techniques discussed in this paper in macroeconomics and central banking. Section 5 concludes.

2. RISK-NEUTRAL PROBABILITY DENSITY FUNCTIONS

Define $P_t(n)$ as the price at time t of an n-period zero-coupon bond that pays \$1 at time $t+n$ and let $y_t(n) = -(1/n)\log(P_t(n))$ denote its yield. Let

$$f_t(n_1, n_2) = \frac{(n_2 - t)y_t(n_2 - t) - (n_1 - t)y_t(n_1 - t)}{n_2 - n_1} \qquad 1.$$

denote a forward interest rate from time n_1 to time n_2 $(t \leq n_1 < n_2)$.

Suppose that we have options with payoffs that are tied to $y_\tau(n)$, an n-period interest rate at time $\tau \geq t$. The payoffs are

$$\max(y_\tau(n) - K, 0) \qquad 2.$$

for different choices of the strike price K. For example, if n is 3 months, this corresponds to a Eurodollar option that is based on a 3-month LIBOR interest rate.[1]

The valuation of this asset at time t is

$$E_t(M(t,\tau)\max(y_\tau(n) - K, 0)), \tag{3.}$$

where E_t denotes the physical expectation and $M(t_1, t_2)$ is the pricing kernel from time t_1 to time t_2. The valuation can alternatively be written as

$$P_t(\tau - t)E_t^*(\max(y_\tau(n) - K, 0)), \tag{4.}$$

where E_t^* denotes the expectation under the forward risk-neutral measure.[2] Henceforth, I refer to the forward risk-neutral measure as the risk-neutral measure, or Q-measure. The objective is to reverse engineer the Q-measure probability density for the future interest rate $y_\tau(n)$ from the observed price of the options.

2.1. Other Derivatives

Many more interest-rate derivatives exist, but these can all be priced using the same principles. Here is a list of some of the most important, which are discussed in depth by, e.g., Brigo & Mercurio (2006) and Veronesi (2010).

1. Interest-rate caps are contracts that at various future dates pay the amount by which the interest rate exceeds a strike price on a notional underlying principal if the interest rate exceeds that strike price, and zero otherwise. These are effectively bundles of call options on the interest rate, with payoffs of the form in Equation 2.
2. Options on Treasury futures confer the right, but not the obligation, to enter into a Treasury futures contract. They are traded on the CME and are American options (early exercise is possible). Treasury futures contracts are complicated, but are structured in such a way that a long position in a Treasury futures contract can be roughly thought of as a contract to buy the shortest-maturity security in the delivery basket,[3] so the futures option is approximately an option on that security. The MOVE Index, constructed by Merrill Lynch, is an index of implied volatilities on 2-, 5-, 10-, and 30-year Treasury futures contracts and is the equivalent of the VIX for interest-rate uncertainty. Since 2011, the CME has traded options on Treasury futures that expire each Friday afternoon. (The holder must enter into a futures position by the expiration day, or else the option expires unused.) Although they are new, these options are quite liquid and can be used to measure uncertainty about specific risk events, such as employment reports (Kim & Wright 2014).
3. A payer swaption gives the holder the right, but not the obligation, to enter into a swap contract in which they pay a particular fixed rate. A receiver swaption gives the holder the

[1]Strictly speaking, Eurodollar options settle not to the interest rate but to 100 minus the interest rate. A call/put Eurodollar option is a bet on falling/rising interest rates, respectively. However, we can think of such options as derivatives with payoffs of the form in Equation 2.

[2]The valuation of the security under the ordinary risk-neutral measure would be the expectation of $\exp(-\int_t^{t+\tau} r(s)ds)\max(y_\tau(n) - K, 0)$, where $r(s)$ is the instantaneous interest rate. The discount factor $\exp(-\int_t^{t+\tau} r(s)ds)$ is random and cannot be pulled through the expectations operator. The forward risk-neutral measure (Jamshidian 2007; Jarrow, Li & Zhao 2007; Li & Zhao 2009) instead takes the $(\tau - t)$-period zero-coupon bond as the numeraire, which is known at time t and so can be pulled outside the expectations operator.

[3]This statement is true for Treasury futures so long as the level of interest rates is below 6%, which has been true for a very long time.

right, but not the obligation, to enter into a swap contract in which they receive a particular fixed rate. Swaptions are typically European. (Bermudan swaptions are also quite common; these can be exercised only on certain specified dates.) If a swaption expires at time τ and the underlying swap contract calls for R payments every Δ years on a notional underlying principal of L, where the swaption has a strike price of i_S and the swap rate at expiration is i_F, then the value of a receiver swaption at expiration is $L\Delta \max(i_F - i_S, 0)\Sigma_{i=1}^{R} P_\tau(i\Delta)$, which is a rescaled version of the payoff in Equation 2.

2.2. Black Model

For an option with the payoffs in Equation 2, a simple approach to reverse engineering the risk-neutral PDF is to posit that the forward rate $f_t(\tau, \tau + n)$ follows the following process under the Q-measure:

$$\frac{\mathrm{d}f_t(\tau, \tau+n)}{f_t(\tau, \tau+n)} = \sigma \mathrm{d}W_t, \qquad 5.$$

where W_t is a standard Brownian motion. Noting that $f_\tau(\tau, \tau + n) = y_\tau(n)$, it follows from Ito's lemma that

$$\log y_\tau(n) \sim N\left(\log(f_t(\tau, \tau+n)) - \frac{1}{2}\sigma^2\tau^*, \sigma^2\tau^*\right), \qquad 6.$$

where $\tau^* = \tau - t$ is the time to maturity. Under this premise, Black (1976) gives an analytical expression for Equation 4 at time t. Given the price of a single option, this can be inverted to obtain the implied volatility, σ. A 95% confidence interval for $y_\tau(n)$ can then be constructed as

$$\left[f_t(\tau, \tau+n)\exp\left(-\frac{1}{2}\sigma^2\tau^* - 1.96\sigma\sqrt{\tau^*}\right), f_t(\tau, \tau+n)\exp\left(-\frac{1}{2}\sigma^2\tau^* + 1.96\sigma\sqrt{\tau^*}\right)\right]. \qquad 7.$$

The implied volatility in Equation 5 is not directly a measure of uncertainty about the level of interest rates. Uncertainty about the level of interest rates can be measured by the width of a 95% confidence interval for $y_\tau(n)$, which is

$$f_t(\tau, \tau+n)\exp\left(-\frac{1}{2}\sigma^2\tau^*\right)\left[\exp(1.96\sigma\sqrt{\tau^*}) - \exp(-1.96\sigma\sqrt{\tau^*})\right]. \qquad 8.$$

The assumption in Equation 5 implies that interest rates can never go negative. Until recently, this seemed quite uncontroversial. However, many benchmark interest rates are negative today, and that cannot be accommodated in this framework. There is an alternative version of the Black formula that assumes that forward rates are normal, not log-normal, and that version allows interest rates to go negative. We further discuss the ZLB and negative interest rates in Section 4.4.

2.3. Brace–Gatarek–Musiela Model

An extension of the Black (1976) model entails specifying that a vector of forward rates $(f(\tau_1, \tau_1 + n), f(\tau_2, \tau_2 + n), \ldots, f(\tau_K, \tau_K + n))'$ follows a multivariate geometric Brownian motion with variance-covariance matrix $V(t) = [v_{ij}(t)]$. This is known as the BGM (Brace, Gatarek & Musiela 1997) model, or the LIBOR market model. The variance-covariance matrix can in turn be specified to depend on a smaller number of parameters. A common parameterization (Rebonato 1999) is

$$v_{ij}(t) = \sigma_i(t)\sigma_j(t)\exp(-\beta|i-j|), \qquad 9.$$

where

$$\sigma_i(t) = (a(\tau_i - t) + b)\exp(-c(\tau_i - t)) + d. \qquad 10.$$

This constrains $V(t)$ to depend on only five parameters. These parameters can be estimated by minimizing the sum of squared deviations between actual and model-implied interest-rate derivatives prices. Having obtained the entire joint risk-neutral distribution of forward rates, the researcher can work out the implied density of many objects of interest, such as the timing of the peak of a tightening cycle. Elliott & Noss (2015) discuss applying the BGM model to such purposes. I illustrate this use of the model in Section 4.[4]

The BGM model is closely related to the well-known HJM (Heath, Jarrow & Morton 1992) model. The difference is that Heath, Jarrow & Morton (1992) consider a law of motion for instantaneous forward rates. Unfortunately, it turns out that log-normal instantaneous forward rates are inconsistent with an absence of arbitrage. For this reason, the BGM model retains the HJM framework but replaces instantaneous forward rates with discretely compounded forward rates, which have the useful by-product of being more directly relevant to market participants, as actual market rates all have discrete accrual periods. Sandmann & Sondermann (1997), Goldys, Musiela & Sondermann (2000), and Jarrow (2009) all discuss this motivation for using discretely compounded forward rates (for a textbook treatment, see Shreve 2004, subsection 10.4.1). Essentially, the BGM model can be thought of as a device that circumvents a technical problem of explosive rates in the HJM model.

2.4. Probability Density Functions at a Given Point in Time

Another approach is to collect a set of option prices for a fixed maturity date and to reverse engineer a PDF for $y_t(n)$ from these prices without making any parametric assumptions. The key insight in doing this is the result of Breeden & Litzenberger (1978) that if $C(K)$ is the price of a call option at a strike price of K on a future interest rate $y_\tau(n)$, then the CDF (cumulative distribution function) of $y_\tau(n)$ is

$$F(x) = -\frac{1}{P(t, t+\tau)} \frac{\partial C(x)}{\partial K}, \tag{11.}$$

and the PDF is

$$f(x) = \frac{1}{P(t, t+\tau)} \frac{\partial^2 C(x)}{\partial K^2}. \tag{12.}$$

We do not observe options at every strike price and so cannot literally compute the derivatives required for these equations. We can, however, work out the Black-implied volatility for each option, interpolate these implied volatilities over an arbitrarily fine grid of points, convert these back into call prices, and then compute the required derivatives numerically. This approach is implemented by Shimko (1993) and Bliss & Panigirtzoglou (2002). Shimko (1993) uses a polynomial in K to smooth the implied volatilities, whereas Bliss & Panigirtzoglou (2002) use a cubic spline. In Monte Carlo simulations, Bliss & Panigirtzoglou (2002) find that this method is reliable even with a small number of options.

Another related approach is the local linear regression of Aït-Sahalia & Duarte (2003). Consider a set of L call options at different strike prices at a given point in time for the same underlying asset. Let C_i denote the price of the i-th option, with a strike of k_i. We seek to approximate the price of an option at a strike price k' in a neighborhood around k by a locally linear function

[4]A different approach, which also gives the joint risk-neutral distribution of future short-term interest rates, is to calibrate models of short-term interest rates, such as the one-factor model of Hull & White (1990) or the two-factor model of Longstaff & Schwartz (1992), to interest-rate derivatives prices. I do not consider this further in this review, but Rebonato (2003) and Brigo & Mercurio (2006) provide extensive discussions of these methods.

$\beta_0(k) + \beta_1(k)(k' - k)$. We estimate the coefficients as

$$\hat{\beta}_0(k), \hat{\beta}_1(k) = \arg \min_{\beta_0(k),\beta_1(k)} \Sigma_{i=1}^{L} \left(C_i - \beta_0(k) - \beta_1(k)(k_i - k)\right)^2 K\left(\frac{k_i - k}{h}\right) \Big/ h, \qquad 13.$$

where $K(\cdot)$ is a kernel function and h is a bandwidth. There are expressions for the optimal bandwidth in terms of minimizing integrated mean squared error, but it is always wise to look at the smoothed option price to visually judge if the degree of smoothing is appropriate. The first derivative of the call option price with respect to the strike price can then be obtained as $\hat{\beta}_1(k)$, and the second derivative can be obtained as $\hat{\beta}_1'(k)$.

A variant on this approach, discussed by Aït-Sahalia & Duarte (2003), is to approximate the price of the option by a locally quadratic function. The second derivative can then be recovered directly from the coefficient on the quadratic term. However, inferring the second derivative from Equation 13 may work better in finite samples (Aït-Sahalia & Duarte 2003).

2.5. Probability Density Functions Smoothed over Time

In the previous section, I considered constructing a PDF on a given day or at a particular point in time. This can be appealing because the researcher can then study how a unique event, such as the introduction of some type of forward guidance by the Federal Reserve, shifts the PDF. However, because of concerns about measurement error or the absence of options at the required maturity and strike price, it may be preferable to pool options prices over a longer period of time. Such an approach is proposed in the semiparametric methodology of Aït-Sahalia & Lo (1998).

In this approach, observed options prices are converted into Black-implied volatilities. Let these options-implied volatilities be $\{\sigma_i\}_{i=1}^{n}$, where n is the total number of options, pooling all call and put options for all trading days, strike prices, and expiration dates. Assume that the implied volatility is a function $\sigma(Z_{it})$ of a state vector Z_{it}, where Z_{it} includes the strike price or moneyness of the option, the maturity of the option, and time-varying variables such as the level and slope of the term structure and/or the options-implied volatility of interest rates. The implied volatility function can be estimated nonparametrically by kernel smoothing or by a local linear regression. Implied volatilities can then be converted back to call options prices, and fitted call options prices can be constructed for any value of the state vector, giving the Q-measure CDF and PDF in Equations 11 and 12. Intuitively, the value of an option on a given day is constructed by smoothing over options with similar strike prices and maturities and over days when the state vector takes on similar values. The advantage of doing this is that the estimation of the state-price density can be made much more precise. The disadvantage is that we have to assume that a low-dimensional state vector provides a good fit to implied volatilities, although, of course, this assumption can be checked by seeing how well the fitted implied volatilities match their actual counterparts. Li & Zhao (2009) apply this methodology to LIBOR derivatives; more recently, Wright (2016) applies it to a new but thin market on exchange-traded options on Treasury inflation-protected securities.

3. PHYSICAL DENSITY FORECASTS

There is a large literature on forecasting interest rates, with a recent comprehensive summary given by Duffee (2013). Most of the emphasis in this literature is on point forecasting. As is well known, nearly all variation in yields reduces to variation in three factors (Litterman & Scheinkman 1991). These are the first three principal components of yields that can be interpreted as level, slope, and curvature, or are equivalently (up to a rotation) the three coefficients in the model of Nelson &

Siegel (1987). Most of the point forecasts for interest rates that are used in the literature amount to using a possibly restricted vector autoregression in these three factors to predict future values of the factors, which in turn imply forecasts of future interest rates. Diebold & Li (2006) propose a dynamic Nelson–Siegel model, fitting an AR(1) to each of the Nelson–Siegel coefficients. This is a good benchmark for interest-rate forecasting, although it should be noted that the record of this and other methods for interest-rate forecasting in out-of-sample prediction exercises is sensitive to the period used for forecast evaluation, and the very simplest forecasting model—a random walk forecast—is hard to beat consistently (Duffee 2013).

In this article, my focus is on density forecasting, not point forecasting. In line with standard terminology, I refer to the physical density forecast as the P-measure density forecast. To construct a nontrivial density forecast (one that is not just a fixed interval around the point forecast), time-varying volatility is needed. Authors studying density forecasts for interest rates include Hong, Li & Zhao (2004) and Carriero, Clark & Marcellino (2014). One prominent approach, following Koopman, Mallee & der Wel (2010), Hautsch & Ou (2012), and Hautsch & Yang (2012), is to construct density forecasts by a dynamic Nelson–Siegel model but with stochastic volatility. Specifically, suppose that the yield curve is

$$y_t(n) = \beta_{1t} + \beta_{2t}\frac{1-\exp(-\lambda n)}{\lambda n} + \beta_{3t}\left(\frac{1-\exp(-\lambda n)}{\lambda n} - \exp(-\lambda n)\right), \qquad 14.$$

where λ is fixed, following Diebold & Li (2006). The $\{\beta_{jt}\}_{j=1}^{3}$ are observed variables that can be inverted from actual yields. Assume that

$$\beta_{jt} = \phi_{0j} + \phi_{1j}\beta_{jt-1} + \sigma_{jt}\varepsilon_{jt}, \qquad 15.$$

$$\ln(\sigma_{jt}^2) = \omega_{0j} + \omega_{1j}\ln(\sigma_{jt-1}^2) + \kappa_j u_{jt}, \qquad 16.$$

where $\{u_{jt}\}$ and $\{\varepsilon_{jt}\}$ are independent and identically distributed standard normal random variables. Bayesian Markov chain Monte Carlo methods can be applied to Equations 15 and 16, as is done by Koopman, Mallee & der Wel (2010), Hautsch & Ou (2012), and Hautsch & Yang (2012). Hence, density forecasts can be obtained by stochastic simulation. The model does not explicitly incorporate the ZLB, although one can naturally truncate the resulting interest-rate forecasts at zero.

The model is already quite a simple and tightly parameterized specification. One could restrict the model further. One possibility is to specify that

$$\phi_{0j} = 0, \quad \phi_{1j} = 1 \qquad \text{for all } j. \qquad 17.$$

This implies that random walk forecasts are used for all the factors, and hence for all the yields (as noted above, random walk forecasts are surprisingly competitive). Another possibility is to specify that

$$\omega_{0j} = \omega_{1j} = 0 \qquad \text{for all } j. \qquad 18.$$

This implies that the innovation variance in Equation 15 is constant at κ_j^2. This in turn means that any density forecast is just a fixed interval around the point forecast.

Here, as in most of the interest-rate forecasting literature, I have considered using only yield curve variables for forecasting. As emphasized by Duffee (2013), barring unusual circumstances, if a factor is relevant for predicting future interest rates, then it should be reflected in bond yields. Nevertheless, many researchers have used macroeconomic variables for interest-rate forecasting, especially in point forecasting but also in density forecasting. For example, Clark (2011) considers density forecasts for the federal funds rate from a vector autoregression with stochastic volatility in GDP growth, unemployment, inflation, and the funds rate.

Whereas Q-measure dynamics are well identified from derivatives prices, P-measure dynamics are hard to pin down. With any of the specifications discussed above, the researcher is basing a density forecast on the historical time-series behavior of interest rates, and that is associated with various econometric problems, including downward bias in persistence estimates and, more importantly, a very flat likelihood. It takes a long sample without structural breaks to precisely estimate mean reversion of persistent data. Motivated by this problem, in the context of point forecasting, Kim & Orphanides (2012) propose incorporating survey forecasts of future interest rates as a way of sharpening identification under the P-measure. They treat surveys as noisy measures of agents' physical expectations and show that this helps a great deal with identification, often preventing the model from giving unreasonable assessments of physical expectations. This remains true even when one allows for considerable measurement error in the surveys. (Discussion on the use of survey forecasts in term structure analysis is also provided by Chun 2011.) The benefits of using surveys are especially great at or near the ZLB, as there is good reason to think that there have been structural breaks. There is virtually no historical experience at such low interest rates to guide a time-series-based model estimation procedure.

The Markets Group of the Federal Reserve Bank of New York (FRBNY) conducts a survey of primary dealers prior to each Federal Open Market Committee (FOMC) meeting, and since 2011 the results have been made public. This survey includes density forecasts for future interest rates. Respondents assign probabilities to the federal funds rate falling into discrete bins, and these probabilities are then averaged over respondents. In light of the great difficulties in constructing physical density forecasts from time-series econometric methods, I think that it is reasonable to view these survey density forecasts as approximating the P-measure density forecasts of investors. At a minimum, they can be useful information in calibrating physical density forecasts. The FRBNY survey is the only survey density forecast for interest of which I am aware. The questions are very specific and change from survey to survey, as the survey is designed to answer questions of current interest to the FOMC rather than for longer-term research purposes. Nonetheless, it is a unique and valuable resource.

3.1. The Pricing Kernel

Armed with the P- and Q-measure PDFs, the researcher can work out the pricing kernel as the ratio of the Q-measure PDF to the P-measure PDF. Given that the data at hand are derivatives prices plus the historical behavior of interest rates, it seems most natural to me to compute the Q-measure PDFs (from derivatives prices) and the P-measure PDFs (typically from the time-series properties of interest rates), and then to work out the pricing kernel as a by-product. This also enables us to exploit the fact that Q-measure PDFs are very well identified and can be estimated with flexible specifications, whereas P-measure PDFs are poorly identified, and tightly parameterized models may be most appropriate for them.

This is not the only possible way to proceed, however. Rosenberg & Engle (2002) estimate physical PDFs and then parameterize a pricing kernel, estimating the parameters of the pricing kernel so as to match options prices. Effectively, this identifies the P-measure PDF and the pricing kernel, and then works out the Q-measure PDF as a by-product.

3.2. Term Structure Models

Affine and quadratic term structure models jointly specify the physical and risk-neutral processes for interest rates and the pricing kernel, and they can also be used to construct P- and Q-measure PDFs for interest rates. Egorov, Hong & Li (2006) consider the use of affine term structure models for interest-rate density forecasting and compare the resulting forecasts with homoskedastic random walk forecasts. They find that whereas the random walk forecasts are more accurate with respect to the conditional mean, the affine term structure model gives better density forecasts, giving some evidence for the importance of modeling volatility.

Term structure models are typically fitted to yields data alone and can fit conditional means quite well, but have trouble with fitting higher moments (Collin-Dufresne, Goldstein & Jones 2009; Jacobs & Karoui 2009). The ability to fit higher moments appears to be sensitive to the sample period. Several authors have documented the importance of allowing for additional volatility factors driving interest-rate derivatives prices that cannot be inverted from yields (Andersen & Benzoni 2010, Collin-Dufresne & Goldstein 2002). This potential phenomenon is generally referred to as unspanned stochastic volatility.

Several recent papers have fitted term structure models to interest rates and derivatives jointly. All of them involve both factors in the conditional mean (effectively level slope and curvature of the yield curve) and additional volatility factors. Allowing for these additional factors, the models are able to fit both interest rates and derivatives prices well. Heidari & Wu (2009) and Cieslak & Povala (2016) consider affine term structure models with conditional mean and volatility factors—Cieslak & Povala also use high-frequency data to obtain precise estimates of the physical second moments of yields. Filipović, Larsson & Trolle (2017) propose a model in which the state-price density is a linear function of a state vector, and they show that it implies that bond yields are ratios of linear functions of those factors. Although these papers have generally focused on obtaining a good in-sample fit, their models might also be useful for density forecasting. It has generally been seen as desirable for a term structure model to impose non-negativity of interest rates—the model of Filipović, Larsson & Trolle imposes non-negative rates,[5] whereas that of Cieslak & Povala does not. However, the case is maybe less clear now than it appeared in the past, as negative bond yields are now common in many countries outside the United States. This is discussed further in Section 4.4.

4. APPLICATIONS

In this section, I turn to some illustrative applications of the methods described above, with special attention to forward guidance and issues raised by the ZLB.

4.1. Options-Implied Probability Density Functions for Short-Term Rates

I first consider Q-measure density forecasts for 3-month interest rates implied by Eurodollar options quotes. Eurodollar options are available expiring each March, June, September and December. For each day from January 2010 to May 2016, I use settlement quotes on call options at up to 41 different strike prices. I linearly interpolated these to constant maturities and then obtained CDFs/PDFs by local linear regression (Equation 13). Eurodollar options are based on LIBOR quotes, which at times incorporate substantial liquidity premia and/or credit risk premia (Hull & White 2013). As a simple attempt to correct for this, I shifted the densities each day by the amount of the LIBOR–OIS (overnight index swap) spread, so they can be thought of as referring to 3-month OIS rates, which can in turn be thought of as pure forward discount rates. I take the CDF at 30 basis points (Equation 11) as the probability of being at the ZLB. When the United States was at the ZLB from 2008 to 2015, the target for the federal funds rate was a range from 0 to 25 basis points, and there was little serious discussion of lowering the funds rate during this period.

[5]Filipović, Larsson & Trolle (2017) find that their model fits swap and swaptions quotes well even during the ZLB period.

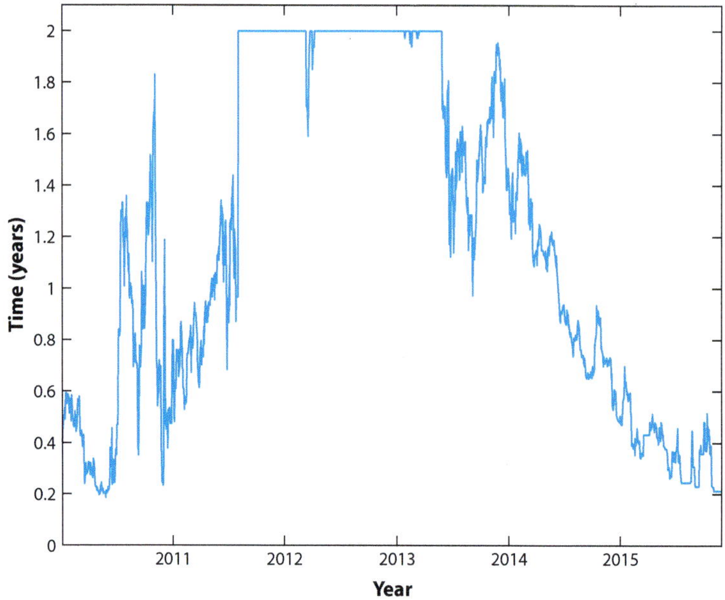

Figure 1

Risk-neutral median time to liftoff. This figure plots the time in years until the (forward) risk-neutral CDF for 3-month OIS rates evaluated at 30 basis points first falls to 0.5, on each day. The time is cut off at 2 years—if the CDF at the 2-year horizon is above 0.5, then the time to liftoff is reported as 2 years. These CDFs are constructed by local linear regressions using Eurodollar options, as described in Section 2.4. The densities are shifted by the amount of the LIBOR–OIS spread so as to be interpretable as PDFs for 3-month OIS rates. Abbreviations: CDF, cumulative distribution function; OIS, overnight index swap; PDF, probability density function.

As a way to condense the information in these PDFs/CDFs, I use them to compute the risk-neutral median time to liftoff, defined as the shortest horizon at which the CDF of 3-month OIS rates at 30 basis points is below 0.5. This is shown in **Figure 1**, from January 2010 to November 2015. It is a measure of how much scope the Federal Reserve had to ease financial conditions via forward guidance, separate from using negative rates or large-scale asset purchases. The risk-neutral median times to liftoff are capped at 2 years (if the CDF at the 2-year horizon is above 0.5) because of the sparsity of options quotes at longer maturities. In 2010, the time to liftoff was very short, at under 6 months. By 2012, it had risen to at least 2 years. This is probably the limit of what forward guidance can credibly achieve, short of an economy being widely perceived to be mired in an intractable slump. Later, the median time to liftoff came back down as the Federal Reserve signaled that the normalization of monetary policy would begin soon.

For a more granular look at two key events, **Figure 2** plots the PDFs at the 1-year horizon for the days before and after August 9, 2011, and June 19, 2013. August 9, 2011, was the day that the FOMC announced that it expected to keep rates exceptionally low at least through the middle of 2013, substantially sharpening its forward guidance. June 19, 2013, was the date that the FOMC announced a plan to taper and end its large-scale asset purchases sooner than had been expected. **Figure 2** allows us to see the effects of these announcements on the entire risk-neutral PDF of interest rates. **Figure 2** shows the PDF for interest rates above 30 basis points and the point mass associated with the ZLB (i.e., the CDF at 30 basis points). I represent the densities in this way

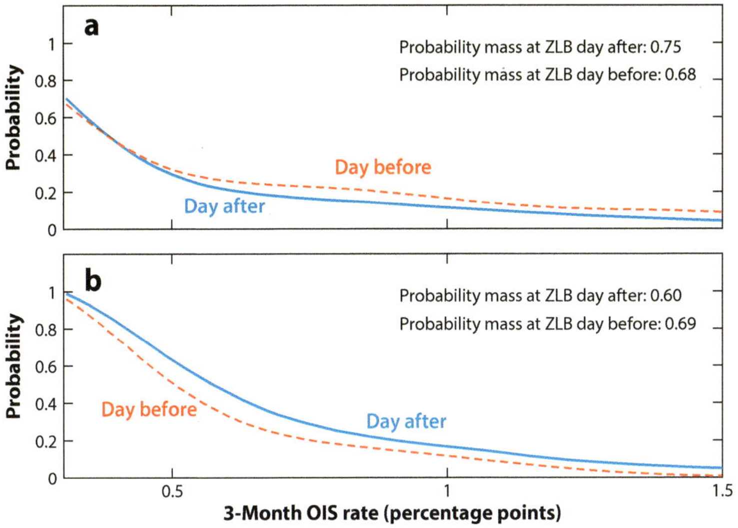

Figure 2

The (forward) risk-neutral PDFs for 3-month OIS rates at the 1-year-horizon as of the days before and after two Federal Open Market Committee meetings: (*a*) August 9, 2011; (*b*) June 19, 2013. These are constructed by local linear regressions using Eurodollar options, as described in Section 2.4. The densities are shifted by the amount of the LIBOR–OIS spread so as to be interpretable as PDFs for 3-month OIS rates. Panels *a* and *b* each show the continuous densities above 30 basis points along with the value of the cumulative distribution function at 30 basis points (probability mass at the zero lower bound). Abbreviations: OIS, overnight index swap; PDF, probability density function.

because the densities put very high probabilities on interest rates just below 30 basis points, clearly corresponding to the target federal funds rate remaining in the range from 0 to 25 basis points. In **Figure 2*a***, it can be seen that the announcement on August 9, 2011, increased the probability of being at the ZLB 1 year hence from 68% to 75%, and the probability associated with a substantial tightening of monetary policy was correspondingly marked down. The forward guidance was therefore quite effective. In **Figure 2*b***, it can be seen that the announcement on June 19, 2013, reduced the probability of being at the ZLB 1 year hence from 69% to 60%. The tapering announcement evidently led market participants to increase their odds of liftoff from the ZLB within 1 year.

This exercise illustrates that we can study the effects of specific announcements—including rather unique one-off announcements such as those considered in **Figure 2**—on risk-neutral PDFs for interest rates. In doing this, it is important that entirely separate PDFs are constructed just before and after the event. Methodologies that pool data over a long period in forming PDFs, as described in Section 2.5, are not well suited to examining the effects of specific events.

The daily variation in the PDF at the 1-year horizon from January 2010 to May 2016 is shown in the **Supplemental Video**.

4.2. Shadow Interest Rates

Clearly the ZLB does not affect only the overnight interest rate; it also affects yields further out the term structure. Swanson & Williams (2014) look at the sensitivity of the term structure of yields to economic announcements to see how far out the term structure the ZLB reaches. Options provide an alternative approach for doing this.

Assume that the 3-month OIS interest rate at time τ is $\max(\underline{s}, s_\tau)$—as in the Black (1995) model—where s_τ, the shadow rate for time τ, is $N(\mu, \omega^2)$, and $\underline{s}$ is the lower bound (taken as 30 basis points). Under the Q-measure, using results on the mean of a truncated normal, the expectation of a 3-month interest rate will be

$$\mu + \Phi(\alpha)(\underline{s} - \mu) + \phi(\alpha), \quad 19.$$

where $\alpha = (\underline{s} - \mu)/\omega$. This will be equal to the futures rate, F. Also, the probability of 3-month rates being at the ZLB is $P_Z = \Phi(\alpha)$, and this can be recovered from options quotes. Rearranging, we can solve for μ:

$$\mu = \frac{F - \underline{s}P_Z - \phi(\Phi^{-1}(P_Z))}{1 - P_Z}. \quad 20.$$

The parameter μ tells us what the futures rate for time τ would be in the absence of the ZLB. I call this a shadow futures rate. It is a different concept of a shadow rate than that conventionally employed in the ZLB literature. Black (1976) defines the shadow rate as what the current level of the short rate would be in the absence of a non-negativity constraint. Wu & Xia (2016) show how to reverse engineer this shadow rate from how close short- and intermediate-maturity yields are to zero. Instead I am defining a shadow futures rate as what the futures rate would be in the absence of a non-negativity constraint, and identifying this from options prices alone.

In **Figure 3**, I plot the futures rate and the shadow futures rate at the 1-year horizon. In 2010 and early 2011, the two were close, as the probability of an early exit from the ZLB was seen as high. From mid-2011 to mid-2014, the shadow futures rate was well below the actual futures rate, as the ZLB was binding further out the term structure. After mid-2014, the shadow and actual

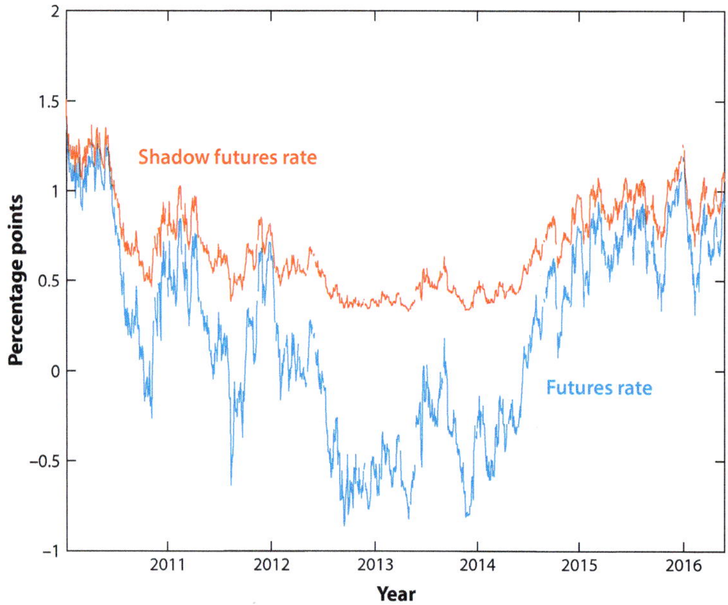

Figure 3

Actual and shadow 3-month futures rates 1 year hence. The actual futures rate is a 1-year ahead rate at constant maturity formed by linearly interpolating between Eurodollar futures quotes, less the current LIBOR–OIS (overnight index swap) spread. The shadow rate is formed from Equation 20 and represents what the futures rate would have been in the absence of the zero lower bound, as implied by options quotes.

Table 1 Risk-neutral probabilities of time to first peak in 1-year yields as of May 31, 2016

Time to first peak (yr)	Probability (%)
<1	44.8
1–2	25.7
2–3	16.1
3–4	6.6
4–5	4.9
>5	1.9

This table shows the probability density function of the time to the first peak in 1-year yields from simulations of a Brace–Gatarek–Musiela model calibrated to swaptions quotes as of May 31, 2016.

futures rates converged once again as liftoff came near. These findings are consistent with those of Swanson & Williams (2014), although they are obtained in a different and perhaps more direct way.

4.3. Calibration of the Brace–Gatarek–Musiela Model

To illustrate the use of the BGM model (discussed in Section 2.3), I took at-the-money swaptions prices on May 31, 2016, from Bloomberg, at m-year exercise dates and n-year underlying swap maturities (for $m, n = 1, 2, 3, 5, 7, 10$), and calibrated the BGM model parameterized as in Equations 9 and 10, so as to minimize the sum of squared swaptions pricing errors. Payoffs were discounted using the zero-coupon yield curve[6] of Gürkaynak, Sack & Wright (2007).[7] The calibrated parameters (a, b, c, d, and β in the notation of these equations) then give a complete characterization of the risk-neutral evolution of future interest rates, which allows questions to be answered that cannot be addressed by looking at a single maturity point in isolation.

To illustrate this, I simulated the calibrated model and computed the Q-measure time until the first peak in 1-year interest rates. **Table 1** shows these probabilities. Interestingly, the implied probability of a peak in 1-year rates within the next 2 years was nearly 70%, meaning that options implied a better-than-even chance of the current Federal Reserve tightening cycle ending before mid-2018.

4.4. Options-Implied Probability Density Functions and Negative Rates

In the United States, the ZLB has consistently kept the federal funds rate above zero and has prevented 3-month LIBOR from falling much below 50 basis points. Occasionally, negative yields were observed in the secondary Treasury bill market, but these were very isolated cases. The approach in the Black model, or in most papers in the ZLB literature (Black 1995, Kim & Singleton 2012, Krippner 2014, Wu & Xia 2016), is to simply rule out negative interest rates. This seems appropriate in the US context. Federal Reserve Chair Janet Yellen stated in Congress (February 11, 2016) that it was unclear if the FOMC had the legal authority to set negative interest rates. That alone makes it quite unlikely that negative interest rates will be used in the United States.

However, other countries grappling with overvalued currencies (especially Switzerland) and/or sustained economic weakness (especially the euro area and Japan) have resorted to negative interest

[6]It used to be market convention to value derivatives using LIBOR rates for discounting. This has changed since the financial crisis, however. Other rates—most often OIS rates—are now sometimes preferred instead (Hull & White 2013).

[7]This uses the Svensson (1994) parameterization of the yield curve. For a discussion of zero-coupon and forward yield curve fitting methods, see Jarrow (2014).

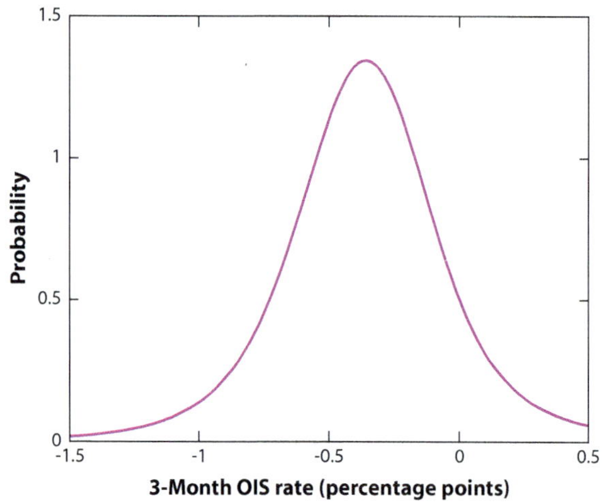

Figure 4

The (forward) risk-neutral PDFs for 3-month OIS rates at the 1-year-horizon for the euro area as of May 31, 2016. These are constructed by local linear regressions using Euribor options, as described in Section 2.4. The density is shifted by the amount of the euro LIBOR–OIS spread so as to be interpretable as a PDF for 3-month OIS rates. Abbreviations: OIS, overnight index swap; PDF, probability density function.

rates. This has come as something of a surprise to many observers. Nonetheless, to date, fears that this would lead to warehousing of large amounts of cash have not proved correct (Rognlie 2016), although there is surely some tipping point that would lead the financial system to develop a new infrastructure to hold enormous cash balances. In these countries, the ZLB seems better thought of as a soft constraint. Options can then be used just as before to measure the market assessment of how far rates might go into negative territory.

Euribor options are the euro-area analog of Eurodollar options. Although most of the literature on options-implied interest-rate densities is applied to the United States, there have been some applications to the euro area (Andersen & Wagener 2002, Ivanova & Gutiérrez 2014). Because of its size and because of negative rates, the euro area is of special significance at present. Consequently, **Figure 4** plots the Q-measure PDF for euro-area 3-month interest rates in 1 year's time, as of May 31, 2016. These were obtained in the same way as for the United States, again with an adjustment for the LIBOR–OIS spread, although that was very modest. On May 31, 2016, the 3-month euro OIS rate was −34 basis points. The PDF implies low odds of rates moving back above zero but substantial odds of rates moving somewhat further into negative territory by mid-2017.

4.5. Physical Interest-Rate Density Forecasts

Generally time-series models are used to construct P-measure interest-rate forecasts. However, in this article, owing to the difficulties discussed in Section 3 pertaining to time-series models of interest rates, especially in the current environment, I instead use the FRBNY primary dealer survey. **Figure 5** plots the PDF for the target federal funds rate at the end of 2017 from the April 18, 2016, primary dealer survey. (The survey asks respondents for the PDF conditional on moving to the ZLB at some point in 2016–2018, the PDF conditional on not moving to the ZLB at any point in 2016–2018, and the probability of moving to the ZLB during that period. **Figure 5** plots the implied unconditional PDFs.) The Q-measure PDF for the OIS rate over a 3-month window centered around the end of 2017, as of the survey date, is also shown in the figure. This

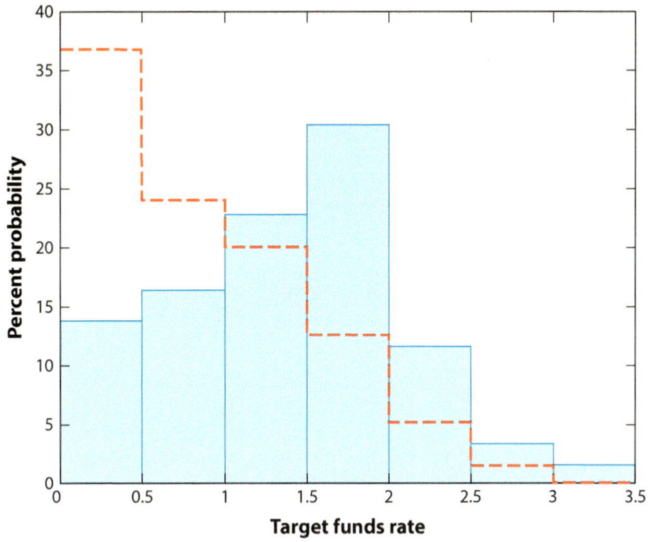

Figure 5

This figure plots survey probabilities for target federal funds rates at the end of 2017 from the Federal Reserve Bank of New York primary dealer survey of April 18, 2016. Probabilities are put into bins that are 50 basis points wide, with the leftmost bin referring to interest rates of less than 50 basis points and the rightmost bin referring to interest rates of more than 3 percentage points. The survey asks respondents for probabilities conditional on a return to the ZLB in 2016–2018, probabilities conditional on no return to the ZLB in 2016–2018, and the probability of a return to the ZLB in that period. The probabilities plotted as bars in this figure are the implied unconditional probabilities. In addition, the figure shows the corresponding risk-neutral PDFs for 3-month OIS rates on November 15, 2017, at the 18-month horizon (*red dashed line*). These are constructed by local linear regressions using Eurodollar options, as described in Section 2.4. The density is shifted by the amount of the LIBOR–OIS spread so as to be interpretable as a PDF for the federal funds rate around the end of 2017. Abbreviations: OIS, overnight index swap; PDF, probability density function; ZLB, zero lower bound.

was obtained from Eurodollar options, as discussed in Section 4.1, and represents an approximate Q-measure PDF for the target funds rate at the end of 2017. This makes the P- and Q-measure PDFs as directly comparable as possible. Another alternative would be to use federal funds futures options, which settle to the average effective federal funds rate for a particular month. These are very illiquid, however, except at the shortest maturities.

The primary dealer survey can also be used to compute the mean forecast of the federal funds rate, whereas most surveys are ambiguous as to whether they elicit the mean, median, or modal forecast (Engelberg, Manski & Williams 2009). In **Figure 5**, the mean survey forecast for the funds rate at the end of 2017 was 1.38%, whereas the corresponding modal forecast was 1.5–2%.

4.6. Pricing Kernel

In **Figure 5**, it can be seen that the survey reported 14% odds of the federal funds rate being less than 50 basis points, with the rest of the probability mass being distinctly away from the ZLB. Also, the Q-measure PDF derived from Eurodollar options puts more mass on very low interest rates. The empirical pricing kernel—the ratio of Q- to P-measure PDFs—is thus downward sloping. **Figure 6** plots the pricing kernel constructed in this way on April 18, 2016, and also on dates in

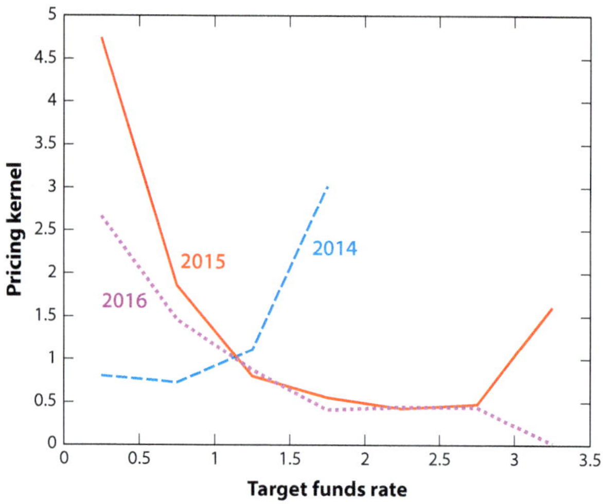

Figure 6

Empirical pricing kernels constructed as the ratio of the risk-neutral PDFs for 3-month OIS rates at the 18-month horizon to the survey probabilities for the target federal funds rate at the end of the following year from the Federal Reserve Bank of New York primary dealer surveys of April 22, 2014; April 20, 2015; and April 18, 2016. Survey probabilities are put into bins that are 50 basis points wide. Risk-neutral PDFs are constructed by local linear regressions using Eurodollar options, as described in Section 2.4. The density is shifted by the amount of the LIBOR–OIS spread so as to be interpretable as a PDF for the federal funds rate around the end of following year. Abbreviations: OIS, overnight index swap; PDF, probability density function.

April 2014 and April 2015, likewise constructed from the primary dealer survey for interest rates at the end of the following year, coupled with Eurodollar options quotes.

Most researchers have found pricing kernels to be U-shaped in interest rates. Li & Zhao (2009) computed the pricing kernel by comparing P- and Q-measure PDFs using interest-rate caps from 2000 to 2004. They found that it was U-shaped in interest rates; both very high and very low interest rates were high-marginal-utility states of the world. Ivanova & Gutiérrez (2014) also found U-shaped pricing kernels using Euribor options data from 2006 to 2012. In **Figure 6**, I also find something of a U-shaped pattern in the empirical pricing kernel in 2014 and 2015. In 2016, however, I find that investors are willing to pay a premium to hedge against low-interest-rate states of the world, but not high-interest-rate states. This may be reasonable, as the predominant macroeconomic worry today is slow growth, deflation, and/or financial instability—circumstances that will be associated with low levels of the federal funds rate (Campbell, Sunderam & Viceira 2009). It is also entirely consistent with the finding that term premia are presently negative in the models of Kim & Wright (2005) and Adrian, Crump & Moench (2013), although those papers focus on the Treasury term premium, not the term premium in short-term money market futures. (At the time of writing, the term premium in short-term interest-rate futures has to be negative in order to give a reasonable expected path of monetary policy.) The differences between my results and those of Li & Zhao and Ivanova & Gutiérrez arise because I use more recent data and take the P-measure PDF from surveys, not from time-series methods. Ivanova & Gutiérrez use 6-year rolling windows of actual interest rates to form the P-measure PDF, and although that might be reasonable in normal times, I prefer to use survey evidence given the unusual recent behavior of interest rates.

5. CONCLUSION

With the wealth of interest-rate derivatives that trade in deep and liquid markets, researchers can identify the state-price density for future interest rates with great precision and minimal assumptions. The physical density is much harder to recover, but progress can be made on that front too, via time-series econometric methods and/or surveys. Depending on the purpose, researchers may be most interested in either the physical or risk-neutral density (Feldman et al. 2015).

In this article, I have reviewed methods for interest-rate density forecasting under both risk-neutral and physical measures. I have shown some illustrative applications, with particular focus on issues relating to the ZLB. The main goal of these applications is to show that forward-looking estimates of interest-rate distributions are important not only to finance practitioners, but also in macroeconomics and monetary economics, where these methods remain regrettably underutilized.

DISCLOSURE STATEMENT

The author is not aware of any affiliations, memberships, funding, or financial holdings that might be perceived as affecting the objectivity of this review.

ACKNOWLEDGMENTS

I am grateful to Tobias Adrian for helpful comments on an earlier draft. All errors and omissions are my sole responsibility.

LITERATURE CITED

Adrian T, Crump RK, Moench E. 2013. Pricing the term structure with linear regressions. *J. Financ. Econ.* 110:110–38

Aït-Sahalia Y, Duarte J. 2003. Nonparametric option pricing under shape restrictions. *J. Econom.* 116:9–47

Aït-Sahalia Y, Lo AW. 1998. Nonparameteric estimation of state-price densities implicit in financial asset prices. *J. Finance* 53:499–547

Andersen AB, Wagener T. 2002. *Extracting risk neutral probability densities by fitting implied volatility smiles: some methodological points and an application to the 3M Euribor futures option prices*. Work. Pap. 198, Eur. Cent. Bank, Frankfurt, Ger.

Andersen T, Benzoni L. 2010. Do bonds span volatility risk in the U.S. Treasury market? A specification test for affine term structure models. *J. Finance* 65:603–53

Black F. 1976. The pricing of commodity contracts. *J. Financ. Econ.* 3:167–79

Black F. 1995. Interest rates as options. *J. Finance* 50:1371–76

Bliss RR, Panigirtzoglou N. 2002. Testing the stability of implied probability density functions. *J. Bank. Finance* 26:381–422

Brace A, Gatarek D, Musiela M. 1997. The market model of interest rate dynamics. *Math. Finance* 7:127–54

Breeden DT, Litzenberger RH. 1978. Prices of state contingent claims implicit in options prices. *J. Bus.* 51:621–51

Brigo D, Mercurio F. 2006. *Interest Rate Models—Theory and Practice*. Berlin: Springer

Campbell JY, Sunderam A, Viceira LM. 2009. *Inflation bets or deflation hedges? The changing risks of nominal bonds*. NBER Work. Pap. 14701, Cambridge, MA

Carriero A, Clark TE, Marcellino MG. 2014. *No arbitrage priors, drifting volatilities and the term structure of interest rates*. Discuss. Pap. 9848, Cent. Econ. Policy Res, Washington, DC

Chun AL. 2011. Expectations, bond yields, and monetary policy. *Rev. Financ. Stud.* 24:208–47

Cieslak A, Povala P. 2016. Information in the term structure of yield curve volatility. *J. Finance* 71:1393–436

Clark TE. 2011. Real-time density forecasts from Bayesian vector autoregressions with stochastic volatility. *J. Bus. Econ. Stat.* 29:327–41

Cochrane JH, Piazzesi M. 2005. Bond risk premia. *Am. Econ. Rev.* 95:138–60

Collin-Dufresne P, Goldstein RS. 2002. Do bonds span the fixed income markets? Theory and evidence for unspanned stochastic volatility. *J. Finance* 57:1685–730

Collin-Dufresne P, Goldstein RS, Jones CS. 2009. Can interest rate volatility be extracted from the cross section of bond yields? *J. Financ. Econ.* 94:47–66

Diebold FX, Li C. 2006. Forecasting the term structure of government bond yields. *J. Econom.* 131:309–38

Duffee GR. 2013. Forecasting interest rates. In *Handbook of Economic Forecasting*, Vol. 2, ed. G Elliott, A Timmermann, pp. 385–426. Amsterdam: Elsevier

Egorov AV, Hong Y, Li H. 2006. Validating forecasts of the joint probability density of bond yields: Can affine models beat random walk? *J. Econom.* 135:255–84

Elliott D, Noss J. 2015. Estimating market expectations of changes in bank rate. *Bank Engl. Q. Bull.* 55:273–82

Engelberg J, Manski CF, Williams J. 2009. Comparing the point predictions and subjective probability distributions of professional forecasters. *J. Bus. Econ. Stat.* 27:30–41

Feldman R, Heinecke K, Kocherlakota N, Schulhofer-Wohl S, Tallarini T. 2015. *Market-based probabilities: a tool for policymakers*. Work. Pap., Fed. Reserve Bank Minneap., Minneapolis, MN

Filipović D, Larsson M, Trolle AB. 2017. Linear-rational term structure models. *J. Finance* 72:655–704

Goldys B, Musiela M, Sondermann D. 2000. Lognormality of rates and term structure models. *Stoch. Anal. Appl.* 18:375–96

Gürkaynak RS, Sack B, Wright JH. 2007. The U.S. Treasury yield curve: 1961 to the present. *J. Monet. Econ.* 54:2291–304

Hautsch N, Ou Y. 2012. Analyzing interest rate risk: stochastic volatility in the term structure of government bond yields. *J. Bank. Finance* 36:2988–3007

Hautsch N, Yang F. 2012. Bayesian inference in a stochastic volatility Nelson–Siegel model. *Comput. Stat. Data Anal.* 56:3774–92

Heath D, Jarrow RA, Morton A. 1992. Bond pricing and the term structure of interest rates: a new methodology for contingent claims valuation. *Econometrica* 60:77–105

Heidari M, Wu L. 2009. A joint framework for consistently pricing interest rates and interest rate derivatives. *J. Financ. Quant. Anal.* 44:517–50

Hong Y, Li H, Zhao F. 2004. Out-of-sample performance of discrete time spot interest rate models. *J. Bus. Econ. Stat.* 22:457–73

Hull J, White A. 1990. Pricing interest-rate derivative securities. *Rev. Financ. Stud.* 3:573–92

Hull J, White A. 2013. LIBOR versus OIS: the derivatives discount dilemma. *J. Invest. Manag.* 11:14–27

Ivanova V, Gutiérrez JM. 2014. Interest rate forecasts, state price densities and risk premium from Euribor options. *J. Bank. Finance* 48:210–23

Jacobs K, Karoui L. 2009. Conditional volatility in affine term-structure models: evidence from Treasury and swap markets. *J. Financ. Econ.* 91:288–318

Jamshidian F. 2007. An exact bond option formula. *J. Finance* 44:205–9

Jarrow RA. 2009. The term structure of interest rates. *Annu. Rev. Financ. Econ.* 1:69–96

Jarrow RA. 2014. Forward rate curve smoothing. *Annu. Rev. Financ. Econ.* 6:443–58

Jarrow RA, Li H, Zhao F. 2007. Interest rate caps 'smile' too! But can the LIBOR market models capture the smile? *J. Finance* 62:345–82

Kim DH, Orphanides A. 2012. Term structure estimation with survey data on interest rate forecasts. *J. Financ. Quant. Anal.* 47:241–72

Kim DH, Singleton KJ. 2012. Term structure models and the zero bound: an empirical investigation of Japanese yields. *J. Econom.* 170:32–49

Kim DH, Wright JH. 2005. *An arbitrage-free three-factor term structure model and the recent behavior of long-term yields and distant-horizon forward rates*. Work. Pap. 2005-33, Finance Econ. Discuss. Ser., Fed. Reserve Board, Washington, DC

Kim DH, Wright JH. 2014. *Jumps in bond yields at known times*. Work. Pap. 2014-100, Finance Econ. Discuss. Ser., Fed. Reserve Board, Washington, DC

Koopman SJ, Mallee MIP, der Wel MV. 2010. Analyzing the term structure of interest rates using the dynamic Nelson–Siegel model with time-varying parameters. *J. Bus. Econ. Stat.* 329–43

Krippner L. 2014. *Zero Lower Bound Term Structure Modeling: A Practitioner's Guide*. New York: Palgrave Macmillan

Li H, Zhao F. 2009. Nonparametric estimation of state-price densities implicit in interest rate cap prices. *Rev. Financ. Stud.* 22:4335–76

Litterman R, Scheinkman J. 1991. Common factors affecting bond returns. *J. Fixed Income* 1:54–61

Longstaff FA, Schwartz ES. 1992. Interest rate volatility and the term structure: a two-factor general equilibrium model. *J. Finance* 48:1259–82

Nelson CR, Siegel AF. 1987. Parsimonious modeling of yield curves. *J. Bus.* 60:473–89

Rebonato R. 1999. *Volatility and Correlation*. Chichester, UK: Wiley

Rebonato R. 2003. *Modern Pricing of Interest Rate Derivatives: The LIBOR Market Model and Beyond*. Princeton, NJ: Princeton Univ. Press

Rognlie M. 2016. *What lower bound? Monetary policy with negative interest rates*. Work. Pap., MIT

Rosenberg JV, Engle RF. 2002. Empirical pricing kernels. *J. Financ. Econ.* 64:341–72

Sandmann K, Sondermann D. 1997. A note on the stability of lognormal interest rate models and the pricing of Eurodollar futures. *Math. Finance* 7:119–25

Shiller RJ, Campbell JY, Schoenholtz KL. 1983. Forward rates and future policy: interpreting the term structure of interest rates. *Brookings Pap. Econ. Act.* 1:173–217

Shimko D. 1993. Bounds of probability. *Risk* 6:33–37

Shreve SE. 2004. *Stochastic Calculus for Finance II: Continuous-Time Models*. New York: Springer

Svensson LEO. 1994. Estimating and interpreting forward rates: Sweden 1992–4. NBER Work. Pap. 4871, Cambridge, MA

Swanson ET, Williams JC. 2014. Measuring the effect of the zero lower bound on medium- and longer-term interest rates. *Am. Econ. Rev.* 104:3154–85

Veronesi P. 2010. *Fixed Income Securities*. Hoboken, NJ: Wiley

Wright JH. 2016. Options-implied probability density functions for real interest rates. *Int. J. Cent. Bank.* 12(3):129–49

Wu JC, Xia FD. 2016. Measuring the macroeconomic impact of monetary policy at the zero lower bound. *J. Money Credit Bank.* 48:253–91

Cumulative Indexes

Contributing Authors, Volumes 2–9

K

L

M

N

O

P

Q

R

S

T

V

W

X

Y

Z

Article Titles, Volumes 2–9

Volume 2 (2010)

Volume 3 (2011)

Volume 4 (2012)

Volume 5 (2013)

Volume 6 (2014)

Volume 7 (2015)

Volume 8 (2016)

Volume 9 (2017)